RACIAL AND ETHNIC RELATIONS

Selected Readings

second edition

edited by

BERNARD E. SEGAL

DARTMOUTH COLLEGE

THOMAS Y. CROWELL COMPANY

New York   Established 1834

RACIAL AND ETHNIC RELATIONS

SELECTED READINGS

L.C. Card 73-165378

ISBN 0-690-66632-2

Manufactured in the United States of America

PREFACE

In second editions of collections of readings, often the changes or additions of just a few selections make the book more current, but otherwise indistinguishable from their predecessors. I have set out, however, to compile and edit a different book, retaining only a small number of selections from the previous edition. I have also tried to edit the present book more tightly and more extensively. Part and selection introductions ground each of the pieces in a broader context and relate them to one another. In addition, I made an effort to select readings that would reflect geographical conditions and regional diversity more than the first edition did, which I had come to think as concentrating too much on the East.

I make no claim for the timeless quality of the older selections that appear again here. I merely think they describe and analyze circumstances and phenomena that are not very different from five years ago. The pieces are still germane and accurate; they fit my predisposition to think of racial and ethnic relations as being carried out on a stage protruding from a massive backdrop of large-scale institutional arrangements that shape men's lives in ways we are too often only dimly aware of. American racism, for example, is a serious pathology in its own right, yet its course has been and continues to affect and be affected by other conditions that influence the over-all state of the body social. I don't want to carry the metaphor too far; we sociologists have already overused organismic analogies. Let me just say, therefore, that I am among those who would rather cure the patient than kill him, and I want to do it before he kills himself.

The new selections reflect changes in our ways of apprehending the American social order. The selections are not *brand* new; lags between completion and publication make it impossible to keep readings up to the minute. As a consequence, I am more convinced every day that texts must concentrate more on analysis and understanding than on description and reportage. There really is no substitute for a good daily newspaper, no way to stay current without it. Similarly, I am persuaded that we cannot grasp the present without knowing the past, and this, in turn, means reading papers a good deal older than yesterday's.

Three issues above all have contributed to changes in how Americans think about their nation and their own places within it. This book is directly concerned with just one of those issues—the assertiveness of racial minorities and their attempts to find power through collective solidarity. The second issue is a war that we have virtually lost. In losing, we discovered that we fought it in the name of one of the most misguided conceptions of self-interest possible to imagine, and so plunged into a chasm separating professions of humanity from quests for security and preeminence based on naked power alone. The third issue is the disaffection of the young, fed by the war and by the outcomes of racism and racial conflict. The disaffection led to mass behavior in the capital and on campus. Perhaps it also led to a lasting shift in cultural standards, although an uncharitable observer might want to conclude that till now the "greening" of America has depended more on spreading around organic fertilizer than on firmly rooting improved new seeds.

Nevertheless, a society is different when it feels different, when many of its people have changed beliefs about it, when they discover that they have to take account of many other people's new expectations and performances. It *is* a change when many people become more aware than they were before that important paradoxes need to be resolved, and that long-term secular trends must be considered and confronted if resolutions are to be found.

Yet should we not also note that consciousness is more volatile than social structure? Consciousness gets transformed more rapidly than old organizations change or new ones find strong grounding. After all, the key structures in a complex industrial society's economy and government combine enormous resources—including human talent—in such a way as to maximize the probability of attaining specific outcomes. They have done so rather well. The proof is that if we take the outcomes one by one—high output, high employment, considerable efficiency, solid predictability—we can see that most people want each of them. Sudden and direct structural change would threaten some of the outcomes most prized by large numbers of groups and individuals. It is hard to tamper with what has been called success, even when the success has been inequitably distributed; or even when, as now, new groups with new values question how reasonable it is to go on measuring the nation's or an individual's success in terms of the dollar-value of outputs and incomes, irrespective of increasingly apparent psychic, environmental, and social cost.

Of course, social structures change too. The United States

is obviously not the same society it was in 1920 or 1940. But structural change is not just a simple response to the skepticism and criticism that so often run ahead of it. The major economic and political organizations of this society are controlled as well by their own system demands. The imperative character of such demands may be likened to an internal gyroscopic mechanism. As a consequence, the directions of the changes that organizations make are predetermined, though not absolutely and with far from complete predictability, by the felt necessity of husbanding and recombining organizational resources for maintaining organizational identity and purpose, thereby leading to organizational growth. What is good for General Motors may not, in fact, be good for the country. Still, a Utopian's dream but an economist's nightmare is to think of the shape the American economy would have to be in for General Motors to be in serious financial difficulty.

In sum, changes in American society have occurred on some levels but not on others. The great paradoxes remain: wealth and poverty, abundance and despoilment, nobly generous claims and petty limiting policies, particularisms of inheritance and the universalization of achievement criteria. The institutional arrangements that lie behind these paradoxes also remain. As compared to five or ten years ago, how different are the patterns for distributing rights, rewards, and privileges that we sociologists call the stratification system? Aside from classrooms here and there, what changes in educational methods or goals have been reflected in students' performances or in the character of the connection between education and employment? Where have the technocracies that are the major resource and the driving engine in both huge corporation and overblown yet overburdened government become any less influential?

The reader is entitled to ask what all that I have said has to do with racial and ethnic relations. On my part, I feel entitled to counsel patience. The answer will become more apparent as he reads more of this book. As he reads, he should also keep reminding himself that the word "society" is in many ways merely a synonym for a social system that has the capacity to maintain and reproduce itself. What happens in social systems depends on the form and character of the different sorts of units that compose that system, and we have already seen that many such units are far larger than individuals or separate families. Moreover, there are connections that link different units (and different kinds of units) to one another. Such connections mean that no single unit is ever completely autonomous. An important part of the sociologist's task is to try to make clear where these connections lie and how strong their effects are. I ask the reader to share this task, at least temporarily, and I hope this book will help him to perform it. All that this book is about, really, is how various American racial and ethnic groups relate to themselves, to one another, to the other kinds of major social units, and to the society as a whole. The key word is "how." It leads to the search for the links that explain. Then, when the explaining is *nearly* done, for the job is never complete, there must arise a second question, inevitably. That question is, simply, "So what?"

Your answers to the second question, dear reader, will depend far more on you than on me.

B. E. S.

Hanover, New Hampshire
December, 1971

CONTENTS

RACIAL AND ETHNIC RELATIONS

Selected Readings

INTRODUCTION

When I was preparing the first edition of this book in 1964 and 1965, I wanted my readers to share with me the intellectual and emotional excitement of discovering how many different cultures and ways of life had contributed to the fabric of our national life. Most of them were, of course, merely threads woven into the background canvas of a predominantly Anglo-Saxon and British heritage, but they were identifiable threads, giving strength and character, as well as variety, to a tapestry that has even now not been finished.

I was also hopeful because there had been some great changes in American race relations over a rather brief span of time. Let anyone who doubts that statement think about what race relations were like in this country in 1940. Better still, let him read about them in Gunnar Myrdal's *An American Dilemma,* or Allison Davis and others' *Deep South,* or John Dollard's *Caste and Class in a Southern Town,* or in many moving passages of *The Autobiography of Malcolm X.* Take just one example of the change, aside from the legal developments with which most of us are now familiar. By 1965, in a variety of different places and circumstances outside of deepest Dixie where people were still being fired for daring to vote, interpersonal caste etiquette had been turned on its head. Black people could be openly contemptuous of white ones and get away with it, could even frighten white people into deferring to them just through the force of their convictions and personalities. The tendency has become more marked in the last five or six years, but it was nearly inconceivable in 1940. Then a black had real reason for being physically afraid of being considered an "uppity nigger." I wonder how many of the present readers of this book would think of daring to use such a phrase to a black man's face now. Very few, I submit, unless given false courage by being part of a rowdy crowd.

Considering the changes in race relations that were taking place, I harbored the wish, along with a good many other liberal academics, that my work might contribute to a broader understanding that would help speed a coming racial and ethnic millennium that I then thought was not very far off. The major social structural arrangement that would bring this millennium about, I thought, was integration in a growing economy. This would offer prospects of upward mobility to people who had not yet been allowed to become fully participating members of the national community. Integration, mobility, more integration, more mobility, and the vicious circle of discrimination would be broken once and for all.

In the long run, that may turn out to be the case. Someday the inhabitants of the ghettoes, the barrios, and the reservations may get to repeat part of the history of the white immigrant ethnic groups and may draw even with them. In the short run, however, the five years between 1965 and 1970 made clear that more time was necessary to wash away the sediment of several centuries of exploitation and discrimination. Not only that, but also changes in the future would have to go faster than they had in the past, even though it was evident that the route to equality was no clear, free-running stream. Though for the first time anyone could now swim in that stream, newcomers couldn't get very far when the channels were clogged by so many others who had already gotten their feet wet. Under the circumstances, to jump in with no choice but to sink or swim didn't seem to be a particularly good way of getting anywhere. Perhaps it would be better to dig new channels, or failing that, to blast them. But either of those courses muddied the water, it seemed, and angered a great many bathers who thought nobody new ought even to think about getting into the stream unless he already knew how to use the currents.

In 1965 I did know, and tried to convey, that the accident of birth led men to be shaped in different ways by being raised in different regions, in different class and ethnic and racial groups, by parents and friends who shared life-styles and beliefs that somehow set them apart from others and at the same time helped them to feel solidarity among themselves. The feelings from these experiences went deep, deep enough so that men would try to build their security and identity upon them. It should have been obvious to me, but it was not, that it was a mistake—all the greater because the society did not really let down the gates—to assume that people from groups never allowed to develop firm identities in this society would not want to discover and create their own. Instead, I was too ready to believe that they would rush to don the garb of a well-behaved, well-intentioned, generous and forgiving, adjusted middle class. I was not alone among liberals of the time. It was not so much that we expected gratitude—though there was some of that—as that we believed in the magnetic pulling force of our shining example. We wished to see the world patterned in the terms of our own expectations, and we were disappointed that ghetto jungles didn't turn into garden cities overnight. White liberals were not the only impatient and disappointed people. In many different places for a few nights at a time, wishes were horses, and beggars did ride, as the tremor of major urban riots shook the nation for four years.

The nation didn't know if the riots would end, and it seemed unable to decide what to do once they did.

It must not have been hard to sympathize with and "understand" Watts from Beverly Hills or UCLA; or Detroit from Grosse Pointe or the University of Michigan; or Newark from Short Hills or Princeton. But when the action got closer to home, sympathies got tested, strained and sometimes snapped. Unlike the gentle, rolling preserves of our suburban peerage, the ivory tower wasn't spared. Were you there, were you part of what happened when the movement hit the campuses? Only rarely was there any more violence than that involved in a building takeover, yet academics and administrators alike were split and disorganized in the face of what many of them took to be a threat to their, till then, taken-for-granted ways of organizing their professional lives.

Pointed fingers raised from clenched fists bristled with anger or quivered with a fear the anger was meant to hide. At emergency faculty meetings, voices boomed from puffed, expanded chests declaiming that they belonged to men of principle who agreed with what their minority students were trying to do, but that their methods could not be countenanced. Later, there were negotiations in which the threat of more disruption and embarrassment generally turned out to win more than prestige and rank. Academics had learned that when confrontation goes to college, politics means more than winning or losing an important committee assignment. Then there was time for examining the roots of the students' complaints. And, among a few, there dawned the realization that the protected quiet eminence of the university and the buzzing, threatening beehive of the ghetto slum were part and parcel of the same society. Tax and endowment dollars had helped make the one great and strong; like so many other dollars—the ones for highways, for space, for defense—they had done nothing to help the other from being disorganized and weak.

From 1966 to early 1968, I lived in Argentina and Chile, during which time I learned what a conflict society is, one in which men are so far set apart by espousing opposed absolute principles that it is impossible for them to get on with the job of building and maintaining the commonweal. Men holding to absolute principles do not compromise, nor do they see that many values—faith, order, property, equality—may have different relative significance when time and circumstance combine to change the character of the society in which they live.

I returned to the United States just before the

assassinations of Martin Luther King, Jr., and Robert Kennedy. I found that consensus was gone. I had returned to a conflict society.

I was not a very good prophet before I left, so it is perhaps just as well that I did not commit myself to any predictions. I did not see that it was possible for personal prejudice to decline at the same time that each new step in race relations seemed to provoke a crisis by threatening that the gains of one group could come only at the expense of another. I did not sufficiently understand that ordinary people worked hard and honestly to establish little islands of security and stability, and so I did not see how tenaciously they would cling to them against the real or imagined onslaught of outsiders who seemed menacing on account of the aggressive or careless lower-class life ways they carried with them or that their groups seemed to represent. I did not see the people who would say what I would hear around me on every side whenever I left my tranquil New England town: "They want too much too fast." "Why don't they go to work?" "I had to sweat for what I've got, why don't they sweat too?" "OK, they're entitled to their rights, just like the rest of us, but why do they have to pick on *me?*" "That's all right for you to say, but your kids don't have to go to school with them." "Of course they can work here, that's the law; it's just that most of them aren't qualified." "No, we don't try to recruit them, but if they apply and meet our requirements they can enter." "One or two nice families, professional men maybe, would be fine, but—."

Though I peered into my crystal ball, I did not see an administration so unequipped to deal with inflation caused by a brutal and meaningless foreign war that it would play on domestic fear and prejudice to try to win votes. I did not see that capital would go on flowing so much to prospective profit and so little to human need, or that the men who controlled capital would not be inventive enough to find ways of meeting human need and maintaining corporate earnings at the same time. I did not see that these were futile hopes when inventiveness was already being bought and paid for by companies, and armies, and governments, and workers, and voters so involved in building missiles and rockets and jet bombers and bullets to protect themselves that they forgot to care much about the fact that they were also protecting hunger and sickness and income inequalities and ignorance and hate. I did not see that these conditions fed a frustration so great that it would lead some to talk of violent revolution and encourage thousands of others to take their talk seriously. I did not see that the coexistence of all these conditions would make men with great power more reluctant to grant conciliatory accommodations, and that henceforth their concessions would be more dependent on the capacity of others to harness and apply the threat of disruption. I did not see a wave of police suppression that could so readily be defended as necessary to preserve domestic tranquillity and so easily denounced as still another demonstration of the perfidy and illegitimacy of constituted political establishments.

Some are better insulated from shock than others. Yet we must all of us have been touched by change by now. How could this edition of my book be the same as its predecessor? The society had changed, and so had my ways of looking at it.

One of many important shifts in my point of view that came from my experience in Latin America was a greater comprehension of how much our economic hegemony over the Western Hemisphere depends upon corporate giants who customarily repatriate their profits here rather than reinvesting them abroad. Only changed political climates in the foreign countries can threaten the giants' investments enough to exact some major concessions from them. However, since a threatening political climate constitutes a severe drawback to the possibility of a foreign country's being able to receive and hold onto the foreign capital that it needs for its development, there is a problem here. American government action and policy, therefore, rush into the breach to try to manage several marionettes with the same set of strings. Development loans, subsidized prices above the world market level for agricultural products, and military aid all help to fill the gap of capital shortage. At the same time, they buy time against the internal forces that are clamoring for basic structural changes in their countries' economies and societies; tie those economies closer and closer to our own; and allow American-owned properties and business practices to continue relatively unmolested. Now all of that does not mean that underdeveloped Latin American countries would find instant harmony and prosperity if only we were to leave them alone. What it does mean is that we try to shape the routes toward progress that they do take, in order to try to insure that they do not conflict with our economic and political interests. Although our span of tolerance for the politico-economic forms they choose is actually pretty wide, it takes in much more of the right than of the left. It gets wider, and we are readier to put up with more genuinely (usually leftist) nationalistic efforts when our hands are tied elsewhere than when they are not.

This is not the place for me to discuss how far I think this policy combination does or does not fall short of satisfying our national interests, or how much it depends upon and has been shaped by considerations of the Cold War. Instead, I merely want to call attention to some parallels between the relations of Latin American nations to the United States, and those of contemporary American racial minorities to American society as a whole. I repeat that these are merely some parallels, for the situations themselves are far from identical. After all, American minorities lack a juridically defined territorial base; do not have legitimate control over the use of force within any such base; do not have elaborate and complex linkages between their own metropolitan areas and hinterland, or between higher and lower status members of their own group. Moreover, they do not control natural resources that are important to the economy (though a few Indian and Eskimo groups are a partial exception); and they are far from having unitary governments that can even claim to represent them. Furthermore, in an economy as capitally intensive as ours, corporate titans do not derive most of their profit from employing minority people as cheap labor; and union power, which protects the jobs of the already employed, keeps minorities from being used as an army of surplus labor. Finally, American minorities do at least have the same formal political rights as all other citizens. They can and do vote on issues that affect them, and increasingly have some impact on the outcomes. There is even a bit of evidence from the 1970 census that for the first time some of them have begun to have an even share of the national income distribution. (Stable non-Southern black families headed by males under thirty years old now have about the same median annual income as their white counterparts.)

After all these differences, where, then, are the parallels? Blacks, Mexican-Americans, Puerto Ricans, Indians are still our cheap labor. Disproportionately, they get low pay for doing the dirty or demeaning jobs no one else wants; and, although they do not control much of the productive process, they constitute a huge market. It seems a strange market when you stop to think about it. These people often can't get jobs in the organizations that sell things to them; despite lower income than others they pay more for such things as housing and furniture and used automobiles. Stranger still, a large number of minority people get other people's tax money in the form of welfare and relief payments, while tax money also supports an enormous, mostly middle-class, bureaucratic apparatus to run the welfare program. Tax money also pays police who help keep minorities in line, making sure when called upon that welfare rules aren't broken. It is absurd. For the sake of the short-run small gain of relatively few, it costs more year by year to keep people in ghettoes than we could all gain if once we fully committed ourselves to making enough resources available to allow the ghettoes and the people in them to develop themselves.

The parallels should be clear now. If not, call welfare checks a foreign-aid loan to take care of restless natives so they won't start an uprising; call appropriations for bigger and better police forces a military-aid grant to put down the natives in case they riot; call radical or communist or subversive anyone who suggests that we ought to do more than tinker with fiscal policy and, instead, get on with the job of questioning the accounts and practices of the titans that dominate the economy. Call a revolutionary anyone who argues that the poor need more resources to stop being poor, but who fails to add that cultural deprivation makes them incompetent to handle the resources themselves, proof of which is that, if they weren't incompetent, they would do something about their situation by themselves. And then, when they do try to do something by themselves, call it a riot, call it a plot, call in the cops, call out the Guard. Call . . . call . . . call. Not all the conflict societies speak Spanish.

As a last note, in case I have not already made it clear, I want to point out that I have no pretensions, as I did at the time of the first edition, of having selected and edited objectively. My objectivity left me when I felt anger over hypocrisy in high places and despair over venality in low. Nevertheless, in this edition, as in the first, I have tried to indicate that complex matters have many different facets, and that it is a mistake to try to oversimplify them. Of course I have also tried to be accurate. Ignorance is not bliss for anyone still conscious enough to be concerned about his own world or involved enough to care about the programs that others may design to help develop their own worlds.

PART I: THEORETICAL PERSPECTIVES

Sociological theory ought to do four things. (1) It should rely on concepts that correspond to or have parallels in what research has shown to be true of the empirical world. (2) It should summarize and explain, through a limited number of propositions, a variety of phenomena, making clear common features and showing relationships. (3) It should extend cognitive understanding by stimulating consideration of additional circumstances which might either corroborate the propositions or suggest additional variables that need to be taken into account to qualify them. (4) It should be susceptible to being *dis*proved.

Theory synthesizes, explains, and attempts to predict. With the selections in Part I, it will be useful to try to maintain a distinction between explanations and predictions on the one hand and recommendations or advocacy on the other. It will not be easy to do so. Yet, if the attempt is not made, then theory will appear to shade into ideology or propaganda. Theory is not necessarily better or worse than ideology or propaganda; but it is different. Its major emphasis is on intellectual grasp, whereas ideology defines the world more normatively, telling what's right or wrong with it and what ought to be done. Propaganda is an even more deliberate shading of evidence and an appeal to emotion, intended to persuade, convince, and call to action.

These terminological distinctions are more than academic. Ultimately, these three ways of viewing the social world refer to questions about what truth is, about where it is to be found, about whether it is the same as justice, and if not, about which is the more important. In social theory, it does not take long before value concerns intrude upon abstract thought. Why?

The knowledge upon which sociological theories are based is never complete; facts do not speak for themselves but are subject to interpretation; and theoreticians themselves differ concerning how directly they think their ideas ought to reflect or affect the world in which they live. Add to these points the possibility of having adopted particular ideological premises without being aware of having done so; consider as well that the audience for theoretical statements includes people suspicious of positions that seem not to take a clear stand and others who are impatient for ideas that will serve as a practical guide to their actions. Under all these circumstances, it is not surprising that some sociological theories induce boredom or antipathy as often as others stimulate purely intellectual challenges that lead to the refinement of thought.

The selections that appear in this section probably won't bore many people. They are examples of "middle-range" theory, quite close to actual situations, "theoretical" in the sense that they try to make generalizations about these situations, but not about abstract concepts such as the nature of culture, or conflict, or social differentiation. The first three selections are more "formal," tending toward the abstract and value-free. But all have clear links to events and conditions with which we are all familiar and in which we probably have been involved. The next three selections will undoubtedly call forth more heated opinions. They bring into question a number of assumptions that have until recently served as comforting rationalizations of the nation's intergroup relations, or as supports for the hope that the transition toward greater equality and interracial justice could be smooth and tranquil.

In the first selection, Williams calls attention to conditions that affect the appearance, the character, and the strength of ethnocentrism, that is, the tendency to assume that the culture and life-style of one's own membership group are valuable in their own right and preferable to those of other groups. An idea that will appear and reappear throughout the book is that groups with an already high status—especially if they also possess the power and income to back it up—have an obvious advantage here. They are able to use the distance between themselves and others as if it proved the correctness of their beliefs and vindicated the propriety of their behavior.

Van den Berghe then uses a fine brush on a broad canvas to compare different types of race relations that appear in societies at different levels of socioeconomic development. His observation that racial inequalities in industrial societies take a competitive form and his judgment that they have disintegrative effects on the society as a whole are immediately germane to the points Blalock makes in the subsequent selection. Blalock attempts to specify the conditions under which black and white workers are most likely to improve their common situation by forming coalitions based upon their discovery that they have common rather than opposed interests. Seen in the context of Van den Berghe's work, Blalock's appears as a means for identifying cooperative possibilities even in a predominantly competitive situation.

The excerpt from Oppenheimer's book makes some order out of the apparent chaos of the different forms of insurrectionary activity that occur among various subordinated groups. Not all violent action is protest; not all violent protest is politically oriented; not all politically oriented violent protest involves massive collective participation. Indeed, these three conditions may never coalesce if dominant groups make significant concessions, or if without making concessions their power remains overwhelming and is held back neither by foreign concerns nor internal scruple. Rather, a massive political insurrection, an attempt at revolution, is an end point of interaction over time between protest on one side and the responses made by the dominant group on the other. Many, perhaps most, protests fail.[1]

The papers by Blauner and Turner both help to show why racial protest is now taking forms that would have seemed inconceivable to most people as short a time as a decade ago. Blauner's paper shows that racism and colonization have been reciprocally reinforcing phenomena. His work analyzes more closely how ghettoes became and remain internal subject provinces of an extraordinarily powerful white state and economy. Turner's paper is more urgent, going beyond explanation and recommendation to justify and call for solidary belief and action. It is, in terms of the way I attempted to distinguish theory from ideology at the outset, the most clearly ideological selection in this section.

[1] Revolutionaries, of course, argue among themselves concerning the tactics and conditions that will increase the probability of successful insurrections. However, they have launched them even against great odds, sometimes out of desperation, at other times out of their conviction that losses are only temporary whereas a victory will be forever.

1. ETHNOCENTRISM

Robin M. Williams, Jr.

In this selection, Williams draws a useful distinction between ethnocentrism and prejudice. An individual can take pride in the accomplishments of his own group without necessarily disparaging the contributions of others; he can understand why other people value their particular norms and life-styles at the same time that he retains his commitment to those of his own group. Indeed, both of these possibilities must be at least partially realized if group relations are to be harmonious in a society that is at once democratic and pluralistic. On the other hand, there are conditions under which ethnocentrism is likely to lead to prejudice—where antipathies are sanctioned by tradition, where there are real or perceived grounds for believing that one is threatened by members of another group, and where opportunities for mutual understanding are limited. Williams shows that these conditions are related, and that no single one is a necessary and sufficient reason for prejudice to accompany ethnocentrism.

Ethnocentrism, says William Graham Sumner, is that ". . . view of things in which one's own group is the center of everything, and all others are scaled and rated with reference to it." [1] It is a fact that men classify their fellows in a variety of ways and react to others as members of social categories. What is the nature of these groups that men form? How do they form them, and why? What is the nature of ethnocentric feelings, and how strong are they? The answers to these questions will constitute the main part of this chapter. We will also con-

[1] *Folkways* (Boston: Ginn & Company, 1906), p. 13.

Source: *Strangers Next Door: Ethnic Relations in American Communities* (Englewood Cliffs, N.J.: Prentice-Hall, Inc., 1964), pp. 17–29. Copyright © 1964. Reprinted by permission of the author and publisher.

ROBIN M. WILLIAMS, JR., author of *American Society* and other well-known works, is Henry Scarborough Professor of Social Science, Cornell University.

sider, in the final pages of this chapter, whether ethnocentrism necessarily results in prejudice.

THE FORMING OF GROUPS

Terminology

The word "group" is used in everyday parlance to refer to anything from a crowd at Yankee Stadium to the members of a family. Although we too may find it convenient to employ the term "group" in our discussion of intergroup relations, it is necessary to understand that there are actually many kinds of groups, which vary from one another in cohesiveness and social significance and which should technically be referred to by some term other than "group." The category of least social importance is the *aggregate,* a collection of human individuals having no relationships among themselves other than those that are intrinsic in occupying geographic space in some proximity. As the distinctiveness, unity, and internal organization of the aggregate increases, we may want to recognize it as a *social category,* then as a *group,* and finally as a *society.* The social category is exemplified by an occupational grouping or a social class, where there is only a vague sense of membership and very rudimentary capacity for any sort of concerted collective action. A fully developed collectivity, on the other hand, is a *people,* and is characterized by 1) a distinctive culture; 2) tests or criteria of membership; 3) a set of constitutive norms regulating social relations both within the collectivity and with outsiders; 4) an awareness of a distinct identity by both members and nonmembers; 5) obligations of solidarity, such as enforced requirements to help members in need and to resist derogation by outsiders; and 6) a high capacity for continued action by the collectivity on behalf of its members or of itself as a

unit. In its most comprehensive development such a collectivity may become a potentially self-sufficient society, able to meet all internal needs from its own resources and to perpetuate itself as a functioning system from generation to generation.

The term "group," then, when used most accurately, refers to a special case of a small-scale collectivity. What traditionally have been called "minority groups" are either social categories or collectivities. However, so long as it is clear from the context "group" (or the compromise term "grouping" when we wish to stress the loose, aggregative quality of some part of the population).

How Socially Significant Groups Form

How do aggregates become collectivities? There undoubtedly are several different major sets of processes. One important general sequence, illustrated by the cases of American Negroes and many immigrant populations, is approximately as follows:

1. By reason of any one of many historical circumstances, there is an initial categorization of persons considered to have some important characteristic in common—for example, they are slaves, newcomers, foreigners, or heathens. An identifying set of symbols is found that gives the category high social visibility: skin color, food habits, religious rites.

2. Persons in the category are typically found (or, are believed to be found) in occupations of other social roles that are recognizably different from those typically associated with persons in one or more other social categories: trade, money lending, domestic service, landlordism.

3. As a consequence of their distinctive social roles, persons in the given ethnic category will develop additional relatively distinctive interests, beliefs, values, and specific modes of behavior.

4. These differences will render

more distinct, reinforce, and elaborate the initial definition of the social category.

5. As a consequence of all these developments, the like-circumstanced members of the social category will come increasingly to have a sense of common identity, which will tend to increase their within-category interaction and to reduce their contacts with outsiders. This closure of interaction will increase the tendency of outsiders to treat them as a unit, and this tendency, in turn, will enhance the new collectivity's cultural distinctiveness and social separateness.

6. If, however, the collectivity so formed is part of and is economically and politically dependent upon a larger social system, it will not become a completely closed social system. Its members must maintain relationships with members of other collectivities and social categories within the same total society.

7. If some other collectivity, or set of collectivities, is economically and politically dominant, the new subordinate collectivity will be forced to accept the dominant grouping's rules of the game. It will be forced into a largely one-way adaptation to a common set of constitutive norms that will regulate the necessary relations between the two groupings. In other words, the subordinates have to accept some of the culture of the super-ordinate grouping, especially the basic rules of the game for vital dealings with the members of the dominant collectivity.

Groups of Greatest Social Significance

Although there are numerous social categories that have social importance (such as enlisted men, union workers, women), the groups that are of greatest social significance and those in which students of intergroup relations are most interested are those collectivities that

have racial, ethnic, and religious distinctions. It is within the ethnic grouping that all individuals form their first relationships, their deepest dependencies, and the most important bases of emotional ambivalence.

Why We Are Ethnocentric

All individuals need group belongingness and group anchorage. Without stable relationships to other persons, without some group ties, the individual becomes insecure, anxious, and uncertain of his identity. In order to receive the emotional support of the group (that is, the family group, the neighborhood or school peer group) the individual must heed the opinions of other group members. In the homogeneous family group he learns definite codes for behavior within the group and for behavior towards other groups. The child discovers very early that agreement with group opinions and codes is rewarding. He learns that the teachings of one's parents and close associates are helpful in getting what he wants and avoiding what he does not want. To the extent to which the child finds the instruction of elders and peers reliable for achieving rewarding results, he learns to give credence to their opinions. The child's need is great for relationships of trust that mediate reality to him. And through group attachments and loyalties he learns also of group antipathies and conflicts. He perceives groups, then, as social units in which he can expect security and love or danger and negative emotional experience.

Secure identity as a member of an ingroup is not a free good, contrary to some first appearances, but is only to be had at a price. Often one must have already established credentials of other group memberships and of personal qualities and achievements. Furthermore, maintenance of a clear, full, and secure identity within the ingroup requires conformity to group norms. More exactly, the price of one's group identity is responsible reciprocity with other members, a reciprocity defined by mutually accepted norms.

The Overlapping of Groups

Particularly in our complex society, most individuals are members of more than one group. The child, aware at first only of his membership in a kinship group, slowly becomes conscious of other memberships. Piaget reports that only at the age of ten to eleven were the children he studied capable of understanding that they could be members of both a locality and a nation, and of understanding what a nation is.[2] By adulthood then, the individual is aware of a plurality of group memberships that help him identify himself. The person is rare in urban America today who feels a clear and strong sense of identification with one and only one grouping or segment of the community and nation. The typical individual is a member of many in-groups (groups of intimate belonging; "we-groups") and may relate himself to many other reference groups (those that matter to him, and upon whose opinions he relies).

It is difficult to realize fully the enormous significance of alternative group memberships. If the individual can belong to only one group, that group inevitably becomes all-important to him. In it all his satisfactions are found and are controlled and limited. It encompasses and constricts all his experiences. However, totalistic character of group

[2] J. Piaget and Anne-Marie Weil, "The Development in Children of the Idea of the Homeland and of Relations with Other Countries," *International Social Science Bulletin*, III, No. 3 (Autumn, 1951), 561–78: ". . . the feeling and the very idea of the homeland are by no means the first or even early elements in the child's makeup, but are a relatively late development in the normal child, who does not appear to be drawn inevitably towards patriotic sociocentricity." (p. 562)

membership diminishes in complex and fluid societies.[3] The growth of alternative possibilities of group membership and group reference depends upon the number and variety of distinctive groupings, but the sheer multiplication of groupings is far from the whole story. Changes in the criteria of membership are accentuated by changes in the functions of groups and by shifts in the alignments among the between groups. The characteristics that actually are statistically typical of a grouping or category at one time cease to be typical later.

· · · · ·

ETHNOCENTRIC FEELINGS

Positive Ethnocentrism

What are the components of the sentiments of ethnocentrism? George Peter Murdock says, "Always the 'we-group' and its codes are exalted, while 'other groups' and their ways are viewed with suspicion, hostility and contempt." [4] It is true that satisfaction with one's own group (Oog) sometimes is accompanied by negative feelings toward other groups, but for the moment let us examine the attitude that ethnocentric groups have toward themselves. The most important are:

1. A belief in the unique value of Oog.
2. Satisfaction with membership in Oog.
3. Solidarity, loyalty, or cooperation with regard to Oog.
4. Preference for association with members of Oog.
5. Belief in the rightness of Oog's relationships with other groups.

[3] Of course we recognize that multigroup societies can be engulfed by political totalitarianism, which enforces a new kind of all-encompassing membership.
[4] "Ethnocentrism," *Encyclopedia of the Social Sciences*, V, 613.

The attitudes toward other groups that often accompany the five sentiments just mentioned are:

1. Judging other groups by Oog's standards.
2. Belief that Oog is superior to other groups, in all ways or in some ways.
3. Ignorance of other groups.
4. Lack of interest in other groups.
5. Hostility toward other groups.

Negative Ethnocentrism

It is not true, as is often assumed, that every group, people, or society considers itself superior in some generalized sense to all others or even to most others. There are many well-documented instances in which positive loyalty to the ingroup goes along with some appreciation of outgroup values and practices. One's own group does provide the norms for judging other groups, and in various particular ways an outgroup may be seen as superior. For instance, a tribe that prides itself upon its skill in the building of boats can recognize that the products of another tribe represent superior craftsmanship. This admission need not result in a general devaluation of Oog; it is negative ethnocentrism only in its admission of specific points of inferiority. One still retains one's ingroup standards and a basic adherence to its values.[5]

Yet, the phenomena of self-hatred and self-deprecation of one's own membership group are common and must be taken into account. History is replete with voluntary exiles, expatriates, outgroup emulators, social climbers, renegades, and traitors. Also, the dominant attitude in a whole people can be one of accepting at least some of the low evaluations of outsiders. Peter A.

[5] Cf. Marc J. Swartz, "Negative Ethnocentrism," *The Journal of Conflict Resolution*, V, No. 1 (March, 1961), 75–81.

Munch has given a fascinating account of such attitudes among the inhabitants of the remote island of Tristan da Cahuna.[6] Among the villagers in southern Italy whose amoral familism has been described by Edward C. Banfield, the desire to emigrate, the awareness of poverty, and the deprecation of the local society are evident.[7] Other examples can be found, as in numerous instances of tribal peoples overwhelmed by conquest and subordinated to technologically advanced rulers. But the most important manifestations of negative sentiments toward the individual's own membership group occur in subordinated minority groups that are objects of prejudice and discrimination. [This negative ethnocentrism is discussed further in later sections of Williams' book. Ed.]

DOES POSITIVE ETHNOCENTRISM NECESSARILY RESULT IN PREJUDICE?

Whether strong negative feelings toward an outgroup always develop along with positive feelings of ethnocentrism is a question that has been explored in numerous studies. On the one hand we have Mary Ellen Goodman's study of Negro and white children, which showed that racial preferences were associated with hostility in only a minority of cases.[8] On the other hand, William Graham Sumner is usually singled out among American sociologists as favoring the idea that ingroup solidarity is related to outgroup hostility. What he says, however, is somewhat ambiguous: "The relationship of comradeship and

[6] *Sociology of Tristan Da Cahuna* (Oslo, Norway: Det Norske Videnskaps-Akademi I Kommisjon Hos Jacob Dywab, 1945).

[7] *The Moral Basis of a Backward Society* (New York: Free Press of Glencoe, Inc., 1958).

[8] Mary Ellen Goodman, *Race Awareness in Young Children* (Cambridge, Mass.: Addison-Wesley Publishing Company, Inc., 1952).

peace in the we-group and that of hostility toward others-groups are correlative to each other." [9] Sumner was thinking primarily of preliterate groups with relatively clear boundaries in situations in which threat and counterthreat affected the group as a whole. Even so, his statement bears the marks of caution: he says "are correlative" rather than "necessarily occur together." The consensus of studies, however, seems to be that continued interaction between culturally distinctive peoples need not result in conflict. One group may be assimilated by another, or there are even rare examples of sustained contacts between two endogamous and ethnocentric peoples with little conflict and little or no assimilation of one culture to the other.[10] Such accommodative relations seem to rest upon an economic interdependence that is mutually advantageous and essentially noncompetitive. Much more common, unfortunately, are asymmetrical relations in which cultural differences become signals for discriminating behavior by members of a more powerful collectivity.[11]

Whether or not prejudice results is dependent on such complicated factors as 1) the nature of the social system of which the groups are a part, 2) the extent to which one group is a threat (economically or otherwise) to the other, and 3) the degree of understanding or misunderstanding of one group toward another. [Other significant factors that are discussed in subsequent chapters are the personality structures and dynamics of individuals within the groups. Ed.]

[9] *Folkways*, p. 12.
[10] The case usually cited as an example has been described by E. J. Lindgren, "An Example of Culture Contact Without Conflict," *American Anthropologist*, XV, No. 5 (October–December, 1938), 605–21. See also: John Gillin, "Race Relations Without Conflict: A Guatemalan Town," *American Journal of Sociology*, LIII, No. 5 (March, 1948), 337–43.
[11] Cf. Hilda Kuper, *Indian People in Natal* (Pietermartzburg: University of Natal Press, 1960).

The Nature of the Social System

When ethnic distinctions have been built into the cultural definitions and the norms of routine behavior in a social system, prejudiced attitudes and discriminatory behavior will be characteristic of normal personalities in that system. The manifestation of prejudice is not necessarily a symptom of unusual psychological needs or of neurotic or psychotic tendencies. When prejudice is normal in a society its manifestations are found among the respectable members of the population who are most firmly embedded in and committed to the legitimate organizations and conventional behavior characteristic of that social system. (Conversely, as shown by the findings in Southport, low prejudice is found most often among persons who are most likely to be free from the most constrained adherence to the general conventions of the community.) That is, when ethnic differences are the result of deeply rooted historical cleavages, it is usual for prejudice to accompany ethnocentrism.

Threat

If for any reason two clearly distinguished social categories or collectivities are so situated in a society that their members frequently come into competition, the likelihood is high that negative stereotyping (a common variety of prejudice) will reinforce a sense of difference and that hostile attitudes will tend to restrict interaction and/or cause conflict. Whether the competition is economic, political, sexual, or for prestige, if one group perceives another as a threat, prejudice results. A central implication of Rokeach's extensive résumé of research on dogmatism is that a closed belief system is a consequence of threat.[12] It is implied by this formula-

[12] Milton Rokeach, *The Open and Closed Mind: Investigations into the Nature of Belief Systems and Personality Systems* (New York: Basic Books, Inc., 1960).

tion that the greater the threat: 1) the more rigid the belief system that develops in response, 2) the more intense the affects supporting the beliefs, and 3) the more punitive the sanctions against disbelief.

Certain individuals and segments of the population will be so located in the social structure as to be especially likely to attach the meaning of threat, injury, deprivation, or punishment to the presence and behavior of one or more ethnic groups. Concretely, this most often means economic competition. For example, a white union member on strike sees "his" job taken by a Negro; a Protestant businessman believes his profits are reduced by the competition offered by a Jewish merchant. Or the so-called realistic threat may be noneconomic, such as when legislation thought to have been passed at the public behest of Catholic spokesmen confronts the Protestant with legal restrictions on dissemination of birth-control information or materials. Another example might be the Mexican-American father who is deeply concerned with the preservation of customary roles of women and fears the example set for his daughters by Anglo-American schoolmates.

When two ethnocentric groups come into a mutually threatening relationship, the stage for group conflict is fully set.[13] Short of the cycle of threat-hostility-threat that is the classical prelude to group conflict—from gang fights, to riots, to global wars—we can observe a quieter prejudice, stabilized in systems of preferential ranking and preferential social access and personal association.

Understanding and Misunderstanding

The notion that understanding will always lead to the reduction of prejudice

and/or the diminution of conflict has limitations that are often overlooked, ignored, or underestimated. Deadly enemies often understand one another all too well. Conversely, some groups manage to live together in a state of uneasy but tolerable accommodation when an accurate and detailed knowledge of each other's real sentiments and intentions would precipitate severe conflict. Understanding will reduce antipathy and the likelihood of conflict only if the groups like or respect what they discover by understanding each other or if one group finds that the threat posed by the other, though real, is not so severe, unalterable, or immediate as previously believed.

When persons feel themselves to be members of a group and identify themselves with that group's corporate views or policies in competition with another group, they necessarily find it difficult to comprehend the other group's position. An ingenious experiment by Blake and Manton[14] suggests that under these conditions a loss in competition leads to hostility both toward impartial judges and toward the winning group, ". . . with feelings expressed that the decision was completely unjustified in the light of the 'evidence.'" Even though the members of the competing groups reported that they understood the competitor's view as well as they understood those of their own group, they, in fact, did not. In all groups, the members knew their own group's position best and were inclined toward distortion in their comprehension of the other group's position.

Misunderstanding another group's beliefs and values / Many observers, noting the relative unimportance of skin

[13] H. M. Blalock, Jr., "A Power Analysis of Racial Discrimination," *Social Forces*, XXXIX, No. 1 (October, 1960), 58.

[14] Robert R. Blake and Jane Srygley Manton, "Comprehension of Own and of Outgroup Positions under Intergroup Competition," *Journal of Conflict Resolution*, V, No. 3 (September, 1961), 309.

color biology—and the failure of scientific studies to produce significant evidence of genetically determined racial differences in intelligence—have been puzzled to observe that many individuals persist in exhibiting prejudice toward those with physical racial characteristics. In studies done by Rokeach it has been revealed that prejudice may not be a result of the fact that the other person is of a different racial category, national origin, or religious group affiliation but a result of the prejudiced person's assuming that the other individual's beliefs and values are incongruent with his own.[15] He found that white students both in the North and in the South prefer a Negro with similar beliefs to a white person with different beliefs. But in most situations many white persons would take it for granted that the Negro person did differ from them in basic ways. Thus misunderstanding or

[15] Rokeach, *The Open and Closed Mind.*

lack of knowledge of the outgroup frequently results in prejudice.

Possibly one can now see why a wide range of concepts and types of data must be dealt with in order to begin to understand the causes and the nature of prejudice. Intergroup behavior involves three great systems of human social action: the culture, the social system, and the personality system. Accordingly, we need to study cultural content—"stereotypes," beliefs, and evaluations; and we need to study personality as related to cultural content and to social interaction. We must analyze interaction both in terms of general patterns of intergroup contact and in terms of specific situations. And even while we deal with each of these sets of factors, we must remember that they all are simultaneously engaged in those person-to-person communications that are conceived by the participants to have an intergroup character.

PATERNALISTIC VS. COMPETITIVE RACE RELATIONS

Pierre L. van den Berghe

Advanced societies place a premium on efficient production for a very large market composed of masses of the population. The goal of high output at low cost theoretically encourages impersonal universalism. That is, for the sake of efficiency and the maintenance of high levels of motivation, people are judged, employed, and paid on the basis of their effort and talent alone. Ascribed status characteristics, such as racial background, tend to become less and less relevant. Furthermore, since the market is also the labor force, but with workers in their roles as family heads and consumers, economic growth will be held back if large portions of the population never get the chance to earn enough to be effective consumers.

It is not only the economy that has to be considered, for the political system and certain not always intentional consequences of advanced industrialization also come into play. For example, aside from whatever values of freedom and equality modern states may have in their heritage, they have an additional incentive for incorporating all of their population in the nationally shared political and social patterns we know as citizenship. Citizenship, with its promise of some control over governmental agencies that regulate the economy and its productive and distributive processes, helps to maintain high motivation levels through the prospect of fair reward for fair effort. It is also a helpful means of insuring high ability levels through universal education. Finally, advanced technology carries with it population concentration and modern methods of mass communication. These conditions favor the development

Source: In its present form, the article appeared for the first time in the previous edition of this volume. It is reprinted with the permission of the author. The original version appeared in *Social Forces*.

PIERRE VAN DEN BERGHE is Professor of Sociology at the University of Washington. Among his writings are *Caneville, Race and Ethnicity,* and *Race and Racism.*

of class, status, or racial consciousness among members of subordinate groups. Frequently these groups are drawn into the modern economy from more laggard sectors and regions, but they do not yet share equally in it or in the social and political benefits that are generally available to the better off.

Because of all these tendencies, race relations that involve the subordination of one group to another constitute a strain for modern societies. In these societies, racial subordination is not as easily managed or as easily rationalized as under the conditions that favor paternalism; also, it seems to make less sense in terms of a strict cost-benefit accounting system that takes the whole society into account.

Nevertheless, not all societies resolve the strain by fully incorporating their subordinate groups, thereby, of course, ending their subordination. The United States is one example. Here in America past patterns of deprivation and exploitation make it more difficult for black and brown people to compete with others in structures and organizations demanding skills that white people have been able to obtain more easily. In addition, some white people do profit directly from continued discrimination. Perhaps among most white people, however, the strongest support for racism's continuation is simply that the economic and prestige costs of wiping out black and brown disadvantage are greater than people are ready to bear and vote for. More than out-of-pocket costs are involved; consider as well an indirect advantage such as being able to insure that one's children will get more and better schooling than other people's children, thereby getting a better crack at a higher-level, higher-paying job.

Nazi Germany provides a more drastic example of how the tendencies that favor full sociopolitical equality in modern societies may not bear fruit. There an entire nation was urged to war. Totalitarian control was both goal in itself and means for assuring the national solidarity that was assumed to be necessary for Nazi world hegemony. A trumped-up notion of racial purity was used to increase a sense of superiority and cohesion among "Aryan" Germans. Nazi anti-Semitism became the most shocking example of genocide the modern world has ever seen. The attempt to impose the "final solution" eliminated not only the German Jewish minority, which had in fact been made up of almost fully participating members of German society before 1930, but also millions of other Jews throughout Nazi-conquered Europe.

These two examples are alone [1] enough to show that

[1] For another example, see Van den Berghe's discussion of the Union of South Africa in his *Race and Racism* (New York: John Wiley and Sons, 1967).

although a shift from paternalistic to competitive race relations may seem a step forward in societal evolution, the industrialization that causes the shift is not sufficient to resolve racial problems originating at an earlier time. Regional political culture, traditional heritages, past and present international relations and foreign policy—all these and other matters must also be considered.

The main thrust of Van den Berghe's paper is his attempt to construct "ideal types" of the paternalistic and competitive forms of race relations. His closely related second aim is to indicate the contexts in which each is most likely to be found.

The author suggests that the paternalistic form of race relations occurs more frequently in traditionalistic societies with one-crop agricultural economies, while competitive forms occur in societies with more advanced techniques of production and more complex divisions of labor.

The forms of prejudice are constructed as "ideal types," that is, as conceptual abstractions emphasizing some common features of empirical phenomena, but not necessarily corresponding to empirical reality in all their specifics. Such types are useful analytical tools, for they call attention to phenomena that may have been overlooked before. In the hands of a skilled builder of typologies, they can also help indicate whether all the features attributed to a particular social phenomenon are necessarily logically associated with it.

Our general contention is that manifestations of racial prejudice have historically polarized around two ideal-types which we shall call *"paternalistic"* and *"competitive."* The choice of labels is always a difficult one. Rather than use arbitrary symbols, and thereby hinder readability, we adopted two words which are in some way descriptive of our two types. Obviously the common sense meanings of the labels do not exhaust the content of the two types.[1]

[1] The labels "paternalistic" and "competitive" will be used in conjunction with the term "prejudice" when the psychological reference is emphasized, and with the term "race relations" when sociological or social system factors are stressed. This paper is a revised version of Chapter Two of my doctoral dissertation: *The Dy-* namics of Race Relations: An Ideal-Type Case Study of South Africa, Harvard University, 1959. An earlier version of the theory was presented in my article: "The Dynamics of Racial Prejudice: An Ideal-Type Dichotomy," *Social Forces,* 37, (December, 1958), 138–41.

THE PATERNALISTIC TYPE: ITS CHARACTERISTICS

The paternalistic type is incompatible with a complex manufacturing economy and with large-scale industrial capitalism. The most congenial form of economy is agricultural, pastoral, or handicraft. Mercantile capitalism and a large-scale plantation agriculture geared at the export of staple products (cotton, coffee, rubber, sugar, etc.) are also compatible with the paternalistic type. This type of economy coincides with an "intermediate" level of differentiation in the division of labour. By "intermediate" is meant here a degree of specialization which has gone considerably beyond a "primitive" division of labour based primarily on sex and age criteria, and yet which is not as complex as in the case of large-scale manufacturing industry.

Typically, in this intermediate stage of the division of labour, the mass of the labour force still consists of a fairly unspecialized, servile or quasi-servile peasantry. But there is already considerable differentiation. Handicraft production is in the hands of full-time specialized artisans. Trading is concentrated in the hands of merchant class, though the latter is often not very powerful. A rudimentary professional specialization is present. Warriors, priests, judges, and officials constitute the ruling group. This "intermediate" stage corresponds to what Weber called the "traditional" type of authority and is exemplified by most large-scale pre-modern societies. This stage implies both urbanization and fairly advanced social stratification. In paternalistic interracial situations with which we are concerned, the division of labour is along racial lines. A servile or quasi-servile racial caste (serfs, slaves, indentured labourers, "recruited" labour, *peones*, etc.) performs the heavy manual labour, in particular, the agricultural tasks.[2]

The dominant upper caste confines itself to such occupations as war, the priesthood, the professions, government, supervision of labour, and commerce. The upper caste is, in fact, a ruling aristocracy, usually a small minority of the total population. This ruling caste

is fairly homogeneous in social status. Class distinctions within the ruling caste are secondary to the paramount caste distinctions between the racial groups.[3]

A wide and unbreachable gap exists between the castes, as indicated by living standards, income, occupations, education, death rates, etc. There is a horizontal colour bar with no inter-caste mobility. Intra-caste mobility is possible but limited, as there is little status differentiation within the castes. A slave can be manumitted, or gain a privileged position as house servant, skilled craftsman, foreman, etc., but he remains in a subordinate position. Spatial mobility is also limited, serfs are attached to the land, slaves and servants to their masters. Such a non-mobile labour is clearly incompatible with large-scale industry, which requires a flexible allocation of resources.

The form of government found in a paternalistic society is aristocratic or oligarchic. Autocratic authority of Weber's "traditional" type prevails, either in a centralized form as in colonial governments, or in a decentralized "feudal" form. The legal system is on the side of the racial *status quo*. The lower caste has a clearly defined legal status which entails both rights and obligations, though the latter are often more numerous than the former. Nevertheless, the lower caste is protected under law and punished within the framework of the law.

Paternalistic attitudes and stereotypes are well integrated in the value system of the society. Elaborate sets of

[2] In agreement with Dollard, Warner, Myrdal and others, we shall call "caste" a group which satisfies all three of the following criteria: 1) endogamy, 2) membership therein by birth and for life, and 3) a position of superiority or inferiority *vis à vis* other such groups.

[3] Professor Parsons suggested to us an important distinction between social stratification as a product of internal differentiation in the social system and social stratification imposed from the outside. In the latter case, the hierarchy is likely to be rigid. In fact, most caste or quasi-caste systems, such as estates, have their origin in conquest. The greater the disparity in physical characteristics, level of organization, technology, etc., between conqueror and conquered, the greater is the likelihood of a caste system to arise. Of course, a caste system may perpetuate itself long after these differences have been blurred, as exemplified by India.

rationalizations come to the defence of the racial *status quo*, and are subjectively, if not logically, consistent with the basic religious and ethical promises of the society. Examples of such rationalizations are the "white man's burden" theory, the "civilizing mission of the West," the "Christianizing of the Heathen," etc. In short, there is no ideological conflict between the existing norms of prejudice and the basic value system of the society.

Racial roles and statuses are sharply defined. An elaborate and rigid etiquette of race relations stabilizes the master-servant relationship. Indeed, etiquette seems to be the primary mechanism of social control to maintain intimacy of contact coupled with status inequality.[4] To borrow Talcott Parsons' pattern variables, roles are based on ascription, particularism, diffuseness, collectivity orientation, and affectivity.

Spacial segregation is minimal because the wide status gap allows close but unequal contact. In other words, spacial distance can be thought of as an alternative mechanism of social control to status distance. Slaves and servants live in close intimacy with their masters, particularly household servants. Although caste endogamy (i.e., prohibition of intermarriage) is rigidly adhered to, miscegenation between upper-caste males and lower-caste females is condoned and frequent. It takes the form of institutionalized concubinage, and is accepted at all class levels within the upper caste. Wealthy masters interbreed freely with their female slaves without any opprobrium or fear of censure. This miscegenation leads to the rise of a group of half-breeds who generally remain in the lower caste but with privileged status.

[4] Cf. Robert E. Park, *Race and Culture*, Glencoe, Ill.: The Free Press, 1950, p. 183; Bertrand W. Doyle, *The Etiquette of Race Relations in the South*, Chicago: University of Chicago Press, 1937; and Pierre L. van den Berghe, "Distance Mechanisms of Stratification," *Sociology and Social Research*, 44, 1960, pp. 155–164.

The half-breeds may, by intermarriage among themselves, constitute an intermediate caste of their own. Some half-breeds can and do, of course, become assimilated to the upper caste through "passing," and when interbreeding has been extensive for several generations, the racial caste system may eventually break down. Such complete interbreeding has only rarely taken place wherever physical characteristics of the groups in presence were widely different. The closest approximation to it is the "colour continuum" situation which prevails in Haiti, Mexico, or to a somewhat lesser extent, in Brazil.

Generally speaking, race relations in the paternalistic type are stable. The lower caste is "accommodated" to its inferior status which it may ever internalize. What Dollard has called "white folks manner," and Kardiner and Ovesey, the "mark of oppression," are illustrations of such internalized subservient status.[5] To use the Southern United States phraseology, the "old time darky knows his place." The converse of accommodation on the part of the lower caste is paternalism on the part of the upper caste. The upper caste adopts an attitude of benevolent despotism towards members of the lower caste whom it treats as perpetual children. Stereotypes of members of the lower caste describe them as immature, exuberant, impulsive, uninhibited, lazy, fun-loving, good-humoured, happy-go-lucky. In short, they are inferior but lovable. They ought to be treated sternly and kindly at the same time. Corporal punishment is to be used as one uses it to keep one's own children in line.

This paternalistic prejudice might also be described as "pseudo-tolerance." The slave, or servant, is acceptable "in his place," even "loved" in a condescending way. It should be fairly

[5] John Dollard, *Caste and Class in a Southern Town*, New Haven: Yale University Press, 1937; Abraham Kardiner and Lionel Ovesey, *The Mark of Oppression*, New York: Norton, 1951.

apparent that this paternalistic "syndrome" bears little relation to "authoritarianism," "high F," etc. The psychological characteristics of the bigot which have come out of research in the United States are, we think, more typical of a competitive situation when the "ethos" of the culture is opposed to prejudice. This is not to say that no "high F's" will be found in a paternalistic situation, but rather that within a paternalistic society the "authoritarian" syndrome will not be a good predictor of racial attitudes, opinions and behaviour. It would also be a misunderstanding of our position to interpret us as saying that psychological variables are not operative in the paternalistic type of prejudice. In fact, we suspect that there might be a corresponding psychological syndrome in the paternalistic type. Roger Bastide, a psychoanalytically oriented social scientist, has suggested that paternalistic master-servant relationships are an extension of the nuclear family situation.[6] He suggests an ambivalent oedipal relationship between master and slave in the plantation situation, and an incest taboo between white mistress and male slaves. We are not equipped to pass judgement on such interpretations. But although our own primary theoretical focus is sociological, we do not deny the operation of psychological factors or the existence of individual differences in the paternalistic situation.

An important note of caution should be added here. The romantic myth of the kindly master who led an existence of genteel leisure on his plantation amidst the happy singing of his slaves, should of course be dismissed. Violence and aggression do occur in the paternalistic type. But they take different forms than in the competitive case. They generally originate from the lower caste, and are not directly and specifically

[6] Roger Bastide, *Sociologie et Psychanalyse*, Paris: Presses Universitaires de France, 1950, pp. 241–245.

racial in character. Slave rebellions and nationalistic, revivalistic, or messianic movements are typical of the paternalistic type, and indicate a lack of complete integration of the society. Such movements are usually repressed with utmost vigor by the upper caste, because if they are allowed to develop, they tend to lead to a violent and cataclysmic overthrow of the "old regime" as exemplified by the Haitian revolution.

Generally speaking, however, the paternalistic type of prejudice can be said to be "adjustive," "functional," or "integrative" for the social system. This statement implies, of course, no value judgement. We simply mean that, barring external influences and other disruptive factors such as industrialization, the more the racial ideology is believed in and practiced in a paternalistic society, the more integrated and stable the social system is. In other words, the more the hierarchial norms have been internalized in the personalities of both upper- and lower-caste members, the greater the stability of the social system, everything else remaining constant. But this inherent stability of the paternalistic type is accompanied by inherent inflexibility and inadaptability, i.e., when the system is attacked from the outside, as is colonialism today, or when internal developments such as industrialization are incompatible with paternalism, the whole social system collapses altogether, or evolves into a competitive situation.

Examples of the paternalistic type of racial prejudice are the slave plantation regimes of the ante-bellum U.S. South, of the West Indies, of Brazil; the "encomienda" or "hacienda" system in various parts of Spanish America; the colonial regimes of the various European powers in Africa, some of which, such as the former Belgian Congo, have survived in fairly pure form to the recent past. All the preceding examples were taken from Western societies because the cases are more familiar. But paternalism is not limited to Western societies. In Ruanda-Urundi (Central Africa) for example, the Watuzi, a group of pastoralists famous for their tall stature, have imposed their domination over an overwhelming majority of shorter and physically quite distinguishable Bahutu. The latter, who were already tillers of land before the Watuzi conquest, have become the serfs of the Watuzi; the situation is typically paternalistic.

Likewise, paternalism as a type of relationship is not limited to interracial situations as we shall see later.

THE COMPETITIVE TYPE: ITS CHARACTERISTICS

In our ideal-type dichotomy, the competitive type is the polar opposite of the paternalistic type. Generally, the competitive type is found in large-scale manufacturing economy based on industrial capitalism. However, competitive prejudice has existed in pre-industrial societies. The case of the Jews in medieval Europe, though not "racial" according to our definition of the word, was competitive. The problem whether the competitive type is linked with capitalism, as a Marxist might contend, is not easy to settle empirically. Ethnic relations in the Soviet Union and Soviet policies toward the "nationalities" are not easy to investigate. However, the U.S.S.R. has known waves of anti-Semitism indicative of competitive prejudice. At any rate, urbanization seems a prerequisite for a competitive situation, and, empirically, the latter is very much associated with an industrial and capitalistic society.

The division of labour is complex and based on "rational" and "universalistic" criteria as required by a differentiated manufacturing economy. The bulk of the labour force is no longer unskilled, and technical competence and efficiency become paramount criteria of selection. Hence any rigid racial division of labour based on ascription and particularism cannot be maintained without entailing serious economic dysfunctions. Racial criteria of selection are not altogether absent, however. Indeed, they can be operative, due to prejudice, but they can only be maintained at a cost to the efficiency of the system of production and the tendency is toward a breakdown of the industrial colour bar. As a corollary of the above factors, there is much mobility, both social and spacial. Any complex industrial economy based on "organic solidarity" requires a spacially and socially mobile labour force, i.e., one which is responsive to the demand for labour and skills. Again, social mobility is hampered by racial prejudice but only at a cost to the production system, and the tendency is towards *"la carrière ouverte aux talents."*

In typical form, the competitive situation is accompanied by a caste system, but the distance between the castes in education, occupation, income, living standards, death rates, etc., tends to diminish, i.e., the colour bar tends to tilt from a horizontal to a vertical position, though the vertical position has never been fully achieved. Within each colour caste, there is more and more class differentiation. In other words, the status gap *between* castes tends to diminish and the status range *within* the castes tends to increase. With the tilting of the colour bar, an upper-class-lower-caste person may have a higher education, occupation, living standard, etc., than a lower-class-upper-caste person. Hence, there often comes about a "status panic" of lower-class persons from the upper caste, who feel threatened by rising lower-caste members as soon as class status and caste status cease to have a one-to-one correspondence. Though threat to status is probably not the whole story, it goes a long way to account for the higher virulence of competitive prejudice among "poor whites" in the United States, for example.

The dominant caste, in the competitive situation, is usually a majority which has within itself great status and class differences. The upper caste is not a homogenous ruling group as in the paternalistic case. On the contrary, a large segment of the upper caste engages in manual labour, and hence is in direct competition with members of the lower caste. The sheer numerical ratio between the castes makes this situation inevitable. A certain percentage of the population must engage in manual occupations, and only a minority can be "on top."

In some interracial situations where miscegenation has been so extensive as to blur physical distinctions, and where the criteria of group membership are at least partly cultural rather than purely racial, the rigid colour caste system has broken down in part. This has been the case to some extent in most of Latin America. In Mexico, for example, a *mestizo* or *ladino* can be a full-blooded Indian, provided he speaks fluent Spanish and is acculturated to Hispanic ways. But that still does not make him a "Spaniard." Prejudice is still present though it is a mixture of ethnic and racial prejudice, and a quasi-caste system exists, though in much less rigid form than in the United States.

The competitive type is usually accompanied by ideological conflict, at least in a Western, "Christian," "democratic," and "liberal" sort of society. This conflict was the central core of Myrdal's analysis of the U.S. situation.[7] Whether the ideological conflict is simply a "superstructural" reflection of the more basic incompatibility between the production system and prejudice, as the Marxist line of argument would run, is an open question, and one which cannot easily be settled empirically.

[7] Gunnar Myrdal, *An American Dilemma,* New York: Harper, 1944, pp. 21, 39, 84–89, 460, 614, 899.

The form of government found in a competitive situation is generally a restricted or partial democracy from which the lower caste is excluded by various means, and to a greater or lesser degree. The lower caste has generally no definite legal status. Discriminatory legislation can be passed but usually without explicitly mentioning race as the basis of exclusion. Devious devices such as poll taxes, re-zoning, and the like are used. Extra-legal sanctions against the minority are resorted to, such as lynching in the Southern United States. The law generally is on the side of the general value system of the society and hence opposed to the prejudice norms. In terms of Max Weber's typology, the form of authority found in the competitive type is "rational-legal."

Racial roles and statues are ill-defined and in a constant state of flux. In terms of Parsons' pattern variables, they are based on achievement, universalism, specificity, self-orientation, and affective neutrality. There is no elaborate etiquette. Rather, members of the lower caste are in constant doubt as to the behaviour expected from them. Conversely, members of the upper caste are in constant difficulty as to how to address educated lower-caste members, for example. The old etiquette is no longer applicable, and no new one has been evolved.

Unequal caste status is constantly assailed by the levelling forces discussed above. Since etiquette has broken down as a mechanism to maintain intimate unequal contacts, spacial segregation is resorted to in order to minimize interracial contacts which threaten to become equal, and which are replete with uneasiness, ambiguity, and tension because of mutual prejudices.[8] Suspicion, hatred,

[8] If one conceives of spacial distance and social distance as alternative mechanisms of social control in a racial caste situation, certain theoretical considerations follow. Both mechanisms are based on the ascriptive criterion of race, and hence involve a "cost" in efficiency, at least in

antagonism prevail between the racial groups. Competition, real or imaginary, for status, for jobs, for women, etc., or the threat of competition, poison race relations. Miscegenation is severely condemned and infrequent. If it takes place at all, it will assume the form of transitory or commercialized contacts between the fringe members of both castes (e.g., between poor whites and Negro prostitutes in the United States). Lasting concubinage is not institutionalized. A few cases of intermarriage will occur, at the cost of much disapproval, and usually among fringe groups (artists, bohemians, political radicals, low-class white immigrants, etc.).

Forms of aggression are numerous and originate both from the upper and from the lower caste. The basis of such aggression involves specifically racial issues. Besides the more violent manifestations of prejudice, such as sabotage, bombing, lynchings, race riots and pogroms, other forms of resistance and antagonism are organized mass protests, strikes, passive resistance, etc. The lower caste often seems to turn also to in-group aggression as a response to frustration. Typical of the competitive situation is a recurrent pattern of increase and decrease in prejudice which is in contrast

with the relatively stable level of prejudice in the paternalistic case. In the competitive case, prejudice against groups seems to build up to a point of dangerous tension in response to such conditions as rapid influx of lower-caste migrants, unemployment, etc. The slightest incident will then trigger off interracial violence. Such a gradual building up of tension seems to precede most race riots, pogroms, waves of terrorism, and the like.

Naturally, competitive prejudice, irrespective of these cyclical trends, can operate at an average level which is lower in one society than in another. (E.g., anti-Semitism is stronger in Germany than in France, but still there has been a Dreyfus affair in France. Anti-Negro prejudice is stronger in the United States than in Brazil, but is far from absent in the latter country).

Stereotypes held about the lower caste are coloured by fear. Lower-caste members are held to aggressive, "uppity," insolent, oversexed, dirty. In short, they are despicable and dangerous as well as inferior. Clearly, stereotypes and prejudice are reciprocal. Lower-caste members describe upper-caste members as overbearing, "bullying," brutal, etc.

It appears that competitive prejudice is linked with "authoritarian" personality variables in members of the upper caste. This relationship is probably even closer when the values of total society are opposed to prejudice. In the United States, this aspect of prejudice has been widely studied and the link between competitive prejudice and sexuality, sadism, "anality," etc., has been established. Scape-goating and frustration-aggression are clearly not complete explanations of prejudice even at the psychological level, but the relevance of these psychological mechanisms is beyond question. One may speak of a personality "need," or, as Allport puts it, of the "functional significance" of prej-

the sense of economic rationality. To quote Linton, "the ascription of status sacrifices the possibility of having certain roles performed superlatively well to the certainty of having them performed passably well." (Cf. Ralph Linton, *The Study of Man,* New York: Appleton-Century, 1936, p. 129). But social distance involves a great measure of functional differentiation insofar as the members of the various castes perform tasks which are largely complementary. Spacial distance, on the contrary, involves a large degree of segmentation without differentiation, insofar as tasks, facilities, and functions are duplicatory rather than complementary. If the above considerations are correct, they may in part account for the greater degree of in-built maladjustment in the competitive type of race relations. An industrial competitive type of society which "needs all the differentiation it can get" can afford the luxury of segmentation even less than a pre-industrial paternalistic society. Yet the tendency is towards spacial segregation as a substitute for social distance. This is one of the inherent paradoxes of the competitive type.

udice for the "high F's." [9] It is still an open question how this relationship between "authoritarianism" and competitive prejudice holds when the values of the society are not openly against prejudice. Fragmentary evidence from the Southern United States suggest, however, that the relationship becomes lesser. In other words, conformity to prejudicial norms in the Southern United States accounts for a good deal of anti-Negro prejudice. [10]

One point stands out clearly from our description of competitive prejudice; it is a highly "maladjusting" or "dysfunctional" phenomenon in an industrial society. Again, no value judgement is implied. Not for a moment would we assert that the paternalistic type is normally "better." By "maladjusting" we mean that the higher the level of competitive prejudice is, the less smoothly the social system will operate. Competitive prejudice, then, is a "luxury" which can only be bought at a price.

The reason for this built-in maladjustive factor in competitive prejudice lies primarily, we think, in the functional prerequisites of an industrial society which conflict with prejudicial norms. Mobility of labour and "rationality" of recruitment based on achievement and universalism are all in conflict with racial prejudice which is ascriptive and particularistic. Competitive prejudice finds itself in the inherently paradoxical position of operating both within a "rational-legal" system and against it.

Some empirical examples of competitive types of prejudice are the anti-Negro prejudice in the United States since the Civil War, the anti-Asiatic prejudice in California, anti-Semitism in Europe and the United States, anti-non-European prejudice in South Africa in recent years, and anti-Negro prejudice in Brazil, at

[9] Gordon W. Allport, *The Nature of Prejudice,* Cambridge: Addison-Wesley, 1954, pp. 285–286.
[10] Thomas F. Pettigrew, *Regional Differences in Anti-Negro Prejudice,* Harvard University, Unpublished Thesis, 1956.

least in the large industrial centers such as São Paulo, Santos, and Rio de Janeiro.

THE TWO TYPES OF PREJUDICE: A SUMMARY AND ANALYTICAL SCHEMA

Such a broad description of the two types of prejudice as we have presented is rather unmanageable for analytical purposes. We shall now attempt to isolate the main variables, classify them for purposes of analysis, and present a schema contrasting the two types side by side to insure that they do indeed constitute polar opposites and differ on the same dimensions.

We propose to classify the main variables of analysis into "dependent," "independent," and "social control" variables. Since these terms call to mind the experimental model, we should immediately emphasize that we are using them, for lack of better words, only in an analogical manner, not in a strict experimental sense. As variables interact, the words "dependent" and "independent" are interchangeable. In the present context, they are only meant to clarify the starting point of our analysis, and to disentangle somewhat the relationship between variables.

We shall call "dependent variables" those that are directly concerned with race relations and prejudice, such as stereotypes, patterns of segregation, psychological syndromes, etc. They are the variables which we shall attempt to "predict" *ex post facto* from the "independent variables." The latter are broader social structure variables, i.e., the social framework within which prejudice expresses itself. They are the type of economy, the division of labour, the social stratification, etc. Lest we be accused of economic, sociological, or some other form of determinism, we must again emphasize that the primacy we give to these "independent" variables is strictly heuristic, and in no way precludes reciprocal causation.

A third set of variables we shall call "social control" variables, though we depart again from the strict experimental model. By "social control" we mean here deliberate attempts to modify, restore, or preserve an existent set of social conditions. This set of variables includes primarily governmental action in its executive, legislative, and judicial forms. Here, then, follows the schema:

A. "Independent" Variables

	Paternalistic	Competitive
1. Economy	Non-manufacturing, agricultural, pastoral, handicraft; mercantile capitalism; plantation economy.	Typically manufacturing, but not necessarily so. Large-scale industrial capitalism.
2. Division of labour	Simple ("primitive") or intermediate (as in pre-industrial large-scale societies). Division of labour along racial lines. Wide income gap between racial groups.	Complex (manufacturing) according to "rational" universalistic criteria. Narrow gap in wages. No longer strictly racial.
3. Mobility	Little mobility either vertical or horizontal (slaves, servants, or serfs "attached" in space).	Much mobility both vertical and horizontal (required by industrial economy).
4. Social stratification	Caste system with horizontal colour bar. Aristocracy vs. servile caste with wide gap in living standards (as indexed by income, education, death and birth rates). Homogeneous upper caste.	Caste system but with tendency for colour bar to "tilt" to vertical position. Complex stratification into classes within castes. Narrower gaps *between* castes and greater range *within* castes.
5. Numerical ratio	Dominant group a small minority.	Dominant group a majority.
6. Value conflict	Integrated value system. No ideological conflict.	Conflict at least in Western, "Christian," "democratic," "liberal" type of society.

B. "Dependent" Variables

	Paternalistic	Competitive
1. Race relations	Accommodation. Everyone in his place and "knows it." Paternalism. Benevolent despotism.	Antagonism. Suspicion, hatred. Competitiveness (real or imaginary).
2. Roles and statuses	Sharply defined roles and statuses based on ascription, particularism, diffuseness, collectivity orientation, affectivity. Unequal status unthreatened.	Ill-defined and based on achievement, universalism, specificity, self-orientation, affective neutrality. Unequal status threatened.
3. Etiquette	Elaborate and definite.	Simple and indefinite.
4. Forms of aggression	Generally from lower caste: slave rebellions, nationalistic, revivalistic or messianic movements. Not directly racial. "Righteous" punishment from the master.	Both from upper and lower caste. More frequent and directly racial: riots, lynchings, pogroms. Passive resistance, sabotage, organized mass protests.

B. "Dependent" Variables (Continued)

	Paternalistic	Competitive
5. Miscegenation	Condoned and frequent between upper-caste males and lower-caste females. Institutionalized concubinage.	Severely condemned and infrequent.
6. Segregation	Little of it. Status gap allows close but unequal contact.	Much of it. Narrowing of status gap makes for increase of spacial gap.
7. Psychological syndrome	Internalized subservient status. No personality "need" for prejudice. No "high F." "Pseudo-tolerance."	"Need" for prejudice. "High F." Linked with sexuality, sadism, frustration. Scape-goating.
8. Stereotypes of lower caste	Childish, immature, exuberant, uninhibited, lazy, impulsive, fun-loving, good-humored. Inferior but lovable.	Aggressive, uppity, insolent, oversexed, dirty. Inferior, despicable, and dangerous.
9. Intensity of prejudice	Fairly constant.	Variable, and sensitive to provocative situations.

C. "Social Control" Variables

	Paternalistic	Competitive
1. Form of government	Aristocratic, oligarchic, autocratic. Either centralized or "feudal." Colonial.	Restricted or partial democracy.
2. Legal system	Lower caste has separate legal status. Law on side of racial *status quo*. Weber's "traditional" type of authority.	Lower caste has no separate legal status. Resort to extra-legal sanctions. Weber's "rational-legal" type of authority.

THE TWO TYPES OF PREJUDICE IN RELATION TO OTHER THEORETICAL SCHEMES

We have already indicated explicitly our borrowings from Parsons and from Weber. Weber's traditional type of authority tends to coincide with our paternalistic type of prejudice whereas his "rational-legal" type of authority both coincides and conflicts with competitive prejudice. Weber's third type of authority, the charismatic one, is unstable and rarely found in a pure state. Insofar as charisma is revolutionary and unstable, it is incompatible with our paternalistic type. An example of competitive prejudice under a system which had strong charismatic elements is anti-Semitism under National Socialism in Germany. But anti-Semitism was already present in the rational-legal Germany of pre-Hitler days. Hence, charisma and the competitive type are not incompatible, but the relationship is not a necessary one.

In our use of Parsons' pattern-variables, we have seen that they polarized along our two types. The pattern-variables are conceived of by Parsons as being *independently* variable, however. That such is the case in many of the possible applications of the scheme, we shall not dispute. But in application to racial roles, there does not seem to be independent variation.

Our dichotomy is obviously related to some of the classical distinctions in sociology. Our competitive type coincides largely with the type of social solidarity which Durkheim called "organic." However, the reverse relationship between paternalism and mechanical solidarity does not hold. Most cases of paternalistic prejudice are found in a functionally differentiated, though preindustrial, society with a division of labour which we have termed "intermedi-

	Paternalistic type	Competitive type
Max Weber's types of authority	Traditional	Rational-legal (occasionally: charismatic)
Parsons' pattern-variables	Ascription, particularism, affectivity, collective orientation, diffuseness.	Achievement, universalism, affective neutrality, self-orientation, specificity.
Durkheim's forms of solidarity	Mechanical-organic mixture	Organic
Toennies	Gemeinschaft	Gesellschaft
Redfield	Folk or urban	Urban

ate." Such a level of differentiation in the division of labour already contains strong "organic" elements, and no longer represents a primitive "mechanical" level of solidarity, at least not in anywhere near a pure state.

Redfield's "folk" *versus* "urban" distinction likewise bears only a partial relationship to our own typology. Although the competitive type is associated with urbanism, and although paternalism is compatible with a "folk" society, the paternalistic situation is also found in urban societies. As regards Toennies *Gemeinschaft-Gesellschaft* dichotomy, the correspondence to our two types is perhaps closer. The paternalistic type has many *Gemeinschaft* characteristics and a *Gesellschaft* society is most compatible with the competitive type.

Subject to the reservations mentioned above we may schematize the relationship between our dichotomy and the distinctions reviewed (see table above).

APPLICABILITY OF THE PATERNALISTIC-COMPETITIVE DISTINCTION AND THE PROBLEM OF "MIXED TYPES"

We must first answer the question: Is our scheme synchronic or diachronic?

The answer is that it is both. Historically, at least in Western societies since the first period of overseas expansion in the fifteenth century, the general tendency has been away from the paternalistic type and toward competitive prejudice. In that sense, then, our scheme is diachronic and evolutionary. But each of the two types can also be viewed as an existing situation in a given society. There is no *necessary* evolution from one type to the other. A competitive situation can prevail without having been preceded by a paternalistic one, as with Jews in medieval Europe; conversely, a paternalistic system can endure, barring disruptive factors, without leading to the competitive type, as between Watuzi and Bahutu in Ruanda-Urundi until the eve of independence.

There is another sense in which our scheme is to be regarded as synchronic. The two types of prejudice can co-exist within different segments of the same society, and toward different groups. One example comes to mind to illustrate this point, though it is not a case of racial prejudice. In medieval Europe, the prejudice against Jews in the cities was competitive, while the feudal lord-serf relationship in the rural areas was paternalistic.

We have already hinted that our scheme was applicable cross-culturally to non-Western societies. The argument that racial prejudice is a recent development limited to Western societies, and intended to rationalize the economic exploitation of subject peoples is only a half-truth. True, the pseudo-scientific theories of racial differences have attained their most thorough elaboration in the Western world with the writings of Gobineau and the popularization of social Darwinism. That such theories provided convenient justifications for the exploitation of "native" labour and slaves in the European colonies is likewise incontrovertible. But the exploitation preceded the development of the theories, and a simplistic view that the theories were devised with the Machiavellian purpose of justifying the colonial system is untenable. The main point, however, is that racial prejudice is much older than Gobineau, and not limited to the Western world. Whenever phenotypical differences have existed between groups of people, racial prejudice seems to have arisen. The Bantu groups of central Africa regard the pygmies who live among them as intermediate between chimpanzees and men. The Japanese express contempt for the bearded Ainu of Hokkaido. The Chinese expressed bewilderment at the sight of the first Europeans who landed in their country, and compared the Europeans to monkeys because of their hairiness. In India, there is considerable evidence that the caste system originated in racial differences between Aryan conquerors and Dravidians, though, of course, race alone does not account for the florescence of caste. In short, physically distinguishing characteristics are generally seized upon to perpetuate group differences, and establish the superiority of one group over the other.

Not only does our scheme apply to non-Western societies. It also applies

mutatis mutandis to forms of prejudice other than racial. The competitive ethnic and religious prejudice against Jews in Europe and the United States is an example of non-racial prejudice. Similarly, the paternalistic syndrome can be found in a wide variety of contexts: between the factory owner and his workers; between the company or ship commander and his men. In this study, however, we shall limit ourselves to specifically racial prejudice.[11]

The problem of "mixed types" is crucial in any ideal-type scheme. As ideal-types are logical constructs, it is important not to reify them. The fact that no empirical situation coincides exactly with one of the types does not invalidate a typology. But, as in any scientific theory, heuristic usefulness is a paramount consideration. A distinction should be made here between schemes that are constructed in terms of a continuum between two or more poles and schemes based on what we may call a "true typology." The first sort of scheme admits of all intermediate positions on the continuum; even a normal distribution where most cases are found in the middle of the continuum, and none at the extremes, is compatible with this sort of scheme.

A true typology, in the restricted sense in which we use that term, implies an empirical polarization of cases around the extremes, and qualitative rather than quantitative differences. "Mixed cases" must be inherently unstable and tend to move towards one of the ideal-types. We believe that our dichotomy

[11] This limitation of our subject matter is heuristic rather than substantive. We do not believe that racial prejudice is fundamentally different from the other forms of prejudice. We conceive rather of racial prejudice as a special case of a more general phenomenon. But the relative permanency of physical characteristics makes for a more rigid definition of groups, and for more clear-cut and enduring situations than in other forms of prejudice. For these reasons, racial prejudice is particularly well suited to scientific inquiry.

satisfies this condition. Societies have moved from the paternalistic to the competitive type of prejudice and hence must have gone through a "mixed" stage. But the social system as a whole tends to continue to evolve until the competitive situation is rather closely approximated. It cannot remain in a stable intermediate position between the polar opposites. Mixed types at the total society level of analysis can only be transitory. But there is another sense in which "mixed types" can occur. Subsystems within the society can belong in different types as in the case of medieval Europe mentioned earlier. Different groups within the same society can be the object of different types of prejudice. Also, in the case of a society in transition, different segments of the total society (e.g., rural *versus* urban) can be in different stages in the process of evolution. The isolated rural areas will tend to remain paternalistic longer than the industrial centers, for example. All these possibilities can make the overall characterization of a total society a complex matter. But again, this does not invalidate the criterion of polarization. It is only a question of defining the boundaries of the social system or sub-system under analysis.

3. LABOR UNIONS AND THE NEGRO

Hubert Blalock

In 1969, of nonwhite and white male workers, respectively, 14 percent and 21 percent were craftsmen and foremen, the census occupational category most likely to include members of craft unions; 28 percent and 19 percent were in the category called operatives, the group most likely to be members of industrial

Source: *Toward a Theory of Minority-Group Relations* (New York: John Wiley and Sons, Inc., 1967), pp. 84–92, with footnotes renumbered. Propositions are numbered as in the original. Copyright © 1967. Reprinted by permission of the author and publisher.

HUBERT BLALOCK is Professor of Sociology at the University of Washington. He is the author of *Social Statistics, An Introduction to Social Research,* and other works.

unions; 18 percent and 6 percent were nonfarm laborers, the blue-collar group least likely to be unionized.[1]

Four conclusions emerge from these figures: (1) Nonwhite minorities are underrepresented at the higher-ranking blue collar jobs, overrepresented at the lower ones. (2) They are therefore in greater need of whatever benefits union membership and organization might be able to bring them. (3) They are in any case only a minority of all the workers at a given level. (4) Hence, in order to improve their bargaining position they must somehow combine with their white peers.

In this selection, Blalock tries to indicate when such coalitions are most likely to occur. He does so through a set of propositions that are derived from "balance theory" on the one hand and knowledge about the American labor movement on the other. In the triad composed of managements, white labor, and black labor, the last group is most often the weakest one. It is therefore not surprising that Blalock's list of propositions contains relatively few based upon circumstances that clearly predict the emergence of majority-minority labor coalitions. However, at least two major national unions (steel and auto workers) are good examples of what happens when Blalock's conditions for coalition formation are met. The leadership of both has devoted considerable effort to providing equal occupational benefits to all the workers in their respective industries.

However, even in unions like the United Auto Workers where leadership ideology and labor force composition favor on-the-job equality, rank and file antipathy toward extending

[1] Bureau of Labor Statistics Report No. 375, *Current Population Reports,* Series p-23, No. 29, "The Social and Economic Status of Negroes in the United States, 1969," Washington, D.C., 1970; G.P.O. #1970—392-367/64. Census categories are useful for grasping general tendencies quickly, but are of more limited value for more specific formulations. For example, the category "professional and technical" includes a range that runs from stripteaser to neurosurgeon. A less absurd and more general point is that there are significant differences in the income and social rank of various professions, and these differences are associated with racial group member-ship. Thus, eliminate teachers and ministers from the category, and the minority professional and technical group would be much more sharply reduced in size than the white one. Leave them in, and the proportion of rather low-paid minority professionals is higher than the white.

Census racial categories also leave something to be desired. American Indians, blacks, and Orientals are "nonwhites," assigned to that category on the basis of census takers' impressions (till 1970, thereafter on the basis of the family head's self-designation on a questionnaire form). Mexican-Americans and Puerto Ricans are quite often treated as if they were non-white by the general population, yet they are officially counted as whites, and then an estimate of their numbers is made on the basis of the number of "Spanish surnames" in the population.

equal rights to blacks off the job is not uncommon.[2] Finally, although blacks have more readily found their way to leadership in unions than in any other major multiracial economic interest type of organization, they are quite underrepresented at the top. Harold Baron reports, for example, that in 1965, when about 20 percent of Cook County's population was black, "We asked several experts on the Chicago trade union movement to list the number of Negroes among the 100 most powerful trade unionists in the area. Among the 100 they named, the number of Negroes ranged from two to five."[3]

As for craft unions, on February 8, 1971, the Equal Opportunity Employment Commission reported that in referral unions, those which place their members on jobs, like most of the building trades unions, minorities were concentrated in unions at the lower end of the wage scale. Just two days later, at their Miami convention, the construction unions vowed to fight against the adoption of proposed new federal regulations requiring them to place a specified proportion of minority workers in their apprenticeship programs.

[2] See Dietrich C. Reitzes, "Union vs. Neighborhood in a Tension Situation," in the earlier edition of this book, pp. 389–96; also, John C. Leggett, *Class, Race and Labor* (New York: Oxford University Press, 1968).

[3] Harold M. Baron, "Black Powerlessness in Chicago," in Jerome Skolnick and Elliot Currie (eds.), *Crisis in American Institutions* (Boston: Little, Brown and Company, 1970), p. 81.

LABOR UNIONS AND THE NEGRO

The general picture of Negro-white labor relations in the United States is relatively clearcut and easily summarized. This is not to say, of course, that there are no exceptions to the rule. But exceptions have been relatively rare, and despite a slight overall trend in favor of upgrading of Negro labor, the relationships among the variables concerned have been remarkably stable over time.

Herbert Northrup's analysis of interracial labor relations in the 1930's and early 1940's can be summarized briefly.[1]

[1] See Herbert R. Northrup, *Organized Labor and the Negro* (New York: Harper, 1944).

(i) Exclusion of Negroes and discrimination are much more pronounced in craft-type unions than in industrial unions.[2]

(ii) Thus, the structure of the industry is a principal determinant of union policy, with those industries that are most conducive to industrial unionism (e.g., mine, steel, and auto industries) showing the lowest degree of discrimination.

(iii) Labor market conditions are another major determinant, with largest Negro employment gains occurring during periods of labor scarcity, as in the

[2] At the time of Northrup's study this distinction coincided reasonably well with the one between AFL and CIO unions.

two world wars, and with tendencies for Negroes to lose ground during periods of labor surplus.

(iv) The philosophy of a union has some significance. Those unions that stress social or fraternal aspects of organization, and those with predominantly Southern memberships are most restrictive.[3]

(v) Strong national control of unions is more likely to work to the advantage of Negroes than is local control.

(vi) Where there are rival unions bidding for membership, Negroes have often benefited, although on occasion a "liberal" union has relaxed its equalitarian policy in order to retain its white members.

A more recent study by Scott Greer points to essentially the same conclusions.[4] Greer tends to play down the significance of ideological factors, but this may reflect a different intellectual orientation from that of Northrup, rather than a real difference in situations. Greer's analysis gives major emphasis to the nature of the industry and work setting as determinants of union policy. This policy toward Negroes and other minorities is taken as a dependent variable, primarily determined by the major problem of maintaining the union in a given setting. A factor of overwhelming importance in influencing the degree to which Negroes and other minorities are employed and upgraded is the condition of the labor market.

Greer's study offers additional insights into the dynamics of union racial policy by showing the nature of the constraints that operate on union leaders as a result of the work setting, union struc-

ture, relations with rival unions, and dealings with employers. Certain of his findings for 21 Los Angeles locals are relevant to our discussion. It should be explicitly noted that *all* of the unions studied by Greer contained at least some minority-group members (primarily Negroes and Mexicans).

(i) Many of the craft unions that do not exclude Negroes and Mexicans involve extremely unskilled work (e.g., janitors, dishwashers). These are often "captive locals" that must depend for bargaining power on more powerful unions. The latter usually consist of more skilled white workers, often being exclusionist trade unions. Even though these captive locals may contain a majority of Negroes and Mexicans, and a predominance of minority leadership, these leaders are relatively powerless.

(ii) Other craft unions at somewhat higher skill-levels are dominated by their respective internationals, which often make higher-level deals with other unions and management. These unions are particularly insensitive to local membership demands and have disproportionately small minority representation among their leadership.

(iii) Industrial unions, on the whole, tend to be more membership dominated. Degree of democratic control, and minority influence as well, depend on the size of the work group. In "plant-oriented" unions there are large numbers of workers in each plant. Shop stewards are responsible to each plant group and hold considerable power. In effect, they constitute an "organizational middle-class" which serves as a check on higher leadership. In "hall-oriented" industrial unions, on the other hand, the size of the local work group is much smaller, and leaders are elected at large rather than by members of their own plants who know them personally. In these unions, Negro and Mexican influence is relatively less strong.

(iv) In industrial unions, organiza-

[3] Since unions having social and fraternal functions were primarily craft unions, it is difficult to disentangle the relative influences of these two kinds of factors.

[4] See Scott Greer, *Last Man In* (Glencoe: The Free Press, 1959). For somewhat similar findings, see William Kornhauser, "The Negro Union Official: A Study of Sponsorship and Control," *American Journal of Sociology*, 57 (March 1952), pp. 443–52.

tion involves the grouping of workers at *different* occupational levels into the same union. In craft unions, however, members are generally drawn from the same level. This difference results in greater occupational mobility for minority members in the former case, where unions are forced to bargain for benefits across the board. But since Negroes and Mexicans tend, on the average, to be concentrated at the lower skill levels in these industrial unions, and since leaders tend to be drawn from the upper levels, minority members are underrepresented among the leadership. On the other hand, in the case of craft unions with very low status (e.g., dishwashers), Negroes and Mexicans have no difficulty becoming officers of the union.

(v) In general, the leadership in all types of unions is constrained by the necessities of dealing with diverse forces, so that individual beliefs and ideologies are unimportant. Most leaders of locals are in insecure positions and in danger of being removed from office or losing membership to rival unions. Only when control is in the hands of the membership does the minority question gain serious attention, even in unions with numerically large minorities.

(vi) Negroes and Mexicans are especially handicapped in those unions in which the "hiring-hall" system gives additional power to union leaders through discretionary work assignments. In general, these involve jobs where the work force is small and temporary and where the employer merely asks for a given number of men to be hired on a day-to-day basis.

In addition to the case of the American Negro and labor, there are many illustrative situations in which organized labor has been overtly hostile toward minorities, and where efforts have been made to control the minority's entrance into the labor force. When unions have lacked economic power, violence has also been prevalent. Such labor reactions have oc-

curred not only within the South, but in the Far West in the case of orientals, and throughout the United States as a reaction against cheap immigrant labor. South African labor has of course also been extremely hostile toward "native" competition and has formed one of the components in the ultra-conservative Nationalist Party.

Of special importance is the problem of identifying the general conditions under which a coalition with the minority labor force is likely. Before stating some propositions based on previously cited facts, let us consider a line of theoretical reasoning that may eventually prove helpful. There have been several recent attempts in the sociological literature to set forth a theory of coalition formation. I shall be concerned with two of such theories, those of Theodore Caplow and William Gamson.[5] Attention will be confined to triad situations (e.g., involving employers, white labor, and Negro labor). Though the theories of Gamson and Caplow differ in some respects, that of Gamson being the more general of the two, I shall treat them together since both make essentially the same predictions in the cases we shall consider.

The initial postulates of the two theories differ somewhat, but they include the assumptions that (1) a given party will seek either to maximize its payoff or to dominate as many of the other parties as possible; (2) belonging to a winning coalition gives one a known and fixed payoff which, however, may be divided unequally among coalition partners; (3) the resources of each party are known or can be accurately assessed; and (4) other motives or "nonutilitar-

[5] See Theodore Caplow, "A Theory of Coalitions in the Triad," *American Sociological Review,* 21 (August 1956), pp. 489–93; Theodore Caplow, "Further Development of a Theory of Coalitions in the Triad," *American Journal of Sociology,* 64 (March 1959), pp. 488–93; and William Gamson, "A Theory of Coalition Formation," *American Sociological Review,* 26 (June 1961), pp. 373–82.

ian" preferences (Gamson's term) are not explicitly considered.[6]

With assumptions such as these, both theories predict that given three parties, A, B, and C, with A more powerful than B, which is in turn more powerful than C: (1) no coalition will form if the combined power of B and C is less than that of A, and (2) a coalition between C and one of the other parties is likely if the power of A is less than that of B plus C. In the latter case, Caplow's theory predicts that the A-C and B-C coalitions are equally likely. Gamson's theory, however, predicts the B-C coalition since the choosing partner C will prefer a coalition with B on the grounds that, since B is less powerful than A, C's position within the winning coalition would be relatively stronger if it were to join with B.

Thus both theories predict the surprising result that the weakest party C is likely to belong to a winning coalition much more frequently than would ordinarily be expected. Both parties would prefer a coalition with C rather than with the stronger rival. If such theories were applied directly to minority-group situations, then we might expect minorities to fare rather well, much better in fact than they ordinarily do.

Before suggesting certain modifications, however, it would be well to point out that these coalition theories may very well provide us with a *necessary* (though not a sufficient) condition for coalition formation with minority labor: namely, the (perceived) combined strength of majority and minority labor must be sufficient to form a "winning coalition," at least in the sense that such a coalition is in a power position to extract important concessions from management.

One rather obvious modification of the above theories, which would be re-

quired before they could be applied to the problem at hand, is that resources of the potential coalition partners may not be additive. In the case of craft unionism, bargaining power depends not on numbers but on exclusiveness and control over access to training. The formation of a coalition between whites and Negroes would therefore not help the bargaining position of white labor. We have a case, here, where in some sense the sum of the separate powers of B and C might be greater than that of A, but when B and C are actually combined, the value of B + C is still less than that of A. This might be contrasted with the case of industrial unionism where strength depends on numbers and where the resources of B and C are therefore approximately additive. Even here, however, it is still possible that a coalition of B and C will be too weak to influence A, in which case the theory would predict a breaking of the coalition. The implication is that a coalition is by no means necessary, even in occupations where industrial unionism would be most appropriate. To the degree that both labor elements are weak, coalitions are unlikely.

The above comments concerning nonadditivity can obviously be handled in terms of the postulates of coalition theory. But certain other qualifications would seem to require the addition of new variables or modification of postulates. One of these concerns the distinction between present and future power, or between the actual exercise of power, on the one hand, and resources or power potential, on the other.[7] Let us consider two quite different situations regarding the weakest party C, which we shall take to be the minority group. In the first situation, C is presently weak, owing to low mobilization of its resources. But its power potential is considerable. Perhaps the "minority" is numerically large but

---

[6] Gamson allows for "nonutilitarian" preferences, but does not treat them systematically. See Gamson, *op. cit.*

[7] This distinction [is] considered in greater detail in Chapter 4. [of Blalock's book].

disorganized. A coalition with C will therefore not add much to the present strength of A or B, but if a winning coalition with C happened to be formed, this would then enhance C's position. Were C's total potential then to be realized as a result of increased mobilization, C might very well come to dominate its coalition partner. In a second situation, we can imagine C' with equal present power to that of C, but with this power being primarily due to a high degree of mobilization rather than large reserve resources. Such a potential coalition partner would be much more attractive to either A or B, since there should be less fear of C' eventually becoming the dominant partner.

The above line of reasoning is of course relevant to coalition formation with numerically large minorities and would seem to help explain the reluctance of Southern whites to unite with Negro labor, even where the experience of Northern labor would indicate a high probability of a successful coalition. The same is true of labor within the Union of South Africa, where the numerical imbalance is even greater. This distinction between present and future power can be handled by including it as a "nonutilitarian" preference in the Gamson scheme. But the distinction should nevertheless be made explicit.[8]

It is this fear of the minority power threat, which will be discussed in Chapter 4, that requires additional qualifications or modifications in the theory for it to be applicable to minority situations. A history of past conflict may, of course, invalidate Gamson's assumption of no differences in nonutilitarian strategy preferences. Both theories, in effect, assume that belonging to the winning coalition is the overriding consideration. They also assume that the total payoff is constant.

[8] The distinction also seems related to Caplow's discussion of continuous, episodic, and terminal coalition situations. See Caplow, "Further Development . . .," op. cit.

But A and B may agree to exploit C and thereby maximize the total gains to both parties. In a sense, then, A and B may form a coalition against C in situations in which there is no outside agent controlling the allocation of rewards to the winning coalition. This has a number of parallels in the real world. Colonial powers, for example, may divide up a given territory and cooperate in the spoils. Similarly, a Southern white elite group may form an effective coalition with poor whites, offering the latter group certain "prestige gains" in the form of Jim Crow regulations or outlets for sexual or aggressive impulses.

Finally, in most real-life situations, it will be exceedingly difficult to assess accurately the relative resources of each party, let alone the degree to which these resources will actually be mobilized in a three-cornered power struggle. Furthermore, since any given party may be only loosely held together, it will also be difficult to foresee whether or not defections will occur. In the case of labor movements, for example, a strong push toward alliances with Negro labor might very well loosen ties with Southern affiliates, thereby decreasing the total union resources. We would expect that the more difficult it is to appraise such factors, the more likely that so-called "nonutilitarian preferences" will determine policy.

Propositions

With these qualifications together with the previous facts in mind, let us state a number of more general propositions.

(33) The greater the perceived need for having the minority as a coalition partner, the stronger the bargaining position of minority labor. The perceived need should be greatest whenever:
(a) the position of the dominant-group labor element is not sufficiently strong to gain concessions from the

employer but strong enough that, when combined with minority labor, the power of this coalition will be sufficient to win demands;

(b) the resources of dominant-group and minority labor are additive owing to the fact that bargaining position depends on numbers rather than on exclusion.

(34) The minority as a potential coalition partner will tend to be:

(a) discriminated against by trade unions which depend on exclusion and control of training;

(b) treated with indifference by unions which are already strong and which do not fear competition of rival unions;

(c) treated with indifference even by industrial unions if the minority is numerically small, unless there are a number of such small minorities similarly situated.

(35) If a minority is sufficiently large, and *if* conditions are such that bargaining power depends on the successful organization of large numbers of workers (e.g., industrial unions), then a coalition between dominant-group and minority labor is likely *unless:*

(a) the minority is so large that it constitutes a potential power threat;

(b) the minority is presently so disunited that it is perceived as a weak coalition partner, with combined power insufficient to influence the employer;

(c) there is a tradition of past cleavage between dominant-group and minority labor; and

(d) there is an agreement between dominant-group labor and management that would offer dominant-group labor tangible gains at the expense of minority labor.

Note: Propositions (34c) and (35a) imply that labor coalitions are most likely with a minority group that is *intermediate* in size.

(36) The more difficult it is to assess the resources of the various parties, the more likely that "nonutilitarian" preferences will prevail, and the less likely that a coalition will be formed between dominant-group and minority labor.

(37) The bargaining position of minority labor will be enhanced in times of a labor shortage (and correspondingly diminished during a labor surplus) because:

(a) the general position of labor will be improved, making it more likely that a coalition between B and C will be powerful enough to influence the employer A;

(b) minority competition will be less threatening to dominant-group labor, thereby lessening the influence of "nonutilitarian" preferences;

(c) the less selective employers will be in hiring and upgrading, and the less the probability of their using "particularistic" criteria (e.g., racial) in selecting from a large pool of equally qualified workers.

Note: In (37a) I assume that dominant-group labor is so weak that it needs to rely on minority support. This proposition therefore applies more to industrial than to craft unions. Hence, periods of labor shortage should produce relatively greater minority gains in industrial unions than in craft unions (and their corresponding occupations).

(38) Once admitted to unions, numerically large minorities will have their greatest leverage, both in terms of job benefits and positions within the union, whenever:

(a) union management is not in a position to use "hiring hall" practices by arbitrarily selecting those members who are to work on a given project;

(b) the local union has a high degree of autonomy with respect to strike power and is not a "captive" of another union or subject to higher-

level agreements by internationals;
(c) lower-rung union leaders (e.g., stewards) are elected by members of their own plant work groups, rather than the membership at large.

Note: As indicated by Greer, each of these conditions is intimately related to the type of union (industrial or craft) and to the nature of the job setting.

(39) The minority's chances for promotion are more likely in unions, membership in which cuts across several occupational levels rather than being at a single level.

4. COLLECTIVE BEHAVIOR

Martin Oppenheimer

What conditions lead to organized insurrectionary action among the members of a subordinate group? What are the varieties of insurrectionary action? Is there a way to compare the types of action? Is there a movement over time such that one of these types supersedes another?

This selection from Oppenheimer's work helps to answer all of these questions in a remarkably brief way. Responding to the first one, Oppenheimer utilizes the concept of "strain," laying special emphasis on perceived economic, political, or social deprivations. To answer the others, he reviews a number of insurrections from different times and places, finding that various combinations of three variables occur in all of them: (1) the setting is either rural or urban; (2) the action is or is not consciously oriented toward a political goal; (3) the action does or does not involve mass participation. Oppenheimer believes that the massive, politically oriented uprising is the last insurrectionary form to develop, but that the United States is

Source: *The Urban Guerilla* (Chicago: Quadrangle Books, 1969), pp. 26–39, with some footnotes omitted and others renumbered. Copyright © 1969 by Martin Oppenheimer. Reprinted by permission of the author and publisher.

MARTIN OPPENHEIMER is Associate Professor of Sociology at the Livingston Campus of Rutgers University.

probably heading toward one now. If it does occur here, it will be urban, for the subordinated racial underclasses of America do not have substantial political or tactical bases in the countryside.

Two items that have a prominent place in later parts of Oppenheimer's book deserve to be mentioned here. One is that he prefers nonviolent to violent revolution, believes it is necessary, and suggests steps that may help to bring it about. The second item is related to the first. Oppenheimer is at great pains to show that the gradual development of an attempt at revolution, as well as the success or failure of that attempt if it does occur, depends upon how superordinate majority groups respond to the protests they can see occurring in their midst. The strategies of police and other agencies responsible for enforcing order and maintaining social control are of particular importance, especially if in their attempts to apprehend or isolate what they consider to be guilty or conspiratorial leaders they also do harm to the innocent. Oppenheimer's comments on the "two-war strategy" near the end of the selection are just a sample of observations he makes at greater length and in fuller detail elsewhere.

KINDS OF STRAIN

What kinds of strain are there, aside from ambiguities among values (for example, "Thou shalt not kill" versus "Thou shalt report for induction"), or between values and conditions (for example, the value of work versus the condition of unemployability)? Several are of particular importance to students of revolution. One concerns ambiguity in the allocation of resources to various sectors of society, that is, what groups get how much of the political, economic, and prestige resources available. This ambiguity has to do with the stratification or class structure of the society. Of course, most societies usually are not ambiguous about this; there is no strain until some large number of individuals see themselves as deprived. Almost always they are those in the sub-ordinate strata, that is, the poor, the oppressed, the "disadvantaged," workers, farmers, or, as seen from "the top," "the dangerous classes" who, in this kind of strain, have an interest in change. As Allan Silver points out, the literature of police work abounds with perennial themes of potential disorder in the urban setting which call for military steps to contain these dangerous classes. The social order is again and again threatened by, variously, the poor, workers, sailors, immigrants, criminals, the lumpen-proletariat, and various combinations of them, and the police have historically had as their mission the control of these elements on behalf of the propertied.[1]

The term "deprivation" is commonly

[1] Allan Silver, "The Demand for Order in Civil Society: A Review of Some Themes in the History of Urban Crime, Police, and Riot," in David J. Bordua, ed., The Police, New York, Wiley, 1967, pp. 23–24.

used to describe ambiguity in the allocation of economic resources, but resources of power and prestige can also be involved. Moreover, it is rarely deprivation as such which accounts for strain. Rather, the deprivation must first be *perceived* by a group, and this can only be done if the group can compare itself with some other relevant group. The group must see itself deprived *relative* to some other group; hence the concept "relative deprivation." This other group may be beneath it, above it, similar to it but in another country, or even itself at an earlier time. And the deprivation may be perceived because the group has become more miserable while its reference group is becoming miserable at a lesser rate; or it is becoming miserable while its reference group is stationary; or it is stationary while its reference group is improving; or it is actually improving, but its reference group is improving faster, as is the case for black Americans in terms of absolute income.

There are strains other than deprivation, and while they are important in creating conditions leading to social movements, they are probably not quite as important as deprivation in leading to revolutionary activity. To mention some of them briefly: there is the ambiguity in society as to how resources will be allocated to fulfill different social tasks (for example, the war on poverty versus the war in Vietnam); there is ambiguity in an organization as to how to keep itself going (shall students be allowed to participate more, or shall they be deprived of participation in order to keep an educational bureaucracy going?); there is the ambiguity stemming from the difference between how one performs and how one is rewarded (do we get what we think we are worth, relative to others like us?); there is the ambiguity stemming from conflict among our many statuses and roles in society (father–employee; emancipated woman–housewife; maturing adult–sheltered stu-

dent; teacher–researcher; black American–middle-class American; and so on); there is the ambiguity of the means by which different sectors of society compete for resources, that is, what is sanctioned by the social and legal structure (if it is all right for the police to murder members of the Black Panther party, why is it not all right for the Panthers to go about armed? If it is all right for university bureaucrats to refuse significant communication by giving people the old bureaucratic run-around, why is it not all right for students to communicate with their bodies by preventing the machinery from functioning until communication takes place?).

Finally, and perhaps inevitably, there is the ambiguity described by Freud: the conflict between individual self-expression and the group's need to survive, that is, the struggle between self and society, id and superego.

. . . . .

Revolutionary movements . . . are largely [but not exclusively] related to that strain stemming from perceived deprivation of society's resources in economic goods and services, political power, or social prestige. Within the field of sociology, the study of such movements has to do with the study of large (secondary) groups along a continuum from informal collective behavior to formal complex-organizational behavior. Now let us look more specifically at paramilitary activities from the sociological viewpoint.[2]

I have already implied that rebellion is one kind of social movement among many, involving a collective effort to create a more satisfying culture or to protect some aspect of the culture against a perceived threat to it. Strain of one

[2] More detailed discussion of social movement theory can be found in, among others, Turner and Killian, *Collective Behavior;* Neil J. Smelser, *Theory of Collective Behavior,* New York, Free Press, 1963; and Hans Toch, *The Social Psychology of Social Movements,* Indianapolis, Bobbs-Merrill, 1965.

kind or another is what motivates individuals to participate in movement; thus the prerequisite to insurrection, too is that the status quo is seen as inadequate to the solution of certain problems as they are felt by some group in the population. In addition, the group must be desperate enough to feel that only a military strategy can bring about, or prevent, the desired, or undesired, change. The tactical issue then often becomes whether the group is capable of accomplishing its goal, especially in the face of the armed opposition of the "establishment."

Armed insurrection can obviously be distinguished from other kinds of collective behavior because it involves violence directed toward the immediate or ultimate overthrow of the established order, or, in the case of defensive insurrections, toward the defense of a subgroup of society against the further encroachments of the established order—two rather different types. But once violence and a posture vis-à-vis the status quo have been established, the picture takes on several other dimensions.

INSURRECTION AS COLLECTIVE BEHAVIOR

One set of variables which may help to clarify the picture and put insurrection into a perspective is that of (a) involvement or interaction and (b) formal organization.

We begin with apathy, disillusionment, or depression. As apathy is dispelled by a particular situation—for example, the development of a movement or the appearance of a charismatic leader —the individual becomes more involved as he seeks to "resynthesize" his way of life, values, behaviors so as to make more sense out of his situation. But there are degrees of involvement—some interaction may be with movements which in fact reject interaction as their goal, or

perhaps as their tactic. For example, religious separatism, the escapism of utopian communities, or some aspects of the drug culture do not seek interaction. Tactically, involvement may be in a movement which advocates a strike or boycott, which is a withdrawal from interaction with an opponent (though not from society). Interaction with an opponent (say, the police, or "the power structure") increases in other kinds of demonstrations such as picket lines, and is brought to an extreme in the tactics of direct action (sit-ins, seizures of plants or buildings, marches on public offices, and so forth). In the same way, interaction with an opponent or at least with his symbolic representations (his property) increases in a riot, but decreases if a mob is dispersed by the authorities. Mobs can therefore move in a focal way, toward an objective, in which case they increase interaction; or they can flee and disperse, in which case interaction is decreased.

But mobs differ from demonstrations in that they are less structured, less organized—hence the dimension of organization. And they differ from inactivity or dispersal—hence the dimension of interaction. Therefore, when we have no organization and no interaction we have apathy or flight; when we have organization but no interaction we have utopian withdrawal, a boycott, or a strike; when we have interaction but no organization we have a mob or a riot; when we have both organization and interaction we have political demonstrations, revolutionary activity, and, sometimes, insurrectionary warfare.

One key to paramilitary or guerrilla warfare is that interaction is sporadic. It includes hit-and-run tactics and withdrawal in the face of superior force. Only at the actual point of seizure of the government (or its attempt), that is, a general outbreak of revolutionary activity possibly as the closing stage of an extended guerrilla war, do we see full interaction with the opponent—unless the opponent chooses to flee at that point, as was the case of Batista in Cuba.

A distinction from nonviolent protest activity needs to be made here as well. Obviously, paramilitary activity involves violence; but it is often combined with various other forms of direct action, some of which, like strikes, can be and often are conducted on a nonviolent or at least on an a-violent basis. Thus civil disobedience sometimes operates in tandem with criminal disobedience (rebellion), although if a paramilitary force is actually operating, all disobedience will be perceived by the authorities as criminal and in the same category with the rebellion, and will be similarly punished. This is an important point, for it largely rebuts recent arguments which say that a little disruption, rioting, and violence does not harm "the movement," and that the movement therefore need not openly disavow violence and explicitly espouse nonviolence. For if a movement is not explicitly nonviolent, it will be treated as if it were its most violent part. Even if a movement is nonviolent it may be perceived and treated as if it were violent. This strategic point will reappear later.

TYPES OF VIOLENT PROTEST

Three dimensions of violent protest are of particular interest: (1) a historical dimension involving the rural-urban continuum; (2) an associated dimension involving degree of political consciousness; and (3) an independent dimension related to the distinction between a coup or putsch and a revolution, that of numbers of people involved. By rural-urban continuum I mean basically the issue of whether the countryside or the city is to be the focus of insurrectionary activity. By political consciousness I mean whether a particular insurrectionary or violent effort has some kind of political ideology, or whether it is basically a pre-political or proto-political endeavor. By the distinction between coup and revolution, and numbers of people involved, I mean generally whether the contemplated social change is to be undertaken by a relatively small number of men, an elite, from the top down, or whether the change is to involve a real movement, masses of people, with the strategy of change being from the bottom up. The latter would include movements led by elites but involving masses of people as the instruments of change in some major way.

There are, as I see it, eight variations on these three dimensions, four in a rural context and four in an urban setting, as shown in outline form at the bottom of the page. (Note that a check mark indicates whether the setting is rural or urban, a plus or a minus indicates the

	Rural/Urban	Political consciousness	Mass participation
social banditry, vendettas, early Mafia	√	−	−
peasant uprisings, revitalization movements	√	−	+
guerrilla bands	√	+	−
guerrilla liberation army (Zapata, FLN, NFL, etc.)	√	+	+
gangsterism, contemporary Mafia, jacket clubs, hooliganism	√	−	−
riots, vandalism, looting	√	−	+
terrorism (selective assassination, possibly leading to a coup)	√	+	−
rebellion or "rising"	√	+	+

presence or absence of political consciousness and mass participation.)

There are four variations within each setting; these show a historical development, that is, the normal historical progression is from the first variation through the second and third type, to the fourth. The first two variations, then, are pre-political or proto-political movements; the second two are more modern, politically oriented revolutionary movements.

Note, too, that each type of movement has an analogy in the other setting, as follows:

Rural		Urban
social banditry	=	gangsterism
peasant uprisings	=	riots
guerrilla bands	=	terrorism
liberation army	=	rebellion or "rising"

In order properly to understand urban paramilitary activity, each of these eight variations or ideal types must be seen in historical context.

The social bandit has perhaps been best described by E. J. Hobsbawm: "A man becomes a bandit because he does something which is not regarded as criminal by his local conventions, but is so regarded by the State or the local rulers." [3] He is a Robin Hood, a Pretty Boy Floyd, a Jesse James, or at least he is so regarded by the local population from which he comes. The social bandit existed as a type in southern Italy as recently as the 1940's; the rise to dominance of an urban-industrial culture usually marks the end of the rural bandit. Bands of such people are usually small, no larger than thirty, and their victims tend to be members or representatives of the upper strata in the society: rich merchants, clergy, lawyers, politicians. Bandits were often successful, being protected by the people of their area; they seldom strayed outside. Occasionally they became prosperous, poor boys who "made good," thus making banditry one road to upper mobility in situations where most other roads were closed to the common man. (There are certain parallels here with James Hoffa, or Adam Clayton Powell, in the urban setting; but they should not be overdrawn, obviously.) A bandit's standard ending was that of death by betrayal, or, on the other hand, to become a thug for the upper class—which is pretty much what happened to a lot of *mafiosi* in Sicily. The bandit, then, is rural and pre-political; his strength is inverse to organized, political agrarian movements, but like such movements it grows with hard times —precisely when the bandit, due to his lack of ideology, is least able to have solutions. The bandit can therefore set limits to oppression (by terrorizing the oppressor), but he cannot really solve it. People with guns but without ideology are bandits; people with ideology but without guns are liberals, and in a rural setting in which the oppressor classes rule with violence, they are impotent.

The analogous social formation in the urban area is the gangster, or, on a less organized level, the juvenile fighting gang. The gangster-racketeer represents an outgrowth of the Mafia, or rather, a more formalized, better-organized and urbanized version of it, but often historically related to the rural and small town Mafia of Sicily.[4] Like the rural bandit, his career begins, often enough, by violating laws not regarded by his neighborhood culture as real violations. He is stigmatized by a criminal record, and legitimate roads to upward mobility are subsequently closed to him. Like the rural bandit, he basically accepts society's system of goals (material rewards),

---

[3] E. J. Hobsbawn, *Primitive Rebels*, New York, Norton, 1965, p. 15.

[4] Robert T. Anderson, "From Mafia to Cosa Nostra," *American Journal of Sociology*, vol. 71 (November 1965), 302–310.

but he must innovate illicit means to attain those goals. He is seldom as "social" (helpful to his people) as the rural bandit, but from time to time urban gangs (mainly juveniles, not racketeers) go "social," that is, abandon fighting and adopt tasks of a "social welfare" character, such as recreation, clean-up campaigns, and so forth.

PEASANT WARS AND URBAN RIOTS

Peasant uprisings (chiefly European) and revitalization movements, their equivalent in the colonial or underdeveloped nation, have been amply described in sociological, anthropological, and historical literature.[5] Semi- or pre-feudal slave uprisings (Nat Turner, for example) would be included in this category. The basic distinction between a peasant uprising and rural banditry is that the uprising is generally of shorter duration (although a series of uprisings can follow one upon another so as to make for virtually a half-century of warfare, as in central Europe from about 1478 to about 1527), has somewhat more specific goals (usually of a revivalistic or historically reactionary sort, that is, oriented toward the restoration of some previous, ostensibly better, condition), and involves significant masses of people on a more or less spontaneous, relatively unorganized basis. The level of political consciousness, given populations that are at best semi-literate, is still fairly low, though individual peasant leaders (Emiliano Zapata in Mexico) or leaders of the peasants (Thomas Münzer, 1498–1525, a theologian) may have more developed ideas.

Incidents having the characteristics of a peasant war took place in the United States as recently as the 1930's. Widespread suffering, especially by day laborers and sharecroppers in the South following a decline in cotton prices, led to a series of strikes, attempted seizures of homes and work implements by sheriffs, and harassment and persecution of union organizers. In response, proto-revolutionary outbreaks, including armed resistance to sheriffs and their deputies, took place on a wide scale. In one incident, armed blacks barricaded a house when police came to seize the property, and in the ensuing gunfight the sheriff and two deputies were wounded and one black killed.[6]

The urban analogy to the peasant uprising, again politically one step advanced from gangsterism, though still a proto-political kind of activity, is the riot. Before full participation in parliamentary democracy in England, the streets had been a more or less legitimate arena in which to make demands on elites; it was a "proto-democratic system." In the eighteenth and nineteenth centuries, the streets were used so that "the unorganized poor . . . might articulately address the propertied classes through riot and disorder." [7] Current debates as to whether ghetto riots are class- or race-based, or whether they are "merely" criminal or more in the nature of rebellions, are a clue to seeing the riot as a "proto-political" development. "The riot," as Tom Hayden says, "is certainly an awkward, even primitive form of history-making. But if people are barred from using the sophisticated instruments of the established order for their ends, they will find another way." [8] There would not be much point here in analyzing urban riots in more detail; the literature has been voluminous in the

[5] For example, Peter Worsley, *The Trumpet Shall Sound*, London, MacGibbon and Kee, 1957; Vittorio Lanternari, *The Religions of the Oppressed*, New York, Knopf, 1963; Frederick Engels, *The Peasant War in Germany*, Moscow, Foreign Languages Publishing House, 1956, first published in 1850; and James, *The Black Jacobins*.

[6] U.S. Department of Labor, *Labor Unionism in American Agriculture*, Bulletin #836, Washington, U.S. Government Printing Office, 1945.

[7] Silver, in Bordua, *The Police*, pp. 23–24.

[8] Tom Hayden, *Rebellion in Newark*, New York, Random House, 1967, p. 69.

last few years.[9] It is enough to say that there is now general agreement on underlying causes and immediate precipitants. Stanley Lieberson and Arnold Silverman "see the riot in terms of institutional malfunctioning or a racial difficulty which is not met—and perhaps cannot be met—by existing social institutions." Anthony Oberschall talks about "the situation of the lower-class urban Negroes outside of the South," and the fact that the civil rights gains of the past years "have not removed the fundamental sources of grievances of a large proportion of the Negro population in the U.S." The "Riot Commission" notes that "Segregation and poverty have created in the racial ghetto a destructive environment totally unknown to most white Americans . . . white society is deeply implicated in the ghetto. White institutions created it, white institutions maintain it, and white society condones it." Riots have provided more than ample data supporting the basic premise discussed earlier, that of "structural strain," as being the single best overall (though perhaps over-general) framework within which to discuss all collective behavior.

What is particularly interesting, however, is that the urban riot (and, by implication, the peasant uprising), is seen by a number of observers as a step in the direction of a more politically conscious movement. Historically, it would seem, urban mobs and riots give way to more sophisticated political forms, such as modern social movements (trade union-

ism, for example, or working-class political parties), where such forms are feasible. In an authoritarian society (czarism, for example) where reforms are not sufficiently forthcoming, or where democratic outlets are excluded, riots are replaced by revolutionary movements involving armed insurrection.

Hayden puts it this way: "Men are now appearing in the ghettos who might turn the energy of the riot in a more organized and continuous revolutionary direction. . . . During a riot, for instance, a conscious guerrilla can participate in pulling police away from the path of people engaged in attacking stores. . . ."[10] And it is only a step from this riot with auxiliary guerrillas to the urban insurrection as such. The transition in the individual's consciousness between urban rioting and insurrection, including guerrilla warfare, is no longer difficult to make. In fact, as Harold Black and Marvin Labes point out, the analogy has been made for some time by police."[11] Ghetto areas are considered enemy territory; the police are "at war" with criminal elements; it becomes less and less possible to differentiate between ordinary citizens and criminals (just as in guerrilla warfare); the innocent thereupon begin to suffer harassment and to identify with "criminal elements," and see the police as a common enemy. Constitutional rights (a domestic equivalent of the Geneva Convention) become hindrances to the police in their "war." Subsequently, better "community relations" are called for—imaginative "social programs" must be developed by the police. But, as in Vietnam or elsewhere, the police are alienated from the population by the fact that these social programs are in tandem with policies of massive repression; so the police, like the Green Berets, are seen as hypocritical, and the social programs as merely a sub-

[9] Hayden, *Rebellion in Newark;* Robert Conot, *Rivers of Blood, Years of Darkness,* New York, Bantam Books, 1967; Russell Dynes and E. L. Quarantelli, "What Looting in Civil Disturbances Really Means," *Trans-action,* vol. 5 (May 1968), 9–14; National Advisory Commission on Civil Disorders, *Report,* New York, Bantam Books, 1968; *American Behavioral Scientist,* vol. 11 (March–April 1968), Special Issue on Urban Violence and Disorder; Irving L. Horowitz and Martin Liebowitz, "Social Deviance and Marginality," *Social Problems,* vol. 15 (Winter 1968), 280–296; Anthony Oberschall, "The Los Angeles Riot," *Social Problems,* vol. 15 (Winter 1968), 322–341; Stanley Lieberson and Arnold R. Silverman, "Precipitants and Conditions of Race Riots," *American Sociological Review,* vol. 30 (December 1965), 887–898.

[10] Hayden, *Rebellion in Newark,* p. 70.
[11] Harold Black and Marvin J. Labes, "Guerrilla Warfare: An Analogy to Police-Criminal Interaction," *American Journal of Orthopsychiatry,* vol. 37 (July 1967), 666–670.

terfuge. The "two-war" strategy fails, both in the ghetto and in the countryside, as a strategy with which to divide the civilian population from "criminal elements" or guerrillas. (And, under this kind of strategy, the line between the criminal or bandit and the guerrilla begins to disappear; the bandit and the criminal become more political, hence revolutionary.)

. . . . .

. . . An urban rebellion is almost invariably accompanied by individualistic, non-political (or pre-political) acts of a gangsterish sort, such as hooliganism, and is frequently also accompanied by what can be called proto-political behavior such as rioting, looting, or even ethnic pogroms. Looting of Jewish-owned stores in black ghetto areas, while not a pogrom in the classical sense, does border on that. On the other hand, looting by police or army units of black-owned stores is a nearly perfect example of the classical pogrom, but this is not done as part of an instruction by the oppressed group; on the contrary, it is done to again, is what the classical pogrom under keep the oppressed group in line, which, czarism in part was intended to do.

5. INTERNAL COLONIALISM AND GHETTO REVOLT

Robert Blauner

England and the American North used profits from the slave trade and from the manufacture of cotton, which slave labor produced, as part of the necessary capital for continuing their industrial revolutions. Meanwhile, like some of today's Latin American countries, the South, where that cotton was grown and sold, was run by a paternalistic oligarchy which earned and maintained its wealth, power, and prestige through extensive land holdings and the control of a large, unskilled labor force that in return for its efforts received only enough to stay alive and go on working. The Civil War changed the pattern but did not destroy it. The end of Reconstruction dashed any hopes for black political power or individual economic autonomy in the South. Debt peonage, backed by force when

Source: *Social Problems,* Vol. 16, No. 4 (Spring 1969), pp. 393–408, with some footnotes omitted. Reprinted by permission of the author and the Society for the Study of Social Problems.

Robert Blauner is Associate Professor of Sociology at the University of California, Berkeley. He is the author of *Alienation and Freedom.*

necessary, replaced chattel slavery, becoming the economic basis for a continuing white supremacy that reached its peak between 1890 and 1920.

By World War I, a trickle of black migration from Southern farm to Northern factory had begun. The trickle became a stream during and after World War II, dependent on the push of technological sophistication in Southern agriculture and the pull of employment opportunities in industry, not only in the North and West, but in the urban South as well. As blacks moved in, whites moved out. Old ghettoes grew larger, and new ones began, like West Side Chicago and Bedford-Stuyvesant in Brooklyn.

In sum, in a century the "transformation of the Negro American," as the title of a 1965 book put it,[1] was a transformation from the predominant status of slave, to that of peasant, to that of unskilled and semiskilled worker. In 1968, median black family income was about $5,400, only 60 percent of the white median. That was not much relative progress from 1950, when the national nonwhite median was 54 percent of the white one. Indeed, although the percentage gap seemed to be narrowing, the white gain was larger than the nonwhite or black one when measured in terms of absolute numbers of dollars of constant purchasing power.

In any case, ghetto residents paid more to get less.[2] Moreover, they had little control over the political system that regulated them, the economic system that employed them, the schools that were supposed to educate them, or the landlords and housing agencies they paid to shelter them. Although progress had taken place, it seemed to be at a painfully slow rate. It was limited by the fact that by 1960 good jobs increasingly depended upon the possession of educational credentials in a way that they had not in 1900, 1920, or even 1940, when it was virtually only the middle class that graduated from high school. Hemmed in, controlled, and dependent, by the middle sixties many ghetto residents became angry and disillusioned over the gap between political promise and the immediate reality of local obfuscation, restriction, and repression. A new, younger group of black intellectuals took note of how the tension and bitterness were played out in Watts and Harlem, Detroit and Newark; of how blacks had externalized the rage that older and tighter racial restrictions and socialization had forced them to turn inward as self-hatred or

[1] Leonard Broom and Norval Glenn, *Transformation of the Negro American* (New York: Harper and Row, 1965).

[2] Many works document this point. One of my favorites is Paul Jacobs, *Prelude to Riot* (New York: Random House, 1968).

displace on members of their own group. The new spokesmen combined their observations with their conviction that the success of collective action in the civil rights movement could be no more than partial, that civil rights efforts and hopes for integration could go no further than what the majority of non-Southern white people were willing to relinquish at no cost to themselves.[3]

In this selection, Blauner acknowledges his debt to some of those people most responsible for new styles of black thought. He begins by showing how a form of colonialism can exist outside of the classic historical case of dominant homeland empire and distant subject province. The key feature of both classic colonialism and American racism is the process of colonization. In terms of the components of this process, Blauner analyzes riots, cultural nationalism, and ghetto control. Then, contrasting whites' historic and present advantage with blacks' disadvantage, he ends by suggesting some steps that have to be taken if black people are to find a place in the society that will be mutually satisfactory for them and for the rest of the nation.

He is not optimistic. Although he thinks changes are imperative, he does not think they will occur easily, and he believes that disorder and strife can be expected to continue for some time. In fact, since the appearance of his article, major locales of confrontation have shifted from ghettoes as a whole (as in the riots), to universities, and now to urban secondary schools.

Like most of the other papers in this section, Blauner concentrates on black-white relations. Later in the book, however, especially in Parts III and IV, many selections and my comments about them concern other groups that have also been treated as if they were racial minorities. That is, the members of these groups have visible physical differences that identify them for subjection to discriminatory behavior "justified" by assumptions about their different biological background. "Ethnic minority" is too general a term to capture much of the connotation of the type and degree of prejudice and discrimination these people have encountered; "quasi-racial minority" is too awkward to read and write again and again (although I do use it once or twice). Therefore, I use the term "racial minority" to describe all of these groups, even though

[3] For a useful review of how black leadership became disillusioned with federal government efforts and with the limits of the civil rights movement, see Lewis Killian, *The Impossible Revolution?* (New York: Random House, 1968).

not all of them have had to cope with equally virulent racism, and even though the term is not quite accurate. For example, light-skinned Puerto Ricans and Mexican-Americans who possess no accent but who do possess the appropriate sorts of cultural accoutrements can easily become part of the white majority if they so choose.

In general, there are two important elements of Blauner's conception of the colonization process which do not apply among other racial minorities to the same degree or in the same way that they do among black people. One of these is forced migration; the other, cultural obliteration. Still, it may be worth emphasizing that these exceptions are matters of degree and not of categorical exclusion. American Indians, for example, first were defeated in battle and *then* were rounded up and moved. Miserable conditions in rural Mexico or San Juan made many people feel that they *had* to move, not merely that they *wanted* to. Moreover, while no culture was destroyed among other groups as much as most traces of African heritage were eradicated among black slaves, the other racial minorities —excepting Oriental Americans—have not, until now, had much chance to equip themselves for coping with the overwhelming dominance of established white America's ways of speaking, feeling, and doing.

Finally, I want to point out that militant and sometimes violent protest is not now, nor has it ever been in American society, limited to racial minority groups. Consider just as examples, the Ku Klux Klan, the labor struggles of the 1930s, and the currently active Jewish Defense League.

. . . . .

For a long time the distinctiveness of the Negro situation among the ethnic minorities was placed in terms of color, and the systematic discrimination that follows from our deep-seated racial prejudices.[1] This was sometimes called the caste theory, and while provocative, it missed essential and dynamic features of American race relations. In the past ten years there has been a tendency to view Afro-Americans as another ethnic group not basically different in experience from previous ethnics and whose "immigra-

[1] This is a revised version of a paper delivered at the University of California Centennial Program, "Studies in Violence," Los Angeles, June 1, 1968. For criticisms and ideas that have improved an earlier draft, I am indebted to Robert Wood, Lincoln Bergman, and Gary Marx. As a good colonialist I have probably restated (read: stolen) more ideas from the writings of Kenneth Clark, Stokely Carmichael, Frantz Fanon, and especially such contributors to the Black Panther Party (Oakland) newspaper as Huey Newton, Bobby Seale, Eldridge Cleaver, and Kathleen Cleaver than I have appropriately credited or generated myself. In self-defense I should state that I began working somewhat independently on a colonial analysis of American race relations in the fall of 1965; see my "Whitewash Over Watts: The Failure of the McCone Report," *Trans-action*, 3 (March–April, 1966), pp. 3–9, 54.

tion" condition in the North would in time follow their upward course. The inadequacy of this model is now clear—even the Kerner Report devotes a chapter to criticizing this analogy. A more recent (though hardly new) approach views the essence of racial subordination in economic class terms: Black people as an underclass are to a degree specially exploited and to a degree economically dispensable in an automating society. Important as are economic factors, the power of race and racism in America cannot be sufficiently explained through class analysis. Into this theory vacuum steps the model of internal colonialism. Problematic and imprecise as it is, it gives hope of becoming a framework that can integrate the insights of caste and racism, ethnicity, culture, and economic exploitation into an overall conceptual scheme. At the same time, the danger of the colonial model is the imposition of an artificial analogy which might keep us from facing up to the fact (to quote Harold Cruse) that "the American black and white social phenomenon is a uniquely new world thing." [2]

During the late 1950's, identification with African nations and other colonial or formerly colonized peoples grew in importance among Black militants.[3] As a result the U.S. was increasingly seen as a colonial power and the concept of domestic colonialism was introduced into the political analysis and rhetoric of militant nationalists. During the same period Black social theorists began developing this frame of reference for explaining American realities. As early as 1962, Cruse characterized race relations in this country as "domestic colonialism." [4] Three years later in *Dark*

Ghetto, Kenneth Clark demonstrated how the political, economic, and social structure of Harlem was essentially that of a colony.[5] Finally in 1967, a full-blown elaboration of "internal colonialism" provided the theoretical framework for Carmichael and Hamilton's widely read *Black Power*.[6] The following year the colonial analogy gained currency and new "respectability" when Senator McCarthy habitually referred to Black Americans as a colonized people during his campaign. While the rhetoric of internal colonialism was catching on, other social scientists began to raise questions about its appropriateness as a scheme of analysis.

The colonial analysis has been rejected as obscurantist and misleading by scholars who point to the significant differences in history and social-political conditions between our domestic patterns and what took place in Africa and India. Colonialism traditionally refers to the establishment of domination over a geographically external political unit, most often inhabited by people of a different race and culture, where this domination is political and economic, and the colony exists subordinated to and dependent upon the mother country. Typically the colonizers exploit the land, the raw materials, the labor, and other resources of the colonized nation; in addition a formal recognition is given to the difference in power, autonomy, and political status, and various agencies are set up to maintain this subordination. Seemingly the analogy must be stretched beyond usefulness if the American version is to be forced into this model. For here we are talking about group relations within a

---

[2] Harold Cruse, *Rebellion or Revolution*, New York: 1968, p. 214.

[3] Nationalism, including an orientation toward Africa, is no new development. It has been a constant tendency within Afro-American politics. See Cruse, *ibid.*, esp. chaps. 5–7.

[4] This was six years before the publication of *The Crisis of the Negro Intellectual*, New York:

Morrow, 1968, which brought Cruse into prominence. Thus the 1962 article was not widely read until its reprinting in Cruse's essays, *Rebellion or Revolution, op. cit.*

[5] Kenneth Clark, *Dark Ghetto*, New York: Harper and Row, 1965. Clark's analysis first appeared a year earlier in *Youth in the Ghetto*, New York: Haryou Associates, 1964.

[6] Stokely Carmichael and Charles Hamilton, *Black Power*, New York: Random House, 1967.

society; the mother country—colony separation in geography is absent. Though whites certainly colonized the territory of the original Americans, internal colonization of Afro-Americans did not involve the settlement of whites in any land that was unequivocally Black. And unlike the colonial situation, there has been no formal recognition of differing power since slavery was abolished outside the South. Classic colonialism involved the control and exploitation of the majority of a nation by a minority of outsiders. Whereas in America the people who are oppressed were themselves originally outsiders and are a numerical minority.

This conventional critique of "internal colonialism" is useful in pointing to the differences between our domestic patterns and the overseas situation. But in its bold attack it tends to lose sight of common experiences that have been historically shared by the most subjugated racial minorities in America and non-white peoples in some other parts of the world. For understanding the most dramatic recent developments on the race scene, this common core element—which I shall call colonization—may be more important than the undeniable divergences between the two contexts.

The common features ultimately relate to the fact that the classical colonialism of the imperialist era and American racism developed out of the same historical situation and reflected a common world economic and power stratification. The slave trade for the most part preceded the imperialist partition and economic exploitation of Africa, and in fact may have been a necessary prerequisite for colonial conquest—since it helped deplete and pacify Africa, undermining the resistance to direct occupation. Slavery contributed one of the basic raw materials for the textile industry which provided much of the capital for the West's industrial development and need for economic expansion-

ism. The essential condition for both American slavery and European colonialism was the power domination and the technological superiority of the Western world in its relation to peoples of non-Western and non-white origins. This objective supremacy in technology and military power buttressed the West's sense of cultural superiority, laying the basis for racist ideologies that were elaborated to justify control and exploitation of non-white people. Thus because classical colonialism and America's internal version developed out of a similar balance of technological, cultural, and power relations, a common *process* of social oppression characterized the racial patterns in the two contexts—despite the variation in political and social structure.

There appear to be four basic components of the colonization complex. The first refers to how the racial group enters into the dominant society (whether colonial power or not). Colonization begins with a forced, involuntary entry. Second, there is an impact on the culture and social organization of the colonized people which is more than just a result of such "natural" processes as contact and acculturation. The colonizing power carries out a policy which constrains, transforms, or destroys indigenous values, orientations, and ways of life. Third, colonization involves a relationship by which members of the colonized group tend to be administered by representatives of the dominant power. There is an experience of being managed and manipulated by outsiders in terms of ethnic status.

A final fundament of colonization is racism. Racism is a principle of social domination by which a group seen as inferior or different in terms of alleged biological characteristics is exploited, controlled, and oppressed socially and psychically by a superordinate group. Except for the marginal case of Japanese imperialism, the major examples of colonialism have involved the subjugation of non-white Asian, African, and Latin

American peoples by white European powers. Thus racism has generally accompanied colonialism. Race prejudice can exist without colonization—the experience of Asian-American minorities is a case in point—but racism as a system of domination is part of the complex of colonization.

The concept of colonization stresses the enormous fatefulness of the historical factor, namely the manner in which a minority group becomes a part of the dominant society.[7] The crucial difference between the colonized Americans and the ethnic immigrant minorities is that the latter have always been able to operate fairly competitively within that relatively open section of the social and economic order because these groups came voluntarily in search of a better life, because their movements in society were not administratively controlled, and because they transformed their culture at their own pace—giving up ethnic values and institutions when it was seen as a desirable exchange for improvements in social position.

In present-day America, a major device of Black colonization is the powerless ghetto. . . .

Of course many ethnic groups in America have lived in ghettoes. What make the Black ghettoes an expression of colonized status are three special features. First, the ethnic ghettoes arose more from voluntary choice, both in the sense of the choice to immigrate to America and the decision to live among one's fellow ethnics. Second, the immigrant ghettoes tended to be a one and two generation phenomenon; they were actually way-stations in the process of acculturation and assimilation. When they continue to persist as in the case of San Francisco's Chinatown, it is because they

are big business for the ethnics themselves and there is a new stream of immigrants. The Black ghetto on the other hand has been a more permanent phenomenon, although some individuals do escape it. But most relevant is the third point. European ethnic groups like the Poles, Italians, and Jews generally only experienced a brief period, often less than a generation, during which their residential buildings, commercial stores, and other enterprises were owned by outsiders. The Chinese and Japanese faced handicaps of color prejudice that were almost as strong as the Blacks faced, but very soon gained control of their internal communities, because their traditional ethnic culture and social organization had not been destroyed by slavery and internal colonization. But Afro-Americans are distinct in the extent to which their segregated communities have remained controlled economically, politically, and administratively from the outside. One indicator of this difference is the estimate that the "income of Chinese-Americans from Chinese-owned businesses is in proportion to their numbers 45 times as great as the income of Negroes from Negro owned businesses."[8] But what is true of business is also true for the other social institutions that operate within the ghetto. The educators, policemen, social workers, politicians, and others who administer the affairs of ghetto residents are typically whites who live outside the Black community. Thus the ghetto plays a strategic role as the focus for the administration by outsiders which is also essential to the structure of overseas colonialism.[9]

[8] N. Glazer and D. P. Moynihan, *Beyond the Melting Pot,* Cambridge, Mass.: M.I.T., 1963, p. 37.
[9] "When we speak of Negro social disabilities under capitalism, . . . we refer to the fact that he does not own anything—*even what is ownable in his own community.* Thus to fight for black liberation *is to fight for his right to own.* The Negro is politically compromised today because he owns nothing. He has little voice in the affairs of state because he owns nothing. The fundamental reason why the Negro bourgeois-

[7] As Eldridge Cleaver reminds us, "Black people are a stolen people held in a colonial status on stolen land, and any analysis which does not acknowledge the colonial status of black people cannot hope to deal with the real problem." "The Land Question," *Ramparts,* 6 (May, 1968), p. 51.

The colonial status of the Negro community goes beyond the issue of ownership and decision-making within Black neighborhoods. The Afro-American population in most cities has very little influence on the power structure and institutions of the larger metropolis, despite the fact that in numerical terms, Blacks tend to be the most sizeable of the various interest groups. A recent analysis of policy-making in Chicago estimates that "Negroes really hold less than 1 percent of the effective power in the Chicago metropolitan area. [Negroes are 20 percent of Cook County's popution.] Realistically the power structure of Chicago is hardly less white than that of Mississippi." [10]

Colonization outside of a traditional colonial structure has its own special conditions. The group culture and social structure of the colonized in America is less developed; it is also less autonomous. In addition, the colonized are a numerical minority, and futhermore they are ghettoized more totally and are more dispersed than people under classic colonialism. Though these realities affect the magnitude and direction of response, it is my basic thesis that the most important expressions of protest in the Black community during the recent years

reflect the colonized status of Afro-America. Riots, programs of separation, politics of community control, the Black revolutionary movements, and cultural nationalism each represent a different strategy of attack on domestic colonialism in America. Let us now examine some of these movements.

RIOT OR REVOLT?

. . . . .

In my critique of the McCone report I observed that the rioters were asserting a claim to territoriality, an unorganized and rather inchoate attempt to gain control over their community or "turf." [11] In succeeding disorders also the thrust of the action has been the attempt to clear out an alien presence, white men and officials, rather than a drive to kill whites as in a conventional race riot. The main attacks have been directed at the property of white business men and at the police who operate in the Black community "like an army of occupation" protecting the interests of outside exploiters and maintaining the domination over the ghetto by the central metropolitan power structure.[12] The Kerner report misleads when it attempts to explain riots in terms of integration: "What the rioters appear to be seeking was fuller participation in the social order and the material benefits enjoyed by the majority of American citizens. Rather than rejecting the American system, they were anxious to obtain a place for themselves in it." [13]

democratic revolution has been aborted is because American capitalism has prevented the development of a black class of capitalist owners of institutions and economic tools. To take one crucial example, Negro radicals today are severely hampered in their tasks of educating the black masses on political issues because Negroes do not own any of the necessary means of propaganda and communication. The Negro owns no printing presses, he has no stake in the networks of the means of communication. Inside his own communities he does not own the house he lives in, the property he lives on, nor the wholesale and retail sources from which he buys his commodities. He does not own the edifices in which he enjoys culture and entertainment or in which he socializes. In capitalist society, an individual or group that does not own anything is powerless." H. Cruse, "Behind the Black Power Slogan," in Cruse, *Rebellion or Revolution, op. cit.,* pp. 238–39.

[10] Harold M. Baron, "Black Powerlessness in Chicago," *Trans-action,* 6 (Nov., 1968), pp. 27–33.

[11] R. Blauner, "Whitewash Over Watts," *op. cit.*

[12] "The police function to support and enforce the interests of the dominant political, social, and economic interests of the town" is a statement made by a former police scholar and official, according to A. Neiderhoffer, *Behind the Shield,* New York: Doubleday, 1967 as cited by Gary T. Marx, "Civil Disorder and the Agents of Control," *Journal of Social Issues,* forthcoming.

[13] Report of the National Advisory Commission on Civil Disorders, N.Y.: Bantam, March, 1968, p. 7.

More accurately, the revolts pointed to alienation from this system on the part of many poor and also not-so-poor Blacks. The sacredness of private property, that unconsciously accepted bulwark of our social arrangements, was rejected; people who looted apparently without guilt generally remarked that they were taking things that "really belonged" to them anyway.[14] Obviously the society's bases of legitimacy and authority have been attacked. Law and order has long been viewed as the white man's law and order by Afro-Americans; but now this perspective characteristic of a colonized people is out in the open. And the Kerner Report's own data question how well ghetto rebels are buying the system: In Newark only 33 percent of self-reported rioters said they thought this country was worth fighting for in the event of a major war; in the Detroit sample the figure was 55 percent.[15]

One of the most significant consequences of the process of colonization is a weakening of the colonized's individual and collective will to resist his oppression. It has been easier to contain and control Black ghettoes because communal bonds and group solidarity have been weakened through divisions among leadership, failures of organization, and a general disspiritment that accompanies social oppression. The riots are a signal that the will to resist has broken the mold of accommodation. In some cities as in Watts they also represented nascent movements toward community identity. In several riot-torn ghettoes the outbursts have stimulated new organizations and movements. If it is true that the riot phenomenon of 1964–68 has passed its peak, its historical import may be more for the "internal" organizing momentum generated than for any profound "external" response of the larger society facing up to underlying causes.

Despite the appeal of Frantz Fanon to young Black revolutionaries, America is not Algeria. It is difficult to foresee how riots in our cities can play a role equivalent to rioting in the colonial situation as an integral phase in a movement for national liberation. In 1968 some militant groups (for example, the Black Panther Party in Oakland) had concluded that ghetto riots were self-defeating of the lives and interests of Black people in the present balance of organization and gunpower, though they had served a role to stimulate both Black consciousness and white awareness of the depths of racial crisis. Such militants have been influential in "cooling" their communities during periods of high riot potential. Theoretically oriented Black radicals see riots as spontaneous mass behavior which must be replaced by a revolutionary organization and consciousness. But despite the differences in objective conditions, the violence of the 1960's seems to serve the same psychic function, assertions of dignity and manhood for young Blacks in urban ghettoes, as it did for the colonized of North Africa described by Fanon and Memmi.[16]

CULTURAL NATIONALISM

Cultural conflict is generic to the colonial relation because colonization involves the domination of Western technological values over the more

---

[14] This kind of attitude has a long history among American Negroes. During slavery, Blacks used the same rationalization to justify stealing from their masters. Appropriating things from the master was viewed as "*taking* part of his property for the benefit of another part; whereas *stealing* referred to appropriating something from another slave, an offense that was not condoned." Kenneth Stampp, *The Peculiar Institution*, New York: Vintage, 1956, p. 127.

[15] Report of the National Advisory Commission on Civil Disorders, *op. cit.*, p. 178.

[16] Frantz Fanon, *Wretched of the Earth*, New York: Grove, 1963; Albert Memmi, *The Colonizer and the Colonized*, Boston: Beacon, 1967.

communal cultures of non-Western peoples. Colonialism played havoc with the national integrity of the peoples it brought under its sway. Of course, all traditional cultures are threatened by industrialism, the city, and modernization in communication, transportation, health, and education. What is special are the political and administrative decisions of colonizers in managing and controlling colonized peoples. The boundaries of African colonies, for example, were drawn to suit the political conveniences of the European nations without regard to the social organization and cultures of African tribes and kingdoms. Thus Nigeria as blocked out by the British included the Yorubas and the Ibos, whose civil war today is a residuum of the colonialist's disrespect for the integrity of indigenous cultures.

The most total destruction of culture in the colonization process took place not in traditional colonialism but in America. As Frazier stressed, the integral cultures of the diverse African peoples who furnished the slave trade were destroyed because slaves from different tribes, kingdoms, and linguistic groups were purposely separated to maximize domination and control. Thus language, religion, and national loyalties were lost in North America much more completely than in the Caribbean and Brazil where slavery developed somewhat differently. Thus on this key point America's internal colonization has been more total and extreme than situations of classic colonialism. For the British in India and the European powers in Africa were not able—as outnumbered minorities—to destroy the national and tribal cultures of the colonized. Recall that American slavery lasted 250 years and its racist aftermath another 100. Colonial dependency in the case of British Kenya and French Algeria lasted only 77 and 125 years respectively. In the wake of this more drastic uprooting and destruction of culture and social organization,

much more powerful agencies of social, political, and psychological domination developed in the American case.

Colonial control of many peoples inhabiting the colonies was more a goal than a fact, and at Independence there were undoubtedly fairly large numbers of Africans who had never seen a colonial administrator. The gradual process of extension of control from the administrative center on the African coast contrasts sharply with the total uprooting involved in the slave trade and the totalitarian aspects of slavery in the United States. Whether or not Elkins is correct in treating slavery as a total institution, it undoubtedly had a far more radical and pervasive impact on American slaves than did colonialism on the vast majority of Africans.[17]

Yet a similar cultural process unfolds in both contexts of colonialism. To the extent that they are involved in the larger society and economy, the colonized are caught up in a conflict between two cultures. Fanon has described how the assimilation-oriented schools of Martinique taught him to reject his own culture and Blackness in favor of Westernized, French, and white values.[18] Both the colonized elites under traditional colonialism and perhaps the majority of Afro-Americans today experience a parallel split in identity, cultural loyalty, and political orientation.[19]

The colonizers use their culture to socialize the colonized elites (intellectuals, politicians, and middle class) into an identification with the colonial system. Because Western culture has

[17] Robert Wood, "Colonialism in Africa and America: Some Conceptual Considerations," December, 1967, unpublished paper.
[18] F. Fanon, *Black Skins, White Masks*, New York: Grove, 1967.
[19] Harold Cruse has described how these two themes of integration with the larger society and identification with ethnic nationality have struggled within the political and cultural movements of Negro Americans. *The Crisis of the Negro Intellectual, op. cit.*

the prestige, the power, and the key to open the limited opportunity that a minority of the colonized may achieve, the first reaction seems to be an acceptance of the dominant values. Call it brainwashing as the Black Muslims put it; call it identifying with the aggressor if you prefer Freudian terminology; call it a natural response to the hope and belief that integration and democratization can really take place if you favor a more commonsense explanation, this initial acceptance in time crumbles on the realities of racism and colonialism. The colonized, seeing that his success within colonialism is at the expense of his group and his own inner identity, moves radically toward a rejection of the Western culture and develops a nationalist outlook that celebrates his people and their traditions.

· · · · ·

Memmi's book, *The Colonizer and the Colonized,* is based on his experience as a Tunisian Jew in a marginal position between the French and the colonized Arab majority. The uncanny parallels between the North African situation he describes and the course of Black-white relations in our society is the best impressionist argument I know for the thesis that we have a colonized group and a colonizing system in America. His discussion of why even the most radical French anti-colonialist cannot participate in the struggle of the colonized is directly applicable to the situation of the white liberal and radical vis-à-vis the Black movement. His portrait of the colonized is as good an analysis of the psychology behind Black Power and Black nationalism as anything that has been written in the U.S. Consider for example:

Considered *en bloc* as *them, they,* or *those,* different from every point of view, homogeneous in a radical heterogeneity, the colonized reacts by rejecting all the colonizers *en bloc.* The distinction between deed and

intent has no great significance in the colonial situation. In the eyes of the colonized, all Europeans in the colonies are de facto colonizers, and whether they want to be or not, they are colonizers in some ways. By their privileged economic position, by belonging to the political system of oppression, or by participating in an effectively negative complex toward the colonized, they are colonizers. . . . They are supporters or at least unconscious accomplices of that great collective aggression of Europe.[20]

The same passion which made him admire and absorb Europe shall make him assert his differences; since those differences, after all, are within him and correctly constitute his true self.[21]

The important thing now is to rebuild his people, whatever be their authentic nature; to reforge their unity, communicate with it, and to feel that they belong.[22]

Cultural revitalization movements play a key role in anti-colonial movements. They follow an inner necessity and logic of their own that comes from the consequences of colonialism on groups and personal identities; they are also essential to provide the solidarity which the political or military phase of the anti-colonial revolution requires. In the U.S. an Afro-American culture has been developing since slavery out of the ingredients of African worldviews, the experience of bondage, Southern values and customs, migration and the Northern lower-class ghettoes, and most importantly, the political history of the Black population in its struggle against racism.[23] That Afro-Americans are mov-

[20] Memmi, *op. cit.,* p. 130.
[21] *Ibid.,* p. 132.
[22] *Ibid.,* p. 134.
[23] In another essay, I argue against the standard sociological position that denies the existence of an ethnic Afro-American culture and I expand on the above themes. The concept of "Soul" is astonishingly parallel in content to the mystique of "Negritude" in Africa; the Pan-African culture movement has its parallel in the

ing toward cultural nationalism in a period when ethnic loyalties tend to be weak (and perhaps on the decline) in this country is another confirmation of the unique colonized position of the Black group. (A similar nationalism seems to be growing among American Indians and Mexican-Americans.)

THE MOVEMENT FOR GHETTO CONTROL

The call for Black Power unites a number of varied movements and tendencies.[24] Though no clear-cut program has yet emerged, the most important emphasis seems to be the movement for control of the ghetto. Black leaders and organizations are increasingly concerned with owning and controlling those institutions that exist within or impinge upon their community. The colonial model provides a key to the understanding of this movement, and indeed ghetto control advocates have increasingly invoked the language of colonialism in pressing for local home rule. The framework of anti-colonialism explains why the struggle for poor people's or community control of poverty programs has been more central in many cities than the content of these programs and why it has been crucial to exclude whites from leadership positions in Black organizations.

The key institutions that anti-colo-

nialists want to take over or control are business, social services, schools, and the police. Though many spokesmen have advocated the exclusion of white landlords and small businessmen from the ghetto, this program has evidently not struck fire with the Black population and little concrete movement toward economic expropriation has yet developed. Welfare recipients have organized in many cities to protect their rights and gain a greater voice in the decisions that affect them, but whole communities have not yet been able to mount direct action against welfare colonialism. Thus schools and the police seem now to be the burning issues of ghetto control politics.

During the past few years there has been a dramatic shift from educational integration as the primary goal to that of community control of the schools. Afro-Americans are demanding their own school boards, with the power to hire and fire principals and teachers and to construct a curriculum which would be relevant to the special needs and culture style of ghetto youth. Especially active in high schools and colleges have been Black students, whose protests have centered on the incorporation of Black Power and Black culture into the educational system. Consider how similar is the spirit behind these developments to the attitude of the colonized North African toward European education:

He will prefer a long period of educational mistakes to the continuance of the colonizer's school organization. He will choose institutional disorder in order to destroy the institutions built by the colonizers as soon as possible. There we will see, indeed a reactive drive of profound protest. He will no longer owe anything to the colonizer and will have definitely broken with him.[25]

Protest and institutional disorder over the issue of school control came to a head in 1968 in New York City.

burgeoning Black culture mood in Afro-American communities. See "Black Culture: Myth or Reality" in Peter Rose, editor, *Americans From Africa*, Atherton, 1969.

[24] Scholars and social commentators, Black and white alike, disagree in interpreting the contemporary Black Power movement. The issues concern whether this is a new development in Black protest or an old tendency revised; whether the movement is radical, revolutionary, reformist, or conservative; and whether this orientation is unique to Afro-Americans or essentially a Black parallel to other ethnic group strategies for collective mobility. For an interesting discussion of Black Power as a modernized version of Booker T. Washington's separatism and economism, see Harold Cruse, *Rebellion or Revolution*, *op. cit.*, pp. 193–258.

[25] Memmi, *op. cit.*, pp. 137–138.

The procrastination in the Albany State legislature, the several crippling strikes called by the teachers union, and the almost frenzied response of Jewish organizations makes it clear that decolonization of education faces the resistance of powerful vested interests.[26] The situation is too dynamic at present to assess probable future results. However, it can be safely predicted that some form of school decentralization will be institutionalized in New York, and the movement for community control of education will spread to more cities.

This movement reflects some of the problems and ambiguities that stem from the situation of colonization outside an immediate colonial context. The Afro-American community is not parallel in structure to the communities of colonized nations under traditional colonialism. The significant difference here is the lack of fully developed indigenous institutions besides the church. Outside of some areas of the South there is really no Black economy, and most Afro-Americans are inevitably caught up in the larger society's structure of occupations, education, and mass communication. Thus the ethnic nationalist orientation which reflects the reality of colonization exists alongside an integrationist orientation which corresponds to the reality that the institutions of the larger society are much more developed than those of the incipient nation.[27] As would be expected the movement for school control reflects both tendencies. The militant leaders who spearhead such local move-ments may be primarily motivated by the desire to gain control over the community's institutions—they are anti-colonialists first and foremost. Many parents who support them may share this goal also, but the majority are probably more concerned about creating a new education that will enable their children to "make it" in the society and the economy as a whole—they know that the present school system fails ghetto children and does not prepare them for participation in American life.

There is a growing recognition that the police are the most crucial institution maintaining the colonized status of Black Americans. And of all establishment institutions, police departments probably include the highest proportion of individual racists. This is no accident since central to the workings of racism (an essential component of colonization) are attacks on the humanity and dignity of the subject group. Through their normal routines the police constrict Afro-Americans to Black neighborhoods by harassing and questioning them when found outside the ghetto; they break up groups of youth congregating on corners or in cars without any provocation; and they continue to use offensive and racist language no matter how many intergroup understanding seminars have been built into the police academy. They also shoot to kill ghetto residents for alleged crimes such as car thefts and running from police officers.[28]

<hr>

[26] For the New York school conflict see Jason Epstein, "The Politics of School Decentralization," *New York Review of Books*, June 6, 1968, pp. 26–32; and "The New York City School Revolt," *ibid.*, 11, no. 6, pp. 37–41.

[27] This dual split in the politics and psyche of the Black American was poetically described by Du Bois in his *Souls of Black Folk*, and more recently has been insightfully analyzed by Harold Cruse in *The Crisis of the Negro Intellectual, op. cit.* Cruse has also characterized the problem of the Black community as that of underdevelopment.

[28] A recent survey of police finds "that in the predominantly Negro areas of several large cities, many of the police perceive the residents as basically hostile, especially the youth and adolescents. A lack of public support—from citizens, from courts, and from laws—is the policeman's major complaint. But some of the public criticism can be traced to the activities in which he engages day by day, and perhaps to the tone in which he enforces the 'law' in the Negro neighborhoods. Most frequently he is 'called upon' to intervene in domestic quarrels and break up loitering groups. He stops and frisks two or three times as many people as are carrying dangerous weapons or are actual criminals, and almost half of these don't wish to cooperate with the policeman's efforts." Peter Rossi *et al.*, "Be-

Police are key agents in the power equation as well as the drama of dehumanization. In the final analysis they do the dirty work for the larger system by restricting the striking back of Black rebels to skirmishes inside the ghetto, thus deflecting energies and attacks from the communities and institutions of the larger power structure. In a historical review, Gary Marx notes that since the French revolution, police and other authorities have killed large numbers of demonstrators and rioters; the rebellious "rabble" rarely destroys human life. The same pattern has been repeated in America's recent revolts.[29] Journalistic accounts appearing in the press recently suggest that police see themselves as defending the interests of white people against a tide of Black insurgence; furthermore the majority of whites appear to view "blue power" in this light. There is probably no other opinion on which the races are as far apart today as they are on the question of attitudes toward the police.

In many cases set off by a confrontation between a policeman and a Black citizen, the ghetto uprisings have dramatized the role of law enforcement and the issue of police brutality. In their aftermath, movements have arisen to contain police activity. One of the first was the Community Alert Patrol in Los Angeles, a method of policing the police

tween Black and White—The Faces of American Institutions and the Ghetto," in Supplemental Studies for The National Advisory Commission on Civil Disorders, July 1968, p. 114.

[29] "In the Gordon Riots of 1780 demonstrators destroyed property and freed prisoners, but did not seem to kill anyone, while authorities killed several hundred rioters and hung an additional 25. In the Rebellion Riots of the French Revolution, though several hundred rioters were killed, they killed no one. Up to the end of the Summer of 1967, this pattern had clearly been repeated, as police, not rioters, were responsible for most of the more than 100 deaths that have occurred. Similarly, in a related context, the more than 100 civil rights murders of recent years have been matched by almost no murders of racist whites." G. Marx, "Civil Disorders and the Agents of Social Control," op. cit.

in order to keep them honest and constrain their violations of personal dignity. This was the first tactic of the Black Panther Party which originated in Oakland, perhaps the most significant group to challenge the police role in maintaining the ghetto as a colony. The Panther's later policy of openly carrying guns (a legally protected right) and their intention of defending themselves against police aggression has brought on a series of confrontations with the Oakland police department. All indications are that the authorities intend to destroy the Panthers by shooting, framing up, or legally harassing their leadership—diverting the group's energies away from its primary purpose of self-defense and organization of the Black community to that of legal defense and gaining support in the white community.

There are three major approaches to "police colonialism" that correspond to reformist and revolutionary readings of the situation. The most elementary and also superficial sees colonialism in the fact that ghettoes are overwhelmingly patrolled by white rather than by Black officers. The proposal—supported today by many police departments—to increase the number of Blacks on local forces to something like their distribution in the city would then make it possible to reduce the use of white cops in the ghetto. This reform should be supported, for a variety of obvious reasons, but it does not get to the heart of the police role as agents of colonization.

The Kerner Report documents the fact that in some cases Black policemen can be as brutal as their white counterparts. The Report does not tell us who polices the ghetto, but they have compiled the proportion of Negroes on the forces of the major cities. In some cities the disparity is so striking that white police inevitably dominate ghetto patrols. (In Oakland 31 percent of the population and only 4 percent of the police are Black; in Detroit the figures are

39 percent and 5 percent; and in New Orleans 41 and 4.) In other cities, however, the proportion of Black cops is approaching the distribution in the city: Philadelphia 29 percent and 20 percent; Chicago 27 percent and 17 percent.[30] These figures also suggest that both the extent and the pattern of colonization may vary from one city to another. It would be useful to study how Black communities differ in degree of control over internal institutions as well as in economic and political power in the metropolitan area.

A second demand which gets more to the issue is that police should live in the communities they patrol. The idea here is that Black cops who lived in the ghetto would have to be accountable to the community; if they came on like white cops then "the brothers would take care of business" and make their lives miserable. The third or maximalist position is based on the premise that the police play no positive role in the ghettoes. It calls for the withdrawal of metropolitan officers from Black communities and the substitution of an autonomous indigenous force that would maintain order without oppressing the population. The precise relationship between such an independent police, the city and county law enforcement agencies, a ghetto governing body that would supervise and finance it, and especially the law itself is yet unclear. It is unlikely that we will soon face these problems directly as they have arisen in the case of New York's schools. Of all the programs of decolonization, police autonomy will be most resisted. It gets to the heart of how the state functions to control and contain the Black community through delegating the legitimate use of violence to police authority.

The various "Black Power" programs that are aimed at gaining control of individual ghettoes—buying up property and businesses, running the schools through community boards, taking over anti-poverty programs and other social agencies, diminishing the arbitrary power of the police—can serve to revitalize the institutions of the ghetto and build up an economic, professional, and political power base. These programs seem limited; we do not know at present if they are enough in themselves to end colonized status.[31] But they are certainly a necessary first step.

THE ROLE OF WHITES

What makes the Kerner Report a less-than-radical document is its superficial treatment of racism and its reluctance to confront the colonized relationship between Black people and the larger society. The Report emphasizes the attitudes and feelings that make up white racism, rather than the system of privilege and control which is the heart of the matter.[32] With all its discussion of the ghetto and its problems, it never faces the question of the stake that white Americans have in racism and ghettoization.

This is not a simple question, but this paper should not end with the impression that police are the major villains. All white Americans gain some

---

[30] Report of the National Advisory Commission on Civil Disorders, op. cit., p. 321. That Black officers nevertheless would make a difference is suggested by data from one of the supplemental studies to the Kerner Report. They found Negro policemen working in the ghettoes considerably more sympathetic to the community and its social problems than their white counterparts. Peter Rossi et al., "Between Black and White— The Faces of American Institutions in the Ghetto," op. cit., chap. 6.

[31] Eldridge Cleaver has called this first stage of the anti-colonial movement community liberation in contrast to a more long-range goal of national liberation. E. Cleaver, "Community Imperialism," Black Panther Party newspaper, 2 (May 18, 1968).

[32] For a discussion of this failure to deal with racism, see Gary T. Marx, "Report of the National Commission: The Analysis of Disorder or Disorderly Analysis," 1968, unpublished paper.

privileges and advantage from the colonization of Black communities.[33] The majority of whites also lose something from this oppression and division in society. Serious research should be directed to the ways in which white individuals and institutions are tied into the ghetto. In closing let me suggest some possible parameters.

1. It is my guess that only a small minority of whites make a direct economic profit from ghetto colonization. This is hopeful in that the ouster of white businessmen may become politically feasible. Much more significant, however, are the private and corporate interests in the land and residential property of the Black community; their holdings and influence on urban decision-making must be exposed and combated.

2. A much larger minority have occupational and professional interests in the present arrangements. The Kerner Commission reports that 1.3 million non-white men would have to be upgraded occupationally in order to make the Black job distribution roughly similar to the white. They advocate this without mentioning that 1.3 million specially privileged white workers would lose in the bargain.[34] In addition there are those professionals who carry out what Lee Rainwater has called the "dirty work" of administering the lives of the ghetto poor: the social workers, the school teachers, the urban development people, and of course the police.[35] The social problems of the Black community will ultimately be solved only by people and organizations from that community; thus the emphasis within these profes-

sions must shift toward training such a cadre of minority personnel. Social scientists who teach and study problems of race and poverty likewise have an obligation to replace themselves by bringing into the graduate schools and college faculties men of color who will become the future experts in these areas. For cultural and intellectual imperialism is as real as welfare colonialism, though it is currently screened behind such unassailable shibboleths as universalism and the objectivity of scientific inquiry.

3. Without downgrading the vested interests of profit and profession, the real nitty-gritty elements of the white stake are political power and bureaucratic security. Whereas few whites have much understanding of the realities of race relations and ghetto life, I think most give tacit or at least subconscious support for the containment and control of the Black population. Whereas most whites have extremely distorted images of Black Power, many—if not most— would still be frightened by actual Black political power. Racial groups and identities are real in American life; white Americans sense they are on top, and they fear possible reprisals or disruptions were power to be more equalized. There seems to be a paranoid fear in the white psyche of Black dominance; the belief that Black autonomy would mean unbridled license is so ingrained that such reasonable outcomes as Black political majorities and independent Black police forces will be bitterly resisted.

On this level the major mass bulwark of colonization is the administrative need for bureaucratic security so that the middle classes can go about their life and business in peace and quiet. The Black militant movement is a threat to the orderly procedures by which bureaucracies and suburbs manage their existence, and I think today there are more people who feel a stake in conventional procedures than there are those who gain directly from racism. For in

[33] Such a statement is easier to assert than to document but I am attempting the latter in a forthcoming book tentatively titled *White Racism, Black Culture,* to be published by Little, Brown, 1970.

[34] Report of the National Advisory Commission on Civil Disorders, *op. cit.,* pp. 253–256.

[35] Lee Rainwater, "The Revolt of the Dirty-Workers," *Trans-action,* 5 (Nov., 1967), pp. 2, 64.

their fight for institutional control, the colonized will not play by the white rules of the game. These administrative rules have kept them down and out of the system; therefore they have no necessary intention of running institutions in the image of the white middle class.

The liberal, humanist value that violence is the worst sin cannot be defended today if one is committed squarely against racism and for self-determination. For some violence is almost inevitable in the decolonization process; unfortunately racism in America has been so effective that the greatest power Afro-Americans (and perhaps also Mexican-Americans) wield today is the power to disrupt. If we are going to swing with these revolutionary times and at least respond positively to the anti-colonial movement, we will have to learn to live with conflict, confrontation, constant change, and what may be real or apparent chaos and disorder.

A positive response from the white majority needs to be in two major directions at the same time. First, community liberation movements should be supported in every way by pulling out white instruments of direct control and exploitation and substituting technical assistance to the community when this is asked for. But it is not enough to relate affirmatively to the nationalist movement for ghetto control without at the same time radically opening doors for full participation in the institutions of the mainstream. Otherwise the liberal and radical position is little different than the traditional segregationist. Freedom in the special conditions of American colonization means that the colonized must have the choice between participation in the larger society and in their own independent structures.

6. THE SOCIOLOGY OF BLACK NATIONALISM

James Turner

In 1969, Gary Marx reviewed all the major national surveys of black attitudes that had been carried out until that time.[1] He was able to conclude that the great majority of black people believed that progress was being made in American race relations and in improvement of the black situation; that the leaders who had the widest recognition and support were established moderates like Roy Wilkins or Supreme Court Justice Thurgood Marshall; and that the most commonly desired goal among black people was full and equal participation through integration. The findings of a more recent major survey done by Louis Harris for the April 6, 1970, issue of *Time* magazine were similar. Despite overwhelming majorities critical of local police, strong distrust of the Federal government, and a rise from 22 percent (1963) to 31 percent (1970) in the proportion believing violence would probably be necessary for blacks to win their rights, two-thirds of the respondents nevertheless felt things were getting better than they had been four or five years before. Respondents reported their satisfaction with increasing numbers of black students in college, with new job opportunities, with new-found black pride, and with increases in the number of black-owned businesses.

In a 1968 study for the National Advisory Commission on Civil Disorders (the Kerner Commission), Campbell and Schuman examined the attitudes of black people in fifteen

[1]Gary T. Marx, *Protest and Prejudice*, rev. ed. (New York: Harper & Row, 1969). See especially pp. 215–42.

Source: *The Black Scholar,* December 1969, pp. 18–27. Reprinted by permission of the author and publisher.

JAMES TURNER is Associate Professor and Director of the African Studies and Research Center at Cornell University.

major cities.[2] They found overwhelming support for statements of positive cultural identity, ranging from a high of 96 percent for taking more pride in Negro history to a low of 46 percent for the desirability of black children studying an African language in school. In contrast, separatist proposals received very little support. Agreement ranged from 5 percent preferring that their children should have only Negro friends to a high of only 18 percent for the proposition that stores in Negro neighborhoods should be owned and operated by Negroes.

From all these data there seem to be a few grounds to doubt that what most black people want falls fully within what an important aspect of American sociopolitical ideology says all groups possess the right to have. Practice often falls short, but in theory democratic pluralism allows different groups wide scope to develop or maintain their cultural heritage.

Black nationalists agree with both parts of the last statement, but they differ on whether practice will ever match theory. Their primary task is to win new followers and maintain old ones in order to go on building black pride and cohesive communities. Difficulties arise when leaders try to create independent organizations to carry out activities that the majority believes ought to be under the control of the *general* community. What makes the task of the black nationalist leader harder still is that he does not know how resilient the majority will be, how much it will accommodate itself to black aspirations without cracking down and closing off the chance for new gains. Furthermore, black nationalism promotes self-discipline and directed effort, qualities that can lead individuals to conventional success. The first of these conditions means that it is difficult to find general agreement among leaders about the best ways of accomplishing rapid and lasting change; the second, that the possibility exists for movement members to be co-opted or otherwise diverted by rewards available in the larger society, thereby diminishing the resources and enthusiasm available to a group seeking less conventional means of change.

Black nationalist thought is not all of a piece. It is a mistake to assume that the solidary tactics that are sometimes employed for winning concessions in a specific situation are paralleled by a universally shared ideology that is equally cohesive. Nevertheless, there are some recurrent ideas in black nationalist thought, and Turner's paper reveals them. The

[2] Angus Campbell and Howard Schuman, "Racial Attitudes in Fifteen American Cities," in *Supplemental Studies for the National Advisory Commission on Civil Disorders* (Washington, D.C.: U.S. Government Printing Office, 1968).

following aims are common: (1) to create bases of self-respect that are not dependent on white criteria; (2) to respond positively to charges that black communities have until now been marked by nothing more than social disorganization, ineffectiveness, impoverishment, violence, and despair; (3) to establish psychological and institutional foundations from which to launch other changes like increased electoral clout and more effective education; (4) to emphasize past heritage, a sense of wider community, and a glimpse of a new spiritually richer future through ties to Africa and the whole third world. In short, black nationalism, like other visionary outlooks, aims at the creation of a "new man," and of the institutions that will shape and be shaped by him.

It is the militantly political wing of black nationalism that receives the most publicity. It probably articulates some feelings shared by many black Americans, though the data reviewed earlier make clear that not very many yet believe that their greatest hopes lie with following the directions it suggests. For example, Black Panther rhetoric denounces capitalist standards of individual mobility and success, threatens revolt, and insists that any responsibility for disruption and possible insurrection lies with the majority. In the words of Huey Newton, Minister of Defense of the Black Panther Party in a September 1970, speech before the Revolutionary Peoples Constitutional Convention in Philadelphia, "We will change this society. It is up to the oppressor to decide whether this will be a peaceful change. We will use whatever means necessary. We will have our manhood even if we have to level the earth." Were this not sufficient to be upsetting to many white Americans, what would doubtlessly make it so is the sympathy the Black Panther Party gets from the white student Left, certain activist sectors of which made "campus violence" the domestic problem most frequently mentiond in public opinion polls in autumn of 1970.

Black nationalism would be hard for many white Americans to understand and accept even if it were never accompanied by threats to tear the whole system down. It indicates to the prejudiced that blacks no longer "know their place"; it unsettles those who, even with good intentions, do not believe that blacks are capable of doing all that the nationalists wish to accomplish; it seems too ready to condone any action that contributes to black pride and consciousness; finally (and this should be no surprise under the conditions of threat and competition that have for so long been part of American race relations), black nationalism is ethnocentric, accompanied by criticism of the dominant out-group, its institutions, and its organizational structure. Turner uses the term "disaffection" and takes pains to distinguish between individual white men (who may be decent) and white men in general (who have not been). Criticism is legitimate, in many ways warranted, and in some ways helpful. But the distinction between criticism and prejudice is sometimes a fine one, and it is easy for either white people or black ones to cross it in the heat of controversy or anger.

Black nationalism is the successor to the civil rights movement. That movement tried to turn anger aside through nonviolent resistance, attempting to capitalize on a capacity for love so great that we usually find it only in the men and women who in dying become our saints and martyrs.

Has black nationalism been a worthy successor? Some might claim to know the answer already, but I recommend suspending judgment. Black nationalism has already been many different things to many different people: a source of new ideas that enrich not only blacks but whites and other minorities as well; a rigidly doctrinaire program for an informed elite's attempts to mobilize the masses; a justification for preparing for revolt; a strategic underpinning for conventional participation in interest-group politics; a basis of pride and sense of direction that has enabled young black people to believe they can accomplish through community action and development what white and Oriental immigrants did using ancestral cultures that had not been stripped away from them. Only events that have not yet occurred will show which if any of these themes became and remained dominant on the day after tomorrow.

The movement of black nationalist ideas is dominated by the collective consciousness of its adherents as members of a minority group, which is subordinated to another and more powerful group within the total political and social order. The ideological preoccupations of black nationalism revolve around this central problem, the black man's predicament of having been forced by historical circumstances into a state of dependence upon the white society considered the master society and the dominant culture. The essential theme of black nationalism can be seen as a counter-movement away from subordination to independence, from alienation through refutation, to self-affirmation. In this respect, such a movement of ideas represents an effort to transcend the immediate conditions of an undesirable relationship by a process of reflection which creates a different (and opposing) constellation of symbols and assumptions. Black nationalism is thus at once an ideological movement of both social-psychological and political portent.

The theme of disgrace and subjugation is the point of departure of the whole ideological expression of black nationalism, which derives from the political and cultural uprooting of black people in general through colonial conquest and enslavement. The overwhelming sentiment that dominates in this connection is the belief that the group is being denied a "true" and unadulterated experience of its humanity as a result of being forced into a social system whose cultural values preclude an honorable accommodation. The black nationalist recognizes himself as belonging to an out-group, an alien in relation to the white society which controls the total universe in which he moves. This sentiment of belonging no longer to oneself but to another goes together with an awareness of being black, which becomes translated in social terms into a caste and class consciousness. The association between race and servitude is a constant theme in Afro-American literature. The economic exploitation and social discrimination which defines persons of African descent as a social category gives many of its members an avid sense of race consciousness as a consequence of mutual humiliation.

Becoming a black nationalist seems to involve a realization that persons of African descent are treated categorically by the dominant group. Subsequently, there develops the firm conviction that Afro-Americans must become transmuted into a conscious and cohesive group. The rationale is that a group giving a unitary response can more effectively and honorably confront the constraining dominant group. Race, color, and mutual resistance to the oppression of the dominant group and its imposed assumptions and definitions about the minority, become the vehicles for realizing conversion from category to group. Loyalty to group cultural attributes and commitment to collective goals provide the adhesive for the group. Black nationalists argue for the exclusive right of members of the group to define, establish, and maintain their own group boundaries.

The black man's principal role and meaning in western history has been as an economic tool.[1] This is what Aime Cèsaire, paraphrasing Marx, has called "the reduction of the black man into an object."[2] However, the prevailing preoccupation of the proponents of black nationalism is with the black people primarily as a "race," and secondarily as a class. They are concerned with the collective image of the black man in American society and his human status in the world. They are concerned about a white racial ideology which defined the black man as inferior, and as a consequence a social relationship between black and white men which acquired the moral values summarized by the writer, Bloke Modisane:

White is right, and to be black is to be despised, dehumanized . . . classed among the beasts, hounded and persecuted, discriminated against, segregated and oppressed by government and by man's greed. White is the positive standard, black the negative.[3]

The cultural and political ascendancy of white men over black men, combined with the active denigration of black men, has thus had the effect of vitiating the latter's self esteem, with the profound psychological consequences which involve shame and self-hatred.[*] Black men throughout the world suffered this negation as human beings. This is

[1] Eric Williams, *Capitalism and Slavery*, London: 2nd edn., 1964.
[2] Aime Cèsaire, *Discourse on Colonialism*, Paris: 1955, p. 22.
[3] Bloke Modisane, "Why I ran away," in J. Langston Hughes (ed), *An African Treasury*, New York: 1960, p. 26.
[*] The psychological implications of racial discrimination for the black man in white society have produced numerous studies. This question seems to have been best summarized by John Dollard: "The upshot of the matter seems to be that recognizing one's own Negro traits is bound to be a process wounding to the basic sense of integrity of the individual who comes into life with no such negative views of his own characteristics," in *Caste and Class in a Southern Town*, New York: 2nd edn., 1949, p. 184.

the external reality with which the ideology of black nationalism is concerned.

Historically, contact between black and white peoples has been seriously influenced by certain cultural assumptions and premises upon which social relations were predicated and legitimized. Slavery and the colonial enterprise were rationalized as a civilizing mission aimed at transforming the black man by his assimilation of the western civilization through education. This implied in most cases a dissociation on the part of black men from the basic social patterns of their original ethnic and cultural environment. This predicament of cultural infusion but systematic social restriction and isolation has been variously referred to as the "dilemma of the marginal man," the "pathology of the uprooted man," and called by R. E. Parks, the "cultural hybrid," [4] a result of culture contact and acculturation, but also of systematic social segregation and denial of human consideration.

Black nationalism becomes, as a result, testimony to the injustices of segregated rule and an expression of the black man's resistance and resentment.

In this respect, one of the most striking social-psychological innovations of black nationalism has to do with the reversal of color association within a dominant, and pervasive white-ideal cultural context. A reversal of white-western symbols implies as well a reversal of the concepts associated with them. Thus, black nationalism is a refusal of those white values which are regarded as oppressive constraints.

In can be noted that, in general, the theme of revolt in the ideology of black nationalism represents a reinforcement of the antagonism created by the caste situation between the white dominant group and the black subordinate minority. The refutation of white political and cultural domination in the ideology

[4] Robert E. Parks, *Race and Culture*, New York: Glencoe, The Free Press, 1950, p. 356.

of black nationalism represents an attempt to sever the bonds that tie the black man to white definitions.

. . . The American Negro can no longer, nor will he be ever again, controlled by white America's image of him.[5]

It is an attempt at toppling what some young black intellectuals call "the dictatorship of definition." The corollary to this claim for freedom from white determination of black identity is a search for new values. Revolt involves not only a confrontation with an oppressive and undesirable social status, but is also an act of self-affirmation and a cogent expression of identity. The following passage is illustrative of this point:

Our concern for black power addresses itself directly to this problem, the necessity to reclaim our history and our identity from the cultural terrorism and depredation of self-justifying white guilt. To do this we shall have to struggle for the right to create our own terms through which to define ourselves. This the first necessity of a free people, and the first right that any oppressor must suspend.[6]

The quest for new values thus leads the black nationalist to the belief that self-definition and self-determination are one and the same, and his new self-perception must of necessity be predicated upon terms that are non-normative or divergent from white-western values.

Indication of this concern was expressed by a group of black women who asked, "Is *Ebony* Killing the Black Woman," in the title of an article they wrote:

Ebony magazine stands today as a classic illustration of middle class negro (small *n* is indicative of general scorn for the term as

[5] James Baldwin quoted by Thomas F. Pettigrew in *Profile of the Negro American*, New Jersey: University of Princeton Press, 1964, p. 10.

[6] Stokely Carmichael, *The Massachusetts Review*, Autumn 1966, p. 639–40.

well as the behavior of the class of people being referred to) attempts to assimilate themselves into the mainstream of white american (small *a* is for symbolic de-emphasis) life. *Ebony* has been a highly successful magazine because it has mirrored the values and standards of the larger, dominant white society. . . . *Ebony* has sought to perpetuate the fallacy and old cliche, "if it's white it's alright." The latest in this long line of insults and abuses was the cover story of the February (1966) issue. Under an article entitled, "Are Negro Girls Getting Prettier," *Ebony* cleverly selected a carefully screened group of girls to represent what they claim is positive proof, that "negro" girls are indeed getting prettier. The great injustice here is that girls chosen by *Ebony* did not nearly reflect a full-cross-section of all black folks.

The psychological effect—on our people —of a publication such as *Ebony,* with its skin bleaching cream and straight hair ads, is demoralizing and tends to reinforce the already evident inferiority and self-hatred complexes of the black community. As a race we have been taught by whites that black is ugly; for example to be "black-listed," "blackmailed" or "blackballed"— everyday phrases—denotes exclusion or alienation. By the same token, the symbols used to extol the virtues of honesty, purity and truth are always white. . . . Thus we come to realize the majority of the masses are moved to act or react by the symbolism of the language they speak. The ideas, thoughts and deeds the oppressor wants us to see and react to, are those ideas which strengthen, defend or assert the goals of the established order. When a supposedly black magazine comes forth with the same ideology as the oppressor, it indicates the extent to which the oppressor has used his symbols, through culture, to psychologically enslave black people. It also indicates how successful the oppressor has been. . . . Every race has its own standards of beauty. Every race maintains a loyalty to its cultural and historical roots. Why then would a publication such as *Ebony* want us to lose our inherent standards of beauty, and substitute in its place a European Criteria??? [7]

The issue of identity is inescapable, and pride in race is playing a crucial part in the new identity; it no doubt will lead—as it already has done—to a considerable degree of racial self-consciousness. Many black men and women are not struggling to become free, simply in order to disappear. . . . Contrary to the liberal argument "that the race problem can be solved in this country only by total integration and complete assimilation and eventual miscegenation," . . . there are Afro-Americans who do not want to disappear and desire to preserve specifically Afro-American values and cultural traits.

Such sentiments are expressed by a female student in Robert Penn Warren's book:

. . . The auditorium had been packed— mostly Negroes, but with a scattering of white people. A young girl with pale skin, dressed like any coed anywhere, in clothes for a public occasion, is on the rostrum. She is . . . speaking with a peculiar vibrance in a strange irregular rhythm, out of some inner excitement, some furious, taut elan, saying, "—and I tell you I have discovered a great truth. I have discovered a great joy. I have discovered that I am black! I am black! You out there—oh, yes, you may have black faces, but your hearts are white, your minds are white, you have been white-washed!" [8]

This exclamation of a sense of new "discovered" identity is a conscious experience of "an increased unity of the physical and mental, moral and sensual selves, and a oneness in the way one experi-

[7] Evelyn Rodgers, "Is Ebony Killing Black Women," *Liberator,* New York: Vol. 6, No. 3, March 1965, p. 12–13.
[8] Robert Penn Warren, *Who Speaks for the Negro?* New York: Harcourt and Brace Co., 1965.

ences oneself and the way others seem to experience us." [9]

Much of the academic research and analysis of the race relations situation during the past three decades seems to accept the liberal assumption of historian Kenneth M. Stampp that, "Negroes are, after all, only white men with black skins, nothing more, nothing less." But black men in America are not simply carbon duplicates of white men; to contend that they are is misleading. Differences in skin color, hair texture and physical features are fact. But the issues are not whether differences exist, but what they mean socially.

Identified as a Negro, treated as Negro, provided with Negro interests, forced, whether he wills or not, to live in Negro communities, to think, love, buy and breathe as a Negro, the Negro comes in time to see himself as a Negro . . . he comes, in time, to invent himself and to image creatively his face.[10]

The Afro-American subculture maintains a subterranean and private world of rituals, symbols, and motifs. Rupert Emerson and Martin Kilson in a discussion of black nationalism make the following observations.

. . . The Black Muslims still represent, at the level of the Negro's subterranean world, a force of ultimate significance. This is found in its influence upon the new stage in the Negro's self-definition. This stage, moreover, has been reinforced by the rise of more rational black nationalist concepts than those represented by the Black Muslims, and all of them have been affected by the Black Muslims, all of them have been affected by the debut of African nationalism on the international scene. . . . There are, however, many other groups of this sort, and they are likely to have a more sustained influence upon the Negro's new thrust for self-realization . . . than the Black Muslims. Unlike the Black Muslims, these organizations are secular in orientation, intellectually capable of coping with the modern world; and they reject naive political goals . . .[11]

According to Dr. St. Clair Drake ". . . increased identification of educated Negroes with some aspects of the Negro subculture and with the cultural renaissance taking place in Africa may become the norm." [12] It is not unusual to find people in the larger urban ghettoes, who were previously wary about identifying themselves with Africa, now proudly proclaiming their blackness and developing interest in African politics, art, poetry and literature. Among the educated, and not so educated, discussions of Negritude are becoming commonplace. Among many young people there is a certain reverence for the memory and image of such men as Patrice Lumumba, Kwame Nkrumah, Jomo Kenyatta and Malcolm X, to name a few. These men are looked up to as black heroes and idols and role models. It is interesting to note, in this regard, that the late Medgar Evers—slain NAACP civil rights field director for the state of Mississippi —had named one of his sons Kenyatta. Ordinary black men and women who a short time ago were processing their hair and using hair-straighteners and skin-bleaches are now wearing the new "Afro" and "natural" hair styles, as well as African style clothing. A few are even taking African names and learning to speak an African language.

Dr. Erik H. Erikson explains such

[9] Erik H. Erikson, "The Concept of Identity in Race Relations" in The Negro American, ed. Talcott Parsons and Kenneth Clark, Boston: Houghton, Mifflin Co., 1966, p. 232.

[10] Lerone Bennett, Negro Mood, Chicago: Johnson Publishing Co., Inc., 1964, p. 49.

[11] Emerson and Kilson, "The American Dilemma in a Changing World, the Rise of Africa and the Negro American," in The Negro American, ed. Talcott Parsons and Kenneth Clark, Boston: Houghton Mifflin Co., 1966, p. 640–41.

[12] St. Clair Drake, "The Social and Economic Status of the Negro in the United States" in The Negro American, ed. Talcott Parsons and Kenneth B. Clark, Boston: Houghton Mifflin Co., 1966, p. 35.

social-psychological phenomena as the development of a conscious identity: "Identity here is one aspect of the struggle for ethnic survival; one person's or group's identity awareness may have to do with matters of an inner emancipation from a more dominant identity, such as the "compact majority." [13] Writer John O. Killens comments on the function and value of the new identity: ". . . one of the main tasks of Black Consciousness is to affirm the beauty of our blackness, to see beauty in black skin and thick lips and broad nostrils and kinky hair; to rid our vocabulary of "good hair" and "high yaller" and our medicine cabinets of bleaching creams. To de-niggerize ourselves is a key task of Black Consciousness." [14]

Thus the black artist who embarks upon a search for new standards and values for his salvation must, among other things, discard the tools presented to him by the social order which has proved to be the number one enemy to his sensibility and conscience . . . if he is committed to his people [he] looks elsewhere for new standards and values, for new identification and allies. [15]

The fundamental question black nationalism raises is whether integration is really desired or, more specifically, whether Afro-Americans "should" want integration. "In the whole history of revolts and revolutions, 'integration' has never been the main slogan of a revolution. The oppressed's fight is to free himself from his oppressor, not to integrate with him." [16] Black nationalist ideology molds a new image of the dominant group. The essential concern becomes "not free from what, but free for what?" There is a radical conception in process which has black men redefining themselves and, of necessity, re-evaluating "the white man." The objective of the process is to wrest the black man's image from white control; its concrete meaning is that white men should no longer tell black men who they are and where they should want to go. The proposition that obtains from such a conception is that black men must no longer be bound by the "white man's" definitions. This is a clear response to the control of communications media by the dominant white group.

In the past, some Negroes attempted to define themselves by becoming counter-contrast conceptions, by becoming, in short, opposite Negroes, opposite, that is, to what white men said Negroes were. [17]

In its crudest and simplest form black nationalism is the assertion that black is good. At its most intellectually sophisticated level of development, it is the affirmation of the validity of traditions and values of black people derived from their peculiar heritage and creativity. This process has been described by one sociologist, "as the backfire of the dynamics of American assimilation which gave rise to an increased sensitivity, on the part of black people, in reacting to the institutionalized nature of bigotry. Also, a subsequent development of a more positive regard for black culture and community, and a determination to reconstitute the basic processes of United States life as they affect black people." He further contends that "the most pervasive trend for today's young black intellectuals is their vigor and degree of self-consciousness about being black." [18]

Black nationalism seeks to achieve the diminution of "the white man"—that is the demise of the idea that because of a certain color of skin one man (or group of men) is ordained to determine

[13] Erikson, op. cit., p. 230.
[14] John O. Killens, "The Meaning and Measure of Black Power," in Negro Digest, Nov. 1966, p. 36.
[15] William K. Kgositsile, "Has God Failed James Baldwin?" Liberator, Vol. 7, No. 1, Jan. 1967, p. 11.
[16] Killens, op. cit., p. 33.
[17] Bennett, op. cit., p. 55.
[18] Gerald WcWorter, "Negro Rights and the American Future," Negro Digest, Oct. 1966, p. 20.

the lives of other men because of their darker skin color.

The basis for understanding black nationalism is in acknowledgement of the historical by-products of the slave system.

The tragedy bequeathed by racist beliefs and practices has in modern times been experienced by no other people, save for the Jews who fell into Hitler's hand, so deeply as by the Negro Americans.[19]

The African and his descendants were conquered, enslaved, demeaned and then converted to accepting their low status. Black men were told that they had no history, no culture, no civilization; and it was, for them, often economically rewarding and socially advantageous to repeat this litany. Some individuals began to realize that this was nonsense and sought to dissipate this lack of self-pride. There becomes an awareness of cultural dispossession, which becomes as equal a concern as the problems of material dispossession. Out of this context black nationalism arises. There develops a pattern of looking inward to historical and social traditions in order to overcome low status and low prestige. Attempts are made to construct a new "vision" predicated upon collective traits of social distinction. This vision, because of the "artificial" character of its development and its cultural equivocation, is not merely ambiguous or difficult, but is ambivalent and often looks irrational.

That black nationalism is based on a vehement racial consciousness can be imputed to racism that grew out of, and which often came to underlie, white domination. Black nationalism can in the final analysis be reduced to a challenge to white supremacy—a refutation of the racial ideology of slavery and segregation. In order to understand certain aspects of black nationalism and its peculiarities, it is important to consider the fact that slavery and segregated rule

[19] Emerson and Kilson, op. cit., p. 638.

was not only a political and economic affair, but that it also imposed a specific social framework for the black man's experience both of the world and of "himself." The fact of political domination created contact between black and white men under conditions that constantly underscored racial and cultural differences. Black nationalism, by confronting white domination with its own racial protest and zealous partisanship of the "black race," does more than draw together sentiments and attitudes that go into a collective black reaction, but embodies them in a heightened form that moves in fact very distinctly towards a racial ideology.

. . . Anti-white sensibilities among black nationalists operate to supply a unifying ideology which transcends the experience of any single individual.

In point of fact, however, black nationalism is much more than a response to white outrages (although it is of course that too). In the hands of such a gifted exponent as Malcolm, black nationalism is a sophisticated and pervasive political ideology based on a generalized understanding of the history of the black man in the United States.[20]

Malcolm X explains himself: "When we Muslims had talked about 'the devil white man,' he had been relatively abstract, someone we Muslims rarely came into contact with. . . ." [21] A frequently repeated statement in many of his speeches was that:

Unless we call one white man, by name, a "devil," we are not speaking of any "individual" white man. We are speaking of the "collective" white man's historical record. We are speaking of the collective white man's cruelties, and evil, and greeds, that have seen him "act" like a devil toward the non-white man. Any intelligent, honest, objective person cannot fail to realize that his

[20] Frank Kofsky, "Malcolm X," *Monthly Review*, Sept. 1966, p. 44.
[21] Alex Haley, *The Autobiography of Malcolm X*, New York: Grove Press, 1965, p. 242–43.

white man's slave trade, and his subsequent devilish actions, are directly responsible for not only the presence of this black man in America, but also for the condition in which we find this black man here. . . .[22]

Undoubtedly, such a broadly general and inclusive ideology directed at the dominant group serves the function of polarizing feelings and inducing conflict in the relationship between the two groups. Lewis Coser * suggests that such external conflict establishes group boundaries and gives identity to the group and strengthens its internal cohesion.

An ideology, when it becomes explicit, is a kind of thinking aloud on the part of a society or a group within it. It is a direct response to the actual conditions of life and has a social function, either as a defensive system of beliefs and ideas which support and justify an established social structure, or as a rational project for the creation of a new order. The latter type of ideology, even when it includes a certain degree of idealism, also implies a reasoned program of collective action; it becomes the intellectual channel of social life.

The ideology of black nationalism is an illustration of the conflict model in intergroup interaction. Black nationalism springs from a desire to reverse an intolerable situation—its adherents view the basis of social life as competition between groups for social and economic power. It is a challenge to the legitimacy of the system which white dominance has imposed on black men, whose experience—dispersal, subjugation, humiliation—generates social strain and tension. A prominent ex-civil rights leader and former activist explains this experience.

The evil of slavery—and to some degree Negroes are still enslaved—is in the way it permitted white men to handle Negroes: their bodies, their action, their opportunities, their very minds and thoughts. To the depths of their souls, Negroes feel handled, dealt with, ordered about, manipulated by white men. I cannot over-emphasize the tenacity and intensity of this feeling among Negroes and I believe any fair-minded person pondering the history of the Negro's enforced posture in a world of white power would concede the justice of the feeling.[23]

The black man's worth was low, indeed, not only in the eyes of his white overlord, but also as a consequence, in his own eyes. He was on the lowest rung of the racial hierarchy which Western civilization had established. As Aime Cèsaire, the West Indian writer and initial conceiver of Negritude, observed ". . . at the top, the white man—the being, in the full sense of the term—at the bottom, the black man . . . the thing, as much as to say a nothing." [24] The black man retained an awareness of his racial differences and was forced to organize his life on a racial basis.

Against this background it is not difficult to understand that such development as Garvey's "Back to Africa" movement in particular was not simply, mere atavistic expression: it was presented not as an escape from America, but as a national return to an original home, as a positive rather than a negative gesture. Garvey appreciated the psychological needs of his adherents, realizing that what they needed in order to struggle for political freedom was "freedom from contempt." [25]

Garvey's revaluation of Africa had the precise function of abolishing the world order created by the white man in the minds of black men. Abram Kardi-

[22] George Breitman, ed. *Malcolm X Speaks*, New York: 1965, p. 269.

* Lewis Coser, *The Functions of Social Conflict*, New York: The Crowell-Collier Publishing Co., The Free Press of Glencoe, 1964, p. 87–88.

[23] James Farmer, "Mood Ebony," *Playboy*, May 1966, p. 126.

[24] Aime Cèsaire, "Toussaint L'Ouverture," *Presence Africain*, Paris: 1963, p. 31.

[25] E. Franklin Frazier, *Race and Culture Contacts in the Modern World*, New York: Alfred A. Knopf, 1962, p. 363.

ner and Lionel Ovesey say as much when they write: "Marcus Garvey saw one important truth: that the Negro was doomed as long as he took his ideals from the white man. He saw that this sealed his internal feeling of inferiority and self contempt." [26] Garvey was among the first to create a "New Vision," based on a revaluation of the African cultural heritage, as a source of inspiration to the blacks in America and in the world.

Two facts stand out clearly from a consideration of the progressive development of black nationalism, seen in broad historical perspective. The first is that it was a movement of reaction against the white cultural domination which is concomitant with political domination. Second, it seems perfectly clear, however, that without the pressure of segregation and the conflicts which it creates and without the historical and social factors which dominate the situation of the black man in America—that is, without the racial factor—the forms of reaction to culture contact among black people summarized here would have had a completely different character. In short, black nationalism is inspired by a wish for freedom from both domination and contempt.

James Farmer writes about the shift in emphasis from integration, which had been largely rooted in the black middle class, to emphasis of race and nationalism, which has been the traditional appeal to the black masses. He gives considerable insight as to motives of this movement:

Almost imperceptibly the demand for desegregation had shaded into a demand for black dispersal and assimilation. We were told, and for a while told ourselves, all Negro separation was inherently inferior, and some of us began to think that Negroes couldn't be fully human in the presence of

[26] Abram Kardiner and Lionel Ovesey, *The Mark of Oppression*, New York: Alfred A. Knopf, 1962, p. 363.

other Negroes. Well, we have since come to learn that all separation need not be inferior in all cases and in all places.

. . . We have learned that what is needed is not "invisibility" but a valid and legitimate visibility. . . . We have found the cult of color-blindness not only quaintly irrelevant but seriously flawed. For we learned that America couldn't simply be color-blind. It would only become color-blind when we gave up our color. The white man, who presumably has no color, would have to give up only his prejudices, but we would have to give up our identities. Thus we would usher in the Great Day with an act of self-denial and self-abasement. We would achieve equality by conceding racism's charge: that our skins are an affliction; that our history is one long humiliation; that we are empty of distinctive traditions and any legitimate source of pride.[27]

He recalls a meeting to reconcile a serious strife between "nationalists" and "integrationists" in CORE chapters in the San Francisco Bay Area:

One fellow, a Negro, immediately said, "Brother Farmer, we've got to dig being black." He kept repeating it over and over again, and I knew exactly what he meant. He meant that blackness of the skin had been accepted as a deformity by Negroes, that it had to cease being that, and had to become a source of pride, and so did all the culture and memories that went with it. . . . Some form of nationalism is necessary, even healthy though the willfully color-blind refuse to acknowledge this. . . . The doctrinaire color-blind often fail to perceive that it is "ideally" necessary for the black man to be proudly black today . . . We have come to realize that we must live here and now rather than in eternity.

. . . The system of segregation was mounted and perpetuated for the purpose of keeping the black man down; that it was and is a conspiracy to instill in the Negro and the white a sense of Negro inferiority.

. . . In a free society many Negroes will

[27] Farmer, *op. cit.*, p. 126, 177.

choose to live and work separately, although not in total isolation. They will cultivate that pride in themselves which comes in part from their effort to make this a free land. . . . In helping themselves they will come to love themselves. And because they love themselves, they will be determined to help themselves.

. . . We will accept, in other words, Malcolm X's insight that segregation will become separation only with a separate effort of Negro heart and soul rejecting the notion of some of the older civil rights organizations—that desegregation and integration "in itself" will accomplish miracles.

Perhaps "independence" is a better term than separation. We shall become independent men." [28]

The cultural position of the black man in America possesses its own specific characteristics; he lives in a symbiotic relationship with the white man and is held in subordinate position by the caste system. Furthermore, he is governed by the secondary institutions imposed or sanctioned by the white dominant group, especially in the areas of religion and social morality. The wish for independent expression finds a ready springboard in those elements of black subculture which segregation had helped to mold into something of a definite structure.

An ironic aspect of black popular movements is the way in which white (Western) elements act as catalysts in the emotional reaction which produce nationalist feelings. Christian egalitarian teaching, for example, helps to show up in the eyes of black converts the fundamental contradiction that separate white domination from the avowed humanitarian principles of Western culture, and to underline the rift between the objective practice and the declared values of white men. A powerful emotional inspiration of nationalism is thus a disaffection

for the white man, just against his own principles.

It is apparent that as the black power movement gains more strength and becomes more aggressive and defines its objective in terms of specific Afro-American interest, and not on (white) liberal terms and is controlled by an increasingly politicized Afro-American element, it will appear more threatening and separatist to the dominant group. It would be a mistake, however, to dismiss such development as a futile and sectarian obsession with self—a kind of black narcissism. In the larger context of Afro-American experience, it represents, for many, the ultimate and perhaps most stable form of self-awareness.

In their search for identity, the adherents of black nationalism have to accept and explore to the full their particular situation. But, although preoccupied with a sectional and limited interest, they are inspired by a universal human need for fulfilment.

Thus, black nationalism can be objectively defined as:

(1) The desire of Afro-Americans to decide their own destiny through control of their own political organizations and the formation and preservation of their cultural, economic and social institutions.

(2) The determination to unite as a group, as a people, in a common community, to oppose white supremacy by striving for independence from white control.

(3) The resistance to subordinate status and demand for political freedoms, social justice and economic equality.

(4) The development of ethnic self-interest, racial pride and group consciousness, and opposition to and rejection of those normative and dominant ideas and values perceived to be incompatible with this objective.

(5) A revaluation of "self," and relationship with the dominant group and the social system in general, and a shift-

[28] *Ibid.,* p. 178.

ing frame of reference (Africa and "Blackism" become significant referents) and change in perspective.

These characteristic attributes of the social phenomena referred to as black nationalism do not represent discontin-uous factors, but are intricately related elements which animate a particular process of interaction; which take the form of conscious cultivation of social and cultural pluarlism and a movement toward political self-determination.

PART II: MINORITIES AMONG THE MAJORITY

An individual's ethnicity refers to his membership by birth in a group that has the following characteristics: (1) a common place of origin; (2) the inclination and ability to trace the history and development of the group back to identifiable progenitors who lived in that place; (3) common cultural patterns not shared by members of other groups, including a unique language or remnants of it; (4) a strong tendency toward group preservation backed up by reserving the most intimate forms of association such as marriage and child rearing to fellow group members; (5) a consequent tendency toward group-limited common heredity; (6) a subjective sense of group distinctiveness resting upon common experience, distinctive cultural patterns, and insiders' views of the group's history; (7) ethnocentric judgments of the life ways of members of other groups, although such judgments may recognize the rights of others to organize their lives and communities as they choose.

Factors that may reinforce the sense of ethnicity are the following: (1) nonmembers of the group emphasize the group's distinctiveness and value its contributions (as in the case of avid seekers of ethnic restaurants); (2) alternatively, nonmembers use the group's distinctiveness as a basis for maintaining social distance from it and excluding it (as in the case of the anti-Semite); (3) visible physical differences provide a way of easily distinguishing the group's members from nonmembers so that cross-group interactions have racial as well as ethnic overtones; (4) members' religion may be different from that of nonmembers.

In American society, the conventional usage of the terms "ethnicity" or "ethnic group" has not met all of these criteria. Instead, when the terms are given a general meaning, they seem to stand for cultural or physical difference from some vague conception of a standard American majority type. In this view, blacks, or Jews, or Irish-Americans, or Minnesota Scandinavians are all ethnics, irrespective of social class, religion, or race. I have no complaint with that usage as long as two other points are kept in mind. The first is that a racial minority may or may not be ethnically distinct. The probability is strong that it will be distinct if only because it is likely to have developed a set of common attitudes about itself in response to the majority's treatment of it. Nevertheless, ethnicity is more a matter of where people come from, what they believe, and how they act than it is of how they look. Thus, the second point is that if ethnicity is used in this general way, it ought also be applied to unquestioned members of the racial majority whose physical appearance tends to correspond to the implicit model of that ideal-typical abstraction I shall call Homo Americanus. If any of the following tend to act ethnocentrically toward others and to have an ethnocentric view of themselves, then the Daughters of the American Revolution, the First Families of Virginia, the townspeople of the hamlets of Eastern Tennessee, and migrant Appalachians are as indisputably ethnic as the third-generation descendants of late-arriving immigrants.

In fact, however, the most common ordinary usage of the term "ethnicity" (it is reflected in the paper by Krickus in selection 16) is as a replacement for the older term "nationality." In that limited, not wholly correct, but nevertheless extraordinary prevalent usage, a member of an ethnic group is, or is the descendant of, someone who was part of a given group of Caucasian immigrants who were predominantly Roman Catholic, but also Jewish, or Eastern Orthodox, who came in the main from Eastern or Southern Europe, but also from Ireland and French Canada. In other words, today's American ethnics, as a newscaster would most often use the term, are the descendants of people who came to the United States in the so-called second or late wave of American immigration, which began shortly after the Civil War and lasted until restrictive immigration legislation based on nationality quotas ended it shortly after World War I.

Not long ago, with the possible exception of Appalachian whites, all the groups discussed in the present section were assumed to be, in varying degrees, part of what it used to be fashionable to call the mainstream of American life. The mainstream was an image pretty much reflected and promoted by television's situation comedies of the late fifties and early sixties. It was a white-collar world, prosperous suburban with lots of green grass, where independent nuclear families (pretty much without relatives except at holiday time) lived in separate houses (not apartments and with too much variation to be parts of ticky-tacky tracts), where they spoke standard English (without a trace of accent), and prepared wholesome meals in sparkling kitchens (with never so much as a trace whiff of garlic).

Though that mainstream existed more in our collective imagination and in dreams of national consensus than it did in reality, it reflected a very important point about ethnic relations in the United States. The country had absorbed and found room in its middle classes for an unprecedentedly large number of the descendants of white immigrants. The combination of generational aging, economic growth, and labor force compositional change led to upward class mobility and larger numbers of people sharing a common status and culture. It is generally true that the longer a white immigrant-based group has been in the United States, the higher is its status; and that, within any particular group, the youngest adult generation tends to have the greatest proportions of higher-status members.

The American Dream was no mere myth for immigrants and their offspring. Indeed, many social scientists, themselves often the children and grandchildren of immigrants, had come to assume that the melting pot was at full boil, so that there was little doubt that at least all white Americans would before long be pasteurized and homogenized. Some once-important differences among them would remain, but everyone would be mutually tolerant, and folks would pay more attention to what even their differences had in common than to the differences themselves. Will Herberg's *Protestant, Catholic, Jew* was an important work in this vein.[1]

Then, in close proximity to one another, there appeared three books that cut such assumptions short. They were Gerhard Lenski's *The Religious Factor,* Nathan Glazer and Daniel Moynihan's *Beyond the Melting Pot,* and Milton Gordon's *Assimilation in American Life.*[2] The last two books showed both that processes of mobility and acculturation had by no means killed off ethnic sentiment or ethnic group solidarity and participation, and that large numbers of white ethnic group members had not yet attained and in the near future probably would not attain middle-class jobs, incomes, life-styles, and aspirations.

Lenski's book actually concerned differences in religious affiliation and racial group membership rather than any more precise delineation of ethnic variations. However, since it was based on the clearest data (probability sample surveys of Detroit); since it did include so many different groups (blacks, white Protestants, Catholics, and Jews); and since it showed that for explaining attitudes about many phenomena (e.g., child rearing and political choices), racial or religious affiliation counted for as much or more than socioeconomic status levels —Lenski's study had much the same impact on the academic

[1] Will Herberg, *Protestant, Catholic, Jew* (New York: Doubleday Anchor, 1955).

[2] Nathan Glazer and Daniel P. Moynihan, *Beyond the Melting Pot* (Cambridge: M.I.T. Press, 1965); Gerhard Lenski, *The Religious Factor* (New York: Doubleday & Co., Inc., 1961); Milton M. Gordon, *Assimilation in American Life* (New York: Oxford University Press, 1964). For a more recent detailed treatment of matters covered by these three books, one should also consult Edgar Litt, *Ethnic Politics in America* (Atlanta: Scott, Foresman and Co., 1970).

world as the other two works that dealt more explicitly with ethnicity per se (even though, within religious groups, Lenski found hardly any important ethnic differences on the attitudes he studied).

Glazer and Moynihan examined ethnicity's role in the history, the economy, the class structure, and even the arts and culture of New York City. They showed that ethnic as well as racial differences were still an important foundation underlying matters like residential location, occupational specialization, and family formation. Moreover, they were particularly concerned with how urban politics, especially Democratic Party politics, had emerged as a patchwork of shifting coalitions among various racial and ethnic groups. In order to elect men who would serve them and to implement policies that would satisfy them, the various groups tended to scale down their own most particularistic considerations. (Don't question my support for Israel, and I won't bug you on abortions.) No middle-class Jewish candidate could go very far without taking account of Irish and Italian labor voters. No Irish candidate could afford to alienate all the voting power represented by Jewish school teachers in his search for the blessing of the Patrolmen's Benevolent Association. Even a Republican, dependent on white Protestants for the bulk of his vote, could not expect to win much without a platform plank or two that would strongly appeal to enough of the ethnic vote to swing an election. Patterns like these led over time to the institutionalization of intergroup accommodation and compromise, of bargaining and negotiation rather than open rivalry and conflict over absolute and rigid principles. Perhaps the best single symbol of such compromise was the balanced ticket, where the slate of candidates' names read as if it were the list of head table guests at a Brotherhood Week dinner. Naturally, to those left out of the arrangement, these compromises looked less like democracy in action and more like back-room deals where insiders decided how they were going to divide up the action. Indeed, in a long new introduction written for the 1970 re-edition of *Beyond the Melting Pot,* Glazer places far more emphasis on racial divisions than he did in the earlier edition. He suggests that a new common interest is drawing together the white ethnic groups, particularly in their working-class sectors and along lines of religion, as they try to defend their share of influence against the blacks and Puerto Ricans whom they see as trying to wrest it from them.

Gordon's book was the shortest and yet the most general of the three I have mentioned. It began by tracing the three predominant American ideologies about the processes and desired outcomes of immigrant absorption. Relating the experience and responses of the immigrants and their descendants to these ideologies, which he typified as "melting pot, Anglo-conformity, and pluralism," Gordon concluded that thirty and forty years before no one had quite foreseen the outcome he took to be the case in America of the sixties. In general, the descendants of the immigrant masses coming here after 1880 had not been fully absorbed. They still retained ethnic sentiments and reserved their most intimate primary group relations for interactions within the group. The pattern was to some extent a result of group members' own desires, but also of their never having been given a completely open reception by native Americans at the top of the society. However, the attitudes, values, and life-styles of members of these ethnic groups were not notably different from those of native Americans. Such differences as existed were most pronounced in the working class, and even there one could easily discern the broad tendency for ethnics of different backgrounds to intermarry, though within the bounds marked by religious faith. Finally, blacks' low status, their late entry into the competitive race, and the much higher level of prejudice and discrimination against them, all meant that they had not yet become a part of this pattern. Like almost all observers around 1960, Gordon did not anticipate the emergence of black nationalism and black culturalism, and in a few scattered passages he tended to dismiss the few sprouts he did see.

It is ironic but also revealing that a book like Gordon's, a harbinger of the resurgent interest in American ethnic identity, gave only scant attention to a development that has been quite important in changing a ripple to a tide. Black solidarity and assertiveness, black political consciousness and muscle-flexing, black art and anger not only awakened other *racial* minorities from the coma of white men's paternalism and their own apathy, but awakened as well many white Americans by nudging the cords that tied them to their own past. The wave of ethnic revival has two parts, and both are related to movements originating in the black American world. The foamy crest of the wave is the desire, following the black example, to find a securely rooted sense of one's own person in his group's history. That is not unimportant in a rapidly changing, increasingly standardized, but still uncertain social world. The dark green thrusting mass of the wave is a chauvinistic emphasis on group virtues. These are meant to justify protecting one's own or his kinsmen's interests, with the effect, if not often with the intention, of withholding benefits from others thought to be too soon too eager to win new rights and privileges for themselves. The Jewish Defense League is a good subject for this metaphorical oceanography, since it clearly shows both parts of the wave. The JDL was established with the purpose of helping New York's lower-middle and working-class Jews defend themselves against black demands and incursions. It was quite literally a defense league, intended to protect Jewish school children and Jewish ghetto merchants—not all of them rich by any means—from real and threatened ghetto intimidation and violence. Recently Meir Kahane, the group's founder and leader, was quoted as having said, "Black is supposed to be beautiful. Well, it is. And Jewish is beautiful too." When one group refuses to be inundated and another thinks it must rip and tear at the dike, is it any wonder that outsiders try to tell both that it would be better not to make waves?

This section begins with Michael Parenti's review of studies that demonstrate the continuing significance of ethnic politics. A decade ago, many political theorists thought that significance had sharply diminished and would ultimately disappear as second-, third-, and fourth-generation ethnics prospered and moved away from older central city areas of ethnic settlement. Today, many practitioners of the "New Politics" hope and work for what these theorists had predicted. Parenti's view of his political scientist colleagues, however, is that they overestimated spatial and class mobility, but underestimated the scope, the variety, and the strength of the new forms of ethnic organization that arose in new settings. The 1970 off-year elections did not decide who was more nearly correct. In the meantime, more traditional analysts of American voting behavior, like Kevin Phillips on the right and Richard Scammon and Ben Wattenberg in the center,[3] are convinced that the devotees of the New Politics are making the same mistaken assessment that the political scientists made before them.

The next pair of papers contrasts two Anglo-Saxon groups that occupy opposite ends on the ladder of social stratification. Hollingshead and Redlich describe New Haven's "Establishment," the city's standard-setter with which newcomers have compared themselves, against which they have fought, and whose favor they have attempted to curry as they sought to loosen its monopoly of prestige and privilege. The following contrasting selection examines a portion of

[3] Kevin Phillips, *The Emerging Republican Majority* (New York: Doubleday Anchor, 1969); Richard M. Scammon and Ben J. Wattenberg, "Strategy for Democrats: Excerpts from *The New Majority*," *The New Republic*, Vol. 163 (August 15, 1970), pp. 17–21.

Appalachia. The region had a brief prominent emergence in the national consciousness after John Kennedy's West Virginia campaign and Michael Harrington's *The Other America* [4] but then faded back into relative obscurity. Caudill's work focuses on the area where he was born and raised, the Cumberland Plateau of Eastern Kentucky. The people he describes are those I mentioned as an exception at the beginning of this introduction. Few would have claimed they were in the mainstream in 1960, and they are not there now.

The next three papers concern American Jews. First, Kramer and Leventman concentrate on generational differences in a midwestern Jewish community. They show that after the efforts and astuteness of the immigrant generation and its offspring had made economic security a less problematic issue, members of the third generation became more concerned with social acceptability. The selection from Benjamin Ringer's work carries forward the same theme, but with more emphasis on social class differences as well. Ringer describes how postwar prosperity made it possible for rather large numbers of middle-class Jews to move into a wealthy suburb where only a small number of fairly well-established upper-middle class Jews had lived before. The latter had assiduously followed the customs and manners of their non-Jewish neighbors, and so felt that their comfortable but fragile accommodation was being threatened by the newcomers whose numbers, manners, and interests would provoke anti-Semitism in the non-Jewish community. Ringer's work shows that their concern was not idle, for the possibility of anti-Semitism was indeed present all along, but became manifest only after the sorts of Jewish people who moved into town appeared in some ways to correspond to conventional ethnocentric stereotypes. The following paper, from Selznick and Steinberg's book, shows that many of these stereotypes have had great staying power in American society. The results of their national sample survey of anti-Semitic beliefs and attitudes show that large numbers of Americans, at all social class levels, still view Jews as being not merely different from other people, but different in a negative way. The selection also compares and contrasts anti-Semitism among black and among white people, and tries to account for some of the differences found and expressed in the two different groups.

Samuels describes majority relations with another group that has shown remarkably high rates of social mobility in a relatively brief span of time, the Japanese-Americans of Hawaii. Among Japanese-Americans there is a close correspondence

[4] Michael Harrington, *The Other America* (Baltimore: Penguin, 1962).

between original Japanese culture and the normative standards that govern performances necessary for prospering in American society. This cultural correspondence, acting as a support for individual effort, has helped enable Japanese-Americans to achieve a great deal, both in Hawaii and on the mainland, despite their racial difference from the white majority and the handicap that mainland Japanese-Americans suffered when they were uprooted from homes and businesses to be placed in internment camps in the Second World War.

Then, in the next paper, Herbert Gans shows the continuing impact of some traditional life-ways among working class Italo-Americans.

Although the first of the final two selections does not deal with ethnicity at all while the second emphasizes it quite heavily, there is an obvious connection between them. Eitzen's paper tries to identify a particular constellation of class characteristics associated with whites' support of George Wallace, a candidate whose views on populism and race are too well known to need reviewing here. What Eitzen says about the concerns of Wallace supporters, people with an educational level relatively lower than their income level, could conceivably apply to others like them—urban construction workers, for example. More data are necessary, however, before concluding that Eitzen's finding ought to be generalized beyond his research site in Lawrence, Kansas.

In the last selection, Krickus raises general questions about the present place and future prospects of the white ethnic lower-middle and working classes in the nation's industrial cities. Krickus praises the ethnic contribution to the character of urban life, but concludes that white ethnic communities are being abandoned both by government and by the private housing interests that government policies support. Members of these communities also feel threatened—when their members cannot afford to flee—by the racial minorities with whom they are coming to share what is left of the residential areas of our central cities.

Eitzen's and Krickus' papers, and Parenti's less directly, provide useful background materials for getting a grasp of one of the most pressing sociopolitical problems of our time. Expanding the opportunity structure to make room for America's racial underclasses depends overwhelmingly on political actions and decisions. Yet many working and lower-middle class people feel that they—or the groups upon which they peg their identities—are threatened by change. The most serious confrontations do not take place in prosperous suburbs protected by zoning ordinances and the great expense of residential property, but in areas that are part of or closer to the central cities. There the white ethnic working-class groups are also concentrated; their areas border on the ghettoes or are their refuge from them. Thus, on the local level, it has become particularly difficult to win enough political support for implementing policies interpreted by the public to mean that they aid one group only at the expense of another. Cases in point are police protection, de facto school segregation, the location of public housing, and the recalcitrance of high-skill trade unions to go beyond token integration.

Changes toward greater equality in all of these could come about largely through the application of authority to back up the force of law, as in the case of diminishing formerly de jure Southern school segregation. But, as in this example I have chosen to illustrate the possibility, successful implementation depends on the existence of a strong outside majority supporting the change. Northern whites have been that majority vis-à-vis the South. Today, however, suburban whites more often seem as if they preferred to avoid the problems of the cities.

Change could also occur if contending groups discovered that they lost nothing by it, or that both could profit from an alliance to bring it about (as in the case of industrial unions discussed by Blalock in selection 3). There are those who believe that hope lies only in establishing such a coalition between lower-status ethnic and racial minority group members, along with the support of convinced liberal and radical members of higher-status groups. Perhaps together they could exact concessions from the more prosperous in general.

It is possible to build coalitions based on the common interests of white ethnic and racial minority groups. Indeed, it is necessary to do so in order to win elections in many major cities or in congressional districts within or near them. Promoters of change and other prospective builders of these coalitions know, however, that the keystone consists in finding shared felt needs, like better housing, more effective schools, higher industrial wages, prepaid plans for comprehensive medical care. In this fashion ethnic concerns can be considered, too, but as part of a broader perspective. It is a serious mistake to ignore those concerns altogether, or to call them outmoded because the need for reform seems so pressing. Generalized appeals for reform, for clean orderly government, for interracial justice, for a definitive turning-out of the old rascals, work very well in upper-middle class and silk stocking

Jewish or Protestant areas. They have less impact in working-class Polish, or Irish, or Italian communities.

As Banfield and Wilson put it, in a reading that was included in the earlier edition of this book:

As voters rise in socio-economic status they attach less value to ethnic considerations, which are part of the immigrant political ethos. . . . [However,] the large city, by concentrating the population, provides a necessary (but not sufficient) condition for ethnic political activity. The various nationality and racial groups are sufficiently large that they believe they have some reasonable chance of affecting the outcome of elections; there are enough members of the group to feel a sense of group solidarity and to support their own political leaders and institutions; and they are sufficiently set apart from other groups to stimulate a sense of competition and even conflict.[5]

All of these remarks are still quite appropriate but, race aside, are better accounts of the situation of fifty and even twenty years ago than of today. They will be less applicable still twenty years from now. Nevertheless, under present conditions, if a racial-ethnic coalition is going to be formed, it has to depend on winning support in a way that considers but does not threaten ethnic concerns. Trumpeters of change who forget that point can be crossed off as menaces, as bungling meddlers, or as distant petty tyrants. If that happens, chances for coalition are that much smaller; the way is cleared for conventional defenders of shopworn slogans; and racial underclasses rapping at the gates to get in become more convinced of the futility of trying to play politics by combining the textbook rules for interest-group formation with whatever occasional administrative favors they can manage to obtain.

[5] Edward C. Banfield and James Q. Wilson, *City Politics* (Cambridge: Harvard University Press, 1963).

7. ETHNIC POLITICS AND THE PERSISTENCE OF ETHNIC IDENTIFICATION

Michael Parenti

Elaborating on a theme first set forth by Milton Gordon, Parenti
here distinguishes acculturation from structural and identificational assimilation. He argues, as Gordon did, that while the
first has taken place, the second two have not. Parenti insists
that despite increasing formal education, higher-ranking jobs,
greater incomes, and suburban residences—in short, despite
upward mobility—a considerable proliferation of ethnic
organizations and structures still exists among the
third-generation descendants of immigrants. True, the forms of
association to be found now differ in kind and often in substance
from their parallels in the immigrant and second-generation
communities, but that is less important than that they still
surround individuals in webs of group affiliation. For example,
intimate ties to relatives and friends are reinforced by the
ethnic character of voluntary organizations; occupational
positions are often obtained through contacts with fellow
ethnics; ethnic flavor, style, and sentiment are prominent parts
of ceremony and behavior at weddings and funerals. These sorts
of reinforcement help to maintain a sense of group identity
implanted in individuals as youngsters, frequently in ways of
which they are hardly conscious at the time.

Parenti's major practical conclusion focuses on what has
been and probably still is one of the dominant themes of

Source: *American Political Science Review,* Vol. 61, No. 3 (September
1967), pp. 717–26, with some footnotes omitted. Reprinted by permission
of the author and the American Political Science Association.

MICHAEL PARENTI is Associate Professor of Political Science at the
University of Vermont. He is the author of the *Anti-Communist Impulse*
and has edited a collection of articles entitled *Trends and Tragedies
in American Foreign Policy.*

American politics: "That many urban and suburban politicians persist in giving attentive consideration to minority social groupings . . . may be less due to their inveterate stupidity than to the fact that ethnic substructures and identification are still extant, highly visible, and, if handled carefully, highly accessible and responsive. The political practitioner who chooses to ignore the web . . . does so at his own risk."

Since early colonial times, nearly every group arriving in America has attempted to reconstruct communities that were replications of the old world societies from which they had emerged. With the exception of a few isolated sectarian enclaves such as the Hutterites, the Amish and the Hasidic, they failed to do so. If culture is to be represented as the accumulated beliefs, styles, solutions and practices which represent a society's total and continuing adjustment to its environment, then it would seem to follow that no specific cultural system can be transplanted from one environment to another without some measure of change. Unable to draw upon a complete cultural base of their own in the new world, and with no larger constellation of societal and institutional forces beyond the ghetto boundaries to back them, the immigrants eventually lost the battle to maintain their indigenous ways. By the second generation, attention was directed almost exclusively toward American events and standards, American language, dress, recreation, work, and mass media, while interest in old world culture became minimal or, more usually, nonexistent. To one extent or another, all major historical and sociological studies of immigration and ethnicity document this cultural transition of the American-born generation.[1]

However, such acculturation was most often not followed by social assimilation; the group became "Americanized" in much of its *cultural* practices, but this says little about its *social* relations with the host society. In the face of widespread acculturation, the minority still maintained a social sub-structure encompassing primary and secondary group relations composed essentially of fellow ethnics. . . .

From birth in the sectarian hospital to childhood play-groups to cliques and fraternities in high school and college to the selection of a spouse, a church affiliation, social and service clubs, a vacation resort, and, as life nears completion, an old-age home and sectarian cemetary—the ethnic, if he so desires, may live within the confines of his sub-social matrix—and many do.[2] Even if he should find

[1] See for instance: Oscar Handlin, *Boston's Immigrants, A Study in Acculturation* (Cambridge: Harvard University Press, 1959, rev. ed.); Oscar Handlin, *The Uprooted* (New York: Grosset and Dunlap, 1951); R. E. Park and H. A. Miller, *Old World Traits Transplanted* (New York: Harper, 1924); W. I. Thomas and F. Znaniecki, *The Polish Peasant in Europe and America*, 5 vols. (Boston: Badger, 1918–20); E. V. Stonequist, *The Marginal Man, A Study in Personality and Culture Conflict* (New York: Scribner, 1937); W. L. Warner and Leo Srole, *The Social Systems of American Ethnic Groups* (New Haven: Yale Univ. Press, 1945); William Foote Whyte, *Street Corner Society* (Chicago: University of Chicago Press, 1943); Herbert J. Gans, *The Urban Villagers* (New York: Free Press of Glencoe, 1962).

[2] See Milton M. Gordon, *Assimilation in American Life* (New York: Oxford University Press, 1964), p. 34; also Erich Rosenthal, "Acculturation without Assimilation? *American Journal of Sociology*, 66 (November, 1960), 275–288; Amitai Etzioni, "The Ghetto—a Re-evaluation," *Social Forces* (March, 1959), 255–262; J. Milton Yinger, "Social Forces Involved in Group Identification

himself in the oppressively integrated confines of prison, the ethnic discovers that Italian, Irish, Jewish, Negro and Puerto Rican inmates coalesce into distinct groups in "a complex web of prejudices and hostilities, friendships and alliances." [3]

Hollingshead, in a study of New Haven, discerned vertical social divisions based on race, religion and national origin along with the expected horizontal cleavages due to income and residence. Cutting across the class strata were the parallel dissections of the black and white worlds, with the latter further fissured into Catholic, Jewish and Protestant components which, in turn, subdivided into Irish, Italian, Polish, etc. Within this highly compartmentalized world were to be found the ethnic associational patterns.[4]

HETEROGENEITY WITHIN THE HOMOGENEOUS SOCIETY

Could not such unassimilated substructures be more representative of a time when urban areas were segmented into ghettos untouched by post-war affluence, upward occupational mobility and treks to the suburbs? . . . In actuality, while individual ethnics have entered professional and occupational roles previously beyond their reach, minority group mobility has not been as dramatic as is often supposed. A comparison of first and second generation occupational statuses as reported in the 1950 national

census shows no evidence of any substantial convergence of intergroup status levels. The occupational differences among ethnic groups, with the Irish as a possible exception, remain virtually the same for both generations, leading C. B. Nam to observe that even with the absence of large-scale immigration, "the importance of nationality distinctions for the American stratification system will remain for some time to come." [5] If today's ethnics enjoy a better living standard than did their parents, it is because there has been an across-the-board rise throughout America. Fewer pick-and-shovel jobs and more white collar positions for minority members are less the result of ethnic mobility than of an over-all structural transition in our national economy and the composition of our labor force.[6]

Furthermore, despite the popular literature on the hopeless homogeneity of suburbia, suburbs are not great *social* melting pots. Scott Greer, after noting the breakup of some of the central city ethnic communities, cautions: "The staying force of the ethnic community (in suburbia) must not be underestimated." The good Catholic, for instance, "can live most of his life, aside from work, within a Catholic environment," [7] in a sub-societal network of schools, religious endogamy, family, church, social, athletic and youth organizations, and Catholic residential areas. Similarly, Robert Wood observes that suburbs tend toward ethnic clusters. In the more "mixed areas," ethnic political blocs are not unknown. As in the city, the tension

---

or Withdrawal," *Daedalus*, 90 (Spring, 1961), 247–262; Y. J. Chyz and R. Lewis, "Agencies Organized by Nationality Groups in the United States," *The Annals of the American Academy of Political and Social Science*, 262 (1949).

[3] M. Arc, "The Prison 'Culture' From the Inside," *New York Times Magazine*, February 28, 1965, p. 63.

[4] August B. Hollingshead, "Trends in Social Stratification: A Case Study," *American Sociological Review*, 17 (1952), 685 f; see also Gans, *op. cit.;* Warner and Srole, *op. cit.*, for further evidence of ethnic sub-societal systems.

[5] C. B. Nam, "Nationality Groups and Social Stratification in America," *Social Forces*, 37 (1959), p. 333. The assumption that Negroes have been enjoying a slow but steady economic advance is laid to rest by Dale Hiestand, *Economic Growth and Employment Opportunities for Minorities* (New York: Columbia University Press, 1964).

[6] See Lewis Corey, "Problems of the Peace: IV. The Middle Class," *Antioch Review*, 5, 68–87.

[7] Scott Greer, "Catholic Voters and the Democratic Party," *Public Opinion Quarterly*, 25 (1961), 624.

between the older resident and the new-comer sometimes reinforces ethnic political alignments and ethnic social identifications.[8] Minority concentrations are less visible in suburban than in urban areas because less immigrant and second-generation persons reside there. Lieberson's study of ten major metropolitan areas shows that the groups most highly segregated from native whites in the central city are also most residentially concentrated in the suburbs, so that suburban patterns bear a strong similarity to those found in the city.[9]

Finally, residential segregation is not a necessary prerequisite for the maintenance of an ethnic sub-societal structure; *a group can maintain ethnic social cohesion and identity, while lacking an ecological basis.* The Jews of Park Forest live scattered over a wide area and "participate with other Park Foresters in American middle-class culture," that is, they clearly are acculturated. Yet in one year a Jewish sub-community consisting of informal friendship groups, a women's club, a B'nai B'rith lodge and a Sunday School had emerged. Similarly distinct Lutheran and Catholic social groupings also had developed in which national origin played a large part. (Religion, according to Herbert Gans, was not the ex-clusive concern of any of the three groups.)[10]

The neighborhood stores, bars, coffee-shops, barber shops, and fraternal club-rooms which serve as social nerve centers in the ecologically contiguous first-settlement urban areas are difficult to reconstruct in the new topography of shopping centers and one-family homes, but they are frequently replaced by suburban-styled church, charity and social organizations, informal evening home-centered gatherings and extended family ties kept intact over a wide area with the technical assistance of the omnipresent automobile. The move to second and third settlement areas and the emergence of American-born generations, rather than presaging an inevitable process of disintegration has led to new adjustments in minority organization and communication. *Even when most of the life-styles assume an American middle-class stamp, these in-group social patterns reinforce ethnic identifications and seem to give them an enduring nature.* Today identifiable groups remain not as survivals from the age of immigration but with new attributes many of which were unknown to the immigrants. In short, changes are taking place in ethnic social patterns, but the direction does not seem to be toward greater assimilation into the dominant Anglo-American social structure.

In addition to the movement of ethnics from first settlement areas to the surrounding suburbs there is a smaller "secondary migration" to the Far West. What little evidence we have of this phenomenon suggests that highly visible acculturation styles do not lead to the loss of ethnic consciousness. The numerous Italian, Aremenian, Greek, Finnish and Jewish sub-societal organizations, to cite the West Coast groups that have come to my attention, suggest that structural assimilation into the Anglo-Protes-

[8] Robert C. Wood, *Suburbia, Its People and Their Politics* (Boston: Houghton Mifflin Co., 1958), p. 178. As impressive as is the trek to the suburbs, more recent developments should not go unrecorded. Of great significance, and hitherto unobserved because it is of such recent occurrence, is the effect of the revised and liberalized national origins quota system of our immigration laws. Direct observation of immigration into several of the Italian and Greek communities in New York during 1965–66 leaves me with the conviction that the ethnic core-city community is far from declining. In certain urban centers, such as the Brownsville section of New York, the gradual depletion of old ethnic neighborhoods is being amply and visibly counterbalanced by new injections of Polish refugees, along with Italian, Greek and Latin American immigrants who not only reinforce the core-city neighborhoods but frequently lend them certain first-generation touches reminiscent of an earlier day.

[9] Stanley Lieberson, "Suburbs and Ethnic Residential Patterns," *American Journal of Sociology,* 67 (1962), 673–681.

[10] Herbert J. Gans, "Park Forest: Birth of a Jewish Community," *Commentary,* 7 (1951), 330–339.

tant mainstream is far from inevitable in the "newer America." Friedman, observing how the Jews in Alberquerque are so well integrated as to be "almost indistinguishable from the community at large," then goes on to describe a Jewish network of social organizations such as Hadassah, B'nai B'rith, Shul, Temple, etc.[11] The strenuous efforts made by West Coast Greek-Americans on behalf of Mayor Christopher of San Francisco, including appeals that reached segments of the Greek community in New York, indicate that old-style political ethnic appeals are not unknown in California. The recent gubernatorial contest in Nevada, with its appeals to Mormons, Catholics and Italians, moved one observer to comment that "the Nevada campaign made it clear once again that American elections more often than not are heavily dependent on a maze of ethnic, religious and minority group voting factors that few candidates discuss in public."[12] At the same time, the emerging political articulation of Mexican-Americans throughout the Far West should remind us that growing acculturation often leads to *more* rather than less ethnic political awareness.[13]

In general terms, the new "affluence," often cited as a conductor of greater assimilation, may actually provide minorities with the financial and psychological wherewithal for building even more elaborate parallel sub-societal structures, including those needed for political action. In prosperous suburban locales, while the oldest and most exclusive country clubs belong to old-stock Protestant families, the newer clubs are of Jewish or varying Catholic-ethnic antecedents. Among Chicago's debutantes, established "society," primarily Anglo-Protestant, holds a coming-out at the Passavant hospital

ball. Debutantes of other origins make do with a Presentation Ball (Jewish), a Links Ball (Negro) and the White and Red Ball (Polish). Similar developments can be observed in numerous other urban and suburban regions.[14] Rather than the expected structural assimilation, parallel social structures flourish among the more affluent ethnics. Increasing prosperity among Catholics has been accompanied by an increase in Catholic institutional and social organizations including a vast parochial education system,[15] and the proliferation in sectarian higher education often means a heightened ethnic consciousness. Thus Lenski finds, after controlling for income and party affiliation, that parochially educated Catholics tend to be more doctrinally orthodox and politically conservative than publically educated Catholics.[16]

If ethnic social relations show this notable viability, it might also be remembered that ethnic sub-cultures have not been totally absorbed into mainstream America. Numerous writers have observed the influence of ethnic cultural valuations on political life, causing one to conclude that not only is there slim evidence to show that assimilation is taking place, but there is even some question as to whether acculturation is anywhere complete.[17] Acculturation itself is a multifaceted process, and even as American styles, practices, language,

[11] Morris Friedman, "The Jews of Alberquerque," *Commentary*, 28 (1959), 55–62.

[12] Tom Wicker, "Hidden Issues in Nevada," *The New York Times*, July 23, 1966.

[13] See Joan W. Moore and Ralph Guzman, "The Mexican-Americans: New Wind from the Southwest," *The Nation*, May 30, 1966, pp. 645–648.

[14] *Cf.*, E. Digby Baltzell, *The Protestant Establishment, Aristocracy and Caste in America* (New York: Random House, 1964), p. 357; and "Life and Leisure," *Newsweek*, December 21, 1964.

[15] John Tracy Ellis, *American Catholicism* (Chicago: University of Chicago Press, 1956), *passim;* also James P. Shannon, "The Irish Catholic Immigration," in Thomas T. McAvoy (ed.), *Roman Catholicism and The American Way of Life* (Notre Dame: University of Notre Dame Press, 1960), pp. 204–210.

[16] Gerhard Lenski, *The Religious Factor* (Garden City, N.Y.: Doubleday, 1963, rev. ed.), pp. 268–270.

[17] Cf. Wesley and Beverly Allinsmith, "Religious Affiliation and Politico-Economic Attitude," *Public Opinion Quarterly*, 12 (1948), 377–389; Lawrence Fuchs, *The Political Behavior of the American Jews*, (Glencoe, Ill.: The Free Press, 1956).

and values are adopted, certain ethnic values and attitudes may persist as a vital influence; for instance, the attitude that fellow-ethnics are preferable companions in primary group relations.

That ethnic sub-cultures may still operate as independent variables in political life can be seen in the recent Wilson and Banfield study. In twenty referenda elections held in seven major cities between 1956 and 1963 for expenditures to pay for public services such as hospitals, schools and parks, it was found that the groups which, because of their income level, would pay little or nothing while benefitting most, were least likely to support such services namely Poles, Czechs, Italians, Irish and other ethnics.[18] Conversely, upper-income White Protestants and Jews, the very groups that would be paying the costs while benefitting least, were the strongest supporters of these proposed expenditures. The correlations are too compelling for one to assume that the voters of all groups were acting out of ignorance of their actual material interests. More likely, the authors conclude, there is something in the White Protestant and Jewish subcultural belief systems which tends "to be more public-regarding and less private—(self or family) regarding" than in the other ethnic sub-cultures. In sum, *cultural belief systems or residual components of such systems may persist as cultural and political forces independently of objective and material factors.*

IDENTIFICATIONAL DURABILITY

From the time he is born, the individual responds to cultural cues mediated by representatives that help shape his personal character structure. . . . Insofar as the individual internalizes experiences from earlier social positions and subcultural matrices, his personality may

[18] James Q. Wilson and Edward C. Banfield, "Public Regardingness As a Value Premise in Voting Behavior," this REVIEW, 58, (December, 1964), 876–887.

act as a determinant—or character interpreter—of his present socio-cultural world. To apply that model to our present analysis: ethnic identifications are no matter of indifference even for the person who is both culturally and socially assimilated to the extent that his professional, recreational, and neighborhood relations and perhaps also his wife are of the wider White Protestant world. A holiday dinner at his parents' home may be his only active ethnic link, or it may be—as Stanley Edgar Hyman said when asked what being Jewish meant to him—nothing more than "a midnight longing for a hot pastrami sandwich"; yet it is a rare person who reaches adulthood without some internalized feeling about his ethnic identification. Just as social assimilation moves along a different and slower path than that of acculturation, so does identity assimilation, or rather non-assimilation enjoy a pertinacity not wholly responsive to the other two processes.

There are several explanations for the persistence of individual ethnic identity in such cases. First, even if the available range of social exposure brings a man into more frequent contact with outgroup members, early in-group experiences, family name and filial attachments may implant in him a natural awareness of, and perhaps a pride in, his ethnic origins. An individual who speaks and behaves like something close to the Anglo-American prototype may still prefer to identify with those of his own racial, religious or national background because it helps tell him who he is. For fear of "losing my identity" some individuals have no desire to pass completely into a "nondescript" "non-ethnic" American status. In an age of "mass society" when the "search for identity" concerns many, an identification which is larger than the self yet smaller than the nation is not without its compensations.

Furthermore, the acculturated ethnic may be no more acceptable to the nativist than the unacculturated. Since the beginning of our nation, the native population has wanted minority groups to acculturate or "Americanize," a process entailing the destruction of alien customs and appearances offensive to American sensibilities. But this was not to be taken as an invitation into Anglo-American primary group relations. . . . Ethnic identifications are, after all, rarely neutral. Few things so effectively assure the persistence of in-group awareness as out-group rejection, and much of the ethnic cradle-to-grave social structure, often considered "clannish," is really defensive.[19] The greater the animosity, exclusion and disadvantage, generally the more will ethnic self-awareness permeate the individual's feelings and evaluations. For groups enjoying some measure of acceptance ethnicity plays an intermittent rather than constant role in self-identity, whereas for those groups which have experienced maximum hostility and oppression—for instance, the Negro American—the question of ethnic identification takes on a ubiquitous quality, there being few instances when, for real or imagined reasons, race does not define, shape or intrude upon both the ordinary business of living and the extraordinary business of politics.

As long as distinctions obtain in the dominant society, and the foreseeable future seems to promise no revolutionary flowering of brotherly love, and as long as the family and early group attachments hold some carry-over meaning for the individual, ethnic identifications and ethnic-oriented responses will still be found even among those who have made a "secure" professional and social position for themselves in the dominant Anglo-Protestant world.

[19] Hansen observes: "When the natives combined to crush what they considered the undue influence of alien groups they committed a tactical error, for the newcomers, far from being crushed were prompted to consolidate their hitherto scattered forces": Marcus Lee Hansen, *The Immigrant in American History* (New York: Harper and Row, 1960 ed.), p. 136.

CONCLUSION

By way of concluding I may summarize my major propositions and discuss their broader political and theoretical applications.

1. . . . From the evidence and analysis proffered in the foregoing pages, there is reason to believe that despite a wide degree of second and third generation acculturation: (1) residual ethnic cultural valuations and attitudes persist; acculturation is far from complete; (2) the vast pluralistic parallel systems of ethnic social and institutional life show impressive viability; structural assimilation seems neither inevitable nor imminent; (3) psychological feelings of minority group identity, both of the positive-enjoyment and negative-defensive varieties, are still deeply internalized. In sum, ethnic distinctiveness, can still be treated as a factor in social and political pluralism.

. . . We can see that (a) increases in education have not necessarily led to a diminished ethnic consciousness; indeed, the increase in sectarian education often brings a heightened ethnic consciousness.[20] (b) Increases in income and adaptation to middle-class styles have not noticeably diminished the viability and frequency of ethnic formal and informal structural associations. Such stylistic changes as have occurred may just as easily evolve *within* the confines of the ethnically stratified social systems, thereby leading to a proliferation of parallel structures rather than absorption into Anglo-Protestant social systems. (c) Geographical dispersion, like occupational and class mobility has been greatly overestimated. Movement from the first settlement area actually may represent a transplanting of the ethnic community to

[20] Lenski, *loc. cit.* Lenski's entire study points to the persistence of sub-cultural religio-ethnic variables in political and economic life. The transition away from the Democratic Party by Catholics is not . . . a symptom of assimilation; in fact, by Lenski's data, it is a manifestation of a growing commitment to religious conservatism.

suburbia. Furthermore, as we have seen, even without the usual *geographic* contiguity, *socially* and *psychologically* contiguous ethnic communities persist. (d) Intergroup contacts, such as may occur, do not necessarily lead to a lessened ethnic awareness; they may serve to activate a new and positive appreciation of personal ethnic identity. Or intergroup contacts may often be abrasive and therefore conducive to ethnic defensiveness and compensatory in-group militancy. Perhaps intermarriage, as a genetic integration (for the offspring) will hasten assimilation; where hate has failed, love may succeed in obliterating the ethnic. But intermarriage remains the exception to the rule, and in the foreseeable future does not promise a large-scale structural group assimilation. Furthermore, in the absence of pertinent data, we need not assume that the offspring of mixed marriages are devoid of ethnic identifications of one kind or another.

2. . . . Given the limited availability of campaign resources and the potentially limitless demands for expenditure, the candidate is in need of a ready-made formal and informal network of relational sub-structures within his constituency. He discovers that "reaching the people" is often a matter of reaching particular people who themselves can reach, or help him reach, still other people.

A growing acculturation may have diminished the salience of the more blatant ethnic appeals, and the candidate knows that a nostalgic reference to the old country no longer strikes the resonant note it did thirty years ago; indeed, it may elicit a self-consciously negative response from the American-born generations. But he also should know that social assimilation (whether he calls it that or not) is far from an accomplished reality, as he finds himself confronted with leaders and members from a wide melange of ethnic associations, be they professional, business, labor, veteran,

neighborhood, educational, church, charitable, recreational or fraternal. Unhampered by any premature anticipations of assimilation, the politician can work with what is at hand. Even if "ethnic issues," as such, do not emerge in a campaign, ethnic social life provides him with ready-made avenues to constituent audiences, audiences which—no matter how well acculturated—are not noted for their indifference to being courted by public figures.

That many urban and suburban politicians persist in giving attentive consideration to minority social groupings in American-born constituencies, then, may be due less to their inveterate stupidity than to the fact that ethnic substructures and identifications are still extant, highly visible and, if handled carefully, highly accessible and responsive. The political practitioner who chooses to ignore the web of formal and informal ethnic sub-structures on the presumption that such groupings are a thing of the past does so at his own risk.

3. Historically, the theoretical choice posed for the ethnic has been either isolated existence in autonomous cultural enclaves or total identificational immersion into the American society. We have seen that neither of these "either-or" conditions have evolved. In 1915, Woodrow Wilson observed: "America does not consist of groups. A man who thinks of himself as belonging to a particular national group in America has not yet become an American." [21] As was so often the case when he addressed himself to the problem of national minorities, Wilson took the simple view. His was the commonly accepted assumption that a person's identity or position in the social system were indivisible qualities; therefore, identity choices were mutually exclusive. But in reality a person experiences cumulative and usually complementary

[21] Quoted in Oscar Handlin, *The American People in the Twentieth Century* (Boston: Beacon Press, 1963, rev. ed.), p. 121.

identifications, and his life experiences may expose him to some of the social relations and cultural cues of the dominant society while yet placing him predominantly within the confines of a particular minority sub-structure. For the ethnic a minority group identity is no more incompatible with life in America and with loyalty to the nation than is any regional, class, or other particular group attachment. A pluralistic society, after all, could not really exist without pluralistic sub-structures and identities.

Ethnics can thus sometimes behave politically as ethnics while remaining firmly American. It may be said that minorities have injected a new meaning into a national motto originally addressed to the fusion of thirteen separate states: *e pluribus unum,* a supreme allegiance to, and political participation in, the commonality of the Union, with the reserved right to remain distinct unassimilated entities in certain limited cultural, social and identificational respects.

8. AN ANGLO-SAXON CORE GROUP

August B. Hollingshead and
Frederick C. Redlich

A minority group in only a numerical sense, old and well-established Anglo-Saxon families rank at or near the top of the status hierarchy of many small and medium-sized American cities. Because of their wealth, power, and prestige, groups such as the one described here have frequently served as models for the aspirations of many upwardly mobile members of minority groups. This selection indicates some of the ways that the core group in New Haven, Connecticut, attempts to maintain its position by controlling exclusiveness and capitalizing on ascribed status criteria that are available to only a relatively few others. The group looks down on minority group

Source: *Social Class and Mental Illness* (New York: John Wiley and Sons, Inc., 1958), pp. 68–79. Reprinted by permission of Professor Hollingshead and the publisher. Copyright © 1958 by John Wiley and Company.

AUGUST B. HOLLINGSHEAD, author of *Elmtown's Youth* and co-author of *Trapped* and other works, is William Graham Sumner Professor of Sociology at Yale University. FREDERICK C. REDLICH is Dean of the Yale Medical School.

members, branding even the successful ones as mere *"arrivistes."* Its tight control over intimate social interaction, especially its restriction of marriage to status equals in New Haven or some other city, helps to keep minority group members at a distance and limits their access to informal sources of power and influence.

Some observers believe that such elite groups can serve an important purpose for American society if their wealth and security, which enable them to provide well-trained and responsible leaders, are coupled with a strong sense of *noblesse oblige.* Others however, holding what is probably the more prevalent view among American sociologists, believe that any restriction of the mobility of other members of the society restricts and ultimately threatens the entire democratic process.

When persons or families are arranged on the ordinal scales included in the Index of Social Position, namely, place of residence, education, and occupation, and their positions on these scales are compared with other cultural items, such as the newspapers they read or the television programs they view, their positions on the Index are correlated significantly with their behavior in regard to most items. Persons who possess particular patterns of consumption, taste, attitudes, and other identifiable sociocultural characteristics that are correlated with the three factors built into the Index of Social Position are the constituent units in the population aggregates which we identify as "social classes." In short, classes, as delineated by the Index of Social Position, are characterized by distinct subcultures. The principal constellation of cultural traits associated with each class will be traced in the ensuing sections of this chapter. The rich details of the subculture for each class are based upon a series of studies Hollingshead and his students have made in the last decade supplemented by data collected for this study.

The specific subcultural traits more or less common to the members of a class are learned through participation in the behavior system peculiar to it. The identification of persons with other persons who share similar cultural values, attitudes, beliefs, and customs produces group solidarity as well as group differences. Persons in a particular class learn almost unconsciously, in the course of their lives, a subtle series of cues which enable them to recognize one another and to identify even strangers as equals or unequals; cues shown by persons in other classes are shared as well. Those who are marked by out-group stigmata are viewed with suspicion, if not with hostility or denegation. Differences in patterns of subcultural traits, and the recognition of them by members of the community, set each class off from the others.

Social Mobility

Social mobility involves a change in the class status of individuals during the course of their lives. The class position occupied by an individual's parental family during his childhood and early adolescence is the base line against which mobility may be measured. Viewed theoretically, an individual either goes through life occupying the class position he inherited from his parental family, or he acquires a different class status through the instrumentality of his own activities. An individual who does not change his class is viewed as being inter-generationally *stable*. An individual who changes his class position is *mobile*. A person who achieves a class status higher than that of his parental family is defined as being *upward mobile*. A person who fails to hold the status occupied by the parental generation and acquires a class position lower than his parents' in the status structure is identified as being *downward mobile*. Generally speaking, upward mobility in the American social structure is approved behavior and downward mobility is unapproved behavior. Mobile behavior is learned in the course of an individual's life, but the details of how mobility or stability are acquired are far from being clear.

The principal requisites for achieving upward mobility are skill, education, and knowledge, particularly in males, and physical beauty, charm, and talent in females. The particular choice of goals of upward mobile persons—power, wealth, or fame—depends on specific values of the individuals concerned.

CLASS I

Status Awareness

Each respondent in the control sample was asked a series of questions designed to elicit his awareness of status. The first question asked was: "Do you think classes exist in the community?" The second was: "What things determine one's class?" Each respondent made his own decision as to his belief in classes and the criteria that placed a person in a class. After responses were recorded from these questions, the interviewer

asked, "To what class would you say you belong?" The interviewer then read slowly eight choices: "upper," "upper-middle," "middle," "lower-middle," "working," "lower," "do not know," and "I do not believe in classes."

The direct questions on "class" brought into focus incongruity between a person's response to a question involving values in the publicly professed dimensions of the culture, particularly if it involves democratic beliefs, and his actions in situations involving in-group codes. A class I matron, who was startled by the question but who identified herself as "upper" class, provided insight into this facet of the social ethic with the acid comment, "One does not speak of classes; they are felt." In spite of such incongruities, over 98 percent of the class I respondents think there are "social classes" in the community: 37 percent identify with the "upper" class, 56 percent classify themselves as "upper-middle" class, and 5 percent as "lower-middle" class. The remaining 2 percent do not believe in classes.

Whereas class status brings its members into contact with one another in many functional relationships in the maintenance of the community's general social life, ethnic and religious differences segment the 3.4 percent of the community's population placed in class I (by the Index of Social Position) into internally organized, almost self-contained, social worlds. A *core group,* composed of pacesetting, commonly recognized "old families," enjoys the highest prestige and power positions in the status system. Revolving around it are satellite groups composed of persons who have "arrived" recently in the business and professional worlds and, in the words of an *arriviste,** "Yale profes-

* By *"arrivistes"* we mean persons who are upward mobile, who have achieved class I positions through their own efforts rather than by inheritance, usually in the current generation. The connotation of unscrupulousness usually associated with the word does not apply in these discussions.

sors who try to play the game on $10,000 a year." Although there are distinct differences in the ability of different groups to "play the game," all groups respect and, in many ways, emulate those who sometimes satirically are referred to by members of fringe groups as "proper New Haveners." "Proper New Haveners" are truly "at the summit" of local "society." Members of these families have been at the summit for two, three, and more generations, and some have been in the "nuclear group" since colonial times.

Fifty-three percent of the adults in this class are stable through two and more generations and 47 percent are upward mobile from their parental families. Stable members of the core group possess a complex subculture which aspirants must acquire before they are admitted into the group. Those who are accorded "accepted" status are the "gatekeepers"; they decide which "new people" are invited into their exclusive organizations. Conversely, the gatekeepers "drop the black ball" on those they do not approve.

Economic Orientation

Executives and professional men head class I families. Those in business are major office holders, such as on boards of trustees, presidents, vice-presidents, secretaries, and treasurers in the larger industries, construction and transportation companies, stores, banks, brokerage houses, and utilities. Two thirds of the men in the professions are in independent practice—lawyers, physicians, engineers, architects, and certified public accountants; the other one third are salaried—professors, clergymen, and engineers for the most part. A few executives receive from $40,000 to $50,000 a year, but more earn from $20,000 to $30,000. The modal range for mature free professionals is from $20,000 to $25,000 per year. However, the median

reported family income, where the male head is the only one gainfully employed, is $10,000. This median is conditioned in large part by the presence of Yale University and its large, comparatively low-paid faculty, as well as the presence of young professionals, widows, and retired people in the sample. In the 8 percent of the households where a wife is engaged in business or a profession, the median income is $15,025 a year.

Families in the core group are, on the whole, wealthy, but there are large differences in their economic positions. A few families are multimillionaires; other families may possess only a quarter- to a half-million dollars. The wealth of the core group has been inherited by two, three, and more generations, whereas that of the *arrivistes* has been acquired during the present or previous generation. Inherited wealth is accorded a higher social value within the core group than "made money." Several generations of inherited wealth attests to the genuineness of the patina on the family's pecuniary escutcheon. A family which possessed the ability to make money in the first place, and to hold it and add to it through the generations, has demonstrated its "true" worth.

A cardinal principle in established families is that capital funds should not be squandered. Each generation should live on income only and add to capital by conservative management. Squandering of capital funds results in the next generation's being faced with the problem of earning its living. An inherited income assures a high standard of living without undue effort of a family head to support his family of procreation. Men are expected to look after their inheritances and those of their wives, but estate managers may be employed and trust departments of large banks relied upon for counsel, if not actual management of securities, trusts, and properties. A man should have an occupation or a profession, although he may not rely too heavily upon it for income. Income from inherited wealth supplemented by income from salaries and fees earned by the male head is the most general pattern.

Persons with private incomes are careful to see that the dollar sign is muted on their possessions and on the things they do. The dollar sign and interest in the dollar sign are stigmata of newly rich strivers. Individuals who accumulate wealth view money as *the* requisite of high social position; those who have inherited wealth look to other things as the sine qua non of position. The core group is not ostensibly interested in money, but a substantial income is necessary to their way of life. This point was brought to our attention sharply by an elderly member of a distinguished family who, in response to a question on income, reported with indignation, "We have it."

Ethnic Origin

Persons able to pass the core group's test of financial means are faced with a more crucial barrier—the lineage test. Lineage is used to protect the group from "social climbers" who are attempting to reach "the summit" on the basis of personal achievement. The upward mobile nuclear family with the right ethnic background is the most serious threat to privileged position, and they are a target for the group's hostile and biting remarks. For example, a man in the core group was discussing local families and their estates when the interviewer commented on the purchase of an estate by an *arriviste* of mixed Irish and Yankee descent in the respondent's neighborhood. The respondent, who was interviewed in his office, straightened in his chair, tapped the desk with a forefinger, and stated emphatically, "Money does not count up there (a hill in a suburb covered with estates). Family back-

ground, who you are—these are the things that count." This man overlooks the simple fact that these families could not live on their estates without wealth. An *arriviste* may manage to purchase an estate "on the hill" and be isolated from the social life of the families who accept one another as equals. The question of who one is, ethnically, places acceptance in the group in a different dimension of the social structure from economic competence. A person is able to do something about his role and function in the economic system, but he is powerless in the ethnic dimension of his life. Here he is dependent upon his ancestors.

The core group ascribes a different and lower status to persons from disapproved ethnic backgrounds—Jews, Irish, Italians, Greeks, Poles, and others from southern and eastern Europe. Core group members tend to lump these national origin groups together; all are undesirable. An industrial leader, when asked why New Haven has such a diverse population, stated, "I should say largely it was an overflow of great tidal waves of these races—Italians, Irish, Jews, Germans, and so on—reaching New York and sliding on to the next place. These races are very gregarious, and they are coaxed easily by a roll of money." A prominent core group matron thought that the "Italians just swarmed into this area. It seemed to be the happy hunting ground. New Haven has become an Italian colony. It's amazing." Another emphasized, "The Poles and Italians gave us our vicious gangs." A prominent attorney accused the "Jewish traders" of "gobbling up fine old companies in trouble" and continuing "their Sheeney ways."

Chronologically, wealth comes first; then one's family background is discovered, and the importance of wealth is pushed into the background. The number of generations a family has been prominent *and* resident in the community is important to the elderly arbiters of power and status. This point was well put by a distinguished matriarch while we were discussing the importance of some families in the life of the city over a number of generations. Such a family was named as an illustration. The respondent closed her eyes, thought for a few moments, and resumed the discussion with, "The————are not really old New Haveners. They first settled in Saybrook (a pioneer settlement on the Connecticut coast) in the 1640s, but the family did not move to New Haven until 1772."

The core group is composed of extended families who trace their ancestry directly to the colonial period and then to England, Scotland, the Netherlands, or to French Huguenot refugees. These well-known "old Yankees" represent 59 percent of this stratum. Persons of Irish descent, who through the years have accumulated wealth and established family positions but have maintained their identifications with the Roman Catholic Church, are a group apart and compose 11 percent of this class. Descendants of other immigrant stocks—German (6 percent), Scandinavian (2 percent), and Italian (9 percent)—who are accumulating wealth through business enterprise and successful professional practices, represent other subgroups. Jews (13 percent) represent a separate hierarchy from the Gentile groups. German-Jewish families as a rule occupy higher prestige positions in the Jewish segment of class I than Jews of Polish and Russian descent.

Religious Affiliation

Ethnic origins and religious affiliations are highly correlated. Viewed overall, the three major religious groups are divided as follows: Protestants—61 percent, Roman Catholics—24 percent, Jews—13 percent, and mixed or no affiliation—2 percent. Within the Protestant group,

61 percent of the families are Congregationalists, 17 percent are Episcopalians, 7 percent are Lutherans, 5 percent are Baptists, 2 percent are Methodists, and other denominations comprise the remaining 7 percent. In each religious group—Protestant, Catholic, and Jewish—the membership is concentrated in a small number of congregations. For example, there are 24 Congregational churches in the community, but over 93 percent of the core group members belong to three of these churches. Episcopalians are clustered in 2 of 19 parishes in the area, and Roman Catholics are concentrated in 4 parishes. Among Jews, the greatest clustering is in the Reformed Congregation. As Russian and Polish Jews have moved upward in the class structure, they have left the Orthodox and Conservative congregations and affiliated with the Reformed Temple founded by German Jews who came to the community a century ago. As these *arrivistes* have become affiliated with the Temple, the descendants of its Germanic founders have tended to withdraw from its affairs except for important ritualistic occasions and high holy days.

Although 98 percent of the respondents claim affiliation with three religions, from 8 to 33 percent are not members of any specific congregation and do not attend services. For practical purposes, these people are "unchurched." Approximately 25 percent of Protestant men and women and 38 percent of Jewish men and women have no congregational ties; only 15 percent of the Roman Catholic men and 8 percent of the women are in this category. These people probably had nominal connections with their claimed denominations at one time in their lives, but currently they are outside the religious participation pattern. The percentage of "unchurched" persons is significantly higher in class I in comparison with the other strata. The "unchurched" men and women in each major religion are upward mobile in significantly larger numbers than those who are stable socially. However, a considerable number of upward mobile persons function actively in selected churches and thereby aid their mobility strivings in a positive way.

Religious identification rather than affiliation and active participation is a salient factor in the organization of this stratum's social life. If a person is identified as a Jew, most Gentile doors are closed to him; moreover if he is a Roman Catholic, lines are drawn around him in Protestant circles, but not so openly. Conversely, Jews and Roman Catholics react in negative ways to Protestants. The three parallel hierarchies of Protestant, Catholic, and Jew, around which all social life of the community, at all levels, is organized, have crystallized in class I with signal force. A core group member made this very clear when he stated, in response to a question about his relationships with Jews, "We have business dealings with them. I sometimes sit next to an eminent Hebrew at a business luncheon." When asked if Hebrews were ever invited into his home, he bristled and said coldly, "In my living room there is never a Hebrew, no matter how eminent he is in professional or business life. Hebrews know."

A distinguished member of a prominent Jewish family described in detail how his family has been discriminated against in its attempts to be accepted into "restricted" clubs and associations. With particular reference to having the "black ball dropped" on his application for membership in a beach club, he remarked with feeling, "My ass is not good enough to sit on their sand."

A housewife whose husband changed his name legally from an easily recognizable Polish-Jewish one to a distinguished New England Yankee one about thirty years ago in the hope that it would enable him, in her words, "to cross over," told how this move failed. They then joined the Temple and became leaders in the Jewish community. She feels strongly that her religion is her "social gospel" but it does not help her make contact with the "white Protestants" who are "the privileged group in New Haven society."

A male member of the "privileged group" who was nominally a Congregationalist but attended church on Easter, Christmas, and only a few other times, did not think religion was too important in his way of life. He commented, "The churches are becoming women's and children's organizations, and, outside of paying the bills, the men don't seem to have much control."

Education

Class I is the most highly educated segment of the population. The median years of school completed by the male heads of families is 17.6. The median for the wives is 14.4 years. One wife in five has the same amount of education as her husband; 43 percent of the husbands have had at least four years more education than their wives, but only 7 percent of the wives have had at least one more year of education than their husbands. The distinct difference in the amount of education between husbands and wives is an outstanding characteristic of this class.

Formal schooling, after the eighth grade, normally is received in a private institution patterned after the English public school. Secondary education in a public school is frowned upon by all segments of the core group; many in this stratum refuse to send their children to the public schools from the earliest years. The core group families send their sons to distinguished New England boarding schools where they spend from four to six years preparing for an Ivy League College. Daughters are sent to well-known boarding schools to prepare them for entrance into a select women's college. Families who cannot afford to send their children to boarding schools enter them in one of the accepted single-sex schools in the community.

The country day and boarding schools are staffed by an elite corps of headmasters and headmistresses of approved Yankee lineages and Protestant faiths, from "upper class" families, who were educated in the aristocratic-value system and are dedicated to preserving and transmitting it. They may close the educational gates to persons who cannot pass both the means and lineage tests, but other criteria are used to justify such actions. They attempt to hire teachers with backgrounds similar to theirs; as this is difficult today, their staffs tend to be made up of upward mobile individuals who have identified with the core group's value system.

Private secondary schooling is preparatory, if not a requisite, to entrance into a one-sex "name" college. The "big three," Yale, Harvard, and Princeton, are the dominant preference for men. The smaller men's colleges occupy secondary positions in the local value hierarchy—Amherst, Williams, Dartmouth, Brown, and Wesleyan. Women should be sent to Smith, Vassar, Wellesley, Bryn Mawr, Mount Holyoke, or Radcliffe to be acceptable in the social world under discussion. Coeducational private colleges such as Swarthmore or Oberlin are respectable but do not carry prestige. Attendance at a state university marks a man or a woman as an *arriviste;* the state university graduate is at best a "fringer" in the elite groups. The vast majority of the upward mobile family heads, whether from old American stock or ethnic groups, were trained in whole or in part at state universities, but they generally do everything within their means to see that their children attend private secondary schools and name colleges.

Lessons to teach the individual how to act in various social situations and how to use leisure time in approved ways are extremely important in the way of life of this stratum. Professional functionaries who sell their skills and talents to class I families run classes for ballroom dancing, tennis, golf, sailing, music, and so on. Several years of formal training in leisure time pursuits prepare the young person for the core group's way of life, as well as the parallel one prevailing among the fringe groups.

Family Constellation

The nuclear group of husband, wife, and dependent children constitutes the primary family and common household unit. This group normally passes through a family cycle which begins with marriage, extends through the childbearing and child-rearing years, and ends in old age through the death of one of the parental pair. Each marriage brings a new family cycle. Upon the birth of their first child, the nuclear pair becomes a family of procreation, but for the child this family of origin is his family of orientation. Thus, each individual who marries and rears children has a family of orientation and a family of procreation.

Each nuclear family is related to a number of other nuclear families by consanguinal and affinal ties. Also, each family in the kin group occupies a position in the status system which may be the same or different from the others. The differences are produced by the mobility of some families. This movement of the individual nuclear family in the status system, while it is approved and often lauded as "the American way," has important effects on kin group relations.

One's ancestors and relatives count for more in the core group than what one has achieved in one's lifetime. Background is stressed most heavily when it comes to the crucial question of whom a member may marry. One of the perennial problems of the established family is the control of the marriage choices of its young men. Young women can be controlled more easily because of the more sheltered life they lead and their more passive role in courtship. The relative passivity of the female, coupled with sex exploitation of females from lower social positions by high level males that sometimes leads to marriage, results in a significant number of old maids in established families. Strong emphasis on family background leads to the selection of marriage mates from within the old-family group in an exceptionally high percentage of cases and, if not from the old-family group, then from the new-family segment of this stratum. The degree of kinship solidarity, combined with interclass marriages, results in comparative stability in the class, in the extended kin group, and in the nuclear family within it.

The core group family is basically an extended kin group, solidified by lineage and a heritage of common experience in the communal setting. A complicated network of consanguinal and affinal ties unites nuclear families of orientation and procreation into an in-group that rallies when its position is threatened by the behavior of one of its members, particularly where out-marriage is involved; this principle will be illustrated later. The nuclear family is viewed as only a part of a broader kin group that includes the consanguinal descendants of a known ancestral pair, plus kin brought into the group by marriage. Divorce is avoided if possible; when it occurs the entire family looks upon it as a disgrace, if not a scandal. The solidarity of the kin group is markedly successful in keeping divorce to a minimum. The ratio of widows and widowers to divorced persons is 27 to 1. This is the highest ratio in the population.

An important factor in the established family's ability to maintain its position through several generations is its economic security. Usually a number of different nuclear families within a kin group are supported, in part at least, by income from a family estate held in trust. Also, because of the practice of intramarriage within the core group, it is not unusual for a family to be the beneficiary of two or more estates held in trust. For example, one extended family group is the beneficiary of a trust established a century ago that yields something over $300,000 annually after taxes. This income is divided among 37 different nuclear families descended from the founder, 28 of whom live in the home community; 23 of these families are beneficiaries of one other trust fund, and 14 receive income from two or more other trust funds. These different nuclear families regard themselves as part of the "Scott" family; moreover, they are so regarded by other established families, as well as by persons lower in the status system who know something of the details of the family history.

The Scott family has maintained its social position for more than two centuries by a combination of property ownership, educational, legal, and political leadership, and control of marriages. Its members are proud that it has never had a non-Protestant marriage in seven generations; only five divorces have been traced, but these are not mentioned; one desertion has been hinted but not confirmed.

The family tradition of Protestant intermarriages had a severe test in recent years. A son of one nuclear family, who had spent four years in the Armed Forces in World War II, asked a class II Catholic girl to marry him. The engagement was announced by the girl's family to the consternation of the Scott family, who immediately brought pressure on the boy to "break off the affair." After several months of family and class pressure against the marriage, the young man "saw his error" and broke the engagement. A year later he married a family-approved girl from one of the other "old" families in the city. Today he is an officer in his wife's family's firm, and his father has built him a fine suburban home.

This case illustrates a number of characteristics typical of the established core group family. It is stable, extended, tends to pull together when its position is threatened—in this instance by an out-marriage—exerts powerful controls on its members to ensure that their behavior conforms to family and class codes, and provides for its members economically by trust funds and appropriate positions.

The *arriviste* family is characterized most decisively by phenomenal economic or professional success during a short interval of time. Its meteoric rise in the social system is normally the personal triumph of the nuclear head of the family. If the head is a businessman, he is busy making a "million bucks"; the family purchases the symbols associated with the wealthy American family: a large house, fine furniture, big automobiles, and expensive clothes. The new tycoon knows the power of money in the market place, and he often attempts to buy high position in the status system. In a professional family, the head is intent on making a "name" in his profession and acquiring some wealth. His family follows the same general pattern of purchasing the outward symbols of success but in a more modest fashion. The new family is able to meet the means test, but not the lineage test of the established families. Consequently, it is generally systematically excluded

from membership in the cliques and associations of greatest prestige. This is resented especially by the wife and children, but less often by the tycoon or professional man.

The new family is unstable in comparison with the established family. It lacks the security of accepted position at the top of the local status system—a position that will come only with time; it cannot be purchased. The stabilizing influence exerted by an extended family group, as well as friends, on the deviant individual is absent. Then too, the adults in the new family are self-directing, full of initiative, believe in the freedom of the individual, and rely upon themselves rather than upon a kin group. (Many upwardly mobile individuals break with their kin groups to aid their mobility.) The result is, speaking broadly, conspicuous expenditure, insecurity, and family instability. Thus, we find divorces, broken homes, and other symptoms of disorganization in a significantly large number of new families. The ratio of widows and widowers to divorced persons is only 5 to 1; this is significantly lower than in the core group. In like manner, the percentage of children under 17 years of age living in broken homes is decidedly higher in the new families (18 percent versus 3.4 percent). Because new families are so conspicuous in their consumption and behavior, they become, in the judgment of the general population, symbolic of "upper class" actions and values to the resentment of established families who generally frown upon such behavior.

9. NIGHT COMES TO THE CUMBERLANDS

Harry M. Caudill

It is a striking irony in the United States today that some
citizens of our oldest and purest Anglo-Saxon heritage find
themselves trapped in poor, empty, and bitter lives. Although
white, they are not part of the white majority in anything but
their color. Instead, they are the victims of what has been the
ruthless exploitation of their land's resources and of technology's shift from one fuel to another. They are the miners
of Appalachia. Many have become migrants and, along with
their families, are now new members of the white working and
lower classes in cities like Baltimore, Chicago, St. Louis, and
Cincinnati.

A half-million of these people still live in Kentucky's Cumberland Plateau, the setting for the present selection. In the
context of this book of readings, Caudill's work may be taken to
show that racism has not been the sole basis of human exploitation in America. The blind course of an unregulated
search for profits that often led to economic growth did not
always stay on an onward and upward course. Instead, it made
some white men, as well as most brown, black, and red ones,
pawns on a board they could not understand, let alone control.

The designation white Anglo-Saxon Protestant (and the
bitter acronym WASP) symbolizes probity, security, strength,
prestige, and snobbishness. That symbolism is a product of our
past and of the yearning of new Americans for full acceptance.
But the circumstances of Appalachia compared to those of
Class I New Haven make clear that no notions of racial differences will ever adequately account for conditions that are
social, the outcomes of historical accident and the exercise of

Source: *Night Comes to the Cumberlands* (Boston: Atlantic-Little,
Brown and Co., 1963), pp. ix, x, and 337–48. Copyright © 1962, 1963 by
Harry M. Caudill. Reprinted by permission of the publisher.

HARRY M. CAUDILL writes widely on the Appalachian area. This
excerpt is from his best-known work.

the will of men who were luckier, craftier, or more powerful than others. Appalachian children do badly in school; their parents show apathy, resignation, alienation, and ignorance. These facts are well enough known. Is any reader ready to suggest that they exist because the people among whom they apply are white?

The Cumberland Plateau region of Kentucky is a serrated upland in the eastern and southeastern part of the state. Its jagged hills and narrow winding valleys cover some ten thousand square miles. It embraces nineteen counties and portions of a dozen others. These units of government were created by the caprice of governors and legislators and, with one exception, were named for the state's heroes of statecraft and battlefield: Bell, Breathitt, Clay, Floyd, Harlan, Knott, Knox, Laurel, Lee, Leslie, Letcher, McCreary, Magoffin, Martin, Owsley, Perry, Pike, Whitley and Wolfe. Few of the heroes deserved so high an honor and few of the counties were worthy of creation. Only Pike County has proved to be sufficiently large and wealthy to discharge even fairly well the responsibilities inherent in local government.

The plateau's half million inhabitants are among the earth's most interesting folk. Their European ancestry and American adventures constitute a remarkable page in the history of mankind. The American public is prone to think of them as quaint hillbillies, a concept sociologists have neglected to explain or explore. In truth, the Kentucky mountaineer is drawn from some of the oldest white stock to be found north of Florida. His forebears had dwelt in or on the edge of the Southern Appalachians for generations before the Declaration of Independence was penned. In their long residence on this continent they left behind a unique, checkered and violent history. Their past created the modern mountaineers and the communities in which they live, and resulted in a land of economic, social and political blight without parallel in the nation. The purpose of this work is to trace the social, economic and political forces which produced the vast "depressed area" of eastern Kentucky.

Much of the region's story is the story of coal. Geologists tell us that two hundred million years ago it was a plain that had risen from the floor of a long-dry inland sea. Then the tortured crust of the earth cracked and "faulted," rearing the Pine Mountain. This long, steep ragged ridge now stretches from the Breaks of the Big Sandy River on the Virginia line some hundred and thirty miles southwesterly into northern Tennessee. It parallels the Cumberland (or Big Black) Mountain, the southern boundary of the plateau. Water flowing away from its base over a great fan-shaped territory carved the channels of three of the state's major streams and chiseled thousands of narrow valleys—the creeks and hollows of today.

After the shallow sea receded it left a vast bog where vegetation flourished, died, piled up in deep beds, turned to peat and finally aeons later, to coal. When the streams carved out the mountains and ridges of today they sliced through magnificent seams of coal, a mineral the steel age would esteem more highly than rubies.

Coal has always cursed the land in

which it lies. When men begin to wrest it from the earth it leaves a legacy of foul streams, hideous slag heaps and polluted air. It peoples this transformed land with blind and crippled men and with widows and orphans. It is an extractive industry which takes all away and restores nothing. It mars but never beautifies. It corrupts but never purifies.

But the tragedy of the Kentucky mountains transcends the tragedy of coal. It is compounded of Indian wars, civil war and intestine feuds, of layered hatreds and of violent death. To its sad blend, history has added the curse of coal as a crown of sorrow.

．　．　．　．　．

A fifty-year-old jobless miner summed up the hopelessness the shoddy schools sometimes engender. He sat in my law office one rainy Saturday afternoon and described his plight:

I hain't got no education much and jist barely can write my name. After I lost my job in 1950 I went all over the country a-lookin' fer work. I finally found a job in a factory in Ohio a-puttin' televisions inside wooden crates. Well, I worked for three years and managed to make enough money to keep my young-'uns in school. Then they put in a machine that could crate them televisions a whole lot better than us men could and in a lot less time. Hit jist stapled them up in big card-board boxes. I got laid off again and I jist ain't never been able to find nothing else to do.

But I kept my young-'uns in school anyway. I come back home here to the mountains and raised me a big garden ever' year and worked at anything I could find to do. I sold my old car fer seventy-five dollars and I sold all the land my daddy left me and spent the money on my children. They didn't have much to eat or wear, but they at least didn't miss no school. Well, finally last spring my oldest boy finished up high school and got his diploma. I managed to get twenty-five dollars together and give it to him and he went off to git him a job. He

had good grades in school and I figured he'd git him a job easy. He went out to California where he's got some kinfolks and went to a factory where they was hirin' men. The sign said all the work hands had to be under thirty-five years of age and be high-school graduates. Well, this company wouldn't recognize his diploma because it was from a Kentucky school. They said a high-school diploma from Kentucky, Arkansas and Mississippi just showed a man had done about the same as ten years in school in any other state. But they agreed to give the boy a test to see how much he knowed and he failed it flatter than a flitter. They turned him down and he got a job workin' in a laundry. He jist barely makes enough money to pay his way but hit's better than settin' around back here.

I reckon they jist ain't no future fer people like us. Me and my wife ain't got nothin' and don't know nothin' hardly. We've spent everything we've got to try to learn our young-'uns something so they would have a better chance in the world, and now they don't know nothin' either!

That his son is not an exceptional example is borne out by the statistics on college freshmen from the plateau. Some, of course, do excellent work in college and have little difficulty in entering the University of Kentucky or colleges outside the state. Most of the hopeful freshmen, however, are shockingly unprepared for college study. The standard College Qualification Test is given annually to seniors in the state's high schools and in those of other states. The test is prepared by the Psychological Corporation, a New York firm, and seeks to measure the high-school graduate's cultural background as well as his scholastic achievement. As its name implies, it is designed to measure the student's preparation for college study. In 1960 students in Virginia and Tennessee averaged above 80 per cent on the test. In areas of Kentucky outside the plateau grades averaged between 55 per cent and 65 per cent out of a possible 100 per cent. If this poor showing is startling what, then, must be one's reaction to the results of the same examination in the counties of the plateau? When the high-school graduates in a broad belt of the coal counties were given the test in 1960, the average grade was only 17.5 per cent.

These undereducated young Americans are the regions fortunate youths, notwithstanding the shortcomings of their schooling. Infinitely worse off are the uncounted children who simply do not go to school. One teacher, for example, began the 1959–1960 school term with fifty-eight enrolled pupils, in four grades. But as the term advanced many difficulties beset her weather-beaten little institution. Some children lived several miles away and had little appetite for the long walk over slippery paths on cold wintry mornings. The drafty building was a breeding ground for cold and influenza viruses and a substantial number were kept away by illness. Most absentees, however, stayed at home simply because their parents could not provide shoes and clothing for them to wear. Consequently, average daily attendance was only thirty-four.

Weak and sporadic elementary-school preparation results in crops of high-school freshmen who are totally unprepared for further studies. Almost one third of the freshmen of 1956 had dropped out of school in 1959.

The incidence of total illiteracy is startlingly high. Every lawyer in the plateau receives clients almost daily who are unable to sign their names to legal documents. On one occasion I went to a coal camp to obtain the signatures of a miner and his wife. Though they were under thirty-six years of age they could not write their names. Under the law their "marks" required attestation by two witnesses. Neither of their nearest neighbors could perform this simple duty and we were compelled to visit the third house before a man and woman were found who could sign as witnesses.

The physical task of providing decent housing for the region's school-children—a prerequisite without which real improvement is unthinkable—is staggering. Though the new retail sales tax is financing the construction of several hundred new classrooms annually, the building rate cannot begin to equal that at which ancient, rickety buildings have to be abandoned. Speaking of the building program in his own county, Pike County Superintendent C. H. Farley told a Congressional committee in March, 1961, that the task of catching-up appeared insuperable without major new sources of revenue. As he termed it, "The hurrieder we go, the behinder we get. Our schools are short on literally everything but children."

The county of approximately thirty thousand people which I have previously mentioned is largely supported by Welfarism of one character or another. As this is written, seven hundred and four Old Age pensioners receive monthly checks from the state capitol. Four hundred and eighty-six families are supported by Aid for Dependent Children checks. Seventy-one blind persons draw checks, and one hundred and twenty-six families are supported because the breadwinner is disabled, has fled or has been imprisoned. Nearly a thousand households receive checks from the United Mine Workers, and more than thirty-five hundred persons draw Social Security checks totalling two million dollars annually. Over a thousand pension and compensation checks reach the county each month from the United States Veterans Administration. At least two hundred families receive compensation checks because the husbands were killed or injured in mining accidents. Two thousand other men are paid unemployment compensation benefits while actively seeking other jobs. On "check days," at the beginning of each month, wastebaskets in county-seat banks are piled high with empty brown envelopes from state and Federal agencies. Sometimes they are inches deep on the floor at the tellers' windows. The millions of dollars thus pumped into the plateau each year keep the people alive and support the merchants and other business establishments. Without such checks a majority of the highlanders would be in abject starvation in a matter of days.

One third of the county's population is on the Commodity Relief rolls. From relatively humble beginnings the commodity distribution program has grown to mammoth proportions. On "giveaway" days queues a hundred yards long form in front of the distribution centers and the huge bags and boxes full of staples are carried to automobiles. Sometimes several people will rent a single car to haul their rations, and its luggage compartment will not hold the entire load.

Other Relief recipients arrive in their own vehicles, ranging from pathetic rattletraps to new Buicks. The late-model cars are the property of miners who were recently idled by layoffs at the rail mines. They worked ten or fifteen years at high wages and still drive cars bought or contracted for in happier times. It is incongruous in the extreme to see a man carry his bag of "giveaway grub" out to a bright red late-model Mercury with synthetic leopardskin seat-covers.

Sixteen hundred of the county's men are still employed in the unionized rail mines (at the height of the Big Boom its rail pits hired ninety-four hundred men), and seven hundred and fifty others work two or three days a week in nonunion truck mines. The county and independent school districts hire nearly five hundred teachers, supervisors, bus drivers, lunchroom cooks, librarians and other personnel for nine months out of each year. Banks, stores, garages, filling stations, machineshops, quarries, sawmills, post offices, restaurants, utilities companies, printers, morticians, railroads and other enterprises provide full or part-time employment to another thirteen hundred men and women. The United Mine Workers' hospital employs a hundred and twenty-five others. Approximately one hundred and fifty persons work for municipalities, the county and the state. Together, the employed support fewer than half the county's population.

An interesting outgrowth of the general aging of the population has been a gradual slipping-away of property from taxation. The old men and women whose children have moved to distant states know their heirs are unlikely to ever return to Kentucky. They know that the houses in which they live are worth only a few hundred dollars. Even a large, renovated camp house with plumbing and central heating will seldom bring more than fifteen hundred dollars.

They "raised" large families and when a twelve- or fifteen-hundred dollar estate is divided among ten or twelve heirs the inheritance is not worth the trouble its settlement will entail. Since the heirs are scattered in several states it is unthinkable that they will hire an attorney to settle an estate which is worth little more than a hundred dollars to each inheritor. Under these circumstances, the aged owners often simply stop paying taxes. They know the sheriffs whose duty it is to collect the levies will not risk the political disfavor enforced collections will bring. If the sheriffs went into the camps and onto the creeks and by attachments and sales compelled people to pay their real-estate taxes they would arouse the animosity of whole communities of voters. Since they have political interests and alliances to protect, they will not hunt trouble. Instead they wait politely in their offices and receive whatever tax payments are brought to them. Hundreds of small parcels of land have now gone for a decade or more without taxes being paid on them.

And when the old couple have died and the house stands empty there is no one to move into it. In lengthening lines deserted houses stretch up the creeks and along camp streets. If a local resident wants to buy such a property the technical difficulties are frequently almost insurmountable. Typically some of the sons and daughters of the last owner have died, leaving children of their own. It is not unusual for a thousand-dollar parcel of real estate to be the property of thirty or forty joint owners, some of whom have not set foot in the county for a decade. Some of them were born in other states and are only five or six years old. The guardians or custodians of such infants cannot convey their land until consent has been obtained from the Circuit Court of the county in which the realty is situated, an expensive, complex and time-consuming process. The state has no effective legislation by which the property can be sold for taxes. Thus as the present owners die off the amount of nontaxpaying property rises, to the increasing detriment of the plateau and of its public institutions.

A trip through the coal counties is a distressing experience. One traverses mile after dreary mile of patched and cratered "highways," their ditches choked with mud and their banks and shoulders thick with weeds. Nearly half the precious bottomland grows nothing more valuable than weeds and broom sage, and some is growing up in thickets. The mountains are strewn with rotted, collapsing coal tipples, chutes and bins and pimpled with ugly slate dumps of every size and shape. The streams have lost their sparkle and are sluggish yellow ropes coiling through the valleys. The hillsides, deserted by hoe and bull-tongue plow, are turning into tangled thickets. In the deep moist coves millions of young poplars have sprung up and constitute one of the region's few potential sources of wealth. But most of the forest land, the points and upper ridges, nourish a disheartening growth of cull gums, beeches, oaks and pines. The generations of wasteful logging and the forest conflagrations that followed in their wake have left little valuable timber. The slashed and burned saplings

that survived live on as unhealthy midgets which in the course of decades have grown scarcely at all. In the summertime their green foliage presents the appearance of a vast young forest, but this casual impression is wholly erroneous. One can climb for miles along the coal benches, across the ridges and through the deep coves without encountering a dozen genuinely healthy trees big enough for the sawmill.

Nowhere in the plateau does a single tract of virgin forest remain. All the titanic trees which once towered over its rippling streams have been "worked up" into lumber, mining props or stave bolts. Only a few tiny sawmills persist in a region that once supported scores of mighty band mills. Even a few acres of unspoiled timberland would constitute a priceless heritage for a nation which increasingly idealizes its robust past, but no such acres remain.

Hundreds of worked-out mines have become subterranean lakes. In wet weather water from the overlying mountains seeps into them and in dips or "swags" rises to the crumbling roofs. The unsealed airways and driftmouths disgorge it in foamy torrents, and during the dry summer months the drained hills dry out and turn adobe-hard. They lose their capacity to retain water in normal quantities for the nourishment of the trees struggling on their slopes. Drained of water, the slopes open in deep fissures. These perennial man-made droughts beset the timbered hillsides every summer and choke off growth. In spring the trees have a short burst of vitality but by July they are arrested and stand pale and desiccated, their roots deep in dry hard clay. They are a curious spectacle, little changed year after year, receiving sufficient moisture to preserve life but not enough to nurture vigorous growth.

Along the serpentine roads are the scores and hundreds of abandoned houses. The windows fall out, the chimneys topple, the roofs leak and in the grip of decay they sag ever closer to the earth. Here and there on high, uncertain stilts stands a dilapidated white frame schoolhouse, its playground a grassless, eroded hillside or an undrained mire.

Thousands of highlanders on job-hunting forays into Michigan, Indiana and Northern Ohio bought cheap "junker" cars which they have brought home in the hope of realizing a profit on them. Eventually, these wind up in roadside scrapyards where they are cannibalized for their parts. The mountaineers are inveterate automobile fanciers, but most of them can afford only worn-out, rattling vehicles of ancient vintage. After the last wheezing mile has been wrung from them they come to rest in automobile graveyards. Piece by piece they are stripped for such usable parts as may remain, then eventually they are loaded on trucks and hauled to Ashland, Kentucky, for sale at the great scrapyards of the American Roller Mills Company. The valleys are sprinkled with hideous car dumps where Fords, Chevrolets, Cadillacs and once magnificent limousines lie piled in rusty array. As eyesores they are second only to the ghastly trash dumps.

These latter eyesores abound on roadside and stream-bank. Trash collections outside the towns do not exist and people simply dump refuse wherever impulse directs, usually in the nearest creek or branch. Ancient car bodies, discarded truck beds, rusty bed springs, rotten mattresses, scraps of building materials, tin cans, bottles and paper are heaved onto road shoulders and into rivers and creeks. On a single trip across Knott, Perry, Leslie and Clay counties I counted more than sixty huge trash dumps, each of them plainly visible from the highway. Even when a municipality sponsors a trash-collection system no effort is made toward genuinely sanitary disposal. Instead, the collectors haul it into some ravine not far removed from the main highway. Acres of stinking waste accumulate, sheltering and feeding monstrous rats and buzzing swarms of flies. As the mounds of trash and garbage rise the collectors dump ever closer to the highway. Soon smoke from burning trash ascends from the shoulder of the road.

The city councils and civic organizations appear to be oblivious of the blight cast on their region by private and public dumps. Men who are reputed to be "public-spirited" will cast trunkloads of old newspapers into the river near their homes.

One town labored hard to persuade state officials to establish a state park near its borders. Delegations of city officials, Lions and Rotarians extolled the natural beauty to be seen from a towering mountain crag. Parks commissioners and news reporters were duly escorted to its summit. Through it all, with perfect aplomb, the city trucks carried daily cargoes of litter and waste to a dumping ground below the lookout point. While the community struggled prodigiously to promote "tourism," smoke from its dump sullied one of the region's most picturesque scenic areas.

In the main public standards are symbolized by public buildings. In the plateau the courthouses and jails are incredibly dilapidated and filthy. They go for years at a time without major repairs or even paint, and today it is scarcely conceivable that such vile and crumbling structures could be found in use in any of the new nations of Africa—not even in the chaotic Republic of Congo. At most seasons of the year they are festooned with garish signs of all shapes and sizes which proclaim the promises of candidates for innumerable town, county, state and Federal offices.

The strippers are tearing to pieces such natural scenic beauty as the dumps leave undefiled. Many of them work around the clock, their activities illuminated by batteries of powerful lights mounted on tall posts. From the air and from high mountain peaks the strip-lines are mazes of looped and tangled scars. Like great yellow snakes they twist over the tortured hills. Ironically, this destruction by the coal industry is rapidly nullifying the careful efforts of its boosters to develop a new source of income for the plateau.

Slashed and battered though they are, the highlands still afford many areas of breathtakingly rugged natural beauty. The gorge of the Red River is a paradise for lovers of wild flowers, and from crags on top of the Big Black and Pine Mountains one can look down on enchanting hollows. Seen from such eminences the lesser hills and ridges appear as gigantic waves on a primordial ocean. Many people, charmed by such beauty, have sought to establish "tourism" as a secondary "industry" for the region. The state government has created seven state parks at strategic points in the plateau and state officials have exhorted the mountaineers to clean up their roadsides, beautify their towns, build hotels and motor lodges and cater to such travelers as may wander into the area. Thus far the movement has made little headway. Despite the natural beauty to be found in some seasons, tourists will not spend their vacations driving over tortuous roads the sides of which are littered with heaps of junk and trash.

Livestock has almost vanished from the plateau. Between 1950 and 1960 more than half the farms were abandoned. The pastures have been surrendered to broom sage and the cornfields to weeds and brambles. Even the vegetable garden is a disappearing institution. The people have discovered that between giveaway and state aid nobody is going to starve anyway, and it is easier to carry it in than to grow it. In short, the ancient corn and pork subsistence agriculture has been abandoned under pressure from soil erosion, the enticement of money wages and a realization that the Welfare state will provide free as much as a man can acquire by backbreaking labor from the soil. Those farmers who learned the new methods of the agricultural agents are also being pushed into surrender. With their reliance upon applications of limestone and fertilizer and better strains of hogs and cattle, they acquired the modern farmer's dependence upon cash crops. They had to sell their cattle, hogs, tobacco and other produce for the dollars without which their families could not live. And at sale time their produce is marketed simultaneously with the tremendous avalanche of meat, grain and fiber which annually pours out of the Great Plains. The steep hillsides and narrow bottoms, no matter how well or intensively used, cannot produce in competition with the big farms in the rich lands of the West and South, and with heartbreaking frequency the mountain farmer is forced to sell at a loss or for a profit that is trifling. The 1960 census revealed the total collapse of the old agriculture with its emphasis on cornfields, plow mules and fattening hogs. In full retreat, too, was the new agriculture. Few farm tractors were discovered anywhere in the plateau and with the coming of the Federal soil bank most farmers "banked" their crop land. By this means virtually as much can be realized by a mountain farmer for not working as he can hope to obtain for his family by plowing, planting, harvesting and marketing.

Most saddening of all are the myriads of men, women and children who sit on the front porches of shacks and houses gazing with listless unconcern at the world. The creeks and yards are littered with tin cans, paper bags and cartons, nearly half of which bear the stenciling of the Commodity Credit Corporation. The cloak of idleness, defeat, dejection and surrender has fallen so heavily as to leave them scarcely more than half alive. Their communities are turning into graveyards peopled with the living dead and strewn with the impedimenta of a civilization which once needed them but does so no longer.

The curse of coal is thus etched indelibly on the land and in the hearts and faces of its inhabitants. Its rapid process of automation and the consolidation of mining operations has stranded as permanently jobless most of its laborers. Those who are physically able to work know no skill except mining, and that skill is now hopelessly obsolete. Neither government nor their former employer feels any responsibility to find work—within their capabilities—for their hands. Thus they sit and brood, cynical and bitter but, in most instances, surprisingly well fed. The dole and the wide variety of union and government checks hold at bay the hollow, physical hunger of the early 1930s.

Hellier is a town on Marrowbone Creek in Pike County. It grew up forty years ago as a trading center for the camps that ringed it—Alleghany, Manco, Greenough and Henry Clay. It was a chartered municipality with city hall, police and fire departments and an impressive little high school.

Most of its customers lived in the huge camp called Alleghany. That mining community was built by Hellier Coal and Coke Company fifty years ago. Its rows of two-story frame houses sheltered a multitude of people whose dollars brought prosperity to the stores, poolrooms, garages, barbershops and dives in Hellier.

In the late 1940s the company went through the routine of "freeing" its camp. Then, a few years later, it sold its tipples and coal veins to Blue Diamond Coal Company. With automation the labor force dwindled sharply, but most of the remaining miners lived in the camp. Retired miners and pensioned widows occupied the other houses. The coal reserves were still large and the miners anticipated many years of uninterrupted work.

Then early in 1960 the directors of Blue Diamond negotiated a sale of their mineral rights to a subsidiary of Bethlehem Steel. The steel company desired to withdraw the coal from the opposite side of the hill. It did not want to inherit the commissaries, shops, tipples, coke ovens and portals of Hellier, nor to assume any responsibility for the inhabitants of the town. The results were highly satisfactory for the two corporations, but fell like a sledgehammer on the people of Hellier and Alleghany.

Without previous warning the miners were suddenly informed that the mine was being permanently closed. They received their final wages and "cut-off slips." A few weeks later workmen arrived in the camp and began tearing down the tipple. They were employed by a company dealing in used mining equipment and machinery. They withdrew the machines and tracks from the mine, demolished the shops, coke ovens and commissaries, and hauled away virtually everything the company owned, excepting only the veins of coal. Within a few weeks a bustling community was reduced to a silent, stunned ghost town. The bewildered people required several months to grasp fully the change of circumstances that had so suddenly overtaken them.

Now the stranded town subsists on checks from the U.M.W. of A. and the Welfare state, and such slender earnings as some of the men are able to acquire at truck or auger mines. Those who move away find few buyers for their homes and then only at pitifully low prices. The little city hall stands empty, the government for which it was built having vanished. Auger operations have ripped the hillsides overlooking the town and rains have brought great heaps of mud and rocks down into its creek bed and onto yards, streets and bridges. Stranded Hellier, forlorn and hopeless, symbolizes the coalfield—indifferent and callous economic masters, helpless and despairing people, a narrow twisting valley dependent entirely upon a single industry which has withdrawn its benefits from the families so long dependent upon it.

10. THE WELCOME HERITAGE

Judith Kramer and Seymour Leventman

Contemporary theorists of social stratification have begun to emphasize that an individual's overall rank in a given stratification system is a composite of the ranks of his various statuses—for example, ethnic, occupational, financial, and educational. Kramer and Leventman examine several aspects of status placement among American Jews. Their treatment of class and life-style is similar to that of Max Weber, who used the first to refer to occupational and financial rank, and the second to refer to rank as based on canons of taste and honorific aspects of prestige. Among American Jews, as this selection points out, trends toward status consistency are apparently emerging now, as the third generation attempts to bolster with its life-style the higher economic status that was won by the second generation. In time, as high-status Jews become less distinguishable from their non-Jewish counterparts, the low ethnic status formerly ascribed to Jews also rises. Indeed, many Jewish religious spokesmen are concerned about threats to the survival of American-Jewish communal and religious identity because they believe that these processes are already occurring and that intermarriage is bound to accompany them.

Source: *Children of the Gilded Ghetto* (New Haven: Yale University Press, 1961), pp. 141–50. Copyright © 1961 by Yale University. Reprinted by permission of Professor Leventman and Yale University Press.

The late JUDITH KRAMER taught courses in sociological theory and method as well as minorities at Brooklyn College. SEYMOUR LEVENTMAN is Professor of Sociology at Boston College.

Several observers of the Jewish scene have suggested that aspirations have changed from second to third generation. The fathers had the ambition to build successful businesses and professional practices, the sons only the ambition to inherit them. In wanting to be like everyone else, the third-generation Jew wants also to feel that he doesn't have to strive unduly for success. He prefers to believe that he doesn't have to prove anything to anybody by earning an ever increasing income, and he is wary of offending his well-adjusted neighbors by any display of aggressive ambition. Like everyone else he knows, he wants comfort and security for himself and his family, and time in which to enjoy the income he does earn. He concentrates on spending his money and finding out what it can do for him rather than on enlarging his income. This permits him to avoid incurring the hostility of his non-Jewish peers.

The decline of economic tensions in the third generation offers evidence that many of the economic problems of the minority situation were solved effectively by the second generation. In large part, however, the lowered economic sights simply reflect the broader changes in goals among the younger generation of all Americans. Brogan observes a general reassessment of values among Americans. "One [new type of value decision] is the decision for leisure rather than for ever-expanding income. The man continually striving loses the chance for leisure. His very recreations are driven by a passion to 'succeed.'" Taking for granted the advantages an older generation struggled to acquire is hardly unique to young Jews. "Few self-made men can resist the temptation to give their sons 'advantages' that they didn't have and these advantages often include an education that alienates the son from his father's simple world." Young Jews and non-Jews alike want the comforts of life without having to pay the high price of overwork. They assume they will come into possession of these comforts as a result of a job they will have no difficulty in obtaining (especially if it's in a family business).

Although the values of the third generation are certainly part of a general climate of opinion favoring "peace of mind" over "success," they also reflect changes taking place within the Jewish community. Kurt Lewin argued that it was the tensions of marginality characteristic of second-generation Jews which served to generate their intense strivings for success; a decline in such tensions produces diminished ambition. The tensions of the third generation have been eased in important ways.

The men of the third generation are, after all, not "marginal men." Because of their acceptable middle-class American background with its mild version of Judaism, they do not experience their Jewishness as a source of much conflict. Since in many respects they feel more accepted by non-Jews than their fathers, they have little cause for self-hatred or embittered striving for membership in the non-Jewish world. With the problems of survival and success solved by earlier generations, the third generation rarely experiences the degree of tension necessary for the ambition of its fathers. Even Marjorie Morningstar could not fail to take note of the new Philistine of her generation, the young Jew who "wants to be a writer or a forest ranger or a composer or anything except what his father is, because he's ashamed of his father being a Jew, or because he thinks he's too sensitive for business or law, or whatever the damned Freudian reason may be—and he winds up in his father's business just the same. . . ."

What members of the younger generation are concerned with is the cultivation of appropriate styles of life. Education has helped to nurture their interest in this area. Even more than money, they want time to consume and to engage in the proper leisure-time activities. "Today's heroes don't lust for big riches, but they are positively greedy for the good life." The consummate dedication of the second generation to business left little time for dabbling in status symbols. The third generation wants to "enjoy life" in a way its fathers did not.

I won't kill myself for a buck. There's more to living than just money. I'm more concerned with the way I want to live.

I like my way of life now. I won't cut out activities I like just to earn another buck.

I make enough to get along—I don't want more money—and the heart attack that goes with it.

I don't know what the goal would be for making more money. . . . There's no goal in just making money. You only know what your goals are when you're doing what you want.

These are the voices of men whose fathers devoted twelve hours a day to work and the other twelve to worry. Their sons see no point in having money you can't enjoy, and they reject the "materialistic" preoccupation of the fathers. They take for granted, however, a "suitable" income and assume they will continue to earn an adequate living. To be concerned with material gain, however, smacks of "money grubbing," a peculiarly Jewish vice in the stereotypes of American society.

Although few are looking for wealth, 39 per cent anticipate increased incomes. Motivation for economic improvement derives from a desire to provide appropriate standards of living for their families.

I want to provide adequately for my family and have as much as others have in comforts.

I want more income since I'm not yet up to the standard of living I'd like to achieve.

These ambitions are eminently reason-

able for young men starting out in careers whose income potential increases with time. Although they will not "grub for money," they expect to make enough in the near future to afford the style of life they want. Only 5 per cent express some dedication to the pursuit of their professional interests, regardless of the possibilities of success, financial or otherwise.

The secure aura of economic well-being is enhanced by the fact that few have been handicapped by their Jewishness. Fifty-two per cent feel that being Jewish had no influence whatsoever on their occupational choice. Another 43 per cent feel that being Jewish influenced them to enter a profession, to be self-employed or in public service, and/or to strive for achievement (whether intellectual or financial). Influences of this sort are not considered restrictive. On the contrary, it is still desirable to be motivated to enter a profession, even if the source of such motivation is one's "Jewishness." Even those who chose self-employment because they thought Jews couldn't get ahead any other way do not feel impeded by this. They reason as follows:

I wanted to be self-employed because of the problem of anti-Semitism impeding advancement.

Being Jewish led me to be a self-employed professional. As a Jewish employee in North City, I couldn't have advanced very far. Jewish businesses are all family businesses and I had no way of getting into them.

North City has had an especially virulent tradition of discriminatory employment which has influenced even members of the younger generation to work for themselves. Nevertheless, they have no cause for complaint. Even in North City, an increasing number of young Jews claim,

I like working for the company. I have security there and I don't feel the need to be self-employed.

Being Jewish is no longer an economic problem to the third generation. Only 17 per cent feel that their religious identity has either restricted their occupational choice, limiting them to fewer and less desirable occupations, or impeded their opportunities for advancement within their chosen fields. Not many of this generation encounter job discrimination; few even apply for positions in local industries reputed to be discriminatory. Some of the older members of the third generation were counselled out of certain fields when they were making their career decisions because of the difficulty of finding employment for Jews.

I didn't go into the scientific field (chemical research) for fear of not being employed in the big industries that do the research. I felt I had to be an independent professional to get ahead and law seemed to permit mobility.

I wanted to be an engineer originally, but I worried about discrimination since Jews are not hired. Even as a self-employed professional, being Jewish affects you since you get mostly Jewish clients and patients.

The salaried professions are increasingly open to Jews as the demand for highly trained personnel grows. But those seeking lower-middle-class white-collar positions without any particular skill or training to offer still run up against discrimination. In this sample, however, there are few men with only high school education. One respondent, looking for a job as an insurance salesman found that,

Being Jewish makes it difficult when you don't have real training. If you have special training, being Jewish doesn't matter.

It is easier for a Jew to sell his "skills" on the job market than his "personality." Consequently, he has more access to jobs requiring professional training or technical expertise than to jobs involving executive managerial capacities.

The members of the third-generation sample are a highly educated and disproportionately professional group for whom economic discrimination has rarely been a problem. Complacent in their security, few feel they must be self-employed to insure their source of livelihood. Most respondents are convinced that being Jewish will in no way limit their opportunities for advancement or restrict the number of their business contacts or clients. Some even find their religious identity an asset; there are people who, for example, prefer Jewish professionals because "they're better."

Although the third generation has experienced few occupational restrictions as Jews, it does recognize some occupations as "more Jewish" than others. Perhaps as a result of this awareness, members of the sample have steered away from "Jewish" occupations which lack more general status in the community. Most frequently mentioned as typically "Jewish" occupations are the independent professions (e.g., law and medicine) and retail proprietorships. Factory worker and corporation executive positions are the occupations considered "least Jewish," i.e., respondents believe fewer Jews are found in them than in the others.

The "Jewishness" of an occupation affects its standing in the wider community. In 1953, the North City Junior Chamber of Commerce published a list of "One Hundred Young Men Selected by the Committee for North City's Future." The list, composed mostly of businessmen and such professionals as clergymen, professors, lawyers, and doctors, suggests the type of Jew held in general esteem. Seven Jews were among the chosen and none, except the rabbi of a high-ranking Conservative congregation (whose modern Ivy League approach to religion qualifies him as a representative young clergyman), was in an occupation traditionally associated with Jews in North City. Two were symphony musicians in no way connected with the local Jewish community, one a newspaper columnist. The others included a research chemist, a municipal judge, and a president of a long established manufacturing firm. There are richer Jews in the city, but these six were distinguished by their occupations, which are not the characteristically marginal occupations of an ethnic group.

The immigrant and working-class status of the first generation created tensions to which its sons responded with a fierce drive for success. The second generation was more likely to advance in class than status, but was able to bestow upon its sons all the advantages of economic security, including a college education. The third generation receives its comfortable heritage with some reservations. Although members of this generation have no conscientious objection to the profit they derive from the economic gains of their fathers, they are critical of the "materialistic" values of the older generation. They permit themselves the illusion that interest in money is a peculiar monopoly of Jews, of which they want no part (except in dollars and cents).

The achievement of the second generation brought with it problems requiring resolution by the next generation. The literary voice of the younger generation asks petulantly whether "upper-middle-class Jewish life is different and worse than upper-middle-class life in general" or just different. Heroines of recent Jewish novels insist upon falling in love with unsuitable young men who represent a different way of life from that of their fathers—a way of life that precludes financial success. Young Jews are less concerned with the accumulation of wealth than with the cultivation of appropriate styles of life. Many a be-

wildered second-generation father has wondered why, if his college educated son is so smart, he isn't rich.

The "materialistic" values and the marginal nature of the occupations of the second generation are a source of tension for its sons. Yet despite any qualms they may have about making money, those of the third generation who are heir to successful family businesses rarely refuse them. They appease an occasionally troublesome conscience by spending their money in different and less "Jewish" ways than their fathers. Those without the "burden" of a family business use advanced education as a key to open the doors of a variety of new occupations. Entry into these occupations is one of the important tension resolutions of the third generation, whose life situation is, in part, a response to the demands of a national economy for increasing levels of expertness among its citizens.

Not all members of the third generation have either the means of access to these new occupations or the motivation. The family business still represents greater security and ease. Nevertheless, these new occupations furnish an escape from social uniqueness for a growing number of young Jews. The occupations are not identifiable as "Jewish" and their status in the general community is high. The impetus for the occupational redistribution of the third generation derives, in part, from the characteristic discrepancy between class and status in the second generation. Entrance into traditionally non-Jewish occupations thus by-passes the tensions inherent in marginal occupations, which are low in status, however profitable they may be.

In sum, we find that members of the third generation have not merely accepted the more successful economic resolutions of their fathers, they have improved upon them. They have achieved considerable occupational mobility and are well satisfied with themselves. Being Jewish has rarely hindered the attainment of their occupational goals, although they are aware of the economic discrimination practiced in North City. They are excluded from the local executive world of "organization men," but they have entered through the back door as salaried professionals and technical experts.

It is quite clear then that the third generation accepts the economic world of its fathers, at least in so far as it is a comfortable world. Here there is no wholesale over-throwing of the goals of the second generation, although accumulation of wealth is exchanged for time to spend it. One generation earns the money, and the next learns how to spend it appropriately. The economic mobility begun by the second generation is extended by its sons, who make their gains in occupational status.

11. THE EDGE OF FRIENDLINESS

Benjamin B. Ringer

Differences in social class still distinguish some groups of American Jews from others.[1] While the point is obviously likely to apply to almost any group of six million people, it may prove helpful to know something more about the origin, development, and implications of some of those differences.

Early Jewish immigrants to the United States were of largely German or other Western European background. They were the predominant American Jewish population until about 1870 or 1880, when the influx of what was to become a much larger number of Eastern European Jews began. The earlier Jewish immigrants, like other people from the north and west of

[1] The United States Census does not include questions on religion. However, a Census Bureau sample survey that did include such a question was carried out in 1957, and some of its tabulations were made available for analysis in 1967. Though somewhat dated, they provide the best available approximation of complete information about the social-class characteristics of American religious groups. In the May 1969 *American Journal of Sociology,* Sidney Goldstein of Brown University published his analysis of these materials under the title, "Socioeconomic Differentials among Religious Groups in the United States." What follows is an abridgement of a portion of his Table 6, p. 622, "Percentage Distribution of Employed Persons 18 Years and Over by Major Occupational Group. . . ." (males only)

	White Protestant	Nonwhite Protestant	Roman Catholic	Jewish
Professionals	10.9	2.6	8.9	20.3
Farmers and farm managers	9.5	5.8	3.8	.1
Managers and proprietors	14.1	2.2	12.5	35.1
Clerical and sales	12.8	4.6	13.2	22.1
Skilled	21.2	9.7	22.5	8.9
Semiskilled and service	24.0	41.1	30.1	12.4
Farm laborers and unskilled	7.6	34.0	9.1	.9

Source: *The Edge of Friendliness* (New York: Basic Books, 1967), pp. 7–9, 74–88. Copyright © 1967 by the American Jewish Committee. Reprinted by permission of the author and publisher.

BENJAMIN RINGER is Associate Professor of Sociology at the Graduate Center of the City of University of New York.

Europe, were more readily acculturated than the later ones. They shared more Western standards and were generally less poor to begin with. They prospered rapidly, and were already well established by the time their coreligionists began arriving in large numbers. In fact, the head start still accounts for some wealth and prestige differences between the two groups, although by this time many of the bases for distinguishing between them have disappeared. It is now quite rare, for example, to find the parents of a girl with a German-Jewish background reluctant to allow her to marry a young man whose grandparents were Russian or Polish Jews.

Later arrivals fled Europe not only for the sake of new opportunity and to escape revolutionary turmoil but also to flee from an anti-Semitism that was more severe in Eastern than in Western Europe. Fear of anti-Semitism was a prominent part of their perspective, yet they encountered it in a milder form upon their arrival here. That was partly because they were merely poor immigrants like the Poles and Italians who were also looked down upon, partly because their religion was so different from that of predominantly Protestant but generally Christian America, and partly because medieval myths about the sinister and conspiratorial character of the Jews had never died, but had planted strong roots among nativist sectors of the majority population.

Anti-Semitism did not disappear as Jews prospered. It was encountered in different forms as citadels of Anglo-Saxon dominance resorted to exclusionary or limiting quotas in universities, corporations, neighborhoods, and clubs as a means of trying to maintain social hegemony. The pattern sharply diminished after World War II, but it has not completely disappeared yet.

The Jews' rapid ascension was both a new basis for anti-Semitism ("They're too ambitious; they stick together too much.") and an additional incentive for Jews' wishing to attain full social equality by being accepted in any quarter of the society. There developed among them an ambivalent set of tendencies: on the one hand pride in the group and its achievements, on the other insecurity about the outbreak of an anti-Semitism strong enough to wipe out their accomplishments. The experience of German Jews before and during the war had made it impossible to be quite certain that Jews were safe wherever they were a minority.

One way Jews sought to resolve the ambivalence was by trying to win as much acceptance as possible without provoking hostility among those members of the majority who seemed to matter most because they were at the pinnacle of the society. Even many well-established Jews saw their status as precarious. Despite having cultivated the style of their non-Jewish neighbors, they felt themselves still not wholly accepted. Such people were hardly delighted at the prospect of being considered part of the same category as other, more recently successful Jews whose life-style was closer to that of urban ethnic communities of lower prestige status, communities that fell somewhere between immigrant origins and exclusive suburbs.

This selection describes a suburban town where all of the aforementioned conditions were brought into play. The concluding portion allows little room for doubting that the longtime Jewish residents of Lakeville were quite right in assuming their non-Jewish neighbors would look down on Jewish newcomers. Whether the early Jewish residents had sufficient justification for assuming much the same perspective themselves is another matter, one that ultimately calls for a judgment of the relative worth of ethnic-group solidarity as compared to maintaining a hard-won general esteem based on the ethnocentric judgments of undoubted members of the successful American majority.

By the end of World War I, Lakeville began to develop as a suburb of Lake City. The population grew from 6,000 to 12,000 during the 1920's. While some of its new permanent residents came from the old summer elite, the majority were middle-class "white Anglo-Saxon Protestants" who preferred a house and garden among congenial neighbors in the suburbs to an apartment in the city. They brought with them the values of responsible family life and citizenship, and they promoted a major expansion and improvement of the educational, religious, philanthropic, and community institutions, so that Lakeville became one of the more attractive and progressive communities in the area. The process of suburbanization lagged during the Depression and World War II, but took on a powerful impetus in the late 1940's. Because of its excellent facilities, particularly in education, and its traditions of leisure and culture, the town was especially attractive to the younger generation of middle-class residents of Lake City, who, like their counterparts throughout the country, were intent upon leaving their urban neighborhoods and making a different life for themselves in the suburbs. A steady stream of new residents entered the community, and though a substantial number of the older residents moved away, the total population increased from 17,000 to 25,000 during the 1950's.

JEWS IN LAKEVILLE

One of the salient characteristics of this influx was that many of the newcomers were Jewish. In good part, this phenomenon was due to the "democratic" tradition in Lakeville. . . . There had always been Jews living in the town, and though their number was never very large, they had been part of each phase of its development. . . .

Their number increased after World War I, but the population growth during these years was predominantly Gentile. Moreover, during this period the elite class of Gentiles who took up permanent residence in Lakeville became increasingly influential in the political and social life of the town. The effect of this development was to make the Jewish group even more isolated in the community, since the main thrust of discrimination came from the Gentile elite. Accepting their marginal position in Lakeville, the Jewish group discreetly kept their distance while making substantial contributions to the cultural, educational, and philanthropic institutions of the community.

The 1920's also saw the tentative beginnings of a Jewish communal life in Lakeville. A number of its residents joined with Jews in nearby suburbs to organize the first Jewish temple in the area. But aside from their activities in the temple and the country club, they remained unwilling to develop a strong Jewish community for fear that it would increase their conspicuousness as an outgroup. They preferred to remain a relatively accepted minority of wealthy and accommodating citizens who had adapted to the norms of the community—one of which was that Jews led a separate social life and did not disturb the prevailing Gentile tone of Lakeville.

These grounds of mutual adjustment were dramatically altered after World War II with the heavy migration of Lake City Jews to Lakeville. Within a decade, the Jewish population grew from an insignificant minority to the stage where one out of every three households in Lakeville was Jewish. Though the Jewish newcomers to Lakeville were generally younger, wealthier, better edu-cated, more urbane, and less ethnocentric than the average new Jewish suburbanite, a majority of them were of Eastern European ancestry rather than from the highly acculturated German-Jewish stock. On the whole they were much less inclined to take an inconspicuous place in the community than their Jewish predecessors in Lakeville had been. They were more willing to play an active role in community affairs, to maintain the manners and mores they had acquired in the urban Jewish neighborhoods, and to organize purely sectarian associations and institutions. They established new temples and founded chapters of several national Jewish organizations. Within a short time, a quite visible and variegated structure of Jewish communal life developed in the town.

During the same period, a significant number of the elite Gentile residents moved out of Lakeville. It is difficult to determine to what extent their departure was provoked by the influx of Jews, by the growth and alteration of the community in general, or by the attraction of a more "ex-urban" rather than suburban environment. There is no question, though, that many of the Lakeville people who remained in the community believed that this exodus was in response to the Jewish migration. Certainly it seems probable that many of the elite families who left would have been no more willing to share their clubs with the Jewish newcomers than they had been to share their clubs with the older Jewish residents. Be that as it may, their emigration, combined with the influx of Jews, inevitably altered the social character of the town. While some wealthy and influential Jews continued to move into Lakeville, many Gentile newcomers tended to be young, middle-class families who did not replenish the ranks of the elite group. In sum, the Jewish influx meant that Lakeville had lost its social *éclat* for the Gentile.

. . . . .

. . . At the time of our study, 19 per cent of Lakeville's Jews had lived there for eleven years or more. Most of them belonged to the prewar community, and some to the original Jewish families that had summered in Lakeville early in the century. Many of the longtime Jewish residents regard themselves as native Lakevillers and choose to identify with the older Gentile residents rather than with the Jewish newcomers. For example, while 59 per cent of the Jewish newcomers believe that they have been a benefit to Lakeville, only 31 per cent of the longtime Jewish residents agree with them, and 40 per cent believe their effect has been noticeably harmful.

THE EFFECT OF THE NEWCOMER ON LAKEVILLE

In analyzing the attitudes of the established Jews of Lakeville toward the newcomers, it is best to begin with the broadest areas of objection: the size of the influx. Thirty-seven per cent of the critics object to the population growth as such and not merely to its Jewish element, a fact which they are often careful to make clear. An elderly architect who has lived in Lakeville for twenty-eight years quietly remarks, "The influx of Jews has helped to change the nature of the community. Any large influx of any group would cause this. I would be the last person to blame it on the Jews." And he goes on to say of the newcomers, "This is life. They are merely seeking for themselves and their children the qualities I desired when I first came here."

As one might expect, the longtime Jewish residents who deplore the influx of newcomers do so on the grounds that Lakeville is losing its traditional sedate character and rural flavor and becoming too large, crowded, urbanized, overtaxed, and so forth. "I hate to say this, but we love to live in the country, but this is not the country," remarks the wife of an insurance executive who is visibly troubled by her resentment of the newcomers. . . .

On the other hand, three out of four of the longtime Jewish residents who object to the Jewish newcomer do so either partly or wholly on the ground that he is Jewish. The most widespread concern is that the population balance between Jew and Gentile is being seriously upset. In the words of an elderly widow who has been active in many non-sectarian organizations in the community: "There is not enough of other people in Lakeville now. I do feel a healthier percentage of all kinds—Jew and Gentile—is important. This is also true on boards and clubs. There should be a good percentage." Some of our longtime Jewish residents, in fact, seem no less apprehensive than their Gentile counterparts that the Jewish influx is already getting out of hand and creating a preponderant and predominant majority group. A woman of sixty who has lived most of her life in Gentile communities remarks: "It's not good for any community to be taken over by one religion. I don't think it's good for children to grow up with all Jews." "There are too many Jews here," says a wealthy resident who has considered moving away because her neighborhood has become predominantly Jewish. "They ought to go to another community where there are fewer Jews. When a community becomes 100 per cent Jewish, it's not good for anyone, for children, or for people who live there."

This response is an extreme one. Most of our Jewish respondents who have lived in Lakeville for eleven years or more do not believe that the community is becoming overwhelmingly Jewish. When asked to estimate the percentage of Jews in the present population and to predict that of the coming decade, they produce an *average* figure of 47 per cent and 67 per cent respectively; the aver-

TABLE 1 Jewish oldtimers' response to the influx of Jews by their estimates of the Jewish population

Per cent of longtime Jewish residents who say that the Jewish influx has been:	Oldtimers' estimates of the present percentage of the Jewish population			
	Less than 30%	30–49%	50–69%	70% and over
Harmful to Lakeville	9%	38%	50%	72%
Beneficial for Lakeville	46	29	27	14
Both equally	18	18	19	14
Neither	27	15	4	0
	100% (11)	100% (34)	100% (26)	100% (7)

age estimate of their Gentile counterparts is 52 per cent and 64 per cent respectively. (The actual percentage of Jews in the present population is approximately 35 per cent.) Most of these Jewish respondents, however, do see a trend toward increasing Jewish proportions, are worried by it, and tend to evaluate the effect in Lakeville of the Jewish influx in terms of its estimated extent. Indeed, there is a strong correlation between speculations about the size of the Jewish population and attitudes toward the Jewish newcomer (see Table 1).

The term that frequently occurs in the response of the established Jewish group is "ghetto"—a word that carries a heavy charge of anxiety. A more or less typical instance of this response comes from a young insurance salesman who has lived in Lakeville all his life:

[The Jewish influx] in harmful only to the extent that the great increase has labeled us, as it will, a Jewish town. I wouldn't like to see that happen. It conjures up in my mind the idea of a "ghetto" and I react against it. I don't know why.

Not all the settled Jews, of course, look upon the newcomers with skeptical or apprehensive eyes. As we have already noted, 31 per cent of this group regards the overall effect of the newcomers as beneficial. Some respondents, for example, believe that the physical character of the town has been enhanced by the new Jewish residents rather than altered and disfigured. A wealthy clothing manufacturer who has lived in Lakeville for twelve years and identifies strongly with the town believes that the newcomers "take better care of their homes than anyone else. A certain type of Jew moves out to the suburbs. They desire their own homes. In the old days you owned an apartment with an income." "A lot of areas have been made beautifully residential that we thought couldn't ever be that pretty," says the wife of a real estate lawyer who takes particular pride in her own gardening. . . .

* * * * *

. . . "Just as Jews take real pride in their homes," says a middle-aged businessman who has lived in Lakeville all his life, "so they will back all civic improvements to the hilt. They will raise money for schools because it is good for children, and [they] won't gripe like the Gentile." This respondent also believes that the "Gentiles still look at Lakeville as a little village. I like the newcomers better. They like progress." Another respondent, who has lived in the town for thirty-four years and belongs to one of the most distinguished and civic-minded of the Jewish families in the area, identifies most of the recent improvements in Lakeville—"better schools, the city manager system, and so forth"—with the influx of Jewish voters. Several other longtime residents are pleased by the broader political changes that have transformed Lakeville from a Republican and conservative stronghold into a more liberal, two-party community. Finally, the positive responses of the older Jewish residents center upon the increased resources and improved leadership that have accrued to the Jewish community itself and strengthened its religious as well as social life.

THE CHARACTER OF THE JEWISH NEWCOMER

As analysis of the negative responses of the established Jews shows, their composite image of the Jewish newcomer is strikingly similar to that of the Gentile community, particularly that of the longtime Gentile residents. Though the objections of the established Jews are often uneasy rather than hostile, the themes of criticism are nonetheless the same as those of our Gentile respondents. "I am forced to say that it is slightly possible that some harmful effects have come about," says a serious, well-informed housewife who is active in Jewish as well as non-sectarian organizations. Appraising the new Jewish population in Lakeville, she goes on to say, "I am dismayed at seeing lots of Jewish names, and also the kind of Jews—the *nouveau riche,* the ostentatious, the materialistic, and the overly Jewish."

Such a response sums up much of the prevailing opinion among the settled Jews of Lakeville concerning the new

breed that has come into their midst. Over half consider them to be a serious problem. Like their Gentile counterparts, these critics view the Jewish newcomer as seriously lacking in propriety, as unduly concerned with material wealth and possessions, as capable of misusing power, and finally as stand-offish and ethnocentric. When asked to describe in detail the "kinds of Jews [that] pose a serious problem for the Jewish community in Lakeville," one out of two of the critical longtime residents mentions those whose behavior is socially improper, while approximately one out of three mentions the materialistic, the power-oriented, or the unassimilated Jew.

In ranking the frequency of these themes, we find a great deal of similarity between the responses of the longtime Jewish residents and those of the Gentile community at large. For example, longtime residents of both groups who have high incomes tend to object most often to the Jewish newcomer's lack of manners. The only significant difference in the two groups is that Gentiles tend to attach somewhat greater weight to the Jewish newcomer's use and abuse of power, though again this objection is more prevalent among the lower-income rather than the higher-income members of both groups.

. . . . .

Somewhat less common are the objections and apprehensions about the values, aggressions, and ethnocentricities of the new Jews. Though these are also taken as signs of nonconformity, they are somewhat less immediately visible and presumably do not weigh quite as heavily on the minds of the established and accepted group. Again, the comments of these respondents often resemble in content and tone the objections of the Gentile critics of the new Jews. For example, a middle-aged woman active in community affairs complains of the spoiled Jewish children in terms that might very well have appeared in our previous chapter on Gentile opinions:

The Jewish newcomers have harmed the future young people in Lakeville. When my children went to school they used to work summers and buy a jalopy. Today children have Cadillacs. It hurts them and makes them materialistic and distorts their sense of values. Just take a look at the parking lot of Lakeville High.

Similarly, there are the typical observations on the aggressiveness of the newcomers, "who demand a lot of things when they have no right to demand them"—a remark which comes from a successful physician who has little use for the old German-Jewish elite circles and, except for this criticism, sympathizes with the hard-working, ambitious newcomers. Antipathy to Jewish behavior in such matters as the traditional celebration of Christmas in the schools is by no means confined to Lakeville's Gentile population. A Jewish saleswoman who has lived in Lakeville for two decades remarks:

The Jews move in and try to take over. One example is the way they try to have the Christmas carols removed from the schools. After all, there has been Christmas carol singing in the Lakeville schools for a lot more years than the Jews have been living here. A Jew should not move in and suddenly demand that the old customs be dropped and the new ones be put in to suit him.

· · · · ·

THE ANXIETIES OF THE ESTABLISHED JEWISH RESIDENT

In the eyes of these critics, the undesirable newcomers do not threaten the Jewish community as such but rather its relations with the Gentile community. Only 21 per cent of those who allude to these effects are worried that the newcomers may seriously disturb existing relations among Jews, while 79 per cent believe that they may damage the existing relations between Jews and Gentiles. By their "loud and flashy" dress and deportment, their "arrogant display of possessions," their overly sensitive and pugnacious natures, their tendencies toward "self-segregation," the Jewish newcomers are felt to arouse the disdain, envy, or hostility, as the case may be, of Lakeville's Gentiles. . . .

Such threats are by no means remote to a majority of the longtime Jewish residents. Some 61 per cent believe that the attitudes of "most Gentiles to the Jews in Lakeville" are now unfavorable; only 19 per cent believe they are favorable, while the rest believe they are neither one nor the other. Their dismay at this new state of affairs is reinforced by the fear that their own record of adjustment to Gentile norms counts for little. They have little faith that the average Gentile distinguishes between acceptable and unacceptable Jews, the settled community or the new one. Speaking of the newcomers, the wife of a stockbroker, who claims to have trouble only with her Jewish neighbors, believes that when "non-Jewish neighbors judge them, they judge us all." This may be due to "the natural tendency toward anti-Semitism which exists among Gentiles," according to a merchandising executive who conducts his business life largely among Gentiles, or simply to the force with which the blatant aggressiveness, impropriety, and clannishness of the newcomers evokes traditional stereotypes. These, in turn, obscure any positive image that may have been created and "distort the picture of the Jews," as a young woman who grew up in Lakeville and was educated at Pembroke remarks. Once the Gentile community begins "to lose respect for this kind of Jewish newcomer," the continuing heavy influx of such Jews serves to extend and exacerbate ill-will until finally "the entire community will feel all Jews are this way."

THE GENTILE IMAGE OF THE ESTABLISHED JEWS

While it is not surprising, then, that the established group of Jewish residents in Lakeville believe their hard-earned status and security is being compromised and threatened, their own picture of Gentile attitudes appears to be considerably more distorted than is the prevalent Gentile picture of them. The truth is that many Gentiles in Lakeville do distinguish between the older group of Jews and the newcomers. Moreover, the longer they have lived in Lakeville the more inclined they are to make this distinction (see Table 2).

Furthermore, such distinctions are almost invariably made in favor of the established Jewish group. Indeed, Gentile respect for its qualities is such that it functions as the norm of Jewish acceptability. In other words, a favorable image of the Jewish newcomer is usually related to his degree of similarity to the longtime Jewish resident, while an unfavorable image of him is almost invariably related to his degree of dissimilarity to the longtime Jewish resident (see Table 3).

As we might expect from our survey of Gentile attitudes toward the Jewish newcomer, the positive group image of Lakeville's Jews turns upon their being of "the better class of Jew," usually with respect to their education and income. And, the Gentiles who approve of Jews —whether they are of the older or newer group—tend to value highly their progressiveness and zeal in community affairs. By and large, the profile of individual responses is virtually the same.

A Gentile who distinguishes between the older and newer Jews of Lakeville is likely to have a fully elaborated and favorable image of the former, along with a highly reductive and negative image of the latter. The chief ground of contrast is in the context of class behavior and status, just as the most frequent theme of opinion is the propriety of the longtime Jewish residents. . . .

. . . . .

It is not the older Jews' wealth that is decisive to most of these Gentile respondents, however; it is their background of established wealth. Explaining why "Jewish longtimers don't get along with the incoming Jew," a salesman married to a native Lakeville woman says that "the Jews have had money for a long time, and newcomers have just made theirs and think they are big shots." An advertising man who lives in a low-prestige area and is himself a newcomer to Lakeville puts it this way: "The older Jew comes from a wealthy, well-established family. New ones are a

TABLE 2   Gentile differentiation of Jews by length of residence

Do Jewish people who have lived in Lakeville a long time seem to be like the Jewish newcomers	Gentile respondents; their length of residence		
	5 years or less	6–10 years	11 years or more
In most respects?	46%	28%	18%
In some respects?	34	25	29
In virtually no respects?	20	47	53
	100% (35)	100% (28)	100% (103)

TABLE 3 Gentile attitudes toward and differentiation of Jewish residents

	Gentile respondents who say Jewish oldtimers are like the Jewish newcomers		
	In most respects	In some respects	In no respects
Per cent whose attitude toward Jewish newcomer is			
Favorable	72%	35%	3%
Neutral or balanced	16	29	12
Unfavorable	12	36	85
	100%	100%	100%
	(43)	(49)	(74)
Per cent whose attitude toward Jewish oldtimer is			
Favorable	73%	74%	94%
Neutral or balanced	16	20	3
Unfavorable	11	6	3
	100%	100%	100%
	(37)	(49)	(73)

class or so below the older ones. The new Jew is about the same class as we are."

In general, Gentile responses tend to gravitate toward two polar images. In direct opposition to the crude, aggressive, *nouveau riche,* ethnocentric newcomers, recently arrived from the ghetto, the longtime resident is imagined to be an aristocratic figure. He is seen as belonging to one of the elite Jewish families in town that have earned the respect of the community over the years by their unostentatious wealth, culture, and refinement and by their fastidious deference to the Christian customs and mores of Lakeville. Thus, speaking of the longtime residents in general, a Gentile newcomer who sees a good many Jews in her social activities quickly associates them with this elite segment. "We have some of the finest old Jewish families here," she says. "They won't have anything to do with these newcomers, you can bet." "The old Jewish settlers . . . seem to be more refined," says a longtime

resident, whose deceased husband refused to associate with Jews. "Probably it's the names. You know that their families are so respected that you just sort of feel that way. I really didn't come into contact with them, just knew that they were here." And in the eyes of a sophisticated clubwoman who has herself lived in Lakeville for thirty-three years, "the Jewish oldtimers are all people of many generations and of background . . . a great addition to any community. I personally couldn't get along without them. They make every possible effort to make their community a better place to live."

As a result of this identification with the prominent and accepted Jewish families, the image of the longtime residents takes on the qualities of a "genteel," "responsible," and "conservative" class. Having earned his status in the community by his record of highly respectable and tactful behavior and by his good civic deeds, he does not try to buy status by means of conspicuous consumption. Instead he lives simply, modestly, tastefully. He takes pride in his possessions, but it is the pride of cultivation and maintenance rather than of mere ownership and display. At the same time he can afford to be casual in his life style because he is attuned to the relaxed rhythm and informal tone of Lakeville's suburban social climate. Having been raised in an atmosphere of culture and responsibility, he can take his attainments for granted and implement his interests in the fine arts and civic affairs without being aggressive. Also, according to the Gentile image of him, he does not adopt an arrogant air of superiority, because he is confident of his acceptance by the Gentile community. He regards his fellow townsmen as equals and does not make class distinctions, except between himself and the Jewish newcomer.

In Gentile eyes the solid, respectable quality of the longtime resident's social behavior also extends to his private life. He trains his children to be respectful, diligent, and unassuming; since he is not viewed as regarding his Jewish identity as a stigma, he has no need to arm his children against rejection by means of arrogance and money. Finally, our Gentile respondents who distinguish between the two groups of Jews are particularly impressed by the longtime resident's acceptance of the individual Gentile, by his adaptation to Gentile customs such as Christmas trees and cards, and by his desire to preserve Lakeville's traditional way of life against the depredations of the newcomers.

Given this gloss of Gentile statements about the longtime Jewish resident, it is not surprising that many of our Gentile respondents should see little or no difference between him and themselves. "I know a number of oldtimer families," reports a sixty-seven-year-old spinster, "and I never even think of them as being Jewish. They seem like the rest of the people who have been here a long time."

"There is no difference between the old Jewish settlers and the Gentiles," says a resident of thirty years who belongs to the DAR. "I've never had any friends among them; however, I feel that they are people we've been used to throughout our whole life. They are polite, considerate, and generous." Or, as another Gentile respondent sums up the prevailing opinion of the established Jews of Lakeville: "They are more Gentile and not so pushy."

THE RISE OF THE OLDER JEWISH GROUP

The image we have been developing of the older Jewish residents would probably come as a surprise to many of them. One of the principal reasons why they are so much concerned about being tarred by the brush of Gentile contempt and animosity toward the new group of Jews is that their own position as an accepted, indeed an elite, class in the community has been only recently won. Indeed, so recently won, that they tend to be quite unaware that they have won it. While there are no community studies of Lakeville's Jews before the influx of newcomers, their status appears to have been much more problematic and marginal than the picture that is currently painted by our Gentile respondents. For example, one of our Jewish respondents, a fair-minded lawyer who has been a close observer of Jewish-Gentile relations in Lakeville for the past twenty-five years, observes that, paradoxically enough, "it was not until after World War II that Lakeville's Jews had any kind of decent place in the social community or were permitted any." It seems evident, then, that if only a few of the old-guard, wealthy, and aristocratic Jewish families were able to gain some measure of acceptance in prewar Lakeville, many more of less prominence must have been at best tolerated, and the Jewish community itself, which was not integrated into the social fabric of Lakeville, must have had little prestige or influence in the life of the town.

The new-found acceptance, esteem, and good will that pervade the present image of the older Jewish residents would seem to be due to the presence of that very figure in their midst—the Jewish newcomer—who arouses so much anxiety among them about their status and security. There is little doubt in our minds that the objectionable traits of the new Jews—presumed or otherwise—have deflected latent anti-Semitism among Gentiles from the settled Jew and have at the same time highlighted his social virtues—presumed or otherwise. In the same way, the antipathy toward the Jewish newcomer as an aggressive interloper, as well as a Jew, reinforces the image of the older residents as representative of the traditional life of Lakeville. Apparently, then, acceptance of the older Jew is a necessary counterpoise in the minds of a good many Gentiles to their rejection of the newer ones, a fact which perhaps explains why so many of our Gentile respondents are quickly moved to assert that the settled Jews dislike the newcomers as much as Gentiles do. Be that as it may, the differences between the two groups of Jews have become inordinately exaggerated to produce in many Gentile minds the diametrically opposed images which we have observed.

The new acceptance and prestige of the settled Jews are not the only benefits that have accrued to them through the influx of their fellow Jews. Their influence in the community has also noticeably increased. First of all, the influx of Jews and the subsequent exodus of many of the elite class of the Gentiles has changed the power structure in Lakeville, so that the prominent Jews in the town, formerly an insignificant minority, now find themselves at least equal in numbers to the remaining Gentile elite. Moreover, as more Jews have entered the community, pressure for Jewish representation in its civic life has mounted. It goes without saying that for Gentiles the more acceptable Jewish candidates have been from the older group, and Gentiles have accordingly helped to elect them to positions on school boards, the city council, and the local judiciary. Furthermore, the longtime Jewish residents have inevitably assumed a number of ambassadorial functions between the Jewish and Gentile communities, a role which has also increased their status in the community.

The negative responses of the majority of longtime Jewish residents to the Jewish newcomer were described earlier in this chapter. There is irony in the fact that they owe to him a good deal of their emergence from relative obscurity and isolation in the community to positions of general acceptance and individual prominence.

12. RACE AND ANTI-SEMITISM

Gertrude Selznick and Stephen Steinberg

Selznick and Steinberg call their book "the first extensive analysis of anti-Semitism based on nationally representative data." The portion I have selected for presentation serves two purposes, since the comparison of white attitudes to those of blacks shows something of the nature and scope of anti-Semitism among both groups.

The data were collected through an opinion survey. Surveys are the most efficient means for gathering standardized information from large numbers of people in a rapid and efficient way. Nevertheless, many surveys do have certain weaknesses, and the present work is no exception.

A common though by no means inevitable problem with survey data is the tendency to measure people's attitudes by seeing how many assertions of a given kind they agree with. For example, a list of statements for measuring anti-Appleism might run as follows:

1. The trouble with apples is that the same kind stick together too much on the same tree.

2. Some apples are all right, but too many of them have worms.

3. Apples usually fool you; they look red and shiny but taste mushy.

4. Ever since Eve in the Garden of Eden, apples have been tempting people to do things they shouldn't do.

The difficulty with such a list is that some respondents, particularly those who have less formal education, are more likely than others to give a "true" or an "agree" response to any assertion. The result, if the attitude in question is measured

Source: *The Tenacity of Prejudice* (New York: Harper and Row, 1969), pp. xiv, xv, 117–31. Copyright © 1969 by Anti-Defamation League of B'nai B'rith. Reprinted by permission of the publisher.

GERTRUDE SELZNICK is in the Department of Sociology at the University of California, Berkeley. STEPHEN STEINBERG is Research Associate, Survey Research Center, University of California, Berkeley.

by the number of such responses, is that one ends up studying not simply the attitude, but some combination of the attitude and what has been called "response" or "acquiescence set."

That kind of problem occurs with the anti-Semitism index used in the present selection. All but one of the statements about Jews that it employs are not dissimilar in form from the ones that I have made above about apples. (Scored as if negative, to be consistent with other items, the exception was "Jews are just as honest as other businessmen.") Thus to some unknown extent, response set helps to account for the present study's finding that less well-educated people are apparently more anti-Semitic than the better educated. Were the study to be repeated, the difficulty could be resolved by including some more nice statements about Jews in the index list, rather than merely negative ones, preferably in random order. Better still would be the use of so-called cafeteria questions, the kind that call for respondents to choose one from among several alternative answers to questions about their attitudes or about what they might do in various hypothetical situations.

Surveys also tend to concentrate on questions about attitudes rather than about actions. In the present study, this means that the major emphasis falls upon an analysis of prejudice rather than upon readiness to discriminate. However, the authors did attempt to approximate a study of actions by the use of questions taking the form, "What would you do if . . . ?" Answers to these questions were associated with those on the anti-Semitism index, but the correlation was only moderate.

The gap between attitudes as measured by a survey and actual behavior may be larger still, for behavior may depend on circumstances that surveys alone are not equipped to handle. For example, an ordinarily nondiscriminating person with unprejudiced attitudes might share in discriminating against outsiders when he is among friends who do discriminate, or if his job prospects seem to depend upon it. (The reverse is also true—avoiding discrimination if it costs.) Finally, even if attitudes alone were all that were in question, it would still be difficult to measure prejudice by survey techniques. It is far easier to try to estimate consumer preferences or political party choices. In these cases, any alternative is likely to be a legitimate one. That is quite a different matter from where the alternative to being considered democratic, or accepting, or tolerant is being considered bigoted.

Why, then, if we end up with so many questions about what survey results really mean, should we use surveys at all to study prejudice? Consider that the strength of prodemocratic ideologies and of conventional definitions of bigotry vary over time. (For instance, the Selznick and Steinberg study also shows that Americans tend to accept anti-Semitic declarations less readily than they did a generation ago.) We assume that when a phenomenon like anti-Semitism is itself less tolerated in a public, then the prospects are less for the development of mass anti-Semitic behavior within it. That is because beliefs or actions that are disapproved or that seem to lack justification tend to be suppressed. Thus, though we must be ready to admit that the correspondence between prejudiced attitudes and discriminatory behavior is far from perfect in the examination of individual cases, it is still important to know what the general attitudinal climate about an issue is like in particular groups at different times.

Be wary of arriving at the conclusion that black people are more anti-Semitic than white ones.[1] In addition to the reservations about the data that I have outlined, the authors themselves make clear that readers have to take into account a number of circumstances that make it hazardous to draw a general conclusion about the differences between black and white anti-Semitism. Among these circumstances are whether the concern lies with economic or noneconomic anti-Semitism, whether the index of anti-Semitism being discussed is one that measures attitudes alone or one that comes closer to estimating readiness to discriminate; whether interest lies in older respondents or younger ones; and, whether one group's objective experience has more effect on its attitudes than is the case in another.

Finally, readers should also know that one of the most extensive opinion studies ever carried out among black people showed that their level of hostility toward Jews was a trifle

---

[1] Readers particularly interested in this topic should see the sources given in footnote 1 to the introduction of selection 17 and could also profitably consult the following articles in *Commentary:* Earl Raab, "The Black Revolution and the Jewish Question," *Commentary*, XLVII (January 1969). Milton Himmelfarb, "Is American Jewry in Crisis?" *Commentary*, XLVII (March 1969), and Nathan Glazer, "Blacks, Jews, and the Intellectuals," *Commentary*, XLVII (April 1969). Of these, Glazer's is the best balanced piece; Himmelfarb's, the most ethnocentric; and Raab's, the most fearful. See also Nat Hentoff (ed.), *Black Anti-Semitism and Jewish Racism* (New York: Richard W. Baron, 1969); Shlomo Katz (ed.), *Negro and Jew* (New York: The Macmillan Co., 1967); and Max Geltman, *The Confrontation: Black Power, Anti-Semitism and the Myth of Integration* (Englewood Cliffs, N.J.: Prentice Hall, 1970). The last book, an outright defense of Jewish interests and a pretty severe condemnation of black culture and aspirations, is of more use as an example of a certain style of thinking than as a reasoned analysis.

lower than their level of hostility toward white people in general.[2]

[2] Gary Marx, *Protest and Prejudice* (New York: Harper and Row, 1969), esp. Chaps. 6 and 7. Now it is not possible to equate attitude scores from one index to those of another, though we can relate them. Marx did find that antiwhite blacks also tended to be more anti-Semitic. As for general levels, he called 24 percent of his sample high or very high on anti-Semitism (pp. 128–31); 23 percent strongly antiwhite (pp. 175–77); however (pp. 138, 139), "among [the] 25 percent of Negroes who made a distinction between Jewish and non-Jewish whites [75 percent did not], Jews were seen in a more favorable light than other whites by a four-to-one ratio [that is, 20 percent to 5 percent]."

This study deals with the differential presence of anti-Semitism in contemporary individuals, not the historic genesis of anti-Semitic beliefs in Western society or the United States.[1] . . . An anti-Semitic ethos has long characterized Western society. But [our task] in this book is to explain, not the origins of this ethos, but its acceptance and rejection at the present time.[2]

. . . It is with the routine anti-Semitism of contemporary American society that this study is primarily concerned. There is a tendency in the literature to see anti-Semitism as a sign of personal psychopathology, and psychoanalysts have offered evidence of this from their clinical experience.[3] While personal psychopathology may explain excesses of anti-Semitism in some individuals, it can throw little light on the ordinary sources and manifestations of anti-Semitism in everyday life.

. . . . .

. . . Interviews were conducted with a representative cross-section of the national population during the three week period preceding the 1964 presidential election.

. . . It should come as no surprise that anti-Semitism exists among Negroes. It would be illusory to think that, because they are an oppressed minority, Negroes reject anti-Semitic stereotypes which, to some degree, characterize every segment of American society. The issue is not whether anti-Semitism is present among Negroes, but the extent to which it exists. A few articles and press reports —even virulent anti-Semitism in extremist groups—tell us little or nothing about the general prevalence of anti-Semitism in the Negro population. Three questions direct this analysis: (1) Are Negroes in fact more anti-Semitic than whites, as is often implied? (2) Does anti-Semitism among Negroes differ in content or kind from that found among whites? (3) Is the quality of Negro-Jewish contacts a factor in Negro anti-Semitism? [4]

[1] For a study of the historic origins of anti-Semitism, see *Léon Poliakov, The History of Anti-Semitism* (New York: Vanguard Press, 1965).

[2] The rate of anti-Semitism in any society or social group is determined by two variables: the extent to which individuals are exposed to an anti-Semitic ethos and the extent to which they are able to resist it. As will be seen, most respondents were familiar enough with anti-Semitic beliefs to have opinions about them. However, it is also true that Americans are differentially exposed to anti-Semitism, a fact about which we shall have much to say in later chapters. The main point to be emphasized now is that anti-Semites do not have to invent anti-Semitism; it is part of the cultural heritage and available to them in the same way as many other beliefs and attitudes.

[3] For example, in Nathan W. Ackerman and Marie Jahoda, *Anti-Semitism and Emotional Disorder* (New York: Harper & Row, 1950).

[4] Other issues regarding Negro anti-Semitism are dealt with in an earlier volume in this series

TABLE 1 Acceptance of individual anti-Semitic beliefs by race.

	Whites	Negroes
Care only about own kind	24%	43%
Use shady practices to get ahead	40	58
Control international banking	28	40
Shrewd and tricky in business	34	46
Not as honest as other businessmen	27	35
Always like to head things	53	60
Have a lot of irritating faults	40	44
More loyal to Israel than to America	30	32
Stick together too much	53	48
Too much power in U.S.	11	9
Too much power in business world	31	19

In order to determine whether Negro and white anti-Semitism differ in content, each of the eleven beliefs in the Index of Anti-Semitic Belief is examined by race (Table 1). . . . Of the five beliefs most overaccepted by Negroes, four are clearly economic in content, and the other—that "Jews don't care what happens to anyone but their own kind"—is consistent with the image of Jews as economically exploitative.[5] However, on

the remaining six beliefs in the Index, Negro-white differences are small or reversed. The data, in other words, allow no blanket comparison between whites and Negroes. In the economic area, Negroes are more anti-Semitic than whites. In the noneconomic area, no consistent differences exist.

This finding contrasts with those for education and age. Earlier we reported that the uneducated and the elderly are more anti-Semitic on *every* anti-Semitic belief in the Index, and it could be stated unambiguously that they are more anti-Semitic than the educated and the young. No such statement can be made about Negroes who are more anti-Semitic with respect to certain beliefs only. This has methodological as well as substantive implications. It means that no index can combine economic and noneconomic items without obscuring the relation between race and anti-Semitism.[6] For this

based on special samples of urban Negroes. See Gary Marx, *Protest and Prejudice* (New York: Harper and Row, 1967), chs. 6 and 7. Our analysis is limited to a comparison between Negroes and whites in the national sample.

[5] Two economic beliefs, not explicitly anti-Semitic and not included in the Index, were also overaccepted by Negroes. The proportion saying Jews have more money than others is 66 per cent for Negroes and 60 per cent for whites; the proportion saying that Jews go out of their way to hire other Jews is 59 per cent for Negroes and 48 per cent for whites. These differences are noteworthy only in the context of Negro-white differences on other economic beliefs whose anti-Semitic content is beyond question.

However, Negroes underaccepted both statements concerning excessive Jewish power. In view of the recent emergence of the Black Power movement and the demand for ghetto autonomy,

these beliefs—especially the belief that Jews have too much power in business—may now be more widespread than they were in 1964. It is interesting to note that young Negroes were as likely as young whites to say that Jews have too much power in the business world. It was only elderly Negroes who greatly underselected this belief: only 11 per cent accepted it.

Like every other major group in American society, Jews are found at all social and economic levels. Comparisons with other religious groups, however, yield substantial differences. The following results are based on data collected in 1957:

	Jews	Protes- tants	Cath- olics	Na- tion
Attended college	33%	19%	14%	19%
Working in professions or as owners, managers, or officials	51	21	19	21
Annual family income of $7500 or more	52	18	18	19

Large differences were also reported among the various Protestant denominations. Episcopalians and Presbyterians exhibit roughly the same distribution as Jews with respect to education, occupatonal prestige, and family income. [Bernard Lazerwitz, "Religion and Social Structure in the United States," in Louis Schneider (ed.), *Religion, Culture and Society* (New York: John Wiley and Sons, 1964), pp. 428–429].

[6] This helps to explain discrepant findings in the literature on the relation between race and

TABLE 2 Economic and noneconomic anti-Semitism by race.

	Whites	Negroes	Percentage difference [a]
High on economic anti-Semitism	32% (1,322)	54% (182)	+22
High on noneconomic anti-Semitism	29% (1,282)	26% (168)	−3

[a] Between Negroes and whites.

reason the Index of Anti-Semitic Belief is divided into an Index of Economic Anti-Semitism, comprising the five economic items overaccepted by Negroes, and an Index of Noneconomic Anti-Semitism, which consists of the remaining six items.

These indexes confirm what was previously observed for individual beliefs. On the index of Noneconomic Anti-Semitism there is essentially no difference between whites and Negroes; 29 per cent of whites and 26 per cent of Negroes have high scores.* Despite their lower level of education, Negroes are if anything less likely than whites to hold noneconomic stereotypes. However, a sharp difference appears on the Index of Economic Anti-Semitism (Table 2). Here 54 per cent of Negroes have high scores in contrast to 32 per cent of whites. Among whites the proportion scoring high on both indexes is roughly the same, but among Negroes twice as many score High on Economic as on Noneconomic Anti-Semitism. Table 2 leaves no doubt that economic beliefs have special appeal for Negroes.

Among Negroes, as among whites,

anti-Semitism. A measure of anti-Semitism heavily weighted with economic items and a measure heavily weighted with noneconomic items will produce different results. For example, using an index combining both economic and noneconomic items, Marx found no consistent difference in anti-Semitism between Negroes and whites (*op. cit.*, p. 146). However, Marx also notes that when items were examined individually, "Negroes were more likely to accept negative economic stereotypes about Jews than were whites" (p. 147).
* [High scores are acceptance of two economic or three noneconomic statements—Ed.]

greater education is associated with lower rates of anti-Semitism (Table 3). Nevertheless, Negroes continue to be higher on economic anti-Semitism even when compared to whites at the same educational level. Though Negroes have had much less education than whites, this does little to explain their greater economic anti-Semitism. It must be recognized, however, that Negroes and whites with the same amount of education have not generally received education of equal quality, and some of the remaining educational differences in economic anti-Semitism may reflect this fact.[7] However, educational differences would not explain why Negroes overselect economic rather than noneconomic stereotypes. Moreover, there is additional evidence that factors peculiar to their situation in American society serve to increase economic anti-Semitism among Negroes.

. . . Reported [elsewhere in our study is] that younger people are less anti-Semitic than the elderly. While true for whites, this is not true for Negroes. One of the more striking findings with regard to Negroes—and one that is consistent with the view that Negro anti-Semitism is rising—is that acceptance of anti-Semitic beliefs is disproportionately high in the youngest as well as the oldest age group. Whereas only 17 per cent of whites under 35 scored as anti-Semitic, among Negroes the figure is 49 per cent.

[7] At every level of education, Negroes have less knowledge of writers and contemporary politicians and score lower on other measures of cultural and intellectual sophistication.

	Whites	Negroes	Percentage difference
	Per cent high on economic anti-Semitism		
Grade school	55% (307)	65% (66)	+10
Some high school	38% (235)	60% (50)	+22
High school graduate	27% (436)	45% (38)	+18
Some college	20% (179)	41% (17)	+21
College graduate	10% (164)	18% (11)	+8
Total	32% (1,321)	54% (182)	+22
	Per cent high on noneconomic anti-Semitism		
Grade school	50% (307)	30% (53)	−20
Some high school	30% (230)	34% (50)	+4
High school graduate	26% (409)	19% (37)	−7
Some college	15% (172)	18% (17)	+3
College graduate	11% (163)	0 (11)	−11
Total	29% (1,281)	26% (168)	−3

† [Not including those with three "don't knows" on noneconomic, and two on economic anti-Semitism—Ed.]

This is higher than the rate of anti-Semitism for middle-aged Negroes (34 per cent), and almost as high as the rate for Negroes in the oldest age group (53 per cent).[8] Though young Negroes are more educated than older Negroes, they are no less anti-Semitic.[9]

On the Noneconomic Index the younger segments of the Negro community scored no higher than do young whites.[10] It is only with respect to eco-

[8] Because it is descriptively interesting to know how many at each age level are anti-Semitic, the figures reported above include the opinionless. If only those with no more than one don't-know response on the Index of Economic Anti-Semitism are considered, the results are essentially the same. The proportions anti-Semitic for young, middle-aged, and older whites are 20, 29, and 50 per cent. The corresponding figures for Negroes are 53, 44, and 70 per cent.
There is a considerable discrepancy in the rate of anti-Semitism among elderly Negroes depending on whether the opinionless are excluded or included. It is 53 per cent when they are included, 70 per cent when only those with one

or no don't knows are considered. This discrepancy occurs because a sizable minority of the elderly were opinionless. In contrast, few young Negroes in the youngest age group were opinionless, and therefore the proportion scoring high on economic anti-Semitism is hardly changed when the opinionless are excluded.

[9] Young Negroes are also more antiwhite than older Negroes (Marx, op. cit., p. 185).

[10] About 20 per cent of Negroes score high on the Noneconomic Index regardless of age. Among whites the figures at the three age levels are: 16, 23, and 37 per cent.

nomic beliefs that younger Negroes score comparatively high. Indeed if Negroes as a group score so much higher than whites on economic anti-Semitism, this is largely, though not entirely, due to the high level of economic anti-Semitism in the younger segments of the Negro population.

. . . . .

Two basic findings have emerged from the analysis so far: first, that Negroes are more anti-Semitic than whites, but only with respect to economic beliefs; second, that their greater economic anti-Semitism goes beyond what can be explained by their generally lower level of education. Both findings are consonant with the view that Negro anti-Semitism is rooted in the special economic relations of Negroes with Jews.

Respondents were asked eight questions concerning different kinds of contact with Jews. Replies to such questions are always suspect and must be treated with caution since, as past research has shown, some respondents over-report their actual contacts. Another study in this series provides a convenient example of the kinds of problems that arise.[11] Respondents in that study were asked whether they had entertained a Jew in their homes during the past year. It was found that those low on anti-Semitism more often said they had entertained a Jew than did those high on anti-Semitism. Taken at face value, this finding suggests either that being free of prejudice encourages friendly contact with Jews, or conversely, that friendly contact with Jews reduces anti-Semitism. However, there was good reason to suspect that unprejudiced respondents were exaggerating their contacts. In the city studied, as well as in many surrounding communities, Jews comprised no more than 1 per cent of the total population. But 26 per cent of the sample

reported that they had entertained a Jew in their home during the previous year. Either Jews in that city spent an extraordinary amount of time visiting with non-Jews or, as was apparently the case, a disproportionate number of unprejudiced respondents were overreporting such contacts. Overreporting among the unprejudiced undoubtedly arises from a desire on their part to show that they are willing to entertain Jews, or from a tendency to interpret even casual encounters with Jews as actual visits. Whatever the reason, lack of prejudice can and does lead to overreporting.

It is also possible that prejudiced respondents overreport their contacts with Jews. A respondent who believes that Jews cheat in business may wish to justify his belief by claiming that it is rooted in actual experience with Jewish businessmen. Or when he encounters dishonest businessmen he may assume that they are Jewish even when they are not. Consequently, a finding that economic contact is associated with anti-Semitism may be false in its implication. Far from showing that contact with Jewish businessmen increases anti-Semitism, it might only reflect a possible tendency of anti-Semites to overreport nonexistent contacts with Jews. To avoid these difficulties, one would need more reliable data than can be obtained from surveys. The ideal method would be to observe interaction between Jews and non-Jews in concrete situations, and to measure its impact on anti-Semitism. While survey data fall far short of this ideal, they may nevertheless shed some light on the role that contact plays in the relation between race and anti-Semitism.

About the same proportion of whites and Negroes (44 per cent and 48 per cent) report contact with Jews in work or business.[12] This small quantitative

[11] Charles Y. Glock, Gertrude J. Selznick, and Joe L. Spaeth, *The Apathetic Majority* (New York: Harper & Row, 1966), p. 192.

[12] This figure appears highly inflated. However, the kinds of people who report having contact with Jews are the kinds who, given the geographical distribution of Jews, have the greatest

TABLE 4 Economic and noneconomic anti-Semitism by race and work contact with Jews.

Work contact	Whites	Negroes
	Per cent high on economic anti-Semitism	
Yes	26%	61%
	(621)	(95)
No	38	47
	(701)	(87)
Total	32%	54%
	(1,322)	(182)
	Per cent high on noneconomic anti-Semitism	
Yes	23%	22%
	(613)	(93)
No	34	31
	(669)	(75)
Total	29%	26%
	(1,282)	(168)

difference between Negro and white contacts with Jews obviously masks a very large qualitative difference. Since Negroes are generally employed at lower occupational levels than are whites, work contact for Negroes often means working for Jews as domestics or in some other menial and poorly paid capacity. Whites on the other hand are reporting contacts in which they meet with Jews as peers or near-peers and in which no invidious social or economic distinctions are implied.

---

opportunity of encountering Jews in their lives. In the rural South and Midwest, where there are few Jews, the proportion reporting contact with Jews in their work of businesses is at its lowest, roughly a quarter. In the urban Northwest and Northeast, where Jews are most concentrated, the proportions reporting work contact are at their highest: 52 and 63 per cent. It also happens that reported work contact steadily rises with greater education, from 28 per cent among grade schoolers to a high of 67 per cent among college graduates. This is as it should be since Jews tend to be of above-average education. That the data conform to expectations does not rule out all difficulties but does increase confidence in their relative validity.

Table 4 shows how work contact relates to anti-Semitism for whites and Negroes. Among whites there is an inverse relation: those with contact are less likely to score as anti-Semitic on both economic and noneconomic anti-Semitism.[13] The same holds for Negroes on noneconomic anti-Semitism. On the Economic Index, however, work contact among Negroes is associated with greater anti-Semitism. For those without work contact, the rate of economic anti-Semitism is 47 per cent; for those with work contact it is 61 per cent.[14] This relation stands up when education is controlled. Regardless of education, Negroes with work contact are higher on economic anti-Semitism than Negroes without such contact.[15]

Essentially the same findings emerge when shopping at a Jewish-owned store is examined. Suspiciously large numbers of both whites and Negroes—65 and 84 per cent—report shopping at Jewish stores are less anti-Semitic than those

---

[13] Analysis shows that among whites the inverse relation of work contact to anti-Semitism is explained by education; it is the more educated whites who are apt to have contacts with Jews.

[14] Marx also reports that among Negroes impersonal contacts with Jews is associated with greater anti-Semitism (*op. cit.*, p. 158).

[15] The figures are as follows: grade school Negroes, 73 per cent versus 68 per cent; high schoolers, 62 vs. 44; college educated, 33 vs. 20.

Earlier we questioned the validity of reports of economic contacts with Jews. The reversal in Table 4, whereby work contact is associated with greater anti-Semitism only among Negroes makes it doubtful that the relations are being seriously affected by overreporting.

An early study found that, among Negroes, females are much higher on anti-Semitism than males, and went on to speculate that Negro domestics working in Jewish homes were contributing disproportionately to anti-Semitism. (Richard Simpson, "Negro-Jewish Prejudice: Authoritarianism and Some Social Variables as Correlates," *Social Problems*, Fall 1959, pp. 138–146.) In contrast, our data show anti-Semitism, both economic and noneconomic, to be more prevalent among Negro males than among females. For economic anti-Semitism, the figures are 62 per cent for males, 47 per cent for females. However, among Negroes who have work contacts with Jews, the proportion high on economic anti-Semitism is about as great for women (59 per cent) as for men (62 per cent).

who do not; the same is true of Negroes when it comes to noneconomic anti-Semitism. But unlike whites, Negroes who report shopping at Jewish stores are higher on economic anti-Semitism than those who do not.[16]

One conclusion that *cannot* be drawn from the findings is that Negroes have worse experiences with Jews than with whites in general. Not only would this be an incorrect inference from the data, logically it could not explain why Negroes are higher on economic anti-Semitism *than are whites*. The opposite contention, that Negroes actually have better relations with Jews than with other whites, also misses the point. In fact, it is irrelevant whether Negroes have better or worse experiences with Jews than with other whites.[17] What is relevant is whether Negroes have worse experiences with Jews than whites have. That Negro contacts with Jews are worse than white contacts with Jews hardly needs documentation. Exploitation and humiliation are built into the situation of most Negroes, and the experiences of Negroes with Jewish employers and shopkeepers are obviously worse than the corresponding experiences of whites. This would remain true even if it could be demonstrated that Negroes are less exploited by Jews than by non-Jewish whites.

Whites and Negroes also come into contact with different kinds of Jews. The Jews with whom Negroes come into contact undoubtedly tend to be older and less educated. Just as these factors contribute to anti-Semitism among non-Jewish whites, they contribute to anti-Negro prejudice among Jews.[18] Furthermore, Negroes and ghetto merchants tend to meet in direct, face-to-face contact that easily engenders personal antagonism. As is frequently argued, while intergroup relations are often improved when contact occurs between peers, prejudices are reinforced when one of the parties in the interaction is defined as inferior. When the merchants are Jewish, personal antagonism is apt to find expression in anti-Semitic stereotypes.

Negroes have heard the anti-Semitic beliefs current in the larger society and, *more than whites,* find them confirmed in their own experience with Jews. Numerous caveats can be appended to this statement: Jews are probably no worse than other merchants in the ghetto; the behavior of Jewish merchants has little or nothing to do with their Jewishness, but is characteristic of marginal businessmen generally; the economic realities of the ghetto, not the personal attributes of ghetto merchants, are responsible for the kinds of business practices that prevail.[19] However valid, these are theoretical niceties that have little relevance to the average Negro in the ghetto, who is relatively uneducated as well as materially deprived. He has heard that Jews are unethical, untrustworthy, and indifferent to the fate of others, and his experience seems to confirm these images. If there were a historic image of Christians as being exploitative and dishonest, Negroes would find abundant grounds

[16] Because so high a proportion of Negroes report shopping at Jewish stores, the analysis has focused on work contact. Insofar as it was possible to analyze the effect of shopping, the findings are similar to those for work contact.

[17] This fact *would* be relevant were we trying to understand why Negroes are more anti-Semitic than antiwhite. *But we have no evidence that anti-Semitism, exceeds antiwhite feeling.* In any event, our main preoccupation is with understanding why economic anti-Semitism is greater among Negroes than among whites.

[18] On every question concerning Negroes, Jews with less than a college education were more likely to give anti-Negro responses than were the college educated. Some examples are as follows: "To be frank, I would not want my child to go to school with a lot of Negroes": "Agree," 29 per cent versus 15 per cent. "Do you think there should be laws against marriage between Negroes and whites?": "Yes," 26 per cent verses 11 per cent. "These days you hear too much about the rights of minorities and too little about the rights of the majority": "Agree," 38 per cent versus 15 per cent.

[19] See David Caplovitz, *The Poor ' Pay More* (New York: Free Press of Glencoe, 1967) for an analysis of the economic and social realities of the ghetto economy.

in their experience for being anti-Christian. The growth of the Black Muslim movement is testimony to the fact that some Negroes are responding to their experiences by becoming anti-Christian as well as antiwhite. The matter boils down to this: the kinds of anti-Semitic beliefs that are current in the larger society provide a meaningful and ready-made framework into which Negroes can place their personal experience with Jews.

The presence of anti-Semitism in our society makes "being Jewish" a salient characteristic of the "bad" Jewish employer, shopkeeper, landlord. But there is no ideology that makes "being Christian" a salient characteristic of the "bad" Christian. Prejudice and superstition resemble each other in many ways. Take, for example, the superstition that if a black cat crosses one's path, some misfortune will certainly occur. The consequence of such a superstition is to make black cats, *but only black cats,* highly visible. Nonblack cats are hardly noticed, since the superstition implies that they pose no danger. The very logic of a superstitious belief discourages its disconfirmation. That ill fortune sometimes occurs when a nonblack cat crosses one's path goes unobserved; but when a black cat crosses one's path, it is a simple matter to find some instance of misfortune, no matter how slight or delayed, in time. Moreover, so long as superstitious beliefs are not ruled out in principle, hearsay evidence concerning the conjunction of black cats and misfortune tends to be credited and accepted. For both superstitions and prejudiced beliefs, rejection seems to depend on a fairly high level of education and intellectual sophistication.

In accepting anti-Semitic beliefs, whether or not supported by contacts with Jews, Negroes are making the same unwarranted generalizations and exhibiting the same gullibility as do whites when they accept anti-Semitic beliefs

(or anti-Negro beliefs for that matter). It is hardly relevant that the same beliefs describe non-Jewish whites as well; who can doubt that, from the Negro's perspective, whites in general tend to be shrewd and tricky, shady, and not very honest in business, that they control banking and are careless of the welfare of others.[20] And, indeed, many Negroes have developed hostility toward whites *qua* whites. It would be astonishing were it otherwise.

Since other groups do not do so, Negroes can hardly be expected to reject pejorative statements about Jews on the sophisticated ground that such pejorative statements hold of shopkeepers or employers in general, rather than of Jews in particular. Jews themselves are not the "cause" of the disproportionate amount of economic anti-Semitism to be found among Negroes. Rather Negro anti-Semitism is traceable to two factors: the historic presence of economic anti-Semitism in our society and the deprivation and exploitation inherent in the situation of the American Negro. The presence of Jews in the ghetto economy—regardless of how they compare to other whites—is enough to bring these factors together, resulting in greater economic anti-Semitism among Negroes.

We do not wish to exaggerate the role of economic contact in Negro anti-Semitism. Many Negroes who have economic encounters with Jews do not subscribe to

[20] There has been little research on Negro images of whites. However, Pettigrew reports several old studies indicating that Negro images of whites closely correspond to traditional anti-Semitic stereotypes (Thomas Pettigrew, *Profile of the Negro American* (Princeton, N.J.: C. Van Nostrand Co., Inc., 1964). And as Marx notes: ". . . where Jews do not predominate in the ghetto, the particular ethnic group that does is likely to be the recipient of economically inspired hostility. . . .Drake and Cayton [*Black Metropolis,* p. 432] note that in New Orleans, where Italians are predominant in Negro areas, they are targets of attack, and in the past, when Negroes had disproportionate contact with the Irish, considerable hostility was felt toward them [B. Berry, *Race and Ethnic Relations,* p. 448]" (*op. cit.,* p. 167).

economic anti-Semitism, and economic anti-Semitism frequently exists among Negroes who have no contacts. Some Negroes exhibit economic anti-Semitism simply because they are Americans and live in a society in which such beliefs remain current. Yet if Negroes had no economic contact with Jews, or if Negroes had the same kind of economic contact with Jews that whites have, Negro-white differences in economic anti-Semitism would be smaller. Negro economic anti-Semitism has an existential element in it that appears to be absent among whites. Among whites, anti-Semitism tends to be largely a hearsay phenomenon, with little or no relation to actual Jews known; it thus tends to be a cognitive phenomenon with education strongly determining the likelihood that an individual will accept or reject the anti-Semitic beliefs he becomes acquainted with. Among Negroes, most anti-Semitism, whether economic or noneconomic, is also a hearsay phenomenon, basically cognitive in nature and dependent on education. However, for Negroes, economic anti-Semitism is also an existential phenomenon involving experience as well as hearsay. This reality element, we have been at pains to reiterate, does not consist in worse treatment of Negroes by Jews than by whites in general. It consists rather in the fact that the traditional beliefs of economic anti-Semitism describe Negro experiences with whites in general, and therefore their experiences with Jews in particular.

DISCRIMINATORY ATTITUDES

On . . . questions concerning [an] anti-Semitic [political] candidate and the anti-Jewish immigration law, the response of Negroes was not markedly different from that of whites. In other respects, despite their greater economic anti-Semitism, Negroes are a good deal less likely than whites to hold discriminatory attitudes. Almost all Negroes— 91 per cent—said that the members of a club do not have a right to exclude Jews; the figure for whites was 69 per cent. Moreover, while only a third of whites (31 per cent) indicated a willingness to combat social club discrimination in practice as well as in principle, twice as many Negroes (68 per cent) did so. More Negroes than whites (68 per cent versus 51 per cent) said they would not be disturbed at all if their party nominated a Jew as President. Even when Negroes scored as extreme anti-Semites, 89 per cent said that employers should hire the best man, whether he is Jewish or not. The corresponding figure for whites is 70 per cent.

The finding that Negroes are comparatively low on support of discrimination is analogous to the earlier finding that Southerners are especially high on social discrimination against Jews. Just as discriminatory feeling against Negroes leads Southerners to a disproportionately greater defense of discrimination against Jews, so Negroes respond to their own circumstances as an oppressed minority by a disproportionately greater rejection of discrimination against Jews.

EVALUATION OF THE FINDINGS

Given the nature of anti-Semitism and the conditions of economic hardship that persist in the ghetto, it is hardly surprising that economic anti-Semitism has special appeal for Negroes. As an ideology anti-Semitism blames Jews for social and economic ills. In a society where anti-Semitic beliefs are indigenous and in which Jews are a prominent part of the ghetto economy, it would be nothing short of miraculous to find Negroes immune to economic anti-Semitism. As among whites, however, the extent of immunity is largely a function of education. It takes intellectual sophistication to resist blaming the economic ills of the ghetto on the immediate agents of exploitation, whether Jewish or not, and to see these ills as products of impersonal social and economic forces that transcend the responsibility of particular individuals.

Does this mean that the Jew is becoming a scapegoat for Negro frustrations and dissatisfactions? According to the scapegoat theory, anti-Semitism is a displacement or redirection of hostility away from groups too powerful or legitimate to attack, and toward a powerless and already maligned group such as the Jews. Anti-Semitism is thus viewed as a secondary hostility stemming from a more basic and primary hostility whose expression is blocked. Two versions of the scapegoat theory can be distinguished, depending on whether the primary object of hostility is seen as too legitimate or too powerful. If it is seen as legitimate, the psychological response is typically guilt; hostility is repressed and passes into the unconscious. There it joins forces with the primitive and sadistic Id, thus accounting for the excessive hatred and violence that has historically been directed against Jews. On the other hand, when the primary object of hostility is seen as too powerful, hostility is blocked out of a realistic fear of retribution, and need not entail an active act of repression. This weaker version of the scapegoat theory would explain the excessive hatred and violence often directed against Jews as an expression of the intense feelings of frustration and powerlessness experienced by submerged groups.

It seems clear that Negroes are not using Jews as a scapegoat in either of these ways. Another study in this series found it rare for Negroes to be anti-Semitic without being antiwhite as well,[21] and, in recent disturbances Negroes have taken action against whites as such, without singling out Jews for special treatment. If Jews are sometimes targets of Negro aggression, they appear to be targets simply in their status as whites. To put the matter another way, being white, they would be targets even if they were not Jewish.

In economic anti-Semitism Negroes find a language for describing their experiences and expressing their resentments. Moreover, as Allport cautions: "What seems like displacement, may, in some instances, be an aggression directed against the true source of frustration." [22] Many Negroes have in mind not the mythical Jew, but Jewish businessmen who are implicated in an economic system that exploits them. So long as this is the case, Negroes and Jews are engaged, in part, not in mutual prejudice, but in a genuine conflict of interests. Such conflict can, and does, spill over into the realm of prejudice. This is true when Jewish businessmen are singled out for blame, when the behavior of Jewish businessmen is seen as somehow derived from their Jewishness, or when resentment against Jewish businessmen is directed against Jews generally. Ironically, in accepting anti-Semitic beliefs Negroes bear witness to their participation in Western culture and its symbols.

[21] Marx, *op. cit.*, Chapter 7.
[22] Allport, *The Nature of Prejudice* (New York: Anchor, 1958), p. 332.

13. THE ORIENTAL IN-GROUP IN HAWAII *

Frederick Samuels

Of the fifty states in the union, only one, Hawaii, has seemingly been able to accomplish genuine and almost equal integration under conditions where different racial groups each constitute a significant part of the population. The article that follows concentrates on relations within and among two of the largest of those groups, Caucasians and Japanese-Americans.

The paper helps to demonstrate some rather important propositions. First, when many members of a particular group are able to acquire higher social status over time, their tendencies to hold close to their own group's cultural values and to stay within their own group for all of their significant social contacts tend to diminish. Second, shifts toward acculturation to the dominant culture are especially strong among the young, particularly in groups with marked intergenerational upward mobility. Mobility and generational change interact to reinforce the same kinds of inclinations. Third, another very strong reinforcement comes to the fore if the members of a previously dominant group find that such changes in a minority have made it seem more socially acceptable.

On the mainland the majority or dominant group frequently placed limits on how much acceptability it was willing to grant to newcomers. Since that was once true in Hawaii too, some observers believe that the example of the breakdown of tight group differences there may be being paralleled, though to a

* This paper is taken essentially from Chapter V of the author's New Haven, 1970 monograph, *The Japanese and the Haoles of Honolulu: Durable Group Interaction.*

Source: *Phylon* (Summer 1970), pp. 148–56.
FREDERICK SAMUELS is Assistant Professor of Sociology at the University of New Hampshire.

lesser degree, among college-educated youth on the mainland, despite the simultaneous countertendency for members of the large racial minorities to do all they can to maintain group coherence and solidarity.

A considerable amount of time will probably have to pass before the mainland will be able to follow Hawaii's lead. The rest of the country has different traditions; a different population composition and distribution; and different associations among race, class, and ethnicity. As a matter of fact, even on the mainland, Japanese-Americans have achieved relatively high social rank rather rapidly; in so doing, they have also come to be rather well accepted by the majority population. They constitute, along with Chinese-Americans, the great exception to the general American pattern of cross-race antipathy and exclusion. Part of the reason why that has been the case is neatly adumbrated in the title of a recent journal article—"Westerners from the East: Oriental Immigrants Reappraised." [1] To spell that out a bit, I quote from my headnote to the paper on Japanese-Americans that appeared in the previous edition of this book.[2]

American and Japanese culture both place a premium on achievement, on the capacity to defer immediate gratification for the sake of greater long-term rewards, and on devoting close attention to practical detail. These parallel values help to explain why individuals raised in Japanese-American communities are often well adapted to American educational and vocational demands. By inculcating the oncoming generation with motivations congruent with American needs and opportunities, first-generation Japanese-Americans made good use of part of their traditional culture to aid the social mobility of their children.

Differential rates of upward mobility within various ethnic groups primarily reflect differences in group standards, and not a differential distribution of native talents. The standards of some groups—along with the Japanese, American Jews and Greeks are notable examples—are better suited than others for teaching an individual group member the steps he must take in order to get ahead through his own efforts. . . . American folklore holds that success is and should be the result of individual effort and ability, [but] it is important to see that not

[1] R. Daniels, in *Pacific Historical Review*, XXXV (1966), pp. 373–83.

[2] Bernard E. Segal (ed.), *Racial and Ethnic Relations: Selected Readings* (New York: Thomas Y. Crowell Company, 1966), p. 77. The headnote introduced William Caudill and George De Vos, "Achievement, Culture, and Personality: The Case of the Japanese-Americans," *American Anthropologist*, LVIII (1956), pp. 1102–25.

*all individuals find themselves in situations in which they learn
effective ways of bringing their capacities to bear.*

I want to add a few remarks to that earlier statement. If the
standards and traditions of some groups are better suited than
those of others for achieving success and respectability
through conventional channels, it is in the nature of the case
that members of the latter groups will do proportionally less
well than members of the former. But until now, we have not
done very well at seeing that goals alternative to individual
material achievement may also have merit; *or* at adapting the
channels of ascent to fit other standards; *or* at encouraging
achievement motivation when it appeared in places or among
groups where we did not expect to find it; *or* finally, at
recognizing that if there were some groups that seemed to be
suffering from a sort of cultural emasculation, that some other
group had to have had a hand in the castrating.

Hawaii is not yet a heaven, and some of these points apply
even there. Caucasians and Japanese are now nearly equals at
the top of Hawaiian society, but note the negative attitudes of
both toward Filipinos.

In-group consciousness is the awareness
in an individual that he belongs to a
particular group distinct from all other
groups of the same order. It involves the
preference for associating with members
of his group. Ethnocentrism is the concept that the norms and values of one's
own group are superior to those of all
other groups. Both of these phenomena
are natural to men. In fact, they are
necessary for group survival. It is only
when they become abnormally exaggerated that dangerous intergroup situations may occur.

In the course of two years of field
research on the two major durable
groups [1] of Hawaii—the Japanese and

the Haoles (Caucasians)—I have recorded frequent descriptions of the Japanese by the Haoles in terms which
suggest the presence of abnormal degrees
of in-group consciousness and ethnocentrism among the Japanese of Hawaii.
Following are two brief examples of this
viewpoint:

The Japanese are family-oriented; they
are clannish.

Many Japanese feel that due to culture
they put themselves above Polynesians.
They feel that they [Japanese] are probably
better, more refined than Haoles.

Japanese, too, often perceive the Japanese as tending to stay within their
own group to an exaggerated degree.

[1] *Durable group* refers to a racial, ethnic, or
religious group which is recognized as an effective, identificational entity by its members and
by outsiders. In Hawaii, the most important
durable groups are: Japanese, Haoles (Caucasians), Haole-Hawaiians, Oriental-Hawaiians, Filipinos, Chinese, Portuguese, Koreans, Puerto
Ricans, Hawaiians, and, although still less than

5,000 in number, and thus the smallest of the
eleven groups delineated, Negroes are beginning
to have some impact upon race relations in Hawaii. In the 1960 census, Japanese formed 32.2
percent of the population of Hawaii; Haoles
were 32.0 percent of the population.

This in-groupness is attributed especially to the older generation:

My parents are clannish. On the plantation people were more narrow-minded. We younger generation Japanese try to be more open.

There are sometimes a problem between the first and second and third generations. In some cases the first generation holds tradition too strongly. They expect us to follow their traditions.

These statements by Makiki [2] Japanese indicate the presence of a strong in-group consciousness and perhaps ethnocentrism in the older generation Japanese and the apparent rebellion and eventual emancipation of the younger generation. There is nothing unusual in this. It is a phenomenon occurring in every immigrant group. The newcomers settle in voluntary ghettos where people's faces, language, customs, and the odors of food cooking are familiar and thus comforting. They eventually feel more secure and begin to move tentatively outward, all the while assimilating into the new culture in a thousand little ways. Their children, educated in the schools along with children of other groups, bring home the new culture in books, in speech, through visiting classmates. If the parents do not leave the ghetto, the children surely will. The Japanese in Hawaii, once they left the plantations, followed essentially this pattern. Why then the cry of "clannishness"? Is there any basis for this accusation against the Japanese?

If a group is clannish there will not be much out-marriage of individuals of that group with members of other durable groups. There will be little opportunity for the intimate association with outsiders necessary to establish potential marriages. Furthermore, even should such a bond develop between a member of a clannish group and an outsider, the

pressures from the family and other in-group members would militate against the marriage taking place. The out-marriage rate for the total population of Hawaii was, in 1965, 38.1 percent. That is to say, of all of the marriages which took place in Hawaii during that year, 38.1 percent were across ethnic or racial lines. The Japanese of Hawaii had in that same year out-marriage rates of 19.6 percent of grooms, and 25.5 percent for brides, both rates clearly below the overall average, and, in fact, the lowest out-marriage rates of all of the groups in the Islands.[3] The Japanese have always had extremely low rates of out-marriage. In the period 1912–1916 (when such statistics first became available), Japanese men married out of the Japanese group at the rate of 0.5 percent per year, and Japanese women married across in-group lines at the infinitesimal rate of 0.2 percent per year. The out-marriage rate for the total population of Hawaii was then 11.5 percent per year, and the Japanese were then, too, clearly the group least prone to marry outside of the durable in-group.[4]

It was actually World War II which set off a trend of more out-marriage for Japanese girls. During that War seven hundred young Japanese men from Hawaii of marriageable age were killed and seventeen hundred were maimed, mostly in the Italian campaign and in France.[5] This contributed to unbalancing the sex ratio in Hawaii to the point that many Japanese girls who otherwise would have been restrained by the wishes of their parents to marry Japanese now found themselves in such oversupply that marriage prospects were dim if restricted to their own group. In fact, because of the death and the crippling of the young Americans of Japa-

---

[2] A working-class, racially integrated section in Honolulu.

[3] See *Statistical Report,* Department of Health, State of Hawaii (1965), p. 59.

[4] See Andrew W. Lind, *Hawaii's People* (3rd ed., Honolulu, 1967), p. 108.

[5] See Daniel K. Inouye, *Journey To Washington* (Englewood Cliffs, 1967), pp. 163–64.

nese ancestry and the emigration of other young Japanese males to the more promising jobs on the west coast of the Mainland, the urban sex ratio in 1950 for Japanese males from 30–34 years of age as compared with Japanese females from 25–29 years of age was 78.0, an abnormally low ratio.[6] Meanwhile, the urban ratio for Caucasians in that same age bracket was 116.9. Since for every one hundred Japanese females in the 25–29 age group there were only 78 Japanese males in the 30–34 age group, and since there was concomitantly a surplus of Caucasian males, it would not be surprising to find Japanese girls marrying Haoles in relatively large numbers. This they did, and the Haole groom-Japanese bride combination is still a very popular one in Hawaii. In 1965, 40.0 percent of all of the out-marriages of Japanese women were to Haole men.[7] Japanese males, rising in occupational status after the War, increased their out-marriage rate rapidly a decade after the Japanese females' spurt. However, although there has been some severance of the tight bonds of Japanese in-groupness, the Japanese are still relatively very low in degree of out-marriage as compared with the other ethnic and racial groups of Hawaii.

I recall the words of a Haole woman from Makiki on this point: "I was engaged to a Japanese man. They accepted me as a friend, but not as a member of the family. It wasn't personal. It was— I don't know." Is the answer to this woman found in the statement of a Kahala[8] schoolgirl? "The Japanese think they're superior to the Haole; they

stick together." Is the answer echoed in the words of another Kahala Haole? "They see themselves as a proud race. They are interested in preserving their culture." Or is the statement of a Manoa[9] Haole closer to the core of the matter? "They stick together because they have faith in each other. They cannot depend on the Haole."

The Japanese are depicted by most Haoles as well as by themselves as being shy and reserved. Is it then simply a matter of shyness and reserve being mistaken for aloofness, vanity, and even ethnocentrism? It is not uncommon in human interaction that such symptoms are perceived incorrectly. It is all too common for the insecure, sensitive perceiver to view another's symptoms of insecurity as symptoms of "felt superiority"; it is all too often that the insecure perceiver sees rejection where only reluctance to be rejected is operative, and this same misinterpretation is usually mutual. The Haoles are hardly pictured as shy and reserved, but are seen as being snobbish and aloof:

They [the Haoles] have a tendency to look down on people, laborers, peons. They are used to high status; they infringe on others' rights.

They think that they are superior to the Japanese. This person was amazed that I could speak English.

Haoles see themselves as being superior to the other races, because they have the blonde hair and the blue eyes and speak better English than anyone else.

The local people are afraid to associate with Haoles. It is not so much being clannish, but being afraid of Haoles. We must try not to be afraid.

Is it then really the Haoles who are the group resisting more intimate contact, or at least the perception which the

---

[6] This method of comparing the category of males with the category of females which is five years younger is attributable to Douglas S. Yamamura. Note: sex ratio = $\frac{\#males}{\#females} \times 100$. Thus a ratio of 100 is perfectly balanced.

[7] Calculated from data in *Statistical Report*, *loc. cit.*, p. 59.

[8] An upper-middle-class, Caucasian section near the Diamond Head area of Honolulu.

[9] An upper-middle-class, racially integrated section in the hills above the University of Hawaii.

Japanese have of the Haoles? It is not only the Japanese, however, who view the Haoles as being somewhat arrogant in their racial attitudes. The following are statements by Haoles:

Haoles are snobs; they think they are superior. The majority of Haoles on the Island feel like this.

The Haoles are obnoxious in strange lands. They look down on people who are different. Too materialistic. This situation has been modified in Hawaii, but Haoles have to make greater effort.

The older group of Haoles is racist. They tend to perpetuate their own customs without blending much.

The Haoles should step down and be more humble.

What is especially interesting here is that while the above were derogatory statements made by Haoles about Haoles, it is apparently not these respondents who are the snobs. If anything, the self-image data reveal both Haole and Japanese to be aware of the faults of their own respective groups. The Haoles are perhaps more self-incriminating and appear to more strongly desire internal improvement in race attitudes, but the younger generation Japanese also display a strong resentment against the clannishness of their own elders. What then is the truth of the matter? Are the Japanese abnormally in-group conscious and even ethnocentric? Or is it essentially a defense mechanism to protect themselves against the overbearing Haoles? The data on contact and on attitudes of preference illuminate this subject.

MEASUREMENT OF SOCIAL DISTANCE

A brief explanation of methodology is necessary. Two hundred and ten Japanese and Caucasian respondents from seven different residential sub-samples were interviewed with respect to racial perceptions, attitudes, and behaviors. The residential areas were selected so as to allow for control of durable group, social class, and residence pattern of the respondents—two variables at a time.[10] In addition to open-ended questions intended to elicit both out-group images and self-image, specific measuring tools were used to determine social distance between the respondent and each of eleven durable groups. Social distance is defined as "the degree of intimacy or understanding which individuals or social groups have achieved."[11] Three different types of social distance were conceptualized—perceptual, attitudinal, and behavioral. Perceptual social distance was measured by the perceived socioeconomic status

[10] The basic design is as follows:

	Integrated	
	Working class	*Upper-middle class*
Japanese	Makiki	Manoa
Haoles	Makiki	Manoa
	Segregated	
	Working class	*Upper-middle class*
Japanese	Moiliili	
Haoles		Kahala

A seventh sub-sample, Waikiki residents (Haole, segregated, working class), is contaminated by intervening variables due to its exposure to the tourist atmosphere of Waikiki, and it is not included in overall statistical comparisons in this study. In choosing within each sub-sample the individuals to be interviewed, the following procedure was followed: A census tract map was used. Within each selected area (selected according to census data on socioeconomic status and durable group distribution), streets were chosen at random by means of "blind" pencil pointing. Then on these streets (in the order of their selection) every fifth house was chosen for interviewing one person. In cases where there was no one home, a refusal, or the occupant was not Japanese or Haole, the next house was chosen, and then the fifth house from that one was the next in line for interviewing purposes.

[11] Robert E. Park, "The Concept of Social Distance," *Journal of Applied Sociology*, VII (1924), 339.

rankings of the eleven groups by the respondents. The higher a group was ranked by the respondent, the less was the perceptual social distance judged to be between him and the designated group. This is realistic when it is realized that the respondents were all either Caucasian or Japanese—the former group whose members generally perceive themselves as being at the top of the heap, the latter group whose members perceive themselves as rapidly approaching the top. Thus groups perceived at a low socioeconomic level are different and generally undesirable to these individuals with upper-middle-class norms and/or aspirations.

Attitudinal social distance was measured by the attitudes of preference index. Each respondent was asked with respect to each of eleven durable groups the degree of approval or disapproval which he felt toward having children of a particular group as playmates for his own children, as guests in the home, and as marriage mates for his children. The question was posed separately for each of the three categories, and the choice of answers (printed on a large card) were: "very much in favor," "in favor," "have no preference one way or the other," "not in favor," "very much opposed." The scoring was 1 for "very much in favor," 2 for "in favor," and so forth. "Very much opposed," thus scored as 5, indicates the greatest attitudinal social distance. Each respondent's score for each of the three potential interaction categories between himself and a particular group were added up, and then mean scores were calculated for each of the residential sub-samples of respondents. Any group receiving a mean score of 3 would thus be at minimum attitudinal social distance from that particular section of respondents. A group receiving 15 would be at the maximum social distance.

Behavioral social distance was measured by the contact index. Each respon-

dent was asked to describe the degree of friendly, unpleasant, and overall frequency of contact which he had had with members of each of eleven ethnic and racial groups. The choices for answers were: "a great deal of," "some," "very little," "none." In the case of both friendly and overall frequency of contact, the scoring was 1 for "a great deal of," 2 for "some," and so forth. In the case of unpleasant contact, the scoring was reversed, thus, 4 for "a great deal of," *et cetera*. Again, the smaller the score, the less the social distance. The three categories were totaled, and means for the several sub-samples were calculated. A mean contact score of 3 for a particular durable group would indicate a minimum of behavioral social distance between the sub-sample of respondents and the group in question; a mean score of 12 would indicate maximum social distance.

DIFFERENCES IN SOCIAL DISTANCE

Behavioral social distance between the Haoles and the Japanese is either infinitesimal or moderately great, depending on which version is accepted. To arrive at this understanding, the total contact index (thus taking into account friendly, unpleasant and overall frequency of contact) is the measure of behavioral social distance which is used. In using this index, there is an element of potential subjective distortion. It is not contact as measured by the researcher, but contact as perceived and evaluated by the subject, which is actually measured. This situation has proved invaluable in the present instance.

It would seem reasonable to assume that if the members of one group evaluate their contact with another group at nearly the same level of intimacy as they view contact within their own group, the two groups would have little behavioral social distance between them. The mean of the Haole scores with respect to contact with the Japanese was 4.22. The mean of Haole in-group contact scores was 3.73. Thus, from the viewpoint of the Haole respondents, there is only a .49 difference between Haole in-group behavior and Haole-Japanese interaction. Haole-Japanese intergroup behavior would appear to be on the positive side.

However, when the Japanese version is examined, a different picture emerges. The Japanese mean score with respect to contact with the Haoles was 5.06; the Japanese in-group contact mean was 3.69. The difference between Japanese in-group social distance and Japanese-Haole social distance is here 1.37, nearly three times what it appeared to be from the Haole's perspective.[12]

It is interesting to note how similar the respective in-group contact scores were, *i.e.*, 3.73 and 3.69. Thus it is clearly the out-group interaction level which is in dispute. The Japanese seem to think that the interaction between themselves and the Haoles leaves something to be desired, while the Haoles scarcely seem to differentiate between other Haoles and Japanese in regard to interaction.[13]

Since behavior is closely related to attitude, a similar disparity might be expected in the attitudes of preference index. The expected difference occurs in Makiki, but not in Manoa. In other words, among the working-class respondents, the Haoles preferred the Japanese more than the Japanese preferred the Haoles as playmates for their children, guests in the home, and potential marriage mates for their children. In the case of the upper-middle class, there was no significant distinction between Japanese and Haole intergroup preference. The same relatively large social distance felt by the working-class Japanese toward the Haoles in Makiki is seen in the ghetto working-class area of Moiliili. It would seem that the Japanese who have moved from Moiliili to the more integrated Makiki have retained the ghetto tendency to stay closely within their own group, at least insofar as attitude toward the Haole is concerned. But what is the in-group of the working-class Japanese. Does it consist of only the working-class Japanese?

THE ORIENTAL IN-GROUP

It is very clear from the data that the working-class Japanese prefer to associate with Orientals. In both Moiliili and Makiki, the Japanese chose Chinese and Koreans immediately after themselves as preferred intimates; Haoles were chosen fourth in each case. In Manoa, Haoles were ranked second behind Japanese, and Chinese and Koreans followed them. Thus, once more, it is seen that the working-class Japanese differ from those of the upper-middle class. The Oriental in-group is a phenomenon predominantly of the Japanese working class. This extended in-group of the working-class Japanese includes Japanese, Chinese, and Koreans. Filipinos may appear to be Oriental to the outsider, but the Japanese perceive them as "dark" people with "Latin traits" of quick-temper, jealousy, and violence. Their Spanish "blood" and their low standard of living also count against them. This was made clear in several of the interviews with Japanese respondents. Filipinos are

[12] A critical ratio test for difference of means of Japanese respondents' contact scores with Haoles and with Japanese, respectively, showed t = 5.27. Therefore, at the .01 level of confidence, there is a significant difference.

Japanese contact scores				
	Mean	Standard deviation	N	Standard error
re Haoles	5.06	1.59	54	.22
re Japanese	3.69	1.01	54	.14

[13] The six sub-samples of the basic design are included in this analysis (see footnote 10).

clearly not perceived as part of the Oriental in-group.

Whereas individual Oriental-Hawaiians may be included in the Oriental in-group—if they are living among Japanese or other Orientals as Orientals—those that live as Hawaiians in Hawaiian neighborhoods with Hawaiian norms and values are excluded.[14] It does not appear to be, then, a matter of biological inheritance, but one of culture. This Oriental in-group tendency of the working-class Japanese is thus not racist in the sense that the Nazi "Aryan" in-group was. The Japanese feel more comfortable with other Orientals because, due to relatively similar norms, values, and customs, they feel that they are more likely to be accepted by Orientals than by people from other cultural backgrounds. A common retort to the question of potential marriage mate was, "As long as he is Oriental, he is okay." That there are problems enough in marriage without bringing in cultural conflict was the explanation invariably given.

This Oriental in-group phenomenon must be seen in perspective. It did not always exist, although there were some indications of it in Masuoka's study in 1931.[15] For example, whereas the awesome Haoles were preferred as playmates, fellow club-members, and guests-in-home, when it came to the potential marriage mate for the Japanese respondents' children, the Chinese were the group most preferred. This preference for Orientals has since fully emerged.

But something beyond this has also begun to crystalize. In Manoa, the Japanese are apparently extending outward beyond the Orientals. These more educated and affluent Japanese have begun

to overcome cultural barriers between themselves and the Haoles, even as their predecessors had to overcome traditional antipathies in order to include Chinese and Koreans in their in-group. It is not unreasonable to expect the circle to widen until all of the ethnic and racial groups in the Islands are at a compatible social distance from the once self-centered Japanese. From one's own durable group to those perceived as most similar, and then to other groups as they appear relatively approachable and non-threatening—this would seem both logical and empirically supported as a pattern of assimilation.

AND WHAT ABOUT ETHNOCENTRISM?

The matter of in-group consciousness has been examined, but what of the stronger charge of ethnocentrism that has sometimes been leveled at the Japanese? The older generation Japanese may indeed be ethnocentric to an abnormal degree—the younger Japanese seem to think so. But this younger generation is itself anything but ethnocentric as Japanese—they are perhaps ethnocentric as Americans. Cultural assimilation, Americanization, could not possibly be more successful than in the case of Hawaii's locally born Japanese. They have enthusiastically grasped everything American from baseball to American-style politics. They "dig" American jazz and smile patronizingly at the Japanese songs crackling out of the radio in old "Mamasan's" barber shop.

The Japanese and the Haoles of Honolulu do not feel comfortable enough with one another. Which group is the more aloof is a matter of perception and interpretation, and varies with the individual perceiver. That each group, or at least many members of each group, desires better relations is evident. That

---

[14] The term *Hawaiians* as used here and elsewhere in this paper does not refer simply to all residents of the State of Hawaii, but rather to the descendants of the original Polynesian inhabitants of the Islands.

[15] See Jitsuichi Masuoka, "Race Attitudes of the Japanese People of Hawaii" (Unpublished master's thesis, University of Hawaii, 1931).

while not completely at ease with each other they are nevertheless far from exhibiting overt hostility is also evident. Japanese-Caucasian intermarriage is increasing, and younger Japanese are both more accepting of Haoles and more accepted by them than in the past. Nevertheless, there is a tendency, predominantly among the Japanese working class, to favor association with Orientals. This Oriental in-groupness is seen as a natural phenomenon and not one fraught with perils for race relations. Assuming continuance of the present trends, it may be viewed as a transitory phase in the process of assimilation.

14. TRADITION AND CHANGE IN ITALO-AMERICAN FAMILY STRUCTURE

Herbert Gans

As I have noted above, although differences among ethnic subcultures in American society tend to become less prominent as higher proportions of group members rise from working-class to middle-class status, traditional ways of life and patterns of social organization often persist in the predominantly working-class ethnic enclaves of major cities. On the one hand, these traditions tend to reinforce ethnic identity, leading the minority group member to define his standards and seek his rewards in his "own" community. On the other, in conjunction with whatever antipathies prevail toward his group outside of his community, they limit his

Source: *The Urban Villagers* (New York: The Free Press of Glencoe, 1962), pp. 209–17. Copyright © 1962 by The Free Press of Glencoe, a division of the Macmillan Company. Reprinted by permission of the author and publisher.

Herbert Gans is Professor of Sociology, Columbia University. Among his works are *The Levittowners* and *People and Plans*.

opportunities for occupational advancement and channels for self-expression.

People who wish to participate more fully in the dominant sectors of American life, but who simultaneously feel bound to honor ethnic obligations, often find their situation stressful. An important reason for this is that ties of ethnic loyalty are formed in families and expressed in norms that emphasize kinship solidarity. It is therefore often guilt-provoking to consider leaving the group behind and striking out for oneself.

Gans's study of a large Italian community in Boston's West End, since displaced by an urban renewal project, shows how older and more traditional Italian family patterns continue to influence other areas of Italo-American culture, even as family structure itself changes as the result of American experience.[1]

[1] A recent book criticizes Gans for treating *working-class* Italian family structure and culture as if it represented the whole of the Italo-American experience. The point is worth keeping in mind, but can hardly destroy claims to validity for findings about the group that Gans did study. For the critique, and for a sense of the broader picture of Italo-American life, see Joseph Lopreato, *Italian Americans* (New York: Random House, 1970).

A comparison of the lives of the West Enders with those of the immigrants suggests a number of other changes. For the West Enders, life is much less of a struggle than it was for their parents. There are more jobs, more secure ones, and better paid as well. As economic conditions improve, the ethos which Banfield calls amoral familism has begun to recede in importance. Most West Enders, for example, no longer need to fear their neighbors and unrelated people as a threat to their own existence. These "others" are no longer competitors for a small number of scarce jobs, but people with whom one can associate. Consequently, social life and mutual aid are not entirely restricted to the family circle; West Enders can and do make friends more easily than their ancestors.[1]

[1] A number of other changes between Italians and Italian-Americans are described as part of a larger study of drinking patterns in G. Lolli, E. Serianni, G. Golder, and P. Luzzatto-Fegiz, *Alco-*

Nor is the outside world as threatening as it was to immigrants. The second generation is not barred from it by language, and it can maneuver in the outside world if absolutely necessary. As a result, the attitude toward caretakers, the law, city government, and other phases of the outside world is no longer based on total incomprehension and fear.

The processes by which these generational changes came to be were of course not always painless. In too many cases, the family circle and other immigrant institutions could not cope with acculturation, poverty, and the other degradations forced on the newcomers and their

hol in Italian Culture, New York: The Free Press of Glencoe and Yale Center of Alcohol Studies, 1958. This study notes, for example, that Italian-Americans go to church more than Italians (p. 22); that they report drinking for social reasons, rather than for their health (pp. 68–69); that they get drunk more often (p. 85); and that unlike Italians they get drunk in the presence of the opposite sex (p. 88).

children by the outside world. Some turned to delinquency, crime, and violence to resolve their difficulties; others were beset by individual and family breakdowns. Although these problems affected only a minority of the population, they too are a part of the transition from immigrant to second-generation status.

THE SLOWNESS OF CHANGE: THE BASIS OF THE PEER GROUP SOCIETY

Some aspects of a group's way of life change more rapidly than others. Moreover, the observer's perception of change is affected by his own perspective, by the indices he uses, and by his own value judgments about the desirability of change per se.

These considerations affect any attempt to summarize the comparison of the West Enders to the generations that preceded them. Clearly, there has been considerable change in the standard of living, and in certain patterns of culture. At the same time, however, the many parallels between Southern Italian society and the West Enders suggest that many basic features of the way of life have not changed. The old social structure has remained intact.

What accounts for the stability of the social structure in the face of what would seem to be a rather drastic change in environment? The static, poverty-stricken, and highly stratified rural society of Southern Italy bears little resemblance to the frequently changing, more prosperous, and comparatively open society of urban-industrial Boston. *A brief review of the three generations may suggest the answer: the environment has not really changed as drastically as it appears.* This review will also make it possible to outline more clearly the basis of the peer group society as a

response to the opportunities and deprivations in the environment.

The Italians who came to America were not farmers or peasants, but town-dwelling farm laborers who worked for absentee owners and managers. Although there was some evidence of the existence of a clanlike extended family, the occupational role of the farm laborer made it impossible for the extended family to function as a unit. The farm laborer, who was paid in wages that barely supported even his wife and children, could exist only in a nuclear family household.

Since people lived under conditions of extreme poverty, and in a static social system from which escape—other than by emigration—was impossible, the overriding goal was the survival of the nuclear family. Moreover, as marriages were contracted to advance—or at least not to retrogress—the economic and social position of the families involved, they had to be arranged. Consequently, husband and wife were usually not as close as in partnerships based on love. Since children had to go to work at the earliest opportunity, they were raised to adult status as quickly as possible, which was accomplished by treating them as small adults from an early age.

The nuclear family is neither entirely self-sufficient nor independent; nor can it satisfy all the needs of daily life. It is particularly handicapped in dealing with emergencies. Consequently, other institutions must be available. But when every family was involved in a struggle to survive—as was the case with the Southern Italian farm laborer—few people could be called on for aid, or trusted to give it when their own families were equally in need. Nor could they be treated as friends and companions, for they might take advantage of this relationship to help themselves in the fight for survival. Moreover, in order to attract friends, one had to be able to make a good impression. This required a dwelling unit to which people could be invited without shame, money to pay the costs of entertaining, and a considerable amount of trust over a long period of time. As one of Covello's respondents put it: "Friends are a luxury we cannot afford." Community agencies, were they churches, schools, or welfare agencies, could not be trusted because they were controlled by the employer. It made no difference when they had been founded for beneficial purposes; they were rejected by their intended clients as a matter of pride.

Under such conditions, relatives were the only source of group life and mutual aid. Being tied to each other by what were felt to be irrevocable ties of blood, they could face each other without putting on appearances, without feelings of shame, and without suspicion that the relationship would be exploited. In a society where no one could afford to trust anyone else, relatives had to trust each other. Moreover, when survival depended on the ability to work strenuously for long hours, older people were at a disadvantage. Possessing no special skills or traditional knowledge not also available to younger people, they had little influence on the group once they had become too old to support themselves. In addition, since relatives had to double as friends, people naturally gravitated to family members with whom they had the most in common. Consequently, they were drawn to peers.

The Southern Italian farm laborers lived not simply in poverty, but in poverty in the midst of a visibly higher standard of living enjoyed by the artisans, the middle class, and the gentry. In some areas they resorted to strikes and to class conflict; in others, to emigration.[2] But until these solutions were possible, most farm laborers lived in a state of extreme relative deprivation, a state made even more painful because of the close proximity of more fortunate people. In such circumstances, the restriction of aspirations was emotionally a most functional solution—at least in the short range—since it prevented the development of frustrations, which were frequently harder to endure than physical deprivation. Parental lack of interest in education, detachment from the larger community, and unwillingness to fight the exploiting powers—all were practical solutions in a society in which mobility was so restricted that there was no reason to expect benefits from schooling, and where the oversupply of labor made it possible to starve out rebellious individuals. While these solutions were harsh and denying, they also reduced stress, and made life as bearable as possible. Since the achievement of object-goals was certain to be frustrated, children were reared to reject them. The development of empathy was also discouraged; too great a sensitivity to the problems of other people would have been hard to endure.

Many of the conditions that gave rise to this way of life accompanied the Southern Italians in their move to America. In Italy, they had labored from sunrise to sunset on the farms of landowners; in America, they worked long hours as laborers for factory owners or contractors. Moreover, since they did not gravitate to the highly mechanized and rationalized assembly line jobs, the nature of their work did not change radically either. Many worked with the earth—pick and shovel in hand—in both countries, although in America, they brought forth construction projects rather than farm products. In Italy, they had lived in densely built-up and overcrowded small towns, barren of vegetation; in America, they moved into equally overcrowded and barren tenement neighborhoods. Indeed, their trip across

[2] John S. MacDonald and Lea D. MacDonald, "Migration Versus Non-Migration: A Typology of Responses to Poverty," paper read at the 1961 meetings of the American Sociological Society.

the ocean took them only from rural towns to urban villages.

Most of these parallels continued into the adulthood of the second generation. Not until World War II, in fact, and the subsequent prosperity of the postwar era, did their economic position differ radically from that of their forebears. Even then, many West Enders have been dogged by unemployment, layoffs, and other forms of economic insecurity. Since they—as well as their parents—have often been employed in marginal industries, they also have felt themselves to be exploited occupationally. Moreover, like their ancestors, they have been beset by serious illness, premature death, infant mortality, and by other of the sudden and unpredictable tragedies that so frequently hit low-income people.

Many other parallels exist between Southern Italy and Boston. The immigrants who settled in Boston found a society stratified not only by class but also by ethnic background and religion. In fact, in Boston—more so perhaps than in other cities—they encountered a hereditary aristocracy that at the time of the Italian influx still held considerable social, economic, and political power. Since then, its place has been taken by the Irish and by other groups, all of them culturally different from the Southern Italians. In short, the world outside the home was and still is dominated by people different in class and culture, by outsiders to be suspected and rejected.

Thus, the environment that the immigrants and the West Enders have encountered in America has differed in degree rather than in kind; it is less hostile and depriving, of course, but it is otherwise still the same. There have been no radical changes in the position of the working class vis-à-vis other classes, or in the position of minority ethnic groups vis-à-vis the majority. As a result, there have been as yet no strong pressures or incentives among the West End-ers for any radical change in the basic social structure with which they respond to the environment.

FROM SECOND TO THIRD GENERATION: SIGNS OF CHANGE [3]

In addition to the changes that have already taken place between the past and present generations, other changes are only now developing. Noticeable among a few West Enders today, they are likely to become more prevalent in the next generation. These changes are the result of processes in the larger society that are creating new opportunities for West Enders. They also will make it more difficult to maintain some of the traditional ways of life.

The major source of opportunities is occupational. A few West Enders are now beginning to move into white-collar technical jobs, actually the modern equivalents of skilled factory work. They are also beginning to enter service occupations, notably in sales, in which their ability for self-display and for competitive group activity is helpful.[4]

The third generation will be able to respond to the new occupational opportunities partly because their parents believe in the need for education as a means of obtaining job security. Parents also can now afford to keep children in school at least until high school graduation. Whether or not the third generation actually will take up these opportunities will depend, of course, on their willingness to stay in school, and to learn

[3] This section is speculative, since it deals with a generation only now reaching adulthood. It is based on observations of West Enders, a few ex-West Enders who had left before redevelopment, and on additional observations made among a handful of Italian families in a suburban community near Philadelphia which I studied after I concluded my field work in the West End.

[4] Whether these opportunities will be available to the third generation in as plentiful amounts as I am suggesting depends on the consequences of automation on the labor market in the coming decades.

what is necessary to compete for stable and secure jobs. I assume that an increasing number of third-generation adolescents will remain in school.

New occupational and educational attainments are likely to have repercussions on the structure of the family, and on the peer group society generally. For one thing, they will create more social and cultural differences between people. This, in turn, will affect the family circle, for relatives who have responded to the widening opportunities may begin to find that they have less in common, and are no longer compatible in their interests. At the same time, since people have fewer children than in previous generations, the number of potential family circle members will be reduced. Consequently, the family circle may be somewhat harder to maintain than in the second generation.

Although someday these trends may even decimate the circle, other changes are likely to attract new recruits. I have already noted that as unrelated people cease to be competitors in the struggle for survival, they can become allies in the search for companionship. Indeed, the desire for companionship combined with the decreasing number of compatible kin can mean that friends and neighbors will begin to play a more important role in the social life of the peer group society.

Meanwhile, other changes are taking place in the nuclear family unit. The decimation of the family circle by differential mobility is one step in a larger social process that brings nuclear family members into a more intimate dependence on each other. For while friends can replace relatives in a number of functions, rarely do they help each other as fully or are they as close as people bound by blood ties. Other changes are reinforcing the cohesion of the nuclear family. With the disappearance of arranged marriages, husband and wife are emotionally closer to each other than were their parents and grandparents. Moreover, the nature of the educational process—both in and out of the classroom—is such that husbands and wives now grow up with a more similar background than was true in previous generations. By and large, both sexes are exposed to the same subjects in school. In addition, they are taught by the school, and by American culture generally, that the man may participate in child-rearing and household duties and in sparetime activities with his wife with no reflection on his masculinity. Given the increasing influence of the wife, and the larger number of common bonds between the marriage partners, the segregation of roles now existing in the family is likely to decrease.

Moreover, as the economic functions of the child have disappeared completely, the child's need to become an adult as rapidly as possible has disappeared also. Indeed, as relatives become less close, parents are likely to discover that the child can help to draw husband and wife together. Thus will begin the shift from the adult-centered family to the child-centered one, and the eventual development of the kind of nuclear family structure now prevalent in America.

Also, relations between parents and children are likely to become closer. With fewer ethnic differences between the second and third generation than existed between the first and second, parents will feel more capable of advising their children. This could result in increased family conflict, if only because questions which were never raised before between parents and children will now be thought of as proper subjects of discussion. Family conflict also may be engendered by the fact that children will make greater demands on their parents, not only for goods but also for freedom to participate in children's and teenagers' activities.

Such a family is also likely to increase its participation in the outside world. Reduced suspicion and a decrease in cultural differences will make it less necessary for the next generation to reject the outside world as strongly as did the second. With more economic security, installment buying will seem less risky, and changing tastes will attract people to the consumer products and services that are now rejected. Already, the desire for modernity has made itself felt among some pioneering West Enders. And while the postwar suburbs have attracted only a few, they are likely to seem less frightening to the next generation. Indeed, it is probable that young mothers who look askance on the life of the street and wish closer supervision over their children's activities will find the attractions of suburban life most advantageous, even should their husbands not share this enthusiasm or their urgency about the children. Even now, the bright and sometimes garish pleasures of California and Florida are luring some West End vacationers, and will do so increasingly in the next generation. I remember how intensely a West End mother in her early twenties spoke of her plan to move to California, if only she could persuade her husband to give up his ties in Boston.

By virtue of the women's greater receptivity to education, and their premarital employment in the white-collar world, they are likely to take the lead in the process of change. The husbands may resist their pressure, and will probably be more reluctant to give up the old ways, especially since these were designed—intentionally or not—to maximize their freedoms and privileges. But because the wife remains subordinate to the husband in most families, because she is thoroughly indoctrinated in her homemaker role, and because she is hesitant about leaving the house to go to work, she may be unable to implement many of the changes of which she dreams. Her traditional role could act as a brake on her aspirations and perhaps as an accelerator on her frustrations.

Moreover, the social forms of the outside world will continue to be less attractive than its products, for the unwillingness and inability to concern oneself with object-oriented ways of behaving is likely to remain, among women as well as men. Churches and formal organizations, civic associations, government agencies, and politicians—all will probably be suspect even in the next generation, and participation in such activities is likely to be notably less among people of Italian background than among others.

Most of the people who will be making these changes are routine-seekers. As life becomes more secure, they no longer need—or want—to live for the gratifications of the moment. Not only is the search for adventurous episodes losing its urgency, but the drawbacks of action-seeking now loom larger than they did before. The lulls between episodes, the depression that sometimes accompanies the waiting, and the negative consequences of action-seeking now make it seem much less desirable. The availability of more predictable forms of gratification within the family and the peer group also takes something away from the pleasures of successful action-seeking. Its attractiveness as a way of life is thus being reduced, especially after adolescence. The parental desire to have children grow up respectably encourages this development, as does the increasing influence of women, who are the more earnest advocates of routine-seeking.

Yet parental desires are not always achieved, and, indeed, parental behavior may contradict them. Thus, some third-generation people will pursue action as fervently as did their ancestors. But increasingly, they will be those people who have grown up in idiosyncratic or pathological surroundings. Therefore the search for action will be a consequence of distinctive—and increasingly deviant —childhood experiences, rather than a prevalent way of life that stems from the economic and social insecurity of an entire group.

15. STATUS INCONSISTENCY AND WALLACE SUPPORT

D. Stanley Eitzen

Status inconsistency is a useful concept, but it should not be overused. American society shows so many combinations of the bases of ascribed status (age, sex, race, ethnicity, religion, region) and achieved status (education, occupation, income) that it seems strange to call a particular combination inconsistent because it does not meet theoretical expectations or because it is not the most common combination in a particular large category of individuals. For example, more than a quarter of nonwhites (a low ascriptive category) in the labor force had at least white-collar jobs (a high achieved category) in 1969, and they totalled more than six million people. Moreover, the alignment of status criteria has been shifting over time. Thirty years ago, white-collar workers were more sharply separated from blue-collar workers in income, fringe benefits, working hours, and racial or ethnic backgrounds.

Nevertheless, the determinants and criteria of status still do tend to hang together. In any case, whether a given status combination is or is not to be considered "consistent" is probably less important than the possibility that it refers to a particular kind of life situation, one that encourages concerns that differ from those of people in other situations. The selection that follows usefully suggests what such concerns may be among white people whose income rank in their community was higher than their education rank. They were the most readily identified supporters in Lawrence, Kansas, of Alabama Governor George Wallace's candidacy for President in 1968.

This article also shows how a bit of inventiveness can lead to some interesting and worthwhile original research despite a

Source: *Social Forces,* Vol. 48, No. 4 (June 1970), pp. 493–98. Reprinted by permission of the University of North Carolina Press.

D. STANLEY EITZEN is Assistant Professor of Sociology at the University of Kansas.

limited budget. We are less certain of findings from this study than we would be with those drawn from a national probability sample, but how many student readers will ever get the chance to design, execute, and analyze such a sample?

There may be some basis for generalizing from Eitzen's findings, but it is not firm. Eitzen's index of Wallace support was the placing of a Wallace sticker on one's car. That is a more involved act, and in some ways a more overt one, than either telling one's candidate preference to an opinion pollster or voting itself. Furthermore, it was from a well-off sector of the working class that most of the Wallace support came in Eitzen's study, yet data from a national sample study of candidate preference show that the difference between upper-working- and working-class Wallace preference was quite small. The difference could have been sampling error; but even if it were real, it seems to have depended heavily on unusually strong Wallace preference among the upper-working-class respondents in the South. Oddly enough, Midwestern Wallace preferences— and Lawrence, Kansas, is in the Midwest—were highest in the upper-middle and working classes, lowest in the upper-working class.

Some of the findings to which I have been referring appear in the following table.[1] Their most notable feature is not the pattern of Wallace preferences, but the well-known relationship between class and voter preference for the two major parties.

Voter preference by social class (in percent).

Class	Humphrey	Nixon	Wallace	Number of cases
Working	52.5	34.5	12.9	640
Upper-working	42.3	42.3	15.1	125
Middle	40.4	51.2	8.3	445
Upper-middle	31.5	60.2	8.2	146
Total	45.3	43.5	11.1	1356

A Gallup poll carried out just after the election asked voters both for whom they had cast their ballots and whether they had considered voting for any other candidate earlier in the campaign. An analysis of the results is cited by Eitzen [2] but does

[1] The ultimate source of these data is the Inter-University Consortium for Political Research at the University of Michigan. The table is a secondary analysis and appears as Table 2 in Hugh Cline and Edmund D. Meyers, Jr., "Problem-Solving Computer Systems for Instruction in Sociology," *The American Sociologist,* Vol. 5 (1970), pp. 365–70.

[2] Seymour Martin Lipset and Earl Raab, "The Wallace Whitelash," *Trans-action,* Vol. 7, No. 2 (December 1969), p. 28.

not contain the cross-tabulations that would be necessary to test his central hypothesis directly. The clearest results of the analysis are that occupation, income, religion, size of place of residence, and age all affected both the Wallace vote and total Wallace sympathy, that is, final Wallace vote plus earlier consideration of him as the preferred candidate. Southern patterns did not always match Northern ones, notably because the Southern data showed much stronger effects for education (with the better educated supporting Wallace less frequently), and hardly any differences by age.

The following is not the whole table, but merely some of the extremes.

Extremes of high and low Wallace sympathy and vote in 1968 by region, occupation, income, religion, size of residence, and age (in percent).

	Non-South		South	
	Wallace sympathy	*Wallace vote*	*Wallace sympathy*	*Wallace vote*
Occupation				
Nonmanual	10	5	36	22
Manual	22	9	59	53
Income				
$3,000–$6,999	19	10	48	44
$15,000 plus	10	3	29	15
Religion				
Jews	3	*	*	*
Baptists	25	16	56	45
Size of Residence Place				
Rural	20	7	49	45
500,000	15	8	15	12
Age				
21–25	20	13	*	*
50 plus	8	3	43	33

* Too few cases for analysis

Since the McCarthy era of the early 1950s social scientists have shown increasing interest in determining the factors which attract some individuals away from moderate political views to those which are more extreme.* There has been a particular interest in those peo-

* The author is indebted to Kenneth Kammeyer and Gary Maranell for their helpful suggestions and criticisms.

ple who have moved to the extreme right on the political continuum. This phenomenon has been analyzed from several perspectives, ranging from societal conditions down to the particular personality traits of individuals. At the societal level, social scientists such as Daniel Bell (1961) and Talcott Parsons (1964) have sought to explain the rise of the radical right in terms of "status anxieties" and "strains" in the society. At the societal level, factors such as upward and downward mobility (Lipset and Bendix, 1966:73–74), social class position (Lipset, 1963:87–126), and occupational type (Trow, 1958) have been shown to be related to adherence to radical right beliefs. Finally, some researchers, most notably Herbert McClosky (1958), have focused on the comparison of the personality traits of conservatives and liberals.

The research reported here examines the effects of a social variable which has already proven to have some explanatory power in the area of political behavior–status inconsistency. The focus will be on the relationship between status inconsistency and support for George Wallace outside the South in the 1968 Presidential election.

STATUS INCONSISTENCY AND EXTREME POLITICAL ATTITUDES

Status is accorded to individuals. People evaluate and rate others on a number of dimensions (e.g., possessions, life style, income, extent of education, race or ethnic background, and type of occupation) and this evaluation constitutes an individual's status in a social system. It is possible that an individual may rate high on some dimensions by which status is judged, but low on others. Such variations in status have been conceptualized by sociologists as status inconsistency (or status discrepancy). Research has demonstrated that this phe-

nomenon affects individuals in a number of ways—symptoms of psychological stress (Jackson, 1962), social isolation (Lenski, 1956), desire for change (Goffman, 1957), upward mobility (Fenchel et al., 1951), prejudice toward minority groups (Fauman, 1968), political liberalism (Lenski, 1954), and political conservatism (Rush, 1967).

A basic assumption of these studies is that status inconsistency is an upsetting condition for the individual confronted by this inconsistency—he is frustrated and uncertain. Individuals faced with such ambiguities characteristically react in one of three ways: withdrawal (apathy), acting to change their unequal status ranks (upward mobility), or activism to change the system (political extremism). The mode selected by the individual will depend upon several factors: (1) the degree to which the individual is persistently identified by others in terms of his lower status characteristic(s) (Segal, 1969); (2) the perceived effects of political decisions upon his status ranks (Segal, 1969); (3) whether the imbalances are between achieved statuses or between achieved and ascribed statuses. The effects of status inconsistency are most dramatic in the latter case (cf. Lenski, 1967; Segal and Knoke, 1968; Segal, 1969); (4) the magnitude of the inconsistency; and (5) the particular configuration of status ranks (e.g., high education coupled with low income will have different behavioral and attitudinal consequences than low education combined with high income).

In previous studies status inconsistents have been found disproportionately in social movements of both the left and the right (cf. Rush, 1967; Ringer and Sills, 1952–53; Lipset, 1967:472–473). This suggests that persons with unequal status attributes will be attracted to political figures and political philosophies that offer a break from the moderate political course.

In the Presidential election of 1968 the

candidacy of George Wallace was an explicit break from moderate middle-of-the-road politics. Whether Wallace's political philosophy is labeled "radical right," "extreme right," or "neo-populism," there is no doubt that the Presidential campaign of George Wallace–Curtis LeMay offered a political alternative to the moderate stance offered by the two major political parties. We therefore hypothesized that among Wallace supporters outside the South there would be a disproportionately large proportion of status inconsistents.[1]

THE APPEAL OF WALLACE TO PARTICULAR KINDS OF STATUS INCONSISTENTS

An important research problem is to ascertain those types of status inconsistency which predispose individuals to an extreme political stance. Although his data were not conclusive, Gary Rush (1967:91) suggested that a combination of high income and low education may predispose individuals to right-wing attitudes. Will this type of inconsistency be predominant among Wallace supporters? We will examine the appeal of Wallace in order to explore this notion further.

Lipset and Raab (1969) have noted that Wallace appealed to two quite different categories of persons outside the South—persons who were members of extreme right groups such as the John Birch Society as well as those persons most threatened by racial integration and urban violence, the working-class whites. The first of these two categories included several types of conservatives (e.g., "ideological" conservatives whose

[1] White southern support for Wallace was not an expression of political extremism as it was considered in the North, but rather normative political behavior. Since Wallace gathered a plurality of votes in most of the southern states, it is assumed that status inconsistency was not the primary reason for his support in that region.

ideas focused on limiting the activities of government; and "preservatist" conservatives whose basic interest was in defending against the erosion of cherished American values such as Christian morality, patriotism, and free enterprise). This segment of Wallace supporters can be characterized as "radical rights." A relatively small proportion of Americans were in this category in 1968.

The second group of Wallace supporters was recruited from the "common man" and therefore constitute a larger segment of the population than his radical right followers. Wallace appealed to these persons through a populist emphasis. Wallace's speeches typically pictured the common man as a victim—a victim of the federal bureaucrats, intellectuals, mass media, student demonstrators, and the welfare chiselers. Wallace's appeal was simple—"us common folks against *them.*"

Rush's contention that high income–low education persons tend toward the radical right would probably hold for those followers of Wallace who were members of various "extremist" organizations, since many were in the *nouveau riche* category (Lipset, 1967:471). Would this type of inconsistency also be found among Wallace's common man followers? There are several possible reasons why high-income inconsistents (and here we include high-income–low occupation as well as high income–low education) might be captured by Wallace's extreme politics.

As noted earlier in this paper, Lipset and Raab (1969) have stated that Wallace appealed to those persons most directly threatened by residential integration and the rising urban violence. It appears legitimate to assume that persons living in lower- and working-class residential areas who had enough income to own property would be the most threatened by these trends. For each of these individuals it was the value of his home that was being devalued; his children who were forced to go to integrated schools; his job that was being threatened by automation or the cheap labor provided by minority group members—problems not faced by the white-collar worker from the suburbs, the policy makers in Washington, or the intellectuals in their ivory towers.

A second possible reason for high-income inconsistents to favor Wallace over the candidates from the two major parties may have been the idea that they had been economically successful despite the limits placed upon them by a low-prestige job and/or a less than average education. Such persons naturally would object to government largesse to those individuals whom they see as having similar backgrounds, but who have been unwilling to exert the effort necessary to achieve economic success.

Finally, feelings of relative deprivation may have been at the core of Wallace's support. Riley and Pettigrew (1969), in an analysis of Wallace supporters in Gary, Indiana, found that the typical Wallace supporter was a blue-collar worker earning between $7,500 and $10,000 yearly. Although "well off," Wallace supporters were more likely than Nixon and Humphrey supporters to feel that the conditions of the average man were getting worse, not better. Riley and Pettigrew (1969:4) interpret this in terms of relative deprivation.

While wage earners of this level have received substantial economic gains since 1960, they perceive their conditions as getting worse, not better. Implicitly they compare their economic gains with those of other groups and feel dissatisfied.

For these reasons, then, we hypothesized that the type of inconsistency most often found among Wallace supporters would be that of income level being higher than education and/or occupational levels. We also expected this to differ significantly from a comparison sample chosen to represent the entire adult population of the community studied.

FIELD RESEARCH PROCEDURES

The field study was conducted during the six weeks prior to the 1968 Presidential election in Lawrence, Kansas. Lawrence is a university community of approximately 35,000 with a number of medium-sized industrial plants. This community, apart from the university segment can be characterized as typically midwestern Republican. The citywide election returns for 1968 showed that Nixon received 52 percent of the vote, Humphrey 34 percent, and Wallace 10 percent.

Faced with the approaching election and inadequate research funds to canvass the entire community for Wallace supporters, we decided to pinpoint the Wallace supporters by getting the license numbers of automobiles sporting Wallace campaign stickers. The license numbers of these cars were taken to the county clerk to ascertain the names and addresses of the owners. Several students and the researcher, aided by colleagues and their families, watched for and recorded the licenses of cars bearing Wallace stickers. Some "systematic" search for "Wallace cars" was conducted by criss-crossing the residential areas, the downtown and outlying shopping areas, and church parking lots at various times over a period of three weeks. We found 104 cars and trucks displaying Wallace stickers. The final sample of Lawrence "Wallacites," however, was 37 (26 cars were owned by persons not living in Lawrence, 27 cars were duplicates in that they were second cars owned by persons in the final sample, 9 persons were not at home on the three occasions we tried to contact them and 5 persons refused to be interviewed). While the final sample is small, the technique used allowed us to isolate a particular type of Wallace supporter—the person willing to "tell the world" of his "extremist" choice.

A comparison sample of Lawrence residents was selected from the automobile registration lists. One hundred car owners were selected randomly from the list of automobile registrations kept by the county clerk. Of these individuals, 83 were interviewed prior to election day (the 17 not interviewed either refused or were not home on three occasions).

The two samples, then, were drawn from the same universe (automobile owners in Lawrence)—one made up of Wallace supporters willing to proclaim their support visibly, and a comparison group composed of a representative sample of the car owners of the community. A check of the comparison sample found all voting precincts represented, a wide range of occupations as well as diversity in income and educational levels. In addition, it might be noted, the comparison sample included 11 persons who declared an intention to vote for Wallace.

Both samples were interviewed during a four-week period immediately preceding the election. The interview schedule included a number of items to ascertain socioeconomic data, age, race, church preference, political party identification, candidate preference in the upcoming election, interest in the election and 32 questions which were designed to get at attitudes on authoritarianism, law and justice, social welfare, internationalism, and civil rights.[2]

THE STATUS INCONSISTENCY OF THE WALLACE SUPPORTERS

Three dimensions of status were utilized in this study—education, occupation of the head of household, and family in-

[2] With respect to political attitudes, the Wallace supporters differed significantly from the respondents in the comparison sample on all but the law and justice scale. The Wallace supporters were found to be more authoritarian ($P < .01$), anti-social welfare ($P < .02$), anti-internationalism ($P < .001$), and anti-civil rights ($P < .001$) than those in the comparison sample.

come. Each status dimension was dichotomized into "high" and "low" on the basis of the median scores of the comparison sample. Table 1 (p. 178) shows the distribution of Wallace supporters and the comparison sample for each of the three status dimensions.

The distributions of the three status dimensions in Table 1 show clearly that the Wallace supporters differ from the comparison sample on each one. The data in this table also show that there is a high proportion of high-income inconsistents among the Wallace supporters. The remainder of the analyses in this study will elaborate on this finding.

The first hypothesis tested was: *Wallace supporters when compared with a representative sample of the population will include a disproportionate number of persons with inconsistent status characteristics.* Utilizing the high and low categories for each status hierarchy as shown in Table 1, the respondents in the two samples were classified as either status consistents (i.e., consistently high on all three status characteristics or consistently low) or status inconsistents. Table 2 (p. 179) gives these data.

Table 2 shows that Wallace supporters when compared with the comparison sample (which included 11 persons favoring Wallace) were found disproportionately in the status inconsistent category. Thus, our first hypothesis is substantiated.

Given the fact that approximately 7 out of 10 Wallace supporters were status inconsistents, the question now becomes: what kind(s) of status inconsistency prevailed in this category. Our second hypothesis was: *among the Wallace supporters who were status inconsistents, a disproportionate number would have high income and low education and/or occupation.* Table 3 (p. 179) compares the Wallace supporters with the comparison sample on type of status inconsistency.

In Table 3 we note that almost half (44 percent) of the Wallace supporters

TABLE 1   The distribution of Wallace supporters and the comparison sample on education, occupation and income (in percentages).

Status	Education category	W	CS	Occupation category	W	CS	Income category	W	CS
High	Master's degree or above	0.00	24.10	High executives, large proprietors, and major professionals	2.70	14.46	$15,000+	2.70	14.10
	College degree	5.41	15.66	Business managers, medium-sized proprietors, and lesser professionals	2.70	10.84	10,000 to 14,999	24.32	21.79
	Partial college	24.32	14.46	Administrative personnel, small independent businesses, minor professionals, clerical and sales	27.03	30.12	7,500 to 9,999	35.14	23.08
	Subtotals	29.73	54.22	Subtotals	32.43	55.42	Subtotals	70.27	58.97
Low	High school	45.95	30.12	Skilled manual employees	40.54	26.51	6,000 to 7,499	13.51	10.26
	Partial high school	21.62	12.05	Machine operators and semiskilled employees	21.62	14.46	4,000 to 5,999	13.51	11.54
	Junior high or below	2.70	3.61	Unskilled employees	5.41	3.61	Less than 4,000	2.70	19.23
	Subtotals	70.27	45.78	Subtotals	67.57	44.58	Subtotals	29.72	41.03
Totals	Percent	100.00	100.00		100.00	100.00		100.00	100.00
	N	37	83		37	83		37	78 *

* Five individuals in the comparison sample refused to divulge their income.

TABLE 2 The distribution of Wallace supporters and the comparison sample on type of status consistency.

	Wallace supporters		Comparison sample	
Type of consistency	N	Percent	N	Percent
Status consistents	12	32.43	45	57.69
Status inconsistents	25	67.57	33	42.31
	37	100.00	78*	100.00

$\chi^2 = 6.4$; $P < .02$; $Q = -.48$

* Five of the respondents in the comparison sample refused to divulge their income.

had a single type of inconsistency—low education, low occupation, and high income. Moreover, all but three of the Wallace inconsistents had high income (88 percent). This is compared with 63 percent of the inconsistents from the comparison sample. The difference between these two percentages is significant at the .04 level. When the distribution in Table 3 is collapsed into a fourfold table (separating low-income inconsistents from high-income inconsistents) it is found to be statstically significant ($P < .05$) with a Q value of $-.61$. This supports our hypothesis that Wallace supporters tend to be high-income inconsistents.

CONCLUSIONS

The results of this study indicate that Wallace supporters as a category tended to be below the community median in education and occupation ranks, but above the median in income. Three-fourths of all the Wallace supporters had a higher income than their educational or occupational levels would appear to warrant. Moreover, our prediction was upheld that there would be a disproportionate number of status inconsistents in the Wallace category when compared to the representative sample.

We cannot say with authority whether these results are peculiar to the subject community or are generalizable to other communities.[3] The tentative conclusion is that higher rewards (income) than investments (educational attainment and/or type of occupation) leads to a particular dissatisfaction which manifests itself in a predisposition toward the political extremes offered by candidates such as George Wallace. If this is true for other communities

[3] The distribution of Wallace supporters in Lawrence on the status characteristics is comparable to that found for pro-Wallace citizens in Gary, Indiana, by Riley and Pettigrew (1969). There appears to be a close similarity also between what we found for Lawrence "Wallacites" and what Lipset and Raab (1969) report for northerners who voted for Wallace.

TABLE 3 The distribution of Wallace supporters and the comparison sample on type of status inconsistency.

Type of status inconsistency	Wallace supporters		Comparison sample	
	N	Percent	N	Percent
Hi educ., lo occ., lo income	1	4.00	5	15.15
Hi educ., hi occ., lo income	2	8.00	4	12.12
Lo educ., hi occ., lo income	0	0.00	3	9.09
Lo educ., lo occ., hi income	11	44.00	9	27.27
Lo educ., hi occ., hi income	7	28.00	7	21.21
Hi educ., lo occ., hi income	4	16.00	5	15.15
Totals	25	100.00	33	99.99

then the Wallace phenomenon is not limited to the particular conditions of 1968. Rather, it would appear that whenever the social system produces people who experience structural imbalances there is likely to be increased support for political movements that break away from the traditional middle-road of political ideology.

REFERENCES

Bell, D., 1961 "Status Politics and New Anxieties: On the 'Radical Right' and Ideologies of the Fifties." Pp. 103–123 in Daniel Bell (ed.), *The End of Ideology*. New York: Free Press.

Fauman, S. J., 1968 "Status Crystallization and Interracial Attitudes." *Social Forces* 47 (September) :53–60.

Fenchel, G. H., J. H. Monderer, and E. L. Hartley, 1951 "Subjective Status and the Equilibration Hypothesis." *Journal of Abnormal and Social Psychology* 46 (October) :476–479.

Goffman, E., 1957 "Status Consistency and Preference for Change in Power Distribution." *American Sociological Review* 22 (June) :275–281.

Jackson, E. F., 1962 "Status Consistency and Symptoms of Stress. *American Sociological Review* 27 (August) : 469–480.

Lenski, G. E., 1954 "Status Crystallization: A Non-Vertical Dimension of Social Status." *American Sociological Review* 19 (August) :405–413.

———, 1956 "Social Participation and Status Crystallization." *American Sociological Review* 21 (August) :458–464.

———, 1967 "Status Inconsistency and the Vote." *American Sociological Review* 32 (April) :298–301.

Lipset, S. M., 1963 *Political Man.* New York: Doubleday.

———, 1967 "Political Sociology." Pp. 438–499 in Neil J. Smelser (ed.), *Sociology.* New York: Wiley.

Lipset, S. M. and R. Bendix, 1966 *Social Mobility in Industrial Society.* Berkeley and Los Angeles: University of California Press.

Lipset, S. M. and E. Raab, 1969 "The Wallace Whitelash." *Transaction* 7 (December) :23–35.

McClosky, H., 1958 "Conservatism and Personality." *American Political Science Review* 52 (March) :27–45.

Parsons, T., 1964 "Social Strains in America." Pp. 209–238 in Daniel Bell (ed.), *The Radical Right*. New York: Doubleday.

Riley, R. T., and T. F. Pettigrew, 1969 "Relative Deprivation and Wallace's Northern Support." Paper presented at the annual meeting of the American Sociological Association.

Ringer, B. B., and D. L. Sills, 1952–53 "Political Extremists in Iran." *Public Opinion Quarterly* 16 (Winter) :689–701.

Rush, G. B., 1967 "Status Consistency and Right-Wing Extremism." *American Sociological Review* 32 (February) :86–92.

Segal, D. R., 1969 "Status Inconsistency, Cross-Pressures, and American Political Behavior." *American Sociological Review* 34 (June) :352–359.

Segal, D. R., and D. Knoke, 1968 "Social Mobility, Status Inconsistency and Partisan Realignment in the United States." *Social Forces* 47 (December) :154–158.

Trow, M., 1958 "Small Businessmen, Political Tolerance, and Support for McCarthy." *American Journal of Sociology* 64 (November) :270–281.

16. WHITE ETHNIC NEIGHBORHOODS—RIPE FOR THE BULLDOZER?

Richard J. Krickus

A word of caution may be useful before reading the selection that follows. The author uses the terms "white ethnics," "ethnic working class," and "white lower-middle class" almost interchangeably. This is not the place for detailed discussion of the intricacies of social-class classification, but it may be worthwhile to try to clarify the matter briefly.

First, most regularly employed people who do manual labor can be considered to be in the working class. Second, most of the people who have desk, pencil and paper, and other nonmanual jobs, but who do not have administrative, technical, or professional positions, are in the lower-middle class. Third, many men with blue-collar jobs and relatively low incomes are married to women who earn relatively low incomes despite having white-collar jobs. Such couples are usually thought of as being in the working class, though their combined income might rank them higher if that were the only factor being considered. Fourth, education is an additional criterion of class placement, sometimes used with other criteria and sometimes alone when the others aren't known. Roughly, less than high-school graduate is working class; high-school graduate with or without some college, but in any case less than the bachelor's degree or its equivalent, is lower-middle class. Laymen's terms for the groups that Krickus is discussing would be "the average man," "ordinary folks." For whatever the distinction is worth, "ordinary folks" more concerned with

Source: Middle America Pamphlet Series, National Project on Ethnic America, American Jewish Committee, pp. 3–27. Reprinted by permission of the American Jewish Committee. Copyright 1970; all rights reserved.

RICHARD KRICKUS writes and lectures widely on the issues and problems of ethnic Americans.

respectability than with employment security and getting by are frequently said to have a lower-middle- or middle-class perspective rather than a working-class outlook.

Krickus is quite sympathetic toward all of these people. He does not say, for example, that they are among the groups that some surveys have shown to be most likely to express prejudiced attitudes toward other minorities. The white ethnics are not saints. Saints would not be so susceptible to frustration over inability to possess shiny new consumer durables; saints would not devote so much effort to maintaining monopoly control over the building trades; saints would not worry about sending their kids to schools black kids go to.

Yet many better-off white Americans expect less of themselves than they do of the white ethnics. The white ethnics have no economic and status cushion upon which to rest liberalism, and their jobs and incomes are more susceptible to downturns in the economy than are those of executives and professionals. Moreover, many of them performed just as badly in school—or had the schools perform just as badly for them —as seems to be the case among black people now. As Peter Schrag puts it: "With the possible exception of the Jews, did the school ever become a major avenue of entry for the ethnic minorities of the urban centers? How effective was it for the Irish, the Italians, the Poles? Was it the school or the street that acculturated our immigrants? A half-century ago American society provided alternatives to formal education and no one became officially distressed about dropouts and slow readers." [1] The white ethnic communities still provide those alternatives—in political jobs, in relatives' businesses, in access to apprenticeship programs. Agencies over which the ethnics have little control now threaten to destroy community territorial bases and to weaken these alternatives by establishing parallel structures in which the new kinds of patronage jobs go to new kinds of people.

Krickus suggests why and in what fashion the ethnic communities ought to be preserved. Are his hopes and plans realistic? Perhaps not, but the alternative is urban sprawl around a central city that may stay a commercial center by day but will be no more than a garrison of and for the poor at night. Money is necessary to avoid that outcome, in amounts so great that it must come from the federal government. Will it be forthcoming without a coalition of blacks and browns and white ethnics who can together exercise enough clout to get it appropriated

[1] Peter Schrag, "Why Our Schools Have Failed," in Marilyn Gittell and Alan G. Hevesi (eds.), *The Politics of Urban Education* (New York: Frederick A. Praeger, 1969), pp. 310, 311.

and spent? Or is it rather the case that without the money no coalition can be built because too many groups have to share too small a pie?

Either way, we shall not likely see solutions to these problems unless there occur both massive shifts in governmental priorities and a more equitable distribution of income and privilege throughout the society as a whole.

City planners and urban analysts have given little thought to the role of the white working class in the restoration of our older urban centers. This oversight is difficult to rationalize. The lower-middle class white ethnics, by virtue of their size and strategic locations, are the single largest white population in our Northeastern and Midwestern cities. At present they are being "pulled" and "pushed" to the suburbs. The cities, in the process, are losing a vital source of social capital. The dissolution of white ethnic communities at the same time often sets in motion a chain of events which induces other whites to flee the center city. Unless this exodus is halted, the cities will lose human and economic resources essential to the restoration of urban America.

The white ethnic communities * are a social commodity our cities cannot afford to lose. Because they are, by and large, healthy social systems in an environment of social disorganization, they are a major source of stability. Nevertheless, white ethnic neighborhoods have been neglected because their housing inventory is old, densities are high, and mixed land uses are prevalent. The result is that they have mistakenly been identified as marginal areas doomed to

become slums. Moreover, with a new level of self-awareness on the part of the white ethnics many observers fear heightened discord. On the contrary, assuming that the proper resources and aid are provided, such awareness may very well be utilized to promote more harmonious relations between the races.

The reasons for the white ethnics' growing alienation which is forcing them to flee the center city need to be identified: they are estranged from government, lack economic resources, have been ignored by the agencies of social change, and feel they cannot possibly preserve the integrity of their neighborhoods.

Under discussion here are some recommendations which, it is hoped, will give impetus to an agenda for action to reduce white ethnic alienation and also to provide pathways for convergence with their black neighbors, thus inducing them to remain in the cities where they presently live in large numbers. This twofold goal must be achieved if the white exodus from our older urban centers is to be checked, and if working class whites and non-white minorities are ever to cooperate in an effective coalition for change.

. . . . .

Although the disparate ethnic groups may be at different stages of the assimilative process, it is clear that in our cities and suburbs they share a common "ethnic group" outlook toward social

* Ethnic groups may be defined as human collectivities based on an assumption of common origin, real or contrived. Hence blacks, Mormons, and Germans comprise ethnic groups which are based upon race, religion, and national origin. In this paper, when we refer to ethnics, we mean the white ethnics of European origin.

change. Even if we accept the proposition that their working class status explains their behavior better than their "ethnicity," it is proper to deal with them as distinct social units in the cities where they reside in large numbers. For they are, to all intents and purposes, the white working class in Gary, Newark, and our older industrial cities.

. . . . .

Andrew Greeley suggests that membership in an ethnic group becomes salient when the group is comprised of a large number of persons, when it is a highly visible minority, or when it suddenly becomes aware of itself as a minority because of heightened organizational activity among other groups in the society. The white ethnics meet Greeley's first and third conditions. Large numbers of them live in Hungarian, Polish, and Italian enclaves in America's industrial cities and blue-collar suburbs. Despite their numbers in these locations, they are a minority nationally and have become aware of their "minority group status" in our contemporary environment of rapid social change. Because they see themselves competing with blacks for the same jobs and living space, the black revolution has heightened their own group awareness.

In their view the Federal government has ignored the problems that beset their communities while it has "squandered" money on the blacks and other non-white minorities. While this perception may be distorted, it nonetheless seems true to the white ethnics, and its objective reality becomes almost a moot point. Perhaps an even more important reason for the deprivation they feel is the fact that the mass media, the universities, and the literary world—the institutions which mold public opinion and help set priorities for public policy—have ignored the lower-middle class with which they identify. As Mitchell Sviridoff has said:

"A phenomenon that social scientists have found among the poor, and particularly blacks, also holds true for lower-middle and middle class whites: aspirations run far ahead of actual improvement in their conditions. They see television commercials, read about the jet set, see some people around them advancing materially while they themselves are not. In their frustrated and angry response, they react much like blacks."

. . . . .

All of these factors explain why the ethnics have suddenly become aware of themselves as a minority group. In addition, since the 1968 election, political pundits and social analysts have rediscovered the white ethnics. This also may have contributed to their new level of awareness.

Heightened group identity engenders cooperation within the group, inspires self-confidence, and thus eventually produces indigenous leadership. These are all prerequisites to the ethnics' becoming an effective component of our pluralistic society. As we have observed vis-à-vis blacks, this new self-awareness may also exacerbate intergroup relations until the ethnics are accepted as competitors to be taken seriously by friend and foe alike. Once they attain this stage of social development, it will alter their social vision and enable them to engage in constructive coalitions with groups who share their problems.

As the ethnics discover that they can effectively influence decisions involving their welfare, problems previously deemed beyond resolution and goals once thought unattainable will become a part of their agenda for change. It is at this point that lower-middle class whites will "discover" that they have many problems in common with their black neighbors. For example, many ethnic whites are poor or earn marginal incomes. Even the more economically secure among them are victims of a regressive tax structure and a legal system that favors the rich and influential. Schools are inadequate and their children do not have easy access to institutions of higher learning. Like the blacks, they seldom possess the resources to influence decisions which profoundly affect the welfare of their communities— whether made by government agencies, lending institutions, or real estate speculators. And as in the case of lower-income whites in the South, the bases for interracial cooperation have been overshadowed by the white ethnics' fear and insecurity.

NEIGHBORHOODS

Working class white ethnic neighborhoods are usually inhabited by long-time residents with a sense of group identity —that is, they feel they belong to or are part of a larger social entity. This is actually what sets them off from lower-income whites in the urban South and in those cities in other parts of the country where the white workers are recent migrants from Appalachia or other rural areas.

. . . . .

In many such communities home ownership is high, absentee landlordism generally low. Homes in these neighborhoods may be deemed sub-standard by the criteria of middle class planners, but they are not necessarily overcrowded and harmful to their occupants. Rents are relatively low, flats are often roomy, and comparable living space at comparable rents cannot easily be found anywhere outside the older neighborhoods.

Furthermore, there is generally a tremendous emotional investment in the cultural and social ties established in these homogeneous communities. It was spelled out by the Rev. Mario Zicarelli, an associate pastor of Our Lady of Mount

Carmel in the Belmont section of the Bronx, when he said: "(The people here) believe in keeping up tradition. . . . We are a city of 25,000 people, 95 percent of them first- and second-generation Italians. We still get in 300 families a year from Italy . . . from the south of Italy. . . ."

Because they enjoy city life and value living close to family and friends, inhabitants of these neighborhoods are not disconcerted by mixed land uses. Indeed, they value the convenience of living close to their places of work. The diversity of street life and the benefits of living among one's family and friends compensate amply for the close proximity of factories or other unsightly structures. Primary value is placed upon the integrity of the community, and the social support it affords group members enables them to ignore the paucity of physical amenities which the more affluent take for granted.

The value of these communities to the cities in which they are located has been largely overlooked. In the eyes of city officials, planners, developers, and bankers, they are unsightly gray areas destined to be bulldozed or "overrun" by blacks and Puerto Ricans. As a result, white working class neighborhoods in the center city are disappearing. In many cases, although the residents value their community highly, they lack political influence and economic resources needed to save their neighborhood and feel forced to move out.

. . . . .

The people who hold the fate of our urban centers in their hands are by training and inclination most concerned about physical and economic problems. Contrary to what they may claim in their speeches and writings, they have failed to appreciate fully the economic, much less the social, implications of a stable community and a community-wide approach to the restoration of our cities.

In the technical criteria of redevelopment programs, they define a slum in terms of aged housing, mixed land uses, and high densities. But the primary characteristic of a slum is social disorganization and not low-rent housing (however unsightly to middle class observers) in neighborhoods which bustle with commerce and street life.

Not only is there a need for re-examining assumptions about center-city neighborhoods in general, there is also a need to become aware of the ethnic diversity contained in those neighborhoods. In a research study of four Connecticut cities supported by the American Jewish Committee, Harold Abramson found considerable ethnic variation in how groups viewed their neighborhoods. Italians and Poles, for instance, were much more likely than other groups to have close friends in their immediate neighborhood, and most of these friends turned out to be relatives. Thus, says Abramson, "the neighborhood can be an extended family," and it "assumes a strength and character which, perhaps, many have tended to ignore."

Abramson concludes: "If this pattern varies and is more important for some ethnic groups than for others, as indeed it is, it is crucial for urban planning and development. The problems of urban renewal seem all the more momentous because they frequently tend to ignore this very kind of consideration."

DECLINE OF THE WHITE ETHNIC COMMUNITIES

There is a consensus among urbanists that the rapid out-migration of whites from our older cities has reached crisis proportions. This exodus of taxpayers deepens the plight of revenue-starved municipalities unprepared to cope with a black underclass desperately in need of welfare assistance, jobs, housing, better educational opportunities, and all the

other amenities so scarce in non-white communities.

. . . . .

. . . The ethnics' estrangement from *local government* has received little attention, but it is an important reason for their failing confidence in the political system. For approximately the first half of the twentieth century, the political machine was the hallmark of urban politics in our industrial cities. A boss was the de facto chief executive of the urban political system. While reformers have depicted bossism as corrupt, graft-ridden and inefficient, it did fulfill the function of bringing together competing interest and associational groups in an effective political coalition. . . .

. . . . .

It was the New Deal and subsequent programs expanding the role of government in providing for the needy which emasculated the bosses. The Federal government henceforth distributed material support and offered services that had once "legitimized" the local political machine. The poor, the indigent, and the unemployed now looked to Washington for the assistance once provided by the boss. The middle class municipal reformers hastened the decline of the political machine when they successfully fought for non-partisan municipal government, at large rather than ward elections, and the replacement of patronage with a civil service system. Thus, through the efforts of Washington and the municipal reformers, working class urban residents were estranged from their local political institutions.

In the name of honest, efficient government, new structures and new processes came into being, with the result that "modernization has meant replacement of Old Machines with New Machines. The New Machines are the professionalized administrative agencies that now run the cities. The career bureaucrat is the new Boss."

Only the well educated, the affluent, and the politically influential know how to operate effectively in this new milieu. The planners, the agency chiefs, the builders, and the bankers now tear down neighborhoods, spike a lower-income community with throughways, and dictate the city's aesthetics, citing social progress, the imperatives of enlarging the tax base, and rational living as excuses for their manipulation of the city dweller and his communities.

. . . . .

Blockbusting

Real estate speculators are inclined to zero in on lower-middle class white communities for the purpose of blockbusting —buying cheap from white residents and selling dear to blacks who cannot purchase elsewhere. Unlike the so-called "marginal" housing discussed above, white neighborhoods involved in block-busting often have better quality housing. Well-kept homes, single or multi-family, with lawns and large yards on tree-lined streets, are the objectives of the real estate speculators. For the potential buyers are middle-income blacks and not poor people.

Living in close proximity to black ghettos, blue-collar residents fear black penetration of their communities. Their anxiety is largely rooted in fact and fancy about the relationship between black neighbors and declining property values. Sometimes speculators set the community up for blockbusting by inducing one home owner to sell at an attractive price and then citing the presence of a black family to his neighbors as evidence that a black invasion of the community is imminent.

The essential elements in this piece are the fearfulness and insecurity of the white community. The tactic is less likely to work where the residents are middle class whites and active participants in community affairs and the local

political system. The estrangement from local government of lower-middle class whites, their inability to work effectively within the complex adminstrative system, and their meager economic resources all conspire to make them susceptible to blockbusting.

Urban renewal, blacklisting, and blockbusting are just a few of the forces "pushing" whites from the inner city. Fear of crime, racial strife, exorbitant land costs and high taxes, plus the decline of the school system—all factors dealt with at length in the literature— are also contributing to the exodus.

At the same time there are forces "pulling" the whites to the suburbs, although the current economic picture has decreased their intensity. The FHA mortgage insurance program, the VA's mortgage guarantee program, and the new highway systems have expedited white out-migration. The availability of relatively inexpensive homes which can be purchased with small down payments and long-term mortgages and the popular belief that the suburbs are nice places to live have contributed to the decline of white communities in the inner city. These "pull" factors are, for the most part, incentives which the Federal government has provided and which have induced whites to move to the suburbs. The time has come to provide incentives to reverse this trend. It may be that the decline in housing construction and the rise in interest rates offer us the opportunity to "save" communities which until recently were in the process of dissolving.

SOME CONCLUDING RECOMMENDATIONS

The recommendations which follow will, it is hoped, encourage deeper and more comprehensive study of white ethnic communities and their role in restoring our cities.

1. New Attention and Involvement

Given their numbers and strategic locations, the white ethnics must play a larger role in any comprehensive strategy to restore our older industrial cities. Yet they, like working class whites throughout urban America, have been neglected. The "melting pot" myth, the misjudgment that they are entrenched in the middle class, and the more desperate plight of the non-white minorities all account for the relegation of working class whites to a low priority on our nation's agenda for social change. Foundations, non-profit research institutions, and universities should devote some of their research resources to the collection of data which detail white ethnic patterns, as well as precise numbers, composition, and socio-economic profiles in American cities.

Federal, state, and local governments must reassess their redevelopment programs to see where lower-middle class whites fit into the restoration of the cities. This is essential if inner-city white populations are to be stabilized and working class whites and blacks are to work together in effective coalitions for change.

2. Urban Planning

Although city planners have begun to appreciate the systemic relationship among social, economic, and physical inputs into their designs, this new sensitivity is not reflected in the programs, either public or private, which are intended to restore our urban centers. Developers, more "hardheaded" economic analysts, and members of the lending institutions with an effective veto over implementation of redevelopment schemes, are even less sensitive to social inputs. This obtuseness is difficult to explain since many cities which have restored their downtown business centers are discovering that these centers are waste-lands at night. The customers have moved to the outer ring of the metropolis. Businessmen should recognize that the flight of the ethnics to the suburbs not only robs them of potential customers for their new downtown shopping plazas, but this exodus also produces a climate of fear that compromises the future of inner-city commerce. A fuller awareness of the unique value of stable lower-middle class communities will not materialize, however, until the Federal government provides incentives and sanctions to compel profit-oriented forces to see their value.

3. Housing

City officials facing the dismal prospect of a diminishing tax base believe that lower-middle class housing cannot produce the revenues so desperately needed by municipalities. The Federal government's generous funding of public housing for the poor reduces concern in that area. It is conceivable, however, that lower-middle class housing can be built to provide the city with sufficient tax revenues. To do so may entail reassessment of the kinds of housing which are feasible in blue-collar neighborhoods. For example, cooperative apartments, inexpensive town houses, and multi-family houses might provide the density necessary to guarantee sufficient taxes while making home ownership available to persons of moderate income. Re-evaluation of housing design dogma and the feasibility of building and/or rehabilitating dwellings for present working class residents is in order.

4. Political Participation

Residents of America's inner cities have lost confidence in the efficacy of local government. Unlike their more affluent neighbors, the working class does not possess sufficient organizational talent, political clout, or capital to come to grips with problems threatening the integrity of their communities. They cannot operate effectively within a highly complex bureaucratic system which is removed from the political process. Local government has to be restructured to permit the lower-middle class to articulate its needs more effectively. Local party organization must be revitalized to enable it to receive and to articulate the demands of the poor and moderate-income groups. Meaningful participation in the urban political system will not materialize for our non-affluent residents until they are able to impose sanctions upon the administrators and technocrats who are at present immune from political pressures.

5. Community Organization

The white ethnics of our cities must organize for group action. Their communities will be neglected by public and private agencies alike until they learn to speak up for themselves. Until then, frustration and alienation will continue to grow in these communities and to foster interracial antagonism. Urban poverty, physical blight, and racial strife will persist until a multi-class, multi-racial coalition can deliver the political clout to eradicate them. Because indigenous change-oriented community organizations and experienced leadership are lacking in many ethnic neighborhoods, foundations and service organizations can make a contribution by funding leadership training courses for potential ethnic leaders. Civil rights and poverty activists, both white and black, are also qualified to train young ethnic community workers. (Unfortunately, white reformers and black leaders harbor as many misconceptions about the ethnics as the ethnics do about them. This gap, however, should not be permitted to preclude the formation of a multi-racial working class coalition.)

Organized labor and the churches, both of which have established rapport with their members and parishioners, should consider it a responsibility to assist the ethnics in community development. Labor unions can provide funds, technical assistance, and organizers to work in those communities where large numbers of their members live. The Catholic Church, because it is often the only effective organization in ethnic communities, should devote a larger share of its resources and personnel to community development work in white center-city neighborhoods.

6. Urban Renewal

In the heart of the metropolitan areas, both the business community and upper-middle class residents have received government assistance to construct business complexes and high-rise apartments. Blacks have benefited from a number of Federal programs geared to improving their living conditions (though results have fallen far short of meeting their needs).

Working class whites, however, have been ignored. Thus, since neither state, municipality, nor private sector possesses the necessary resources, the Federal government should meet their housing needs. A program specifically designed for blue-collar communities is essential to the stabilization of our inner-city white populations; such a program should incorporate the following considerations:

Scope / The focus must be broad, encompassing the total community, in order to preserve its integrity and to prevent the dissolution of the social system which results from wholesale out-migration. Related federal, state, and local agencies must integrate or coordinate their efforts with the program for a truly meaningful community approach to such local needs as:

☐ Rehabilitation and/or building of

neighborhood facilities, such as playgrounds;

☐ New housing, in inexpensive row housing, garden apartments, apartment houses, or multi-family units, on an ownership or rental basis;

☐ Space for small businesses and parking lots;

☐ Housing for the elderly and indigent;

☐ Rent subsidies or incentives to landlords to maintain rents close to their former scale;

☐ Upgrading public utilities and services, such as street lighting;

☐ Improvement of the local school system.

The original conception of the Model Cities program included all these elements, but it was diluted in administration and has yet to be adequately tested.

. . . . .

The trend toward racial imbalance in our older industrial centers, however, will not be halted or reversed until center-city blacks are given the option to locate in the suburbs. Until they can do this, the black population will continue to grow and, in their search for living space, to exert pressure on the remaining inner-city white communities. Here, too, the state is a key unit of government action. Only the state can enact the necessary legislation governing land use, codes, and intergovernmental cooperation, which would overcome the restrictions most suburban communities have placed on high-density, low-cost housing development.

Finally, there is consensus among urbanists and the public at large that our cities are too dense and crowded; hence population decentralization is urgent. In the future the suburbs and "new towns" —and not the center city—must absorb the surplus population. This orthodox view of America's use of land deserves to be reassessed, for the suburbs in the in-

dustrial states are gobbling up land at an alarming rate. There is a direct correlation between the growth of the suburbs and America's ecological crisis. If the trend goes on unabated, we may anticipate hundreds of metropolitan areas becoming mini-Los Angeleses. Our public policy is encouraging private developers to make this smoggy nightmare come true.

New towns must be constructed to meet the demands of our growing population, but they are only a partial, expensive answer to the problem. Most of our cities are not too dense, despite the oft repeated assertion that they are. One need only compare them with denser urban centers in Western Europe—that is, cities which provide quality living for their inhabitants—to see the fallacy of this assertion.

There is also much unused and underused land in our cities, and costs for comparable water, transportation, and other public utilities are lower than they are in the suburbs. It will be more efficient to take care of the housing needs of a large segment of our population by raising the densities of center cities; it can be done with the aid of such measures as have already been outlined. It is neither unfeasible nor unrealistic to support a strategy to maintain racial balance in America's cities by deferring white out-migration; it is simply prudent public policy.

BIBLIOGRAPHY

Abramson, Harold J.: *Ethnic Pluralism in the Central City*, The American Jewish Committee, New York, 1970

Fried, Marc: "Grieving for a Lost Home: Psychological Costs of Relocation," in James Q. Wilson: *Urban Renewal*, Massachusetts Institute of Technology Press, Cambridge, 1967

Gans, Herbert: *The Urban Villagers*, The Free Press, New York, 1963

Greeley, Andrew M.: *Why Can't They Be Like Us?* Institute of Human Relations Press, The American Jewish Committee, New York, 1969

Herman, Judith Magidson: *Housing for the Other America: A Fifty-State Strategy,* The American Jewish Committee, New York, 1969

Jacobs, Jane: *The Death and Life of Great American Cities,* Vintage Press, New York, 1961

Kaplan, Harold: *Urban Renewal Politics,* Columbia University Press, New York, 1963

Krickus, Richard J.: "Our 40 Million Ethnics," *The Washington (D.C.) Post,* August 31, 1969

Lowi, Theodore J.: *The End of Liberalism,* W.W. Norton, New York, 1969

Merton, Robert K.: *On Theoretical Sociology,* The Free Press, New York, 1967

Parenti, Michael: "Ethnic Politics and the Persistence of Ethnic Identification," *The American Political Science Review,* September 1967

Sviridoff, Mitchell: "A Perspective on the Seventies," *The Ford Foundation Annual Report 1969*

Whyte, William H.: *The Last Landscape,* Doubleday and Company, Garden City, New York, 1968

PART III: GHETTOES OF DIFFERENT HUES

All the groups described or analyzed in this part have been set aside from and by other Americans. All but the Jews as described in Rischin's historical account are marked by visible physical differences that white people have used as grounds for attributing to them fixed hereditary qualities that were assumed to necessitate or justify discriminatory treatment. Is there such a thing as race? Are there specific racial characteristics that determine specific cultural patterns? Is the presence of any identifiable touch of minority racial ancestry sufficient grounds for assuming that an individual is fundamentally different from others whose complexional tint is one of the approved off-white shades of most Caucasians?

The first question is a legitimate one. Race exists, but it is less a thing in itself than it is a concept. Race is an abstraction properly used only to denote the frequency with which in a given population certain as yet unknown genetic factors determine the appearance of clusters of physical characteristics commonly associated with one another. The second two questions are ridiculous. We could answer "No" to both and dismiss them at once, except that so many white Americans have assumed that the questions were important and that the answer to both was "Yes." In fact, only in recent years have most Americans stopped thinking of Jews in racial terms, despite their obviously Caucasian appearance. The blunt fact is that niceties of terminological distinction and scientific classification have not stopped Americans from acting in a racist fashion whenever physical or even cultural differences between groups seemed to be clear and prominent.

The white majority has always had the advantages of greater political power, more control over military or industrial technology, and larger numbers, and these three advantages have been enough to allow it to treat as inferior all the people who looked different: Chinese coolies, Indian warriors, black slaves and sharecroppers, and Puerto Rican and Mexican migrant laborers. However, because the nation's ethos and creed were supposed to be egalitarian, it was necessary to rationalize discriminatory treatment.

One of the rationalizations was that the same hereditary conditions that determined how people looked also determined inferiority and superiority. Another was that opportunities were open to all (with the success of white immigrant groups as evidence), so that if the members of racial minorities did not get ahead the fault was obviously their own. Still a third, less old-fashioned than the first, is the notion that any part of a group's reluctance to adopt the majority culture is at best a weakness, at worst a willfully stupid form of resistance. These rationalizations back up what has been racism *in fact,* and it would not matter whether we called the shadowy imagined biological determinant lurking in the background "race" or "onions." A root by any other name would smell as foul.

A second point that applies among the racial minority groups studied in this part of the book is that so many of their members are actually recent migrants to modern urban industrial society. As early as 1900, whites had about a generation's head start over blacks in being introduced to urban society. But two generations later, in 1969, although the black population was in general more urban than the white, a larger proportion of urban blacks than of urban whites was of rural origin.[1] The two other large racial minority groups are urban too. Eighty percent of Mexican-Americans and probably an even larger percentage of mainland Puerto Ricans are city dwellers.

Now even in the absence of conscious discrimination, members of these groups would have found upon their arrival in the great cities only the oldest housing, the lowest-ranking jobs, and, at best, the paternalistic concern of members of other groups who had made it. So far that seems no worse than

[1] Consider the following quotations. The first comes from E. Franklin Frazier, *The Negro in the United States* (New York: The Macmillan Company, 1957), and the second from *Current Population Reports,* Series p-23, No. 33, "Trends in Social and Economic Conditions in Metropolitan and Nonmetropolitan Areas," Washington, D.C., September 3, 1970.

"From 1900 to 1940 the proportion of whites living in urban areas increased from 43 percent to 57.8 percent. During the same period the proportion of the Negro population resident in urban areas increased from 22.7 to 48.2 percent. Between 1900 and 1930, about two and a quarter million Negroes left the farms and small villages of the South for the cities." (Frazier, p. 191.)

"It is within metropolitan areas of 1,000,000 or more that differences between white and Negro population trends are most apparent. As the proportion of the white population residing in these largest metropolitan areas remained constant (34 percent) between 1960 and 1969, the pro-portion of the Negro population living in these areas increased from 37 percent to 44 percent. Only 13 percent of the white population, but 35 percent of the Negro population were residents of central cities within the largest metropolitan areas in 1969. In 1969, 21 percent of the central city population was Negro, up from 16 percent in 1960. During this same time, the proportion of Negroes among residents of the suburban rings remained at 5 percent." (*Current Population Reports,* pp. 4–5.)

The New York Times of March 4, 1971, featured a story reporting on 1970 census data showing that black migration out of the South has been fairly steady over the past thirty years. From 1940 till now, at ten-year intervals, the proportion of all blacks living in the South was 77, 68, 60, and 53 percent. The proportion of all Southern people who were black declined less, from 24 percent in 1940 to 19 percent in 1970.

the situation faced by many white immigrants as late as, say, 1920. Thus, in certain circles one sometimes hears that more members of the racial minorities could also make it if they were more like Jews or Oriental Americans.

True on its face, the assertion loses sight of the fact that although conscious discrimination is diminishing, it has by no means disappeared. Furthermore, there are other circumstances that make it necessary to qualify the suggestion drastically indeed.

1. Despite exceptional performances by a few ethnic groups, most of the late-arriving *white* immigrants to the United States are only now, in the third and fourth generations, moving up from the working class in very large numbers. As Krickus pointed out in Selection 16, the white ethnics (along with more recent white migrants from the rural South and Appalachia) *are* the white urban working class. People who flee from a disorganized society bringing only a peasant culture with them do not become, nor do they train their children to become, entrepreneurs or professionals overnight.

2. At present, low-skill jobs once abundantly plentiful to immigrants are in short supply. Besides, they pay so little, offer so few prospects for advancement, and provide so little in the way of occupational security that they are particularly unattractive in a society become so affluent that its mass media ooze prosperity at the turn of a knob.

3. Most new jobs are not opening up close to where the racial minorities live. The Census Bureau estimates that between 1960 and 1970 two out of three new jobs were in the suburbs, not the central cities.

4. The opportunities most avidly sought by young minority-group members are actually quite appropriate in a society so advanced that many observers have taken to calling it post-industrial. Millions of minority youngsters know that educational credentials are more important than they have ever been for getting any employment at all, and especially for starting any place above the bottom. To damn their assertiveness at finding new ways of opening up educational opportunities, or to urge them instead to devote themselves assiduously to the cultivation of mobility techniques that were far from a sure thing thirty, forty, and fifty years ago—these are almost equivalents of asking for humble, patient waiting until continued economic growth and the general upgrading of the labor force gets around to them.

They are not waiting. For example, in the spring of 1969, City College and other units of the City University of New York were rocked by a series of confrontations led by black and

Puerto Rican young people seeking more openings for minority students in the tuition-free system. These youngsters were unwilling to accept the counterarguments that their entrance in large numbers might bankrupt the system, or lead to lower standards, or that the training they had received in fraudulently inferior ghetto high schools did not qualify them for admission. The result?

In September, 1970, freshman enrollments in the City University were 75 percent higher than they had been in the year before. The freshman class was an estimated 21.7 percent black and 11.7 percent Puerto Rican. These figures nearly doubled the respective proportions of 13.8 percent and 5.9 percent of 1969; taken together, they more than tripled the 6.5 percent and 4 percent of 1967. True, disruptions and the threat of personal violence occurred before a reluctant faculty, administration, and city began to move more rapidly toward an accommodation. True, the long-term outlook is still unpredictable. Still, it does not seem likely that students who worked so effectively to find ways to get into the university will long tolerate lowered standards that would unfavorably affect their later employment prospects.

The first of the papers that follow is Moses Rischin's historical account of the Lower Side, for more than forty years after 1880 the largest Jewish ghetto in the United States. Notwithstanding the tendencies of some later writers to idealize and romanticize what conditions were like then, the ghetto was not a very glamorous place, and the people who lived in it did not all have especially noble or richly rewarding lives. Rischin's account is straightforward. It can serve as a take-off point for considering some questions of how today's ghettoes are different from yesterday's.

The pair of papers that follow describe aspects of the culture and life-style of a group composed in large measure of more contemporary immigrants, the Puerto Ricans of New York. Lewis, an anthropologist, presents his materials almost without editorial comment. Hammer, a journalist, recapitulates an interview with a young resident who comments on and analyzes conditions on his block and whose sensitivity and feelings are prominent throughout the piece.

The next three selections, respectively, examine three different kinds of Mexican-American communities: one in a small midwestern city; the next in a small Texas town; and the third in Los Angeles, site of the largest Mexican-American barrio in the United States. The three different settings represent in turn the situations of an immigrant community, the traditional pattern of a subordinate caste living nearby a paternalistic superordinate one, and a contemporary urban ghetto.

Then William Moore examines life in a black-occupied public housing project. Rainwater's work probes more deeply into the circumstances and values of lower-class black families.[2] Werthman's observations, based on his study of mostly black delinquent boys, reminds us of the complex transactions that occur as family, school, and peer or street culture impinge upon one another.

Two different kinds of segregated areas are settings for the next two papers. In the first, Fong considers adjustment problems of recent immigrants from Hong Kong who live in San Francisco's Chinatown. In the second, Dumont and Wax analyze differences between the apparent and implicit interchange that goes on between teachers and Indian children in Eastern Oklahoma.

The last two selections are comparative investigations involving several of the groups that earlier papers described. As a three-year resident of the community he studied in Chicago, Suttles carried out his investigations and drew his conclusions from the viewpoint of a participant-observer. The paper by Irelan, Moles, and O'Shea is based on survey research. Suttles's technique has the advantage of allowing an in-depth knowledge of a relatively few people; survey research, on the other hand, allows rapid and efficient collection of information from a much larger number of people, but does not allow much possibility of probing the nuances of the participants' particular social contexts. For reading pleasure, I prefer Suttles's kind of research and reporting, for it is a product of more direct personal involvement. In some ways it is perhaps the more valid research, but it is less general and certainly much less frequently used for making policy decisions.

[2] For the most complete recent comparison of rates of family stability among whites and nonwhites, see Reynolds Farley and Albert I. Hermalin, "Family Stability: A Comparison of Trends between Blacks and Whites," *American Sociological Review*, XXXVI (February 1971), 1–18. Some of the data from their Table 8, on page 14, are as follows: In 1960, among whites, 92 percent of children to age thirteen lived with both parents; among nonwhites, 68 percent. In 1968, the respective figures were 91 percent and 61 percent. The authors arrive at this final conclusion about their findings: "The evidence suggests that family instability is associated with somewhat lower levels of [subsequent education and occupational rank]. . . . At the same time, the differentials are modest; often the effect of the instability factor is much less important than other factors examined in the works cited, and by itself the family stability variable does not go far in accounting for differences between the races. . . . Programs designed to strengthen black family structure in the hope of thereby improving the socioeconomic status of blacks may be less effective than alternate strategies." (p. 16.)

17. THE LOWER EAST SIDE

Moses Rischin

Because societies and their component parts change over time, history can provide the other social sciences with important materials for comparative studies. The present selection clearly demonstrates that point and would be worth including in this collection on that ground alone, quite aside from its intrinsic interest as an account of the "entry status" and institutions of a significant group of white immigrants. Jews are no longer generally poor in America. Once they were, and they lived in slums, though with a culture so distinctively their own that some Jewish institutions, like the Yiddish press and theater, flourished more in New York than they had ever done in Europe.

Some readers may not know that the word "ghetto" was originally applied to Jewish settlements in the Middle Ages. Then, by extension, it was used as the name for any large settlement of Jews, especially poor ones. It was only about a decade ago that I first heard the word used to describe areas of black settlement. By now, "ghetto" is more general still, as if referring to any residential area with a particularly intense concentration of people of subordinate status who are members of racial or ethnic minority groups.

Although the Lower East Side ghetto was the largest and most famous Jewish immigrant district in the world, areas like it existed as well in Chicago, Boston, Philadelphia, Detroit, and elsewhere. Strictly speaking, these areas were not ghettoes in the European sense. People lived in them out of the press of economic circumstances and their desire to stay with what they knew best and wished to cling to; Jews were not *forced* to live

Source: *The Promised City: New York's Jews, 1870–1914* (Cambridge: Harvard University Press, 1962), pp. 79–94, with end notes omitted. Copyright © 1962 by the President and Fellows of Harvard College, and reprinted with their permission.

MOSES RISCHIN is Professor of Jewish History at San Francisco State College.

in them, were not prevented from living elsewhere as had been the case in most of Tsarist Europe when massive Jewish emigration began about 1880.

As American Jews began to prosper, and as the locations of their work places changed, they moved into what Louis Wirth called areas of "second settlement." Still predominantly Jewish, these areas were also more obviously American. Yiddish was giving way to English; synagogues were established more on the basis of where Jews lived in their new city rather than on where they had come from in the old country; and religion became less an arbiter of the total round of life and more a separate sphere, though it still retained great ritual significance, especially in matters involving family observance and solidarity.

By now, in many American cities, the Jewish areas of second settlement are now areas of black population concentration. The movements of both of these groups, Jews first and blacks now, reveal one of the enduring features of the American urban scene. In the competition for space, poor groups impinged on the better off, taking the housing they could get. As they did so, first on the edges of areas that were already in economic decline because of their age, the presence of the new groups made the old neighborhoods seem less desirable still to the old-timers still living in them. Italians and Jews succeeded Germans and Irish, who had previously succeeded native Protestants. Now, blacks, Puerto Ricans, and Mexican-Americans succeed them all, finding what space they can in the by-now old and less desirable second-settlement areas of their predecessors. In fact, in New York City, Puerto Ricans have been moving into the Lower East Side, in some cases into housing that was already inadequate in 1900. (Not all American ethnic groups have followed this pattern. Scandinavians, for example, settled predominantly in rural areas of the northern Midwest, while some groups of Eastern European origin, like the Slovaks in Cleveland and the Poles in Chicago, moved to their second-settlement areas, bought their homes there, and stayed. Such groups as the latter two, often composed of people who are now rather old or without solid financial resources, often do not wish to think very seriously about moving away again, this time to the suburbs. People like them were considered in depth by Krickus in the previous selection.)

What are some of the parallels and differences between the kind of ghetto discussed in the present selection and the kind that is currently represented by the racially segregated areas of our major cities? Although the question is considered elsewhere in other editorial comments, it ought to be answered broadly here, without comparing the particular cultures of given groups. (See also Selection 5.) Parallels are obvious: the immigrants were poor, lived in miserable overcrowded conditions, and started out taking whatever jobs they could find. If their clothes didn't set them apart from others, their accents did. In any case, they too set out being looked down upon and discriminated against by the better-off.

Differences between old and modern ghettoes may be harder to spot at first glance, but they are of great significance. Among the most prominent is the strictness of residential segregation. Immigrants who were more or less financially successful were able to move out of their ghettoes to new areas; in today's pattern, the ghetto spreads around its own periphery. Middle and stable working-class members of the racial minorities, therefore, find it difficult to obtain suitable housing at a reasonable price, so as to be able to establish solid and substantial residential areas. Moreover, immigrants came here with their ancestral cultures more or less intact, while blacks had theirs destroyed. While that is less true of the two large Spanish-speaking minorities, Puerto Ricans and Mexican-Americans, their distinctive cultures are denigrated rather than praised by an English-speaking majority that is larger than ever before. Consider, too, shifts in the economy, in the labor force, and in local politics. The economy is now more clearly dominated by giant firms; without outside sources of capital and credit, small firms have a proportionately smaller chance of getting started and growing, and of thereby providing intraghetto sources of employment and training. Skill levels, occupational ranks, and educational credentials are enormously higher than they were in 1900 or even 1920. That means one has to wait longer *preparing himself* to be a part of the labor force, if he wishes to attain a reasonable level within it. Note, too, the great increase in the number and proportion of employed women in the labor force, especially in the lower white-collar ranks. Today's minority males, therefore, confront not only a lower demand for low-skill people but also a greater supply of majority women, better trained than they, who are available to take some of the jobs they might otherwise get. Finally, in local politics, the boss—a personalistic product of ethnic constituencies—has nearly disappeared, replaced by middle-class dominated "reform" administrations or cadres of trained professionals operating out of federal agencies. It is probably cleaner government; it might even be more efficient, but it doesn't give much of a sense of self-generated power to the people who need it most.

Points of difference between old and new American

ghettoes receive a lot of attention from advocates of community control. In a broad context, this signifies that just as the conditions surrounding and affecting minority groups have changed, their leaders' responses to those conditions have also changed. Community control is one suggestion for how to cope with today's conditions, but by no means the only one. In this volume, Cohen's and Tumin's papers, Selections 30 and 37, assess some of the relevant circumstances affecting the choices that contemporary minorities are making from among alternative available strategies. Particularly interested readers should also refer to Alan Altshuler's recent book, *Community Control,* which sets forth, clarifies, and evaluates many of the major arguments that are involved in present racial controversies.[1]

[1] Alan Altshuler, *Community Control: The Black Demand for Participation in Large American Cities* (New York: Pegasus, 1970). For a rich account of the history of New York's Jews since 1920, see Judd F. Teller, *Strangers and Natives* (New York: Delta, 1970). Teller's last chapter has some cogent observations on relations between blacks and Jews in the New York area, and on anti-Semitism among some militant black groups in particular. On these last points, see also Selection 12 in the present book; the introduction to the revised edition of Nathan Glazer and Daniel Moynihan's *Beyond the Melting Pot* (Cambridge: M.I.T. Press, 1970), and Seymour Martin Lipset's essay, "Anti-Semitism: The Socialism of Fools," in *The New York Times Sunday Magazine,* January 3, 1971.

Only after 1870 did the Lower East Side begin to acquire an immigrant Jewish cast. In the early years of the century a small colony of Jewish immigrants had lived there. Dutch, German, and Polish Jews had settled on Bayard, Baxter, Mott, and Chatham streets in the 1830's and 1840's. Shortly thereafter, German and Bohemian Jews took up quarters in the Grand Street area to the northeast and subsequently Jews of the great German migration augmented their numbers. Except for highly visible store fronts, Jews made little impress on the dominantly German and Irish neighborhood. But practically all East European immigrants arriving after 1870 initially found their way to the Lower East Side. Virtually penniless upon their arrival in the city, they were directed to the Jewish districts by representatives of the immigrant aid societies, or came at the behest of friends, relatives, or employers.

The changes brought about by the great Jewish migration forced the district's middle-class Germans and Irish, living in predominantly two- and two-and-one-half story dwellings, to retreat to less crowded quarters. By 1890 the Lower East Side bristled with Jews. The tenth ward (loosely coinciding with the Eighth Assembly District), closest to the central factory area, was the most crowded with 523.6 inhabitants per acre; the adjacent wards, the thirteenth and seventh, numbered 428.6 and 289.7 persons per acre respectively. Exceeding 700 persons per acre by 1900, the tenth ward was the most densely settled spot in the city; residential block density was even more appalling as factories and shops crowded tenements. In 1896 a private census counted 60 cigar shops, 172 garment shops, 65 factories, and 34 laundries in the tenth ward. In 1906, of fifty-one blocks in the city and over 3000 inhabitants each, thirty-seven were on the Lower East Side. On Rivington Street, Arnold Bennett remarked, "the architecture seemed to sweat humanity at every window and door." Hardy, older, or improvident remnants of the region's earlier Irish residents and a floating seafaring population still clung to the river edges along Cherry and Water streets; at the turn of the century, Italian immigrants crossed the Bowery on Stanton and East Houston streets and crowded into the lower reaches of East Broadway. But in the second decade of the new century, the Lower East Side from the Bowery to within a stone's throw of the East River, and from Market Street to 14th Street, had become a mass settlement of Jews, the most densely packed quarter in the city. In 1914 one sixth of the city's population was domiciled below 14th Street upon one eighty-second of the city's land area; most of New York's office buildings, and factories that employed over one half of the city's industrial workers were located in this district.

Once the immigrants had come to rest on the Lower East Side, there was little incentive to venture further. Knowing no English and with few resources, they were dependent upon the apparel industries, the tobacco and cigar trade and other light industrial employments that sprang up in the area or that were located in the adjacent factory district. Long hours, small wages, seasonal employment, and the complexity of their religious and social needs rooted them to the spot. It was essential to husband energies, earnings, and time. Lodgings of a sort, coffee morning and evening, and laundry service were available to single men for three dollars a month. Bread at two and three cents a pound, milk at four cents a quart,

a herring for a penny or two, and apples at from one to five for a cent, depending on quality, were to be had. Accustomed to a slim diet, an immigrant could save much even with meager earnings and still treat himself to a bracing three-course Sabbath dinner (for fifteen cents). Thrift and hard work would, he hoped, enable him in time to search out more congenial and independent employment. Until new sections of the city were developed at the turn of the century only country peddlers were to stray permanently beyond the familiar immigrant quarters.

There was a compelling purpose to the pinched living. Virtually all immigrants saved to purchase steamship tickets for loved ones and many regularly mailed clothing and food parcels to dependent parents, wives, and children overseas. The power of home ties buoyed up the spirits of immigrants wedded to the sweatshop and peddler's pack, whose precious pennies mounted to sums that would unite divided families. Among the early comers women were relatively few, but the imbalance between the sexes soon was remedied. In 1890 an investigation by the Baron de Hirsch Society into the condition of 111,690 of an estimated 135,000 Jews on the Lower East Side counted 60,313 children and 22,647 wage-earners, with 28,730 unspecified, mostly women. Undoubtedly, the proportion of women and children in New York was far greater than it was elsewhere. In 1910 women exceeded men among Hungarians and Rumanians, were equal among Austrians, and made up 47 per cent of the Russians. As non-Jews from these countries were heavily male, Jewish women clearly outnumbered men, accentuating the group's domesticity. Among the major ethnic groups of New York, only the Irish, 58 per cent female, exceeded the Jewish ratio.

A nondescript colony of Jews in the 1870's swelled into a center of Jewish life by the turn of the century, the drama of whose fortunes and passions was closely followed by fellow immigrants throughout the country as well as by those in the lands they left behind. A highly visible knot of Jews "huddled up together" around Baxter and Chatham streets had been engulfed by an influx that saturated the whole region with its flavor and institutions.

THE TENEMENT BOOM

Ever since the 1830's New York's housing problem had been acute. Manhattan's space limitations exacerbated all the evils inherent in overcrowding, and refinements in the use of precious ground only emphasized the triumph of material necessities over human considerations. New York's division of city lots into standard rectangular plots, 25 feet wide by 100 feet deep, made decent human accommodations impossible. In order to secure proper light and ventilation for tenement dwellers twice the space was needed, a prohibitive sacrifice considering real estate values. No opportunity was overlooked to facilitate the most economical and compact housing of the immigrant population. To the improvised tenements that had been carved out of private dwellings were added the front and rear tenements and, finally, the dumbbell-style tenement of 1879.

With the heavy Jewish migration of the early 1890's, the Lower East Side, still relatively undeveloped compared to the Lower West Side, became the special domain of the new dumbbell tenements, so called because of their shape. The six- to seven-story dumbbell usually included four apartments to the floor, two on either side of the separating corridor. The front apartments generally contained four rooms each, the rear apartments three. Only one room in each apartment received direct light and air from the street or from the ten feet of

required yard space in the rear. On the ground floor two stores generally were to be found; the living quarters behind each had windows only on the air shaft. The air shaft, less than five feet in width and from fifty to sixty feet in length, separated the tenement buildings. In the narrow hallways were located that special improvement, common water closets. In 1888 a leading magazine described typical dumbbell tenements on Ridge, Eldridge, and Allen streets.

They are great prison-like structures of brick, with narrow doors and windows, cramped passages and steep rickety stairs. They are built through from one street to the other with a somewhat narrower building connecting them. . . . The narrow courtyard . . . in the middle is a damp foul-smelling place, supposed to do duty as an airshaft; had the foul fiend designed these great barracks they could not have been more villainously arranged to avoid any chance of ventilation. . . . In case of fire they would be perfect death-traps, for it would be impossible for the occupants of the crowded rooms to escape by the narrow stairways, and the flimsy fire-escapes which the owners of the tenements were compelled to put up a few years ago are so laden with broken furniture, bales and boxes that they would be worse than useless. In the hot summer months . . . these fire-escape balconies are used as sleeping-rooms by the poor wretches who are fortunate enough to have windows opening upon them. The drainage is horrible, and even the Croton as it flows from the tap in the noisome courtyard, seemed to be contaminated by its surroundings and have a fetid smell.

As if the tenement abuses were not degrading enough, the absence of public toilet facilities in so crowded a district added to the wretched sanitation. It was reported that "in the evening every dray or wagon becomes a private and public lavatory, and the odor and stench . . . is perfectly horrible."

Conditions became almost unendurable in the summer months. Bred in colder and dryer climates, tenement inhabitants writhed in the dull heat. Added to the relentless sun were the emanations from coal stoves, the flat flame gas jets in lamps, and the power-producing steam boilers. Inevitably, roofs, fire escapes, and sidewalks were converted into sleeping quarters, while the grassed enclosure dividing Delancey Street and Seward Park supplied additional dormitory space. Late July and early August of 1896 were especially savage. Between August 5 and 13, 420 New Yorkers perished from the continuous heat, "the absolute stagnation of the air, and the oppressive humidity," noted Daniel Van Pelt, although the temperature averaged 90.7 degrees and never reached 100.

Fire and the possibilities of fire brought added terror to the inhabitants of overcrowded tenements. "Remember that you live in a tenement house," warned insurance agents. In 1903, 15 per cent of the tenements in the district still were without fire escapes. Of 257 fatalities in Manhattan fires between 1902 and 1909, 99 or 38 per cent were on the Lower East Side, all victims of old-law tenements.

Few families could afford the privacy of a three- or four-room flat. Only with the aid of lodgers or boarders could the $10 to $20 monthly rental be sustained. The extent of overcrowding in the tenements, reported a witness before the United States Immigration Commission, was never fully known.

At the hour of retiring, cots or folded beds and in many instances simply mattresses are spread about the floor, resembling very much a lot of bunks in the steerage of an ocean steamer. . . . The only way to properly determine the census of one of these tenements, would be by a midnight visit, and should this take place between the months of June and September, the roof of the building should not be omitted.

However trying tenement living proved

to be for adults, for children it was stultifying, concluded a settlement worker. "The earlier years of the child are spent in an atmosphere which . . . is best described by a little girl, 'a place so dark it seemed as if there weren't no sky.' "

Evictions for nonpayment of rent and rent strikes were perennial. Uncertainty of employment, nonpayment of wages, unexpected obligations, dependents, and adversities contributed to the high incidence of evictions. In the year 1891–1892 alone, in two judicial districts of the Lower East Side, 11,550 dispossess warrants were issued by the presiding magistrates. In 1900 the absence of mass evictions was regarded as a mark of unexampled well-being.

Earlier residents of the Lower East Side and hereditary property owners profited from the overcrowding. The rise in real estate values, exorbitant rents, and the low upkeep provided tenement owners with ample returns upon their investments. Even allowing for losses due to nonpayment of rent and an average occupancy of ten months in the year, landlords earned ten per cent. By more studied neglect, a resourceful agent might reap even higher returns. The Lower East Side tenements soon came to be recognized as the most lucrative investment in the city. Nowhere else did the speculator's market in tenement properties flourish as luxuriantly as it did here, where earlier immigrants had learned to exploit the misery of later comers.

In 1901 the further construction of dumbbell tenements was prohibited. The Tenement House Law of that year set new standards for future housing and attempted to correct the worst abuses in the existing buildings. All new tenements were to have windows that opened at least twelve feet away from those opposite. Toilets and running water in each apartment, unobstructed fire escapes, and solid staircases were required. In the old buildings modern water closets were to be installed in place of the outside privies. Finally, a Tenement House Department was established to supervise and enforce the provisions of the law. While the law never was effectively enforced, its initial achievements proved encouraging.

Many new tenements were quickly built according to the new specifications. In the fiscal year ending July 1, 1903, 43 per cent of New York's new tenements were located on the Lower East Side. Its inhabitants eagerly welcomed the brightly lighted rooms, bathtubs, and other improvements. At first, landlords on the Lower East Side were more prompt to make alterations in old-law tenements than landlords elsewhere in the city, for the heavy pressure of population made even remodeled properties attractive. The years 1905 to 1909 saw an unparalleled boom throughout the city with houses to fit every taste, from tenements to palatial mansions for chance customers, at unprecedented prices ranging up to $500,000. "It is doubtful if New York City, or in fact any other city of the world, ever before witnessed the expenditure of so many millions of dollars in the construction of tenement houses during a similar period."

While new housing was on the rise, the fast developing clothing trades also were relocating and building. As the heavy settlement of East Europeans decisively affected the housing of the city's earlier residents, so the new growth of the apparel industry, manned by Lower East Side Jews, helped to transform the city's business districts. Once legislation and the advent of electric power combined to reduce Lower East Side sweatshops, thousands of garment shops and factories pushed up the axial thoroughfares of Lower Manhattan. By 1910 the continued march uptown found the garment industry intruding upon once fashionable Madison Square, the site of New York's tallest skyscrapers. Brownstones and brick residences were razed to be dis-

placed by 16- to 20-story steel-girdered loft buildings trimmed with granite and marble and housing scores of clothing shops. In the course of this displacement, the city's central retailing district and its theater and hotel district were forced northward. The main retailing center, at 14th Street in 1880 and at 23rd Street in 1900, became anchored at 34th Street by 1910.

DISEASE AND CRIME

Superficially, East European Jews seemed ill-prepared to contend with the demands that tenement living thrust upon them. "Their average stature is from five feet one inch to five feet three inches, which means that they are the most stunted of the Europeans, with the exception of the Hungarian Magyars." Shortest were the Galicians, tallest and sturdiest, the Rumanians. Undersized and narrow-chested, a high proportion were described as "physical wrecks." Centuries of confinement, habituation to mental occupations, chronic undernourishment, and a deprecation of the physical virtues ill-fitted them for heavy labor. Between 1887 and 1890 nearly five thousand immigrants were returned to Europe labeled physically "unfit for work." Seemingly helpless and emaciated, they were to exhibit exceptional capacity for regeneration; traditional moral and religious disciplines were to serve them in good stead.

Despite the trying conditions under which the immigrants lived, they showed a remarkable resistance to disease. With the highest density of tenants per house in the city, the tenth ward had one of the lowest death rates. Indeed only a business ward and a suburban ward surpassed it in healthfulness. Dr. Annie Daniel, a pioneer in public health, volunteered her interpretation of this before the Tenement House Committee:

The rules of life which orthodox Hebrews

so unflinchingly obey as laid down in the Mosaic code . . . are designed to maintain health. These rules are applied to the daily life of the individuals as no other sanitary laws can be. . . . Food must be cooked properly, and hence the avenues through which the germs of disease may enter are destroyed. Meat must be "kosher," and this means that it must be perfectly healthy. Personal cleanliness is at times strictly compelled, and at least one day in the week the habitation must be thoroughly cleaned.

True, only some 8 per cent of Russian Jewish families had baths, according to a study of 1902, and these often without hot water. Yet the proliferation of privately owned bathhouses in the city was attributable largely to the Jewish tenement population. "I cannot get along without a 'sweat' (Russian bath) at least once a week," insisted a newcomer. In 1880, one or two of New York's twenty-two bathhouses were Jewish; by 1897, over half of the city's sixty-two bathhouses (including Russian, Turkish, swimming, vapor, and medicated bathhouses) were Jewish. If standards of cleanliness were not as faithfully maintained as precept required, the strict regimen of orthodoxy, even when weakened, contributed to the immigrant's general well-being.

Nevertheless, close crowding and unsanitary conditions made all communicable diseases potentially contagious. Despite great apprehension between 1892 and 1894, Jewish immigrants did not carry to New York the cholera and typhus epidemics raging at the European ports of embarkation. But in 1899 the United Hebrew Charities became alarmed by the Board of Health's report of the mounting incidence of tuberculosis in the city. That Jewish immigrants might become easy victims of the "White Plague" was hardly to be doubted. "As many as 119 Jewish families have lived in one tenement house on Lewis Street within the past five years." Hundreds of flats had been occupied by fifteen successive families within a brief period. "Many of these houses are known to be hotbeds of the disease, the very walls reeking with it." Increasingly, the dread disease with its cough and crimson spittle took its toll. Ernest Poole, an investigator, frequently heard the plea of the afflicted. "Luft, gibt mir luft—Air, give me air." Especially susceptible were the intellectuals, whose often shattered spirits, overwrought minds, and undernourished bodies fell prey to the killer. Yet so great was the immigrant's concern for health that the mortality rate from tuberculosis was lower on the East Side than in the city's prosperous districts. Venereal diseases, previously almost unknown among Jews in Eastern Europe, became progressively more common among young men, as restraints were weakened by exposure to new temptations.

Alcoholism, a prime contributor to poverty, ill-health, and mortality among other national groups, was unusual among Jewish immigrants. As Jews replaced the earlier inhabitants, the many saloons of the Lower East Side, trimmed with shields that proclaimed them "the workman's friend," declined. Those that survived drew few clients from a neighborhood addicted to soda water, "the life-giving drink"; they depended on the throng of transients that passed through the district. Jews did not abstain from drink. Yet only upon religious festivals and during the Sabbath ritual when the Kiddush cup was emptied did alcohol appear in the diet of most immigrants. In 1908, $1.50 a year for holiday and ritual wine seemed adequate for a family of six. "The Day of Rejoicing of the Law and the Day of Purim are the only two days in the year when an orthodox Jew may be intoxicated. It is virtuous on these days to drink too much, but the sobriety of the Jew is so great that he sometimes cheats his friends and himself by shamming drunkenness," Hutchins Hapgood noted. Jews habitually imbibed milder beverages. Russians were notorious tea drinkers. Hungarians were addicted to coffee. The less austere Galicians and Rumanians tippled mead and wine respectively. But in the New World all fell victim to the craze for seltzer or soda water with its purported health-giving powers. In his long experience, reported the president of the United Hebrew Charities in 1892, he had known only three chronic Jewish drunkards.

Neurasthenia and hysteria, however, took a heavy toll of victims. Their sickness was the result of a history of continual persecution and insecurity, intensified by the strains of settlement in unfamiliar surroundings. Diabetes, associated with perpetual nervous strain, was common. Suicide, rarely recorded among the small-town Jews of Eastern Europe, also found its victims in the tenements of New York. Despair, poverty, and the fears generated in the imagination led some immigrants to take their own lives. "Genumen di gez" (took gas) was not an uncommon headline in the Yiddish press. Yet in the late 1880's only the city's Irish showed a lower suicide rate than did Russian Jews.

However desperate the straits in which Jewish immigrants found themselves, confirmed paupers among them were few. The rarity of alcoholism, the pervasiveness of the charitable impulse, the strength of ties to family and *lanslite,* and a deep current of optimism preserved the individual from such degradation.

Prior to the 1880's only the Rubinstein murder case spotted the record of New York's Jews. Upon the testimony of doubtful witnesses, Rubinstein was sentenced to death for the slaying of his girl cousin, but cheated the hangman by taking his own life. The first crime of violence attributed to a Jew in the city's annals, its very novelty gave rise to the popular street song, "My name is Pesach Rubinstein." So unassailable was the peaceful reputation of the Jewish dis-

tricts that it was a matter for continual commendation. In 1878 Jews numbered 7 in a workhouse population of 1178; 8 among 485 prison inmates; and 12 among 1110 house-of-correction inmates.

The obloquy attached to the strident Jews of Baxter and Chatham Streets; to the Canal Street clothing shop puller-in and the Division Street millinery shop pulleress; to Michael Kurtz, better known as "Sheeney Mike," reputedly the "champion burglar of America"; and to "Marm" Mandelbaum, unmatched receiver of stolen goods, did not detract from the high repute of the city's Jews. The two dozen Bowery pawnshops were owned by Americans or earlier immigrants who catered to the needs of a heterogeneous population and were not part of the immigrant community.

The major crimes and violence in the area did not stem from the immigrants. They were its victims. The Lower East Side had always attracted much of the city's criminal element to its margins. By the last decades of the nineteenth century, it had shed the ferocity of earlier years when the "Bowery B'hoys" and the "Dead Rabbits" terrorized the area. But Mayor Hewitt's reform drive in 1887 inadvertently reinforced the district's frailties by forcing criminals and prostitutes from their accustomed uptown resorts into the less conspicuous tenements of the tenth ward, where they remained, undisturbed even by the Parkhurst crusade. The Raines Law, which provided that only hotels could serve liquor on Sundays, worsened the situation. In 1896, of 236 saloons in the tenth ward, 118 were Raines Law hotels, while 18 were outright houses of prostitution. In the first decade of the twentieth century, crusading District Attorney William Travers Jerome kept open house in his special office on Rutgers Street, at the hub of the Lower East Side, and the most salient features of criminality were forced underground. By 1905 the "peripatetic sisterhood" had been driven from the Bowery, and Captain Godard's Anti-Policy Society's campaign banished gambling from the thoroughfare. But the criminal elements soon returned.

Crime was endemic to the Lower East Side. The close collaboration between police officers, politicians, and criminals, revealed in detail in the Lexow and Mazet investigations of the 1890's, had turned the district into a Klondike that replaced the uptown Tenderloin as a center of graft and illicit business. Invariably the culprits in these activities were not immigrants, but Americanized Jews learned in street-corner ways and shorn of the restraints of the immigrant generation. "It is not until they have become Americanized, have adapted themselves to the environment of the district and adopted its ways and vices, that they become full-fledged wretches," commented Dr. I. L. Nascher. In the early years of the twentieth century the effect of such conditions upon the young deeply disturbed those anxious for the public weal. In 1909 some 3000 Jewish children were brought before Juvenile court and in the next few years Jewish criminals regularly made newspaper headlines. The appearance of an ungovernable youth after the turn of the century was undeniable and excited apprehension.

The violations of the law that characterized the immigrant community differed from the crimes of the sons of the immigrants. The former were an outgrowth of occupational overcrowding, poverty, and religious habits. Straitened circumstances contributed to the large number of cases of family desertion and nonsupport. Concentrated in marginal commerce and industry, Jews were prone to transgress the codes of commercial law. "The prevalence of a spirit of enterprise out of proportion to the capital of the community" gave rise to a high incidence of felonious larceny, forgery, and failure to pay wages. Peddlers and petty shopkeepers were especially vulnerable to police oppression for evading informal levies as well as formal licensing requirements. Legislation controlling business on Sunday found Jewish immigrants natural victims. In so congested a district, the breaking of corporation ordinances was unavoidable and the slaughtering of chickens in tenements in violation of the sanitary code proved to be a distinctly Jewish infraction.

The Bowery, way-station of derelicts, transients, and unsuspecting immigrants, attracted the less stable and wary of the immigrant girls. The dancing academies that sprang to popularity in the first decade of the twentieth century snared impetuous, friendless young women. Lured by promises of marriage, they soon were trapped by procurers for the notorious Max Hochstim Association and other white slavers who preyed upon the innocent and the unsuspecting. The appearance of prostitution, previously rare among Jewesses, alarmed the East Side.

The Lower East Side, girded by the Bowery with its unsavory establishments and Water Street with its resorts of ill-fame that catered to the seafaring trade, was surrounded by violence. Bearded Jews often were viciously assaulted by young hoodlums, both non-Jews and Jews, the area adjacent to the waterfront being especially dangerous. In 1898 and 1899, the newly organized American Hebrew League of Brooklyn protested a rash of outrages in the wake of the Dreyfus affair. Nevertheless there was only one instance of mass violence: the riot of July 30, 1902 at the funeral of Rabbi Jacob Joseph. This incident, the only one of its kind, can be attributed to the stored-up resentment of the Irish who were being forced out of the area by the incursion of Jews.

SIGNS OF CHANGE

Gradually the miseries and trials of adjustment were left behind. For those who had inhabited the hungry villages of Eastern Europe, the hovels of Berditchev, and the crammed purlieus of Vilna and Kovno, the factories and sweatshops of New York provided a livelihood and possible stepping-stone. Despite unsteady and underpaid employment, tenement overcrowding and filth, immigrants felt themselves ineluctably being transformed. The Lower East Side, with its purposeful vitality, found no analogue in the "leprous-looking ghetto familiar in Europe," commented the visiting Abbé Félix Klein. Physical surroundings, however sordid, could be transcended. Optimism and hope engulfed every aspect of immigrant life. For a people who had risen superior to the oppressions of medieval proscriptions, the New York slums acted as a new-found challenge. Each passing year brought improvements that could be measured and appraised. Cramped quarters did not constrict aspirations. "In a large proportion of the tenements of the East Side . . . pianos are to be seen in the dingy rooms." And soon the phonograph was everywhere. "Excepting among the recent arrivals, most of the Jewish tenement dwellers have fair and even good furniture in their homes."

The East Europeans began to venture beyond the boundaries of the Lower East Side into other areas where employment was available on terms compatible with religious habits. Brooklyn's German Williamsburg district, directly across the East River, where Central European Jews had been established for some decades, was settled early. In the late 1880's a few clothing contractors set up sweatshops in the languid Scottish settlement of Brownsville, south and east of Williamsburg. The depression delayed further expansion for a decade despite the extension of the Fulton Street El in 1889. Then the tide could not be stemmed. Between 1899 and 1904 Brownsville's population rose from ten thousand to sixty thousand. Land values soared as immigrants came at the rate of one thousand

per week. Lots selling for two hundred dollars in 1899 brought five to ten thousand dollars five years later. As the real estate boom revolutionized land values, many a former tailor was suddenly transformed into a substantial landlord or realtor who disdained all contact with shears and needles of bitter memory.

The mass dispersion of Jews from the Lower East Side to other parts of the city was in full swing in the early 1890's, as the more prosperous pioneers hastened to settle among their German coreligionists in Yorkville between 72nd and 100th streets, east of Lexington Avenue. For many a rising immigrant family in this period of swift change, it was judged to be a ten-year trek from Hester Street to Lexington Avenue.

The unprecedented flow of immigrants into the old central quarter, exorbitant rents, and the demolition of old tenements incidental to the building of parks, schools, and bridge approaches drastically reduced the area's absorptive capacity and spurred the search for new quarters. The construction of the Delancey Street approach to the Williamsburg Bridge in 1903 displaced 10,000 persons alone. The consolidation of the city and the growth and extension of rapid transit facilities connected what were once remote districts with the central downtown business quarters. In the new developments, cheaper land made possible lower rents that compensated for the time and expense of commuting. On Manhattan Island, the construction of underground transit opened to mass settlement the Dyckman tract in Washington Heights and the Harlem flats. The new subway also opened the East Bronx to extensive housing development. In Brooklyn, in addition to the heavy concentrations in Brownsville, Williamsburg, and South Brooklyn, Boro Park with "tropical gardens" and "parks" became increasingly accessible. Even distant Coney Island was brought into range by improved transit facilities.

With 542,061 inhabitants in 1910, the Lower East Side reached peak congestion. Thereafter, a decline set in. By 1916 only 23 per cent of the city's Jews lived in the once primary area of Jewish settlement, compared to 50 per cent in 1903 and 75 per cent in 1892. By the close of the first decade of the twentieth century the Lower East Side had lost much of its picturesqueness. In tone and color, the ghetto was perceptibly merging with the surrounding city. East European Jews had scattered to many sections of the city and were swiftly becoming an integral, if not as yet a fully accepted, element in the life of the community.

In 1870 the Jews of New York were estimated at 80,000, or less than 9 per cent of the city's inhabitants. By 1915 they totaled close to 1,400,000 persons (nearly 28 per cent), a number larger than the city's total population in 1870. Before 1880 the Jews of the city were hardly more than a subject for idle curiosity. But thereafter, the flow of East European Jews quickened the city's industrial life, helped to transform its physical shape, and contributed a varied and malleable people to the metropolis. Despite poverty and great numbers, these immigrants created no new problems. But their presence accentuated New York's shortcomings in the face of unprecedented demands upon its imagination and resources. In the early years of the new century, their voice would be heard. The problems of industrial relations and urban living accentuated on the Lower East Side were to become the focus for major reforms.

18. A STUDY OF SLUM CULTURE

Oscar Lewis

Oscar Lewis's *La Vida* is probably a better-known book than
the one from which the present selection has been
taken. *La Vida* consists of Lewis's reconstructions of unusually
extensive interviews with a limited number of informants whose
own words describe and contrast the lives of Puerto Ricans in
New York City and in Puerto Rico. In that book, Lewis limited
his own writing to an introduction, one of the places where he
formulated the central themes of what he named "the culture of
poverty." Many of those themes appear in this reading, too.
Among them are the following: having to do low-skill work for
low pay and with virtually no chance for upward mobility;
contact with the larger society limited to exchanges with
official agencies or landlords and bosses; a high incidence of
broken or temporarily disorganized families; difficulty in
establishing secure trust and confidence that extend much
beyond the immediate family and occasional groups of intimate
friends.

All of the patterns are more than mere correlates of poverty.
In one sense, they help to perpetuate it, for if one's life is
organized around such standards, it is difficult for him to prosper
in a competitive society. In another and larger sense, however,
these patterns are products of poverty, attempts to find ways of
achieving some order and predictability in one's life under
unusually difficult and anxiety-provoking circumstances.

Some of the difficulties Puerto Ricans encounter had to be
faced by other immigrant groups before them. Problems of
language and of the decline of paternal authority in a shift from
a traditional to a more egalitarian and youth-oriented cultural

Source: *A Study of Slum Culture: Backgrounds for La Vida* (New
York: Random House, 1968), pp. 109–11, 144–53, 182–85. Copyright ©
1968 by Oscar Lewis. Reprinted by permission of the publisher.

The late OSCAR LEWIS was one of the best known of American
anthropologists. Many of his works are cited in the footnotes of
Selection 29.

setting were common. Some other difficulties are more unique to Puerto Ricans and to the time of their arrival in the United States. For example, American majority preferences for people with lighter skin mean not only that many dark Puerto Ricans encounter racial discrimination, but also that the racial prejudices of the majority intrude upon Puerto Rican group solidarity. Moreover, Puerto Ricans face competition for jobs and living space with black Americans. In addition, as late arrivals, Puerto Ricans find no other groups following them and pushing them up the ladder by occupying the bottom spaces, while increased technological complexity has meant that there is no ready market for people without highly developed skills in any case. Finally, heroin, with its overtones of adventure and quick escape from a meaningless and oppressive situation, has been widely available in ghetto and barrio areas only since about twenty-five years ago. It is a temptation and crippler that was not there for the young men who lived in earlier immigrant neighborhoods.

In the next two selections, Lewis and Hammer examine these points in greater detail. Quotations from Lewis's informants enliven and amplify his presentation, putting flesh on the skeleton of spare description and cold statistics. Hammer's article places even more emphasis on how the Barrio feels to someone who lives there. Both of these readings are important background for helping to explain the emergence of Puerto Rican militance, a phenomenon examined in its own right in Selection 35.

Our survey of Puerto Ricans in New York in 1964–1965 was limited to 50 families because of the difficulty of doing fieldwork in that city. These families had a total population of 198 individuals, 99 males and 99 females, all of whom were related to families studied in Puerto Rico. To make more valid comparisons between the families in New York and Puerto Rico, it was desirable to compare persons who had been raised together or under similar circumstances in Puerto Rico before their separation resulting from the migration to New York. . . .

. . . . .

It should be emphasized that the families we studied were all first-generation migrants to New York. This was implicit in the research design and to a great extent explains their conservatism. For most of them, the process of adjustment and of assimilation was slow and painful. Indeed, the most striking finding was the relative lack of change in habits, customs, and world outlook, even among adults who had been in New York for as long as forty years.

LOCATION OF SAMPLE FAMILIES

In New York, the sample families lived in three of the five city boroughs: Manhattan, the Bronx, and Brooklyn. Twenty-five families lived in Manhattan, fourteen in the Bronx, and eleven in Brooklyn. They tended to settle in districts already heavily populated with Puerto Ricans, namely, the Bedford-Stuyvesant and Flatbush sections of Brooklyn; the south Bronx; and, in Manhattan, the area from East 100th Street to East 116th Street between Second and Fifth Avenues (the so-called Barrio, or Spanish Harlem), and from West 60th Street to West 90th Street between Columbus Avenue and West End Avenue.

These neighborhoods formed little islands within the city where the Spanish language and many Puerto Rican customs were perpetuated. Our families had few contacts with North Americans and found it difficult to relate to them because of the language barrier and also because, for many, the only contacts were with landlords, employers, or doctors—people who, they felt, were exploiting them.

The household heads in the sample had lived in New York for an average of 11.3 years, ranging from eight months to forty-three years. The median length of residence in New York City is eleven years. Three-fourths of the household heads had been in the United States less than fifteen years, although only 12 percent had arrived within the four-year period preceding our study.

EMPLOYMENT AND INCOME

The families in our sample found that the range of employment opportunities open to them in New York was very limited and, on the whole, at the bottom of the socioeconomic ladder. This was true even when compared with other Puerto Ricans in New York. In our sample, 86 percent of the employed males and about 96 percent of the females were in low-status jobs (see table below). Among all Puerto Ricans in New York, however, 70.6 percent of the employed males and 78.2 percent of the females were in this category.

There was a general feeling among

Occupations of men and women in the New York sample families, 1964.

Occupation classification *	Males		Females	
	Number	Percentage	Number	Percentage
Operatives	25	58.1	20	83.3
Nonhousehold service	9	20.9	1	4.2
Craftsmen, foremen	3	7.0	0	0.0
Laborers, nonfarm	2	4.7	0	0.0
Merchant marine	2	4.7	0	0.0
Farm laborers	1	2.3	0	0.0
Professional	1	2.3	0	0.0
Private household workers	0	0.0	2	8.3
Clerical, sales	0	0.0	1	4.2
Total	43	100.0	24	100.0

* This classification is used by the U.S. Bureau of the Census.

our informants of being exploited and discriminated against—mainly, they believed, because of their language handicap.

Hispanos are the only ones in New York who have to work for practically nothing. The colored people are a bit better off than the Hispanos because at least they know English. Negroes are the laziest people you'll find here. They're born lazy. A colored man gets a job in a factory and the boss explains clearly to him what he is supposed to do. But suppose he's working at something and the boss says, "Look, hand me that piece of paper." He'll tell the boss, "Pick it up yourself," and go on with what he is doing. With an Hispano it's different. Like if the boss says, "The only thing you have to do here is to dust that little chair," you can be sure that before he's through they've made him scrub the floor, clean the toilet, wash down the walls. And if there's a heavy package to be carried, it's the Hispano who has to carry it. And all for the wages he was offered for dusting the little chair!

What else can he do? He doesn't know the language and if he quits the job he will have a hard time finding another one. All because he doesn't know English. That's what keeps us down. In a factory we have to do all the odd jobs because we don't have the advantage of speaking English, and the Hispanos who do know English get the best of the others and hold them back instead of helping them out. When a boss tells an Hispano who knows English to order another man to do something and the other says, "Tell the boss that if I am to do that he should pay me more," the first will come back at him, "If you don't like the pay, you can quit." A man of one's own race!

(Demetrio)

The median annual income of our New York families was $3,678, which was below the median figure for all Puerto Ricans in New York. In 1959, 33.8 percent of all Puerto Rican families in New York had annual incomes of less than $3,000, as compared to the 1964–1965 figure of 34 percent of our sample. Also in 1959, 53.7 percent of the Puerto Ricans in New York had less than $4,000 annual income, while the corresponding percentage for our families five years later, when wages and prices had risen, was 56 percent. In view of the fact that in New York the Puerto Rican group as a whole ranked below the income level of both Negroes and whites, our sample families were among the very poorest in the city. A further breakdown of income categories showed that 6 percent of our sample earned under $2,000 a year. However, 16 percent earned $7,000 or more and 4 percent had incomes of $10,000 or more. . . .

· · · · ·

The unemployment rate in the sample families was about the same as that for all Puerto Ricans living in New York. Among males fourteen years and older in the New York labor force (that is, men who were not students, were not disabled, were not on relief, etc.), 9.1 percent in our families were unemployed, compared with 9.9 percent for the entire Puerto Rican population in New York.

· · · · ·

Although the incomes of the families tended to rise through the years, there was no signficant correlation between family income and the number of years a family had been in New York. The families above the median income level and those below it had all been in New York an average of 11.3 years. The highest income families had been in the city for an average of 10.6 years and the lowest for 11 years.

The lack of correlation between family income and years spent in New York City is explained by the severely limited earning capacity of the unskilled laborer. However rapidly or slowly wages may rise over the years, the wage ceiling for unskilled labor is reached very quickly.

The Puerto Rican migrant who had been in New York since 1950 was usually not earning much more, if any more, than the man who had arrived only recently. For the sector of the economy that includes factory workers, laborers, dishwashers, and similar occupations, wage increases tend to be general.

Low income households in our sample tended to be associated with separation, abandonment, and divorce. Some 40 percent of the below-median income households were characterized by a missing spouse. Seven of the ten individuals (mostly women) who had separated from their spouses were drawing relief payments. A study of the case histories revealed that low income women who had been abandoned or divorced and were living on relief usually had a previous history of unstable marriages, sporadic employment, illiteracy, and frequent appeals for public assistance.

· · · · ·

Only three of the ten families receiving relief payments in New York had been on welfare in Puerto Rico. On the other hand, several families who had been on relief in Puerto Rico were not receiving welfare payments in New York.

In general, the migrants did their best to keep off relief. Only two of the informants admitted that welfare payments influenced their decision to come to New York. One of these explicitly stated that relief was the prime motive for her migrating to New York.

· · · · ·

The migrants usually found their first job through a friend or relative; 83 percent of initial employment of informants in New York was obtained with such help. A relative helped in 38 percent of the cases, and a friend in 45 percent. The remaining jobs were found through newspaper ads, employment agencies, and "help wanted" signs. There was less reliance upon friends and

relatives for subsequent employment. Less than half (48 percent) of the migrants depended upon these personal contacts to get their second job, and the others tended to rely upon newspaper ads and employment agencies. A review of the work histories of our informants revealed that 63 percent of all their jobs were obtained through the aid of a friend or relative—34 percent through friends, 29 percent through relatives. The remaining jobs (37 percent) were obtained through more formal channels.

For those without relatives or friends to help them find a job, the search was often discouraging and frustrating, particularly when the person did not know any English. One man gave the vivid account that follows:

Well, so you're looking for a job and you start walking. Man, how long, how long are the streets of New York! You can walk and walk and never get to the end of them. While you walk you keep your eyes peeled for places where they might hire someone. You go into a shop. "Do you need a man to work here?" In some places they tell you, "No." In other places they say, "I don't speak Spanish." You just walk on and on and on. One time, you know what happened to me? I went to this place and they had a Latino there, the son of a bitch. I knew he was a Latino, so I went and talked to him in Spanish. I said, "Muchacho, you know, I'm down and out. I'm broke, see, and I'm looking for a job."

This son of a great whore answered in English, "Wat you min? I no spik Spanish." I'm telling you, it's the Puerto Ricans themselves who'll be your worst enemies in New York.

So you keep on walking until you finally land a job. At least that's the way I got mine, at a brassiere factory. I was hired as shipping clerk for $40 a week. I had ambition, you know, that thing that makes a man want to earn more, and I paid attention and learned my job and was promoted to another department and another and another. Five years I worked there. The most I ever earned was $75 a week and I had to work hard for it. Because in New York you have to work, really work, see?

When you land a job they give you a form to fill out. You look at it and think, "What's this all about?" You have to fill it out, see? So you read it, if you can read English. If you can't you're out of luck. They ask you your name, where were you born, are you single or do you have a couple of children and a wife to support. Two children plus a wife makes three, right? That's four people to support counting you, because you support yourself too. You start with a salary of $42. If you have four people to support, they won't deduct a cent, not one single cent, from your pay check. But if you mark that bit of paper with a circle around the word "Single," then you're done for. Out of $42, all you'll get your hands on is $32. Out of those $32, you'll pay $10 for a room if you're lucky. And you won't have it to yourself You'll be sharing it with the rats. You can't expect a nice room for $10 a week. Then there's the laundry, and breakfast, lunch, and dinner. How much will be left after you pay all that? Just figure it out.

By that time you'll be wanting to go back to Puerto Rico, but you haven't been able to save a cent to pay your fare. So you write, "*Mami,* things are bad here and I want to go back. Send me money for my fare."

Suppose when you filled in that little paper you said you had a family to support. The police come around to investigate, to see if you told the truth. If it turns out you're single, man! you have to return every cent they were supposed to deduct. All the tax money. If not, you'll land in jail. So, which would you choose? No, man! *Deja eso.* Leave New York alone. You can't live there. You can't live. You get swallowed by a horse!

(Héctor)

Most of the men and women in our sample worked in factories, a new ex-perience for almost all of them. There was a general feeling of discontent with working conditions in the factories. The following complaint was typical:

That's the way they work you in the factories here—worse than animals. You have to stick to your job every single minute and don't have a chance to take time off for anything at all. The boss won't allow you even a fifteen-minute break. It's work here, work there, work everywhere, any place you turn to. And if you don't like it, get out!

A man with a family to support can't be jumping from job to job because if you are out of work for a week, where are you going to get money for food and money to pay the installments you owe? All of those things pile up while you are looking for another job. So what is a man to do?

There's a lot of difference between the bosses here and those in Puerto Rico. For one thing, the same blood as your own runs through the veins of your boss in Puerto Rico, so he'll treat you like one of the family, so to speak. My boss in Puerto Rico treated me as if I were his son. . . .

(Ramón)

ATTITUDES TOWARD AMERICANS AND OTHER PUERTO RICANS

The families in our sample were evenly divided in their opinions about the attitudes of Americans toward Puerto Ricans. As many believed that the Americans viewed the Puerto Rican favorably as believed that the Americans were hostile. A smaller number thought that the attitude of the Americans was neutral or evenly balanced between those who were favorable and unfavorable. In several cases, the American Negro was considered to be an exception to otherwise favorable attitudes on the part of Americans. The hostility of the Negroes was attested to by many informants and was heartily reciprocated.

The Puerto Ricans tended to view Americans favorably, except for the

Negroes. Although sixteen Puerto Ricans said they had experienced hard feelings, misunderstanding, or more serious difficulties with Americans, most stated that they had never had any trouble with them.

Our informants were very critical of the manner in which Puerto Ricans behave toward each other. Although some insisted that there is no friction among Puerto Rican migrants, many others lamented their lack of unity and the presence of discrimination and exploitation within the group.

The Hispanos also have a little—let's say a little—discrimination among themselves. Not actually because of color, you understand, but because some Hispanos are in better positions, they live in better sections of the city and earn more money than the rest of us. This class may own a business and wants to segregate itself from the other Hispanos. Sometimes they even disown us. They say that they're not Hispanos but South Americans or something like that. So after they get ahead they want to belittle the other Hispanos. There's no cooperation among us. The Hispanos here are very distant from one another, like about from New York to Puerto Rico.

If we had any kind of unity all those things that happen to us here wouldn't occur. Instead of offering a hand, the ones that come first try to keep the others down. If a veteran Hispano is working as a salesman, he goes from door to door to exploit his compatriots rather than going to the houses of Americans who have the money. Here we Hispanos are after each other's necks so we have to be on our guard.

. . . . .

Like a boy I know who signed some papers to buy something on the installment plan. The papers he signed said the goods were worth $200 and then they wanted to charge $450 for them because of these charges and those charges and I don't know what charges. My friend refused to pay so they called up the place he worked and told the boss to take the installments out of his paycheck. The boss said the boy had to agree to that or to quit his job.

They do that here all the time; they send a letter to the boss saying that so-and-so owes them money. Then he goes to an Hispano lawyer and says, "Look, I need your help in this case," and the lawyer will say, "If you bought it you have to pay for it, but don't worry, pay for it as you can, little by little."

When you hear something like that you don't even feel like working any more. You lose your faith in work and feel dispirited and think, "Here the thieves live better than the men who do honest work; what they steal they get free, gratis, for nothing. But a working man has to leave his very guts in his job just to earn a living."

. . . . .

You see, if you talk back to a Jewish foreman and he insults you, well, if the boss comes to see what it's all about you always have the excuse that you didn't understand him and he probably didn't understand you. But an Hispano speaks your own language. That way you don't have much chance, see? If it were a Jew, he would say, "O.K. Forget it and go do something else." But an Hispano will threaten to fire you right away. What does he care? The boss goes to him and says, "I'll give you a raise of $5 or $10." He comes out ahead and the hell with the others. They can go rot for all he cares.

A friend of mine told his Hispano foreman, "I need to earn more money. Tell the boss to give me a raise, *bendito,* or let me work overtime." And do you know what the foreman did? He went and told the boss that the boy was no good. So one day the boss called my friend to the office and fired him. Then the foreman brought in a friend of his to fill the job for less pay.

Yes, those Hispanos are the worst. We can never get ahead here, never.

(Valentín)

19. REPORT FROM A SPANISH HARLEM FORTRESS

Richard Hammer

To the commuter or tourist briefly passing through, a slum-like
ghetto often seems simply an unpleasant place in which
to live. Seeing one, the resident of a more comfortable area
may feel some relief because he has been able to place his own
family in a cleaner, safer, and more acceptable community.
But to a ghetto resident, apparent signs of physical decay and
visible indications of human failure are symbols of systematic
social deprivation. We know that many ghetto residents feel
trapped and hostile, angry at the profit others make from their
cheap labor, discouraged because there seems so little hope
that those who hold power will use it in any way that might
effectively ameliorate the lot of the ghetto as a community and
of the individuals who live in it. This selection helps explain
why they feel as they do.

Source: *The New York Times Magazine,* January 5, 1964, pp. 22, 32,
34, 37, 39. Copyright © 1964 by *The New York Times* Company.
Reprinted by permission of *The New York Times* Company and the author.
RICHARD HAMMER is a writer-editor with The Week in Review
Section of *The New York Times* and author of (among other books)
One Morning in the War: The Tragedy at Son My.

The people will tell you that his block
is a fortress: Its walls are invisible; they
are inside the mind, built by the people
who live on the block and by society
outside. But the walls are as real as if
they were made of mortar and stone;
they keep 3,000 people locked up inside,
afraid, and they keep most outsiders
away, afraid.

The block is in the middle of Spanish
Harlem, a section of New York that runs
roughly from 96th Street to 118th Street
between Fifth Avenue and Park Avenue.
As events constantly make clear, the area
is seething. To the outsider, it is a strange
and unfamiliar and often frightening
world—one he can never know on his
own and one he can understand only

partially even with the most expert help.

Recently I met a young man, 18 years old, for whom Spanish Harlem is home. He was born on the block on which he lives and has spent his entire life on it, in the same small apartment he now shares with his mother, widowed for 10 years, three brothers, three sisters and three other relatives. From all outward signs, Hiram Gonzales (this is not his name) could be a typical 18-year-old from his block. He has grown up in its poverty and faced discrimination all his life because his skin is dark and he is recognizably of Puerto Rican descent. Twice he has dropped out of high school, once from vocational high school in Brooklyn and later from an academic high school in Manhattan.

But Hiram is articulate beyond his education and background, made so by self-education and by an innate brightness and intelligence, and he has thought long and hard about what it is like to grow up and live in Spanish Harlem. He also has a goal and the talent and determination to realize it; he wants to be a professional photographer and he is driven by a desire to return to school and then go on to college. And he has the sensitivity to see into and beneath the sights and sounds and texture of the life around him.

For several nights, we sat together and talked. At first, he was hesitant and wary, looking for something in the interviews other than interest in him and his problems. "To tell you the truth, man," he said later, "I dislike white men because I feel all the injustice that I, my family, my mother, my friends . . . you know, that all of us have gone through." Later, as respect and trust grew, Hiram led me through his world.

"When you walk through my block," he said, "probably the first thing you realize is that there are a lot of people on the streets all the time, from early in the morning to late at night. You'll see that the buildings are old, almost falling apart, but a lot of people have hung curtains in the windows.

"If you are an observing person, you'll notice prostitutes waiting for guys with money, most of them white men from downtown. You'll see drug addicts just moving nowhere; you'll see dope peddlers practically passing the stuff right out in the open. You'll see incidents of theft, you'll just walk along and see them. You'll see a lot of things that are wrong by moral standards and by the moral laws of the rest of society.

"But, man, ever since I was a little kid, this was my block, the block of the fellows who live in it. It was our property and we govern it and we make our own laws and no outsider or no people who don't live in the block can tell us what to do. There are a lot of people who come up and they try to tell us. But, man, they don't understand, they're living in some kind of dream.

"Their standards and ideas don't belong on this block. Because we've been made to feel like we're different, like we don't fit, like we don't belong any place but on our own crummy little block. And there's nobody up here who's going to listen until the white man lets us become a part of his society outside, and I don't mean just a couple of guys who are really exceptional, who've got a lot of brains, but I mean everybody who can make it."

One of the things the rest of society has to understand, Hiram thought, was that the people on his block are not different or strange. "To live on my block," he said, "is to live anywhere where there are a lot of people who are poor and who don't have any place else to go. There's a lot of pain and a lot of sorrow, but underneath there's also a lot of glory and happiness and love. Sure, there are a lot of problems on my block, and maybe more problems than a lot of other places. And everybody on the block knows that you think we brought all the problems with us. Well, man, we didn't. The problems were all here before the people came, or anyway, the things that made the problems. For every unjust act done by the people in my neighborhood, there was an unjust act, directly or indirectly done to these people by society."

By indirect, Hiram meant the often unthinking attitudes of whites. "There was this white woman from downtown," he said, "who sometimes came into the neighborhood to help my mother when she was sick. One day, this woman said to me, 'Now, I don't have anything against the Irish or the Italians, but I just don't like most Negroes and I don't like most Puerto Ricans.'

"Now, man, even though she was helping us when we needed help, I got damn mad. 'Now just a minute,' I said to her, 'how many Puerto Ricans or Negroes do you know? How many do you associate with? Where do you come off saying something like that?'

" 'Well, she told me, 'I see lots of Negro and Puerto Rican boys hanging on the street corners who look tough, and I'm afraid of them.'

" 'You go out to Bedford-Stuyvesant and you'll see plenty of white boys who are just as tough; you go anywhere where people have to live in this kind of filth and you'll see the same damn thing. When you and your kind first came here, you weren't any better.' "

Later, Hiram said, "You know, I'd like to move all the people from Scarsdale, N.Y., right into my block, into the same apartments where some of them have to pay maybe $70 for a couple of crummy little rooms for 10 or 11 people and have to share a bathroom in the hall with the door falling off. Let them live in a place where somebody throws a tire in the furnace and stinks out the place and then the cops come along and tell you that it's nothing and laugh when they're telling you.

"I'll tell you, I think they'd make just as much of a mess as we do, maybe more, because we're used to it, we're used to dodging those weak spots in the floors and not leaning on the wall because it will fall in.

"I don't think those people from Scarsdale could take it. In Scarsdale, the first things the kids learn are how to read and write; that's taken for granted. In my neighborhood, the first things the kids learn are how to fight and steal and not take any crap from anyone. We grow up knowing about narcotics, I mean we don't even remember when we didn't know about them, and everybody just takes that for granted.

"In my block, there are five places where you can buy marijuana cigarettes and I know, even though he's never said anything, that my little brother who's 14 knows where most of them are, that he's known for a long time."

I suggested that nobody forces the kids to use narcotics. "Of course, nobody comes up to us and says, 'Man, here's some pot, you *got* to take a drag; man, here's some horse, you *got* to shoot.' But, man, these little kids look at the teen-agers who are using, and they *look* bigger, and, man, they can laugh and forget everything that's around. So, the little kids think, 'That's a tough man; he's great.' And then they see the pushers and racketeers in their $50 shoes and $100 suits, driving a big car, and they think, 'Man, he's tough; he's into some money and he's doing good.' So, when the pusher talks, they listen."

Hiram told me that by the time the boys on the block get to be 20 probably 95 per cent of them have tried some kinds of drugs and about 40 per cent of them are hooked.

"We aren't fooling ourselves," he said, "when we try drugs. We know what can happen. When I was 13, I saw somebody die of heroin. I went up to the roof of the house next door . . . I think it was to fly my kite . . . anyway, when I came out the door I nearly fell over these addicts who were sort of sitting around in the hallway next to the door. They saw I was only a kid, so they kept right on shooting.

"All of a sudden, I heard a lot of rumbling and this one guy leaped out through the door and started running and turning and jumping all over the roof. Man, he still had the needle sticking in his arm. His friends, and they were still half asleep, sort of staggered out and grabbed him and held him down until he was quiet; then they started walking him back and forth to keep him awake. After a while, they sent me downstairs to get some milk, and more people began coming up to try to help. But nobody could do nothing, and by the time the ambulance got there, he was dead."

Most of the young people in Spanish Harlem are bitter and disillusioned. They sit on the stoops because there isn't anything else most of them can do, and they play cards and they joke. "Our goal is to have a good time, to keep having fun so we don't have to think," said Hiram. "You know what we're doing? We think we're sending the world on its own way while we go on ours. But we know, and, man, that's the trouble, we know that we can't send the world away, that we're part of the world and the world is looking down at us and snarling and laughing at us."

Isn't there, I asked, a desire to get out of the block and into that world to stop that sneering?

"Man, when I was a kid, I used to have dreams that maybe I'd be a scientist and discover all kinds of things. But they were only dreams; when I woke up, there wasn't anything real about them, there couldn't be anything real about them. I've never seen a scientist; I don't understand anything about them; there aren't any scientists, or anybody else who has a big job, on my block so I haven't got the least idea of what they're like. It's hard to even picture them mentally. These things are so far above us they

aren't real. They're like a cloud that looks solid until you grab onto it and find it falls apart in your hands."

The boys on the block feel that even with an education they have no hope of realizing any dreams. "I know guys with a diploma who start looking for jobs. You know what they can get? A stockboy or a delivery boy or something like that, but not something where they feel they can move ahead.

"I've got a friend who wants to be a mathematician and he's a real smart guy. But when he graduated from high school, an academic one, too, not a lousy vocational one like most of us dropped out of, he went looking for a job so he could make the money to go to college. Nobody had nothing for him. Finally, he answered an ad for a lousy bus boy's job in a crummy cafeteria.

You know what they told him? They told him that he had too much education, that they were afraid he would quit. Now this kid would have worked like hell because he needed the money; but he couldn't even get that crummy job, a job any fink who didn't even know how to read could handle."

So most of the boys just sit. They are convinced that if they went back to school, it would not assure them of a decent job; besides, they are disenchanted with the schools themselves. "When I reached sixth grade, I couldn't read," said Hiram. "The teachers, most of them didn't give a damn."

The school, instead of revealing the world, merely mirrored the world the young people from the block already knew. "But when I was in seventh grade, I went to a Catholic school for a year. They put a kind of wrench in my mind and opened it a crack and I began to see that there was a world outside my block. Man, that school cared, about me and about everybody, and they wanted to teach and wanted me to learn.

"Then I went back to public school because, man, the work just got too hard and I wasn't ready for it. In public school, the only thing the teachers wanted was quiet. If they thought we didn't want to learn, they'd sit there smoking and reading and if you got out of line, sometimes they'd curse at you: 'You little spic, sit down.' "

But in that school Hiram's horizons were broadened by one teacher of a subject he hated, English. "One day, the teacher came in and played us 'The Three Penny Opera,' and there was something about this 'Mack the Knife' character that really hit us. We asked him to play it over and over, and the next day he brought in 'West Side Story,' and every day he played us records for a while. Then he began to read to us. He read 'The Old Man and the Sea,' 'The Most Dangerous Game,' and lots of others.

"Now, man, we weren't angels after that; we still carried on, maybe even more because we were getting some freedom, but when that man asked for silence, he got it, and when he began to suggest things, they began to move."

While there were some who managed to get an education, Hiram explained that they paid a terrible price for it. They had to be the teacher's pet, and this put them at the mercy of their fellows, who were not slow to deal out fitting punishment. For most, however, "this was the white man's education, taught the way the white man wanted it taught, without giving it any meaning for us. It was routine, do this and do that, and today we try to escape routine all the time. And it was using things from the white man's world which didn't mean anything to us or things that were so completely against everything we knew that we laughed at them. They even had books telling us what great guys the cops are.

"Now look, man, I know that most cops are just doing their jobs and trying to protect people most of the time. But I've grown up admiring people, I mean *admiring*, who would fight back at cops;

to some extent I still admire them. Why, I think that if right now, right this minute, a cop walked into this room and told me to do something, I don't think I'd do it, just because he was a cop."

This is the way Hiram and his friends see the law. "In my neighborhood the cops feel that they're superior to the people, and, man, they let us know they think they're better than us. They walk into our homes and look around and tell us to open up, and we're afraid, and I mean afraid, to do anything or say anything. We just do what the cops say.

"And they'll come walking down the street and see us sitting on the stoop, and you know what they do? They come up to us asking us who we're going to rape next and what job we're planning to pull, and then they tell us to get moving. Man, it can be our stoop, right in front of our house, with our mothers watching out the windows, and the cops are cursing and, man, even demanding that we show them identification."

Another group of "outsiders," youth board and social workers, also rank low in the opinion of the block, Hiram said. "They're all around the neighborhood and most of them are rat fink types. They act like they think that we're not human. They think they've got all there is and all they've got to do is convert us to think and do what they think and do. Then, everything will be just great. But, man, these jerks pop up in the morning with their little briefcases and they cut out for their homes a hell of a way away around 5 or 6 at night, and that's it. If you ever are nuts enough to go to one of them, they hand you the old crap, 'Now, son, you shouldn't feel that way.'

"Now, look, I don't think these guys mean any harm. I think the least thing they want is to do any harm. But harm comes in many forms."

So Hiram and the people on the block have come to distrust those who arrive with good words and offers of help. They feel that they have only themselves to depend on, that only within their group is there reliability.

"As bad as things are here," Hiram said, "in my lifetime I have seen more good things on this block than I have seen bad. On my block, people help each other and most of them do the right things, for themselves and for everybody. Man, I have seen thieves help other guys; I have seen guys who have to rob for a living, and I mean really rob because they don't have any other way, I have seen them give their money to make another guy a little happier.

"I have seen an addict—and this guy was nearly crying for a fix and practically running across the street to get one —stop and shove his last $3 in the shirt pocket of another guy who was married and had a lot of kids but who couldn't find a job and didn't have any money. And this junkie went walking away, kicking himself and cursing, 'Now, why the hell did I do that?'

"Now, man, this may not sound like much, but that one incident, for me, could equal 50 unjust things, because it shows that these people do have concern about each other, even though it may be hard for them to show it or express it or maybe even to understand it."

The people on the block are not unconscious of the horror and the filth and destitution around them. They know that it is bad and, at times, they talk of leaving it, though few ever do. But now, today, most of them are afraid. They are afraid because their block is going; all around, new housing projects have risen and this is almost the last block to remain unchanged. It will not remain so for long, and the people know it. Hiram said that most of them would not be able to get into the new projects; some because they wouldn't be able to afford the rents, some because they have an addict or a criminal in the family and the rules of projects forbid such tenants.

"The people are going to have to move, like up to the Bronx, and the landlords know that these people are going to need houses, so instead of $50 they'll make it $70 or $100 an apartment; they're already doing it.

"Man, this is the end of my block," said Hiram. "This is something that we all evade; like, this has been going on for five years. All the other blocks have been going, and this has been in my mind, in everybody's mind, but I haven't really given it any thought, but it scares me. I fear it. But wherever, any place, there is poverty and minorities like us, you will find another block like this one, with all the same horrors that we have. Maybe that's where we will have to go. Forget it, man, let me live in this rathole that I have now, that I know, instead of some other new rathole that I don't know."

20. MEXICAN-AMERICANS IN A MIDWEST METROPOLIS

Julian Samora and Richard Lamanna

Mexican-Americans are not an easy group to name or to count correctly. Some people of essentially the same ancestral background as today's residents of, say, Mexico City have been American citizens since the Mexican War. Such people are sometimes called, and call themselves, Spanish-Americans, and live mainly in southern Colorado and New Mexico. In the latter state they may constitute as much as 20 percent of the population, and some belong to families that have been rich and eminent for generations.

Sometimes "Latin American" or merely "Latin" are used, but these terms are too general because Cubans and Puerto Ricans, not to mention people from South America who also live here, are also Latin Americans. "Spanish-speaking" does not work either, for the same reason as well as because many American-born citizens with parents or grandparents who emigrated here from Mexico speak Spanish poorly or not at all. Compounding the difficulty is the inadequacy of using physical appearance as a means of classification, particularly in the absence of cultural cues. The Census relies on an unsatisfactory compromise, estimating the numbers of Mexican-Americans in terms of "Spanish surnames," thus missing people like quarterback Jim Plunkett of the New England Patriots football team.

As long as these terminological difficulties are understood, I see no reason to hesitate in using "Mexican-American" as the most general and accurate term, employing it in the same

Source: University of California at Los Angeles, Mexican-American Study Project, Advance Report No. 8, July 1967. Reprinted by permission of the Regents of the University of California and the authors.

JULIAN SAMORA is Professor of Sociology and RICHARD LAMANNA Associate Professor of Sociology at The University of Notre Dame. Samora is the author of *Los Mojados: The Wetback Story*.

sense as "Italo-American," "Polish American," or "Jewish American." I shall also follow the rather inaccurate but useful Western and Southwestern convention of using the term "Anglo" to refer to the white (that is, non-Mexican, nonblack, non-Oriental, non-Indian) majority. And at times, I shall use "Chicano," a contraction of the Spanish pronunciation of "Mexicano." The term was once derogatory when Anglos used it, but it has now taken on proud connotations. Young Mexican-Americans in particular use it to describe their own group and to differentiate it from people who are citizens of Mexico.

Half of all the Mexican-American people in the United States are American-born children of American-born parents, only about one out of seven having been born in Mexico. In 1960, 80 percent of the population lived in just five states: Arizona, California, Colorado, New Mexico, and Texas. Their number then (according to the Spanish surname count) came to three and a half million people; it is now more than four million, and it has been shifting from Texas (the Mexican-American's Mississippi) to California (his Illinois).

Puerto Ricans and Mexican-Americans are the two large American minority groups based on recent emigration from outside the continental United States. Mainland Puerto Ricans are a smaller group, about a million people, concentrated (although not exclusively) around metropolitan New York. Puerto Rican immigration did not become appreciable until after World War II, while the peak early years for Mexican immigration were 1920–1929. Another difference is that Puerto Ricans became residents of huge cities like New York and Chicago almost immediately upon their arrival. More Mexican-Americans spent some time in rural areas or in the small urban centers serving the agricultural regions where they worked as farm laborers. A final difference concerns ancestry. Puerto Ricans are a composite population, with touches of black and Spanish white along with a trace of Caribbean Indian. Mexican-Americans are generally mestizos, that is, a mixture of Spanish white and Mezo-American Indian.

The most obvious similarities between the two groups are that both share the Spanish language—though many of today's youngsters do not speak it; the predominance of the Roman Catholic faith; and some features of Latin (actually Western Mediterranean) culture such as the paternalistic family and individualistic conceptions of dignity resting on personal honor and pride. Another parallel is that immigration of members of both groups continues. Continued immigration along with the proximity of Mexico and Puerto Rico mean that it is relatively easy for the immigrant to stay up-to-date with developments in those places. The point is not irrelevant. Puerto Rican criticisms of American ethnocentrism and cultural dominance expressed in the Puerto Rican independence movement strike a harmonious note with Mexican-American pride in the Mexican nation's recent rapid economic growth and its conscious emphasis on ancestral indigenous heritage.

It is not farfetched to claim that there are also parallels between Mexican-Americans and blacks. Mexicans were never slaves, but most Mexican immigrants who came to this country were poor and unlettered *campesinos,* peasants who for subsistence worked land over which they had some hereditary-use rights but which they could not own because it belonged to extensive *latifundios* that were the holdings of wealthy *patrones.* The overwhelming majority of Mexican nationals were landless peasants until President Cárdenas' administration (1934–1940) extended agrarian reform and consolidated the Mexican Revolution. In this country the Mexican immigrants were used as cheap labor, and many returned or were driven back to Mexico during the depression of the thirties. They were strikebreakers and unskilled labor, migrant farm workers who found industrial jobs in World War II. In the last few years, potential immigrants have been simultaneously strikebreakers and migrant workers in California's grape and lettuce fields. Growers still hire Mexican citizens for wages Mexican-Americans are beginning to refuse to accept.

Through all of this, Anglos did not hesitate to show their distaste for what they considered an alien culture and inherent racial inferiority. The 1964 Civil Rights Act stopped Texas advertisements for a "neat dependable Anglo short-order cook," or "Waitresses, Colored or Latin." [1] It did not stop, however, Houston's 1970 plan for public school integration, a plan that calls for black and Mexican-American children to go to school together while white children continue having their own schools to themselves.[2] Nor did it stop—until a 1970 court order—the California practice of giving placement tests in English to kids whose home language was Spanish, and then placing them in classes for the retarded if they did not score well.

[1] Paul Bullock, "Employment Problems of the Mexican-American," in John H. Burma (ed.), *Mexican-Americans in the United States* (Cambridge: Schenkman, 1970), p. 154.

[2] I have read that a court ruling has quashed the same sort of plan in Corpus Christi, Texas, but do not know if that ruling will be applied across the state.

Today many Mexican-Americans believe that they may profit from adopting some of the same strategies that have earned new recognition and self-respect for and among black people. Nevertheless, there are also contrary currents of opinion in the group as a whole. For one thing, centuries of oppression in Mexico encouraged a fatalistic perspective in Mexican culture, along with a dependence upon the hope of favors paternalistically granted by those at the top. For another, the assertion of group independence means calling attention to group distinctiveness. Older Mexican-Americans resented the discrimination practiced against them; some tried to insist that they were, after all, Caucasians. Finally, Mexican-Americans share with blacks the tendency of almost all American minority groups to look down on others whom the majority does not accept. Thus, since neither group has a well-established or deep-seated trust and respect toward the other, the possibility of more than temporary black-Chicano alliances seems limited.

In the first of this section's three consecutive papers on Mexican-Americans, Samora and Lamanna describe an atypical community. It is old and well established, but outside the main area of Mexican-American settlement. Many features of the community and its history are similar to those that could have been found in ethnic minority communities around industrial centers as recently as a generation ago. There is concentrated residential settlement stemming from community members' desire for the familiar, from the prohibitive cost of more comfortable housing, and from the resistance of local populations to letting a minority spread. There is a perceived need for children to take education more seriously and to raise their aspirations, but this desire is countered by the possibility of their leaving school early for an initially attractive but ultimately dead-end job. There is the ethnic Catholic parish as the locale of rituals like christenings, weddings, and funerals that bring together family, faith, and group culture even though (and this is also common) adult men are not especially careful about attending mass regularly. There is the combination of parents knowing that their children will face a different world from the one they faced, and wanting to prepare them for it, without quite knowing the most effective ways of doing so.

Nevertheless, one should be wary of assuming that this community is wholly representative of ethnic communities in general. One reason is continuing immigration which helps to maintain traditional culture. Even more important is a continuing pattern of prejudice and discrimination that goes beyond mere ethnic antipathy. Poles were not given boat fare and sent back to Poland, nor Greeks to Greece; and when Irish and Italian students went to the same parochial school, they did not attend segregated classes.

Samora and Lamanna conclude with the observation that the decreased intensity of discrimination should lead to greater assimilation. They are probably right, but there is also the possibility that even as acculturation continues, new Chicano solidarity will make assimilation seem less desirable.

Not far from the "Main Street of the Midwest"—the Indiana East-West Toll Road—in the industrial city of East Chicago, the unsuspecting traveler is likely to be surprised to find a large, well-established colony of Mexican-Americans. Many of us associate Mexican-Americans almost exclusively with the Southwestern states; others assume that all Mexican-Americans outside the Southwest are migrant farm laborers or at least that they got wherever they happen to be in this country by way of the migrant stream. Is it also frequently assumed that this movement of population is of fairly recent origin.

The Mexican-American colony of East Chicago, Indiana, located in that part of the city known as Indiana Harbor, sharply differs from this stereotype. For one thing, it is located in the midst of one of the world's greatest urban-industrial complexes,[1] and the great majority of its residents are employed in manufacturing and heavy industry. Secondly, the colony was founded by Mexicans who were recruited to work in these industries almost half a century ago. Thirdly, unlike any other colony outside the Southwestern states, the Mexican-American settlement of East

[1] Although the population of East Chicago itself is only 57,669 it is part of a larger complex of almost 7 million. The Gary-Hammond-East Chicago Standard Metropolitan Statistical Area had a population of 573,548 in 1960 and the Chicago SMSA a population of 6,220,913.

Chicago has constituted a substantial portion of the total population of the community.

The early Mexican immigrants to the Calumet region came principally from the area north and northwest of Mexico City and "leap-frogged" over the United States's border states to our northern interior. From a small colony of 20 to 30 persons in East Chicago before World War I, it gradually increased and expanded, becoming in time one of the largest concentrations of Mexicans outside the Southwest. This development grew out of the employment opportunities that opened up during World War I, and as industry grew and expanded in the area, so did the number of Mexicans who were recruited and attracted to it. By 1930 there were 5,343 Mexicans in East Chicago, and they constituted 10 percent of the city's population.

Later, during the depression of the 1930's, a mass repatriation of Mexicans took place. A plan was devised for expediting and subsidizing the exodus, at the suggestion of the American Legion of East Chicago. The Legion pointed out that it would cost less to send the Mexicans back home than to keep them on the relief rolls, that the city would be spared the expense of educating their children, and that when conditions improved, the Mexicans would not be on the scene to compete for jobs with American citizens. The Mexicans were more than willing to return to their homeland. The first train left East Chicago in May, 1932, and by the end of the year about 1,800 Mexicans had been sent back to their homeland from East Chicago and almost 1,500 from nearby Gary.[2]

Allowing ourselves a digression, we should like to point out that this massive repatriation was a dramatic example of one of the distinctive features of the Mexican immigration to the United States. Unlike other ethnic minorities in this country, the Mexicans have been able to and have gone back and forth across the border or to the Southwestern states. The Mexican immigrants have frequently not intended to become permanent residents of the United States, or they have been engaged in seasonal work, so that returning to their homeland has been relatively normal for them. Other immigrant groups have sometimes come with the intention of returning to their place of origin but they rarely had similar opportunities, and even more rarely did they avail themselves of the opportunities when they had them.

A change introduced by the Bureau of the Census of 1940, in the racial classification of Mexicans, has made it difficult to establish the number of Mexicans in East Chicago at the time, but 1,358 persons were listed as having been born in Mexico. This population increased steadily during the following two decades—in 1950, 1,867 gave Mexico as their country of birth, and the 1960 Census lists 6,532 persons of Mexican stock (first and second generation), 11.3 percent of the population of East Chicago. However, since Mexicans have resided in the Calumet region for some time, and since many have migrated there from other areas of the United States where they had resided for several

generations, the "foreign stock" group very likely represents only a part of the total population of Mexican ancestry. A more realistic picture of the colony's size can be obtained by considering the ethnic composition of the public schools. In 1965, close to 22 percent of the school children were clearly of Mexican ancestry. Almost two-thirds of these came from homes where Spanish was the customary language. Another 9 percent of the school population was of Puerto Rican background. This means that in 1965, except for the Negro minority (38 percent), the Spanish stock minority constituted the largest (31 percent) single ethnic category in the East Chicago public schools.

Among the first families to settle in East Chicago, in 1838, were to be found the following national groupings: Irish, German, Dutch, Swiss, and native-born Americans. These settlers were followed almost immediately by Russians, Croatians, Hungarians, and the English. By 1895, Greeks, Austrians, Italians, Rumanians, Slovaks, Serbs, Lithuanians, the French, and other national groupings had come to the city. By 1910 more than half (53 percent) of the population of East Chicago was foreign-born representing almost every nationality among the people who had come to the United States. The most heavily represented nations were: Poland, Czechoslovakia, Yugoslavia, Hungary, Rumania, and Mexico. There were few Negroes (28 in 1910) in East Chicago until World War I restricted the flow of the European labor supply. By 1920 there were 1,424 Negroes; 5,088 by 1930; and 13,766 by 1960. The number of Asiatic residents has always been small in East Chicago. Although at various times some Chinese, Japanese, Filipinos, and Indians have lived there, they have never constituted a significant proportion of the population.

Ethnic heterogeneity is still a striking characteristic of the community. The

[2] Paul S. Taylor, *Mexican Labor in the United States: Chicago and the Calumet Region* (Berkeley and Los Angeles: University of California Press, 1932), p. 209.

foreign-born population is dropping off rapidly; however, an examination of public school records indicating the birth place of students and their parents shows some 47 states, the District of Columbia, Puerto Rico, and 36 foreign countries are represented. Included among the foreign countries are such unusual places as China, Turkey, Peru, Egypt, and Argentina. From the United States, Texas, Alabama, and Mississippi have been major points of origin, while Puerto Rico and Mexico have been the biggest sources outside the continental United States. Almost one out of every ten of the students enrolled in 1965 were foreign-born or born in Puerto Rico. The proportion of foreign-born parents is of course much higher. It is apparent that the community is still attracting a considerable number of interregional and international migrants seeking greater economic opportunity.

Residential segregation was in part due to preference for reasons of convenience (proximity to the steel mills) and choice (the tendency for immigrants to prefer areas inhabited by their countrymen), but it was also due to discrimination. Taylor has reported that in practically every major colony of Mexicans in the region there were efforts to drive them out or to isolate them by restricting the boundaries of their residence.[3] The reasons given for opposition to the Mexican were diverse, but they included charges that they were given to fighting and annoying their neighbors, that they were dirty and poor housekeepers, that they were racially undesirable, that they depreciated property values, or simply that the intrusion of another nationality was unwanted. Competition for jobs and women also contributed to the hostility which at times expressed itself in physical assaults and even killings. Incidentally, many of the objections to Mexicans that Taylor has reported were repeated almost verbatim in the comments we heard (in

[3] Ibid.

1965) from Mexican-Americans regarding the Puerto Rican newcomers.

It is apparent that the Spanish surname population—both Mexican-American and Puerto Rican—is highly concentrated in a small part of the total area of East Chicago. One census tract (31) has over 35 percent of all the Mexican-American population in East Chicago and 39 percent of all the Puerto Rican population, while another 44 percent of the Mexican-American population and 39 percent of the Puerto Rican live in three adjoining tracts (30, 32, 34). Almost 80 percent of East Chicago's Spanish surname population resides in these four tracts which constitute only a part of the Indiana Harbor section of East Chicago. The remaining tracts have relatively few Spanish surname persons, but they are likely to have a relatively greater number of more assimilated persons who have been socially mobile and are not recorded by the census as being of Spanish stock, because they are neither first nor second generation Mexican-Americans. It is noteworthy, however, that—just as Taylor noted in 1928 —while there is a considerable amount of segregation, there are some Spanish stock persons residing in each of the tracts of the city and in no tract are they more than 51 percent of the total population.

Although Spanish is still the dominant language of the home even among those of native parentage (64 percent of the Mexican-American students report Spanish as the language at their homes), it appears that this, too, will change in time. For one thing, it is impressive that 8 percent of the students from English-speaking homes were born in Mexico (40 percent of their fathers and 28 percent of their mothers were born there). This indicates that at least some make a rather rapid transition at least as far as language is concerned. It is also apparent that the language of the home is more likely to be English if the students and their parents were born in the United States.

The obvious implication is that the current predominance of Spanish is likely to decline with the passing of the foreign-born generation. Its complete disappearance, however, is far from imminent.

The picture that emerges from an analysis of demographic characteristics is one of a community with an excess of single, unrelated adult males, but also with a substantial number of stable families with very high fertility. It appears from the data we have analyzed that Mexican-American family life in East Chicago has in some ways changed considerably since the 1920's, but that in other ways it has changed very little. The population is still demographically abnormal, and consequently prostitution, divorce, gambling, alcoholism, narcotics addiction, and other dysfunctions are still a problem. On the other hand, family and kinship are still very important. In our discussion with informants, they generally "place" persons in the community by noting to whom they are related, and family connections are still regarded important in the establishment and operation of local businesses. Parental control, moreover, continues to be extreme by American standards. Nevertheless, the family's solidarity reflected in its stability, self-sufficiency, and cultural distinctiveness after so many years in the industrial urban center of East Chicago is quite impressive. It seems clear, the Mexican-American family in East Chicago has held up quite well under the impact of urbanization, industrialization, and acculturation. It still constitutes the major reservoir of the traditional culture and the major link with the mother country. It also constitutes the major focus of conflicts between the old and the new, between the Mexican heritage and the American experience, between the traditional family structure and the demands of an urban-industrial social system. Thus, the family has done well in maintaining the continuity with the past in the face of massive social changes.

A distinct pattern of providing parishes and religious services for nationality groups developed within the Catholic churches in East Chicago. Each group, whether Polish, Slovak, Croatian, Rumanian, Negro, Mexican, or Italian, felt a need to have its separate church, its own pastor who could give services in its native language, or its own idiom (Negro)—and eventually its own schools. Thus, a separatism was created which continues to the present time. While it might have been a good idea in the beginning to create such parishes and such schools to keep the faith intact and to transmit the cultural heritage, it is obvious that such a system has tended to retard the eventual assimilation into the larger community of the various national groups. However, in none of the parochial schools which remain today is the instruction conducted in the native language of the particular group and no significant attempt is made to teach its cultural heritage. To some extent the walls of nationalism are breaking down, though more so among Protestants than among Catholics, Eastern Orthodox people, or Jewish residents; and this is a trend that will continue in the foreseeable future.

[In fact] until very recent years, the Catholic Church in the United States had initiated few special programs or organizations to minister to the large Spanish-speaking population. Where there have been large concentrations of Catholics of Mexican descent, the Church has provided a national church or churches in particular neighborhoods (making them almost segregated churches), but in most instances the loyalty to the Church of the minority population has been taken for granted because of its long tradition of Catholicism. Protestants, on the other hand, have worked actively among this population in the city slums, the small towns, the agricultural migrant streams, providing welfare programs in the form of food, clothing, health clinics, recreational facilities, adult education, and child care centers. The almost complete neglect on the part of Catholic organizations has contrasted dramatically with the active Protestant programs and this contrast has resulted in a number of conversions among Mexican-Americans to the Protestant faith. It would be difficult to estimate the number of converts for any particular region or city, but popular opinion suggests that, although the number is relatively small compared to those who remained Catholics, the number of converts to Protestantism among this population is growing at an increasing rate.

[Still,] many writers who have addressed themselves to the subject of Latin Americans and their relationship to the Catholic church have commented on the deeply religious character of the people and their devotion to the Faith. Most writers have also suggested that this population is at least nominally Catholic and makes efforts to receive and see that their children receive the basic sacraments. Burma states that most Mexican-Americans are nominally Catholic, being baptized, married, and buried in the church. It is chiefly women, old men, and young children, however, who attend church regularly. Adolescents, young adults, and males in general are likely to be indifferent but will not relinquish their bond to the Church.[4] The members of Our Lady of Guadalupe, the local Mexican-American Parish, appear to fit this generalized description. A knowledgeable informant stated that less than 5 percent of the people attended Mass. This percentage is similar to that of participation of the parishioners in voluntary associations.

The present pastor has attempted a number of programs to aid the people in becoming more integrated into the larger society, such as, the parochial school, adult education classes, and English language training, with varying degrees of success.

The dilemma faced by this parish is a familiar one and has confronted most national churches: on the one hand, it was important and necessary in the development of the parish to minister to the people in their native language, showing cognizance of their culture and building the bridge between the parishioners and the dominant society: on the other hand, the persistent use of the native language and the reinforcement of the culture presented a formidable barrier to the eventual assimilation of the people. There is no easy solution to this dilemma. Other national churches in East Chicago and elsewhere have resolved it rather effectively by diminishing the use of the native language, by insisting upon educational achievement, and by establishing programs aimed more at the youth than at the older generation.

Our Lady of Guadalupe, however, has problems that are not easily solved; they will continue in the foreseeable future. Unlike other national parishes, whose immigrant stream dried up years ago, this parish continues to attract immigrants daily, either directly from Mexico or from the southern part of Texas. The open international border has its effect in East Chicago, thousands of miles away. The other contributing factor aggravating this situation is social and geographical mobility. By and large, the more successful and the better educated move from this parish, leaving behind the older, the less successful, and the newly arrived. The pastor and his assistants have had to begin all over again, almost every year, the slow and arduous task of attempting to integrate foreign-culture immigrants into the larger society—a task which normally confronts other national parishes only once. Thus, the failures and successes of this Mexi-

4 John H. Burma, *Spanish-Speaking Groups in the United States* (Durham, N.C.: Duke University Press, 1954), p. 31.

can-American parish must be viewed in the light of the special circumstances in which it was born and had had its being.

The adjustment of the Mexican-American to East Chicago can be described in terms of four major processes on stages:

1. Accommodation

The initial adjustment of Mexican-American migrants was facilitated by the circumstances of their migration. Since they came during periods of labor shortage and, in many cases, were recruited by the employers, there was no question of their acceptance in the community. Moreover, the practices of using them in more or less segregated work crews and providing group quarters for them limited their contact with other groups and enabled them to get by with a minimum of difficulty. The Mexican-Americans, for the most part, stayed out of trouble, and the other residents, although not exactly friendly, refrained from overt hostility except during periods of economic stress (e.g., when Mexican-Americans were used to break the steel strike of 1919 and during the depression of the 1930's). The preponderance of young unmarried males, however, did present some problems in the early years. But, all in all, the group accommodated smoothly to the new situation.

Individuals and families who have since migrated to East Chicago have also managed the transition smoothly—due in no small part to the pattern of chain-migration that in effect puts each arriving immigrant in touch with a circle of friends and relations who can provide him with material, social, and psychological support until he gets settled. New immigrants, on the other hand, can count on little assistance from the dominant community in getting settled. The data on the poor performance of recent migrants on the selective service examinations and the virtual absence of special English-language courses or adult education programs suggest that the new immigrant can count on little more than a handout from the township-trustees office.

2. Economic Integration

The Mexican-American immigrants have been quickly and smoothly integrated into the economy of East Chicago. The availability of good-paying, steady, unskilled and unionized employment opportunities in the steel mills have provided them with the economic security so necessary for further advance. The general consensus has been that the Mexican-Americans have made excellent workers and that in some cases they have been much preferred as workers to members of other ethnic groups. With the notable exception of the mass repatriation to Mexico in the 1930's and during the occasional recessions in the steel industry in recent years, the Mexican-Americans of East Chicago have had little difficulty adjusting to the economy of the region. However, because of the character of that economy and the limited educational achievement of the group, its economic integration has remained more or less frozen at this basic level. Mexican-Americans employed in East Chicago have been concentrated in a few industries, and at the lower pay and status levels. This has, in part, been due to the limited range of occupational opportunities available in a place like East Chicago and the fact that individuals who qualify for other types of positions simply leave the community. But, compared to the income and occupational distribution of other groups in the community, it is apparent that Mexican-Americans have not been very successful in obtaining higher level positions in industry and business. This has undoubtedly been due in part to a past and present discrimination, but perhaps more importantly to the social and cul-

tural characteristics of the group involved—that is, language, education, and
motivational problems.

3. Cultural Integration

The cultural integration of the Mexican-
American follows a rather mixed pattern
and is strongly related to recency of
migration and age. One still finds in the
community many cultural elements reminiscent of situations in the society which
the immigrants left and which may be a
hindrance to certain aspects of cultural
integration. The services of the ethnic
churches (both Catholic and Protestant)
are a case in point. The Spanish-lan-
guage newspapers, movies, and radio
programs, the dances, music, Mexican
Independence celebrations, the restaurants and stores featuring Mexican food,
and the work of the consular officials,
still make the group and its culture very
"visible," although many of these services, activities and cultural elements
become pervaded with the "American" influence. Facility in the English language
is still a problem for a considerable number, and even many Mexican-American
natives of East Chicago have pronounced
accents and distinctive gestures. Social
roles, although they have undergone
some changes, have remained remarkably
traditional—especially the parental roles
and the role of women. They have not
as yet acquired, to any great extent, the
achievement motivation so prominent in
the larger society. The problems in educational performance (age-grade retardation, high drop-out rate, non-academic
curriculum, and limited higher education) reflect both the community's failure to meet the needs of this group and
the group's failure to adapt its values
and aspirations to the host society. But
there are signs of change—the strain
noted in family relations and the increasing value being placed on education, as
evidenced by the publicity and fuss made
over youngsters who graduate or go to

college—these suggest a growing amount
of acculturation on the part of the Mexican-Americans. However, there remain
sharp and clearly visible cultural differences between them, as a group, and the
rest of the community. Individuals who
learn to think and act like Anglos are
more likely than not to drift off to a
larger city in the United States, to seek
greater opportunity, thus depriving the
remaining residents of the small community of role models and assimilating
leadership.

Although residents take pride in the
cosmopolitan character of the Mexican-
American community, there is actually
not much evidence of other groups adopting elements of the Mexican culture. Assimilation for the most part means con-
forming to Anglo-American models.

4. Social Integration

The structure of social relationships in
the Mexican-American community of
East Chicago is still for the most part
separate and distinct from that of other
groups. Except in the area of employment and the unions, Mexican-Americans tend to restrict their informal interactions to other Mexican-Americans and
to belong almost exclusively to ethnic organizations and groups. Many of them
lack citizenship, and there is a great deal
of sentimental nationalism still expressed. Voting participation is low even
among the native born, and they have
not as yet succeeded in developing any
significant power or influence in the political arena. In the estimation of most
observers there has been a significant
decline in prejudice and discrimination
against the Mexican-Americans but this
has not resulted as yet in any major
change in the patterns of social interaction. There is an increasing amount of
residential dispersion but the group is
still highly concentrated and consequently tends to be institutionally segregated (e.g., churches, schools). Volun-

tary associations and friendship groups still generally follow ethnic lines, and the amount of intermarriage remains insignificant. In short, ethnicity remains an important, if not the most important, status-defining characteristic for Mexican-American as well as most other groups in East Chicago. The assimilation process in East Chicago has resembled a mixing bowl rather than a melting pot. There has been a surprising amount of success in preserving the social and cultural identity of the different immigrant groups that have settled there. The signs of change, however, are also apparent. The breakage of ethnic neighborhoods, the decline of the national parishes and their parochial schools, the declining number and proportion of foreign-born persons—all suggest that the population will undergo more assimilation, but it remains problematic how much and what kind.

FACTORS INFLUENCING THE PACE OF ASSIMILATION

Some writers have in fact been somewhat naive in discussing the problem. McWilliams, for example, writing in 1948, claimed that: "It is a foregone conclusion that the northern Mexican settlement will have largely vanished in another generation," [5] and Burma, writing in 1954, stated that: "the adult Mexican immigrant keeps his old ways because he does not know any other," but that he rapidly takes on the Anglo culture when given the opportunity.[6] Both of these statements are questionable, as we have shown.

It would be useful to examine the experience of Mexican-Americans in East Chicago in the light of factors generally assumed to influence the assimilation process. As Heller notes: "Although the limited assimilation and acculturation of Mexican-Americans have often been commented on by social scientists, there are very few scholarly studies of the factors accounting for this situation." [7] We have attempted in this study to make a contribution to the isolation of the factors of which Heller speaks. The summary of our findings follows.

CHARACTERISTICS OF THE MEXICAN IMMIGRANTS

1. Goals and Intentions

An immigrant who does not intend to settle permanently will usually make little effort to integrate. It is clear that most of the early settlers in East Chicago intended to return to Mexico; moreover, the group as a whole, both then and now, has not been clearly committed to an assimilationist goal. It has generally made the minimal changes necessary to cope with the East Chicago situation, but it has never really questioned the value or desirability of preserving its separate existence. In this respect, as others have noted, the Mexican-American is somewhat differently oriented in terms of ideology than most American minority groups.[8] Its expectations have been more or less limited to economic ends.

2. Predisposition to Change

Coming from a folk society, Mexican-American immigrants were little prepared to accept rapid social change, in general, and assimilation, in particular. Even more recent migrants have come from more stable and traditional communities that do not predispose them to accept the changes that assimilation implies.

[5] Carey McWilliams, *North From Mexico* (Philadelphia: J. B. Lippincott Co., 1948), p. 223.
[6] Burma, *op. cit.*, p. 125.

[7] Celia S. Heller, *Mexican American Youth: Forgotten Youth at the Crossroads* (New York: Random House, 1966), p. 19.
[8] McWilliams, *op. cit.*, p. 207.

3. Size of the Group

The group, almost from the beginning, because of the organized nature of the migration, was large enough to provide mutual reinforcement and to eventually support the full range of separate community institutions. Moreover, because of its size, it encountered more organized resistance to its dispersion in the community. A smaller migration or settlement would likely have undergone more assimilation.

4. Physical "Visibility"

The physical "visibility" of most Mexican-Americans was probably also an obstacle to assimilation, especially at the individual level, although their success in "redefining" themselves as Caucasians eliminated this barrier at least formally.

5. Socioeconomic Status

Immigrants are generally of a lower status than the host population, but in the case of the Mexican-Americans there is no doubt that their extremely low educational, income, and occupational levels presented especially severe obstacles to their assimilation.

6. Marital and Family Status

Although Humphrey contends that single persons acculturated faster than married immigrants, it appears to us that the excess of unmarried males tended to retard the assimilation of the group.[9] The children of married migrants, exposed as they are to the dominant culture, act as bridges between the two cultures. Single adults, on the other hand, are likely to be more isolated from the dominant group and to retain their original culture longer.

[9] Norman D. Humphrey, "The Changing Structure of the Detroit Mexican Family: An Index of Acculturation," *American Sociological Review,* 9 (1944), 622–627.

7. Kinship Ties

Strong ties of sentiment to the extended family, the *Compadrazgo* system, and place of origin account for both the continued contact with Mexico, the Southwest, and things Mexican, and the pattern of chain migration that replenishes the immigrant colony. The familial ties also partially account for the persistence of the residentially segregated colony. Moreover, a well-integrated, self-sufficient group is less susceptible to change than a less integrated one.

8. Proximity and Access to Homeland

It is generally felt that the greater the proximity and access to the homeland, the slower the rate of assimilation. There is little question but that this has made a difference. In comparison to the Southwest, the Mexican-American in East Chicago has been relatively isolated from Mexico; but in comparison to European immigrant groups, the homeland is physically and psychologically much closer.

9. The Pattern of Migration

The rapid initial influx and continued chain migration is a pattern that is likely to maximize the "holding" power of the old culture. The open border makes this cultural influx possible.

10. Length of Residence

Assimilation, as we noted, is a slow, gradual process. The longer an immigrant group is in a country, the more assimilated it is likely to be. Even though the first Mexicans arrived some time ago, the bulk of the population is of fairly recent origin, as evidenced by the birthplaces of school children and their parents. The host society has literally not yet had an opportunity to make a great impact on the bulk of this population.

11. Fertility

The relatively high fertility of the more unassimilated Mexican-Americans also has a retarding effect on the assimilation of the group. A relatively young population consisting of large households is not socially mobile nor economically independent enough to make certain decisions toward assimilation.

12. Reaction to Prejudice and Discrimination

The fierce pride and sensitivity of the Mexican-American leads him to react to slights and hostile sentiments by withdrawing and cultivating pride of "La Raza," which further deters his assimilation. Many, for example, think Negroes are foolish "to want to go where they are not wanted—we're too proud for that." Even when there is no desire to be excluded, one cannot detect any great desire by this minority to be included.

13. Value Orientation

The very nature of some of the value orientations of the Mexican-Americans presents a barrier to their rapid assimilation. There is a note of fatalism and resignation in the attitudes and behavior of the residents and an orientation to the present (not unlike that described by Kluckhohn in connection with the Southwest) that would have to change somewhat before they could be expected to achieve significant changes in their social situation.

14. Individualism and Leadership

Individual leaders can frequently make a great deal of difference either in opposing or encouraging assimilation, but in a fragmented community, like the East Chicago Mexican-American one, one is tempted to conclude that it remains unassimilated by default—no one does or can lead effectively. This lack of organization and cohesion has other consequences as well. Assimilation becomes an individual matter—individuals pursue their goals and, if they succeed, they move up and out of the community. There is no concerted effort to change the position of the group comparable to the civil rights activities of Negro organizations.

The voluntary organizations, although oriented to greater participation of their membership in the dominant community, have yet to put together significant programs which are meaningful to the members and would help them realize their goals in the broader community.

15. Religion

Although the national church is quite concerned that its members become integrated in the community, the Catholicism of the immigrant does not predispose him to active participation in the Church programs. The continual new immigration also forces the Church to offer services and programs which are not conducive to full assimilation (e.g., services in Spanish and ethnic sodalities).

The Protestant church appeals more to the lower socioeconomic classes, and its services and programs are even less assimilative.

CHARACTERISTICS OF THE EAST CHICAGO COMMUNITY

1. The Recency and Rapidity of Development

East Chicago grew very rapidly, and the Mexicans arrived at a fairly early point in the development of the community and were aided by the steel industry in their adjustment to the new situation. The subsequent stabilization of the population and the economy, however, has ended this early opportunity, and group assimilation is likely to be very slow and difficult in the future, especially if automation leads to the displacement of large numbers of unskilled steel workers.

2. General Socio-Cultural Features

It is generally agreed that modern urban industrial communities, which ask the immigrants to fulfill more universal roles, afford a better climate for immigrant assimilation than rural folk societies. East Chicago has provided a situation in which an incredible variety of people have integrated into a productive community.

3. Cultural Heterogeneity

The fact that East Chicago has included such a conglomeration of ethnic groups has made it that much easier for newcomers to have their differences respected, or at least tolerated. But it has also complicated the matter of assimilation—when virtually everything and everyone is in some sense "foreign," there is no point in giving up one's native culture only to take up someone else's "foreign" attributes.

4. Ecological Structure

The peculiar ecological structure of East Chicago has also retarded the assimilation of Mexican-Americans. Normal dispersion out of the area of first settlement has been impeded by the physical barriers that fragment the community. Such "natural" barriers tended to box in the various subcommunities, increase the residents' consciousness of differences, and make access to other parts of town more difficult.

5. Industrial Specialization

The limited types of employment opportunities in the area have given the community a very special character. There have been relatively few middle class white-collar type positions and relatively few opportunities for women. Consequently, the better-educated are encouraged to leave the community, and women are forced to restrict themselves to the domestic role, both of which tend to retard the assimilation of the group.

6. Absence of Formal Assistance

The assimilation of Mexican-Americans could have been facilitated by the provision of formal programs to aid them in making the transition. Little was or is being done in the way of adult education, family guidance, compensatory education for Spanish-speaking children, vocational education. Some of the agencies dealing with this population do not even have staff members who are fluent in Spanish.

7. Unfavorable Attitudes

The hostility of many elements of the community—not as pronounced now as in the past—is still a factor in the cultural and social isolation of the group. It is difficult to assess the extent to which discrimination has actually held back the group, but it seems certain to have slowed the process of assimilation—as, for example, the segregation of classes in the parochial school at the insistence of the Polish group when the two schools were merged.

RELATIONSHIP BETWEEN THE MEXICANS AND THE COMMUNITY

1. Cultural Differences

It is generally felt that the more nearly alike the host and immigrant cultures, the easier and more thorough the assimilation. We found support for Kluckhohn's contention that the slow rate of

Mexican-American assimilation is, at least in part, the result of sharp differences between the "deeply rooted" value orientations of the original Mexican culture and the value orientations of the newer dominant American society.[10] The differences in language and even religion have also proven formidable. The Catholicism of the Spanish is both socially and ideologically differentiated from that of the European immigrants of East Chicago.

2. The Ratio of the Two Groups

The larger ratio of the minority group to the resident population, the slower the rate of assimilation. This seems to be true for two reasons: a large ratio is likely to prove threatening to the resident population and elicit hostility from them, and, on the other hand, a larger proportion is likely to give the minority the internal resources and confidence to maintain its identity and distinctiveness. In East Chicago, assimilation does not seem to be as extensive as in many Northern centers, where the migrants constitute a very small part of the total population, but it seems to be more extensive than in the border counties, where Anglos are in a minority.

3. Contact and Isolation

Generally speaking, the greater the contact between immigrant and host community members, the greater the degree of assimilation. The contacts between Mexican-Americans and other residents of East Chicago have been severely limited by a number of factors: First, language problems have caused employers to assign workers to homogeneous work crews, sometimes even supervised by a member of their own group. Second, traditional values and limited work op-

portunities have kept women in the home and close to their traditional domestic role. Third, the strong preference for Mexican brides has kept intermarriage at a much lower level than one would have expected considering the sex ratio of the group. Fourth, the pattern of settlement, making for a high degree of concentration in separate neighborhoods even in the age of the automobile, has encouraged exclusiveness and has limited social contacts with others. Finally, institutional segregation in the schools and churches has had the same consequence. Although the schools are not as rigidly segregated as in some parts of the Southwest, the enrollments are ethnically imbalanced in both the public and parochial schools. The crucial importance of this factor is pointed up by Heller's Los Angeles study showing that school integration was the most salient factor associated with ambition among Mexican-American youth.[11] The organization of the churches in East Chicago has also contributed to this isolation. Unlike the Southwest, however, the non-Spanish Catholic population is large in East Chicago, and there is some evidence that, under pressure from the Bishop, in time both schools and parishes will cease to be organized along national lines. The discontinuation of the Our Lady of Guadalupe School and the increasing tendency on the part of Mexican-Americans who live outside the colony to affiliate with the nearest parish are encouraging signs.

4. Crisis Situations

Two crises situations also played a role in retarding the assimilation of Mexican-Americans. Both were related to situations in which the newcomers suddenly posed a threat to the economic security of the older resident population. The first came with the steel strike of 1919 and the use of Mexicans as strikebreak-

[10] Florence R. Kluckhohn and Fred Strodtbeck, *Variations in Value Orientation* (New York: Row, Peterson, 1961), pp. 175–257.

[11] Heller, *op. cit.,* pp. 86–87.

ers—this soured relations for some time. The second, and more serious, was the mass repatriation in the early 1930s, when several thousand unemployed Mexicans and Mexican-Americans were loaded on trains and returned to Mexico. Although many returned later, this action seriously disrupted the community and wiped out much of the progress which had been made up to that time.

The East Chicago Mexican-American community is in many important respects unique, and, although we hope that our study will be of some help in understanding the situation of Mexican-Americans in general, we remind the reader that this is by no means a typical community. It differs from most Northern colonies in that its population is less transient, that it is *not* composed of agricultural workers who dropped off the migrant stream, and, finally, that the settlement is older, larger, and constitutes a larger proportion of the total population than in most other places in the North.

Compared to the Southwest, the settlement is more intensely urban, smaller in terms of aggregate numbers, further from the border, more heavily industrialized and economically secure. The Mexicans are immigrants rather than indigenous, the dominant groups are of European immigrant stock and not "old" Americans, many of the "others" are also Catholic, in contrast to the predominantly Protestant Anglos of the Southwest, and the intergroup situation is more complex compared to the Southwest.

It appears that group assimilation has been limited and slow. Individual assimilation appears to have been more extensive, but, because of its nature and the nature of the community, its extent is difficult to gauge. . . . It appears that East Chicago functions as a way station on the road to *individual* assimilation—a place where families can find employment and economic security that satisfies most and provides the resources and motivation for a few to attain more. The community currently lacks the "holding power" to train its more assimilated elements, and, given the nature of East Chicago, this is unlikely to change. Moreover, as long as the colony continues to be fed by a stream of new migrants and as long as its fertility remains high, Mexican-Americans as a group cannot expect to assimilate much more than they have. A crisis brought on by the latent conflict between the high drop-out rate and shrinking employment opportunities for the unskilled, could, on the other hand, radically change the picture by encouraging a new emphasis on education and, perhaps, by generating the motivation for a social movement that would seek improvement in the group's position.

21. THE MUTUAL IMAGES AND EXPECTATIONS OF ANGLO-AMERICANS AND MEXICAN-AMERICANS

Ozzie Simmons

In the selection that follows, Simmons compares the attitudes of two groups toward one another. Rather than presenting quantitative data, he describes group members' feelings and beliefs, showing how they relate to the groups' cultures and relative social statuses. The dominant Anglo-Americans think that Mexicans are inferior, incapable, or unmotivated to improve themselves. The Mexican-Americans, especially those in the middle class, call attention to the hypocrisy implied in the Anglo definition of the situation and see no reason why they should not try to retain enough of their own traditional culture to have the best of both worlds. Simmons clearly reveals two important reasons why neither group understands the other. Both groups have their perceptions rooted in different basic values, and these differences are reinforced by the attempts of Anglos to maintain their actual material advantages and their sense of superiority.

Source: *Daedalus,* Vol. 90, No. 2 (Spring 1961), pp. 286–99. Reprinted by permission of the American Academy of Arts and Sciences.

OZZIE SIMMONS, Program Advisor for the Ford Foundation has written widely on Latin American topics and is also co-author of *The Mental Patient Comes Home.*

A number of psychological and sociological studies have treated ethnic and racial stereotypes as they appear publicly in the mass media and also as held privately by individuals.[1] The present paper is based on data collected for a study of a number of aspects of the relations between Anglo-Americans and Mexican-Americans in a South Texas community, and is concerned with the principal assumptions and expectations that Anglo- and Mexican-Americans hold of one another; how they see each other; the extent to which these pictures are realistic; and the implications of their intergroup relations and cultural differences for the fulfillment of their mutual expectations.[2]

THE COMMUNITY

The community studied (here called "Border City") is in South Texas, about 250 miles south of San Antonio. Driving south from San Antonio, one passes over vast expanses of brushland and grazing country, then suddenly comes upon acres of citrus groves, farmlands rich with vegetables and cotton, and long rows of palm trees. This is the "Magic Valley,"

an oasis in the semidesert region of South Texas. The Missouri Pacific Railroad (paralleled by Highway 83, locally called "The longest street in the world") bisects twelve major towns and cities of the Lower Rio Grande Valley between Brownsville, near the Gulf of Mexico, and Rio Grande City, 103 miles to the west.

Border City is neither the largest nor the smallest of these cities, and is physically and culturally much like the rest. Its first building was constructed in 1905. By 1920 it had 5,331 inhabitants, and at the time of our study these had increased to an estimated 17,500. The completion of the St. Louis, Brownsville, and Mexico Railroad in 1904 considerably facilitated Anglo-American immigration to the Valley. Before this the Valley had been inhabited largely by Mexican ranchers, who maintained large haciendas in the traditional Mexican style based on peonage. Most of these haciendas are now divided into large or small tracts that are owned by Anglo-Americans, who obtained them through purchase or less legitimate means. The position of the old Mexican-American landowning families has steadily deteriorated, and today these families, with a few exceptions, are completely overshadowed by the Anglo-Americans, who have taken over their social and economic position in the community.

The Anglo-American immigration into the Valley was paralleled by that of the Mexicans from across the border, who were attracted by the seemingly greater opportunities for farm labor created by the introduction of irrigation and the subsequent agricultural expansion. Actually, there had been a small but steady flow of Mexican immigration into South Texas that long antedated the Anglo-American immigration.[3] At present, Mex-

[1] See John Harding, Bernard Kutner, Harold Proshansky, and Isidor Chein, "Prejudice and Ethnic Relations," in Gardner Lindzey (ed.), *Handbook of Social Psychology* (Cambridge, Addison-Wesley Publishing Company, 1954), vol. 2, pp. 1021–1061; and Otto Klineberg, *Tensions Affecting International Understanding*, New York, Social Science Research Council, 1950, Bulletin 62.

[2] The term "Anglo-American," as is common in the Southwest, refers to all residents of Border City who do not identify themselves as Spanish-speaking and of Mexican descent. The Anglo-Americans of Border City have emigrated there from all parts of the United States and represent a wide variety of regional and ethnic backgrounds. The terms "Mexican-American" and "Mexican," as used here, refer to all residents of Border City who are Spanish-speaking and of Mexican descent. The term "Spanish-speaking" is perhaps less objectionable to many people, but for present purposes is even less specific than Mexican or Mexican-American, since it also refers to ethnic groups that would have no sense of identification with the group under consideration here.

[3] For the historical background of the Valley, see Frank C. Pierce, *A Brief History of the Lower Rio Grande Valley*, Menasha, George Banta Publishing Company, 1917; Paul S. Taylor, *An American-Mexican Frontier*, Chapel Hill, University of

ican-Americans probably constitute about two-fifths of the total population of the Valley.

In Border City, Mexican-Americans comprise about 56 percent of the population. The southwestern part of the city, adjoining and sometimes infiltrating the business and industrial areas, is variously referred to as "Mexiquita," "Mexican-town," and "Little Mexico" by the city's Anglo-Americans, and as the *colonia* by the Mexican-Americans. With few exceptions, the *colonia* is inhabited only by Mexican-Americans, most of whom live in close proximity to one another in indifferently constructed houses on tiny lots. The north side of the city, which lies across the railroad tracks, is inhabited almost completely by Anglo-Americans. Its appearance is in sharp contrast to that of the *colonia* in that it is strictly residential and displays much better housing.

In the occupational hierarchy of Border City, the top level (the growers, packers, canners, businessmen, and professionals) is overwhelmingly Anglo-American. In the middle group (the white-collar occupations) Mexicans are prominent only where their bilingualism makes them useful, for example, as clerks and salesmen. The bottom level (farm laborers, shed and cannery workers, and domestic servants) is overwhelmingly Mexican-American.

These conditions result from a number of factors, some quite distinct from the reception accorded Mexican-Americans by Anglo-Americans. Many Mexican-Americans are still recent immigrants and are thus relatively unfamiliar with Anglo-American culture and urban living, or else persist in their tendency to live apart and maintain their own institutions whenever possible. Among their disadvantages, however, the negative attitudes and discriminatory practices of the Anglo-American group must

be counted. It is only fair to say, with the late Ruth Tuck, that much of what Mexican-Americans have suffered at Anglo-American hands has not been perpetrated deliberately but through indifference, that it has been done not with the fist but with the elbow.[4] The average social and economic status of the Mexican-American group has been improving, and many are moving upward. This is partly owing to increasing acceptance by the Anglo-American group, but chiefly to the efforts of the Mexican-Americans themselves.

ANGLO-AMERICAN ASSUMPTIONS AND EXPECTATIONS

Robert Lynd writes of the dualism in the principal asumptions that guide Americans in conducting their everyday life and identifies the attempt to "live by contrasting rules of the game" as a characteristic aspect of our culture.[5] This pattern of moral compromise, symptomatic of what is likely to be only vaguely a conscious moral conflict, is evident in Anglo-American assumptions and expectations with regard to Mexican-Americans, which appear both in the moral principles that define what intergroup relations ought to be, and in the popular notions held by Anglo-Americans as to what Mexican-Americans are "really" like. In the first case there is a response to the "American creed," which embodies ideals of the essential dignity of the individual and of certain inalienable rights to freedom, justice, and equal opportunity. Accordingly, Anglo-Americans believe that Mexican-Americans must be accorded full acceptance and equal status in the larger society. When their orientation to these ideals is uppermost, Anglo-Americans believe that the assimilation of the Mexican-Americans is only a matter of time, contingent solely

North Carolina Press, 1934; and Florence J. Scott, *Historical Heritage of the Lower Rio Grande*, San Antonio, The Naylor Company, 1937.

[4] Ruth D. Tuck, *Not with the Fist*, New York, Harcourt Brace and Company, 1946.
[5] Robert S. Lynd, *Knowledge for What?* Princeton, Princeton University Press, 1948.

on the full incorporation of Anglo-American values and ways of life.

These expectations regarding the assimilation of the Mexican are most clearly expressed in the notion of the "high type" of Mexican. It is based on three criteria: occupational achievement and wealth (the Anglo-American's own principal criteria of status) and command of Anglo-American ways. Mexican-Americans who can so qualify are acceptable for membership in the service clubs and a few other Anglo-American organizations and for limited social intercourse. They may even intermarry without being penalized or ostracized. Both in their achievements in business and agriculture and in wealth, they compare favorably with middle-class Anglo-Americans, and they manifest a high command of the latter's ways. This view of the "high type" of Mexican reflects the Anglo-American assumption that Mexicans are assimilable; it does not necessarily insure a full acceptance of even the "high type" of Mexican or that his acceptance will be consistent.

The assumption that Mexican-Americans will be ultimately assimilated was not uniformly shared by all the Anglo-Americans who were our informants in Border City. Regardless of whether they expressed adherence to this ideal, however, most Anglo-Americans expressed the contrasting assumption that Mexican-Americans are essentially inferior. Thus the same people may hold assumptions and expectations that are contradictory, although expressed at different times and in different situations. As in the case of their adherence to the ideal of assimilability, not all Anglo-Americans hold the same assumptions and expectations with respect to the inferiority of Mexican-Americans; and even those who agree vary in the intensity of their beliefs. Some do not believe in the Mexican's inferiority at all; some are relatively moderate or skeptical, while others express extreme views with considerable emotional intensity.

Despite this variation, the Anglo-Americans' principal assumptions and expectations emphasize the Mexicans' presumed inferiority. In its most characteristic pattern, such inferiority is held to be self-evident. As one Anglo-American woman put it, "Mexicans are inferior because they are so typically and and naturally Mexican." Since they are so obviously inferior, their present subordinate status is appropriate and is really their own fault. There is a ready identification between Mexicans and menial labor, buttressed by an image of the Mexican worker as improvident, undependable, irresponsible, childlike, and indolent. If Mexicans are fit for only the humblest labor, there is nothing abnormal about the fact that most Mexican workers are at the bottom of the occupational pyramid, and the fact that most Mexicans are unskilled workers is sufficient proof that they belong in that category.

Associated with the assumption of Mexican inferiority is that of the homogeneity of this group—that is, all Mexicans are alike. Anglo-Americans may classify Mexicans as being of "high type" and "low type" and at the same time maintain that "a Mexican is a Mexican." Both notions serve a purpose, depending on the situation. The assumption that all Mexicans are alike buttresses the assumption of inferiority by making it convenient to ignore the fact of the existence of a substantial number of Mexican-Americans who represent all levels of business and professional achievement. Such people are considered exceptions to the rule.

ANGLO-AMERICAN IMAGES OF MEXICAN-AMERICANS

To employ Gordon Allport's definition, a stereotype is an exaggerated belief associated with a category, and its function is to justify conduct in relation to that category.[6] Some of the Anglo-American images of the Mexican have no ascertainable basis in fact, while others have at least a kernel of truth. Although some components of these images derive from behavior patterns that are characteristic of some Mexican-Americans in some situations, few if any of the popular generalizations about them are valid as stated, and none is demonstrably true of all. Some of the images of Mexican-Americans are specific to a particular area of intergroup relations, such as the image of the Mexican-American's attributes as a worker. Another is specific to politics and describes Mexicans as ready to give their votes to whoever will pay for them or provide free barbecues and beer.[7] Let us consider a few of the stereotypical beliefs that are widely used on general principles to justify Anglo-American practices of exclusion and subordination.

One such general belief accuses Mexican-Americans of being unclean. The examples given of this supposed characteristic most frequently refer to a lack of personal cleanliness and environmental hygiene and to a high incidence of skin ailments ascribed to a lack of hygienic practices. Indeed, there are few immigrant groups, regardless of their ethnic background, to whom this defect has not been attributed by the host society, as well as others prominent in stereotypes of the Mexican. It has often been observed that for middle-class Americans cleanliness is not simply a matter of keeping clean but is also an index to the morals and virtues of the individual. It is largely true that Mexicans tend to be much more casual in hygienic practices than Anglo-Americans. Moreover, their

[6] Gordon W. Allport, *The Nature of Prejudice,* Cambridge, Addison-Wesley Publishing Company, 1954.

[7] For an analysis of Mexican-American value orientations and behavior in the occupational and political spheres, see Ozzie G. Simmons, Anglo-Americans and Mexican-Americans in South Texas: A Study in Dominant-Subordinate Group Relations (unpublished doctoral dissertation, Harvard University, 1952).

labor in the field, the packing sheds, and the towns is rarely clean work, and it is possible that many Anglo-Americans base their conclusions on what they observe in such situations. There is no evidence of a higher incidence of skin ailments among Mexicans than among Anglo-Americans. The belief that Mexicans are unclean is useful for rationalizing the Anglo-American practice of excluding Mexicans from any situation that involves close or allegedly close contact with Anglo-Americans, as in residence, and the common use of swimming pools and other recreational facilities.

Drunkenness and criminality are a pair of traits that have appeared regularly in the stereotypes applied to immigrant groups. They have a prominent place in Anglo-American images of Mexicans. If Mexicans are inveterate drunkards and have criminal tendencies, a justification is provided for excluding them from full participation in the life of the community. It is true that drinking is a popular activity among Mexican-Americans and that total abstinence is rare, except among some Protestant Mexican-Americans. Drinking varies, however, from the occasional consumption of a bottle of beer to the heavy drinking of more potent beverages, so that the frequency of drinking and drunkenness is far from being evenly distributed among Mexican-Americans. Actually, this pattern is equally applicable to the Anglo-American group. The ample patronage of bars in the Anglo-American part of Border City, and the drinking behavior exhibited by Anglo-Americans when they cross the river to Mexico indicate that Mexicans have no monopoly on drinking or drunkenness. It is true that the number of arrests for drunkenness in Border City is greater among Mexicans, but this is probably because Mexicans are more vulnerable to arrest. The court records in Border City show little difference in the contributions made to delinquency and crime by Anglo- and Mexican-Americans.

Another cluster of images in the Anglo-American stereotype portrays Mexican-Americans as deceitful and of a "low" morality, as mysterious, unpredictable, and hostile to Anglo-Americans. It is quite possible that Mexicans resort to a number of devices in their relations with Anglo-Americans, particularly in relations with employers, to compensate for their disadvantages, which may be construed by Anglo-Americans as evidence of deceitfulness. The whole nature of the dominant-subordinate relationship does not make for frankness on the part of Mexicans or encourage them to face up directly to Anglo-Americans in most intergroup contacts. As to the charge of immorality, one need only recognize the strong sense of loyalty and obligation that Mexicans feel in their familial and interpersonal relations to know that the charge is baseless. The claim that Mexicans are mysterious and deceitful may in part reflect Anglo-American reactions to actual differences in culture and personality, but like the other beliefs considered here, is highly exaggerated. The imputation of hostility to Mexicans, which is manifested in a reluctance to enter the *colonia,* particularly at night, may have its kernel of truth, but appears to be largely a projection of the Anglo-American's own feelings.

All three of these images can serve to justify exclusion and discrimination: if Mexicans are deceitful and immoral, they do not have to be accorded equal status and justice; if they are mysterious and unpredictable, there is no point in treating them as one would a fellow Anglo-American; and if they are hostile and dangerous, it is best that they live apart in colonies of their own.

Not all Anglo-American images of the Mexican are unfavorable. Among those usually meant to be complimentary are the beliefs that all Mexicans are musical and always ready for a fiesta, that they are very "romantic" rather than "realis-tic" (which may have unfavorable overtones as well), and that they love flowers and can grow them under the most adverse conditions. Although each of these beliefs may have a modicum of truth, it may be noted that they tend to reinforce Anglo-American images of Mexicans as childlike and irresponsible, and thus they support the notion that Mexicans are capable only of subordinate status.

MEXICAN-AMERICAN ASSUMPTIONS, EXPECTATIONS, AND IMAGES

Mexican-Americans are as likely to hold contradictory assumptions and distorted images as are Anglo-Americans. Their principal assumptions, however, must reflect those of Anglo-Americans—that is, Mexicans must take into account the Anglo-Americans' conflict as to their potential equality and present inferiority, since they are the object of such imputations. Similarly, their images of Anglo-Americans are not derived wholly independently, but to some extent must reflect their own subordinate status. Consequently, their stereotypes of Anglo-Americans are much less elaborate, in part because Mexicans feel no need of justifying the present intergroup relation, in part because the very nature of their dependent position forces them to view the relation more realistically than Anglo-Americans do. For the same reasons, they need not hold to their beliefs about Anglo-Americans with the rigidity and intensity so often characteristic of the latter.

Any discussion of these assumptions and expectations requires some mention of the class distinctions within the Mexican-American group.[8] Its middle class, though small as compared with the lower class, is powerful within the group and performs the critical role of intermediary

8 See *ibid.,* for a discussion of the Anglo-American and Mexican class structures.

in negotiations with the Anglo-American group. Middle-class status is based on education and occupation, family background, readiness to serve the interests of the group, on wealth, and the degree of acculturation, or command of Anglo-American ways. Anglo-Americans recognize Mexican class distinctions (although not very accurately) in their notions of the "high type" and "low type" of Mexicans.

In general, lower-class Mexicans do not regard the disabilities of their status as being nearly as severe as do middle-class Mexican-Americans. This is primarily a reflection of the insulation between the Anglo-American world and that of the Mexican lower class. Most Mexicans, regardless of class, are keenly aware of Anglo-American attitudes and practices with regard to their group, but lower-class Mexicans do not conceive of participation in the larger society as necessary nor do they regard Anglo-American practices of exclusion as affecting them directly. Their principal reaction has been to maintain their isolation, and thus they have not been particularly concerned with improving their status by acquiring Anglo-American ways, a course more characteristic of the middle-class Mexican.

Mexican-American assumptions and expectations regarding Anglo-Americans must be qualified, then, as being more characteristic of middle- than of lower-class Mexican-Americans. Mexicans, like Anglo-Americans, are subject to conflicts in their ideals, not only because of irrational thinking on their part but also because of Anglo-American inconsistencies between ideal and practice. As for ideals expressing democratic values, Mexican expectations are for obvious reasons the counterpart of the Anglo-Americans'—that Mexican-Americans should be accorded full acceptance and equal opportunity. They feel a considerable ambivalence, however, as to the Anglo-American expectation that the only way to achieve this goal is by a full incorporation of Anglo-American values and ways of life, for this implies the ultimate loss of their cultural identity as Mexicans. On the one hand, they favor the acquisition of Anglo-American culture and the eventual remaking of the Mexican in the Anglo-American image; but on the other hand, they are not so sure that Anglo-American acceptance is worth such a price. When they are concerned with this dilemma, Mexicans advocate a fusion with Anglo-American culture in which the "best" of the Mexican ways, as they view it, would be retained along with the incorporation of the "best" of the Anglo-American ways, rather than a one-sided exchange in which all that is distinctively Mexican would be lost.

A few examples will illustrate the point of view expressed in the phrase, "the best of both ways." A premium is placed on speaking good, unaccented English, but the retention of good Spanish is valued just as highly as "a mark of culture that should not be abandoned." Similarly, there is an emphasis on the incorporation of behavior patterns that are considered characteristically Anglo-American and that will promote "getting ahead," but not to the point at which the drive for power and wealth would become completely dominant, as is believed to be the case with Anglo-Americans.

Mexican ambivalence about becoming Anglo-American or achieving a fusion of the "best" of both cultures is compounded by their ambivalence about another issue, that of equality versus inferiority. That Anglo-Americans are dominant in the society and seem to monopolize its accomplishments and rewards leads Mexicans at times to draw the same conclusion that Anglo-Americans do, namely that Mexicans are inferior. This questioning of their own sense of worth exists in all classes of the Mexican-American group, although with varying intensity, and plays a substantial part in every adjustment to intergroup relations. There is a pronounced tendency to concede the superiority of Anglo-American ways and consequently to define Mexican ways as undesirable, inferior, and disreputable. The tendency to believe in his own inferiority is counterbalanced, however, by the Mexicans fierce racial pride, which sets the tone of Mexican demands and strivings for equal status, even though these may slip into feelings of inferiority.

The images Mexicans have of Anglo-Americans may not be so elaborate or so emotionally charged as the images that Anglo-Americans have of Mexicans, but they are nevertheless stereotypes, overgeneralized, and exaggerated, although used primarily for defensive rather than justificatory purposes. Mexican images of Anglo-Americans are sometimes favorable, particularly when they identify such traits as initiative, ambition, and industriousness as being peculiarly Anglo-American. Unfavorable images are prominent, however, and, although they may be hostile, they never impute inferiority to Anglo-Americans. Most of the Mexican stereotypes evaluate Anglo-Americans on the basis of their attitudes toward Mexican-Americans. For example, one such classification provides a two-fold typology. The first type, the "majority," includes those who are friendly, warm, just, and unprejudiced. For the most part, Mexican images of Anglo-Americans reflect the latter's patterns of exclusion and assumptions of superiority, as experienced by Mexican-Americans. Thus Anglo-Americans are pictured as stolid, phlegmatic, cold-hearted, and distant. They are also said to be braggarts, conceited, inconstant, and insincere.

INTERGROUP RELATIONS, MUTUAL EXPECTATIONS, AND CULTURAL DIFFERENCES

A number of students of intergroup relations assert that research in this area has yet to demonstrate any relation between stereotypical beliefs and intergroup behavior, indeed, some insist that under certain conditions ethnic attitudes and discrimination can vary independently.[9] Arnold M. Rose, for example, concludes that "from a heuristic standpoint it may be desirable to assume that patterns of intergroup relations, on the one hand, and attitudes of prejudice and stereotyping, on the other hand, are fairly unrelated phenomena although they have reciprocal influences on each other . . ."[10] In the present study, no systematic attempt was made to investigate the relation between the stereotypical beliefs of particular individuals and their actual intergroup behavior; but the study did yield much evidence that both images which justify group separatism and separateness itself are characteristic aspects of intergroup relations in Border City. One of the principal findings is that in those situations in which contact between Anglo-Americans and Mexicans is voluntary (such as residence, education, recreation, religious worship, and social intercourse) the characteristic pattern is separateness rather than common participation. Wherever intergroup contact is necessary, as in occupational activities and the performance of commercial and professional services, it is held to the minimum sufficient to accomplish the purpose of the contact.[11] The extent of this separateness is not constant for all members of the two groups, since it tends to be less severe between Anglo-Americans and those Mexicans they de-

[9] Robert K. Merton, "Discrimination and the American Creed," in R. M. MacIver (ed.), Discrimination and National Welfare (New York, Harper and Brothers, 1949), pp. 99–128; John Harding, Bernard Kutner, Harold Proshansky, and Isidor Chein, op. cit.; Arnold M. Rose, "Intergroup Relations vs. Prejudice: Pertinent Theory for the Study of Social Change," Social Problems, 1956, 4: 173–176; Robin M. Williams, Jr., "Racial and Cultural Relations," in Joseph B. Gittler (ed.), Review of Sociology: Analysis of a Decade (New York, John Wiley and Sons, 1957), pp. 423–464.

[10] Rose, op. cit.

[11] Simmons, op. cit.

fine as of a "high type." Nevertheless, the evidence reveals a high degree of compatibility between beliefs and practices in Border City's intergroup relations, although the data have nothing to offer for the identification of direct relationships.

In any case, the separateness that characterizes intergroup relations cannot be attributed solely to the exclusion practices of the Anglo-American group. Mexicans have tended to remain separate by choice as well as by necessity. Like many other ethnic groups, they have often found this the easier course, since they need not strain to learn another language or to change their ways and manners. The isolation practices of the Mexican group are as relevant to an understanding of intergroup relations as are the exclusion practices of the Anglo-Americans.

This should not, however, obscure the fact that to a wide extent the majority of Mexican-Americans share the patterns of living of Anglo-American society; many of their ways are already identical. Regardless of the degree of their insulation from the larger society, the demands of life in the United States have required basic modifications of the Mexicans' cultural tradition. In material culture, Mexicans are hardly to be distinguished from Anglo-Americans, and there have been basic changes in medical beliefs and practices and in the customs regarding godparenthood. Mexicans have acquired English in varying degrees, and their Spanish has become noticeably Anglicized. Although the original organization of the family has persisted, major changes have occurred in patterns of traditional authority, as well as in child training and courtship practices. Still, it is the exceedingly rare Mexican-American, no matter how acculturated he may be to the dominant society, who does not in some degree retain the more subtle characteristics of his Mexican heritage, particularly in his conception of time and in other fundamental value orien-

tations, as well as in his modes of participation in interpersonal relations.[12] Many of the most acculturated Mexican-Americans have attempted to exemplify what they regard as "the best of both ways." They have become largely Anglo-American in their way of living, but they still retain fluent Spanish and a knowledge of their traditional culture, and they maintain an identification with their own heritage while participating in Anglo-American culture. Nevertheless, this sort of achievement still seems a long way off for many Mexican-Americans who regard it as desirable.

A predominant Anglo-American expectation is that the Mexicans will be eventually assimilated into the larger society; but this is contingent upon Mexicans' becoming just like Anglo-Americans. The Mexican counterpart to this expectation is only partially complementary. Mexicans want to be full members of the larger society, but they do not want to give up their cultural heritage. There is even less complementarity of expectation with regard to the present conduct of intergroup relations. Anglo-Americans believe they are justified in withholding equal access to the rewards of full acceptance as long as Mexicans remain "different," particularly since they interpret the differences (both those which have some basis in reality and those which have none) as evidence of inferiority. Mexicans, on the other hand, while not always certain that they are not inferior, clearly want equal opportunity and full acceptance now, not in some dim future, and they do not believe that their differences (either presumed or real) from Anglo-Americans

[12] For cultural differences and similarities between Anglo-Americans and Mexicans, see Simmons, *op. cit.*; Tuck, *op. cit.*; Lyle Saunders, *Cultural Difference and Medical Care*, New York, Russell Sage Foundation, 1954; Munro S. Edmonson, *Los Manitos: A Study of Institutional Values* (New Orleans, Middle American Research Institute, Tulane University, 1957, Publication 25), pp. 1–72; and Margaret Clark, *Health in the Mexican-American Culture*, Berkeley, University of California Press, 1959.

offer any justification for the denial of opportunity and acceptance. Moreover, they do not find that acculturation is rewarded in any clear and regular way by progressive acceptance.

It is probable that both Anglo-Americans and Mexicans will have to modify their beliefs and practices if they are to realize more clearly their expectations of each other. Mutual stereotyping, as well as the exclusion practices of Anglo-Americans and the isolation practices of Mexicans, maintains the separateness of the two groups, and separateness is a massive barrier to the realization of their expectations. The process of acculturation is presently going on among Mexican-Americans and will continue, regardless of whether changes in Anglo-Mexican relations occur. Unless Mexican-Americans can validate their increasing command of Anglo-American ways by a free participation in the larger society, however, such acculturation is not likely to accelerate its present leisurely pace, nor will it lead to eventual assimilation. The *colonia* is a relatively safe place in which new cultural acquisitions may be tried out, and thus it has its positive functions; but by the same token it is only in intergroup contacts with Anglo-Americans that acculturation is validated, that the Mexican's level of acculturation is tested, and that the distance he must yet travel to assimilation is measured.[13]

CONCLUSIONS

There are major inconsistencies in the assumptions that Anglo-Americans and Mexican-Americans hold about one another. Anglo-Americans assume that Mexican-Americans are their potential, if not actual, peers, but at the same time assume

[13] See Leonard Broom and John I. Kitsuse, "The Validation of Acculturation: A Condition to Ethnic Assimilation," *American Anthropologist*, 1955, 57: 44–48.

they are their inferiors. The beliefs that presumably demonstrate the Mexican-Americans inferiority tend to place them outside the accepted moral order and framework of Anglo-American society by attributing to them undesirable characteristics that make it "reasonable" to treat them differently from their fellow Anglo-Americans. Thus the negative images provide not only a rationalized definition of the intergroup relation that makes it palatable for Anglo-Americans, but also a substantial support for maintaining the relation as it is. The assumptions of Mexican-Americans about Anglo-Americans are predominantly negative, although these are primarily defensive rather than justificatory. The mutual expectations of the two groups contrast sharply with the ideal of a complementarity of expectations, in that Anglo-Americans expect Mexicans to become just like themselves, if they are to be accorded equal status in the larger society, whereas Mexican-Americans want full acceptance, regardless of the extent to which they give up their own ways and acquire those of the dominant group.

Anglo-Americans and Mexicans may decide to stay apart because they are different, but cultural differences provide no moral justification for one group to deny to the other equal opportunity and the rewards of the larger society. If the full acceptance of Mexicans by Anglo-Americans is contingent upon the disappearance of cultural differences, it will not be accorded in the foreseeable future. In our American society, we have often seriously underestimated the strength and tenacity of early cultural conditioning. We have expected newcomers to change their customs and values to conform to American ways as quickly as possible, without an adequate appreciation of the strains imposed by this process. An understanding of the nature of culture and of its interrelations with personality can make us more realistic about the rate at which cultural change can proceed and about the gains and costs for the individual who is subject to the experiences of acculturation. In viewing cultural differences primarily as disabilities, we neglect their positive aspects. Mexican-American culture represents the most constructive and effective means Mexican-Americans have yet been able to develop for coping with their changed natural and social environment. They will further exchange old ways for new only if these appear to be more meaningful and rewarding than the old, and then only if they are given full opportunity to acquire the new ways and to use them.

22. NO SIESTA MAÑANA

Anthony Gary Dworkin

The largest concentration of Mexican-American population in the United States confronts many of the same issues as the small Mexican-American community in East Chicago, Indiana. Cultural, linguistic, economic, educational, and residential barriers separate the minority from the Anglo majority. However, Dworkin's work shows that in a large metropolitan area these problems are compounded many times. First is the matter of scale. For example, families may be able to band together to overcome the effects of unemployment if only a few individuals are involved and neighbors all know one another pretty well. Public agencies have to come into the picture when unemployment strikes thousands. In general, the larger the size of a given community of relatively poor people, the greater their dependence on public agencies. Although public agencies can and have limited the scope of personal prejudice and discrimination, they are frequently so bound up in complex sets of general rules and regulations that they are

Source: Raymond Mack (ed.), *Our Children's Burden: Studies of Desegregation in Nine American Communities* (New York: Random House, 1969), pp. 392–99, 414–23, 439, with some footnotes omitted. Copyright © 1969 by Raymond Mack. Reprinted by permission of Raymond Mack, the author, and the publisher.

ANTHONY GARY DWORKIN is Assistant Professor of Sociology at the University of Missouri.

not especially well equipped to deal with individuals who neither understand their rights nor know the provisions for appeal.

Furthermore, in a small city like East Chicago, when upwardly mobile members of the Mexican-American community move away, they do not move very far. They may still be available to provide skills and leadership to fellow group members remaining in the older community. But if Mexican-Americans move from East Los Angeles, they move farther away, and in large enough numbers to be more concerned about their own place in their new residential areas than about the one they left behind.

Another difference between the two situations concerns the significance of education. It counts for less in East Chicago because of the relatively easy accessibility of local industrial jobs. In a growing city like Los Angeles, however, not only are the available jobs likely to be far from where people live, but jobs created by normal market processes to accommodate young people just entering the labor market tend increasingly to be white-collar jobs. These occupations (as well as many manual ones) now call for educational credentials like high school diplomas. Dropouts don't get steady work.

Finally, large cities tend to attract not just one but several minorities. We have already noted one or two reasons why it may be difficult for blacks and Chicanos to work together. Here are some others. Los Angeles' Mexican-Americans, of course, wish to improve their position relative to that of Anglos, but they are also fearful that black gains will come at Chicano expense. Cultural differences keep the groups apart, along with the fact that Mexican-Americans were the first of the racial minorities migrating from within the United States to settle on the West Coast, thereby contributing to a feeling that they ought to get priority. For such reasons as these, the leadership of both groups depends more on furthering particularistic group interests than on fostering a more general concern for the minority situation. Were all that not enough, a final numerical fact must also be considered: taken together blacks and Mexican-Americans are only a sixth of the total population of Los Angeles County. There is therefore no guarantee that together they would be any the less outvoted and outmaneuvered than they are now when representatives of the majority try to play one group off against the other.

THE MEXICAN GHETTO TODAY: THE HARD DATA OF DISCRIMINATION

There are more individuals of Mexican descent in Los Angeles than in any city in the world except Mexico City. Mexican-Americans comprise Los Angeles' second largest minority group, and represent 11.5 per cent of the city's 2.5 million residents.[1] Only the Negro, who makes up 14 per cent of the city's population, is larger in numbers. However, for the county of Los Angeles,[2] Mexican-Americans are the largest minority group. Of the county's 6 million residents, 9.6 per cent are Mexican-Americans, while 7.6 per cent are Negro. The Mexican population increases on the average by 2,250 new residents per month.[3]

[1] Statistical data on the city of Los Angeles are taken from Fair Employment Practice Commission report, "Los Angeles City Schools," October, 1964.

[2] Statistical information on the county of Los Angeles and for the Mexican-American ghetto are derived from the Research Department of the Welfare Planning Council, Los Angeles Region report, "Background for Planning," 1963.

[3] The United States Census does not adequately differentiate the Mexican-American population from other Spanish-speaking groups. The term "Spanish surname" is employed instead by the census. Hence, Mexican-Americans, Puerto Ricans, Cubans, and Central and South Americans comprise Los Angeles population of 576,716 people with Spanish surnames. However, this does not present too much of a problem. Over 90 per cent of the Spanish-surname population of Los Angeles are Mexican-Americans, and so the data on Spanish surnames are fairly accurate for Mexican-Americans as well. If anything, the data present a more conservative estimate of the Mexican-American plight as the Cuban population, most of whom are escapees from Castro's regime and were former professionals in Cuba, are better educated, earn better incomes, and have better jobs. However, because the Spanish-surname population who are not of Mexican descent represent only a small fraction of the total category, the discrepancy between statistics on Mexican-Americans and on all Spanish surname groups is slight. If anything, the total number of Mexican-Americans with Spanish surnames is an underestimate of the total Mexican-American population because some Mexican women change their surname by marriage to Anglo men, and some Mexican men Anglicize their surnames.

· · · · ·

. . . As might be expected the Anglo's condition is considerably better than the Mexican-American's. More Anglos are married; but fewer people of Spanish surname are widowed or divorced. The divorce rate among the Mexican-American is considerably higher, however, than the statistics or Catholicism would indicate. As one Mexican-American newspaperwoman noted:

Today, as never before, women are going down to Mexico to get divorces from their husbands if they are not satisfied. Before, the woman would just endure, but now women are freer. They go to Mexico for a divorce and it never gets recorded by the State of California. Therefore, population figures could never tell you anything about the shifts.

The Anglo, however, has a higher income (a median of $7,433 for the Anglo and $5,759 for the Mexican-American); he is better educated (the Anglo has completed 12.2 years of school while the Mexican-American has completed only 9); the Anglo is less affected by unemployment (5.1 per cent of the Anglos are unemployed as compared to 7.6 per cent of the Mexicans). And finally, the Anglo lives in a better home; the Anglo's home is worth $16,900 while the Mexican's is worth $13,100; further, 19.8 per cent of the Mexican homes are dilapidated or deteriorated, while only 6.8 per cent of the Anglo homes are in such condition.

The present paper is based upon research in one of the ghettos in the county—East Los Angeles and Boyle Heights. Within this area reside 180,000 people, of whom 67 per cent are of Spanish surname. This ghetto represents the largest single concentration of Mexican-Americans, is a center of Poverty Program work, produces the most militant Mexican-Americans, and is an area in which social scientists have been studying for the past twenty years, thus providing an invaluable storehouse of data.

It was in this area that the 1943 "zoot-suit riots" raged. Here in East Los Angeles and Boyle Heights, situated on the east and traditionally the wrong side of the Los Angeles River and Southern Pacific Railroad tracks, is the infamous Flats. The Flats has been the home of gangs and the repository for successive waves of immigrants. From the 1880s to the post-World War II period the Flats has been occupied by newly immigrated Irish, Armenians, Molokans, Slavs, Jews, and finally Mexicans. Each group turned the Flats into an interstitial area plagued with problems of crime, delinquency, tuberculosis, and human decay—physical, psychological, and social.

In order to make this report more meaningful, at times we shall not restrict our discussions simply to the ghetto itself. Instead, we shall discuss the ghetto in relation to the county as a whole, the Anglo communities to which the successful Mexicans migrate, and Watts, one part of the Negro ghetto.

There is a distinct path taken by the mobile Mexican family as it flees the ghetto. The stages seem to be as follows: out of the ghetto to El Sereno, then to Montebello and Monterey Park, and then, often with the name change and complete Anglicization, into eastern San Gabriel Valley and other Anglo areas. In terms of social class, as judged by income, education, occupation, living conditions, delinquency rates, property values, etc., the class shift is roughly from lower-lower to upper-lower to lower-middle to upper-middle. As one sociologist who has worked with East Los Angeles Mexicans for fifteen years notes:

There is a mass exodus from East LA to El Sereno. While East LA is lower class, El Sereno is upper-lower and lower-middle class. Thus, as the Mexicans get more money they move out of the LA ghetto and into the El Sereno ghetto. Another reason for the movement to El Sereno is the fact that it has a powerful Catholic church and parochial school. The pattern of migration is into East LA, to El Sereno, and then finally into Montebello and Monterey Park and east.

Table 1 presents the 1960 statistics on population density and ethnic concentration. It should be noted that there exists a linear relationship between these characteristics and the progressive movement out of the ghetto into successively higher socioeconomic levels. That is, as one moves out of the Mexican ghetto of East Los Angeles and Boyle Heights, population density and percentage of ethnicity decrease. In addition the ratio of Mexican-Americans to Anglos decreases.

TABLE 1   1960 Census, population density, and ethnic distribution.*

Area	1960 population	Persons per sq. mi.	Per cent Negro	Per cent other	Per cent Spanish surname	Per cent all minorities
East Los Angeles	105,464	12,379	<1.0	3.8	67.1	70.9
Boyle Heights	75,065	14,463	3.7	8.0	66.8	78.5
El Sereno	29,477	6,110	1.2	3.8	37.4	42.4
Montebello	32,097	4,312	<1.0	1.6	22.6	24.2
Monterey Park	37,821	5,352	<1.0	2.9	13.1	16.0
Watts (comparison population	72,203	13,818	85.7	<1.0	8.8	94.5
L.A. County	6,038,771	1,479	7.6	2.0	9.6	19.2

* Compiled from Tables 2 and 7 of *Background for Planning*, Research Department of the Welfare Planning Council, Los Angeles Region, Research Report No. 17, February 1964.

Furthermore, while Watts has approximately the same high population density as the Mexican-American ghetto, it is more segregated. East Los Angeles is 70.9 per cent and Boyle Heights is 78.5 per cent ethnic, while Watts is 94.5 per cent ethnic. Further, Watts is more homogeneously ethnic. Eighty-five per cent of Watts is of the same race (Negro), while only 67 per cent of the Mexican ghetto is of the same ethnic group (Spanish surname).

The traditional indices of social rank and socioeconomic status also demonstrate a linear relationship between the progressive steps taken out of the Mexican ghetto and increasingly favorable economic, educational, and occupational conditions. The median incomes for the ghetto and the three steps beyond are as follows: the ghetto of East Los Angeles and Boyle Heights, $5,437 and $5,053, respectively; El Sereno, $6,461; Montebello, $7,351; Monterey Park, $7,650. In comparison, the median income in Watts is $4,365, a figure even lower than in the Mexican ghetto.

The median school years completed for East Los Angeles and Boyle Heights are eight each; for El Sereno it is ten years; for Montebello it is eleven years; and for Monterey Park it is twelve years. The educational level in Watts is nine years, and thus is higher than in the Mexican ghetto. As will be discussed later, the difference between the ghetto and Watts may be attributed to an extreme difference in the value system of the Mexican ghetto and that of the school system.

Unemployment rates also demonstrate the linear relation and the fact that conditions in the Mexican ghetto are somewhat better (except for education) than in Watts, the Negro area. In East Los Angeles and Boyle Heights the unemployment rates are 6 and 6.6, respectively; while the values for El Sereno, Montebello, and Monterey Park are 3.7, 3.5, and 3.9, respectively. The apparent deviant case of Monterey Park is confounded by the higher percentage of college students in the area. This group enters the ranks of the unemployed during the school year. Unemployment in Watts is much higher than in the Mexican ghetto. In fact, it is 50 per cent greater, with a 9.4 per cent rate.

Lastly, we note that housing conditions and values improve as we move out of the ghetto into the three other areas. In East Los Angeles and Boyle Heights, respectively, 29 and 23.5 per cent of the homes are deteriorated or dilapidated, and median property values are $11,861 and $11,563, respectively. In El Sereno 17.8 per cent of the homes are deteriorated or dilapidated, and the median property value is $12,581. In Montebello only 4.5 per cent of the homes are deteriorated or dilapidated, while the median property value is $17,833. Fewer homes in Watts (22.6 per cent) are deteriorated or dilapidated than in the Mexican ghetto; however, property value ($10,208) is less than in the Mexican ghetto. All of these statistics indicate that the path taken by the Mexican-American as he leaves East Los Angeles and Boyle Heights is one of upward mobility, as measured by these traditional indices.

While no statistics are available on the actual number of Mexican-Americans who escape from the ghetto, we can be sure that the percentage is small. One index is the relatively low percentage of people with Spanish surnames found in the more Anglo areas. Even the phenomenon of passing and name changing is not sufficiently frequent to allow us to conclude that most Mexican-Americans escape the ghetto. Rather, we must conclude that the majority of Los Angeles' Mexican-American population is destined to remain in the ghetto where one may live and die without the need for English, without knowing that the world outside is any better, without leaving the "culture of poverty."

"BUT THEY'RE JUST DIFFERENT" [4]

The educational level of the Mexican-American in the ghetto is lower than in the more disadvantaged Negro ghetto of Watts, because the Mexican value system is so much more at odds with the school system than is that of the Negro. In this section we shall discuss the cultural factors which make the Mexican seem so strange to the Anglo teachers.

There is a sharp split between the Anglo's and Mexican's culture. The Anglo is secular, practical, objective, competitive, materialistic, and future-oriented. Traditionally the Mexican was not.[5] The new Mexican-Americans are changing, but a viable culture, reinforced by generations of ghetto life and discrimination, and centuries of life in Mexico does not die easily. A conglomeration of Spanish, Indian, and Roman Catholic in origin, the Mexican-American culture has served as a defense against the exploitation by the Anglo. . . .

. . . . .

Mexican-Americans want their children also to learn about the Anglo way

[4] A frequently heard statement among Anglo teachers in the Mexican-American ghetto in Los Angeles. One teacher elaborated on the statement by pointing out that "the reason Mexican kids get into so much trouble is that they are born Mexican."

[5] Of the sociological models available to explain the differences between the Mexican and Anglo societies, the most frequently used among researchers in Mexican-Anglo relations is that of the Folk-Urban asymtotic dichotomy. Born in the nineteenth-century tradition of Tönnies, Maine, and Durkheim, the distinction was tested empirically by Redfield, with data from villages in Mexico. Redfield characterized the ideal-typical folk society as follows: "Such a society is small, isolated, nonliterate, and homogeneous, with a strong sense of group solidarity. The ways of living are conventionalized into that coherent system which we call 'a culture.' Behavior is traditional, spontaneous, uncritical, and personal; there is no legislation or habit of experiment and reflection for intellectual ends. Kinship, its relationships and institutions, are the type categories of experience, and the familial group is the unit of action. The sacred prevails over the secular; the economy is one of status rather than of market." (Robert Redfield, "The Folk Society," *American Journal of Sociology*, 52, 1947, p. 294.)

of life, but not at the expense of the Mexican-American heritage and a knowledge of the Spanish language. This, however, creates a difficult problem. It is the dilemma of difference, the conundrum of cultural pluralism. If the Mexican-American wishes to retain his cultural ties to Mexico, many Anglos, including some teachers, will offer resistance. Some school administrators are unwilling to support demands by Mexican-Americans for enriched educational programs which will compensate for the child's academic deficiencies and at the same time give instruction on the contributions of Mexico to American society to make the child feel proud of his ancestry. These administrators feel that this will encourage the child not to want to "become an American." One teacher complained, "These Mexicans want to have their cake and eat it, too. They want to be Mexicans and they want to be accepted as members of our society, too." Much of the prejudice and discrimination centers around this issue.

There is considerable evidence that some Anglo administrators and teachers in the Mexican-American ghetto resent the community's attempts at cultural pluralism. Primarily through a misunderstanding of the Mexican culture and Mexican intentions, hostile attitudes, . . . pervade the schools in the ghetto. The principal of one of the major high schools in the area begins his orientation session for each new group of teachers with the following statement:

There are two or three cultures here. The kids run from the disciplined Japanese to the unconcerned Mexican race. If there are any doubts in your mind, you had better think it over before signing on to this school. Teaching at ———— High School is an asset. If you have been successful here, you can teach anywhere. You don't get things put on a silver platter here for you. This is not a gravy school. There are few top kids in this place. You have to be a super teacher to get anything out of Mexicans. If you fail at ——— High School, it doesn't mean that you were not a good teacher. You could be a good teacher in a "white school."

. . . . .

The Language Barrier

One of the most frequently mentioned complaints by both the schools and the Mexican-American community concerns the issue of the use of Spanish in schools. Spanish is the language of *La Raza,* and is the binding factor in the community. Thus, the Mexican-American activists demand that Spanish be permitted and taught in the schools, especially since it is the native and sometimes the only tongue of the entering children. In the past the schools have ignored the requests. However, even though there has recently been some token acceptance of the Spanish heritage in East Los Angeles schools, there is still resistance. As one Mexican-American educator observed:

If it is true, that the schools reflect the norms and values of the community, then perhaps it is equally true that its prejudices are also reflected, through acts of commission as well as omission. Few school systems can, or do, gear their curricula to the needs of this segment of the population. Few know, empirically, what the needs are. It is easier and safer to prohibit the speaking of Spanish on the school ground and in the school [the need being to learn English] than to take the imaginative step of teaching both English and Spanish to both Anglos and Spanish-speaking beginning in the elementary school. As a consequence, the "educated" Spanish-speaking person who has survived the school system is likely also to be one who has been stripped of his native language, or at best speaks and writes it imperfectly. To the enlightened, this situation is such a waste of human resources; to others, including some school teachers, the burden of proof is on the shoulders of the minority: "If you want to be American, speak American!" [6]

[6] Julian Samora, "The Education of the Spanish-Speaking in the Southwest: An Analysis of

In most schools in the ghetto the faculty does not speak Spanish, and the children when they enter elementary school do not speak English. I asked one teacher what this meant. Her reply was:

. . . for the first two years the teacher looks at the child and the child looks back. They don't speak to one another because neither understands the other's langauge.

In some schools the Anglo teachers do communicate via translators to the Mexican children who speak no English. A principal said that some of the teachers in her school use the bilingual Mexican kids to help them with their teaching. She observed:

. . . the bilingual students translate the lessons from the teacher to their Spanish-speaking classmates. The teachers tell the bilingual kids and then they in turn translate the lectures.

There are few Anglo teachers who speak Spanish and few Mexican teachers in the school system. Of the eight thousand in-service training teachers in Los Angeles today only seventy-five are Mexican-American.[7]

The schools have met the demand by Mexican-American community leaders for more Spanish-speaking teachers, especially for the primary grades, with a token gesture. In one elementary school, for example, a teacher with a knowledge of Spanish comes once a week to talk to the children. In one of the high schools only five of the hundred and twenty faculty members speak Spanish. While most Mexican-American students in high school do speak English, many of them have only a minimal grasp of the language—a factor which contributes to the high dropout rate.

the 1960 Census Materials." A mimeographed copy of a paper delivered at the Mexican-American workshop, Careers for Youth of the Mexican-American Community, Phoenix, Arizona, January 18, 1963.

[7] Statistics taken from the Castro Report of the Council of Mexican-American Educators, 1965.

The Anglo teachers frequently do not realize that many high school students in the ghetto do not understand English well enough to achieve any satisfactory level of academic success. One teacher in an East Los Angeles high school demonstrated the lack of awareness of the Mexican's problem when he maintained that:

Most of the Mexican kids really do speak English well, but they use their Mexican heritage as an excuse to get out of doing homework. They just pretend that they don't understand English.

Besides the actual linguistic handicap, many members of the Mexican-American community have also protested that the text books are culturally biased against Mexican-American children. Books used in the predominantly lower-class Mexican schools do not portray a life-style with which the children can identify. The traditional Dick and Jane reader, which portrays an upper-middle-class Anglo family, is foreign to the children, and hence the reading material is not readily comprehensible. Mexican-American leaders have protested, but to no avail. One community representative in the Mexican ghetto pointed out:

Another example of poor handling of Mexicans is the revision of the elementary school reader. They have changed the Dick and Jane book. They are Negroes and their father is portrayed as a laborer rather than as a businessman. Also, they have a next-door neighbor who is a Chinese girl. However, there are no Mexicans in the book. Once again the Mexican has been left out. The Council on Mexican-American Affairs has protested to the state, but nothing has been done. I guess one reason why they don't write more about Mexicans is that there is really very little information available about the Mexican. Thus, few textbooks have anything other than that the Mexican is a grape picker. That's the popular stereotype which is common in the press. When the State of California did publish a pamphlet on Mexicans entitled *Californians of Spanish Surnames,* published by the FEPC, it came out about two years after all the literature on Negroes came out.

Some teachers in the schools also acknowledge the problem, but the question of textbooks is an administrative decision farther along the chain of command than the teacher's authority. A high school math teacher notes:

The textual material is not the best for the culture of the kids. They are some of the best books you can get; but just because they are some of the best books does not mean that they are best for a particular culture. The books don't communicate with the student. They are foreign to his experience and his culture.

Teacher Hiring

In a 1963 conference on Mexican-American education, a member of the board of education stated:

A major problem of the Mexican-American lies in the fact that there is a great lack of adequate recruitment by the Mexican-American community of Mexican-American teachers. There should be more encouragement of Mexican-Americans by Mexican-Americans to become teachers.

That year the Fair Employment Practices Commission (FEPC) noted that:

In November, 1963, only 2.2 per cent of teachers were Mexican-American while pupils of that ethnic group represented more than 16 per cent of school enrollment.
. . . The disparity between the proportion of Negro teachers and Negro pupils was far less severe with Negro teachers amounting to 13.3 per cent of all teachers, and Negro pupils 18.1 per cent of total enrollment.[8]

In one elementary school surveyed in 1962 there were five Mexican-American teachers, nine Negro teachers, seven Jap-

[8] California Fair Employment Practices Commission, *op. cit.*

anese-American teachers, and ten Anglo teachers. Such ethnic ratios prompted certain activists in the Mexican-American community as well as members of the board of education to attempt Mexican-American teacher recruitment programs. An indication of the success of the endeavor may be seen in the 1966 restudy of that school. There are ten Anglo teachers, ten Japanese teachers, twelve Negro teachers, and no Mexican-American teachers. This elementary school, which has a total enrollment of one thousand children, is 92 per cent Mexican-American and is representative of the elementary schools in the ghetto.

The reasons there are so few Mexican-Americans in education are complex, and probably not attributable to blatant discrimination in hiring practices by the board of education. If anything, the board of education will sometimes waive certification requirements to hire Mexican teachers. One educator noted that:

. . . the few Mexicans who do go into teaching are usually those who can't make it elsewhere. The board of education often scrapes the bottom of the barrel to get teachers, and sometimes is even willing to accept a Mexican-American with normally unacceptable grades in college for a credential.

While the board of education frequently attempts to attract Mexican teachers, some administrators in the high schools attempt to prove to the board that attracting Mexican teachers would solve no problems. One teacher related the following example:

To prove to the Mexican community that even if you got a lot of Mexican teachers in the school you would still have great discipline problems with the Mexican kids, they gave the four Mexican teachers in our school the most difficult kids to teach. The principal proved that the teacher with the best knowledge of Spanish had the most discipline problems.

By so manipulating the situation, the principal could not avoid verifying his foregone conclusion.

In general, however, Mexican-Americans with a college education are scarce and in great demand, especially since the advent of the Poverty Program. Teaching salaries do not compare favorably with government and industrial wages. One newspaperwoman put it like this:

You know, it's becoming profitable and favorable to become a Mexican. At least if you're a Mexican with a college degree and can speak Spanish. There are very high federal salaries for such persons. I was offered a job for $17,000 per year, but most Mexicans don't qualify since only a few per cent get more than a high school education. Those with a college degree used to go into teaching, but school salaries don't compare with what you can get elsewhere.

Another and traditionally important reason why there are so few Mexican teachers relates to *machismo*. Public school teaching is viewed by Mexicans as an effeminate profession. Consequently, very few men entertain the idea of becoming teachers. Furthermore, Mexican girls are not encouraged either to stay in school or to seek a career. A woman's place, according to most Mexican males, is in the home, satisfying the wants of her husband and tending her children. In many cases a Mexican girl who seeks to become a public school teacher alienates herself from her family.

Because the school has remained a symbol of Anglo authority and a place where Mexican-Americans have suffered failures, the college graduate of the East Los Angeles ghetto is hesitant about entering public school teaching. As a result the teachers in the ghetto schools are primarily Anglo and Negro. If it appears that the Mexican-American is hostile toward the Anglo, his anger is even greater toward the Negro. Many Mexican parents have said:

I can tolerate my kid having a Negro teacher in first grade, but when he has another Negro teacher in second grade and in third grade, it just burns the hell out of me.

In an editorial from a now defunct East Los Angeles newspaper, *The Eagles,* an organ of the vocal Anglicized Mexican-American population, appeared the following example of Mexican hostility toward Negroes:

The Negro in California finds himself in the unique position of being a minority who is in the minority and who, furthermore, cannot claim to be the only or worst victim of discrimination. . . .

Many a Mexican-American still remembers when he had to go to a separate section in the movies; when there were schools for "Mexicans" and schools for "whites"; when municipal swimming pools were out of bounds for Mexicans; when lynchings took place; when a Mexican had to step down the curb when a policeman walked toward him; when restrictive deeds, excluding Mexican-Americans from the purchase of land or house, were in effect.

It must be realized, then, that the Mexican-American paved the way for the Negro and that, if for no other reason, the Negro leadership should be extremely careful not to step on Mexican-American toes. . . .

If the Rumford Act is repealed by a comparatively narrow margin and the Mexican-American precincts vote heavily against the Act, perhaps then a second, hard look will be taken by the Negro leadership, for it will become evident that the Negro cannot win without the help of the Mexican-American.[9]

By election time "YES ON PROPOSITION 14" stickers became a common sight on walls, fences, and telephone posts in the ghetto. A "yes" vote meant the repeal of the Rumford Act and the end of a fair housing law in California. The Mexican ghetto voted overwhelmingly in favor of the proposition as did the Anglo community. The Rumford Act was dead

[9] *The Eagles,* Vol. I, No. 10, July 3, 1964, pp. 2–3.

and so was equal opportunity housing law in California. Such is the hostility of the Mexican-American toward the Negro. Rather than help the Negro cause, the Mexican is willing to destroy his own hopes for integrated housing.

If there is a paucity of Mexican-American teachers, there is an even greater shortage of Mexican-Americans in higher administrative positions. An FEPC report indicated that for the whole Los Angeles School System, "ninety-four per cent of all principals and vice principals are members of the majority group."

In 1962 an Anglo-American principal of one elementary school pointed out to me that:

While it is not official administrative policy, positions as principal and vice-principal are generally not open to Mexican-Americans, regardless of their seniority or academic degrees.

There are no Mexican-Americans on the board of education. Educators in the Mexican-American community have frequently stated that equal educational opportunities cannot be guaranteed until Mexican-Americans are placed on the school board. However, as one board of education member observed:

It is very difficult for a member of a minority group to get elected to the school board. A Mexican must not only win the election in East LA, but also in the rest of the city. And you know quite well that the rest of the city will resist voting for a Mexican.

· · · · ·

EPILOGUE: MAÑANA IS TODAY

Appearing in the ghetto for the first time is a new kind of Mexican. There are more young men who are staying in school than ever before. This new Mexican is not content to live in poverty. A Mexican-American newspaper reporter hinted at this change when he said, "The ghetto is somehow different. Two years ago if you stepped on a Mexican's foot he would apologize for being in your way. Now if you did that, he would ask you why you stepped on his foot and demand that you apologize. Mexicans are not afraid to protest any more. The community is changing."

The community *is* changing. The community has rallied an impressive grass-roots support of the Delano Farm Worker's Association, the group of Mexican-American agricultural laborers who have gone on strike in protest of less than minimum wages and substandard housing conditions provided by the Anglo growers of Delano, California. Nearly every automobile in the Mexican ghetto bears the bumper sticker *"Viva la Huelga!"* ("Long live the labor strike!"), and for several months the ghetto families have refused to buy fruit from the Anglo merchants who own markets in the ghetto.

The resistance is having an effect. The Anglo is vulnerable in his pocketbook, and that is where the Mexican-American is directing his challenge against a century and a quarter of discrimination in California. Because of the economic sanctions applied, many of the Anglo merchants have begun offering Mexican-American students part-time after-school jobs. This has helped several to stay in school.

The walls of prejudice are difficult to scale, but the first foothold has been made. The Mexican-American is still confined to the ghetto by cultural, linguistic, economic, and educational barriers, but tomorrow he will be free. *No siesta mañana*—no sleep tomorrow.

23. THE VERTICAL GHETTO

William Moore, Jr.

Blackmoor is a series of eleven-story buildings standing in the center of a ghetto in a large Midwestern city. It is a public housing project where more than ten thousand people have their homes. It is not dilapidated and it is rat-free, but it is overcrowded and noisy and its public areas are dirty. Its facilities for laundry and waste disposal are inconveniently located and inadequate, and there is not enough children's play

Source: *The Vertical Ghetto* (New York: Random House, 1969), pp. 111–20, 227–31. Copyright © 1969 by Random House, Inc. Reprinted by permission of the author and the publisher.

WILLIAM MOORE, JR., former President of Seattle Central Community College, is on the Faculty of Higher Education Administration of Ohio State University. He has also written several books on the character of community college student bodies and administration.

space. Blackmoor's new brick and cinderblock enclose and hide poverty; they do not eradicate it. The people who live there stay because it's the best they can get for what they can afford.

In April, 1967, of the 2,100 families in Blackmoor, 90 percent were black; 57 percent had annual incomes of less than $3,000; 79 percent, of less than $4,000; 1,166 families were on public assistance. In comparison, in the United States as a whole in 1968, among nonwhite and white families, respectively, only 23 percent and 9 percent had annual incomes under $3,000; 45 percent and 20 percent, under $5,000. Those few numbers are enough to show how the housing authority that built Blackmoor conserved city space by stacking poor blacks atop one another, segregating them by class as well as race.

Moore spent nine months in Blackmoor, learning what life there was like from the points of view of the hundred families he interviewed intensively. Most of his book concentrates on "telling it like it is." His final chapters, however, are devoted to suggestions for change. His ideas do not call for such great expense as to make it seem impossible to locate the necessary funds and so ought to appeal to even the most "practical" of men. I have included one set of his recommendations as a conclusion to the other part of his book that is reprinted here.

Through boom and depression, the bleak economic facts of life remain the same for Blackmoor's tenants. More than 63 percent of the homes are without adult males who bring in income. Those tenants who do find work (male and female) work at menial tasks, for minimum or subminimum wages. The unemployment rate for the city's Negro population as a whole is about 12 percent, but Midwest City's housing authority says that the adult male unemployment rate in Blackmoor is over 40 percent. Every resident in the housing project has heard the reports and statistics about his economic plight and has stopped listening to them. He is more sensitive to his stomach, which tells him he is hungry. His baby's crying is the biting rhetoric that holds his attention. His empty hands clenched in his empty pockets tell him he has no money for adequate shelter or decent clothes or health service.

The lack of employment and its consequence, the lack of money, is the problem of major magnitude in the disadvantaged home. This home is characterized not only by financial deficit due to insufficient income but also by a lack of skill to increase the income. Moreover, employment opportunities for the disadvantaged are fragmentary and tentative. If there is room at the top in employment, the tenants in the housing project know that it is not intended for the rank and file, which they represent. Most of Blackmoor's tenants are denied access to employment because of inadequate skill, social stigma, and racism, with all its attentive inequities (discrimination in hiring, bigotry, denial of entrance into labor unions and apprenticeship programs, crippling schools that do not offer adequate training). These are the reasons why tenants have come to regard the pronouncements of the alleged room at the top as being inundated in hypocrisy.

The traditional idealism of honor in poverty has been refuted by today's needs of poor people. Poverty and pride in contemporary society have been assessed by Blackmoor's residents as two separate entities—one, primarily physical; the other, primarily emotional—and they see little reward for having them coexist. The economic inequities encountered by the disadvantaged wage earner in the housing project are never corrected. Many things about Blackmoor describe the economic frustrations of the people. The fact that a person lives in the housing project in the first place reveals that he is a person whose income falls within certain limits. Only 12 households in 1,700 earn as much as $7,000. In the sample of the 100 families used in this book, only one family had an annual income of more than $3,999 (Table 1).

TABLE 1   Income of 100 sample families.

Income	Number
Under $1,000	1
$1,000–$1,999	32
$2,000–$2,999	46
$3,000–$3,999	20
$4,000–$4,999	1
$5,000 and over	0

Families have very small incomes in Blackmoor. Fifty-five of the households had no earning power, they were recipients of aid to dependent children. In no case did any family's income exceed an annual salary of $4,600. The total number of children reported in these families numbered as many as fifteen and as few

as two. In view of the income limitations and the family size, the poor economic conditions that prevail in most families create situations that make desirable adjustment in the family and society a monumental task and survival a difficult and uncertain goal. Dorothy Rogers (1962) contends, "Economic frustrations have serious detrimental effects upon personalities of adults and children." These frustrations often destroy rather than strengthen character and appear to have a particularly deleterious effect upon the black father as a wage earner.

THE FATHER AS A WAGE EARNER

The father in the disadvantaged home is usually a sporadic wage earner. Possessing few skills, he is forced to take whatever kind of employment is available to him. In the labor market, he is expendable. He is never in a position to bargain. The few skills that he has to market have long since reached the point of diminishing returns in the technological stream of our culture.

Historically, the Negro male has not been the source of complete support of his family. There have been working wives in these families for generations. As Maurice R. Davis (1949) noted, "Negro working-class women always hold the purse strings. Ill-paid and irregularly employed, the masses of Negro men have not succeeded in becoming steady providers for their families . . . Negro women are actually or potentially economically independent."

Lack of adequate employment is one of the many sources of psychological stress for the father in the slum culture. This father rarely establishes or maintains a position of respect in the family; furthermore, he seldom becomes a good model for his children, especially the boys, and finally, his stimulus value seems so low that his own ego structure is in constant jeopardy. Israel Woronoff summarizes these observations effectively:*

The husband, if present, is often an ineffective family leader. The boy growing up in a Negro family frequently perceives his father with a low-status job, who is regarded with indifference or varying degrees of hostility by members of the outgroup. In short, the lower-class Negro adult male is seldom regarded as a worth-while masculine model for the boy to emulate.

This problem of identification with a sound male model is of the utmost importance to a male youngster. Emotionally the boy who grows up surrounded and dominated by women readily develops a sense of role confusion which is often crippling. Such a youngster has problems of handling aggression, making decisions, accepting responsibility, and executing leadership, in addition to syndromes of neurotic behavior (ie., panic, extreme self-centeredness, hypochondriasis, irritability, depression).

A strong back and a willingness to work are no longer adequate criteria for employment for culturally disadvantaged males; skill is also necessary. Most men in the ghetto are willing to do almost anything, but they are without skill. There are some men in this housing project who work from day to day when they can find work. They can frequently be seen distributing handbills, working on coal trucks, unloading produce, and "junking" (selling rags, glass, bones, and paper). They work as janitors, dishwashers, and shoeshine boys.

Many of the traditional jobs done by unskilled men are now gone. Midwest City has not kept pace with other urban communities of its size in industrial expansion or in attracting new industry —and thus new jobs—into the area. In fact, there has been a decline in the textile, apparel, stockyard, and warehousing industries in the Midwest City community. These were the industries

* "Negro Male Identification Problems and the Educational Process," *Journal of Educational Sociology*, 36 (Sept., 1962), 30-32.

that were low paying and labor intensive and required relatively unskilled workers. It was to these industries that historically, immigrants and other minorities initially tended to attach themselves. The demand for unskilled labor has been declining in the inner city, while the size of the work force has increased. The suburban communities surround Midwest City like a white collar around a dirty neck. Unlike the city, the suburbs have experienced a rapid expansion in transportation, electrical, chemical, and service industries. The skills required in the *growth industries* and the amount of training necessary are considerably higher than in the *declining industries*. There are, however, some job opportunities for the unskilled and uneducated individual. The problem is that workers in the city have no way of getting from the inner city to the suburb. The cost of public transportation is such that the small salary that they could earn would become even smaller. (This condition exists in several major cities: Los Angeles, Chicago, and St. Louis.) Even when the unskilled do secure employment, it is frequently terminated after a few days, sometimes a few weeks, at most a few months. It is therefore understandable why a group of unemployed men sitting in a state employment agency made these remarks. One said:

I'm the best hod carrier you can find—but who needs a hod carrier? I've been carrying hod since I was fifteen. I don't know how to do nothin' else.

Another, obviously trying to preserve his dignity, related:

I set here day by day—I know I ain't going to get no job but I keep on coming and setting. *I have to keep going through the motions of being a man.*

And another tried to explain or rationalize his lack of skill:

I didn't get no education because I didn't

need no education then—in Mississippi—what for? Down there they had more college-trained elevator operators than they did professors.

Still another said:

I have been from one end of this city to the other—walking. I'm willing to do any kind of work. I'll do anything short of stealing, but it looks like I'm gonna have to do that.

The depth of another's feelings are characterized in this statement:

I used to hate the alarm clock because I knowed I had to meet "the Man." Now it'd sound like Gabriel's horn. If I could just do it a week, so I'd know how it feels to get up and go to work again, to smell stinking, sweat and joke with other fellows, to draw down a paycheck. I'd rather hear the old lady fussing because I had spent part of the money on whiskey than to have her go along and just say nothing.

Only three of the husbands in the families surveyed reported knowledge of some special skill. Out of the three, one, a tailor, was actively engaged in his trade. Another, a baker, was employed as a cook; and the third, a mechanic, was employed as a janitor. The majority of the males in the families surveyed worked in some type of janitorial service. Five of the husbands were employed as day laborers in construction work. These workers *did not* live with their families. Their salaries were well over the limits set by the housing authority and thus would render their families unqualified for residency in public housing. The rationale for separate residency of the men was simple: it was better for the male to live away from home and let the family continue on the welfare rolls than it would be to go back home and have their families removed from the welfare rolls. The men knew that construction work for them was seasonal and unstable; therefore, they could not run the risk of being laid off and moving away from home again so that their families could receive relief. Four of the five did contribute significantly to the mother for the care of the children. These four fathers became transient or visiting fathers.

Many men physically withdraw from the home although they *have not* deserted their families. They exhibit all the behavior of the deserting husband, but they frequently leave by mutual agreement with the mother for the economic benefit of the entire family. The father will rarely be seen in the project community; nevertheless, he is "there." Although there are many women without husbands, there are fewer divorces among project residents than any other group in the city as a whole, and legal separation is seldom requested or authorized.

The social worker is often the only one who is expected to believe that the husband has deserted; and he knows better. He may also know that a man is employed and his family is still receiving welfare payments. He has heard the following type of statement many times.

We don't desert our families—we hide. I probably spend more time with my family than a lot of other men. It was real hard at first for a man like me to see his family take handouts and couldn't do nothin' 'bout it. But then I learned how to act like I don't give a damn. That helped a little.

He has also heard the pragmatic view:

Don't make no kinda sense to go running back home soon as you draw one paycheck. You know you ain't gonna be drawing it long. So, you better off to pay five bucks a week for a room somewhere and help your family out all you can while money is coming in.

Whereas some may consider some of this activity as having really dishonest aspects, many men say that the economic practicality dictates their behavior. Each male the author talked to indicated that he would rather help provide for the family the way he was doing it than have his wife be the lone breadwinner all the time.

THE MOTHER AS A WAGE EARNER

The mother in the disadvantaged home does not encounter the same employment problems as the father. She can usually do domestic work or "day work" if she has someone to care for her children, although she usually expects her children to care for themselves. In like manner, if she is without a husband, she can apply and qualify for aid to dependent children. One young mother's response to "Do you have difficulty finding employment?" was

Naw, I don't have no trouble finding work— none of the women do. It's the men and boys that can't find nothing to do. Our only problem is to find somebody to take care of the children.

An older, rather candid mother who "tells it like it is" explained:

As long as folks are too lazy to clean up after themselves, I'll have a job. Have you ever heard of a status symbol? Well, I'm it. I heard Mrs. J. talking to a friend of hers on the phone and she was saying, "Well, darling, you know that we really can't afford her, but she's one of the status symbols that we all have to ad-here to." That *her* that they was talking about was me.

Numerous women in this environment work as waitresses, barmaids, hotel workers, and nurses' aides. These jobs provide more than salary. The mother can frequently bring foodstuffs and other items home that will help her provide for her children. She is also in a better position to save her own money for her own entertainment. Her sex is also an important fact in her securing employment, because employers do not have to pay women the same salaries as men, although the women are frequently expected to do the same job.

The mother in Blackmoor who is compelled to work to augment her income seems frequently to encounter family disorganization. Robert C. Weaver calls the incidence of family disorganization to urbanization an indicator of social disorganization. The disorganization permeates the entire family. School-age siblings are expected to get their own meals and take care of the needs of the smaller children. Older children frequently do not attend school regularly but remain at home in the mother's absence to entertain friends in the apartment. An investigator in the project environment can pick almost any building at random and find groups of elementary school children and teen-agers assembled at some apartment during school hours playing the "soul sounds."

Disadvantaged preschool children get very little attention when the mother is employed. After work, parents rarely have the time or energy to provide desirable training and experience for the small children. Except in families where there was a grandmother, there were only nine cases where the female parent was employed and the children had a hot breakfast prepared for them. The parent who must report to work early frequently leaves her children in bed and expects the older ones to arise and care for the younger ones. Many older siblings perform this task well. Others neglect the small children. Many mothers recognize this problem. As one said:

You know, mister, it's really a matter of choosing; what I mean by that is, I've either got to go to work and feed them or stay home and watch them hungry. Some folks wouldn't even call that a choice. There is a lot of things I'd like to do for them and with them, but I got to depend on the big children to do it. You know how children are—they don't always do what you say. When you get right down to it—they ain't responsible for them. I just found out that when I go to work in the morning and leave money with my oldest daughter to buy food and cook breakfast for the little children, she doesn't do it. She has been giving the little kids a few cents and they have been buying donuts, potato chips, and candy bars for breakfast from them street peddlers and them little gyp stores up and down the street in the neighborhoods and eating on the way to school.

Mothers who have children too young to look after themselves often leave them with relatives and friends while they work. Others sometimes keep school-age siblings at home to care for the children. One employed mother of ten rotated her children as baby-sitters by keeping a different one home from school each day to baby-sit with the three preschool children. No one child was absent from school enough consecutive days to attract the immediate attention of the welfare authorities.

There is little doubt that some working mothers in this environment neglect their children, for there is constant evidence of this neglect. It is common to see preschool and some young school-age children without socks and with shoes unlaced. One observes the comedy of dress as he sees children with their shoes on the wrong feet. This lack of attention would not, in itself, be unusual for many preschool children. However, the fact that some school-age children receive so little attention that they reach school in this condition provides an example of neglect and lack of parental supervision.

Items of clothing such as sweaters may be worn by children until one side is filthy and then turned and worn on the reverse side until they develop offensive odors. Some say that these examples definitely indicate neglect. Parents say, however:

When they ain't got no clothes—that ain't neglect. Have you ever tried to get six children out in the morning without a good suit of underwear among them? Half of them can't find their shoes. You need to wash every day with a family this big, but you got to wash when the schedule says— so if the children don't have changes of clothes, and you can't wash them they got every day, they just have to wear them.

Lawd today! Here we go with that again! Expecting us to do with seven or eight what a lot of other folks can't do with one—and I leave mine at home to go there and help them with that one. I expect they would be in the same fix without a husband, with one bathroom, six kids, and poor. They probably couldn't do as well.

Many mothers apparently do not have the skill, know-how, or desire to develop routines and schedules designed to make their families function more effectively; yet some try. Others simply do not accept parental responsibility. The household tends to fall apart from lack of leadership and direction.

Although the mother in Blackmoor must assume many responsibilities that are not normally undertaken by a woman in a privileged home or in a home where there is a male spouse, she does not always develop good qualities of leadership. Many things happen to her as she plays the numerous roles incumbent upon her. Frequently, she has had too little education to deal with some of her children intellectually. Sometimes she has encountered many frictions and abrasions in dealing with merchants who have attempted to exploit her. These encounters make her skeptical and suspicious; thus, she may fail to instill in her children a sense of trust. If she lives in a house without an adult male, her children will have little or no opportunity to see her react emotionally to a member of the opposite sex. She recoils at the moral myopia of people in the mainstream who criticize her and expect a code of behavior from her that she feels is too difficult and too absurd for her to follow. Consequently, she may not always set a good example for her children. Many mothers fail to become effective leaders because they do not know what their rights are and what resources are available to them. Mothers in Blackmoor have lived with the many and varied evils of the ghetto—human congestion, filth, crime, exploitation, low income, lack of dignity—which have made them cynical. Too many are hostile. Hostility in a mother does little to develop in children a positive attitude.

Household heads in the housing project spend their time providing for the basic needs and have little time to devote to developing their own leadership or to giving direction to their children. Being poor is an all-consuming and full-time job.

. . . . .

The outlook is not good in Blackmoor. Unemployment is still there. Welfare, with all its attending inequities and antiquation, is still there. The deprived conditions of the housing project are still evidenced. Children still go to bed hungry. The housing project remains the same or gets worse. Many are concerned with trying to make it better. Plans are born, die and are born again—and die. The road ahead has only the signs of pessimism. The people seethe. One angry woman marching on City Hall with a protest group from Blackmoor told a TV reporter:

They pay more a day for a monkey's family out there in the city zoo than they pay me in welfare—and they don't ask the monkeys to pick themselves up by their bootstraps. The monkey house out in the park got all of the windows in it—they got enough janitors to keep it clean. Ain't we as good as monkeys? I don't want nothing free; I want to work. But where? Can't we

come up with some kind of workable idea to solve some of the problems in Blackmoor?

WELFARE AND NEW JOBS

There is one plan that the author would propose for consideration as a possible solution for some of the dilemmas of the tenants, especially the male tenants. The plan would require cooperation from many areas of the community—labor unions, employers, welfare agencies, the state employment agency, and the local housing authority. Most significant, the plan would require active participation of the tenants.

In the state where Midwest City is located, a new bill for aid to dependent children of unemployed fathers is expected to be passed by the state legislature. If such a bill becomes law, an unemployed father may remain in the home while his family continues to receive welfare assistance. The author would propose that these men become part of a maintenance force for the housing project. They would work under the supervision of a union painter, glazier, or landscaper during the periods they were out of work. Their jobs would be to keep the project clean and in good repair. They would not be expected to earn full union scale, but they would receive pay and would receive on-the-job training. While this inhouse work force was learning a new skill, the state employment service would seek placement for them. If steady work was located, either using the skill for which they were receiving training or doing some other work, they would be free to take the new employment.

It would have to be absolutely understood that this program would not be just a source of cheap labor for the housing authority but a training program where men could learn a useful skill. It is envisioned that trainers of this labor force would determine areas where the most frequent demands for workers are made. The whole maintenance supervision area would be explored. It is further envisioned that some attempts would be made to find a job that would fit the particular interest, abilities, and skills of the worker. Those tenants, for example, who have rural backgrounds, like to work out of doors, and have no specific academic skills, may wish to do landscape work. This does not mean that a brigade of men with broomsticks with a nail on the end who go out and pick up paper would be considered landscapers. Rather, the training would be intensive and broad, including planting, pruning, fertilizing, transplanting, using insecticides, landscape designing, and any other skills that would help a man learn the exterior management of homes. A college degree is not needed for this type of work. A survey conducted by one of the local newspapers in Midwest City revealed that 80 percent of the men doing landscape work and 73 percent of those working in professional plant nurseries in the Midwest City area have less than a high school education. Moreover, most of the subdivisions are maintained by men who said that they learned the trade by trial and error plus the experiences they had while living in rural communities. There is a need for landscape workers during the entire year. The amounts of money they can earn are limited by their initiative, the equipment they can accumulate and use, and the time they wish to spend doing the work.

On the other hand, young men who do not enjoy working out of doors, who have a high school diploma or some previous educational training, and who have the interest and motivation may be offered stipends to attend adult classes or the local community college on a full- or part-time basis and work for the housing authority as part-time workers.

Older men in the housing project may choose to become trainers of new tenants as they move into the housing project.

They may also become permanent members of the maintenance staff who, in fact, could move about and work in other public housing throughout the city. The important thing is that every man in the project have a job. It is obvious that a plan of this nature would require a monumental task of coordination. However, if the expertise of an entire city is brought to bear on this problem and if the facilities of the colleges and universities that in the past have been used to study the housing projects, and their tenants are utilized and if the resources of the federal government are available, the job of coordination should and could become routine.

Many benefits could accrue from a plan of having tenants partially responsible for maintaining their own homes. Some of the benefits would be in the interest of the housing authority, some would be of a financial and practical nature that would profit both the tenants and the housing agency; the whole city would certainly have much to gain. The tenants, however, would get the greatest return on their investment of themselves to improve their own lot and that of their children. The advantages would be as lofty and ideal as people developing pride in themselves and as practical and ordinary as workers not having a problem of transportation to and from work because they would reside at their place of employment. The fathers would be in the home and could assume more of the roles expected of them. Men could take more pride in their homes because their efforts would be essential to the maintenance of them. Children would see their fathers go to and from work and could watch them as they painted the walls in apartments, repaired the locks on washrooms, and completed other jobs. More specifically, children would be able to observe how the work habit is developed, nurtured, and maintained. The cost of day-to-day operation of the housing project would be greatly reduced. Project children and persons from the outside would be less likely to destroy property with adult males around, especially those males responsible for keeping the property in good repair. Adult males in the ghetto have an immediate and direct way of handling aggressive and destructive behavior on the part of teen-agers and other young adults. By comparison, the prolonged and nondirective approach of teachers, social workers, and psychologists for handling this behavior is considered ineffective by adult males in the project. If we follow this argument to some of its logical conclusions, we can also see that such an arrangement as having tenants in the project become its maintenance force can have a positive effect on the total community. Perhaps, for the first time, fringe benefits could come to a ghetto. These benefits would accrue to the schools, merchants in the area, churches, and other agencies. These men might also prove to be deterrents to the winos, gamblers, robbers, rapists, and other persons and questionable activities found in the housing project. Just the presence of a male head in the majority of the 2,100 families in Blackmoor would certainly change the character of the entire area.

Like most plans, this one has its problems. It would probably be severely criticized by many as keeping poor people (black and white) in menial tasks with a pipeline only to obsolescence. Union people could justifiably say that union scales were not being paid and that some dues-paying union workers were being denied employment. Many would suggest that the workers would not be placed on a job even if they learned skills. Some of the project males would have arrest records.* These factors would prevent many employers from hiring workers from the Blackmoor labor pool of workers and trainees. There are also problems of compensation for the injuries of workers if accidents should occur, and, of course, some would. There is a whole cadre of other problems— legal, moral, social and practical—that would have to be thought through. There is also the possibility that the men in the housing project would not be interested in this plan. In spite of everything done, there are tenants who by choice, circumstances, obstinacy, and lack of initiative prefer the status quo. This is a part of the price of innovation, especially when one group of men attempts to plan the lives and the use of the time of other men.

The problems in the housing project, as we have seen, will not be solved by using a single approach—if they can be solved at all. Housing agencies across the country approach the problem of public housing in varying ways. None of the methods has been successful where the tenants are poor, where the number of ADC families exceeds more than 20 percent, where they are located in an inner-city ghetto, where the ethnic occupancy is more than 90 percent, and where all the other symptoms and problems of the ghetto are present. Blackmoor meets all these criteria and they affect the tenants in a negative way, especially the children. The unfavorable effects of living in the housing projects on children in particular are reinforced when the children leave the total influence of the home and go to school in the ghetto.

* A record of arrest does not mean that a man has been convicted or even committed a crime.

24. CRUCIBLE OF IDENTITY: THE NEGRO LOWER-CLASS FAMILY

Lee Rainwater

This note is for the two following selections. They provide further glimpses into aspects of life-style in the poorest sectors of the black urban ghetto. Rainwater probes further than Moore did in the preceding selection into issues of family organization and values. Then Werthman shows some of the interplay between delinquent boys' perspectives and those of their parents and schools. The complementarity between Rainwater's and Werthman's works suggests that when rewards and satisfactions are not available through conventional settings that are approved in the larger culture, people tend to seek them elsewhere, building up their own codes and standards that channel and govern the behavior that occurs in the directions that are open. Then the pull or attraction of the alternative reward systems makes it more difficult still to go on settling for the few and uncertain long-range satisfactions that conventionally approved conduct might lead to.

Let's leave the words and world of sociology for a while to daydream as someone else might do. Imagine that you're fourteen years old, and that you live in an overcrowded flat where your mother keeps the kitchen light on all night to discourage rats from coming out. The water is rusty, and maybe this is one of the mornings that a cockroach is in the cereal box. A wino slept the night in the hall of your building; when you pass him you vaguely note that he stinks of urine. On your way to school you notice a few junkies and pass a whore or two coming back from work pretty late. School is where they tell you

Source: *Daedalus,* Vol. 95, No. 1 (Winter 1966), pp. 172–216, with some footnotes omitted. Reprinted by permission of the author and the American Academy of Arts and Sciences.

LEE RAINWATER, author of *And the Poor Get Children, The Moynihan Report,* and *The Politics of Controversy,* and other works, is Professor of Sociology at Harvard University.

to keep on working hard, and that if you're good you can make something of yourself, whatever that means. It all seems so far away. How are you going to be able to put up with four or eight or twelve more years of having to stay quiet and learn about things that don't mean much to you because you never had any experience with any of them, just so you can get to be a high school graduate, a college man, a lawyer? How can you do that for so long when you have so much on your mind now, like that chick on the block who's got big eyes for you; like how sore your old man gets whenever your mom says anything to him about what a lousy place you have to live in; like how she's trying to keep you off the street when all the other guys are out there; like how you've got to get yourself some money somehow because without it you can't feel like you're anybody; like if maybe you could grow six inches quickly you could get to be a big basketball player? Your little sister is your mother's darling because she does well in school. She even *likes* it. How does she do it when there's nobody to talk to about what you're learning—as if you learn anything anyway after the sixth grade. Like you've had two years of Spanish, but you can't understand a word of what those Puerto Ricans are talking about. Your folks have never been to the school since your mom took you to kindergarten—seems like they were ashamed not to know what to say or how to say it. Anyhow, they're either out working or tired when they get home. It isn't their fault; they came up from down South when they were little, without anybody who could teach them anything either. It isn't their fault, and it isn't yours. But what can you do? That's a big world out there, and one little kid isn't going to change it. That just about decides it. Why not just raise a little hell tonight? If you have to, you can sleep it off tomorrow in that stupid old school anyhow.

Come back now to the abstractions of academe. The vignette you've read is not the whole story of ghetto early adolescence. In the black middle class, life is much more like what most of you reading this book know from your own experience. Moreover, I have tried to describe a fairly sensitive boy from a stable working-class family. He might—or might not—pick up the pieces of his existence and get his life together. There are real people who have far less choice than he. For in the black lower class, life is more depressing and experience more frustrating than what I have written. It is of the lower class that Rainwater writes, of families that are not merely financially and materially impoverished, but without informational and emotional resources as well.

In most of American society, families are expected to provide children with values and attitudes that keep behavior from being too far out of line, with psychic and material resources that help to build and maintain self-confidence, with acquired drives that motivate curiosity and support efforts to achieve. Slum families of whatever color fail at all of these tasks more frequently than more prosperous families do. That is not disputable. A weak family structure, combined with the socioeconomic handicaps confronted by each family member, is related, both as symptom and as partial cause, to school failure, to delinquency, to unemployment, to addiction, to infant mortality and high rates of sickness in general—in short, to the whole gamut of ills that is one of the hallmarks of the urban slum.

What *is* disputable is expecting that slum families be able to perform the tasks expected of them as well as other families do. Slum families have to overcome severe handicaps to meet these goals. The resources at their disposal for trying to do so are meager in comparison to what most of the rest of the society has to work with. Just trying to carry out those tasks is a source of strain and tension. Clearly, the weak family system of poor urban black people is more a product of its history and circumstances than it is a starting point to be taken *in itself* as cause for those indices of social disorganization that are obviously higher in black and other poor areas than among the better-off.

The most perplexing thing about the poor black slum family is not that it is an anachronistic urban relic of a kinship system created by slavery but nonetheless able to function more or less effectively in the conditions of the postbellum rural South. Nor is the major issue that our society acts as if it were pure and Puritan when assessing the immorality of its underclasses, while at the same time relaxing its own sexual codes and becoming expert in the use of legal, institutionalized means of ending marriages and dissolving family units. Nor is the key that we are reluctant to consider the possibility that healthy and fulfilling family systems might be built on the base of a tradition different from our own; one which (through necessity rather than choice, to be sure) has not subjugated women and mothers to male standards, but has rather depended upon them for strength, stability, and authority.

All those points are relevant, but for me they are not the crux of the matter. The essential paradox, as I see it, is obvious. On the one hand, the rewards and satisfactions of the dominant culture and of its family system have been there for poor black people to see and to desire. On the other hand, the glimpse of security and stability has not been backed up by routes of access to the facilities, the resources, and the opportunities that would let the bottom-ranking third or so of American black males get a solid grip on the bootstrap that plays so large a role in our folklore and in the actual history of our white immigrant groups.[1] The social problems of the ghetto do not originate in the family system of poor black people. They originate in the history that created that family system. They lie in the school systems that do not know how to deal with it. They fester in politico-economic arrangements that provide their own justification for the developed world's most disparate distribution of absolute purchasing power. They are an implicit concomitant of a refusal to come to terms with the fact that only by letting everyone who wishes to work earn a living standard high enough to buy some of the pegs that decency and security hang on, shall we be able to clear away the tangled growth of ignorance and apathy, frustration and anger that have flourished under three centuries of enslavement, peonage, oppression, and disdain. One need not dream of utopias. Without making crime and conflict disappear completely, other Western nations have done far more than us to foster equal life chances and conditions. Admittedly, their populations are smaller and more homogeneous and have had lower material expectations. Taking account of those qualifications, however, ought to make us pause to consider whether we can rest at all satisfied with where racism and acquisitiveness have led us.

I pointed out above that a weak family system is part of a larger pattern that also includes a highly elaborated street culture. Particularly for young males, the street and the peer groups to be found upon it provide satisfactions and opportunities that are not readily found elsewhere, in home or school. Delinquency is an active, striving way of meeting the street culture's norms. As Werthman shows, when other channels are clogged, delinquency offers a route to comradeship, adventure, fun, excitement. It is a way of displaying courage, autonomy, intelligence, and leadership skills, of attaining a bit of fleeting fame. Not least important is that it is also a method of obtaining money. A few of the brightest and hardest working delinquents continue longer at illegal activities, taking advantage of so-called illegitimate opportunities by finding good semipermanent hustles. More fall victim to the scourge of addiction, and to support their habit become chronic and careless lawbreakers. Most will ultimately leave delinquency behind, will settle down to one or another or a series of humdrum jobs.

Currently we occasionally hear of attempts to endow ghetto

---

[1] Few others have argued these points as convincingly as Elliot Liebow in his *Tally's Corner* (Boston: Little, Brown and Company, 1967).

delinquency with intrinsic political significance, seeing street gangs, for example, as a nascent form of organization for race-oriented protest. In my judgment, such statements are still far off the mark.[2] Victims of black delinquents are disproportionately other blacks; and delinquent acts are still usually carried out by groups of two or three youngsters after adventure, prestige, and profit. Racism maintains the conditions that spawn delinquency, but in the narrower, more circumscribed situation in which most delinquent acts take place, racial vindication is often merely one of the anticipatory or post hoc rationalizations that are part of the delinquent's world view.[3]

The ghetto street-world operates pretty much under its own informal rules except when property is threatened, or when legal or administrative rules (such as those of welfare departments) are too openly broken, or when mass outbursts break out, or when the authorities feel threatened by prospects of sedition. Then arrests and forceful suppression occur. Little people, or perhaps a few well-known "militants," get rounded up. The big men whose organizations manage drugs and gambling, funneling the major profits outside the ghetto, go untouched. Narcotic addiction is a plague in the ghetto; [4] the

[2] This is not to say that gangs do not exist. Indeed, they do, and in some cities they have a surprisingly elaborate and extensive network. For a description of one such network see R. L. Keiser, *The Vice Lords* (New York: Holt, Rinehart and Winston, 1969). The best comparative study of lower-class black and white gang and nongang boys and of middle-class nongang boys is James Short, Jr., and Fred Strodtbeck, *Group Process and Gang Delinquency* (Chicago: University of Chicago Press, 1965).

[3] Of course, many black delinquents feel discriminated against—why not?—but so do many "straight" black youngsters. The sociological theory of delinquency that gives the greatest scope to racial barriers is Richard Cloward and Lloyd Ohlin, *Delinquency and Opportunity* (New York: The Free Press of Glencoe, 1960). As for the ways delinquents define their world and explain their acts, the best book is still, despite a difficult style, David Matza, *Delinquency and Drift* (New York: John Wiley & Sons, Inc., 1964).

[4] "More striking . . . was the residential pattern of addiction. Nearly half the city's [Washington, D.C.] addicts live in a 7.7 square mile area that is the most densely populated part of the city—the 'inner city,' or black ghetto. Within that large area lies the three-square-mile 'Model Cities' sector, just a few blocks north of the White House. In the Model Cities sector, 36 percent of all young men between twenty and twenty-four years of age and 24 percent of all youths between fifteen and nineteen are heroin addicts."—Tom Wicker, "A Tale of Two Cities," *The New York Times,* February 7, 1971, p. E-13.

In Washington, so high an addiction rate struck authorities as surprising. In certain areas of New York and Chicago, in contrast, it is already old hat. Rates that high constitute epidemics. There were addiction epidemics as long as twenty years ago, too, though the rates were lower then,

numbers game, one of its favorite pastimes. Both are illegitimate; both are controlled by whites at the top; both depend on whatever influence they can muster over local police and political officials, and both are as colonialist as the near lily-white and snow-pure downtown bank that sooner lends money to a profitable real-estate speculator than to an uncertain ghetto family seeking a home-improvement mortgage.

and there was far less concern about them. After all, the disease seemed to be quarantined, stuck in the bottle by the same cork that kept black people from doing any more than trickling out into white residential areas.

As long as Negroes have been in America, their marital and family patterns have been subjects of curiosity and amusement, moral indignation and self-congratulation, puzzlement and frustration, concern and guilt, on the part of white Americans.[1] As some Negroes have moved into middle-class status, or acquired standards of American common-man respectability, they too have shared these attitudes toward the private behavior of their fellows, sometimes with a moral punitiveness to rival that of whites, but at other times with a hard-headed interest in causes and remedies rather than moral evaluation. Moralism permeated the subject of Negro sexual,

marital, and family behavior in the polemics of slavery apologists and abolitionists as much as in the Northern and Southern civil rights controversies of today. Yet, as long as the dialectic of good or bad, guilty or innocent, overshadows a concern with who, why, and what can be, it is unlikely that realistic and effective social planning to correct the clearly desperate situation of poor Negro families can begin.

This paper is concerned with a description and analysis of slum Negro family patterns as these reflect and sustain Negroes' adaptations to the economic, social, and personal situation into which they are born and in which they

[1] This paper is based in part on research supported by a grant from the National Institutes of Mental Health, Grant No. MH-09189, "Social and Community Problems in Public Housing Areas." Many of the ideas presented stem from discussion with the senior members of the Pruitt-Igoe research staff—Alvin W. Gouldner, David J. Pittman, and Jules Henry—and with the research associates and assistants on the project. I have made particular use of ideas developed in discussions with Boone Hammond, Joyce Ladner, Robert Simpson, David Schulz, and William Yancey. I also wish to acknowledge helpful suggestions and criticisms by Catherine Chilman, Gerald Handel, and Marc J. Swartz. Although this paper is not a formal report of the Pruitt-Igoe research, all of the illustrations of family behavior given in the text are drawn from interviews and observations that are part of that study. The study deals with the residents of the Pruitt-Igoe housing projects in St. Louis. Some 10,000 people live in these projects which comprise forty-three eleven-story buildings near the downtown area of St. Louis. Over half of the households have female heads, and for over half

of the households the principal income comes from public assistance of one kind or another. The research has been in the field for a little over two years. It is a broad community study which thus far has relied principally on methods of participant observation and open-ended interviewing. Data on families come from repeated interviews and observations with a small group of families. The field workers are identified as graduate students at Washington University who have no connection with the housing authority or other officials, but are simply interested in learning about how families in the project live. This very intensive study of families yields a wealth of information (over 10,000 pages of interview and observation reports) which obviously cannot be analyzed within the limits of one article. In this article I have limited myself to outlining a typical family stage sequence and discussing some of the psychosocial implications of growing up in families characterized by this sequence. In addition, I have tried to limit myself to findings which other literature on Negro family life suggests are not limited to the residents of the housing projects we are studying.

must live. As such it deals with facts of lower-class life that are usually forgotten or ignored in polite discussion. We have chosen not to ignore these facts in the belief that to do so can lead only to assumptions which would frustrate efforts at social reconstruction, to strategies that are unrealistic in the light of the actual day-to-day reality of slum Negro life. Further this analysis will deal with family patterns which interfere with the efforts slum Negroes make to attain a stable way of life as working- or middle-class individuals and with the effects such failure in turn has on family life. To be sure many Negro families live *in* the slum ghetto, but are not *of* its culture (though even they, and particularly their children, can be deeply affected by what happens there). However, it is the individuals who succumb to the distinctive family life style of the slum who experience the greatest weight of deprivation and who have the greatest difficulty responding to the few self-improvement resources that make their way into the ghetto. In short, we propose to explore in depth the family's role in the "tangle of pathology" which characterizes the ghetto.

The social reality in which Negroes have had to make their lives during the 450 years of their existence in the western hemisphere has been one of victimization "in the sense that a system of social relations operates in such a way as to deprive them of a chance to share in the more desirable material and non-material products of a society which is dependent, in part, upon their labor and loyalty." In making this observation, St. Clair Drake goes on to note that Negroes are victimized also because "they do not have the same degree of access which others have to the attributes needed for rising in the general class system— money, education, 'contacts,' and 'know-how.' " [2] The victimization process

started with slavery; for 350 years thereafter Negroes worked out as best they could adaptations to the slave status. After emancipation, the cultural mechanisms which Negroes had developed for living the life of victim continued to be serviceable as the victimization process was maintained first under the myths of white supremacy and black inferiority, later by the doctrines of gradualism which covered the fact of no improvement in position, and finally by the modern Northern system of ghettoization and indifference.

When lower-class Negroes use the expression, "Tell it like it is," they signal their intention to strip away pretense, to describe a situation or its participants as they really are, rather than in a polite or euphemistic way. "Telling it like it is" can be used as a harsh, aggressive device, or it can be a healthy attempt to face reality rather than retreat into fantasy. In any case, as he goes about his field work, the participant observer studying a ghetto community learns to listen carefully to any exchange preceded by such an announcement because he knows the speaker is about to express his understanding of how his world operates, of what motivates its members, of how they actually behave.

The first responsibility of the social scientist can be phrased in much the same way: "Tell it like it is." His second responsibility is to try to understand why "it" is that way, and to explore the implications of what and why for more constructive solutions to human problems. Social research on the situation of the Negro American has been informed by four main goals: (1) to describe the disadvantaged position of Negroes, (2) to disprove the racist ideology which sustains the caste system, (3) to demonstrate that responsibility for the disadvantages Negroes suffer lies squarely upon the white caste which derives economic, prestige, and psychic benefits

[2] St. Clair Drake, "The Social and Economic Status of the Negro in the United States," *Dædalus* (Fall 1965), p. 772.

from the operation of the system, and (4) to suggest that in reality whites would be better rather than worse off if the whole jerry-built caste structure were to be dismantled. The successful accomplishment of these intellectual goals has been a towering achievement, in which the social scientists of the 1920's, '30's, and '40's can take great pride; that white society has proved so recalcitrant to utilizing this intellectual accomplishment is one of the great tragedies of our time, and provides the stimulus for further social research on "the white problem."

Yet the implicit paradigm of much of the research on Negro Americans has been an overly simplistic one concentrating on two terms of an argument:

White cupidity ⟶ Negro suffering.

As an intellectual shorthand, and even more as a civil rights slogan, this simple model is both justified and essential. But, as a guide to greater understanding of the Negro situation as human adaptation to human situations, the paradigm is totally inadequate because it fails to specify fully enough the *process* by which Negroes adapt to their situations as they do, and the limitations one kind of adaptation places on possibilities for subsequent adaptations. A reassessment of previous social research, combined with examination of current social research on Negro ghetto communities, suggests a more complex, but hopefully more vertical, model:

White cupidity

creates

Structural Conditions Highly Inimical to Basic Social Adaptation (low-income availability, poor education, poor services, stigmatization)

to which Negroes adapt

by

Social and Personal Responses which serve to sustain the individual in his punishing world but also generate aggressiveness toward the self and others

which results in

Suffering directly inflicted by Negroes on themselves and on others.

In short, whites, by their greater power, create situations in which Negroes do the dirty work of caste victimization for them.

The white caste maintains a cadre of whites whose special responsibility is to enforce the system in brutal or refined ways (the Klan, the rural sheriff, the metropolitan police, the businessman who specializes in a Negro clientele, the Board of Education). Increasingly, whites recruit to this cadre middle-class Negroes who can soften awareness of victimization by their protective coloration. These special cadres, white and/or Negro, serve the very important function of enforcing caste standards by whatever means seems required, while at the same time concealing from an increasingly "unprejudiced" public the unpleasant facts they would prefer to ignore. The system is quite homologous to the Gestapo and concentration camps of Nazi Germany, though less fatal to its victims.

For their part, Negroes creatively adapt to the system in ways that keep them alive and extract what gratification they can find, but in the process of adaptation they are constrained to behave in ways that inflict a great deal of suffering on those with whom they make their lives, and on themselves. The ghetto Negro is constantly confronted by the immediate necessity to suffer in order to get what he wants of those few things he can have, or to make others suffer, or both—for example, he suffers as exploited student and employee, as drug user, as loser in the competitive game of his peer-group society; he inflicts suffering as disloyal spouse, petty thief, knife- or gun-wielder, petty con man.

It is the central thesis of this paper that the caste-facilitated infliction of suffering by Negroes on other Negroes and on themselves appears most poignantly within the confines of the family, and that the victimization process as it operates in families prepares and toughens its members to function in the ghetto world, at the same time that it seriously interferes with their ability to operate in any other world. This, however, is very different from arguing that "the family is to blame" for the deprived situation ghetto Negroes suffer; rather we are looking at the logical outcome of the operation of the widely ramified and interconnecting caste system. In the end we will argue that only palliative results can be expected from attempts to treat directly the disordered family patterns to be described. Only a change in the original "inputs" of the caste system, and structural conditions inimical to basic social adaptation, can change family forms.

. . . . .

Household groups function for cultures in carrying out the initial phases of socialization and personality formation. It is in the family that the child learns the most primitive categories of existence and experience, and that he develops his most deeply held beliefs about the world and about himself.[3] From the child's point of view, the household *is* the world; his experiences as he moves out of it into the larger world are always interpreted in terms of his particular experience within the home. The painful experiences which a child in the Negro slum culture has are, therefore, interpreted as in some sense a reflection of this family world. The im-

[3] Talcott Parsons concludes his discussion of child socialization, the development of an "internalized family system" and internalized role differentiation by observing, "The internalization of the family collectivity as an object and its values should not be lost sight of. This is crucial with respect to . . . the assumption of representative roles outside the family on behalf of it. Here it is the child's family membership which is decisive, and thus his acting in a role in terms of its values for 'such as he.'" Talcott Parsons and Robert F. Bales, *Family, Socialization and Interaction Process* (Glencoe, Ill., 1955), p. 113.

pact of the system of victimization is transmitted through the family; the child cannot be expected to have the sophistication an outside observer has for seeing exactly where the villians are. From the child's point of view, if he is hungry it is his parents' fault; if he experiences frustrations in the streets or in the school it is his parents' fault; if people are aggressive or destructive toward each other it is his parents' fault, not that of a system of race relations. In another culture this might not be the case; if a subculture could exist which provided comfort and security within its limited world and the individual experienced frustration only when he moved out into the larger society, the family might not be thought so much to blame. The effect of the caste system, however, is to bring home through a chain of cause and effect all of the victimization processes, and to bring them home in such a way that it is often very difficult even for adults in the system to see the connection between the pain they feel at the moment and the structured patterns of the caste system.

Let us take as a central question that of identity formation within the Negro slum family. We are concerned with the question of who the individual believes himself to be and to be becoming. For Erikson, identity means a sense of continuity and social sameness which bridges what the individual *"was* as a child and what he is *about to become* and also reconciles his *conception of himself* and his community's recognition of him." Thus identity is a "self-realization coupled with a mutual recognition."[4] In the early childhood years identity is family-bound since the child's identity is his identity *vis-à-vis* other members of the family. Later he incorporates into his sense of who he is and is becoming his experiences outside the family, but always influenced

[4] Erik H. Erikson, "Identity and the Life Cycle," *Psychological Issues,* Vol. 1, No. 1 (1959).

by the interpretations and evaluations of those experiences that the family gives. As the child tries on identities, *announces* them, the family sits as judge of his pretensions. Family members are both the most important judges and the most critical ones, since who he is allowed to become affects them in their own identity strivings more crucially than it affects anyone else. The child seeks a sense of valid identity, a sense of being a particular person with a satisfactory degree of congruence between who he feels he is, who he announces himself to be, and where he feels his society places him.[5] He is uncomfortable when he experiences disjunction between his own needs and the kinds of needs legitimated by those around him, or when he feels a disjunction between his sense of himself and the image of himself that others play back to him.[6]

"Tell it like it is." / When families become involved in important quarrels the psychosocial underpinnings of family life are laid bare. One such quarrel in a family we have been studying brings together in one place many of the themes that seem to dominate identity problems in Negro slum culture. The incident illustrates in a particularly forceful and dramatic way family processes which our field work, and some other contemporary studies of slum family life, sug-

gests unfold more subtly in a great many families at the lower-class level. The family involved, the Johnsons, is certainly not the most disorganized one we have studied; in some respects their way of life represents a realistic adaptation to the hard living of a family nineteen years on AFDC with a monthly income of $202 for nine people. The two oldest daughters, Mary Jane (eighteen years old) and Esther (sixteen) are pregnant; Mary Jane has one illegitimate child. The adolescent sons, Bob and Richard, are much involved in the social and sexual activities of their peer group. The three other children, ranging in age from twelve to fourteen, are apparently also moving into this kind of peer-group society.

When the argument started Bob and Esther were alone in the apartment with Mary Jane's baby. Esther took exception to Bob's playing with the baby because she had been left in charge; the argument quickly progressed to a fight in which Bob cuffed Esther around, and she tried to cut him with a knife. The police were called and subdued Bob with their nightsticks. At this point the rest of the family and the field worker arrived. As the argument continued, these themes relevant to the analysis which follows appeared:

1. The sisters said that Bob was not their brother (he is a half-brother to Esther, and Mary Jane's full brother). Indeed, they said their mother "didn't have no husband. These kids don't even know who their daddies are." The mother defended herself by saying that she had one legal husband, and one common-law husband, no more.

2. The sisters said that their fathers had never done anything for them, nor had their mother. She retored that she had raised them "to the age of womanhood" and now would care for their babies.

3. Esther continued to threaten to cut Bob if she got a chance (a month later they

[5] For discussion of the dynamics of the individual's *announcements* and the society's *placements* in the formation of identity, see Gregory Stone, "Appearance and the Self," in Arnold Rose, *Human Behavior in Social Process* (Boston, 1962), pp. 86–118.

[6] The importance of identity for social behavior is discussed in detail in Ward Goodenough, *Cooperation and Change* (New York, 1963), pp. 176–251, and in Lee Rainwater, "Work and Identity in the Lower Class," in Sam H. Warner, Jr., *Planning for the Quality of Urban Life* (Cambridge, Mass., forthcoming). The images of self and of other family members is a crucial variable in Hess and Handel's psychosocial analysis of family life; see Robert D. Hess and Gerald Handel, *Family Worlds* (Chicago, 1959), especially pp. 6–11.

fought again, and she did cut Bob, who required twenty-one stitches).

4. The sisters accused their mother of favoring their lazy brothers and asked her to put them out of the house. She retorted that the girls were as lazy, that they made no contribution to maintaining the household, could not get their boy friends to marry them or support their children, that all the support came from her AFDC check. Mary Jane retorted that "the baby has a check of her own."

5. The girls threatened to leave the house if their mother refused to put their brothers out. They said they could force their boy friends to support them by taking them to court, and Esther threatened to cut her boy friend's throat if he did not co-operate.

6. Mrs. Johnson said the girls could leave if they wished but that she would keep their babies; "I'll not have it, not knowing who's taking care of them."

7. When her thirteen-year-old sister laughed at all of this, Esther told her not to laugh because she, too, would be pregnant within a year.

8. When Bob laughed, Esther attacked him and his brother by saying that both were not man enough to make babies, as she and her sister had been able to do.

9. As the field worker left, Mrs. Johnson sought his sympathy. "You see, Joe, how hard it is for me to bring up a family. . . . They sit around and talk to me like I'm some kind of a dog and not their mother."

10. Finally, it is important to note for the analysis which follows that the following labels—"black-assed," "black bastard," "bitch," and other profane terms were liberally used by Esther and Mary Jane, and rather less liberally by their mother, to refer to each other, to the girls' boy friends, to Bob, and to the thirteen-year-old daughter.

Several of the themes outlined previously appear forcefully in the course of this argument. In the last year and a half the mother has become a grandmother and expects shortly to add two more grandchildren to her household. She takes it for granted that it is her responsibility to care for the grandchildren and that she has the right to decide what will be done with the children since her own daughters are not fully responsible. She makes this very clear to them when they threaten to move out, a threat which they do not really wish to make good nor could they if they wished to.

However, only as an act of will is Mrs. Johnson able to make this a family. She must constantly cope with the tendency of her adolescent children to disrupt the family group and to deny that they are in fact a family—"He ain't no brother of mine"; "The baby has a check of her own." Though we do not know exactly what processes communicate these facts to the children it is clear that in growing up they have learned to regard themselves as not fully part of a solidary collectivity. During the quarrel this message was reinforced for the twelve-, thirteen-, and fourteen-year-old daughters by the four-way argument among their older sisters, older brother, and their mother.

The argument represents vicious unmasking of the individual members' pretenses to being competent individuals.[7] The efforts of the two girls to present themselves as masters of their own fate are unmasked by the mother. The girls in turn unmask the pretensions of the mother and of their two brothers. When the thirteen-year-old daughter expresses some amusement they turn on her, telling her that it won't be long before she too becomes pregnant. Each

[7] See the discussion of "masking" and "unmasking" in relation to disorganization and reequilibration in families by John P. Spiegel, "The Resolution of Role Conflict within the Family," in Norman W. Bell and Ezra F. Vogel, *A Modern Introduction to the Family* (Glencoe, Ill., 1960), pp. 375–377.

member of the family in turn is told that he can expect to be no more than a victim of his world, but that this is somehow inevitably his own fault.

In this argument masculinity is consistently demeaned. Bob has no right to play with his niece, the boys are not really masculine because at fifteen and sixteen years they have yet to father children, their own fathers were no goods who failed to do anything for their family. These notions probably come originally from the mother, who enjoys recounting the story of having her common-law husband imprisoned for non-support, but this comes back to haunt her as her daughters accuse her of being no better than they in ability to force support and nurturance from a man. In contrast, the girls came off somewhat better than the boys, although they must accept the label of stupid girls because they have similarly failed and inconveniently become pregnant in the first place. At least they can and have had children and therefore have some meaningful connection with the ongoing substance of life. There is something important and dramatic in which they participate, while the boys, despite their sexual activity, "can't get no babies."

In most societies, as children grow and are formed by their elders into suitable members of the society they gain increasingly a sense of competence and ability to master the behavioral environment their particular world presents. But in Negro slum culture growing up involves an ever-increasing appreciation of one's shortcomings, of the impossibility of finding a self-sufficient and gratifying way of living.[8] It is in the family first and most devastatingly that one learns these lessons. As the child's sense of frustration builds he too can strike out and unmask the pretensions of others.

[8] See the discussion of self-identity and self-esteem in Thomas F. Pettigrew, *A Profile of the Negro American* (Princeton, N.J., 1964), pp. 6–11.

The result is a peculiar strength and a pervasive weakness. The strength involves the ability to tolerate and defend against degrading verbal and physical aggressions from others and not to give up completely. The weakness involves the inability to embark hopefully on any course of action that might make things better, pratically action which involves cooperating and trusting attitudes toward others. Family members become potential enemies to each other, as the frequency of observing the police being called in to settle family quarrels brings home all too dramatically.

The conceptions parents have of their children are such that they are constantly alert as the child matures to evidence that he is as bad as everyone else. That is, in lower-class culture human nature is conceived of as essentially bad, destructive, immoral.[9] This is the nature of things. Therefore any one child must be inherently bad unless his parents are very lucky indeed. If the mother can keep the child insulated from the outside world, she feels she may be able to prevent his inherent badness from coming out. She feels that once he is let out into the larger world the badness will come to the fore since that is his nature. This means that in the identity development of the child he is constantly exposed to identity labeling by his parents as a bad person. Since as he grows up he does not experience his world as particularly gratifying, it is very easy for him to conclude that this lack of gratification is due to the fact that something is wrong with him. This, in turn, can readily be assimilated to the definitions of

[9] Lee Rainwater, Richard P. Coleman, and Gerald Handel, *Workingman's Wife* (New York, 1959), pp. 44–51. See also the discussion of the greater level of "anomie" and mistrust among lower-class people in Ephriam Mizruchi, *Success and Opportunity* (New York, 1954). Unpublished research by the author indicates that for one urban lower-class sample (Chicago) Negroes scored about 50 per cent higher on Srole's anomie scale than did comparable whites.

being a bad person offered him by those with whom he lives.[10] In this way the Negro slum child learns his culture's conception of being-in-the-world, a conception that emphasizes inherent evil in a chaotic, hostile, destructive world.

Blackness / To a certain extent these same processes operate in white lower-class groups, but added for the Negro is the reality of blackness. "Black-assed" is not an empty pejorative adjective. In the Negro slum culture several distinctive appellations are used to refer to oneself and others. One involves the terms, "black" or "nigger." Black is generally a negative way of naming, but nigger can be either negative or positive, depending upon the context. It is important to note that, at least in the urban North, the initial development of racial identity in these terms has very little directly to do with relations with whites. A child experiences these identity placements in the context of the family and in the neighborhood peer group; he probably very seldom hears the same terms used by whites (unlike the situation in the South). In this way, one of the effects of ghettoization is to mask the ultimate enemy so that the understanding of the fact of victimization by a caste system comes as a late acquisition laid over conceptions of self and of other Negroes derived from intimate, and to the child often traumatic, experience within the ghetto community. If, in addition, the child attends a ghetto school where his Negro teachers either overtly or by implication reinforce his community's negative conceptions of what it means to be black, then the child has little opportunity to develop a more realistic image of himself and other Negroes as being

damaged by whites and not by themselves. In such a situation, an intelligent man . . . [might] say with all sincerity that he does not feel most Negroes are ready for integration—only under the experience of certain kinds of intense personal threat coupled with exposure to an ideology that places the responsibility on whites [might] he begin to see through the direct evidence of his daily experience.

To those living in the heart of a ghetto, black comes to mean not just "stay back," but also membership in a community of persons who think poorly of each other, who attack and manipulate each other, who give each other small comfort in a desperate world. Black comes to stand for a sense of identity as no better than these destructive others. The individual feels that he must embrace an unattractive self in order to function at all.

We can hypothesize that in those families that manage to avoid the destructive identity imputations of "black" and that manage to maintain solidarity against such assaults from the world around, it is possible for children to grow up with a sense of both Negro and personal identity that allows them to socialize themselves in an anticipatory way for participation in the larger society.[11] This broader sense of identity, however, will remain a brittle one as long as the individual is vulnerable to attack from within the Negro community as "nothing but a nigger like everybody else" or from the white community as "just a nigger." We can hypothesize further that the vicious unmasking of essential identity as black described above is least likely to occur within families where the parents have some stable sense of security, and where they therefore have less need to protect

[10] For a discussion of the child's propensity from a very early age for speculation and developing explanations, see William V. Silverberg, *Childhood Experience and Personal Destiny* (New York, 1953), pp. 81 ff.

[11] See Ralph Ellison's autobiographical descriptions of growing up in Oklahoma City in his *Shadow and Act* (New York, 1964).

themselves by disavowing responsibility for their children's behavior and denying the children their patrimony as products of a particular family rather than of an immoral nature and an evil community.

In sum, we are suggesting that Negro slum children as they grow up in their families and in their neighborhoods are exposed to a set of experiences—and a rhetoric which conceptualizes them— that brings home to the child an understanding of his essence as a weak and debased persons who can expect only partial gratification of his needs, and who must seek even this level of gratification by less than straight-forward means.

Strategies for living / In every society complex processes of socialization inculcate in their members strategies for gratifying the needs with which they are born and those which the society itself generates. Inextricably linked to these strategies, both cause and effect of them, are the existential propositions which members of a culture entertain about the nature of their world and of effective action within the world as it is defined for them. In most of American society two grand strategies seem to attract the allegiance of its members and guide their day-to-day actions. I have called these strategies those of *the good life* and of *career success*.[12] A good life strategy involves efforts to get along with others and not to rock the boat, a comfortable familism grounded on a stable work career for husbands in which they perform adequately at the modest jobs that enable them to be good providers. The strategy of career success is the choice of ambitious men and women who see life as providing opportunities to move from a lower to a higher status, to "accomplish something," to achieve greater than ordinary material well-being, prestige, and social recognition. Both of these strategies are predicated on the assumption that the world is inherently rewarding if one behaves properly and does his part. The rewards of the world may come easily or only at the cost of great effort, but at least they are there.

In the white and particlarly in the Negro slum worlds little in the experience that individuals have as they grow up sustains a belief in a rewarding world. The strategies that seem appropriate are not those of a good, family-based life or of a career, but rather *strategies for survival.*

Much of what has been said above can be summarized as encouraging three kinds of survival strategies. One is the strategy of the *expressive life style* which I have described elsewhere as an effort to make yourself interesting and attractive to others so that you are better able to manipulate their behavior along lines that will provide some immediate gratification.[13] Negro slum culture provides many examples of techniques for seduction, of persuading others to give you what you want in situations where you have very little that is tangible to offer in return. In order to get what you want you learn to "work game," a strategy which requires a high development of a certain kind of verbal facility, a sophisticated manipulation of promise and interim reward. When the expressive strategy fails or when it is unavailable there is, of course, the great temptation to adopt a *violent strategy* in which you force others to give you what you need once you fail to win it by verbal and other symbolic means.[14] Finally, and increasingly as members of the Negro slum culture grow older, there is the *depressive strategy* in which goals are increasingly constricted to the bare necessities for sur-

[12] Rainwater, "Work and Identity in the Lower Class," *op. cit.*

[13] *Ibid.*

[14] Short and Strodtbeck see violent behavior in juvenile gangs as a kind of last resort strategy in situations where the actor feels he has no other choice. See James F. Short, Jr., and Fred L. Strodtbeck, *Group Process and Gang Delinquency* (Chicago, 1965), pp. 248–264.

vival (not as a social being but simply as an organism).[15] This is the strategy of "I don't bother anybody and I hope nobody's gonna bother me; I'm simply going through the motions to keep body (but not soul) together." Most lower-class people follow mixed strategies, as Walter Miller has observed, alternating among the excitement of the expressive style, the desperation of the violent style, and the deadness of the depressed style.[16] Some members of the Negro slum world experiment from time to time with mixed strategies that also incorporate the stable working-class model of the good American life, but this latter strategy is exceedingly vulnerable to the threats of unemployment or a less than adequate pay check, on the one hand, and the seduction and violence of the slum world around them, on the other.

Remedies / Finally, it is clear that we, no less than the inhabitants of the ghetto, are not masters of their fate because we are not masters of our own total society. Despite the battles with poverty on many fronts we can find little evidence to sustain our hope of winning the war given current programs and strategies.

The question of strategy is particularly crucial when one moves from an examination of destructive cultural and interaction patterns in Negro families to the question of how these families might achieve a more stable and gratifying life. It is tempting to see the family as the main villain of the piece, and to seek to develop programs which attack directly this family pathology. Should we not have extensive programs of fam-

ily therapy, family counseling, family-life education, and the like? Is this not the prerequisite to enabling slum Negro families to take advantage of other opportunities? Yet, how pale such efforts seem compared to the deep-seated problems of self-image and family process described above. Can an army of social workers undo the damage of three hundred years by talking and listening without massive changes in the social and economic situations of the families with whom they are to deal? And, if such changes take place, will the social-worker army be needed?

If we are right that present Negro family patterns have been created as adaptations to a particular socioeconomic situation, it would make more sense to change that socioeconomic situation and then depend upon the people involved to make new adaptations as time goes on. If Negro providers have steady jobs and decent incomes, if Negro children have some realistic expectation of moving toward such a goal, if slum Negroes come to feel that they have the chance to affect their own futures and to receive respect from those around them, then (and only then) the destructive patterns described are likely to change. The change, though slow and uneven from individual to individual, will in a certain sense be automatic because it will represent an adaptation to changed socioeconomic circumstances which have direct and highly valued implications for the person.

It is possible to think of three kinds of extra-family change that are required if family patterns are to change; these are outlined as pairs of current deprivations and needed remedies. (See p. 288) Unless the major effort is to provide these kinds of remedies, there is a very real danger that programs to "better the structure of the Negro family" by direct intervention will serve the unintended functions of distracting the country from the pressing needs for socioeconomic re-

[15] Wiltse speaks of a "pseudo depression syndrome" as characteristic of many AFDC mothers. Kermit T. Wiltse, "Orthopsychiatric Programs for Socially Deprived Groups," *American Journal of Orthopsychiatry,* Vol. 33, No. 5 (October 1963), pp. 806–813.

[16] Walter B. Miller, "Lower Class Culture as a Generating Milieu of Gang Delinquency," *Journal of Social Issues,* Vol. 14, No. 3 (1958), pp. 5–19.

Deprivation effect of caste victimization	Needed remedy
I. Poverty	Employment income for men; income maintenance for mothers
II. Trained incapacity to function in a bureaucratized and industrialized world	Meaningful education of the next generation
III. Powerlessness and stigmatization	Organizational participation for aggressive pursuit of Negroes' self-interest
	Strong sanctions against callous or indifferent service to slum Negroes
	Pride in group identity, Negro *and* American

form and providing an alibi for the failure to embark on the basic institutional changes that are needed to do anything about abolishing both white and Negro poverty. It would be sad, indeed, if, after the Negro revolt brought to national prominence the continuing problem of poverty, our expertise about Negro slum culture served to deflect the national impulse into symptom-treatment rather than basic reform. If that happens, social scientists will have served those they study poorly indeed.

Let us consider each of the needed remedies in terms of its probable impact on the family. First, the problem of poverty: employed men are less likely to leave their families than are unemployed men, and when they do stay they are more likely to have the respect of their wives and children. A program whose sole effect would be to employ at reasonable wages slum men for work using the skills they now have would do more than any other possible program to stabilize slum family life. But the wages must be high enough to enable the man to maintain his self-respect as a provider, and stable enough to make it worthwhile to change the nature of his adaptation to his world (no one-year emergency programs will do). Once men learn that work pays off it would be possible to recruit men for part-time retraining for more highly skilled jobs, but the initial emphasis must be on the provision of full-time, permanent un-

skilled jobs. Obviously, it will be easier to do this in the context of full employment and a tight labor market.[17]

For at least a generation, however, there will continue to be a large number of female-headed households. Given the demands of socializing a new generation for non-slum living, it is probably uneconomical to encourage mothers to work. Rather, income maintenance programs must be increased to realistic levels, and mothers must be recognized as doing socially useful work for which they are paid rather than as "feeding at the public trough." The bureaucratic morass which currently hampers flexible strategies of combining employment income and welfare payments to make ends meet must also be modified if young workers are not to be pushed prematurely out of the home.

Education has the second priority. (It is second only because without stable family income arrangements the school system must work against the tremendous resistance of competing life-style adaptations to poverty and economic insecurity.) As Kenneth Clark has argued so effectively, slum schools now function

[17] This line of argument concerning the employment problems of Negroes, and poverty war strategy more generally, is developed with great cogency by James Tobin, "On Improving the Economic Status of the Negro," *Dædalus* (Fall 1965), and previously by Gunnar Myrdal, in his *Challenge to Affluence* (New York, 1963), and Orville R. Gursslin and Jack L. Roach, in their "Some Issues in Training the Employed," *Social Problems,* Vol. 12, No. 1 (Summer 1964), pp. 68–77.

more to stultify and discourage slum children than to stimulate and train them. The capacity of educators to alibi their lack of commitment to their charges is protean. The making of a different kind of generation must be taken by educators as a stimulating and worthwhile challenge. Once the goal has been accepted they must be given the resources with which to achieve it and the flexibility necessary to experiment with different approaches to accomplish the goal. Education must be broadly conceived to include much more than classroom work, and probably more than a nine-month schedule.[18]

If slum children can come to see the schools as representing a really likely avenue of escape from their difficult situation (even before adolescence they know it is the only *possible* escape) then their commitment to school activities will feed back into their families in a positive way. The parents will feel proud rather than ashamed, and they will feel less need to damn the child as a way to avoid blaming themselves for his failure. The sense of positive family identity will be enriched as the child becomes an attractive object, an ego resource, to his parents. Because he himself feels more competent, he will see them as less depriving and weak. If children's greater commitment to school begins to reduce their involvement in destructive or aimless peer-group activities this too will repercuss positively on the family situation since parents will worry less about their children's involvement in an immoral outside world, and be less inclined to deal with them in harsh, rejecting, or indifferent ways.

Cross-cutting the deprivations of poverty and trained incapacity is the fact of powerlessness and stigmatization. Slum people know that they have little ability to protect themselves and to force recog-

nition of their abstract rights. They know that they are looked down on and scape-goated. They are always vulnerable to the slights, insults, and indifference of the white and Negro functionaries with whom they deal—policemen, social workers, school teachers, landlords, employers, retailers, janitors. To come into contact with others carries the constant danger of moral attack and insult.[19] If processes of status degradation within families are to be interrupted, then they must be interrupted on the outside first.

One way out of the situation of impotence and dammed-up in-group aggression is the organization of meaningful protest against the larger society. Such protest can and will take many forms, not always so neat and rational as the outsider might hope. But, coupled with, and supporting, current programs of economic and educational change, involvement of slum Negroes in organizational activity can do a great deal to build a sense of pride and potency. While only a very small minority of slum Negroes can be expected to participate personally in such movements, the vicarious involvement of the majority can have important effects on their sense of self-respect and worth.

Some of the needed changes probably can be made from the top, by decision in Washington, with minimal effective organization within the slum; but others can come only in response to aggressive pressure on the part of the victims themselves. This is probably particularly true of the entrenched tendency of service personnel to enhance their own sense of self and to indulge their middle-class *ressentiment* by stigmatizing and exploiting those they serve. Only effective protest can change endemic patterns of police harassment and brutality, or teachers' indifference and insults, or butchers'

---

[18] See Chapter 6 (pages 111–153) of Kenneth Clark, *op. cit.*, for a discussion of the destructive effects of ghetto schools on their students.

[19] See the discussion of "moral danger" in Lee Rainwater, "Fear and the House-as-Haven in the Lower Class," *Journal of the American Institute of Planners,* February 1966 (in press).

heavy thumbs, or indifferent street cleaning and garbage disposal. And the goal of the protest must be to make this kind of insult to the humanity of the slum-dweller too expensive for the perpetrator to afford; it must cost him election defeats, suspensions without pay, job dismissals, license revocations, fines, and the like.

To the extent that the slum dweller avoids stigmatization in the outside world, he will feel more fully a person within the family and better able to function constructively within it since he will not be tempted to make up deficits in self-esteem in ways that are destructive of family solidarity. The "me" of personal identity and the multiple "we" of family, Negro, and American identity are all inextricably linked; a healthier experience of identity in any one sector will repercuss on all the others.

25. SOCIAL DEFINITIONS IN DELINQUENT CAREERS

Carl Werthman

See editor's note for preceding selection, p. 273.

Source: *Task Force Report: Juvenile Delinquency and Youth Crime* (Washington, D.C.: Government Printing Office, 1968), pp. 155–70.

CARL WERTHMAN is Assistant Professor of Sociology and Research Associate at the Center for the Study of Law and Society, University of California, Berkeley.

The moral career of the lower class juvenile gang boy often begins at age 6, 7, or 8 when he is defined by his teachers as "predelinquent" for demonstrating to his friends that he is not a "sissy," and it ends between the age of 16 and 25 when he either takes a job, goes to college, joins the Army, or becomes a criminal.[1] Although much of his behavior during this period can be seen

[1] The concept of a moral career has been defined by Erving Goffman as "the regular sequence of changes that career entails in the person's self and in his framework of imagery for judging himself and others." See Erving Goffman, "The Moral Career of the Mental Patient," in *Asylums* (New York: Doubleday & Co., Inc., 1961), p. 128.

and is seen by him as a voluntary set of claims on one of the temporary social identities available to him as a lower class "youth," his final choice of an "adult" identity will depend in large measure on the way his moral character has been assessed, categorized, and acted upon by his parents, teachers, and officials of the law as well as on the attitudes and actions he has chosen in response. How the boys embrace these identities, how adults tend to define and treat them for doing so, and how the boys respond to these definitions and treatments is thus the subject of this paper.[2]

THE IDENTITY MATERIALS OF THE DELINQUENT

Although the special conditions of youth as a status do not dictate, provoke, or account for "delinquent" behavior, these conditions constitute the structural possibilities that allow it to exist; and, as suggested by the fact that most gang boys leave the streets as soon as they are forced to make a living, one of these conditions concerns the way young people are related to the economy.[3] Since they are required by law to attend school until the age of 16 or thereabouts, they are virtually forced to remain financially dependent on their parents

during these years, and this state of dependence diminishes the magnitude of their responsibilities considerably. They do not have to support themselves or a family, and the schools are equipped to run quite well, if not better, without them. Unlike adults, they are thus left relatively free to organize their lives around noneconomic pursuits. Looked at another way, however, they are also deprived of occupational categories and activities as ways to differentiate themselves from one another.

In the adult world, occupations are the major source of social identity. The jobs themselves are used to classify and rank, while the norms governing performance are the principal criteria by which competence and character are judged. In the world inhabited by youth, however, identities must be constructed from other materials; and on the whole, these materials are limited to the activities that take place in schools and those engaged in and around them.[4] The school provides a number of instrumental training roles for those who wish to pursue them, but if a student is neither academically nor politically inclined, these roles are likely not to have much meaning. Particularly in elementary and junior high schools, it is not so much what you *do* that counts but rather what you *are*, since everyone tends to be doing about the same things.

In the absence of occupational titles, a rich vocabulary of identity categories tends to emerge, a vocabulary that often includes referents to physical or anatomical features, clothing styles, places, possessions, special membership groups, and and a general relationship to the administration of schools.[5] In addition, each of

[4] Although the family can be seen as an important source of emotional support for the various contests that go on outside it, there is little important contribution it can make to the genesis of public identities since most young people do not spend time together in the same home.

[5] Just prior to the completion of this study, for example, the high school population of San

these categories tends to be associated with certain skills and attributes of character as well as with the activities in which these skills and character traits are generally displayed.

As Erving Goffman has elegantly made clear, however, there are certain skills and attributes of character, particularly those most prized by gang boys, that can only be claimed by aspirants to them in social situations where something of consequence is risked; and since the school facilities available for non-academic character construction are generally limited to games, it is not surprising that boys who wish to play for higher stakes tend to use each other, the law, and sometimes even school officials in order to demonstrate their claims.[6]

It is impossible to prove that one is cool, courageous, or "smart," for ex-

ample, without a situation in which there is something to be cool, courageous, or "smart" about, just as it is difficult to gain a reputation for being "tough" unless the skills involved are occasionally put to a test. In situations where it is possible to claim possession of these attributes, the reward won or utility gained, in addition to whatever material goods may be at stake, is an increment in status or reputation, a commodity that youth, like adults, spend a sizable amount of time attempting to obtain and protect. Conversely, the risks include the possibility of damaging the body or the pocketbook as well as the chance of being shown to lack whatever skills or attributes of character the situation calls for. In addition, when the law is being used to prove possession of moral character, there is also the probability of being observed or discovered and thus sanctioned by the State. Goffman further suggests that risky situations should be entered voluntarily if a person wishes others to grant him possession of the desired attributes without any contingent doubts: and when this happens, he says, there is "action" to be found.[7]

Claiming title to these character traits can be more difficult than it may first appear, however, since risky situations do not arise very often in the course of an average day. In fact, as Goffman points out, most people manage to arrange their lives so that matters of consequence such as physical safety and a money supply are protected from unnecessary risk, although as a result these people encounter few situations in which the most heroic of social virtues can actually be claimed rather than assumed.

Yet if someone with an adult status actually decides he desires "action," there is always Las Vegas or a risky job, while a lower class gang boy is more or

Francisco had divided itself into four major groups. The lower and working class Negroes, Spanish-speaking minorities, and whites were referred to as "bloods," "barts," and "white shoes," respectively, while the fourth group, the "Ivy Leaguers," contained the middle and lower middle class segments of all three races. The relationship to schools in this vocabulary is obvious, and all four groups were easily identifiable by uniform. The "bloods," "barts," and "white shoes" were further broken down into gangs by districts and each gang had its own jacket. Moreover, the district and gang distinctions took precedence over race in racially integrated districts so that the lower class Negroes and whites living in predominantly Spanish-speaking areas wore the "bart" uniform and were referred to by members of their own race as such.

In the city of Albany on the other side of the San Francisco Bay, the vocabulary adopted by the students in the all-white high school is devoid of ethnic references but certainly no less to the point: the students who congregate during recess on plots of land in the middle of the school have been entitled the "quadrangles"; the students who meet in the parking lot outside the school are called just that, "parking lots"; and the remainder of the student body is referred to as "uncommitted," presumably because they occupy the territory between the parking lot and the quadrangle that surrounds the school on four sides.

[6] I am indebted to a recent unpublished paper by Goffman for much of the analysis of gang activity that follows. See Erving Goffman, *Where the Action Is: Or, Hemingway Revisited,* Center For the Study of Law and Society, University of California, Berkeley, 1965.

[7] As Goffman puts it, "action" can be located "wherever the individual knowingly takes chances that are defined as voluntary, and whose conduct is perceived as a reflection on character." Goffman, *op. cit.,* p. 48.

less forced to create his own. If he wishes to prove that he is autonomous, courageous, loyal, or has "heart," not only must he take a chance, he must also construct the situation in which to take it; and for most gang boys this means that risky situations must be made from whatever materials happen to be available on the streets and at schools.[8]

On the streets, the various activities defined by law as "thefts" provide perhaps the best examples of the way gang boys use laws to construct and claim identities. In order to become usable as identity materials, however, the situations in which laws against theft are broken must be carefully selected to insure that sufficient risk is present. Unlike the professional thief who takes pride in knowing how to minimize the occupational risks of his trade, most younger gang boys create risks where none need be involved.[9] Joyriding, for example, is ideally suited for this purpose since "cool" is required to get a stolen car started quickly; and once started, the situation contains the generous though not overwhelming risk of detection. Moreover, given the wide range of risky activities that can be engaged in once the cars are stolen, joyriding is viewed as an abundant source of the anxiety, excitement, and tension that accompanies the taking of risks for its own sake, a complex of emotions often referred to as "kicks."

(Did you guys do much joyriding?) Yeah. When I was about 13, I didn't do nothing but steal cars. The guy that I always stole with, both of us liked to drive so we'd steal a car. And then he'd go steal another car

[8] It was largely on the basis of an argument such as this that Norman Mailer suggested "medieval jousting tournaments in Central Park" and "horse races through the streets of Little Italy" as delinquency prevention programs for the City of New York. See Norman Mailer, *The Presidential Papers* (New York: Bantam Books, 1964), p. 22.

[9] See Edwin H. Sutherland, *The Professional Thief* (Chicago: The University of Chicago Press, 1937).

and we'd chase each other. Like there would be two in our car, two in the other car, and we'd drive by and stick out our hands, and if you touch them then they have to chase you. Or we'd steal an old car, you know, that have the running boards on it. We'd stand on that and kick the car going past. Kind of fun, but, uh, it's real dangerous. We used to have a ball when we'd do that other game with the hands though.

In addition to joyriding which was almost always done at night, the younger gang boys I studied also located two risky daytime situations in which to engage in theft. On Saturday afternoons, they would delight in trying to steal hubcaps from a packed parking lot next to a local supermarket, and on special occasions, they enjoyed breaking into gum and candy machines located in a crowded amusement park. In the parking lot, the challenge consisted of making away with the hubcaps without being seen, while in the equally crowded amusement park, the risk consisted of darting through the customers and away from the police after making sure that the theft itself had been observed.

(What else did you guys used to do when you were in Junior High School?) Well, we would sometimes, three or four of us, maybe go to Playland and rob the machines. That would be a ball cause, see, what we'd do is maybe have two guys start fighting or maybe jump on a sailor or something like that. In the meantime, the other two guys would go back in there while the police was, you know, chasing the others, while we was back there breaking the machines open, you know. There was about five or six of them machines. So then the cops would always see us cause somebody would yell for them. So they would stop chasing the other guys and start chasing us. We had a lot of fun up there.

Even among the younger boys, however, thievery was sometimes undertaken for motives other than "kicks" or "fun."

Shoplifting, for example, was viewed as a more instrumental activity, as was the practice of stealing coin changers from temporarily evacuated buses parked in a nearby public depot. In the case of shoplifting, most of the boys both wanted and wore the various items of clothing they stole; and when buses were robbed, either the money was divided among the boys or it was used to buy supplies for a party being given by the club.

Like we'd give a party on a Friday night. Well, we know the bread man come Thursday. And we know what time he leaves, so we know what time to be there to get the bread. And then we know where to get the tuna fish and the Kool Aid. That's simple. Just walk into any store and steal that. I used to call everybody so they get up. Let's say two gonna go get the bread. The other two gonna go out to the streetcars cause early in the morning they just leave their money on the bus cause there ain't nobody around. Get some coffee at the Fire Department. So they go on and hit the streetcar and get the money, something like that.

Yet these thefts were not perceived as exclusively instrumental. Practically as soon as the gang was formed in elementary school, its identity system differentiated into "thieves" and "fighters," and both types of boys were perceived as performing some function for the group. Thus, even when the purpose of theft was defined as instrumental, the act itself was quickly communicated to the other gang members since it was a source of identification as well as party supplies.

Our club was organized. We had a mutual understanding between us. Everybody in the club had something good about them or something bad. Everybody had some kind of profession. Like Ray, he was the fighter, always throwing his weight around when we had a fight or something. Little Johnnie and Ronnie, they were what we called the thieves. They was the best! I mean those two could steal anything. Then, like Arnold couldn't spell his name. He couldn't spell Arnold. I mean, boy he needed help.

As the members of a gang get older, their perception and use of theft become increasingly instrumental; and if they are still in the gang after graduating or getting expelled from high school, theft turns into a particular version of the "hustle." These hustles still involve risks, but the risks are no longer incurred exclusively for what can be demonstrated about the self by taking them. The possible sanctions faced are much more serious than they were in junior high school. Moreover, the boys now need the money. Without it they would find themselves hard pressed to sustain a daily round of socializing with ease. Thus, their relationship to the risky situation changes as both positive and negative outcomes become more consequential; and as this shift takes place, the actual thefts themselves are talked about less and less. Where a boy happens to be getting his money becomes his own private business, a policy that gradually evolves as attempts are made to cut down the probability of detection.

Yet the boys still do not see themselves as professional thieves, even after they have graduated from high school. As long as they can rely on their parents for room and board, the hustle is viewed as a transitory, impermanent, and part-time way of simply getting by. It is not conceived of as an "adult" training role, even though it is an instrumental relationship to the economic world. On the other hand, if the boys remain on the streets after 18, they are no longer stealing for "kicks."

The laws against theft are not the only materials used by gang boys to demonstrate moral character. On the streets, they also tend to use each other for this purpose, activities that Goffman has called "character games."

I assume that when two persons are in one another's presence it will be inevitable that many of the obligations of one will be the expectations of the other (and vice versa), in matters both substantive and ceremonial. Each participant will have a personal vested interest in seeing to it that in this particular case the rules the other ought to obey are in fact obeyed by him. Mutual dependence on the other's proper conduct occurs. Each individual necessarily thus becomes a field in which the other necessarily practices good or bad conduct. In the ordinary course of affairs, compliance, forebearance and the mechanisms of apology and excuse insure that showdowns don't occur. None the less, contests over whose treatment of the other is to prevail are always a possibility, and can almost always be made to occur. The participants will then find themselves committed to producing evidence that will cause a re-assessment of self at the expense of the assessment that will come to be made of the other. A "character game" results.[10]

Goffman further suggests that a claim to possess "honor" is what intiates most character games, honor defined as "the property of character which causes the individual to engage in a character contest when his rights have been violated and when the likely cost of the contest is high." [11] Like other forms of "action," then, character games are played at some risk but also presumably for some reward. As Short and Strodtbeck have pointed out, fighting is perhaps the classic example of a gang activity that is best understood with this model.[12] After observing gang boys in Chicago for a number of years, these authors concluded that most fights take place either when a "rep" for toughness is suddenly challenged by a situation that the gang boy cannot avoid confronting or when a challenge to within-group rank appears,

either from inside or outside the gang. In the first instance, the gang boy is handed a chance to appear "honorable," perhaps even a chance he did not want; while in the second instance, the boy will provoke a character contest to reaffirm or reclaim his status in the gang after it is challenged by a streetworker or another boy, sometimes during an absence in jail.

Although it is quite true that most older gang boys will only fight when their reputations or ranks are threatened, the younger boys can sometimes be found initiating fights even though they have not been provoked. These fights are consciously sought out or searched for in an attempt to build a reputation where none existed before, and the boys are referred to as "looking for trouble" because they are "coming up." In these situations, an attempt is often made to select the target carefully. Not any rival gang will serve as a suitable object on which to build a rep, and thus, as in the following case, a gang invading "rival territory" may decide to go home if the members cannot find boys who are big or important enough to prove a case.

Remember when them guys from Hunters Point came over looking for us? Man, it got real bad there. Cause when we made the papers, you know, everybody thought we was something. So then they all come lookin' for you. Gonna knock off the big boys. So a whole bunch of these little kids from Hunters Point came lookin' for us one night. They was coming up, and they figured they could beat us or something. (Did you fight?) No. We wasn't in the neighborhood that night. They found a bunch of guys their age but they wasn't interested in that. They just went home.

Particularly among younger boys, a great deal of bullying is apparently also inspired by attempts to build rather than protect reputations. For example, a schoolteacher in Washington, D.C., recently told me that her fourth grade

10 Goffman, op. cit. n.6, p. 60.
11 Goffman, op. cit. n.6, p. 63.
12 James F. Short, Jr., and Fred L. Strodtbeck, *Group Process and Gang Delinquency* (Chicago: The University of Chicago Press, 1965), pp. 248–264; also J. Short and F. Strodtbeck, "Why Gangs Fight," *Trans-Action*, 1, 1964.

class already contained a boy who had earned the nickname "tough cat," a nickname that was apparently achieved by beating up younger, older, bigger, and smaller boys virtually at random.[13] After the nickname was given to a single boy, it then became a free-floating identity aspired to by others in the class and could be claimed for the same activity. Once the boys get to high school, however, this sort of fighting tends to be perceived as "unfair."

When I was in Junior High some kids called me king of the school, and there was about seven of us. You know, we ran that school. Those girls, they kinda looked up to us. We didn't let nobody go with nothing. It ain't nothing now, but we all would get in front of the line—Get out the way, let us through—you know. There wasn't about seven of us. Want some money, just ask for it and they glad to give it to you cause they scared. It was just that we was seven bullies I guess. Cause we'd snap our fingers and they'd do what we tell them. See, that was when we was younger. The girls, they went for all that cause they didn't know no better than you. They liked to see somebody being bad then. Big show-offs. Somebody who's a lot of fun. See, they like that then. But now that you get older, they don't go for it so much no more.

There may be a parallel here between the apparently "senseless violence" engaged in by very young boys and the more serious instances of "random violence" some times found among gang boys at the very end of their "delinquent" careers. In the oldest gang I worked with, all of whose members were between 20 and 25, a few of the boys would occasionally stab strangers miscellaneously, ostensibly for having received a "dirty look." Most of these stabbings seemed to occur when the boys were in the process of bragging about their past exploits and their virtually nonexistent "reps."

[13] I am indebted to Ethel Rosenthal for this observation.

It is possible that for very young boys, the task of building a "rep" can involve creating an audience for this behavior where none previously existed, and this task may involve selecting targets miscellaneously in order to establish the rules. In the case of older boys, however, the instances of random violence seem to occur just after most of the real audience for this behavior abandons this source of identity for an occupation, at which point the boys who still wish to retain an identity by engaging in acts of violence may choose to imagine that this audience still exists. Although the consequences of these audience creation problems are clearly more serious among older boys than among younger ones, both tend to be defined as "disturbed" by their immediate audience of peers.

Regardless of whether fights are entered into voluntarily or involuntarily and regardless of whether they take place in situations that are imagined or real, the basic principle involved in this mode of identity construction seems to be clear: the fight is defined as a situation in which reputation or rank can be won or lost. Whether a particular fight will be entered into depends on the expected values of the various outcomes, and these values can vary considerably from boy to boy. It is no accident, for example, that situations involving violence are often perceived as "turning points" by ex-gang members when contemplating their past careers. Particularly among older boys, it is easy to see how reputations can get large enough so as not to be worth the risk of defending.[14] Similarly, in areas where it is tacitly understood that certain affronts can only be revenged by attempting to kill the offender, the person offended may simply decide to leave town

[14] I encountered two boys who dropped out of gang activity for this reason. In one case, the boy decided it was time to leave after he was shot at twice in 1 week from passing automobiles driven by members of different rival gangs.

rather than run the risk of being sent to jail or killed in defense of his honor.[15]

In addition to fighting, there are also other activities in which gang boys use each other to claim and construct identities. The behavior described by Miller as "verbal aggression," also known variously as "ranking," "capping," or "sounding," seems to involve some of the same principles found in fights.[16] As Matza has pointed out, this activity amounts essentially to a process of testing status by insult, and thus honor is the quality of moral character at stake.[17] Goffman has called these encounters "contest contests," situations in which someone forces someone else "into a contest over whether or not there will be a contest." [18] Like fighting, it involves risk and can thus have a bearing on status. Unlike fighting, however, it is not engaged in to demonstrate toughness or courage but rather to display a type of verbal agility that gang boy's call "smart."

Short and Strodtbeck have also suggested that the "utility-risk paradigm" might shed some light on the high percentage of illegitimate pregnancies that gang boys produce while engaged in another type of "interpersonal action" discussed by Goffman, namely "making out." [19] Sexual activity sometimes begins very early among gang boys, and there is typically a great deal of it throughout a career. Most of the Negro boys claimed to have lost their virginity around the age of 8 or 9, and some were having intercourse regularly in junior high school. During most of the years spent in a gang, girls are seen primarily as objects for sexual play, and it is not until the age of 16 or older that they are sometimes treated with anything resembling respect. Ultimately, however, it is marriage that takes most boys out of the gang, thus providing one of the few available legitimate excuses for leaving the streets.[20]

Although Short and Strodtbeck suggest that two separate risks are involved in illegitimacy, the first being the probability of engaging in sexual intercourse with a given frequency and the second being the probability that these actions will eventuate in parenthood, only one of these risks is used as a source of identity. Success or failure at "making it" with a girl is socially risky since the outcome affects status in the gang, while it is doubtful that the risks involved in gambling without contraception are considered a source of pleasure independent of the act itself.

The gang boy thus aspires to an identity that puts him in a special relationship to risk. When he is around his friends, he often creates the situations in which he chooses to exist, an act of creation that involves selecting out certain features of the social environment and then transforming them into the conditions that allow him to define a self. In part, these risks are taken for their own sake since a reputation can be built on this capacity alone and the emotional reward is a "kick." In part, there are also honor, courage, and loyalty involved, special attributes of moral character that can only be demonstrated in situations of risk. Taken together, however, these risks seem to represent a set of special claims to the status of "men," a status they are culturally and structurally forbidden to occupy until the "delinquent career" comes to an end. Why gang boys rather than others decide to take these

[15] Claude Brown, *Manchild in the Promised Land* (New York: The Macmillan Co., 1965), p. 171.

[16] W. B. Miller, H. Geertz, and S. G. Cutter, "Aggression in a Boy's Street-Corner Group," *Psychiatry* (November 1961), pp. 283–298.

[17] David Matza, *Delinquency and Drift* (John Wiley & Sons, 1964), pp. 42–44.

[18] Goffman, *op. cit.*, p. 68.

[19] Short and Strodtbeck, *Group Process, op. cit.*, n. 12, pp. 44–45, 249–250.

[20] Walter B. Miller, "The Corner Gang Boys Get Married," *Trans-Action*, vol. 1 (November 1963), pp. 10–12.

risks is a difficult if not impossible question to answer. Yet it is possible to look at how the gang boy deals with the mechanisms that ordinarily prevent these risks from being taken.

THE GENESIS OF AUTONOMY

Although the absence of adult economic responsibility can be seen as conducive to the development of unconventional identity formations among youth, young people are also politically dependent on adults. A person under age 18 is always in the legal custody of someone; and if he proves to be beyond control by parents, he can always be adopted by the State. In effect, this means that young people can be ordered to obey the rules established for them by their parents since the law can be appealed to if these commands are not obeyed.

In most instances, however, this parental power develops into authority. As a rule, young people simply assume that parents are a legitimate if sometimes difficult source of rules and thus obey them voluntarily.[21] Perhaps more important, it is precisely this authority relationship that allows at least the preadolescent to define himself as "a child." He implicitly surrenders all autonomy and thus does not exercise whatever capacity he might have to make his own decisions. In return, he can afford to feel "protected."

In addition to establishing their own authority, parents also have a vested interest in endowing school teachers with temporary "title to rule." This legitimacy is sometimes conferred in subtle ways but most techniques are easy to observe. Parents caution their offspring to behave and get good grades, then teachers are visited to determine whether there is a dispute between teacher and child, parents rarely voice criticism to a

son or daughter—however much the teacher may be castigated for ruining the future of the family in the privacy of a bedroom.

To further insure that the authority of school personnel is legitimated, boys and girls are made aware that these officials can and do inform parents of their misadventures. Parents, teachers, and other adult officials thus see to it that children are not allowed to segregate roles. Since parents typically have the ultimate power, they become the center of a communications network for other adult authorities. Whether the child is at school or on the streets, he is made to feel that none of his behavior can be hidden from his parents.[22]

The youngsters who define themselves as dependent do not mind being the subjects of this friendly conspiracy and most would feel very insecure without it. They often cannot tolerate a segregation of roles, even when the communications network is broken by accident and thus they often feel the need to confess their sins in order to relieve themselves of the responsibility for hiding information. These "confessionals" are considered rewarding moments for parents who take pride in constructing leakproof systems of surveillance over their offspring. They are looked upon as indicators of "trust."

Precisely how this network of authority is cultivated and maintained remains something of a psychosocial mystery. Yet the fact remains that as long as parents can manage to have their ideals about the behavior of their offspring either aspired to or even vaguely achieved, there is precious little chance, as we will see, that policemen and probation officers will end up defining them as "delinquents," provided, of course, that the number of crimes committed is

[21] Max Weber, *The Theory of Social and Economic Organization,* translated by A. M. Henderson and Talcott Parsons (Glencoe: The Free Press, 1947).

[22] It is largely for this reason that vehicles for public transportation such as buses become scenes of mass confusion when children ride them unsupervised to and from school. The bus drivers do not have access to parents and the children know it.

kept to some reasonable limit. Although I encountered a great many parents who had come to look upon the trip to jail as "routine" by the time their sons were 16, I found none who said that at an earlier point in life they had not hoped for something better. In practically every case, it was possible to locate a set of expectations that was perceived by parents either to have broken down or never to have developed, despite the fact that many had also come to view the news of "trouble" as a more or less "normal" event.

The situation that these parents find themselves it can perhaps best be described with a vocabulary developed by Harold Garfinkel for the analysis of how stable social activity systems are "constituted," become "disorganized," and are "reconstituted." [23] Garfinkel suggests that routine social activities are defined in the most fundamental sense of that word by a set of "constitutive" or "basic" rules, i.e., rules that are used to make behavior recognizable as an act or event in some known order of events. Unlike institutionalized norms (or "preferred rules" as Garfinkel calls them), the "basic" rules do not specify how a person is to act in an activity but only the range of possible acts he could perform as well as the social category of person he is if he takes part in them. As examples of "basic rules," Garfinkel cites those that "constitute" the game of tic-tactoe: "Play is conducted on a three by three matrix by two players who move alternatively. The first player makes a mark in one of the unoccupied cells. The second player, in his turn, places his mark in one of the remaining unoccupied cells. And so on. The term 'tictactoe player' refers to a person who seeks to act in compliance with these possible events as constitutively expected ones." [24]

[23] Harold Garfinkel, "Some Conceptions of and Experiments with 'Trust' as a Condition of Stable Concerted Actions," MS.
[24] Garfinkel, op. cit. n. 23, p. 6

Garfinkel further suggests that in order for an activity system to be "stable," the people involved in the activity must "trust" each other, "trust" defined as a condition in which the participants expect one another to act in compliance with the basic or constitutive rules. If these rules are violated, the activity is in danger of becoming "confused" or "disorganized" since people will find themselves without a context in which to interpret the meaning of the act committed by the violator and thus will not know how to respond to him. In addition, there is often a feeling that the condition of "trust" has been broken and the people who believe themselves to be participants in the activity are likely to get anxious, frustrated, or angry.

In groups such as families, friendships, and businesses where participants are quite committed to one another for personal, economic, and legal reasons, some attempt is usually made to "normalize" the situation. This can mean that there is a renewal of belief in the other person's commitment to the previous rules or that the rules will change, in which case an act or event that was not previously understood will come to be perceived as "normal" or "routine." If a "basic" rule is added or subtracted, however, the result is a new activity.

Following this conceptual scheme, we can see that where the participants in an activity include an "authority" as well as others who are seen as "subordinates," the set of basic rules establishing the activity will always include a rule which constitutes this relationship. From the point of view of a subordinate, moreover, this rule will be one that says: I choose to obey all the preferred rules or norms that are established for me in this activity by the category of person who is designated the authority, say a parent, a teacher, or perhaps even all adults.

In addition, we can predict that where an authority has a part in some activity, it will be important to him that his subordinates act in compliance with the basic rule establishing the source of preferred rules, or, put another way, that his subordinates "trust" him. From the point of view of the authority, moreover, the important issue about all acts becomes not whether they are being performed in accordance with a particular rule but whether they are being performed in accordance with the rule establishing who it is that properly establishes the rule themselves.

This problem is frequently and simply illustrated among the parents of preadolescent and "predelinquent" boys, many of whom are described as simply "out of control." In these cases, what the parents seem to be describing are situations in which no stable pattern of mutual expectations has developed at all. Whatever preferred rules they attempt to establish as a way of ordering the activities of the family are more or less randomly ignored by their offspring. In the neighborhood where this study was done, for example, there were always a certain number of boys on the streets who, from the point of view of their parents, had "suddenly disappeared." They were usually classified as "runaways" after failing to appear for 1, 2, or 3 consecutive nights, but since they only rarely proved to be more than 10 blocks away from their houses at any time and during an absence might even faithfully attend school, this classification was sometimes not adopted until a week of absence had elapsed. In some cases, the inability to predict an appearance was almost total. These parents could rarely count on their sons either to be at school, at home for meals, or sometimes even in bed. For example:

(How do you handle Melvin when he gets into trouble?) Well, we figure that weekends are the main times he looks forward to—parties and going out. So we'd say, "You can't go out tonight." You know, we'd try to keep him from something he really wanted to do. But he usually goes out anyway. Like one night we was watch-ing TV, and Melvin said he was tired and went to bed. So then I get a phone call from a lady who wants to know if Melvin is here because her son is with him. I said, "No, he has gone to bed already." She says, "Are you sure?" I said, "I'm pretty sure." So I went downstairs and I peeked in and saw a lump in the bed but I didn't see his head. So I took a look and he was gone. He came home about 12:30, and we talked for a while. (What did you do?) Well, I told him he was wrong going against his parents like that, but he keeps sneaking out anyway. (What does your husband do about it?) Well, he don't do much. I'm the one who gets upset. My husband, he'll say something to Mel and then he'll just relax and forget about it. (Husband and wife laugh together.) There's little we can do, you know. It's hard to talk to him cause he just go ahead and do what he wants anyway.[25]

The initial response of most parents to this behavior is anger, a sense of betrayal, and a feeling that the family situation has become "disorganized." After a while, however, this lack of predictability becomes virtually "routine." Passing one of these mothers on the street, she might report that "Charles is gone again." Only wistfully would she ask me whether I had seen him or happened to know where he was. She already knew

[25] The family being described here is perhaps a classic example of a "disorganized" activity system since the son himself could rarely count on the appearance of his parents. Both worked, the father as a free-lance garage mechanic and the mother as an Avon saleslady, and both enjoyed taking spur-of-the-moment trips to Las Vegas. This meant that when the boy disappeared, he often returned to find his parents gone and vice-versa. Moreover, given the fact that random disappearances tend to stop around age 12, these family situations are often as unpredictable to sociologists as they are to the family members involved. The boy being discussed, for example, had an older brother on the honor roll at a local San Francisco high school during the same period that he asked his streetworker whether he could be admitted "voluntarily" to Juvenile Hall when he felt that his family situation was unmanageable at home, a desire that is not uncommon although rarely acted upon by the younger boys.

that by and large Charles made up his own mind when to come and go. Since she did not know where, however, she was curious.

Although it is often hard to judge how the absence of parental trust is perceived by the boys involved, in most cases it seems to be taken as a simple matter of fact. When the very young boys are asked why they "ran away," they often do not seem to know; and when they are asked on the streets why they do not return home, their answer is usually, "because when I do I'll get a beating."

These children, most between the ages of 6 and 10, were the most puzzling people I met on this study. Their behavior always seemed to make perfect sense to them, but it also seemed to make so much sense that they could not produce accounts for it. Although they sometimes exhibited a touch of bravado, they were only rarely defensive, and most managed to carry themselves with what can only be described as miniature adult poise. When they were not in motion or suddenly running away, they assumed the posture of "little men," often shouldering their autonomy with great dignity but rarely with perfect ease.

These children are a testimony to the fact that basic rules about authority are not accepted automatically, even among the young. The assumption of dependence must be cultivated before it can be used as a basis for control, and this becomes quite clear when for some reason this assumption is never made. In these cases, the children often demonstrate a remarkable capacity to take care of themselves. In fact, one could argue that the preadolescent who does not conceive of himself as dependent on his parents also does not really conceive of himself as "a child," particularly when he loses his virginity at 8 and supports himself on lunch money taken from classmates. Once the authority rule is rejected the family as an activity system becomes

an entirely new game. Politically the child is not an adult, but sociologically it is hard to argue that he is still a child.[26]

When the gang boy gets on in years, there is often a violent showdown with a father; and regardless of whether these fights are won or lost, most parents simply resign themselves to viewing "trouble" as "normal" or "routine."

My father don't get smart with me no more. He used to whup me, throw me downstairs, until I got big enough to beat him. The last time he touch me, he was coming downstairs talking some noise about something. I don't know what. He had a drink, and he always make something up when he start drinking. He was trying to get smart with me, so he swung at me and missed. I just got tired of it. I snatched him and threw him up against the wall, and then we started fighting. My sister grabbed him around the neck and started choking him. So I started hitting him in the nose and everything, and around the mouth. Then he pushed my mother and I hit him again. Then he quit, and I carried him back upstairs. Next morning he jump up saying, "What happened last night? My leg hurts." And all that old bullshit. He made like he don't know what had happened. And ever since then, you know, he don't say nothing to me.

Similarly, mothers also seemed to resign themselves quite quickly to the possibilities of future "trouble." Where there was no father in the house, they often placed the blame for their son's behavior on his absence. But even in situations where the father was present, they continued to offer what advice and support they could, once it became clear that punishment was no deterrent. On a day-

[26] Herb Gans notes the tendency among working class Italians in Boston to treat their children as "little adults." It could well be that the posture of the boys described in this paper is simply an exaggerated version of lower class socialization generally. See Herbert J. Gans, *The Urban Villagers* (New York: The Free Press of Glencoe, 1962), p. 59.

by-day basis, whatever efforts at direction were exerted tended to be directed at keeping the boys in the house on weekday evenings, at least until they did their homework, and trying to get them home at a reasonable hour on Friday and Saturday nights. In most instances, however, even these attempts at control gradually broke down, particularly among the older boys and those who were either suspended or permanently out of school. As time wears on, a long unexplained absence from home as well as phone calls from the police become socially expected parts of the family activity system itself.

Well, like last week, you know. Last Saturday I came home about 4 o'clock and they got kind of excited. And they didn't say nothing that night. But the next morning they kept talking "where you been" and all this. And I told them where I had been and they said okay. They told me to stay in this weekend but they didn't say nothing about it this weekend so I went out last night and tonight. (When she tells you not to do something, do you go along with her or what?) Like you mean stay or something? Oh, if she say stay in, I talk to her about it for an hour or two and then she get mad and say, "Oh, get out of the house. Leave." That's what I been waiting for.

Not only is the assumption of autonomy the important issue at home, it also has important implications for the way gang boys are defined and treated by school officials as well as for the ways they often fight back. Most young people adopt a posture of deference in the presence of adult authorities because this posture is a taken-for-granted assumption about the self. To gang boys, however, this posture becomes a matter of choice. They can defer or not defer, depending on their mood, their audience, and their feelings about a teacher; and for many teachers, the very existence of the assumption that submissiveness is a matter of choice becomes sufficient grounds for the withdrawal of "trust."

. . . . .

AUTONOMY AND THE SCHOOLS

Recent sociology on gang boys has been very hard on the schools. Cloward and Ohlin suggest that lower class delinquents suffer from unequal *"access* to educational facilities;" [27] Cohen points to their *"failures* in the classroom;" [28] and Miller and Kvaraceus argue that a *"conflict* of culture" between school administrators and lower class students is precipitating delinquent behavior.[29] Although there are many differences between contemporary sociological portraits of the lower class juvenile delinquent, the same model of his educational problem is used by all authors. Regardless of whether the delinquent is ambitious and capable,[30] ambitious and incapable,[31] or unambitious and incapable,[32] the school is sketched as a monolith of middle class personnel against which he fares badly.

Yet data collected by observation and interview over a 2-year period on the educational performances and classroom experiences of lower class gang members suggests that pitting middle schools against variations in the motivation and capacity of some lower class boys is at best too simple and at worst incorrect as a model of the problems faced by the delinquents.

First, some of the "trouble" that gang boys get into takes place on school grounds but outside the classroom. There

[27] Richard A. Cloward and Lloyd E. Ohlin, *Delinquency and Opportunity* (Glencoe: The Free Press, 1960), p. 102.

[28] Albert K. Cohen, *Delinquent Boys* (Glencoe: The Free Press, 1965), p. 116.

[29] Walter B. Miller and William C. Kvaracus, *Delinquent Behavior: Culture and the Individual*, National Education Association of the United States, 1959, p. 44. See also Walter Miller, "Lower Class Culture as a Generating Milieu of Gang Delinquency," *Journal of Social Issues*, vol. XIV, 1958.

[30] Cloward and Ohlin, *op. cit.* n. 27.

[31] Cohen, *op. cit.* n. 28.

[32] Miller, *op. cit.* n. 29.

is some evidence, for example, that gang boys tend to view the rules against fighting, smoking, and gambling the same way they view the laws against theft, as opportunities to demonstrate courage in situations that entail some risk. As suggested in the following quote, the boys sometimes sound thankful for these rules.

(What do you guys do when you cut school?) Well, like everybody, you know, everybody get together and say, "Everybody cut Friday and we'll go to Luigi's house." So, you know, a lot of boys and girls go up there and we have a party. Drinking. Having a good time. Otherwise if we have a day off from school, you know, during the weekend, and we gave that, it probably wouldn't be too much fun cause it'd be almost legal. You know, when I first went to Gompers, we used to be able to smoke in the halls cause the ends of the halls was all concrete. We used to be able to smoke there. I didn't hardly ever smoke there though. We used to go smoke in the bathroom. It seemed like, you know, smoking was better to me since I had to hide to do it. It seem like everything at that school, you have to do it backwards to make it seem more better to you.

Second, during middle adolescence when the law requires gang members to attend school, there seems to be no relationship between academic performance and "trouble." Gangs contain bright boys who do well, bright boys who do less well, dull boys who pass, dull boys who fail, and illiterates.

Finally, the school difficulties of these boys occur only in some classes and not others. Good and bad students alike are consistently able to get through half or more of their classes without friction. It is only in particular classes with particular teachers that incidents leading to suspension flare up. We thus need to see how the same gang boy may become a "troublemaker" in one classroom and an "ordinary student" in another. To do this, it is again worth using

Garfinkel's scheme to look at the classroom as a place where a range of possible activities or "constitutive orders of events" can take place, including the most common and mutually related set known as "teaching and learning." This is not the only activity that can take place in classrooms, however, as suggested by the fact that many young people, including gang boys, tend also to see the classroom as a place to see friends, converse by written notes, read comic books, eat, sleep, or stare out the window. For example:

If I'm bored then I have to do something to make it exciting. First, second, and third ain't too bad because I get me two comic books and they last me three periods. (You read comic books for the first three periods?) Yeah. See in my first three periods I got typing, English, and some kind of thing—Social Studies I think. In them three periods I read comic books, and the next three periods I got Shop and I got Gym and then I got that Math. Them last three periods I don't read comic books because I only bring two, and they only last three periods.

Friday we had a substitute in class named Mr. Fox, and I had a headache so I went to sleep. (Why were you sleeping? Were you out late the night before?) No, I wasn't. I just had a headache. And I went to sleep cause my head was hurting. They wasn't doing nothing but talking. About this and that, Sally and John, and I just went to sleep. The class wasn't doing nothing but fussing, fooling around, talking, so I went to sleep.

When it becomes clear to a teacher that he is in the presence of people engaged in activities other than "teaching and learning," there are a number of ways he can choose to respond to this observation. One thing he can do, for example, is decide to overlook whatever other activities besides "learning" are taking place and decide to "teach" with those people who show signs of wanting to learn. In these classrooms there is rarely "trouble."

(Have you ever had any good teachers, Ray?) Yeah, Mr. F. and Mr. T. in junior high school. (What made them good?) They just help you, you know. They didn't want you always working all the time. As long as you keep your voices down, you know, and don't be talking out loud and hollering, you could go on and talk in groups and have a good time. (They let you have a good time. Did they flunk you?) Yeah, they flunked me. But I mean it was my fault too cause they gave me all the breaks, you know. Anything I asked for, they gonna give me a break. But, you know, I just never do right anyway.

One possible danger of ignoring people who engage in activities other than "learning" is that these people will always be overlooked, even when they decide to enter the "learning" activity. When this happens, there is the possibility that the person overlooked will resent not being allowed to enter the activity.

Like this one stud, man, he don't try to help us at all. He just goes on rapping (talking) to the poop-butts (squares), and when we ask a question he don't even pay no attention. I don't think that's fair. We there trying to learn just like anybody else! (All the time?) Well, sometimes.

The teacher may also, if he wishes, agree to participate in the activities preferred by the other people in the classroom, in which case either a different order of events or some mixture of this order and "teaching" gets constituted. Activities such as "talking to friends," "having fun," and "horsing around" then become "normal" events that can go on at different times in the same room. In these classrooms also there is rarely "trouble."

Like my Civics teacher, he understands all the students. He know we like to play. Like,

you know, he joke with us for about the first 15 minutes and then, you know, everybody gets settled down and then they want to do some work. He got a good sense of humor and he understand.

When confronted with activities other than "learning," however, there are also teachers who tend to feel not only that their rights to teach are being violated but also that the basic rule establishing their authority is being broken. In addition to perceiving that their honor has been challenged, these teachers are also likely to conclude that "trust" is no longer warranted; and when these feelings are communicated to gang boys, the result is almost always defined as "getting smart." In some cases, the teacher will insult them in return; but in most cases he will resort to the imperative and begin to issue "commands." This is a sure sign to gang members that the teacher no longer trusts them to comply with the basic rule establishing his authority. Conversely, however, the boys tend to view these commands as abridgments of their own rights to autonomy, and thus the prospect of a "character contest" arises.

The teachers that get into trouble, they just keep pounding. You *do* this! You know, they ain't gonna ask you nice. You just do this or else, you know, I'm gonna kick you out of school. All that old foul action. Like in Math class, this teacher always hollers. He always raises his voice and hollers, "Do this work!" All that old shit. Everybody just looks at him. Don't say shit, and just sit down, talk, wait around, you know.

This breakdown of trust on the part of teachers does not always occur as one event in a developmental sequence as suggested by the examples quoted above. There are also teachers whose previous experience has led them to define their students as "untrustworthy" right from the start, and they will thus communicate this lack of trust on the first day of class. Similarly, by the time the boys have been through junior high school, they have experienced enough teachers to know that this category of person also cannot always be trusted to honor their claims to a choice about the activities they wish to engage in. Most gang boys will therefore test the limits of the classroom situation before making up their minds whether a teacher can be trusted. This is done by purposely violating a rule preferred by the teacher in such a way as to suggest that their participation in the classroom is a voluntary act and should be acknowledged as such with the proper amount of respect. If the teacher responds to this move by becoming either angry or afraid, the boys know they are dealing with someone who is either "tough," "smart," or "lame." On the other hand, if the teacher responds by acknowledging the right while insisting that the rules still be obeyed, he is considered "straight."

26. IDENTITY CONFLICTS OF CHINESE ADOLESCENTS IN SAN FRANCISCO

Stanley L. M. Fong

The readers of this book who have read Selections 14, 17, and 20 have become familiar with some of the kinds of findings that appeared in the classic urban community studies carried out a generation ago by members of the "Chicago school" (for example, Wirth's *The Ghetto,* Thrasher's *The Gang,* Thomas and Znaniecki's *The Polish Peasant in Europe and America*). There are some striking parallels in the present selection, too. Immigrant parents work for long hours at low

Source: Eugene B. Brody (ed.), *Minority Group Adolescents in the United States* (Baltimore: The Williams & Wilkins Company, 1968), pp. 111–23, 132, with some footnotes omitted. Copyright © 1969 by The Williams & Wilkins Co. Reprinted by permission of the author and publisher.

STANLEY L. M. FONG is Assistant Professor of Psychology at California State College, Long Beach.

pay in a culture they do not understand and in which it is hard for them to prosper. Meanwhile, their children are freed from their control and learn a new language and a new set of behavioral standards at school and on the street. The traditional patterns of discipline, of personal forms of social control, and of the respect of young people for their elders and their established ways of doing things all diminish in the new community.

Despite these contemporaneous similarities to historical processes, once far more common than they are today in the United States, there is every probability that the offspring of today's residents of Chinatown will not be ghettoized. On the contrary, they should have every prospect of being able to move from a poor and overcrowded racially segregated living area. By now, many Chinese-Americans have achieved middle-class status and are considered quite acceptable by the white majority. The capacity of Chinese-Americans to achieve mobility by conventional means even under adverse conditions is not at issue. Even if it were, the existence of a large group of successful Chinese-American predecessors would nevertheless open opportunities and contacts for the Chinese immigrants of today. Chinese immigrants also bring with them, as did their predecessors (and also Japanese-Americans, as Selection 13 shows), cultural approval and a family system strong enough to support the pattern of present personal self-abnegation and effort for the sake of future reward, particularly through children's success in the educational system.

Groups able to put that pattern to work have always been able to prosper in American society as early as the second generation. Indeed, their success has been used to support the idea that the society's institutions were open, despite the contrary conclusion suggested by the general situation of America's larger racial minorities. In a sense, then, the successes of people like the Chinese-Americans and Japanese-Americans in the West and Hawaii, or the earlier successes of people like Jews in the East and Midwest, served as rationalizations postponing the critical test of whether American institutions were intrinsically democratic or whether instead they were receptive only to those able to demonstrate that they had already met certain prior cultural conditions.

Somewhere in the distance I hear a plaintive sigh and a comment, perhaps from a tired teacher who knows that Chinese children are good, well-behaved kids who do well at their school work. The comment is simply, "Oh, if only all the others could be like *them*."

When visitors come to San Francisco, one of the first sights they want to see is Chinatown. When they walk along Grant Avenue after a morning of shopping at Macy's, Roos-Atkins, and the City of Paris, the street suddenly narrows and they see swaying strings of Oriental lanterns, dazzling Chinese signs, and curving pagoda roofs. To many, Chinatown seems picturesque and exotic, a city within a city—a feeling of being in the Orient. It is populated by some 36,000 Chinese, but at night, surprisingly, it seems to be peopled by tourists. The strollers shop in the numerous curio shops, eat in Chinese restaurants, some finely decorated in modern Chinese, and walk by a few impressive banks with Chinese motifs and plate glass doors and walls. But they rarely see or are aware of life behind these buildings. It is on this that this article will focus.

To get a good perspective, one has to go back into the pages of time to the origin of Chinatown. The very first Chinese pioneers to California were merchants, selling food and Chinese goods such as tea and silk. Their early success, in the 1840's, prompted others to follow, but their numbers were still small. Then the cry of gold was heard and the rush was on. At sea ports, Chinese clamored and crowded into the ocean-going vessels of the day. Hitherto, the trans-Pacific passage had been one of trade in goods; henceforth, human cargo was to form a large part of the trade. But unlike the immigrants from Europe, most of these men were married, leaving their wives and children at home; those who were unattached were often quickly married off under the auspices of their parents before they set off to sea. Thus, parents hoped to ensure the return of their sons to the land of their ancestors. They dreamed of finding gold, free for the taking, and returning to China to retire in luxury. "Gold Mountain" was the name they gave to America. Many did not find it. After the gold rush was over

Chinese continued to come. This time it was the call of the transcontinental railway to lay down tracks, and tens of thousands of Chinese "coolie" laborers came. (Chinatowns were often started by men who left the tracks in various parts of the country.) Then the depression came and agitation against Chinese miners and laborers grew. Many laws were passed against aliens to keep them from staking claims or to trouble them in other ways, and many Chinese left the mine fields throughout California and withdrew in the Chinese ghetto. A great many returned to China and the population of Chinese in America started to decline. Others stayed and hoped to glean a small fortune, by peddling or washing clothes, before returning to their fatherland—this was to take a lifetime for some. But a fortune was made by some and they returned to live the lives of wealthy gentlemen in their villages; others, when money ran out, left for America to make more for the next visit, often taking a growing son to help out. The habit of sending their savings across the sea followed.

What are the reasons at home that brought about the immigration of the Chinese? To begin, it is important to say that these Chinese did not come from all parts of China but from one in particular. This was the coastal province of Kwangtung, of which Canton is the best known city. It was once a prosperous area, but it became the most densely populated region in China. In the last century its population outran its food supply and famine and poverty followed. There were also floods. In the north, a most terrible flood occurred in 1847 when the 3000-mile long Yangtze River overran its course. There were also floods in the rivers to the south. Hundreds of thousands of peasants were left homeless and flocked to the cities to find relief and new means of sustenance. The cry of gold on the other side of the Pacific was heard and stirred up great hopes.

After a few decades in America it became popular for Chinese to send for their wives or acquire, with the aid of relatives, picture brides. Slowly families began to appear on the Chinatown scene, a ghetto once geared for units of homeless men. . . .

THE FAMILY

In the traditional Chinese family the father is considered to be the head of the house and has authority over the family members. The wife is considered to be subordinate to the husband. It is for the wife to serve also as a servant to her in-laws. Her status is improved immeasurably when she gives birth to a son, although some recognition does come from giving birth to a daughter. The offsprings are taught to respect their parents and show obedience in the form of filial piety. The children are also taught to respect their relatives near and far. It is the custom of the culture to venerate the elders. In fact, the husband is expected to yield to the authority of his parents and older relatives. . . .

. . . . .

Undoubtedly, the family image these immigrants brought over with them was based on the Chinese model. The child-rearing practices in Chinatown were patterned after this traditional ideal. The growing number of relatives in Chinatown helped maintain the extended family to some extent. But the kinship system was never completely duplicated in America, for such personages as the grandparents and other elders were left behind in the old country. Coupled with this, there were other social forces in the ghetto which made it difficult to preserve, in all aspects, the traditional form of primary family relationships. In moving from the past to the present, from a village setting to an urban one, the style of life changes. In Chinatown the common man usually works over 8 hours a day, 6 days a week, as cook, waiter, dishwasher, and clerk, which are the chief occupations of the ghetto. The work entails working into the evening and it is common practice for employees to eat supper at work, away from their families. The wages are low, and often mothers, especially ones with large families, need to work in a sewing factory to supplement the meager family income. There are about 170 garment factories in Chinatown which make use of this source of labor, hiring about 3000 women in all.[1] (Attempts to unionize the garment factories in the ghetto seem doomed to failure as it would endanger their thin thread of existence. They are grateful for their little extra income and are fearful that their employers would not be able to compete successfully with the larger society if labor cost goes up.) The conditions of life in the ghetto, thus, make it difficult for many parents to perform their roles as agents of socialization. (The case is quite different in a village community.) Family life is weakened even further by the fact that the children go to Chinese classes, after coming home from American public schools, and do not return until after seven o'clock in the evening. Fatigue may set in and it is not surprising that a large number of Chinese youths resent going to Chinese school. It seems, at times, that "they are seldom home except to eat and sleep."[2] But most Chinese parents want their children to learn the language, customs, and manners of their ancestors. In a manner, they have given the Chinese school the task of socializing their children. Many of the youths react negatively to this experience. Mischief in

[1] G. A. DeVos and K. A. Abbott, The Chinese Family in San Francisco: A Preliminary Study. A group masters' thesis under direction of G. A. DeVos and K. A. Abbott, University of California, Berkeley, Calif., 1966.
[2] L. G. Yung, *Chinatown Inside Out* (New York: Barrows Mussey, 1936), p. 115.

school is not uncommon and playing "hookey" is a recognized pastime. Only a small number complete all six grades of Chinese elementary school and a handful finish the Chinese junior high program. . . .

. . . . .

On the whole, though, the respect and obedience that Chinese children give to authority figures elsewhere are, to a large extent, observed in schools also. In the American school system, Chinese children rarely misbehave. They have the reputation of being the best behaved pupils in the city, as teachers at Commodore Stockton Elementary School in Chinatown will attest. Evidently, the attitudes of many youths toward Chinese and American schools are different. The appeal of the Chinese classroom is much less than the American one. Some resent going to Chinese classes when they see a few peers who do not, such as boys and girls from more westernized homes or their American playmates. A number of children develop very strong feeling against learning Chinese. . . .

When the child goes to American public school, he learns a new language, and he acquires greater facility as he goes through school. The time will soon come when he speaks mainly in English with his peers. He speaks English increasingly at home with his brothers and sisters. The parents may soon find that they are losing contact with their children and some communication problems develop. Many parents at this point try to learn the new language to keep up with their children. At school, the child also learns new skills and social values which may be foreign to those of the parents. At this age, the school teachers begin to serve as respected models of social behavior. These behaviors which the child observes and learns may however, be different from those at home. It is common, in the American culture, to teach the child to fend for himself,

to make his own decisions, and to stand on his own feet. Instead of being led by an authoritarian figure, the pupil is encouraged to be self-reliant and independent. In fact, the child may be encouraged to assert himself. I can remember an episode in my grammar school days. I heard a boy crying and turned around. The lady teacher rushed up and yelled at the bully to stand still and asked the small one to hit him back. The little boy stopped crying immediately and shook his head slightly, and a faint smile grew on his face. When I looked back on this, he must have been just as astonished as I was. His smile must have been one of surprise at such a novel approach to discipline. A traditional child would have been told by his family to run home when there is danger and let the family take care of matters through the proper channels.

The seeds of cultural conflict may be sowed, then, at a very early age and the mind of the sprouting child may be bent, at some point, by the winds of perplexities. In a more psychological language, the child may develop some conflict-laden identifications with two social worlds, the one of parents and the other of teachers and peers. In most instances, as the child grows older, the peer values grow stronger and override many parental sanctions. One of the common complaints of Chinese parents is that their child does not obey them—at least not as submissively as before. One wonders if the desire of Chinese parents to enroll their children in Chinese school is to some extent to maintain cultural continuity with their children.

With some immigrants, who are in the lower rung of the economic ladder, they may feel insecure in their tenuous position; the incipient loss of the formerly strict obedience of their children may threaten their status even more. To reinstate their prerogatives, the parents, usually the father, may even demand greater obedience. It may be recalled that in Chinese culture, the behavior of the child reflects on the parents, who will be accused of not having taught their children to behave properly. Hence his status is intimately tied into the behavior of his offsprings. The child, on the other hand, is growing to be more American and independent. Authority based on arbitrary grounds, to the child, is not well received. This area of conflict with his parents may lead to inner turmoil for the child. In speaking about another ethnic group, Erikson mentions that the "weakest relationship . . . seems to be that between the children and their fathers, who cannot teach them anything and who, in fact, have become models to be avoided." [3] In turn, the parents may feel helpless, isolated, and insecure with the disintegration of a former way of life which they have left behind in China. The rapid change in social roles may be damaging to the self-image of these parents. The parents may turn their hopes to the Chinese schools and take greater interest in the progress of their child. However, the report cards are often a shock to even the most sympathetic parents.[4]

STREET CLUBS AND GANGS

There is a growing number of street clubs or gangs in Chinatown. Many of these teen-agers come from families where both parents are working or perhaps bereaved, or from a disturbed family. Instead of going home to an empty house, physically or emotionally, they loiter in coffee shops, street corners, or pool halls. These street clubs separate into the American-born boys and the foreign-born boys, mostly new arrivals from Hong Kong. There is animosity between these two sorts of Chinese teen-agers

and they do not have much to do with each other. They do not even speak the same language. The American-born, clubs go by the name of "The Raiders," "The Sultans," and "The Immortals" and may be identified by their club jackets. The group of about 150 China-born boys is called the "Bugs." The Bugs made the news lately for their part in burglarizing stores, both in and out of Chinatown, by crawling through narrow transoms.

· · · · ·

A look at police records, from the years 1961 to 1964,[5] shows a growth in juvenile delinquency. The number, however, is still small, the second lowest in the city (the lowest is the Japanese). About 160 delinquent Chinese a year go through the halls of the San Francisco Juvenile Bureau. Most of these cases (75%) are either dismissed or placed under informal supervision. Typically, the anti-social behavior of these youths does not involve physical assault, as is true of many other groups, but it does involve stealing, either from home or from stores. The girls usually steal from home. (Could this be a token attempt to get something of value from the home, i.e. affection which is usually given to her brothers first? Or are they so desperately trying to find an identity that a negative one is better than none at all?) For both boys and girls, the trial observation of Abbott [6] is interesting: in the delinquent group, about half of the youths have working mothers, away mainly in sewing factories to make ends meet.

To the unsuspecting tourist, Chinatown presents a picture of swarming activities and growing prosperity. Behind its facade of glittering signs and modern front, however, it has many social and economic problems. It is considered a slum by the city and receives aid from

[3] E. H. Erikson, *Childhood and Society*, 2d ed. (New York: Norton & Company, Inc., 1963), p. 160.

[4] Yung, *op. cit.*

[5] DeVos and Abbott, *op. cit.*

[6] K. A. Abbott, personal communication to author, 1966.

the Anti-Poverty Act. It is short on housing and many rooms are over-crowded. Once the Chinese ghetto was mainly a community for isolated, homeless men and was built along these lines. Today many of these tenements are condemned by the Public Health Department and a number of owners are trying to sell their property instead of trying to renovate them because of the extensive repairs needed. These strains contribute to the adjustment problems of refugees in America.

· · · · ·

. . . The different camps of Chinese adolescents are motley and disharmonious. On the one side are the China-born; its constituents, a cacophonous one: southerners and northerners, rice-eaters and wheat-eaters. On the other side are the American-born, a cleavage of bilinguals and a lesser number to whom the Chinese tongue is a foreign one. In wrestling over their identity—their place in the world—they are grappling with each other. A number of them, fortunately, emerge from the fray with a clear definition of themselves. It has been said by Kipling, "East is East, and West is West, and never the twain shall meet." But the twain shall meet, in the minds of the Chinese youths.

27. CHEROKEE SCHOOL SOCIETY AND THE INTERCULTURAL CLASSROOM

Robert V. Dumont, Jr., and
Murray L. Wax

By the midsixties, education had become the nation's great hope for maintaining continued stability and orderly growth. Schools would develop skills, create commitment to national core values, and provide access to new opportunities for whatever children needed them (or at least for

Source: *Human Organization,* Vol. 28, No. 3 (Fall 1969), pp. 217–26, with some footnotes omitted. Reprinted by permission of the Society for Applied Anthropology and Professor Wax.
    ROBERT V. DUMONT, JR., is Professor, Department of Indian Studies, University of Minnesota. MURRAY L. WAX is Professor of Anthropology at the University of Kanas.

those who seemed to have initiative enough to take advantage of them). The first Soviet Sputnik caused some skepticism about whether or not American education was as good as had been thought, but its total effect was to spur greater efforts to strengthen the educational system without really questioning the twin assumptions that teachers and schools knew the things that ought to be taught, and knew and applied the best methods for getting children to learn those things.

Both assumptions were shaken but not dislodged by the discovery that schools were failing in poor areas, where children simply were not learning very much. Government reports documented the findings (see Selections 30 and 37). Moreover, a number of more impressionistic and more readable books appeared, based on the experiences of people who were new recruits to teaching in ghetto schools.[1] These books had a narrower focus than the national scene, concentrating on particular classrooms in particular schools. All showed how teachers continued to rely on the idea that children were obligated to be interested in standard curriculum materials selected by distant officials; how teachers denigrated the backgrounds from which poor children came; how teachers turned away from children who didn't have enthusiastically eager shining faces, clean clothes, the faculty of staying (or looking) busy in one place for long periods of time, and the capacity either to withhold aggression or transform it into proper modes of hand-raising competitiveness. In sum, conventional classrooms were not very effective with unconventional children; and the more serious the attempts to reward conformity and punish deviance in terms of conventional standards, the less effective the educational process turned out to be.

That did not mean ghetto elementary schools were becoming blackboard jungles. Far from it. What most frequently happened is that children became discouraged, lost. They were promoted from one grade to another not because they had learned very much but because other younger students were coming along, and laws made school attendance mandatory for all of them. What ghetto pupils did manage to learn was what they had to do to stay out of trouble, how to put in their time and get out. Implicitly they banded together to protect themselves against the demands the school was making on them. Through a passive resistance that was at once a defense

[1] Jonathan Kozol, *Death at an Early Age* (Boston: Houghton Mifflin, 1967); Herbert Kahl, *Thirty-Six Children* (New York: World Publishing Co., 1967); James Herndon, *The Way It Spozed To Be* (New York: Simon and Schuster, 1968).

against encroachments and a barely tolerable expression of sullen resentment, they turned off. Many teachers did not see this withholding of emotional and intellectual commitment as the defense it was; instead, they interpreted it as evidence of pure hostility, or of laziness, or of ignorance—or of any of a number of qualities commonly found in stereotypes of the particular groups from which the children came.

The selection that follows shows this process at work, not in an urban ghetto, but in classrooms for poor Cherokee Indian children. The process begins with the teachers' implicit cultural assumptions that are usually ethnocentric, and sometimes openly racist; these assumptions then confront the different culture and different social reality of the Indian children. Later, teachers continue to fail to take their students' concerns into account, and the students band together to thwart their teachers' attempts to remake them. Finally, teachers arrive at the knowledge that they have failed to teach well despite their own best efforts and so blame the children or the children's background. But the authors also found a few other classrooms where interchange took place because teachers let it happen, where Indian children's initial eagerness to learn was not snuffed out, turned aside, and forgotten.

A final more didactic note is that the social sciences still have no substitute for what trained observers can see by taking time to watch. That is made clear not only in this selection but in the one that follows as well.

TRIBAL CHEROKEE COMMUNITIES

The consequence of the various reformative and educational programs aimed at the Indian peoples has been not to eliminate the target societies but, paradoxically, to encourage an evolution which has sheltered an ethnic and distinct identity, so that today there remain a relatively large number of persons, identified as Indians, and dwelling together in enclaved, ethnically and culturally distinctive communities. The Tribal Cherokee of contemporary northeastern Oklahoma are not untypical.[1]

Like other Indian communities, they have lost to federal, state, and local agencies the greater measure of their political autonomy. Many contemporary Indian

[1] We take the term "Tribal Cherokee" from the research reports of Albert Wahrhaftig, which, in addition to whatever information may be inferred from the tables of the U.S. Census, constitute the best recent source on the condition of the Cherokee of Oklahoma. See, e.g., his "Social and Economic Characteristics of the Cherokee Population of Eastern Oklahoma" and "The Tribal Cherokee Population of Eastern Oklahoma," both produced under sponsorship of the Carnegie Cross-cultural Education Project of the University of Chicago, 1965 (mimeographed); and "Community and the Caretakers," *New University Thought*, Vol. 4, No. 4, 1966/67, pp. 54–76. See also, Murray L. Wax, "Economy, Ecology, and Educational Achievement," Indian Education Research Project of the University of Kansas, Lawrence, Kansas, 1967 (mimeographed), and Angie Debo, *The Five Civilized Tribes of Oklahoma: Report on Social and Economic Conditions*, Indian Rights Association, Philadelphia, Pa., 1951.

peoples do have "Tribal Governments," but these do not correspond to traditional modes of social organization or proceed by traditional modes of deliberation and action. In the specific case of the Oklahoma Cherokee, for instance, the Tribal Government is a nonelected, nonrepresentative, and self-perpetuating clique, headed by individuals of great wealth and political power, while the Tribal Cherokee are among the poorest denizens of a depressed region, whose indigenous associations are denied recognition by the Bureau of Indian Affairs.

The Cherokee of Oklahoma once practiced an intensive and skilled subsistence agriculture, which has all but disappeared as the Indians have lost their lands and been denied the opportunity to practice traditional forms of land tenure. The rural lands are now used principally for cattle ranching (often practiced on a very large scale) and for tourism and a few local industries (e.g., plant nurseries, chicken processing), or crops such as strawberries, which require a cheap and docile labor supply. Until the recent building of dams and paved highways and the concomitant attempt to develop the region as a vacationland, the Tribal Cherokee were able to supplement their diet with occasional game or fish, but they now find themselves harassed by state game and fish regulations, and subjected to the competition of weekend and vacation sportsmen.

Like the other Indian societies of North America, the Cherokee have been goaded along a continuum that led from being autonomous societies to being a "domestic dependent nation" and thence to being an ethnically subordinated people in a caste-like status. In Oklahoma there is a distinctive noncaste peculiarity, since a vast majority of the population proudly claim to be of "Indian descent" as this signfies a lineage deriving from the earliest settlers. To be "of Cherokee descent" is, therefore, a mark of distinction, particularly in the northeast of Oklahoma, where this connotes such historic events as "Civilized Tribes" and the "Trail of Tears." [2] Yet, paradoxically, there exist others whose claim to Indianness is undeniable, but whose mode of life is offensive to the middle class. The term "Indian" tends to be used to denote those who are considered idle, irresponsible, uneducated, and a burden to the decent and taxpaying element of the area. Within northeastern Oklahoma, these "Indians" are the Tribal Cherokees, and their communities are marked by high rates of unemployment, pitifully low cash incomes, and a disproportionate representation on relief agency rolls. Perhaps the major respect in which the Cherokee Indians differ from groups like the Sioux of Pine Ridge is that the latter, being situated on a well-known federal reservation, are the recipients of myriads of programs from a multiplicity of federal, private, and local agencies, whereas the Cherokee are still mainly the targets of welfare

[2] Responding to contact and intermarriage with the European invaders, the Cherokee were one of several tribes noteworthy during the 18th century for their adoption of foreign techniques. By 1827 they had organized themselves as a Cherokee Nation, complete with an elective bicameral legislature and a national superior court. Meantime, Sequoyah had been perfecting his syllabary, and in 1828 there began the publication of *The Cherokee Phoenix*, a bilingual weekly. Developments of this character led to the Cherokee and several neighboring tribes of the southeastern U.S. being called, "The Civilized Tribes;" nevertheless, this did not protect them from the greed of the white settlers, particularly in Georgia. When the Indian nations would not cede their lands peaceably, Andrew Jackson employed federal troops to herd the Indian peoples westward into the region which subsequently was to become Oklahoma. There the survivors of the terrible journey ("The Trail of Tears") incorporated themselves once again as a Cherokee Nation and remained such until dissolved by act of Congress early in the present century. Today, books, museums, and pageants commemorate these events and highlight for the tourists the high-cultural aspects of upper-status life in the Cherokee Nation. Judged by that historical standard, the life of contemporary Tribal Cherokee constitutes a blot on a record otherwise cherished by Oklahomans of Cherokee descent.

workers, sheriffs, and aggressive entrepreneurs.[3]

In this essay we wish to focus on the schools attended by Indian children in the cases where they are the preponderant element of the school population. This condition is realized not only on reservations, where the federal government operates a special school system under the administration of the Bureau of Indian Affairs, but also in other regions by virtue of covert systems of segregation. As in the case of Negro/white segregation, the basis is usually ecological. Thus, in northeastern Oklahoma the rural concentrations of Tribal Cherokee along the stream beds in the hill country predispose toward a segregated system at the elementary levels. But the guiding principle is social, so that there is reverse busing of Tribal Cherokee children living in towns and of middle-class white children living in the countryside. Within the rural elementary schools, the Indian children confront educators who are ethnically and linguistically alien, even when they appear to be neighbors (of Cherokee or non-Cherokee descent) from an adjacent or similar geographic area.

Such classrooms may be denominated as "cross-cultural," although the ingredients contributed by each party seem to be weighted against the Indian pupils. The nature and layout of the school campus, the structure and spatial divisions of the school buildings, the very chairs and their array, all these are products of the greater society and its culture—indeed, they may at first glance seem so conventional that they fail to register with the academic observer the significance of their presence within a cross-cultural transaction. Equally conventional, and almost more difficult to

apprehend as significant, is the temporal structure: the school period; the school day; and the school calendar. The spatial and temporal grid by which the lives of the Indian pupils are organized is foreign to their native traditions, manifesting as it does the symbolic structure of the society which has encompassed them.

The observer thus anticipates that the classroom will be the arena for an unequal clash of cultures. Since the parental society is fenced out of the school, whatever distinctive traditions have been transmitted to their children will now be "taught out" of them; and the wealth, power, and technical supremacy of the greater society will smash and engulf these traditionalized folk. Forced to attend school, the Indian children there must face educators who derive their financial support, their training and ideology, their professional affiliation and bureaucratic status, from a complex of agencies and institutions based far outside the local Indian community. The process is designed to be unidirectional; the children are to be "educated" and the Indian communities thus to be transformed. Meanwhile, neither the educator nor the agencies for which he is a representative are presumed to be altered—at least by the learning process.

CHEROKEES IN THE CLASSROOM

The classrooms where Indian students and a white teacher create a complex and shifting sequence of interactions exhibit as many varieties of reality and illusion as there are possible observers. One such illusion—in the eyes of the white educator—is that the Cherokee are model pupils. Within their homes they have learned that restraint and caution is the proper mode of relating to others; therefore in the classroom the teacher finds it unnecessary to enforce discipline. As early as the second grade, the children

[3] Cf. Murray L. Wax and Rosalie H. Wax, "The Enemies of the People," in Howard S. Becker, et al. (eds.), Institutions and the Person: Essays Presented to Everett C. Hughes, Aldine Press, Chicago, Illinois, 1968, pp. 101–118.

sit with perfect posture, absorbed in their readers, rarely talking—and then only in the softest of tones—and never fidgeting. Even when they are marking time, unable to understand what is occurring within the classroom, or bored by what they are able to understand, they make themselves unobtrusive while keeping one ear attuned to the educational interchange. They respect competence in scholastic work, and their voluntary activities both in and out of school are organized surprisingly often and with great intensity about such skills. Eager to learn, they devote long periods of time to their assignments, while older and more experienced students instruct their siblings in the more advanced arithmetic they will be encountering at higher grade levels.

To the alien observer (whether local teacher or otherwise), the Cherokee children seem to love to "play school." The senior author, for example, recalls talking during one recess period with an elderly white woman who had devoted many years to teaching in a one-room school situated in an isolated rural Cherokee community and who now was responsible for the intermediate grades in a more consolidated enterprise that still was predominantly Cherokee. "You just have to watch these children," she said. "If you don't pay no mind, they'll stay in all recess. They like to play school." And, as if to illustrate her point, she excused herself, went back into the school building, and returned with a straggle of children. "They told me they had work they wanted to do, but it is too nice for them to stay inside. . . . You know, I forgot how noisy students were until I went to [the County Seat] for a teacher's meeting. It's time for me to ring the bell now. If I don't, they will come around and remind me pretty soon."

Given the seeming dedication of her pupils, the naive observer might have judged this woman an exceedingly skilled and effective teacher. Yet in reality, she was a rather poor teacher, and at the time of graduation the pupils of her one-room school knew scarcely any English—a fact so well known that parents said of her, "She don't teach them anything!"

Like many of her white colleagues, this woman was interpreting Cherokee conduct from within her own culture, as is evident in her description of the intensive involvement of her pupils in learning tasks as *"playing* school." In kindred fashion, other teachers describe the silence of the students as timidity or shyness, and their control and restraint as docility. Most teachers are unable to perceive more than their own phase of the complex reality which occurs within their own traditions, being the products of rural towns and of small state teachers' colleges, and now working within and limited by a tightly-structured institutional context. Certainly, one benefit of teaching Indians in rural schools is that the educators are sheltered from observation and criticism. Except for their own consciences and professional ideologies, no one cares about, guides or supervises their performance, and little pressure is exerted to encourage them to enlarge their awareness of classroom realities.

Even for ourselves—who have had much experience in observing Indian classrooms—many hours of patient and careful watching were required, plus the development of some intimacy with the local community, before we began to appreciate the complexities of interaction within the Cherokee schoolroom. The shape assumed by the clash of cultures was a subtle one. At first, it could be appreciated most easily in the frustration of the teachers; the war within the classrooms was so cold that its daily battles were not evident, except at the close of the day as the teachers assessed their lack of pedagogical accomplishment. Those teachers who defined their mission as a "teaching out" of native traditions were failing to make any headway; and some of these good people had come to doubt their ability to work with such difficult and retiring children (actually, as we soon discovered, their classes contained a fair share of youngsters who were eager, alert, intelligent, and industrious). A few teachers had resigned themselves to marking time, while surrendering all notions of genuine instruction.

As these phenomena began to impress themselves upon us, we began to discern in these classrooms an active social entity that we came to call "The Cherokee School Society." Later still, we were surprised to discover in other classrooms, which we came to call "Intercultural Classrooms," that this Society remained latent and that instead the teacher and students were constructing intercultural bridges for communication and instruction (these will be discussed in the next section).

In order to comprehend the complexity of classroom interaction, we need to remind ourselves that the children who perform here as pupils have been socialized (or enculturated) within the world of the Tribal Cherokee as fully and extensively as have any children of their age in other communities. In short, we must disregard the material poverty of the Tribal Cherokee families and their lower-class status and avoid any of the cant about "cultural deprivation" or "cultural disadvantage." These children are culturally alien, and for the outsider (whether educator or social researchers) to enter into their universe is as demanding as the mastering of an utterly foreign tongue. In the compass of a brief article, we can do no more than indicate a few of the more striking evidences of this distinctive cultural background.

· · · · ·

In any educational transaction, the Cherokee School Society is actively judging the competence of the teacher and allowing him a corresponding function as leader. Their collective appraisal does not tolerate the authoritarian stance assumed by some educators ("You must learn this!") but rather facilitates the emergence of a situation in which the teacher leads because he knows ("I am teaching you this because you are indicating that you wish to learn . . ."). A consequence of this configuration (or, in the eyes of an unsympathetic observer, a symptom) is that the Cherokee students may organize themselves to resist certain categories of knowledge that the school administration has formally chosen to require of them.

We must bear in mind that within the Tribal Cherokee community, the reading or writing of English, calculating arithmetically, and even speaking English have minor employment and minimal utility. By the intermediate grades, the students perceive that, with no more than a marginal proficiency in spoken or written English, their elders are nonetheless leading satisfactory lives *as Cherokees*. Attempts to exhort them toward a high standard of English proficiency and a lengthy period of time-serving in school are likely to evoke a sophisticated negative reaction. After one such educational sermon, a ten-year-old boy bluntly pointed out to his teacher that a Cherokee adult, greatly admired within the local community—and senior kin to many of the pupils present—had only a fifth-grade education. When the teacher attempted to evade this rebuttal by suggesting that the students would, as adults, feel inferior because they lacked a lengthy education and could not speak good English, the pupils were again able to rebut. To the teacher's challenge, "Who would you talk to?" the same boy responded, "To other Cherokee!"

Orienting themselves toward the community of their elders the Cherokee students respond to the pressures of the alien educators by organizing themselves as The Cherokee School Society. As the teacher molds the outer forms of class procedure, the children exploit his obtuseness as a white alien to construct the terms on which they will act as students. But, while among the Oglala Sioux this transformation is effected with a wondrous boldness and insouciance,[4] here among the Cherokee it is with an exquisite social sensibility. A gesture, an inflection in voice, a movement of the eye is as meaningful as a large volume of words would be for their white peers. By the upper elementary grades, the result is a multiple reality according to which the adolescent Cherokee appear now as quiet and shy, or again as stoical and calm, or yet (apparent only after prolonged observation) as engaged in the most intricate web of sociable interaction. Such delicacy of intercourse, so refined a sensibility, reflects and requires a precision of movement, a neat and exact ordering of the universe.

Interestingly, the Cherokee School Society does not reject the curricular tasks formulated by the alien educational administrators. In fact, the pupils proceed with their usual patient intensity to labor at assignments that can have no bearing on their tradition or experience. The fact that they are unable to relate these materials meaningfully to life within the Cherokee community acts as an increasing barrier to their mastery of them. In particular, the fact that most students have acquired no more than rudimentary proficiency in spoken English means that the involved patterns of the printed language in the advanced texts are beyond their most diligent endeavors; neither the language nor the topics can be deciphered.

So far, we have emphasized that the

[4] Cf. Murray L. Wax, Rosalie H. Wax, and Robert V. Dumont, Jr. *Formal Education in an American Indian Community*, The Society for the Study of Social Problems, Kalamazoo, Michigan, 1964, Chapter 6.

Cherokee students are interested in learning and that, from the viewpoint of the educator, they are docile pupils. Yet the cultural differences noted, and the basic social separateness and lack of communication, ensure that conflicts will develop and become more intensive as the students mature. The school cannot proceed along the trackways established by educational authority, nor can it be switched by the students into becoming an adjunct of the rural Cherokee community. Hence, as the children mature, the tension within the schoolroom becomes more extreme. Since the participants are one adult and many children, and since the latter are imbued with a cultural standard of nonviolence and passive resistance, open confrontations do not occur. Instead, what typically happens is that, by the seventh and eighth grades the students have surrounded themselves with a wall of silence impenetrable by the outsider, while sheltering a rich emotional communion among themselves. The silence is positive, not simply negative or withdrawing, and it shelters them so that, among other things, they can pursue their scholastic interests in their own style and pace. By their silence they exercise control over the teacher and maneuver him toward a mode of participation that meets their standards, as the following instance illustrates:

Teacher: "Who was Dwight David Eisenhower?"

Silence.

Teacher: "Have you heard of him, Joan?" She moves her eyes from his stare and smiles briefly.

Very quickly, the teacher jumps to the next person. There is something in his voice that is light and not deadly serious or moralistic in the way that is customary of him. He is just having fun, and this comes through so that the kids have picked it up. They respond to the tone, not to the question, "Alice?"

Alice leans back in her chair; her blank stare into space has disappeared, and her eyes are averted. She blushes. Now, she grins.

The teacher does not wait, "Wayne?"

Wayne is sitting straight, and his face wears a cockeyed smile that says he knows something. He says nothing.

Seeing the foxy grin, the teacher shifts again, "Wayne, you know?" This is a question and that makes all the difference. There is no challenge, no game-playing, and the interrogation mark challenges Wayne's competency. But Wayne maintains the foxy grin and shakes his head, negative.

Quickly, the teacher calls on another, "Jake?" He bends his head down and grins but says nothing.

Teacher (in authoritative tone): "Nancy, tell me." But she says nothing, keeping her head lowered, although usually she answers when called upon. The teacher switches tones again, so that what he is asking of Nancy has become a command. Perhaps he catches this, for he switches again to the lighter tone, and says; "Tell me, Debra."

The only one in the room who doesn't speak Cherokee, Debra answers in a flat voice: "President."

As soon as the answer is given, there are many covert smiles, and Alice blushes. They all knew who he was.

To most educators and observers, such an incident is perplexing. Who within that classroom really is exercising authority? Are the students deficient in their comprehension either of English or of the subject matter? Are they, perhaps, flexing their social muscles and mocking the teacher—because they don't like the lesson, they don't like him to act as he is acting, or why? For the Cherokee School Society has created within the formal confines of the institutional classroom another social edifice, their own "classroom," so that at times there appears to be not simply a clash of cultural traditions but a cold war between rival definitions of the classroom. Such

tension is not proper within Cherokee tradition, since the Tribal Cherokee value harmonious social relationships and frown upon social conflict.[5] Moderate disagreement is resolved by prolonged discussion interspersed, wherever possible, by joking and jesting, while severe disagreement leads to withdrawal from the conflict-inducing situation. Given the compulsory nature of school attendance, however, the students cannot withdraw from the classroom, much as they might wish to, and the teacher can withdraw only by losing his job and his income. Thus, an unmanageable tension may develop if the teacher is unable to recognize the Cherokee pupils as his peers who, through open discussion, may share with him in the decisions as to the organizing and operating of the school.

The unresolved conflict of cultural differences typifies these classrooms. Within them, there is little pedagogy, much silence, and an atmosphere that is apprehended by Indians (or observers of kindred sensibility) as ominous with tension. The following incident, participated in by Dumont, exhibits all these features in miniature:

The classroom was small and the teacher had begun to relate a joke to Dumont. Not far away were seated four teenage Cherokee, and the teacher decided to include them within the range of his ebullience: "Boys, I want to tell you a joke. . . ." It was one of those that played upon the stoical endurance of Indians in adapting to the whimsical wishes of whites, and to narrate it in the classroom context was highly ironic. The plot and phrasing were simple, and easily apprehended by the students. But when the teacher had finished, they merely continued looking toward him, with their eyes focused, not upon him, but fixed at some point above or to the side of his

[5] See the discussions of "The Harmony Ethic," in John Gulick, *Cherokees at the Crossroads*, Institute for Research in Social Science, the University of North Carolina, Chapel Hill, N.C., 1960, pp. 135–139 *et passim*.

eyes. As he awaited their laughter, their expressions did not alter but they continued to stare at the same fixed point and then gradually lowered their heads to their work.

The Cherokee School Society maintains a rigid law of balance that says, in effect, we will change when the teacher changes. If the teacher becomes involved in appreciating the ways of his students, then they will respond with an interest in his ways. Needless to say, the older the students become, the higher their grade-level, the less is the likelihood that this reciprocity will be initiated by their educators. There is thus a deep tragedy, for it is the students who lose and suffer the most. Yet the School Society is their technique for protecting themselves in order to endure the alien intrusiveness of the teacher and the discourtesy and barbarity of the school. Occasionally, observer and students experience a happier interlude, for some teachers are able to enter into a real intercultural exchange. Unfortunately, they are as rare as they are remarkable. And they are sometimes unaware of their truly prodigious achievements in establishing what we term the Intercultural Classroom.

THE INTERCULTURAL CLASSROOM

Within the Intercultural Classroom, Tribal Cherokee students do such remarkable things as engaging in lengthy conversations with the teacher about academic subjects. For this to occur, the teacher must be responsive to the distinctive norms and expectations of the students; but, strikingly, he need not abide by these nor accept norms as long as he is able to persuade the students of his willingness to learn about them and to accommodate to them. This attitude places the teacher on a plane of parity such that he must learn from his students the most rudimentary Cherokee cultural prescriptions. Naturally, both parties experience conflicts in this reshuffling of teacher/learner roles. Certainly, such interaction is not what the teacher has been trained to sustain. Yet there arise structured devices for reducing these conflicts.

For instance, to bridge the social breaches that are always opening, the Cherokee students urge forward one of their members—not always the same person—to mediate and harmonize. Then if the teacher, by an unconscious presumption, disrupts the harmonious flow of class activity, it is the mediator whose deft maneuver reduces the intensity of the tension and relaxes the participants. In a sense, what the mediator does is to restore parity between teacher and students by removing the nimbus of authority from the teacher, thus allowing the students to work out with the teacher a compromise which redirects class activities and so permits them to regain their proper tempo. The teacher is freed to pursue the subject matter, but as scholastic assistant rather than classroom tyrant. With this in mind, let us examine the sequence of events which ended in a conversational repartee already quoted:

They are reading about important men in history and have just finished with a section about adult educators.

Teacher: (Referring to the observers.) "We have two distinguished educators here. Does this make you feel proud?"

It is quiet for the first time in the room. It is likely that the students are all thinking, how could we be proud of educators! As observer, I am uneasy and expectant; I wonder who will break the silence and how he will handle the delicate situation.

John: "I don't like schools myself." (!)

Teacher: "Would you quit school if you could?" (He's asking for it!)

John (a firm answer): "Yes."

Teacher: "Suppose that your dad came

and said you could quit, but he brought you a shovel and said, 'Dig a ditch from here to Brown's house,' since you weren't going to school."

John: "Okay."

Another student: "He might learn something."

Everyone finds this humorous; the class is in good spirits and is moving along.

John, too, is quick to reply: "Might strike gold." The topic has been discussed earlier in class. (The interaction develops and others become involved, including the more reticent students.)

Here it is John who has played, and most successfully, the role of mediator. The teacher had ventured into a delicate area that had the potential of disrupting the classroom atmosphere. The responding silence was a token of the social peril, and John, who so often among his peers had assumed the mediating role, moved forward first, boldly countering with a declaration as strong as the teacher's. As a consequence, he redefined the structure of the interaction and became the initiator of the exchange, while the teacher merely sustained it. A cultural bridge was thereby constructed, accessible alike to students and teacher; and John's "Okay" is his consent to the conditions of the structure.

The mediating role becomes less necessary as the teacher grows more attuned to the interactional norms of Indian society; it becomes more difficult (if more essential) if the teacher insists on maintaining a tyrannical control over the classroom. Yet, even as the teacher is attuned, some function is reserved for a mediator, for the teacher tends to proceed in terms of work to be done by an abstract student, while the mediator explores how the task can be redefined within the framework of the Cherokee student. His is a work of adaptation, and insofar as he is successful, the classroom becomes *intercultural*—a locus where persons of different cultural traditions

can engage in mutually beneficial transactions without affront to either party.

What must the teacher do to foster the emergence of an intercultural classroom within the cross-cultural situation? The answer would require another essay at least as long as the present one, but it may be helpful to quote the remarks of one teacher in the region:

"I can't follow a lesson plan, and I just go along by ear. I've taught Cherokee students for six years in high school, and this is my first [year] in elementary school." Referring, then to his experiences as a high school coach, he continued, "The thing you have to do, if you get a team, is that you got to get them to cooperate. . . ."

At first glance, this appears at odds with our earlier assertions about the spontaneous emergence of the Cherokee School Society, not to mention contradictory to the conventional notions that Indians will not compete with each other. But what he is explaining is that unless the teacher chooses to recognize the social nature of the classroom and to work toward integrating his teaching with that life, he will not be able to elicit active learning experiences from his pupils. Or, to put it negatively, if the teacher does not work with his Indian students as a social group, their union will be directed toward other goals. Yet the teacher can secure their response only if he "gets them" to cooperate; he cannot "make them" do so.

CONCLUSION

The foregoing report provides the basis for judgments and hypotheses on a variety of levels. On the practical level, it would seem that ethnic integration is not an essential precondition for satisfactory education of groups from a low socioeconomic background. The Tribal Cherokee certainly are impoverished and poorly educated. Nevertheless, we would predict that the consolidation of rural schools into larger, better-staffed, and better-equipped schools in northeastern Oklahoma may actually lead to deterioration rather than improvement of the educational condition. Given the ethos of the Tribal Cherokee, consolidation may mean the irremediable loss of many opportunities for assisting their children educationally.

On the methodological level, we are reminded of how sociologically valuable it is for researchers to focus on the frontier situation "where peoples meet." [6] The resulting accommodations, adaptations, and divisions of labor are an enlightening and fascinating phenomenon, which especially deserve to be studied as a corrective to those theoretical systems which regard the national society as an integrated social system. On the methodological level also, our study illustrates anew the value of ethnographic observations of classroom activities. Basic and simple as it may seem, and unpretentious in the face of modern testing procedures, direct observation still has much to teach us.[7]

[6] Everett C. Hughes and Helen M. Hughes, *Where Peoples Meet: Ethnic and Racial Frontiers,* The Free Press, Glencoe, Illinois, 1952.

[7] Consider for example, the impact and contribution of such recent books which rely either on direct observation or participation observation of classrooms as John Holt, *How Children Fail,* Delta, New York, 1964; Harry F. Wolcott, *A Kwakiutl Village and School,* Holt, Rinehart

Finally, on the substantive level, the research reported here cautions against the erosion of our conceptual armamentarium when researchers allow their research problems to be defined by educational administrators. When that happens, the educational situation of peoples such as the Indians tends to be conceived in terms of individual pupils and their "cultural deprivation." The researcher then is asked to assist the administration in raising these disadvantaged individuals to the point where they can compete in school in the same fashion as do white middle-class children. Our research is a reminder that such styles of conceptualization neglect the social nature of the classrooms and the social ties among the pupils. They also neglect the tension between teacher and pupils as a social group, and the struggles that occur when the teacher presses for individualistic achievement at the expense of group solidarity.[8]

and Winston, New York, 1967; Wax, Wax, and Dumont, *op. cit.;* Estelle Fuchs, *Pickets at the Gates,* The Free Press, New York, 1966; G. Alexander Moore, *Realities of the Urban Classroom: Observations in Elementary Schools,* Doubleday Anchor, New York, 1967; Elizabeth M. Eddy, *Walk the White Line,* Doubleday Anchor, New York, 1967.

[8] Such phenomena were clearly noted by Willard Waller in his *Sociology of Teaching,* first published in 1932, reprinted by Science Editions, John Wiley, New York, 1965. It is unfortunate to see the neglect of such elementary sociological considerations in much of the more recent literature of the "sociology of education."

28. COMMUNICATIVE DEVICES IN THE ADDAMS AREA

Gerald D. Suttles

Three of the four groups that occupy the area described by
Suttles in this selection are "nonwhite" minorities. Each
of the four groups has its own style of expression and
self-presentation, though within each group there are
prominent distinctions between the behavioral style and
deportment of older and younger people. Such modes of
presentation of the self, repeated as part of a pattern in a
particular group, help to create and maintain the impressions
that outsiders have of that group. Arts of impression
management are sometimes practiced consciously within the
group as well. Among younger people in particular they may
become bases of esteem as well as modes of self-expression.

Different vehicles all convey messages: language, gesture,
clothing, music, and the dance. Outsiders often grasp only the
explicit messages such instruments convey; insiders know the
implicit ones as well. Thus, since the total "language" is both
explicit and implicit, misunderstood messages are not
uncommon when members of the different groups interact. Such
misunderstanding frequently leads to tension and antipathy on
the streets of the Addams area. It occurs elsewhere, too, with
equally serious implications, when a physician misreads
symptoms and has trouble arriving at an accurate diagnosis, or
when a teacher finds that she has been made uncomfortable
through an inability to establish rapport with minority-group
students.

Conventions of style, appearance, and manner can be used

Source: *The Social Order of the Slum* (Chicago: The University of
Chicago Press, 1968), pp. 9, 10, 61–72, with some footnotes omitted.
Copyright © 1968, by The University of Chicago Press. Reprinted by
permission of the author and University of Chicago Press.

GERALD D. SUTTLES is Associate Professor of Sociology at the State
University of New York at Stony Brook.

by members of almost any group both to reinforce their own identity and to keep outsiders at a distance. Any reader who has already been involved in, or has thought much about joining, the battle of long hair or bare feet is already familiar with both sides of the proposition. He is probably also aware of how much emotion some members of given groups are willing to invest in their own standards of rightness and propriety. Such standards have also been used as a yardstick for estimating social acceptability among members of many different minority groups who found their access to employment or residence or education blocked because they talked funny or dressed strangely, or in general did not have the kinds of manners that "maketh man."

The Addams Area

The Addams area consists of four different ethnic sections occupied predominantly by Negroes, Italians, Puerto Ricans, and Mexicans. Each of these ethnic sections falls into a somewhat different stage in its development of a provincial order. At one extreme is an old Italian population slowly being displaced by Mexicans, Negroes, and Puerto Ricans. Among the Italians, people from all walks of life are drawn together in a well-knit series of peer groups that range from childhood to the upper realms of adulthood. Both the "church people" and the racketeers are bound together in a common collusion at "impression management" [1] and are equally safe in each other's presence. Local business establishments, street corners, and other public facilities are categorized according to their proper "hangers-on," the license they may enjoy, and the behavior appropriate to "outsiders."

At the other extreme are the Negroes who, like the three ethnic groups, form a small but compact residential group. They are the most recent to invade the

[1] Erving Goffman, *The Presentation of Self in Everyday Life* (Garden City, N.Y.: Doubleday, 1959).

neighborhood and remain the most estranged from one another. Anonymity and distrust are pervasive, and well-established peer groups are present only among the adolescents. Sometimes those residents who are most "respectable" carry on a futile and divisive attack on those who are not so respectable. Occasionally they are incited and encouraged in this endeavor by the social welfare agents who find their neglect of public morality incomprehensible. Local businesses, street locations, and other spatial settings, with the exception of adolescent hangouts, are not well-differentiated according to who can be there and what behavior is required of them. In large part this seems due to the placement of the Negroes in public housing and the lack of private facilities within which the other groups can retire to practice their provincial morality. . . . The local integration of the Negro population seems to have been stymied by their inclusion in public housing. [See Selections 23 and 31.—Ed.]

The Mexicans and Puerto Ricans seem to occupy a middle ground. The Puerto Ricans make up such a small and compact group that the problems of anonymity are less pressing; practically everyone can be known "as an individual." The Mexicans are most numerous and have well-developed peer groups among the adolescents. Beyond this age group, adult affiliations are tenuous although several Mexican adults have been absorbed into the older Italian groups and a few of the adult males have made incipient gestures toward forming groups of their own. All the same, the Mexicans who support public morality and those who violate it have not been entirely reconciled to one another. Unlike the Negroes, however, both the Puerto Ricans and the Mexicans have developed many local establishments and spatial boundaries where a limited range of persons may congregate and find a reliable code for deciding what can or cannot be done.

Despite these differences, all four ethnic sections share many characteristics and seem headed along the same social progression. The overall pattern is one where age, sex, ethnic, and territorial units are fitted together like building blocks to create a larger structure. I have termed this pattern "ordered segmentation" to indicate two related features: (1) the orderly relationship between groups and (2) the sequential order in which groups combine in instances of conflict and opposition. This ordered segmentation is not equally developed in all ethnic sections but, in skeletal outline, it is the common framework within which groups are being formed and social relations are being cultivated.

My own experiences within the Addams area and the presentation of this volume are heavily influenced by the ordered segmentation of the neighborhood. I took up residence in the area in the summer of 1963 and left a little less than three years later. At the outset the most evident finding was the distinctiveness of the Addams area and its opposition to adjacent neighborhoods. Since I had unwittingly settled near the boundary between the Italian, Mexican, and Puerto Rican sections, I soon became acquainted with some of the territorial, institutional, and communication arrangements that prevail between ethnic sections. . . .

. . . . .

COMMUNICATIVE DEVICES

Ethnicity is the major basis of division within the Addams area, but practically every resident has at least one acquaintance in another ethnic group. These relationships are usually rather superficial and often consist of little more than a nod between adults living in adjoining buildings. Occasionally, the host-guest relationship advances to become an acquaintanceship that is acknowledged beyond the establishment where it started. Sometimes there is common membership in a street corner group. More rarely, there is an open covenant such as a marriage, business partnership, or landlord-renter relation.

Relations between ethnic groups, however, are like an off-color joke: they are not recommended for others, they are seldom publicly revealed, and they are taken as a kind of promissory note toward still other "irregularities." Parents who have friends in another ethnic group discourage their children from following the same practice for fear of trouble. Almost all the youngsters in the area have acquaintances outside their ethnic group and place a considerable value on "being in" with another ethnic group. Italian boys brag that they know the Poles up on "Milwaukee"; Mexican girls protest that they know the guys in the projects and "they won't hurt me"; sometimes the Puerto Ricans insist that they personally have safe passage on Laflin street. These are relations, however, which are hidden from adults and seldom expressed in a public form such as a common group membership. Inter-ethnic relations in the Addams area are a very private matter and a part of the neighborhood's "underlife."

Once under way, inter-ethnic relations are subject to a number of misunderstandings and may follow an abortive course. If a Mexican girl is friendly with Negro boys, she is apt to be seen as "on the make." A Negro boy who is friendly with Italians is typically received in one of four ways: (1) he is "conning you," (2) he is different from other Negroes, (3) he is gullible about ethnic group distinctions, or (4) he is the hope of his race.

Often the residents interpret the unconventional character of inter-ethnic relations as an invitation to further unconventionalities. Italians sometimes ask friendly Negroes to procure prostitutes and marijuana for them. Negroes may solicit an Italian's help in fixing a traffic ticket or bad check. Neither party may be able to furnish the expected service, but a person willing to engage in inter-ethnic relations is thought willing to try almost anything else.[2]

These barriers to inter-ethnic relations in the Addams area are common to all the groups in the area and arise chiefly from ethnic stereotypes that are widely shared throughout the United States. Even after an inter-ethnic relationship has surmounted these hurdles, however, it encounters an additional set of obstacles in the different communicative devices used by each local ethnic group.

Each ethnic group in the Addams area has a set of cultural practices unfamiliar to the others. Traditionally

this sort of social misunderstanding between ethnic groups has been called "culture conflict." The cultural differences that divide Addams area residents, however, usually do not extend to an obvious and uncompromising contradiction of basic norms of values. Mexicans, Negroes, Italians, and Puerto Ricans all believe that killing, fighting, stealing, and insolence are "bad." Similarly, they almost invariably agree that cleanliness, motherhood, education, money, and kindness are "good." [3] The differences that become serious in local relationships, then, are not so much in norms, goals, or general standards, but in the *notational devices* that each group relies upon to express and encode their adherence to these basic social rules. In this regard, the participants are like schoolboys using different number systems while trying to explain to one another the same arithmetic problem. Behind their misunderstanding is the same mathematical system and possibly the same answer. However, unless they can make the necessary transformations, they cannot possibly agree. Quite possibly, there is also a correspondence between the meanings attached to the gesture of Italians and Negroes. Yet, so long as each group does not know how to translate this correspondence they go on misunderstanding one another and incorrectly interpreting each other's behavior.

For purposes of this study, it might as well be assumed that each minority group subscribes to exactly the same general norms, even if this is not quite true. The approach here has been narrowed down to specific differences in the behavioral code that each group depends upon to serve notice of its good or bad

[2] During my stay in the Addams area there were at least three instances of flagrant sexual misbehavior. All of them involved members of two or more ethnic groups. There were many more instances of sexual misbehavior, and some of them occurred among members of the same ethnic group. Generally, however, these were fairly discreet affairs carried out with considerable secrecy. What was outstanding about the first three instances was the overt manner in which they were carried out—almost as if they were being endorsed as the norm rather than the exception.

[3] These statements are little more than tautologies. Of course, all these groups value such things as kindness, because one of the bases on which we determine what is considered "kindness" in different cultures is whether or not its particular occurrences are regarded as "good." If they were not defined as good, then we would call them something else.

intentions, its goals, and its beliefs. The question whether each of these notational systems can be translated into the same or completely different normative systems is relatively unimportant because in any case local residents usually cannot bridge the gaps between them.

Language

The most obvious restriction on communication between the ethnic groups in the Addams area is their differences of language and dialect. For many of the older residents, Spanish and Italian are still the working languages for everyday life. Even within each of these speech communities, however, the dialects are often so far apart that they lead to grave misunderstandings, invidious comparisons, and mutual avoidance. Where English is spoken, the range of common understanding is not much greater. With the older Italians, Mexicans, and Puerto Ricans, their English is often badly broken and is either a source of embarrassment or a tool by which only the bare rudiments of communication can take place. All the subtleties that are usually incorporated into speech are suddenly lost. Thus persons are left adrift without the ordinary innuendos, graces, overtones, and insinuations that play such a critical part in the constant reassurances they furnish one another.

Lacking these essentials, verbal behavior often loses the easy continuity that we call spontaneity and takes on a halting and rehearsed manner that is usually attributed to calculation. At the same time, the participants are reduced to presenting only the most mundane and blatant information about themselves and their intentions. It becomes almost impossible to hint at one's objectives before fully broaching them, to use circumlocutions or idioms that evade overt admission of vulgarity, and to employ metaphors that protect the par-

ticipants from the full light of social exposure. A more subtle but no less important deficiency is that inflection and intonation cease to be dependable indices that persons can use to judge the appropriateness of their own reactions. For the older residents, this last shortcoming means that they cannot reliably distinguish between demands, questions, and polite requests. A common greeting by the older Italians and Mexicans, for example, is a bland, "Whadda you want?" Since members of the various groups in the area prefer to be requested rather than required to meet each other's expectations, such an inability to detect nuances in speech is a serious handicap to comfortable social relations.

When the residents are reduced to speech patterns that are coarse, abrupt, and lacking in polite forms, their own self-presentation becomes equally coarse, abrupt, and impolite. Since they can be no more than the shared symbols that represent them allow, most Addams area residents would be embarrassed and humiliated to appear as such crude and incomplete persons or to have to deal with someone who can only be overt, uncompromising, and impolite. Thus, it is not surprising that those among them who depend upon broken English either avoid those encounters requiring communication in English or at best submit to them with considerable uneasiness.

Linguistic embarrassment is most acute among the older residents, and they are most likely to apologize for their language. Italians explain that they speak a "dialect" rather than "real Italian." As for their English, the older people only laugh at their broken English if you are a good friend; otherwise they avoid you and say as little as possible. The Puerto Ricans tell you that their Spanish is not quite "right." Their English is a new and somewhat uncertain way of getting people to understand them. The older Mexicans have a good deal of confidence in their Spanish but regard their English as something of an experiment.

Among the younger people, English is almost invariably spoken, although a few of the Mexicans and even more of the Puerto Ricans maintain varying degrees of familiarity with Spanish.[4] Both the Mexican and Puerto Rican youngsters seem to have learned a dialect of English very similar to that of the Italians. The Negroes, on the other hand, still preserve a measure of several different southern dialects along with their accompanying vocabulary and syntactic forms.[5] Sometimes the Negroes and whites will "make fun" of each others' English, but this is not common.

More often there is an acceptance of the historical origins of their language differences. Both Negroes and whites, for example, will simply point to their regional origins to explain why their language is different. Unfortunately this does not much help them to assign any interpretation to these differences. Like most people, Addams area residents are not likely to dismiss speech differences simply because they are "justifiable." Their life, safety, self-enhancement, and knowledge of the other person's intentions all depend upon being able to decipher these differences. At times, no doubt, these differences between Negro and white speech may not be significant even within their own speech communities. But Addams area residents do not know this. All they know is that differences do exist and, so long as they cannot understand their significance, they are hesitant to expose themselves to a relationship with no recognizable guidelines.

For the most part, syntactic and phonological differences divide the white and Negro residents in the area. An interesting departure is the use of "jive." This special vocabulary of argot or "slang" terms is restricted according to both age and ethnicity, but its usage overlaps the Negro-white distinction. Negro boys are most expert at this sort of discourse, but the English-speaking Mexican and Puerto Rican boys are also somewhat conversant with "jive." The Italians seldom use any of this vocabulary even to the point of not understanding it.[6] In the case of "jive," however, the Italians do not regard language differences so much as an unexplained phenomena as an attempt to talk behind someone's back, "show off" one's knowledge of urban ways, or display one's emancipation from the homely virtues of family, ethnic group, and neighbors. To the Italians, the use of "jive" often indicates a person who has scuttled the surest signs of human feeling and concern for the bonds that secure personal

---

[4] In all the Mexican street corner groups, English is used, and most of the boys cannot speak adequate Spanish. Quite a few of the Puerto Rican boys use Spanish among themselves and speak English with differing degrees of success. However, even in most of their groups, English is the common language, and they differ in their ability with Spanish. All the Italian groups use English, and it is rare to find a member who knows Italian. Incidentally, it is quite common for a child to grow up in a household where Spanish or Italian is used and never come to speak that language. Apparently the children learn most of their language from their peers.

[5] For example, the use of the present tense and the use of the first person verb form with all pronouns. See Raven McDavid and Virginia McDavid, "The Relationship of the Speech of American Negroes to the Speech of Whites," *American Speech*, 26 (February, 1951): 3–17.

[6] Once it was suggested to me that this showed that the Italians no longer need to rely upon secrecy to disguise their underlife. However, this is very unlikely because they are certainly the most involved in the rackets and the most difficult for an outsider to approach. Indeed, it seems that their withdrawal from the wider community and their provinciality are the major reasons for not bothering with the fads of language. The Negroes, Puerto Ricans, and Mexicans are very eager to show they are hipsters, familiar with the most advanced of urban speech, clothing styles, and learning. The Italians, lost in their own provincial world, just don't seem to care. More than any other group, they ignore the fads and fashions that attest to one's place in the forefront of urban life. Whether or not they were always equally indifferent to these new modes of expression is something I have not been able to determine.

relations within the neighborhood. To the Negroes, and less so among the Mexicans and Puerto Ricans, a familiarity with this youthful jargon is only a sign of a willingness to expand the magic circle of trust beyond that of family, ethnic group, and territorial compatriots. . . . There is good reason for the Italians backwardness. More than any other ethnic group in the area, they are firmly ensconced in a network of kinfolk, family friends, and intergenerational relations. Among themselves, they are hardly ever anonymous and can ill afford to flaunt their emancipation from traditional relations.

Gestures

Language differences between each ethnic group are often exacerbated by nonverbal acts which accompany or supplant speech. First-generation Italians, for example, have an entire repertory of gestures that are not even fully understood by their own children. Negro boys, in turn, have a "cool" way of walking ("pimp's walk") in which the upper trunk and pelvis rock fore and aft while the head remains stable with the eyes looking straight ahead. The "pimp's walk" is quite slow, and the Negroes take it as a way of "strutting" or "showing off." The whites usually interpret it as a pointed lack of concern for those adjacent to the walker. Negro girls provide a parallel in a slow "sashay" that white males sometimes take as an unqualified invitation to their attentions.

These subtle differences in posture, stance, and gestures are the source of considerable interest among Addams area residents. The other ethnic groups think it odd that a group of Mexican men should strike a pose of obliviousness to other people and even to their nearby wives and children. Puerto Ricans, on the other hand, are disparaged because they stand painfully close during a conversation and talk in such a voluble

manner as to "jabber." Whites say that Negroes will not look them in the eye. The Negroes counter by saying the whites are impolite and try to "cow" people by staring at them.

The residents do not report these gestural differences as a part of each other's cultural heritage or as a general attribute common to all members of a single ethnic group. Often it is useless for an investigator to ask informants to make a blanket statement about the gestural behavior of another ethnic group. They will simply say that "there's really no difference." [7] When asked about a specific historical event, however, they often provide an account in which ethnic social types are almost always joined to specific gestures. The most subtle accounts are those which describe almost entirely nonverbal encounters: "When I went over to the Negro nurse, she didn't even look up"; "I'd go again (to an Italian restaurant) but they really stare you down"; "Those Mexican men were just standing there while the kids ran in the street and, you know, one of them was their father!" "I was walking by the Projects, and those Negro girls were just sitting there, their legs all sprawled all over, and I didn't feel right."

If asked to generalize from their own

[7] Negro informants seem to be especially unwilling to generalize about differences among the four minority groups in the area. The other groups, however, also insist upon qualifications that exempt at least some members of each minority group. In this respect, Addams area residents are truer to the facts than most investigators who have dealt with the problem of minority groups. They recognize that the members of any minority group are both exceptional and typical. This point was once brought home to me by an Italian lady who, pointing to another woman, said, "Do you see that woman? She is Mexican but she is a wonderful person." The Italian lady went on to tell me why the Mexican woman was so wonderful. Later I found out that the two were close friends. Nonetheless, the Italian lady continued to confide to me her sorrow at seeing the Mexicans move into the area. Incidentally, as a landlord, she steadfastly refused to put a "for rent" sign in her window for fear that she might have to rent to a Mexican or Puerto Rican family.

commentaries, the residents protest that no gestural forms are general or even common to another ethnic group; it is just that some members in a single ethnic group behave this way. Thus, while particular gestural forms are thought to be restricted to a single ethnic group, their use is not usually regarded as a custom or habit but as a calculated and voluntary individual act. Unlike language differences, then, gestural differences are taken as an intentional affront. As one Negro informant put it, "I can understand why those guys (older male Italian street group) can't half speak English, but, dammit, why they gotta eyeball everybody walk past?"

These fragmentary observations on gestural forms only serve to illustrate how nonverbal communications estrange ethnic groups in the Addams area. Often these differences are rare and hardly perceptible, but they do not escape the experienced scrutiny of the local residents. Nonetheless, the residents are no more able than contemporary sociologists at divining the import of these communicative signs. Unlike sociologists, however, Addams area residents cannot afford the academic curiosity that a distant observer might entertain. Many of these gestural forms precede inter-ethnic encounters and thus become the first warning received of the subsequent course of interaction. After the initiation of inter-ethnic relations, gestural behavior is constantly referred to as a source of corroborating or contrary evidence for judging a person's verbal claims. Such subtle and minor signs loom large when evaluated against the residents' suspicions of other ethnic groups.

Clothing, Grooming, and Personal Display

. . . . .

In general these observations on clothing seem to warrant two separate conclusions.[8] First, insofar as these differences are not understood by all ethnic groups, they constitute another occasion for wariness and avoidance between ethnic groups. Second, each style of clothing tends to reiterate local ethnic differences that have been observed elsewhere. The Negro boys do not have a distinctive costume for purely local situations but address themselves to a wider audience. The style of dress associated with the Italians can be worn only locally and governs a self-presentation that can be appreciated only within their own ethnic section. The Puerto Ricans and Mexicans lie between the other two ethnic groups. A few items in their wardrobe seem to be a part of their traditional culture and might appeal to other Mexicans and Puerto Ricans all over Chicago. Otherwise the Mexicans and Puerto Ricans selectively share various items that are provided by the Italians or Negroes. Differences in clothing, then, reflect the degree of provincialism prevalent in each ethnic group.

Dance styles show similar levels of provincialism in each ethnic group. Negro teenagers are almost invariably a step or two ahead of the Italians in the kinds of dances and music with which they are familiar. Between April 1962 and June 1964 at least ten different dance styles passed through the Addams area. At all times the Negroes were at least one dance style ahead of the Italians. Generally, the Mexicans and

[8] Talcott Parsons ("Age and Sex in the Social Structure of the United States" in *Essays in Sociological Theory* [Glencoe, Ill.: Free Press, 1954], pp. 82–103) states that expressive variations in dress are mostly restricted to women, while men still wear something like a uniform. His observations, however, seem restricted to a segment of the American public where males are drawn into multiple loyalties while females are left with the task of expressing the consumer preferences of the nuclear family. In the Addams area, males are divided into quite discrete segments and thus become the main standard bearers of the ethnic sections to which they belong.

Puerto Ricans were in between the Negroes and the Italians in their current dance styles.

In general, then, the Italian and Negro boys seem to be at opposite poles in their use of clothing and dances as communicative devices. Those elements shared by the Italian boys declare either a commitment to their own ethnic section or an indifference to wider social rulings. The Negro boys seem to lack any specific ways of expressing a similar prejudice for local acquaintances and to have a surplus of emblems that can be used beyond the local neighborhood. The Negro boys were, as one white woman put it, "always dressed up like they thought they were going somewhere."

This same pattern of self-presentation was present in the earlier observations on language, gestures, and grooming. The Negroes are very "hip" to linguistic novelty, "jive," and the avant-garde of personal appearance. The Italians are not so venturesome in their language, and many of the adults draw back into a dialect that can be understood only by their local *paisani*. Their gestures are either drawn from a past tradition or are indicative of the informality and intimacy of their ethnic section. Grooming among the Negroes is often meticulous and stylish; in contrast the Italians seem ordinary and "square." [9] Drugs and other "far out" experiences are most prominent among the Negroes. The Italians lay equal emphasis on a domestic round of "basement parties," *paisani* picnics, and wine-making.

On their own part, the Mexicans and Puerto Ricans either represent an intermediate case or an accommodation to the adjacent Italians and Negroes. Both the Mexican and Puerto Rican boys pick up some of the dance styles and "jive" after they have been introduced by the Negroes. Mexican and Puerto Rican clothing is either like that of the Italians or carries its own distinctive stamp.

No doubt some of these differences between ethnic groups are drawn from their separate cultural traditions. In the South the Negroes were a country peasantry [10] with almost no level of organization beyond that of the nuclear family and the church. Even then, their churches were tiny operations with no standing relation among them. Subsequently, the urban Negro has been the most transient and least capable of all the ethnic groups of gathering around kinfolk, people from a common region, or persons of the same religious denomination. Sicilians and Southern Italians were townspeople who brought with them all the petty distinctions, collusions, and trivial skills that townsmen seem to cultivate. Their churches were large enough to serve a sizeable settlement, and a common faith brought them together into a single local establishment. Like the Negroes, the Sicilians and Southern Italians were an oppressed minority, but they reacted jointly as a community rather than as independent domestic units.

Within the Addams area, however, the continuity of traditional expressive orders seems less important than the way each communicative device is fitted into the area's ethnic segmentation. These differences in gestures, language, and style are not simply a barrier to convenient communication; they are emblems of each ethnic group's position in the Addams area and its stance toward the wider community. The daily life of the Italians is heavily restricted to their own

[9] Negro hair styles are either very neat and unobtrusive or tailored to advanced styles by use of the "process" ("conk"). Italian haircuts are either ordinary or show signs of neglect. In the case of adult Negroes, a thin, well-trimmed mustache is the rule; among the Italians it is the exception.

[10] Even today, one of the worst insults is to say something like, "Man, you're real 'country.' Like forty acres and a mule."

local business places, church, and ethnic section. Historically and politically they are still closely identified with the area. The Negroes are regarded as recent invaders and have little political control over the area. In their daily rounds Negroes must spend a good deal of time in establishments and institutions that are not identified with them. Less attached to the local area, the Negroes are thereby more able to borrow cultural forms from the wider society.

The Mexicans and Puerto Ricans are intermediate in ethnic status and share territorial boundaries with both the Negroes and Italians. Much of their daily life can be spent in their own establishments, but they fall far short of the Italians in their control over a full complement of ethnic institutions. Also the Puerto Ricans and Mexicans are caught in the cross fire when the Negroes and Italians are drawn into conflict. Usually the Puerto Ricans and Mexicans avoid taking sides and try not to offend either group. In their predicament it is useful to share some of the communicative devices of both the Italians and the Negroes.

Thus, when examined in the full context of the Addams area, cultural variations in communicative patterns seem to reflect different levels of sociocultural integration within each ethnic group.[11] The Italians are much involved in their local ethnic neighborhood and tend to ignore the fads and fashions of the wider society. The Negroes are far less dependent on their coresidents and are quick to orient themselves to at least some national patterns of dress and style. Each group may have derived some of its distinctive communicative devices from traditional sources and borrowed others from diverse sources. Whatever their source, however, these communicative devices form a composite that conveys an appropriate image of how each group balances its relations to the local neighborhood and the wider community.

[11] Julian H. Steward, *Theory of Culture Change* (Urbana: University of Illinois Press, 1955), pp. 43–63.

29. ETHNICITY, POVERTY, AND SELECTED ATTITUDES: A TEST OF THE CULTURE OF POVERTY HYPOTHESIS

Lola M. Irelan, Oliver C. Moles, and Robert M. O'Shea

The headnote to Selection 18, Oscar Lewis, "A Study of Slum Culture," briefly referred to Lewis' formulation of the nature of the culture of poverty. The present selection examines that formulation in greater detail through a study of the attitudes of poor men in California who were members of three different racial or ethnic groups: Mexican-American, black, and Anglo-American. The technical form of the presentation involves testing the hypothesis that the culture of poverty is a unitary phenomenon that is essentially similar among poor people of whatever racial or ethnic group. The authors conclude that the hypothesis has to be rejected. The attitudes of poor men toward dependency, familism, fatalism, social alienation, and the value of work vary in accordance with their racial or ethnic membership, with whether or not their families are receiving welfare payments, and with the interaction of racial group with welfare receipt. In general, the Mexican-Americans seemed closest to Lewis' original

Source: *Social Forces,* Vol. 47, No. 4 (June 1969), pp. 405–13, with some footnotes omitted. Reprinted by permission of the senior author and the University of North Carolina Press.

LOLA M. IRELAN, editor of *Low Income Life Styles,* is Director of the Longitudinal Retirement History Study in the Office of Research and Statistics, Social Security Administration; OLIVER C. MOLES is Research Psychologist, Office of Planning, Research and Evaluation, Office of Economic Opportunity; and ROBERT M. O'SHEA is Assistant Professor, Department of Sociology, State University of New York at Buffalo.

formulation, perhaps on account of similarities between their culture and those of the Mexican nationals and Puerto Ricans Lewis had studied before.

Two precautions should be kept in mind as you evaluate these research results. First, they depend on attitude survey data that display some of the same difficulties as the instruments discussed in the introduction to Selection 12.

Second, the authors have not disproved that poverty leads to, reflects, or at a minimum merely accompanies a constellation of attitudes and performances which, despite variations in specific manifestations among various groups of poor people, is nevertheless systematically different from patterns of feeling and action that would be encountered among the better-off.

. . . In 1958, Walter Miller described a lower-class cultural system: . . . "a long established, distinctively patterned tradition with an integrity of its own." [1] Subsequently, Oscar Lewis further suggested that there is a culture of poverty which "transcends national boundaries and regional and rural-urban differences within nations. Wherever it occurs, its practitioners exhibit remarkable similarity in the structure of their families, in interpersonal relations, in spending habits, in their value systems, and in their orientation in time." [2]

Thus carefully phrased, the concept invites testing which it has not yet received. . . .

Both the Miller and Lewis statements imply, at the least, the simple hypothesis that very poor people from groups characterized by different major cultures are markedly similar to each other in certain attitudes, values, and patterns of behavior.

It has been possible to take a first step in the testing of this hypothesis. . . .

[1] Walter Miller, "Lower Class Culture as a Generating Milieu of Gang Delinquency," *Journal of Social Issues,* 14 (July 1958), p. 5.
[2] Oscar Lewis, "The Culture of Poverty," *Scientific American* (October 1966), p. 19.

DATA

Data used were collected in California during 1964 in the course of research into characteristics associated with receipt and non-receipt of public assistance funds by economically deprived families.[3] Respondents were the male heads of 1,156 intact families, each of whom could be classified as either Spanish-speaking American, Negro-American, or Anglo-American. The three ethnic groups were represented in approximately equal numbers (440, 316 and 400 respectively). Approximately half of each group were selected from recipients of Aid to Families of Dependent Children with Unemployed Parents (AFDC–UP). The rest were drawn from contacts, in the same counties, of various social service agencies. None of these latter families were receiving public assistance

[3] Sponsored cooperatively by the Welfare Administration of U.S. Department of Health, Education, and Welfare (CRD Grant #207) and the California State Department of Social Welfare. Principal investigators were Robert C. Stone, San Francisco State College, and Frederic T. Schlamp, California State Department of Social Welfare. We are grateful to these investigators for making their data available to us.

at the time of the interview. Each consisted of at least a father, mother, and one minor child. Two primarily rural and two primarily urban counties were represented. Respondents were distributed about equally among the four counties.[4]

All respondents were pcor. Median reported income was $3,306 annually, and median family size was 6.8 persons. An income scale matching the AFDC–UP payment levels for families of different sizes was used to select the non-recipient families (e.g., $2,492 for 4 persons), but in order to reach the quota in urban areas some were included whose income was as much as 30 percent above these figures Thus, non-recipients as a whole had slightly higher income. A large majority of the men reported either unskilled or semiskilled occupations. In general, respondents' families were without savings, insurance, or pension coverage. Seventy-six percent were in debt for an average amount of $1,572.

HYPOTHESIS

The general hypothesis stated above was operationalized as a null hypothesis. . . . No significant difference will be found between Anglo-American poor, Spanish-speaking American poor, and Negro-American poor in their responses in eight specific areas.

ANALYSIS PROCEDURES

The data are additive summaries of responses to attitude items (3- and 5-point scales) in several attitude domains. As such, they meet the requirements of the

[4] The proportion of respondents from rural and urban counties did, however, differ among ethnic groups. The rural counties contained 65 percent of the Spanish-speaking and 62 percent of the Anglos, but only 16 percent of the Negroes. This was not an important variable for the present analysis, since Lewis' theory specifically posits no differences between the poverty culture of rural and urban groups.

Kruskal-Wallis nonparametric one-way analysis of variance by ranks. A probability level of .05 was specified as significant and sufficient to reject a stated null hypothesis.

To utilize the full possibilities of the data, responses of men who had received public assistance were tabulated and tested separately from those of men with no such experience. The hypothesis was thus tested on two levels of poverty.[5]

RESULTS

Results of the 16 applications of the Kruskal-Wallis test are summarized as follows. In 14 cases, differences among the three ethnic groups were found to be significant at the .05 level or better. Eleven were significant at the .001 level. In 2 applications nonsignificant differences were found. Considerable doubt is thus cast upon the validity of the culture of poverty concept. The results will now be discussed in more detail.

Dependency

Lewis has stated in several publications that dependency is a notable characteristic of the culture of poverty.[6] Two sets of dependency questions, measuring dependent feelings and dependent behavior, were included in the questionnaire of the original study.[7] Both

[5] Lewis has suggested that receipt of public assistance serves to perpetuate the culture of poverty. See Oscar Lewis, La Vida (New York: Random House, 1965), pp. xlv, xlvi; his unpublished report to the Social Security and Welfare Administration, The Culture of Poverty in Puerto Rico and in New York (Cooperative Research Grant No. 127), p. 8; and Lewis, 1966, op. cit., p. 21.
[6] Oscar Lewis, "The Culture of Poverty," in Te Paske and Fisher (eds.) Explosive Forces in Latin America (Columbus: Ohio State University Press, 1964), p. 154; Lewis, 1965, op. cit., p. xlvii; and Lewis, 1966, op. cit., p. 23.
[7] These scales were drawn from Arthur Lamphere, "The Relationship between Dependency Factors and Goal Setting in Duodenal Ulcer Patients," unpublished Ph.D. dissertation, Univer-

TABLE 1 Dependency feelings and behavior among low-income Anglo, Spanish-speaking, and Negro recipients and non-recipients of public assistance.

	Percent of persons agreeing with item among:					
	Public assistance recipients			Non-recipients		
	Anglo	Spanish-speaking	Negro	Anglo	Spanish-speaking	Negro
	(N = 210)*	(N = 212)	(N = 165)	(N = 189)	(N = 227)	(N = 151)
Dependency Feelings Items						
I secretly wish I were a child again	34.0	39.9	23.2	19.7	41.4	17.3
I feel a person must "play politics" to get promotions or increases in pay and jobs	25.4	30.6	33.1	22.3	41.3	39.7
I feel out of sorts if I have to be by myself for any length of time	33.7	43.7	30.5	20.2	39.2	27.2
Average score for all items *	4.3	5.4	4.1	3.0	5.3	3.7
Dependency Behavior Items						
I feel afraid of being alone or of not being wanted	31.6	32.2	27.3	25.5	35.4	23.8
I do a great many things just to avoid criticism	40.0	52.6	56.1	38.3	51.3	50.7
Because I want to be liked, I tend to be apologetic and won't stand up for what I know are my real feelings	26.3	39.6	31.1	20.1	44.2	24.5
Average score for all items †	4.6	5.6	4.8	3.9	5.5	4.4

* Based on each person's total score derived by combining all responses. Average scores may range from 1 to 13. All items were 5-point scales with *strongly disagree* and *strongly agree* as the extreme low and high point responses.
† Total number of respondents on which percentages were based are approximately the same for all tables. For some percentages numbers are slightly smaller because of missing data.

"acceptable" and "unacceptable" dependency questions were included but it was decided to use only the acceptable items. They could be expected to separate more and less dependent persons more clearly (Table 1).

The reliability of differences which emerge here is quite high. For both recipients and non-recipients of public assistance, ethnicity is significant at the .001 level as a trait associated with the extent of dependent feelings and depen-

sity of Washington, 1953. Items were originally selected on the basis of judgment by clinical psychologists.

dent behavior. In both cases average scores indicate that Spanish-speaking respondents were most dependent, and that Anglos and Negroes were similar in their lesser dependency.

Family Related Attitudes

Lewis believes that poverty has a strong effect upon family organization, behavior, and attitudes. Repeated emphasis is placed by him on the detachment which characterizes husband–wife relations, the mother-centeredness of families, the lack of protective and cher-

TABLE 2 Family related attitudes among low-income Anglo, Spanish-speaking, and Negro recipients and non-recipients of public assistance.

| | Percent of persons agreeing with item among: | | | | | |
| | Public assistance recipients | | | Non-recipients | | |
	Anglo	Spanish-speaking	Negro	Anglo	Spanish-speaking	Negro
Items on Primacy of Family of Orientation						
The responsibilities of taking care of his wife and children should not keep a husband from spending plenty of time with his own parents	35.9	57.5	50.9	40.5	50.4	47.7
There is no excusing a wife who tries to come between a man and his parents	45.4	50.0	47.8	47.8	57.3	41.6
A man should be careful that his marriage doesn't result in his losing interest and close contact with his own mother and father	48.5	67.6	67.5	55.1	73.8	71.5
Average score for all items *	6.2	7.7	7.1	6.5	7.4	6.8
Items on Child Autonomy						
If children plan their own work and do it without the direction of parents they are more willing to help, and they do more	65.9	54.3	77.0	67.6	46.9	67.3
Parents should keep out of children's activities as much as possible so that children can learn to do things on their own	41.9	47.1	58.5	44.1	44.9	57.0
Managing their own affairs without interference develops responsible children	59.2	50.2	68.3	53.5	49.8	57.0
Average score for all items	7.0	6.3	8.0	6.8	6.0	6.8
Items on Responsibility for Child Behavior						
No matter what the parents try to do, there are children who don't change at all in the way they behave (Percent disagree)	23.1	23.9	16.0	26.7	18.6	19.9
When neighbors or teachers complain about the behavior of a child this shows that the parents haven't done a good job	47.1	58.2	50.3	38.4	66.8	40.4
Problems in children come out of trouble inside the family	77.0	73.6	69.9	71.3	79.7	59.7
Average score for all items	6.2	6.5	5.8	6.1	6.7	5.4

* Average scores may range from 1 to 13. All items were 5-point scales with *strongly disagree* and *strongly agree* as the extreme low and high point responses.

ishing attitudes toward children, and, withal, the strong verbal emphasis upon family solidarity.[8] It is logical, then, to use measures of a man's attachment to his own parents contrasted with ties to his wife and children, attitudes toward autonomy of children, and beliefs about responsibility for children's behavior to test this aspect of the culture of poverty hypothesis.[9]

The lack of agreement on items relating to these areas is documented in Table 2. The statistical significance of ethnicity as a determinant was, in all instances, well under the 5 percent level. Ethnic variations again are similar to those for the dependency area. Spanish-speaking men stand out among both assistance recipients and non-recipients for the greater importance they attach to their parents (the family of orientation), the lesser concern they have for children's development of autonomy, and their more common belief that parents are responsible for children's behavior. Negro men stand second in relative attachment to parents. They also tend most often to view the child as autonomous and, perhaps consequently, to believe least often that parents are responsible for children's behavior.

Fatalism

The fatalistic outlook of the poor, their resignation to an uncontrolled future in the face of which they feel helpless and for which, therefore, they see no point in

[8] Lewis, 1964, *op. cit.*, p. 153; Lewis, 1965, *op. cit.*, p. xlvii; and Lewis, 1966, *op. cit.*, p. 23.
[9] Primacy of family of orientation and attitudes toward child autonomy were measured by items taken from the Parental Attitude Research Instrument developed by Earl Schaefer and Richard Bell, "Development of a Parental Attitude Research Instrument," *Child Development* (September 1958). Beliefs about responsibility for child behavior were assessed by applying the scale reported by Gildea, Glidewell, and Kantor in "Maternal Attitudes and General Adjustment in School Children," in John C. Glidewell (ed.), *Parental Attitudes and Child Behavior* (Springfield, Illinois: Charles C. Thomas, 1961).

planning—these are repeatedly pointed out as traits of the poverty culture.[10] The questionnaire included four items related to an orientation of fatalism. Distribution of agreement and disagreement with each item are recorded in Table 3. Treated as a simple additive scale, these questions elicited no significant differences among Anglos, Spanish-speaking Americans, and Negroes who had received public assistance. Conversely, an ethnic difference significant at the .001 level was demonstrated for the respondents who had not received assistance. The relationship of fatalism and ethnicity is not a consistent one. Considered individually, there is only one item, "the wise person lives for today and lets tomorrow take care of itself," on which the assistance recipients agreed more highly than their nonassisted ethnic counterparts. Even that agreement was less than a majority of each group. A second item, "Saving for a rainy day," showed almost nobody disagreeing. It thus contributes little variation to the total scores. The remaining two items are a mixture of directional differences. Finally, when the average scores of the groups are compared, they are consistently lower for Anglo and non-recipients, the economically better-off poor respondents. It would seem that, indeed, the more extremely deprived (public assistance recipients) do resemble each other closely in the extent of their fatalism—but only the Spanish-speaking among them show more fatalism than do the less extremely deprived.

Social Alienation

Social alienation and cynicism are nominated by Lewis as outstanding characteristics of the culture of poverty.[11] Four attitude items from the original

[10] Lewis, 1964, *op. cit.*, p. 153; Lewis, 1965, *op. cit.*, p. xlviii; and Lewis, 1966, *op. cit.*, p. 23.
[11] Lewis, 1964, *op. cit.*, p. 154; Lewis, 1965, *op. cit.*, p. xlvi; and Lewis, 1966, *op. cit.*, p. 23.

TABLE 3 Fatalism and alienation among low-income Anglo, Spanish-speaking, and Negro recipients and non-recipients of public assistance.

	Percent of persons agreeing with item among:					
	Public assistance recipients			Non-recipients		
	Anglo	Spanish-speaking	Negro	Anglo	Spanish-speaking	Negro
Fatalism Items						
Planning only makes a person unhappy, since your plans hardly ever work out anyway	55.0	69.2	66.7	50.0	70.5	56.0
It is always a good idea to put away some of your money for a rainy day (Percent disagree)	2.4	.5	—	2.6	1.3	1.3
When a man is born, the success he is going to have is not already in the cards; each makes his own fate (Percent disagree)	5.3	7.2	9.1	10.3	11.1	7.3
Nowadays, with world conditions the way they are, the wise person lives for today and lets tomorrow take care of itself	38.3	48.6	44.8	24.5	46.3	37.7
Average score for all items *	5.0	5.6	5.6	4.3	5.5	4.8
Alienation Items						
In general, lots of things are going downhill. Lots of people have less today and less chance than was true in the past	54.1	53.8	51.5	33.5	49.8	37.1
Nobody cares whether you attend church or not except the clergy (ministers)	49.0	66.8	57.3	46.6	62.5	42.0
Cheating on income tax is nobody's business but the government's	40.9	57.3	48.5	33.3	66.1	39.1
People who go out of their way to help a personal friend are usually disappointed	47.4	56.0	74.8	39.9	57.3	59.7
Average score for all items	8.3	10.0	9.6	7.0	9.7	7.6

* Total scores may range from *1* to *17*. All items were 5-point scales *strongly disagree* and *strongly agree* as the extreme low and high point responses.

TABLE 4 Occupational values among low-income Anglo, Spanish-speaking, and Negro recipients and non-recipients of public assistance.

	Percent of persons giving positive replies among:					
	Public assistance recipients			Non-recipients		
Items	Anglo	Spanish-speaking	Negro	Anglo	Spanish-speaking	Negro
Would you take or stay in a job if it would require you to move around the country a lot?	36.8	40.6	46.1	31.7	42.9	44.7
Would you take or stay in a job if it would require you to leave your friends?	87.6	89.6	93.3	83.6	87.1	85.3
Would you take or stay in a job if it would mean you'd have to learn a new routine?	90.4	92.5	93.3	85.6	91.1	90.7
Would you take or stay in a job if it would mean you'd have to work harder than you are now (or harder than most)?	81.3	73.6	80.0	77.7	63.6	74.8
Would you take or stay in a job if it would mean you'd have to take on more responsibility?	84.2	80.1	87.8	87.6	76.9	83.4
Average score for all items *	8.1	7.9	8.4	7.9	7.8	8.0

* Total scores may range from *1* to *11*. All items were *3*-point scales with *would be less likely* and *wouldn't matter* as the extreme low and high point responses.

questionnaire allow measurement of this theme. They are displayed in Table 3. On both levels of poverty—that at which self-sufficiency has been maintained and the more extreme level at which public help has been necessary—ethnic groups remain reliably distinct from each other. Ethnically associated variety in responses appears to be greater among non-recipients.

Value of Work

The evaluation of work has not been specifically mentioned as a point of divergence between poverty's culture and the larger ones which surround it. It is implied, though, in suggestions that (1) the culture of poverty is most likely to manifest itself in a society which prizes

thrift and upward mobility,[12] and that (2) a prominent characteristic of a particular poverty culture is its antipathy to the larger culture's values.[13]

In the data which were analyzed, five items tested the men's willingness to take jobs which would make certain demands upon them. If poverty induces attitudes similarly at variance with an achievement-oriented society's evaluation of work, it should also produce similar responses when people are asked to choose between work and certain other values.

Table 4 lists the items analyzed and variations in response to them. Public assistance recipients are ethnically distinct

[12] Lewis, *op. cit.*, 1965, p. xliii, xliv; and Lewis, *op. cit.*, 1966, p. 21.
[13] Lewis, *op. cit.*, 1964, p. 154; Lewis, *op. cit.*, 1965, p. xlvi; and Lewis, *op. cit.*, 1966, p. 23.

from each other in reported attitudes. Non-recipients are not, in terms of statistical significance. Again, as with fatalistic attitudes, there is a suggestion that extent of deprivation among Negroes makes some difference in orientation. Two points are of special note about these findings. First is the high level of preference for taking and keeping jobs when such alternate values as friendship, easy work, familiar routines, and level of responsibility are considered. Second is the even higher degree of preference among public assistance recipients. Far from being content with living on welfare money and being unwilling to apply themselves, as they are often pictured, a large majority of men receiving AFDC–UP gave support to every job question but one. That single exception asked about willingness "to move around the country a lot," a condition very disruptive to established social and family relationships.

DISCUSSION

. . . It was found that, in 14 out of 16 tests, ethnic groups differed significantly from each other. . . . In total, half of the tabulated average score comparisons indicate at least moderate divergence. There is much less similarity of viewpoint than the cuture of poverty concept implies. Its tenability, as it has heretofore been used, is questionable. The null hypothesis stated at the beginning of this paper must be rejected.

It is striking to note that the Spanish-speaking have demonstrated most strongly the traits associated with the culture of poverty concept. In a slight majority of the comparisons Negroes were second, although their average scores tend to look more like those of the Anglos than of the Spanish-speaking. Taken together, these findings suggest that a systematic consideration of ethnic groups other than the Spanish-speaking

might have led Lewis to different conclusions about the existence, scope, and intensity of the culture of poverty.

Besides ethnic variations, there are some consistent differences between assistance recipient and non-recipient men of the same ethnic groups. In particular, expressions of dependency feelings and behavior, fatalism, and alienation are higher among Anglo and Negro recipients than among their non-recipient counterparts. These values are central to the culture of poverty concept and, while no significance tests are offered, the size and consistency of the differences warrant comment. The fact that there is little difference among the Spanish-speaking again suggests that the culture of poverty concept, largely developed through experience with persons of Latin-American origin, may have limited general utility and should be reexamined.

It would seem more profitable to examine the impact of poverty, welfare dependency, and related phenomena on values and attitudes in the context of the particular cultures of interest. Perhaps, for some societies and ethnic groups, optimism and the belief in one's own efficacy are diminished by poverty but not necessarily reduced to a common level with the poor of all cultures. However, the evidence from the Spanish-speaking men warns against a too general application of this idea since many of their attitudes were not noticeably altered by receipt of public assistance. Perhaps the language handicap in an English-speaking society was enough to make them fatalistic and dependent. Or are these attitudes general Latin cultural values?

There is no doubt that prolonged economic deprivation, wherever it occurs, influences many aspects of total life outlook as well as specific attitudes. The limited analysis reported here does, however, raise serious doubt that poverty overrides basic cultural orientations as an attitude and value determinant.

Conclusive evidence can, of course, come only from larger scale, cross-societal studies. Such studies would need to include a wider variety of attitude areas, as well as family life patterns and other behaviors. Other deprived ethnic and nationality groups should be included. Each should be similarly disadvantaged economically in a society where others are much more favored. A control group of higher status persons should be included for each ethnic category. With such a design it would be possible to tell whether any similarities reflect a culture common to the poor or one more broadly based in individual societies.

PART IV: MAKING THE SCALES WEIGH TRUE

On October 12, 1970, the United States Civil Rights Commission presented a report to the President. The report was based on the commission's survey of the federal government's civil rights activities in its roles as employer, purchaser, and regulator of industries. The report pointed out that enforcement of the provisions of the major civil rights acts passed between 1957 and 1968 has been lax and unenthusiastic, and in some cases nonexistent, during both the Johnson and the Nixon administrations. Commenting on the report, *The New York Times* noted:

The Office of Federal Contract Compliance is "grossly understaffed" and patently reluctant to use its authority. It has never terminated a contract or debarred a contractor from further government work because of racial discrimination. Between 1965 and 1970 it referred only eight cases to the Justice Department for litigation. The Equal Employment Opportunity Commission relies passively on injured parties to file complaints. It rarely initiates an attack on job bias on its own. . . . If such passivity has been characteristic of two agencies specifically charged with combating racial discrimination, it is not astonishing that most of the regular departments and commissions have done an even worse job.[1]

We in North America have often looked down on many of the Latin American countries because of their lack of orderly government and what appears to be their lack of public respect for their own governmental agencies. Ironically, however, two Latin American aphorisms seem especially applicable to the present case. One comes from the colonial period, when authorities in the New World found it was possible, convenient, and profitable to go about business as usual without paying attention to edicts from Spain that were intended in part to mitigate the colonialists' exploitation of native populations. *"Se obedece, pero no se cumple"*; they said, "One obeys, but he does not carry out or follow through." The other saying is more contemporary. *"Hecha la ley, hecha la trampa,"* which means "As the law is made, so is deception."

If laws were all that was necessary for the attainment of equal civil rights in the United States, we should have had enough of them by 1870, by which time the Thirteenth, Fourteenth, and Fifteenth amendments had been ratified. Who, then, are deceived by the law in today's United States? Perhaps some of the legislators themselves, if we can assume, giving them the benefit of the doubt, that they share the naive but extraordinarily prevalent notion that passing a law suffices to

[1] *The New York Times*, October 13, 1970, p. 42.

solve a pressing problem. Perhaps the public deceives itself, for many people feel no twinge of conscience in avoiding the dictates of laws felt to be unreasonable and believed to be unenforceable. (Such people can use a convenient Yankee aphorism if they choose, the one that goes, "Laws are made to be broken.") Perhaps the ultimate irony is that members of minority groups are sometimes willing parties to deception, too, if they believe as they were taught, as all of us were, that this is a government of laws and not of men.

Consider for a moment that members of racial or quasiracial minority groups have to depend on specific laws or administrative rulings merely to secure rights that most of the rest of us take for granted: rights to vote, to open housing, to equal employment and educational opportunities. Consider, too, that higher proportions of these minorities than of other population sectors are poor. They must, therefore, come to terms with other sets of rules that have far less impact on others: minimum wages, work safety policy, housing authority regulations, welfare department stipulations. Indeed, it is because laws and rules count so very heavily among minority people that the general failure of law to accomplish more rapid change and the specific failures of inequitable enforcement have led to widespread disenchantment and bitter recrimination.

For example, between 1954 (the Warren Court's school desegregation decision in *Brown* v. *Board of Education*) and 1965 (the Voting Rights Act), black people had come to depend upon the federal government to frame and carry out the rules and procedures that would make equal rights securely available to all citizens. But by late 1965, disaffection toward the government had already set in. As noted earlier, in the remarks preceding Selection 5, James Killian, in a book that reviews these matters, goes so far as to say that by then the federal government had come to be perceived as the enemy by even well-established black leaders.[2] Complaints about Albany or Sacramento, Springfield or Austin, Jackson or Trenton, were probably better founded and deeper seated. Yet it was Washington that was supposed to come up with answers to problems being played out in local areas that were either ill-equipped or disinclined to handle them. Thus, federal failures counted for more in the long run. Besides, Washington was symbolic of the total nation and its institutions. Washington was where hope had been placed, but its frequent response was to appoint commissions to study problems rather than to make changes that might help to solve them.

[2] *The Impossible Revolution?* (New York: Random House, 1968), esp. Chap. 5.

I have alluded briefly to the fact that higher proportions of racial minorities than of other Americans are poor. Sometimes, as if to make us forget that poverty is not democratically distributed, we are reminded that many poor people (about three-quarters of all of them) are white rather than black or brown. That is true, but like many statistics it takes on a different implication when placed in a different context. For instance, in 1968, 28 percent of all families in what the Bureau of the Census calls "Negro and other races," as compared to just 8 percent of white families, fell below the poverty line, then set at $3,553 annually, for the urban family of four. Or perhaps a more significant figure, because more general, is that 62 percent of the former group and only 34 percent of the latter had combined family annual incomes of less than $7,000. Or possibly we ought to center our attention on the major metropolitan areas, where both whites and blacks tend to earn the highest average incomes. In those areas in 1968, black male workers, as compared to white ones, were (1) less likely to be employed at all; (2) if employed, less likely to have jobs for the full year; (3) when fully employed for the whole year, still less likely to have high-ranking jobs (69 percent of fully employed white workers as compared to 35 percent of fully employed black workers had jobs at the level of skilled worker or higher); and (4) less likely to earn as much even when fully employed at the same level as white workers.[3]

Viewing such matters as these more generally, the English sociologist Michael Banton has written, ". . . where ethnic alignments run counter to class alignments, they hinder one kind of social fissure from opening up; where they run in the same direction, they make the cleavage deeper." [4] In other words, where minority-group or majority-group members are themselves divided in terms of social-class position, it will be more difficult for them to act uniformly and collectively in order to further predominantly ethnic or racial interests. Such actions may run contrary to the class interests of many members of the group. Correlatively, the American experience has also been one in which racial and ethnic differences have often split the working class, helping to make class conflict a much less seriously divisive issue than in most countries of, say, Western Europe. But the part of Banton's hypothesis that may be most important for the present discussion is also the most difficult to demonstrate clearly. It depends upon the idea that only minority

[3] *Current Population Reports,* Series p-23, Nos. 29 and 33 (Washington, D.C., 1970), are the sources for all these data.
[4] Michael Banton, *Race Relations* (New York: Basic Books, 1967), p. 337.

segments of the population will find themselves kept from substantial upward mobility, while the majority continues to prosper by improving its occupational status, its income, and its life-style. As Banton puts it:

. . . Negroes tend to inherit the economic status of their parents because their whole social background puts so many of them at a disadvantage in a highly competitive society. A new kind of colour line appears, though hardly anyone desires it. This tendency for the lines of ethnic group and social class membership to merge is likely to strengthen in the immediate future.[5]

If Banton were correct, the implication would be that *racial* antipathy toward black and other similarly placed minorities would be reinforced or might even be replaced by antipathy toward minority-group members' poorer life-styles or lower-class behavior patterns. Indeed, there are doubtless many white people who even now vehemently deny that their distaste for black or brown people has any racial basis at all. They claim instead that their concerns are objective and reasonable, based on class differences set in the context of American emphases on respectability and success as legitimate signs of worth and virtue.

Still, Banton is not entirely correct. For one thing, although the absolute gap in constant dollar incomes between the racial minorities and the white majority has increased since, let us say, 1920, the social-class gap as based on occupational level and education has become far smaller. For another, there is no doubting the existence of a large and growing middle class among blacks, Mexican-Americans, and Puerto Ricans. It is simply impossible to conclude that the members of all these minorities are condemned to a status no higher than that of the working class while all the remainder of the population rises to the middle class and beyond.

It is therefore useful to consider the views of another foreign observer, an English sociologist like Banton, the late J. P. Nettl. Nettl agreed that class-based explanations of race relations in modern societies were important for increasing our understanding of the issues at play, but he also held that class considerations were not sufficient for arriving at a full comprehension of these issues. Rather, Nettl believed, the immediacy and intensity of racial identification among both the majority and the minority, or minorities, living alongside it made what he called the sociologists' "collectivist notions" seem

[5] *Ibid.,* p. 345.

inadequate for the explanatory task at hand.[6] The industrial metropolitan setting that theory says "ought" to be dominated by issues of class is in fact beset by problems that both stem from, and continue to contribute to, castelike distinctions arising from real or assumed, natural or artificial, visible racial differences.

With Nettl's observation in mind, it may be easier to understand that in a modern industrial society it is not necessary for all of a minority group's members to have a class status lower than all of the members of the majority in order for minority identification to become the preeminent basis of solidarity among the minority's members. What is sufficient for that result to occur is that there be a set of conditions of the kind that now obtain in the United States. They include the following:

1. A higher proportion of minority- than of majority-group members who have low status, including a certain number (the proportion now is about 30 percent, but there is no way to set higher and lower limits about what it has to be) for whom channels for upward mobility are simply not available, either because of present discrimination or because of past discrimination, which has been responsible for their failing to develop skills and confidence.

2. A substantial proportion of the majority holding to the assumption that any member of the minority is essentially or ultimately inferior or undesirable; and a substantial proportion of the majority able to put prejudice into practice by keeping most of the minority segregated and limited to inferior facilities. (As the late Malcolm X put it, "You know what they call a Negro with a Ph.D.? . . . Nigger." A bit of wry folk wisdom makes the same point in different words, "Down South it don't matter how close you get, long as you don't get too big. Up North, don't matter how big, long as you don't get too close.") It is not necessary that such discriminatory outcomes always be consciously linked to prejudice, or that there invariably be a clear intent to maintain relative superiority and inferiority. The result is the same even where majority performances are predicated on nothing more than a willingness to tolerate others' discrimination merely to avoid upsetting them, as we avoid upsetting relatives, friends, neighbors, or business associates.

3. Politically mobilizing factors affecting the minority, such as residential concentration in massive urban agglomerations,

[6] J. P. Nettl in Colin Leys (ed.), *Politics and Change in Developing Countries* (Cambridge, England: Cambridge University Press, 1969), p. 31.

increasing education without correlative boosts in income, actual or threatened employment layoffs, and rapid means of mass communication.

4. Relative deprivation, which is sensed most severely when absolute deprivation has lessened and when erasing remaining inequities seems to be neither quite possible nor wholly impossible.

It may be true that today there are more opportunities for noncompetitive interracial contacts in equal-status personal relations, contacts of the kind past research has shown lead to greater mutual understanding and tolerance among majority- and minority-group members.[7] It also seems to me, not on the basis of systematic research but merely as one more observer, that I encounter more use of exemption mechanisms than I used to. (An exemption mechanism assumes a negative stereotype of a given group, but specifically sets some few members of the group apart from the rest, as in the statements, "Some of my best friends are Negroes" or "They're a *nice* Mexican family.") Neverthelss, it is clear that the factors I outlined above far outweigh these slight tendencies in the direction of mutually harmonious and satisfactory race relations. The easily visible lower-status minority population concentrations provide all the evidence that is necessary for many members of the majority to go on clinging to racial stereotypes (though in the past twenty years the majority may well have become too sophisticated to accept statements of the kind that begin with or imply that *all* x's are y) and to go on avoiding intimate personal contact with minority members who increasingly call for demonstrations of trustworthiness before welcoming majority members' overtures anyhow.

Issues of class and issues of race are different but intimately related. They mutually strengthen one another in American society, intensifying the cleavage between the white majority and the racial minorities. Recall that when Banton wrote of these matters he spoke of "the immediate future." That means tomorrow, the day after, next year. American minorities are competing not only against the majority but also

---

[7] See, for example, Madeline Radke Yarrow, "A Study of Desegregation," *Journal of Social Issues,* Vol. 14, No. 1 (1958), pp. 8–28; Daniel M. Wilner *et al.,* "Residential Proximity and Intergroup Relations in Public Housing Projects," *Journal of Social Issues,* Vol. 8, No. 1 (1952), pp. 45–69; and Vincent Jeffries and H. E. Ransford, "Interracial Social Contact and Middle-Class White Reactions to the Watts Riot," *Social Problems,* Vol. 16 (Winter 1969), pp. 312–24. The last study compares Los Angeles whites who had and had not previously been friendly with blacks, showing that the former were less critical of the Watts riot and more likely to explain its occurrence as black people did.

against time as well. They believe they must find ways to catch up quickly, or never catch up at all. The first group of papers in this section concerns areas where minorities are still held back; the second group concerns efforts now being made by the minorities themselves to exact the sorts of institutional changes that will provide them with more chances to take on this competitive society on its own terms. Those efforts may fail. There are some who are already convinced that they have already failed. The next step is being taken now, and it involves attempts to change the very terms by which the society actually runs itself. We are on our way to the arena; we can hear the sounds of clamor within. Some of us will remain spectators; many others, like the police that the spectators would hire to do their fighting for them, will not.

The first selection in this part refers to research findings from the Coleman Report, *Equality of Educational Opportunity.* In one sense, the report documents the obvious by showing that children who are from poor minority-group families do not perform as well in school as children from better-off families. The report's documentation of this finding is so firm, so extensive, that it is impossible to dispute. What is in dispute is the explanation of how the condition arose and what ought to be done about it. Adding fuel to the fires of controversy are other report results showing that there is relatively little about the schools per se which seems to have very much to do with the quality of their students' academic performances. Far more depends upon the pupils' socioeconomic backgrounds and the strength of their belief in their own capacity to order their world.

Cohen's paper on the New York City controversy over community control of schools refers to these and other Coleman Report findings. Rather than merely relying upon and translating the study's results, Cohen tries to place them in the context of political and economic as well as sociological and educational considerations. Research findings, Cohen shows, have quite different meanings and implications depending on the group interests of the various constituencies that have to interpret and act upon them.

Housing and the police are two of the other matters (along with education and employment) about which the members of racial minorities are most concerned. Lowi's paper shows how conscious prejudice shaped an urban planning design, and then how the broad framework and easily penetrated loopholes of federal directives made possible continued discrimination not merely by perpetuating but by in fact adding to a city's residential segregation. The selection is also a demonstration of how what passes for an improvement in an urban Southern pattern of race relations may actually be nothing more than a shift to a more sophisticated, more Northern type of racial isolation and separation.

The next article is taken from a presidential task force report that reviews many of the most important studies made on the racial attitudes of policemen and police force administrations. The tone of the report is moderate and measured, even dry, as if the staff that wrote it did not anticipate or did not wish to exacerbate a delicate situation that has by now become dominated by threats of terrorism on the one side and threats of massive forceful repression on the other. It is still an open question whether police forces will change in a way that will make them more effective in putting down ghetto militance, or in a way that will better accommodate minority interests and answer to minority complaints. My interpretation of events till now leads me to guess that the former is by far the likelier possibility.

The last four papers of this part of the book concern four different types of minority militance in three different settings. The first pair of papers examines some of the steps Mexican-Americans are now taking in their own behalf. The first selection, set in the grape fields of California, is about an agriculturally based movement, Cesar Chavez' United Farm Workers' Organizing Committee. Group action among Chicanos is running through a history similar to that of recent black group action. That is, as the focus of the movement shifts from more traditional smaller towns and cities to larger major metropolitan areas, a more open anger replaces earlier restraint; riots occur along with nonviolent resistance. Reflecting this shift, the second selection is set in Denver.

Continuing in an easterly direction, the next reading describes the aspirations of the Young Lords, militant young Puerto Rican activists in Chicago and New York City. In both cities the Lords have moved into power vacuums, drawing some inspiration from Cuba as well as using some of the ideology and techniques of black activists before them. The vacuum the Lords try to fill exists because city agencies have not met the needs of poor Puerto Ricans in a satisfactory way and because the Puerto Ricans in formally established leadership positions have customarily emphasized the importance of using conventional respectable measures to reach conventional respectable status levels. In the meantime, poor Puerto Ricans had had to go on living in inadequate housing, have had to go on seeking inconvenient and indifferent medical care, have had to depend upon alien police protection, and have had to run the risk of seeing their sons turn out to be junkies. The Lords try to respond to some of these issues directly, and to others by trying to organize their communities to exert greater collective influence. They rely on tight quasimilitary discipline and demeanor, and on revolutionary ideology and rhetoric. These help to explain the Lords' internal solidarity and much of the effectiveness they have had until now. But the Lords have also been weakened by disputes over leadership, by fear among the general Puerto Rican population over their gang origins and reputations, and by the uncertainty most nonrevolutionaries feel over whether revolution is a desirable or even necessary method for definitively attaining benefits people need and believe are their due.

The last paper in this part does not describe any specific place. It could be applicable to any large, predominantly white university that was open enough for an organization of black students to be formed. Edwards is not simply describing black university students. He is also appealing to them to act in terms of what he sees as their group interests. They should not and will not, he feels, simply follow their own personal inclinations or accommodate themselves to the traditional definition of the general welfare of the university community. Edwards' writing helps to account for a constellation of cynicism and bitterness combined with pride and courage sometimes encountered among some black students. Many white students and university administrators have found such outlooks inexplicable in an environment they had thought to be warm and inviting.

Readers may not agree with Edwards' formulations and characterizations, may in particular wish to insist that the ambiance of their own university is far different from what Edwards describes. Agree or not, anyone who does not take this reading seriously will simply not be able to comprehend events like those which occurred at Cornell and Michigan in 1969, at Syracuse in the fall of 1970, or future ones which could arise on any of hundreds of other campuses that have felt themselves sufficiently just and open to have been spared from racial crisis until now.

30. THE PRICE OF COMMUNITY CONTROL

David Cohen

Equality of Educational Opportunity, popularly known as
the Coleman Report after the name of its senior author,
James Coleman of The John Hopkins University, is the
most extensive study of the characteristics and outcomes of
public education ever carried out in the United States. The
report was submitted in response to the call of the 1964 Civil
Rights Act for a study of "the lack of availability of equal
educational opportunities for individuals by reason or race,
color, religion, or national origin in public educational
institutions at all levels. . . ." The study attended to differences
among American Indians, Oriental Americans, mainland Puerto
Ricans, Mexican-Americans, Southern and non-Southern
blacks, and Southern and non-Southern whites. More than
645,000 primary and secondary school students were
surveyed. (About 30 percent of the schools selected did
not participate. Including some of them, like Chicago's, might
have increased the estimates of the disparities between
minority and majority student performances, or affected other
findings. The report notes however, on page 8, "an analysis
of the nonparticipating schools indicated that their inclusion
would not have significantly altered the results of the survey.")

At the time of the study, the academic year 1965–1966, the
national findings were that nearly 80 percent of all white students
in the first and twelfth grades attended schools that were
from 90 to 100 percent white. In tandem with this finding was
one showing that more than 65 percent of all black pupils in the
first grade went to schools that were between 90 and 100
percent black. It is difficult to tell how much these figures have
changed in four or five years, for figures out of Washington
usually concentrate on the South rather than on the country as

Source: *Commentary,* Vol. 48, No. 1 (July 1969), pp. 23–32. Copyright ©
1969 by the American Jewish Committee. Reprinted by permission of
the author and the American Jewish Committee.

DAVID COHEN is Executive Director, Center for Educational Policy
Research, Graduate School of Education, Harvard University.

a whole. There is no doubt that formal and open segregation has sharply decreased in the South. For example, according to information made available by HEW Secretary Richardson on January 14, 1971, a reporter was able to write that "80 percent of school-age black children and eleven Southern states were in public schools that white children also attended. The proportion (38.2 percent) of black children in public schools where most of the children were white was higher in the South than it was anywhere else in the country." [1]

Certainly that is a considerable step away from the legally enforced "separate but equal" systems that were the standard Southern pattern before 1954. Nevertheless, it appears that Southern districts will tend to fall into the Northern and Western patterns of *de facto* school segregation that depend upon *de facto* residential segregation. Most black children will therefore continue to go to school with mostly black classmates, and most whites, with whites. For example, consider another pair of the Coleman Report's findings, this time based on regional rather than national data. In 1966, in the metropolitan areas of the North and West, over 90 percent of white first graders were in schools that were at least 80 percent white; and nearly 65 percent of black first graders were in schools that were at least 60 percent black. (Elementary schools are more segregated than secondary schools, for they are a more nearly direct reflection of neighborhood population compositions.) Thus, without changes in the demographic and administrative conditions that presently surround and govern neighborhood school districts in most of the country, there is little reason to anticipate that the report's findings for the non-South in 1966 would be much different in 1971, or five years from now, in 1976. By then, the South's pattern of segregation, as well as its statistics, may be even closer than now to what obtains in the rest of the country.[2]

Large sections of the report are statistical or deal with technical methodological issues. The report is already one of the "best known" but least read technical studies ever carried out. But summarizing a portion of it, in an admittedly simplified way, I hope to encourage some readers to search out the original. The diagram (p. 356) may help to understand the

[1] John Osborne, "The Nixon Watch: Call It Desegregation," *The New Republic,* January 30, 1971, p. 12.

[2] Recent court decisions on busing, and particularly a Richmond, Virginia, ruling that suburbs must also be included in school integration plans, may lead to more open patterns. Still to be seen, however, is how much support will be given to changing de facto segregation in contrast to the greater legal attention til now given to places and school systems where segregation previously had been decreed by law.

major results of the report. The summary results are as follows:

1. Background characteristics are strongly associated with the kinds of schools children go to, with children's attitudes about themselves, and with their achievement.

2. After a control for background characteristics (that is, statistically eliminating its effects on the relations of any of the other variables to one another), *only* the attitudes children have about themselves make an appreciable difference in their achievement. Background characteristics, however, continue to be strongly related to achievement even after other variables have been controlled.

3. Of all school factors that were measured, after the control for the effects of background characteristics, there was only one with as much as a slight association to achievement: the status composition of the school student body as a whole—a cumulative measure of the background characteristics of all of the students in a school. Thus, racial integration helped the achievement scores of minority children to a slight

Initial Condition	Second Condition	Third Condition	Fourth Condition	Fifth Condition
Group membership	*Background characteristics*	*Self-attitudes*	*School factors*	*Achievement*
White, black, Oriental, etc.	Parents' income, occupation, education; employed or not; whole or broken family, etc.	Mastery of environment, self-concept,* school interest.*	Budget per student, curriculum, level of teacher training, student body composition, etc.	Math and reading test scores

* A suprising finding was that these factors did not differ appreciably by race. However, for all groups, self-concept and school interest were closely related to school achievement.

degree, because the presence of white students raised the background characteristic level of the school as a whole.

4. Therefore, although it quite clear that minority students do not achieve as well as majority students (in general), the reason is not their group membership per se, but rather the lower socioeconomic status of their own families and, to a lesser extent, that of the families of other minority students with whom minority children are likeliest to go to school.

5. As a final summary, in the plainest terms I can manage, the study shows (a) minority kids are likelier to be poorer kids; (b) poorer kids think they have less control over their fate, go to worse schools, and do worse at them; (c) most

surprising, poorer kids do a bit, but not much, better if they go to better schools; and better-off kids don't do much worse if they go to worse ones; (d) poorer kids do better, in good schools or bad, if they believe they can take charge of their own lives' circumstances.

What are the Coleman Report's policy implications? That is a difficult question to answer, for different contending groups can find results supporting their respective viewpoints. However, some implications are discussed at length in this selection, Cohen's analysis of New York City's community control controversy. And, as this book goes to press, new desegregation decisions involving busing and *de facto* segregation may spell out guidelines that both Southern and non-Southern school systems will have to follow in the future.

Cohen's work is an attempt (1) to explain how and why community control became so important an issue among black educators and in black communities; (2) to show the effect that majority attitudes and actions have had on the development of this issue; (3) to evaluate some policy implications of the Coleman Report in light of the contentions of the different groups most concerned with the issue; and (4) to suggest some new directions urban education could take if a sufficiently broad political consensus provided will, organizational skill, and monetary resources.

What was the initial impetus for community control? Like most observers, Cohen believes that it began with the failure to end *de facto* segregation and with the at-best equivocal results of insufficiently funded and indifferently staffed compensatory programs. Neither of these worked, because neither received enough support from a divided electorate and its consequently inconsistent educational leadership, especially in large cities already hard pressed for funds enough to run essential municipal services.

We tend to think of public education as a public right. We place great hopes on education, viewing it not only as mere training but also as a major means for assuring equal opportunities. Less often, we see it as a way of narrowing gaps in outcomes, as generally effective performances open up more occupational possibilities to more people. Such impressions help to veil the strong self-interest that permeates the educational process. Teachers, principals, and administrators work hard at protecting their jobs and their occupational prerogatives; and it is they who control channels of advancement in the educational establishment. Parents choose places to live that have "good schools," when what they mean is "better schools," the kinds that will give their children advantages that other children do not have. Finally, neighborhood schools serve children of similar class or ethnic character. The social composition of their student bodies varies correlatively with the social composition of the school area; a change in either causes changes in the other.

From the perspective of black communities, these forces seemed so strong that they could not be overcome. Furthermore, there arose the conviction that instead of finding useful ways to overcome social handicaps that no one doubted were present among black students, white-dominated school systems were placing the blame for black students' lower performance levels on "cultural deprivation," or "the weaknesses of black family structure." The students' culture of poverty became the basis for the teachers' culture of defeat, their feeling that nothing could be done with children who seemed unsuited for being taught in the traditional ways. Sometimes this feeling reflected sincere disappointment; at other times it was nothing more than a poor, weak disguise for underlying racist attitudes.

In sum, political, organizational, and educational tendencies came together in an outcome that was racist in effect even when not racist in intention. To many, black control over black schools seemed the only viable solution to overcome that racism. Black educators in particular became convinced not only that black community control was necessary but also that it would work. It may indeed, but the evidence is still unclear. Equally unclear is whether the frequently obvious political character of the ideology and practice of community control —important and as controversial as it may be in its own right—is necessary or even helpful in finding ways for letting black children learn more effectively.

In the meantime, many white people are extremely critical of what they call separatism, segregation in reverse, or black racism. It may not be amiss to remind them that the society as a whole was not prepared to work and pay for, and to tolerate, genuine integration and educational experimentation. It chose a cheaper way by default, only to find that it didn't get itself off the hook after all.

Hard evidence on the effectiveness of educational strategies has never been easy to come by. Until 1966, for example, when the Coleman Report was published,* virtually no direct evidence existed on the relationship between a school's racial composition and how well its students performed. What the Coleman Report revealed turned out to be at some variance with integrationist ideology: Negro students in mostly white schools were indeed higher achievers

* James S. Coleman, et al., Equality of Educational Opportunity, Washington, 1966.

than those in mostly Negro schools, but this apparently bore no intrinsic relation to a particular school's racial composition. Rather, in those mostly white schools where Negroes performed well, the white students were typically from more advantaged homes; Negro students in a middle-class white school would do no better than Negro students in an equally middle-class Negro school. As a practical matter, integrationists could reassure themselves that the relative lack of a Negro middle class meant that social-class integration would inevitably entail racial integration as well, but in view of this finding they could no longer embrace the notion that a school's racial composition *per se* affected achievement.

Of course, the absence of unequivocal evidence on achievement was never the main obstacle to school integration, and in many communities where integration was tried, achievement gains seem indeed to have followed. In most communities, however, the attempt was never even made. The blame for this may be placed primarily on the indifference, inertia, and oposition of school officials, and on the general political sentiment which they reflected. Although committed educational leadership in places like Berkeley, Evanston, and Syracuse showed that organized white resistance could be overcome, most school systems—in the hundreds of communities whose size and demography put integration within easy reach—never reached that stage. Even fewer efforts were made in the large cities, where national attention was riveted.

Integrationists responded to this situation by devising a strategy which promised to reduce white opposition by coupling integration with a variety of beguiling educational attractions: educational parks, magnet schools, special education centers, and the like. If most white parents, the reasoning went, were forced to choose between inferior all-white schools and educationally superior integrated facilities, they would not hesitate to choose the latter. The problem was that educational innovations are as expensive as school budgets are tight; the strategy required new legislation which would allocate much more money to city schools.

In any event, the strategy was never really tried, since most professional educators chose a different response altogether. They saw that Negro parents wanted better schools and higher achievement, and therefore offered programs of remedial and compensatory education in the existing segregated schools. When this counter-strategy was embodied in local programs, and in Title I of the Elementary and Secondary Education Act of 1965, it put a premium on the perpetuation of segregated schools. It paid educators to maintain schools in the slums rather than create the integrated, educationally superior facilities envisioned in integrationist rhetoric.

Thus it is incorrect to say that school integration failed; what failed was the politics required to bring it about. Like most liberal strategies for social change, integration is politically viable only on the assumption that it is in the interest of whites to reduce the status disparity between themselves and Negroes. Inducing whites to choose integration by creating educationally irresistible schools was a clever effort to create such an identity of interest. The only flaw was that before white parents could be presented with the choice, vast new funds would have had to be appropriated, with the explicit proviso that they would be used to create these schools. And naturally the money itself could not be obtained without substantial white support. In political terms this meant that in order to make the strategy work one had to presume the prior existence of that very identity of educational interests which the strategy was designed to bring into being. In this case, circular reasoning proved to be as deadly in politics as it usually is in logic: only a few of the integrationists' schools have ever been created.

The concept of compensatory education favored by most educators represented an effort to avoid this fatal circularity. Since compensatory programs operated only in slum schools, they seemed indeed to offer a happy political alternative. Whites could assume a progressive stance by supporting improved ghetto education—and better schools for poor whites, too—while opposing or remaining neutral on demands for busing, Princeton plans, and other politically volatile integration tactics. For these reasons—to say nothing of the substantial Negro support the remedial programs enjoyed—a powerful coalition of moderate and liberal reformers and schoolmen came together behind such legislation as Title I of the Elementary and Secondary Education Act.

How did these programs fare? Over the past two years a succession of evaluations has been unable to find much evidence of improved achievement. To be sure, their sponsors have proclaimed the programs a success: the litanies of praise that have been issued cite improved school conditions, brighter attitudes, better attendance, reduced vandalism, happier teachers, etc. Nonetheless, to judge by the main criterion the programs were designed to satisfy, the general absense of gains in achievement makes all these claims seem trivial or disingenuous.

What accounts for this unhappy record? In a strict sense the question cannot be answered, for as long as we don't know what works, it is impossible to make the comparisons which might suggest the reasons for failure. Comparisons aside, however, one *can* assess in a general way the actual impact on slum schools of the millions of federal dollars that have been appropriated for their improvement. Title I increased instructional expenditures for each participating child by about $60 a year in 1966–67, and last year by about $65. Since the nation annually spends an average of about $450 per pupil for instruction, the increment (10 to 15 per cent) from Title I can only be described as modest. The simplest way to figure the amount of educational improvement that an increase like that can buy is in terms of the time a teacher devotes to her children. If a teacher has thirty students and works a five-hour day (and if we imagine that she divides the day into a series of tutorials), then each student receives a ten-minute daily tutorial. An increase of 10 per cent in the teaching staff would add one minute to the daily individual attention a student receives. That does not exactly constitute an educational revolution.

There is more. For one thing, the compensatory moneys have often been used to make up for existing differences between black and white schools, rather than for creating better-than-equal black schools. For another, the funds made available under Title I frequently have been so dispersed that their budgetary impact—which is clear enough on a balance sheet—is undetectable in the target schools themselves. As a result, in many cases the infusion of money has had the opposite effect from the one intended. If, on the one hand, the funds are concentrated only on the neediest children, a noticeable change does occur in these children's school program, but only for an hour or so a day, or a day a week. Teachers who work in the school but not in the program often become hostile or jealous, and those who do work in the program, since their colleagues are unfriendly and their students unsuccessful, grow frustrated and discouraged. They explode and leave, or somehow adjust cynically to the situation; neither reaction is particularly productive. If, on the other hand, the funds are diffused widely over a variety of children and schools, intense frustration on the part of a few teachers is traded off for a more generalized low level of despondency or indifference. Then there is the added problem of turnover in both teaching staff and in the programs themselves, which occurs partly as a result of the conditions I have just outlined, partly for political or administrative reasons. Continuity is rare and knowledge non-cumulative: the same basic lessons are often learned over and over again, either by new teachers in the same program, or by the same teachers in new programs. No one benefits perceptibly.

There have been a few experiments which involved rather larger sums than those provided by Title I, but here too one would be hard put to say unequivocally that they resulted in improved achievement. Some interpretations of evidence from the More Effective Schools program in New York City, for example, suggest that there may have been achievement gains for children who were exposed to the program over long periods of time, but other interpretations suggest the opposite; similarly with the tutoring program conducted by New York's Mobilization for Youth and a few other programs. In all cases, reports of improvement are open to serious question.

Finally there are pre-school programs, which vary in content and direction from traditional classroom situations, to parent-training programs, to programs giving individual attention to two-year-olds. A number of these programs have reported substantial gains. Two things, however, should be noted about them. The first is that the gains appear to dissipate quickly if things are allowed to return to normal; the second is that those programs which are school-centered are very expensive, costing between $1,000 and $1,500 per child per annum. Now, research on pre-school education seems to indicate that it is indeed

possible, although it is by no means easy, to affect patterns of intellectual development if pervasive changes in a child's environment are instituted a good deal earlier than the age at which schooling now begins, and if they are continued on into the elementary school years. But the prospect of undertaking such a course of action raises many problems in its turn. One of these relates to the political and cultural implications of further extending the schools' dominion over children; I will take this up later. Another is suggested by the price that is likely to be exacted for such reform: if the cost of improving achievement will be an additional one or two thousand dollars per pupil per year, and if our main goal is to eliminate racial disparities in adult income and occupation, then why not spend the money directly on family income maintenance, or on creating socially useful and important jobs? Perhaps the best way to change existing inequalities in income and occupation is to change them, not to use schooling as a means of deferring reform.

The costliness of programs of intensive education in early childhood is politically crucial in another way, too, for a ghettoized approach to school improvement assumes that whites will trade off the programs' cost for the maintenance of segregation. Although to some extent that is doubtless true, there is no guarantee that the commitment of whites to existing patterns of segregation will stretch to the point where they would be willing to spend on black children two or three times what is typically spent on whites. It is precisely here that the "failure" of compensatory education resides. As a recent publication of the U.S. Office of Education dolefully pointed out, a really serious effort in compensatory education would ". . . require a mobilization effort more far-reaching than any now envisioned by any community." It would, in other words, imply a level of white support for ghetto development which—in light of the past eight years' experience—is as difficult to conceive as the amount of white support that would be required for integration.

What has failed, then, is not the traditional "liberal" educational technologies—whether of the integrationist or compensatory variety; these technologies have been tried too sporadically and haphazardly to permit careful assessment. Rather, the deficiency lies in the absence of operational political strategies which would bind up the interests of blacks and whites in such a way as to elicit white support for programs that would improve the relative status of black children. That is a primitive political defect, an inability to apply what might be called the politics of common interest to basic social reform.

But if it is incorrect to say that integration and compensatory education have been tried and found wanting, politically it all seems to amount to the same thing: the relative educational status of Negro and white children in metropolitan areas is little different now from what it was in 1954. The persistence of this dreary contrast has in recent years provided a major impetus to movements for decentralization and community control.

Decentralization and community control refer to a variety of notions about schooling and school reform, not all of them related to the problem of disparities in achievement. One of these is that the potentially effective components of city school systems—parents, teachers, and inquisitive children—are walled off from each other by a Byzantine bureaucratic maze; before the elements can function to the children's best advantage, the argument runs, the walls must be broken down and the bureaucracy brought under control. Another view is that the entire educational system is racist, from the way it allocates resources, to the attitudes of its teachers and the character of its textbooks; according to this view the remedy is not to make the system more accessible but to transfer control of the enterprise altogether: until the schools are operated by the parents of their young black clients (or those who legitimately stand *in loco parentis*), they will not be responsive to the needs of Negro children. A third view is that the problem resides in the psychological consequences of powerlessness. As things now stand, it is argued, the central fact of life for black Americans is that they do not control their personal and collective destinies. All the significant ghetto institutions—schools, government, welfare, etc.—are controlled by whites. Unless these whites are replaced by Negroes, black children will lack a sense that the world will respond to their efforts, and their achievement will languish as a consequence. The last two ideas roughly comprise the meaning of community control, the first, decentralization.

Of the three, the notion that the root problem is bureaucracy probably has the broadest appeal. For one thing, the complexity and unresponsiveness of many big-city school systems is legendary; no client of any class or color happily accepts the reign of the clerk, and increasing numbers reject the inflexible style and pedagogy of the schools. For another, we have long been accustomed to the idea that the very size of institutions inevitably produces a king of social arteriosclerosis, and assume that the remedy lies not in reaming out the conduits, but in reducing the distance between the vital organs and the extremities. Finally, the anti-bureaucratic critique is almost always couched in irresistible contrasts between extreme situations—Scarsdale as opposed to Bedford-Stuyvesant, or Winnetka as opposed to the West Side of Chicago.

Unfortunately, however, there is no

evidence that the level of parent partici- pation in schools is related to students' achievement. It is true that parents in suburban communities are somewhat more likely to participate in school af- fairs than those in central cities, but this seems to have more to do with the conse- quences of affluence than with anything else; analysis of the data in the Coleman Report fails to reveal any association between the level of parental participa- tion and achievement. Nor is there any evidence that smaller school districts— which we all presume to be less bureau- cratized and more responsive to parents and children—produce higher levels of achievement than larger ones. With a few outstanding exceptions, public educa- tion in the U.S. runs on the assump- tion that administrative decentralization, small and homey school districts, and lo- cal control are educational essentials; literally thousands of school jurisdic- tions stand as testimony to this creed, against only a handful of urban mono- liths. Yet here again there appears to be no relation whatsoever between the size of a school district (or whether its board is elected or appointed) and the achievement of the students in its schools.

On the other hand, there is abundant evidence that parents who are involved in a direct way in their children's educa- tion tend to have children who achieve at higher levels. Involvement of this sort includes reading to children, taking them to libraries, talking to them, explaining things, and otherwise providing lots of cognitive stimulation and support for intellectual accomplishment. Thus, when poor parents are trained to behave toward their children in the way middle- class parents do, the children's level of achievement rises. This should not come as a surprise, except perhaps to those hardy souls who believe that the intel- lectual deprivation associated with pov- erty can be traced exclusively to genetic

makeup. It does, however, argue for the establishment of parent-training efforts, like the one that has been operating in Ypsilanti, Michigan, rather than pro- grams aimed at eliminating bureaucracy in schools.

Advocates of community control (as opposed to administrative decentraliza- tion) might raise the objection here that the source of underachievement is not bureaucratic inertia in the first place, but institutional racism. There is, in fact, no dearth of evidence that city school systems discriminate against the poor in general and Negroes in particu- lar. Studies of resource allocation almost always reveal that predominantly black schools suffer by comparison with white schools, in terms of such things as teacher experience, tenure, and certifica- tion. In addition, the attitudes of many teachers are influenced by class and ra- cial antagonisms; in the Coleman sample of Northern urban elementary schools, between 10 and 20 per cent of teachers in ghetto schools overtly expressed a preference for schools with all or nearly all white student bodies. It should be noted, however, that Negro children whose teachers are as good as or better than the average for whites and have better than average racial attitudes, do not show higher achievement than their less fortunate counterparts in ghetto schools.

Here it may be countered that it is not a teacher's racial attitudes which affect performance, but his expectations of his students' academic success. And indeed, this idea appears to make in- tuitive good sense. It seems reasonable to believe that bigoted white teachers— or Negroes who accept white stereotypes —will somehow communicate to their students the sense that black children are academically less capable. If that is so, then it might well follow that the most efficient way to deal with such teachers, short of large-scale psychotherapy, would be to sharpen dramatically their responsibility to the parents of Negro children, on the theory that they would then have to shape up or ship out.

Let us assume for the moment that this hypothesis is correct.* Let us also grant that community control would transform academic expectations that have been distorted over the years by bigotry or brainwashing. Would it also eliminate underachievement in ghetto schools? The latter is unlikely, for most achievement differences appear to be related not to a student's race or to his school's racial composition, but to factors having to do with social class. Correcting the consequences of racist distortions in teachers' expectancies is not the same thing as correcting the vast class differentials which produce differences in achievement in the first place. The notion that bigoted teachers depress the academic performance of black children is based on the premise that these teachers fail accurately to perceive and/or to act upon the children's real potential, *because the children are black.* Yet it has been shown that differences in achievement are of roughly the same magnitude at grade six or nine as they are at the time children enter school, and are relatively insensitive to variations in *anything* about schools. All the research of the last four decades points to the conclusion that differences in nutrition, general health, and access to intellectual and cognitive stimulation—which, of course, vary widely by social and economic status, and therefore by race—are the chief environmental determinants of children's intellectual performance. Eliminating racial distortions in teacher expectations would improve

* It has been argued most persuasively by Robert Rosenthal and Lenore Jacobson in *Pygmalion in the Classroom* (Holt, Rinehart & Winston, 1968). In a review published in the *American Educational Research Journal.* (November 1968), Robert L. Thorndike cast serious doubt on the authors' research.

ghetto education, but it would probably not eliminate disparities in achievement that are ultimately due to differences in social class.

Both of the theories that I have discussed so far suffer from the obvious defect of presuming that schools have an impact upon students' achievement, when most evidence on this point tends in the opposite direction. The third—the fate-control theory—does not so presume. Its premise is the notion that the central educational problem for black children is not poor pedagogy, but powerlessness, a political condition in the ghetto which is not at all unique to the schools. Now, it takes only a modicum of political insight to notice that Negroes do not control most of the institutions which directly affect their lives, and little ideological originality to argue that hence they are a subject people, dominated in colonial fashion by a foreign white ruling class. This argument has been advanced with increasing strength since World War II, but until publication of the Coleman Report there was no way to link the political fact of powerlessness with students' performance in school. One of that report's major findings, however, was that the extent to which black students felt they could master their destiny was a powerful determinant of their achievement, more important than all the measures of family, social, and economic status combined.

That provided the necessary link. If a student's sense of environment control strongly influenced his achievement, black control of ghetto schools, it seemed to follow, would produce a sense of personal efficacy which would in turn lead to improved performance. The idea now enjoys enormous popularity, primarily because it seems entirely consistent with reality. First of all, political and cultural emasculation has been a dominant element of the black experience in America. Secondly, all the precedents of

American ethnic history are supposed to demonstrate that group political and economic solidarity is the touchstone of personal status and mobility. Finally, it seems to make eminent sense that people who feel in control of their destiny will be high achievers; the sense of mastery leads to mastery.

But try it the other way: mastery leads to the sense of mastery; high achievers are more likely to have a stronger sense of environment control than low achievers. It sounds just as persuasive one way as the other, a perplexity which is amply reflected in research. Some studies suggest that the sense of efficacy causes achievement, some suggest that it works the other way around, and others find no association whatsoever. We have no studies of the relationship between parents' political efficacy (or their sense thereof) and their children's test scores; the few studies that relate parents' general sense of environment control to their children's achievement are inconclusive and contradictory. Here as elsewhere, the results of scientific research provide a firm basis for nothing but further research.

In summary: a good deal has been made of the various ways in which decentralization and community control will improve achievement, but a review of what we know turns up confused, contradictory, or discouraging evidence. This does not mean that greater participation, less bureaucracy, greater openness, and more accountability are not worthwhile goals; I happen to think they are crucial. In my view, however, these are essentially political and administrative issues, and one's assessment of their significance or desirability should be determined by theory and evidence particular to those realms of experience. The one thing my brief review of the educational evidence *does* mean is this: if one were guided solely by research on achievement and attitudes, one would not employ community control or decentralization as the devices most likely to reduce racial disparities in achievement.

But the gathering momentum for community control and decentralization is unlikely to be diminished by this news. On the contrary, advocates of these policies argue that evidence derived from the existing situation is not simply inadequate but altogether inapplicable. More important, the major pressures for decentralization and community control now have less to do with the failure of educational strategies than with the failure of what I referred to earlier as the politics of common interest.

As a historical matter, it is of course true that one of the underlying causes of the movement for community control has been the persistence of racial disparities in achievement. Yet the nature of the current situation is best illustrated by the fact that within the last year, the persistence of these disparities has not simply produced more militant demands for higher achievement but has created a profound crisis of authority in ghetto schools, a sense that these schools lack legitimacy as educational institutions. This feeling is strongest among Negroes —especially the young, the activists, and the professionals—but it is reinforced by the many middle- and upper-middle-class whites who reject the public schools' regimentation and authoritarianism for other reasons. For some blacks and whites, the notion that only parents and community residents are legitimately empowered to operate schools rests on what is taken to be the objective inadequacy of those in authority; scarcely anyone with access to print denies that the schools have failed to correct ghetto educational problems. Repeated for years, this assertion has led effortlessly to the idea that the established agencies lack the special competence upon which most educational authority is assumed to rest.

There is, however, more to the crisis of authority than that. The illegitimacy of ghetto education is more and more often proclaimed to reside not in the failure of that education to produce achievement equal to that of white schools—had it done so, according to the earlier logic, the criterion of legitimacy need never have been challenged—but in the defective nature of the social contract between black and white America. One manifestation of this position is the attack that has been launched on the instruments—achievement test results, rates of college acceptance, etc.—typically used to determine if the older, "rational" criterion of authority was being satisfied; not only that, but the intellectual and cultural content of those instruments has been dismissed as irrelevant or antithetical to the black community's political and cultural aspirations. A second, and politically more explosive, manifestation of this view is the assertion that school officials and teachers whose ideas or activities suggest the absence of political and cultural identification with the black community therefore also lack the qualifications requisite to educate black children. This is entirely consistent with the new criterion of authority, which assumes that the task of educators in the ghettos is to establish the basis for a valid social contract between Negroes and the institutions in their communities. Hence it becomes not at all strange to substitute for the old, "rational" tests of educational competence a subjective test of political consensus, for in a sense the situation is presumed to have reverted to the precontract state of nature, wherein the main issue is one of defining the body politic that is about to come into being, and deciding who shall be its citizens.

This "anti-colonial" position is, in the technically correct sense of the term, revolutionary; it asserts that the established authorities and the principles upon which their dominion rests are fundamentally and irreparably illegitimate, and that the only way they can continue to command is by the use of naked power. In such a situation the minimum task of the revolutionary is to bring that fact into the open, to "expose" the illegitimacy by provoking the authorities to violence.

Although only a relatively few Negroes consciously hold this position, their political strength is multiplied enormously by the fact that there are very few who explicitly hold the opposite view. Most blacks have an acute sense of the injustice which white society has visited upon them, so that if white authorities should attempt to suppress an openly revolutionary cadre, the best response they could hope for from the general community would be one of sullen hostility. In the case of the struggle over the schools, this makes it functionally impossible to distinguish those who want community control as a means of fulfilling the achievement critierion from those who want it as the basis for a new social contract. The two groups will remain pretty much identical so long as the achievement criterion remains unsatisfied.

It is easy to see why the anti-colonial position is anathema to the established authorities. Among other things, in selecting school personnel advocates of this position seek to substitute what amounts to a test of political loyalty for a series of universalistic "professional" standards. In last year's school dispute in New York, for example, the Ocean Hill Board was accused of racism and of violating due-process guarantees for teachers, but whether or not this was true, the real issue was the Board's effort to apply a test of political consensus to educators. Since—as in Africa—there are always whites who can pass such a test, the Ocean Hill Board could maintain that it was not guilty of racism at the same time that it sought to expel teachers for what *it* called racism—i.e., non-consensus.

But whatever the local variations, the crucial fact is that the crisis in urban education is passing into a phase in which only a change in the locus of authority will bring peace. How long the present transition period will last is hard to say, but the main elements of the domestic political situation appear to favor an increase rather than a diminishing of the anti-colonial impulse. Those elements include: the inability of the liberal/labor/civil-rights coalition to secure legislation that would mount a broad and basic attack upon black-white disparities in income and occupation; an unprecedented (but hardly unheralded) upsurge of black nationalism; the emergence of a black professional class in Northern cities as a political force.

Since the collapse of the Johnsonian consensus on domestic affairs, which can be roughly dated to the 1966 White House Conference "To Fulfill These Rights," these three elements have come into high relief, reinforcing one another. After the White House Conference, it became increasingly clear that Congressional liberals were light-years away from the political strength required to legislate fundamental change in the economic and social status of Negroes. The resources lost to the war effort in Vietnam were of course partly to blame, but there was more to it than that: as the White House Conference report suggested, fundamental change would require social spending on an absolutely unprecedented scale. Even without a war in Vietnam the Congressional struggle would have been titanic in its proportions; it was clearly impossible under conditions of large-scale defense spending.

In the cities, therefore, where no real effort has been made to deal with the underlying problems of jobs and income, attention remains where it has been since 1954. The schools are visible and accessible, in the sense that the political nexus of employment and housing is not; their performance has been obviously out of harmony with the ideology of education expounded by all moderates and liberals since *Brown* vs. *Board of Education;* and the inability in the last decade to effect widespread educational reforms has insured that existing frustrations would grow as performance fell farther and farther behind expectations.

As a result, the primary urban activity since late 1967 has been a struggle for the division and control of what already exists. Although one may argue that this is a rational response if one belives there is no hope for new social legislation, it has the notable drawback of creating political divisions which even further diminish the likelihood of such legislation. The greatest division of this kind has occurred between Negroes and white liberals. (To be sure, the peace between them had never been easy. Aside from the inevitable element of paternalism—whites in the movement were cooperating to solve what was typically seen as "the Negro problem"—there was the problem generated by rivalry for jobs and leadership once the movement began to score some successes.) In the recent disasters in New York City, many of the same white liberals who had championed the cause of civil rights suddenly found themselves under attack because they happened to inhabit those institutions toward which urban Negroes were now turning with hungry eyes. In a sense, the social-welfare bureaucracies—schools, welfare, anti-poverty programs—were the least strategic places to attack. They have, after all, been among the most liberal institutions, they have a common interest with blacks in the expansion of social-welfare legislation, and they are typically populated by whites who are noticeably more liberal than the average. But they were close at hand, they were the institutions Negroes knew about, they were (or seemed) easier to approach than others more remote and conservative, they were located in the ghettoes rather than downtown, and they were even sympathetic to the situation which produced the movement for black control.

Add to this the politicization of the cultural and psychological upsurge known as black nationalism, which began in the mid-1960's and was well underway long before black power became a political and ideological reality. Renewed interest on the part of blacks in Afro-American culture and "Negritude" produced basic and legitimate demands upon white America, in the schools and elsewhere. The written materials of education are typically bigoted, and there is virtually no important aspect of public education in the cities, from the distribution of money to the attitudes of teachers, which is untouched by discrimination or racial antagonism. These problems, however, are as amenable to remedy by integration as by black separatism.

But in the absence of genuine integration, or of much evidence of fundamental economic and social change, nationalism became wedded to the demand for a piece of the action, and was forged into a program for change. This is not the place to argue the merits of the position as a general matter; what is important is that black nationalism offered a system of ideas which seemed to correspond with the interests of the emerging class of black professionals, and to explain the need for black community control. Even in itself integration is a difficult path: it promises strain, tension, and unfamiliarity to black and white administrators and teachers equally, and hence it has never inspired real enthusiasm except among a few. Community control, on the other hand, avoids these pitfalls. It offers concrete gains long overdue—jobs and promotion to administrative and supervisory positions, without the accompanying discomfort of venturing into foreign schools and neighborhoods —under the ideological aegis of assisting in the development of one's own community. A more perfect coincidence of ideology and self-interest can hardly be imagined.

The coming-of-age of the black professional class, a potent aspect of the struggle for community control, may turn out in the end to be the most important element in the battle over the schools, more significant than the substitution of parent for citywide boards, or community for bureaucratic control. Then franchisement of a black elite, long overdue, should indeed help to improve education. In the short run, however, it has poured fuel on an already raging fire. Frustration, hostility, ambition, and concern for children long neglected is a potent combination, especially when applied generously to the complicated gear-works of big-city civil-service labor relations. The results have been spread depressingly over more editions of the *New York Times* than one cares to contemplate. As the struggle continues—and it surely will—the Lindsays of the world will seek to maintain civil peace—and their positions—by accommodating as many black demands for a slice of the action as they find possible, while the Albert Shankers will seek to maintain life by holding on to what they have. In so doing, the Lindsays will find themselves alienating lower-class and sometimes liberal white constituents, and the Shankers will find themselves making alliances with and concessions to conservative elements. The liberals will find themselves in the position of having to defend those portions of the social-welfare bureaucracies they control against black demands; all they can do, aside from hanging on for dear life, is to assume a principled position against segregation and for the application of vastly greater resources. However one may sympathize with that position, it is no more likely to be useful in the next day's struggle to keep afloat politically than it is either to reduce segregation or to increase the available resources.

Is there a way out of our present morass? The difficulty here is twofold. One might still imagine that a massive assault on status disparities would shift attention away from the question of legitimacy, but it is hard to conceive of such an assault being mounted. Producing the needed legislation would require sustained political mobilization of blacks and whites, a prospect which seems remote so long as: a) they are so fatally preoccupied with each other; b) new money cannot be found to reduce the competition and allow recruitment of a broader constituency; and c) many powerful whites and ambitious blacks, for their separate reasons, prefer a political settlement to economic and social justice.

I do not mean to imply, however—and this is the second difficulty—that the way out would be clear if only more resources were available. That, unfortunately, is only the converse of the argument for decentralization: it makes no more sense to pretend that removing social and economic disparities will solve all the problems of city schools than to argue that political rearrangement will eliminate achievement disparities. The point can be conveniently illustrated: the liberal ideology of educational improvement tells us that since schooling is the least divisive and best way to insure equal chances for jobs and income, we should provide more of it for Negroes. School reforms based on this notion typically include heavy doses of those disciplined activities which are thought to yield high scores on achievement tests. But the same middle-class liberals who advocate this medicine for the poor often cannot stomach administering it to *their* children; they enroll them instead in more open, permissive, and pedagogically diversified

private schools. This paradox suggests in practice what many advocates of school reform cannot admit as a matter of principle: that there exists presently a fundamental tension between the sorts of educational changes which are thought to improve achievement, and those designed to diversify pedagogy, reduce routine, and allow for individual and cultural creativity.

As an ideological matter, school reformers have dealt with this tension by placing exclusive stress on either diversity or achievement; the practical political consequence has been to behave as though solving one problem would solve the other. Many liberals have therefore supported programs designed to extend the dominion of the schools over children's lives, and have advocated such things as twelve-month school years, preschools and kindergarten for all, afternoon school centers, and the like. Under any circumstances serious questions could be raised about the desirability of a further intrusion of state institutions into a child's cultural and intellectual development; given the current circumstances—in which the institutions in question suffer from an advanced form of political, cultural, and pedagogical atrophy—the problems are terrific. Although one can easily imagine a program of extended schooling being executed well, with concern for diversity and individuality, there is a big difference between what one can imagine and what one can actually do with the materials at hand. The extension of schooling means the extension of the schooling that happens to exist, as the history of Headstart and Title I—to say nothing of the compulsory education movement—makes abundantly clear. Thus, liberals who advocate such measures run the risk of overtly or covertly subverting other educational values they hold dear.

In the case of decentralization—as the recent events in New York reveal—the same insistence on unitary solutions to separate problems has led to the widespread idea that political and administrative change will remedy racial achievement differences, an idea which, as I have tried to show, flies in the face of all past experience and knowledge concerning the determinants of achievement. As for the aim of creating diversity in the schools, decentralization and community control can be described only as half-hearted and incomplete attempts in that direction.

Consider the various proposals for decentralizing the New York City schools. All, from the Bundy plan to the most radical proposals for community control, assume that the necessary and sufficient condition for producing diversity is the imposition of new control on existing institutions and resources. But this amounts to nothing more than a system of educational laissez-faire, which is hardly the same thing as diversity, especially when schools are segregated by race and class. In the competition for school resources, the net effect of such a system would be to institutionalize the political disadvantages of blacks and poor people, isolate them in the competition for money, and thereby establish in custom, law, and administrative code those failures of the politics of common interest which led to the demands for control in the first place.

More important, however, is the fact that the need for diversity—for alternative cultural and pedagogic styles in schooling—cannot be satisfied by racial division or changes in administrative structure alone. Diversity and excellence in schools are qualities not likely to appear unless a premium is put upon them. Creating such diversity would entail the recruitment of new people to education, and new institutions to schooling: not just neighborhood boards, but universities, labor unions, churches, and voluntary associations formed for the purpose of education. The business of attracting, organizing, funding, and maintaining such institutions cannot be accomplished by further provincializing the existing structure, any more than regulating it can be left to essentially free competition.

Real diversity would be costly both politically and fiscally, and would require a somewhat different view of the relationship between the state and the schools from the one now regnant. At the moment we think of the state not only as the sole regulator of public education, but as exclusive operator of the schools; this greatly restricts, for political and constitutional reasons, the extent to which the schools can be diverse. Were the state to continue its role as regulator but take less of a hand in actually running the schools, greater diversity might be possible; under such conditions the state would concern itself with maintaining essential principles of interest regulation, civil liberties, civil rights, and educational standards.

The form that such an arrangement would take is uncertain. There have been proposals to put money on the heads of children—or in the pockets of their parents—but they raise problems related to segregation, and to the well-known fact that the poor usually exercise choice in a less strategic fashion than do the affluent. Another proposal has been to create alternative institutions; this might obviate the problem of choice to a certain extent, but like the tuition proposals, it raises questions about the interests of parties that are presently involved in the educational enterprise.

All these alternative proposals deserve careful consideration, whether one is concerned with pedagogy, political participation, or the possibilities for a democratic culture. They deserve consideration not only as to their intrinsic merits, but because they serve as a counterbalance to the idea that diversity and openness in the schools can be produced solely through political arrangements designed to settle an authority crisis arising from long-standing grievances of quite another sort. One might also hope that a discussion of these issues would contribute to repairing some of the deep political divisions within the democratic Left. These fissures have sprung in part from the fact that organizations and individuals that would in a more civilized atmosphere have tended to take different stands on different issues—racial identity, pedagogic diversity, political participation, reduction of racial disparities in income and occupation—have in the current climate been forced to take a single stand on all at once. The resulting schizophrenia has been widely displayed in the columns of all serious publications which either originate in or recognize the existence of New York City.

Finally, attention to alternative forms of education might help to set in clear relief another idea currently simmering at the edges of the liberal political consciousness, namely that the best way to reduce racial disparities in children's school achievement might be to reduce the disparities in their parents' social and economic status. Support for this notion, as I pointed out earlier, arises from a variety of considerations: the dependence of achievement on parental status; the potential political, cultural, and emotional dangers of extending the system of schooling that now exists; the inherent risks of presuming that profound social change can be purchased cheaply with a bit of improved schooling.

It should be plain by now that I myself am persuaded by the soundness of this analysis, yet I am also aware that its intellectual cogency is strongly and negatively related to its chances for political life and prosperity. We are presently at an important crossroad, both in education and in race relations, and the path we take will probably influence the shape of things for many, many years. Roughly speaking, the issue is how to settle an increasingly severe crisis of authority. On the one hand, by carving up existing institutions and resources in such a way as to arrange a viable contract between blacks and the institutions in their neighborhoods, we can work out a political settlement of the tensions that have arisen from a long-standing failure to remedy basic social and economic injustice. Thereby, perhaps, we can purchase peace, or, if not peace, at least the confinement of the conflict and noise within the ghetto. On the other hand, we can resolve the authority crisis by attacking the fundamental disparities which produced it.

It would be easy to overestimate in alarmist fashion the consequences of choosing the easier path; a good deal of this has unfortunately already been done. It would be silly, or worse, to argue that educational disaster will ensue from whatever decentralization and community control can be politically arranged. There will be problems, but there are problems now. It seems to me much more likely that under community control the basic disparities would remain more or less intact, while the atmosphere and conduct of the schools would show improvement.

A good deal has also been said to the effect that the movements for decentralization and community control are provoking a general rightward trend in American politics. That such a trend exists is clear, and it also seems reasonable to believe that it feeds upon the wilder and more vociferous elements in the movement for community control. But we should remember that this trend was first noticed years ago as a reaction to the movement for integration, and that it probably manifests the underlying reality of white attitudes in a limited-resource situation, not a response to particular strategies. It is unhappy and frustrating to witness the present spiral of distrust, and the struggle for control of what exists; these contribute their share to the general poisoning of the political atmosphere. But they are symptoms of the underlying political weakness, not its primary cause.

Of the two alternatives, it takes no great vision to see where the political chips lie. The second alternative is costly, whether we measure cost in dollars allocated, status lost, stereotypes shattered, or political effort expended. The first has a certain political price— as the convulsions in New York revealed —but it gives the appearance of costing little otherwise. In addition to this enormous political advantage, it has behind it the gathering momentum of profound changes in black politics, culture, and society.. Although the politicization of these forces, and their arrangement behind the banner of community control, results chiefly from the failure of the society at large to deal directly with social and economic inequality, political facts cannot be wished away, either by dreams of what might have been or strategies on paper about what might be: unless the inequalities are swiftly attacked, these forces will not be denied.

31. RESEGREGATING IRON CITY

Theodore Lowi

It is one thing to claim that "urban renewal is Negro removal"; it is another to prove it. Lowi's paper documents this contention by tracing the history and implementation of an urban redevelopment plan in a Southern city. For the cynical, this selection could serve as a set of lessons on the building of a residential ghetto by the creation of new forms of *de facto* segregation to replace and be added to old forms of *de jure* segregation. It is a case study of how federal government policies that start out seeming noble in design turn out sullied when implemented by local officials.

Lowi's remarks on the way that federal mortgage agencies

Source: *The End of Liberalism: Ideology, Policy and the Crisis of Public Authority* (New York: W. W. Norton & Company, Inc., 1969), pp. 250–66. Copyright © 1969 by W. W. Norton & Company, Inc. Reprinted by permission of the author and the publisher.

THEODORE LOWI is Professor of Political Science at the University of Chicago.

have worked to promote the profits of developers taking advantage of the middle-class exodus from the central cities are similar to some of Krickus' observations in Selection 16. Another reading in this book, Moore's account of Blackmoor in Selection 23, also takes on added meaning in the context of Lowi's analysis of the motivations of the men responsible for the design and building of public housing projects. Readers especially interested in the problems of low-cost housing location and construction might wish to refer back to the two earlier papers after reading this one, keeping in mind that about half of all the people who live in public housing in the United States are black.

HOUSING POLICY IN IRON CITY: HAVE A PLAN WHEN YOU PLAN

Iron City is an urban-industrial area whose corporate boundary surrounds nearly 60,000 residents and whose true metropolitan area includes about 100,000. The name of the city has been fictionalized to avoid embarrassing the local officials. They are guilty as charged but no more so than thousands of mayors, councilmen, planners, realtors, and builders all over the country. Iron City presents a single well-documented case. The case situation itself is extreme and unrepresentative, but it will soon be clear that that is precisely why it offers an ideal laboratory for discovering the nature and limitations of modern Federal enabling legislation. Iron City is a southern city, and its official development plan promulgates a set of explicit racial goals. In so doing, however, Iron City officials only stated, as the innocent child in Hans Christian Anderson's "The Emperor's New Clothes," the awful truth about the land-use goals of cities all over the country. The explicitness of Iron City simply documents beyond doubt the extraordinary permissiveness of Federal urban policy; for these official development plans provided the local

facts and proposals upon which the Federal allocations were based.

Interlarded Neighborhoods: *Status Quo Ante*

In 1950, over 20 per cent of Iron City's population were Negroes. But there was something peculiar about these Negroes, peculiar at least to those acquainted only with northern cities. In 1950 they did not live in a ghetto. The largst concentration was in the north-central section, "across the tracks." (Note shadings on map p. 374.) There was another large neighborhood in the south-central section. However, there were neighborhoods of Negroes in virtually every section of town. There was a narrow strip along The River, and several strips in the west-central and western sections, in easy walking distance from the steel and textile mills.

This has been the typical Negro residential pattern in southern cities, especially stable, middle-sized cities. Beginning in the 1920's, relatively slow growth of the city and slow but steady immigration of Negroes from outlying rural areas contributed to a patchwork pattern. Rather than a single Negro section, there were interlarded neighbor-

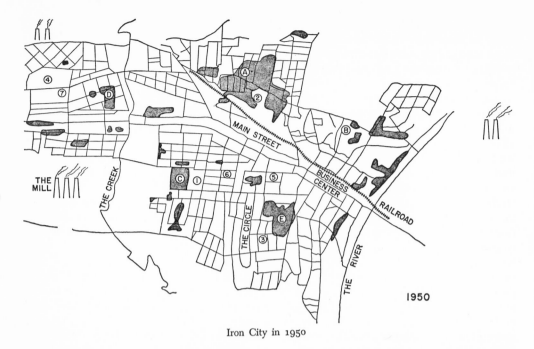

Iron City in 1950

hoods of black and white.[1] This pattern was supported by the needs of the wealthier whites for domestic servants. "Close quarters" was literally the predominant feature. For example, the Negro neighborhoods east and north of The Circle were surrounded on three sides by the wealthiest homes in Iron City.

Although the residents of Iron City tolerated the proximity of the races, in fact encouraged it in many ways, they could in no way be accused of living in an integrated community. There was of course no Harlem. The very word and its implications suggest the recency as well as the non-southern origin of systematic housing discrimination. On the other hand, each Negro neighborhood was pure. There were no black-white-black-white house patterns (although there were a number of instances where several Negro families lived directly

[1] Iron City extends to the east beyond The River as well as to the north. And Negro neighborhoods are interlarded with white ones in those sections as well. However, they need not enter significantly into the case here.

across the street from or "alley to alley" with a larger number of white families). In good urban fashion, Negroes and whites learned to ignore each other, yet to profit from the proximity wherever possible. Negroes accepted their back-of-the-bus status. And indeed they received certain privileges unavailable to whites. Merchants and newsboys were more permissive in granting or extending petty credit. Crimes committed within the race were not as a rule investigated or prosecuted with utmost vigor. The raising of a pig or a goat was usually allowed, in violation of public health regulations. Negro bootleggers (legal sale of liquor has for years been forbidden in the county) had freer rein—and were often patronized by the insatiably thirsty white middle class. And the rents tended to run considerably lower.

This was the dispersed and highly status-bound social situation as recently as 1950. At that time most Southerners could see a racial crisis approaching, and for them the problems inherent in the residential pattern were immediately clear. In almost no direction away from the major public schools could one walk without encountering at least a strip of Negro housing and a collection of school-age children. Central High School received all white children in grades 9 to 12 who lived east of The Creek (Fig. 1). Rebel High (No. 4) was for all white children in grades 9 to 12 who lived west of The Creek, including some areas not shown on the map. Washington High School (No. 2) was exclusively for the Negro children in grades 7 to 12 from the entire city and surrounding county. Note how perilously close were Negro families, with eligible children, to both of the white high schools, most particularly to Central, where virtually all of the children of upper middle- and middle-class families attended. Note also how far a good half the Negro children commuted to Washington High and also how many of them actually crossed the paths to Rebel and Central in the course of commuting. The same problem obtained for the junior highs (No. 3 and 7) and elementary schools (No. 5, 6, 7). Another junior high and elementary complex was similarly situated in an unmapped area east of The River.

The Plan

Into this situation stepped the Iron City Planning Commission in 1951. The Commission's first step was a thorough analysis of housing, land use, economic facilities, and deterioration. In 1952 they produced a handsome and useful Master Plan, the emphasis of which was upon the need for measures ". . . for arresting beginning blight and correcting advanced blight." On the basis of the master plan, a more intensive investigation was ordered, toward ultimate production of a Rehabilitation Plan to guide actual implementation and financing. The result was a careful study published in a very professional three-color, glossy-paper, fully illustrated booklet, *Iron City Redevelopment*. This plan centered upon three areas in which blight had made urban redevelopment necessary. On the map these are designated A, B, and E. Area E the plan identified as "occupied by Negroes, but the number is too few to justify provision of proper recreational, school, and social facilities. . . . The opportunity to reconstitute the area as a residential district in harmony with its surroundings was the main reason for its selection as the number one redevlopment site." The second area on the map, B, was chosen because "a relatively small amount of housing—standard and substandard—exists there"; therefore it would serve "as a companion project to . . . [Area E] . . . thus affording home sites for those occupants of [Area E] who are not eligible for relocation in public housing or who, for reasons of their own, prefer single-family or duplex dwellings." Area A, as shown by the intensive survey and the maps published with the Plan, contained as much dilapidated and blighted housing as Area E; but Area A was not designated an urban redevelopment area in the Plan. Although "blighted and depreciating," it was the "center part of the area . . . growing as the focal point of Negro life." Along the Main Street of this area, extending into area B, the Plan proposed the building of an auditorium, a playfield, and other public facilities "to serve [Iron City's] Negro community." Sites were inserted by the redevelopment of Area E.

The Plan was clearly a Negro removal plan. All of the projects proposed in the Plan are explicit on this point, as the selection of quotes from the document clearly demonstrates. The underlying intent of the Plan can be further identified, if need be, in the inconsistencies between the design for Area E and that for Area A. The latter possessed as much blighted housing as Area E, and yet the standard of blighting was not applied to it. There the Plan called for intensification of use rather than renewal.

The Plan Is Implemented

Even before the completion of *Iron City Development,* implementation projects had begun in Iron City. These were expanded as financing allowed. The first steps, quite rationally, were toward expansion of housing replacements for those families to be displaced by renewal. Consistent with the types of people to be most affected by the Plan, those first steps were the construction of public housing. There had been some public housing construction under depression legislation, but it is of no concern here. Iron City built four public housing projects under the Housing Act of 1949. On the map they are the actual letters A, B, C, and D, and these designations have been placed as close as possible to their actual locations within each area.

Each public housing project was placed carefully. Project A was built in the middle of the largest Negro area. Project B was built in a sparse area, about 50 per cent Negro, but marked out in the Plan as the area for future expansion of the Negro community. (In the Plan, the proposed sites for the three new "colored churches" and the "colored auditorium" were strung along the area around Project B.) Project C, an exclusively white project, was built literally on top of the Negro area around it. While it is the smallest of the projects, as measured by the number of housing units, the structures were so designed to be spread over the entire 8-square-block area. It was, according to the executive director of the Greater Iron City Housing Authority, "a rather unique design, known in the architectural trade as a crankshaft design; thus providing both front and rear courtyards." This project was cited professionally as an outstanding example of good design and utility.

TABLE 1   Public housing projects in Iron City.

Project	Size (no. of units)	% Negroes in project	Composition of original area	Development cost
A	160	100	Negro	$1,491,000
B	224	100	Mixed	$2,491,000
C	146	0	Negro	$1,595,000
D	220	0	Negro	$2,300,000

And no wonder. Its maximum utilization of space, although it was a low-rent project, made it a combination of public housing and slum (and Negro) removal project par excellence. Project D was also built on top of a blighted Negro neighborhood. However, although it is a relatively large project it did not alone eliminate every Negro in the area.

By 1955 the public housing projects had been completed and were occupied. From the start there was never any controversy over the racial distribution. The Plan was being implemented smoothly and in every respect. Projects A and B were 100 per cent Negro; Projects C and D were 100 per cent white. Meanwhile, but at a slower pace, renewal of the central city had begun. It was not until 1956 that implementation projects were fully designed. Two areas were marked out in the Plan for intensive renewal, the shaded Areas around B and E. The important one was Area E, a 56-acre area relatively tightly packed with rickety frame houses, outside toilets, corn and potato plots, and Negroes. In the official Plan proposals, Area E included the unconnected Negro neighborhood just north of The Circle as well as the entire shaded area due east of The Circle. Area B, as noted before, was relatively sparse. A few shacks needed removing, and in some of those shacks were white unemployables.

Within three years the two urban renewal projects were declared 100 per cent

TABLE 2

Accomplishment	Activity	For Area E	For Area B
100%	Land Acquisition, No. of Parcels Acquired	168	39
100%	No. of Families Relocated	176	24
100%	No. of Structures Demolished (Site Clearance)	236	33

accomplished. In the official report to the Urban Renewal Administration (HUD) the results were as shown in Table 2.

In Area E, every trace of Negro life was removed. As the executive director of the Greater Iron City Housing Authority put it, "In this project, all of the then existing streets were vacated and a new land-use map was developed." One entirely new street was put in, several of the narrow lanes (e.g., "St. James's Alley") were covered over, and through connectors were built for a dead-end street or two.

All of Area E has become prime property. Most of the area was zoned for single-family residences, and, as of mid-1967, the boom in construction of houses in the $25,000–$40,000 range in the area was still in progress. One large supermarket and several neighborhood businesses are operating on renewal land purchased from the Authority. A 95 per cent white elementary school, with lighted ballfield and large playground, occupies most of the eastern section. It is a consolidation of elementary schools No. 5 and No. 6, which no longer exist. With the 95 per cent white junior-high (No. 3), an impressive campus resulted.

Area B also enjoys a new elementary school, with fieldhouse, lighted ballfield, tennis court, and playground. The city also built a swimming pool in this area, but it and the original municipal pool

on The River had been closed for several years to avoid integration of public facilities. As mentioned earlier, three of the redevelopment sites in Area B were set aside for the three churches demolished in the redevelopment of Area E. Each of the churches ultimately chose locations elsewhere in the Negro community. Except for the 224 units of public housing, most of the relocating Negroes chose the more densely populated and blighted Area A. Area B remains underutilized. The major part of Area B extends north of Project B toward the mountain, where although "some of the terrain is steep," reports *Iron City Development*, "much of it is gently rolling and well drained. . . . In most southern cities there is a scarcity of vacant land located close to schools and churches and shopping districts and served by city utilities and transportation, land that is suitable and desirable for expansion of Negro neighborhoods or creation of new ones. [Area B] is such an area." But apparently the Negroes did not agree, and most of the area remains a graded but raw expanse of red southern earth on the side of the mountain. This is the one part of the Plan that went wrong; this was the voluntary part of the Plan, *the part unfinanced by Federal agencies.*

The result, despite frustrated expectations in the north part of Area B, was overwhelming success for the Plan. Well before the 1960 Census the large Negro area in Area E had been reduced to 5.1 per cent of the entire census tract, and this was comprised of a few shanties behind the bottling works and the western edge of the Area along The River. In Area C, the removal process immediately around Central High was complete with Public Housing Project C. After 1960 some 10 per cent of the area was still nonwhite, but other families continued to move out. Removal from Area D was approaching totality. By 1964, removal from all areas west of The Creek was

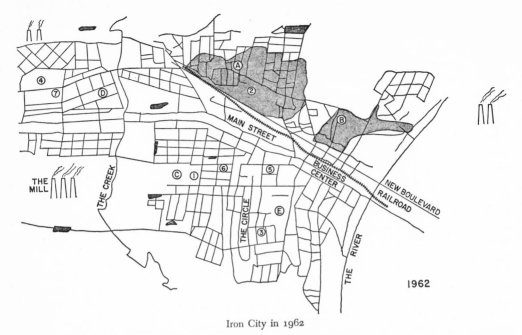

Iron City in 1962

given further assistance by the completion of one federally supported arterial running east-west through the city, and the inauguration of Iron City's portion of the new north-south Interstate Highway. That brought the nonwhite proportion in the western sectors of the city down to about 3 per cent.

This is how the situation stood by the end of 1967: west of The Creek and north of Main Street (all around Area D), there remained six Negro families. When a nearby textile mill was closed down some years before, they, as employees, were given the right to buy their houses, and they have chosen to remain. West of The Creek and south of Main Street (the area including The Mill) fewer than 5 per cent of the housing units were occupied by Negroes. Virtually every one of these houses is located in isolated and sparse sections along The Creek and behind The Mill, where one can still plant a plot of sorghum, catch a catfish, and, undisturbed, let a 1948 Chevrolet corrode into dust. East of The Creek and south of

Main Street, closer to the center of things, the 1960 distribution of Negroes continues to be reduced. Every last shack is gone from Area E and the entire central area of the white city. Three small pockets remain in the western portion near Area C, and that is all that remains in all of the white city. The last remaining Negro neighborhood of any size, a group of shanties running along The River south of Main Street, was removed by the construction of a city hall–police department–YMCA complex. Area B remains completely nonwhite and underdeveloped. Area A now fills the entire triangle pointing north. It is a ghetto.

The Secret of Success

The Plan enjoyed strong consensus among officials and white citizens. It enjoyed at least the acquiescence and tacit consent of the Negroes, who were, in any case, tenants whose landlords were white. But the Plan would have had little chance of success, consensus or not, without outside financial assistance. The assistance came from Federal programs. It was allocated, and continues in 1967 to be allocated, by Federal agencies whose personnel could and did have access to the Renewal Plan, the Master Plan, and all the project plans. Nothing was kept a secret in Iron City. What we have seen here is an honest, straightforward job of physical and social planning. And despite Iron City's open approach to *apartheid*, Federal assistance was never in question. Relative to Iron City's size, and especially the size of its annual public sector budget, Federal aid was quite substantial. And the results were dramatic. Perhaps only New Haven, Connecticut, a town famous for redevelopment, has had a higher per capita success ratio.

Direct Federal assistance for public housing in Iron City amounted to slightly over $280,000 for fiscal 1966. Each year since the completion of the four projects the city received about the same, or perhaps a slightly smaller amount. The figure varies and cannot be broken down among the four projects, because it is *computed* on the basis of the "development costs" (given above) and granted as a lump sum. The Public Housing (recently changed to Housing Assistance) Administration of HUD is authorized by law to grant *each year* to any housing authority the difference between expenses (governed by development costs) and income from public housing. Such a subsidy arrangement enabled authorities like Iron City's to borrow from private banks and to refinance through sale of relatively cheap housing authority bonds. What is even more significant is that under the formula, Iron City is authorized to receive a maximum grant of nearly $305,000 per annum. It is a point of pride at the Greater Iron City Housing Authority that the full amount available under the law was never needed or requested. At a minimum estimate of $250,000

per year, Federal grants to help carry the public housing have amounted to $3,000,000. And federal public housing grants are never-ending. Each year the total to Iron City goes up another $250,000 or more.

Federal assistance was also indispensable for the urban renewal projects in the Plan. Between 1957 and 1961, by which time virtually everything but land disposition was completed, Iron City received just short of $1,600,000 from the Federal government under the urban redevelopment laws. This amounts to a Federal subsidy of $400,000 per annum.

This Federal assistance of at least $300,000 for each year since 1954 or 1955, and of at least $700,000 during the years of peak planning activity (1957–62), constitutes the secret of the Plan's success. *It amounts to almost exactly 20 per cent of Iron City's total annual government budget.*

To this should of course be added an undetermined amount of Federal highway assistance which helped remove Negroes from the western edge of Iron City. There are also FHA and VA, which have been helping provide financing for the lovely homes being built in Area E. At this writing it has not yet been possible to determine whether Federal community facilities funds helped remove the Negroes from The River, where now stands the new city hall complex. It has also not been possible to determine whether the local banks balked at extending FHA and VA homeowner credit to Negroes for building on the mountainside north of Area B. But these facts would affect the meaning of the case only marginally.

Implications

First, the case bears out the contentions of two decades that slum removal means Negro removal. It supports the even more severe contention that the ultimate effects of Federal urban policies have been profoundly conservative, so much so as to vitiate any plans for positive programs of integration through alteration of the physical layout of cities.

Second, it supports the general thesis of this book, that policy without a rule of law will ultimately come to ends profoundly different from those intended by their most humanitarian and libertarian framers. It supports, still further, the contention of the book that some of the most cherished instruments of the positive state may be positively evil, and that the criterion by which this evil outcome can be predicted is absence of public and explicit legislative standards by which to guide administrative conduct.

Third, the case supports, especially by virtue of the explicitness of the racial policy, the main contentions [made earlier in the book]. It shows precisely how and why Federal policy is ill-equipped to govern the cities directly. The case confirms beyond doubt the contention that the present disorder in the cities is properly explained by the failure of government and politics rather than by the inferiority of Negro adjustment. The case shows how national legitimacy can be tarnished to the degree that it is loaned to the cities for discretionary use, and how a crisis of public authority was inevitable as long as the virtue made of an untutored political process ended in the abuses cataloged in Iron City. In sum, it helps show why liberal governments cannot achieve justice.

Every Negro in Iron City knew what was happening. Every Negro in Chicago and New York and Cleveland and Detroit knows the same about his city too, but since these northern Negroes are not so docile, does that leave any possibility that Federal imperium was used completely differently outside the South? True, planning authorities would never so deliberately pursue racial planning. True, few social plans could be as extensive or as successful as Iron City's.

Nonetheless, misuse of Federal programs in ways indistinguishable on principle from Iron City has been widespread and undeniable.

Martin Anderson, for example, estimated in 1964 that about two-thirds of all people displaced from urban renewal homes were Negroes, Puerto Ricans, or members of some other minority group.[2] In public housing the record is even more somber, first, because the pattern is even clearer, and second, because these projects stand as ever-present symbols of the acts of discrimination by which they were created.[3] As of 1965, only three of New York City's 69 public housing projects were officially listed as all-nonwhite or all-white in occupancy, but 10 of Philadelphia's 40 projects were all-nonwhite, and 21 of Chicago's 53, 5 of Detroit's 12, 4 of Cleveland's 14, and all of Dallas' 10 projects were listed as either all-nonwhite or all-white.[4] The rest of reality is hidden, because the Public Housing (renamed Housing Assistance) Administration defines an "integrated project" as one in which there are "whites and more than one nonwhite, including at least one Negro family." [5] Not only is it impossible to determine the real number of truly integrated projects; this system of reporting, as permissive as the law itself, was ideally suited for local racial policies and local individual racial prejudices.[6] Until July, 1967, the agency even followed a rule of "free choice" allowing eligible tenants to wait indefinitely for an apartment, which allowed them also

[2] Martin Anderson, *The Federal Bulldozer* (Cambridge: M.I.T. Press, 1964), pp. 6–8.

[3] See James Baldwin's observations, quoted at the beginning of Part III. [The reference is to an earlier portion of Lowi's book. Ed.]

[4] Source: Public Housing Administration (HUD), *Low-Rent Project Directory,* December 31, 1965.

[5] *Ibid.,* p. v.

[6] *Cf.* a study by Bernard Weissbrourd which concluded: ". . . most cities have followed a deliberate program of segregation in public housing. . . ." *Segregation, Subsidies and Megalopolis* (Santa Barbara: Center for the Study of Democratic Institutions, 1964), p. 3.

to decline a vacancy on racial grounds. Thus, while the whole story cannot be told from official statistics, every urban Negro knows it.

The Civil Rights Act of 1965 was supposed to have put an end to such practices, but there is little evidence that it can or will improve the situation in public housing in particular or city housing in general. It was not even until July of 1967 that the rule of "free choice" was replaced with a "rule of three," plan whereby an applicant must take one of the first three available units or be dropped to the bottom of the eligible list. All this has produced so far is undeniable testimony that the practices all along had constituted a "separate but equal" system of federally supported housing. As of June, 1967, therefore, following three years under the 1964 Civil Rights sections and following more strenuous efforts by the Johnson Administration, 2 of Detroit's 5 segregated projects became "integrated," by virtue of the fact that in each case exactly one white family had moved into a totally black project. At the same time at least 11 of New York's projects were classified as "integrated" when in fact fewer than 15 per cent of the units were occupied by families of some race other than the 85 per cent majority in that project.[7]

A month after the belated 1967 directive on public housing, the Federal Housing Administration (FHA) instituted a *pilot* program to increase FHA support for housing finance in "economically unsound" areas. This was an official confession that for 33 years FHA has insured over $110 billion of mortgages to help whites escape the city rather than build it. This step and others

like it will not erase the stigma of second-class citizenship placed upon the residents of Federal housing programs nor remove the culpability of Federal power in the American local government policy of *apartheid*. These remedial steps came five years after President Kennedy's famous "stroke of the pen" decision aimed at preventing discrimination in publicly supported housing, and three years after the first applicable civil rights act. But all of the efforts surely suggest that mere remedy is never enough for bad organic laws, because bad organic laws literally possess congenital defects.

Better not to have had the housing at all than to have it on the Iron City pattern and at the expense of national legitimacy. Some would argue that the problem was actually one of mere timidity and that the answer is a proper expansion of public housing.[8] Judging from the patterns reviewed here, more could hardly have been better. Other writers and officials, including highly placed officials, have proposed solutions ranging from semipublic [9] to private [10] financing of public, low-cost housing. These proposals focus on the mere details of financing and offer further examples of the ignorance present liberals have of the implications of forms of law and administration for the achievement of simple, ordinary justice. Regardless of the means of financing, these programs will produce no lasting social benefit without a rule of law that states unmistakably what is to be achieved and what is to be forbidden. That is the moral of the Iron City story.

[8] *Cf.* Michael Harrington, *The Other America* (New York: Macmillan, 1962), pp. 139 ff.

[9] President Johnson, for example.

[10] Senators Charles Percy and Robert Kennedy, for example.

[7] Source: Computer printouts provided by the Housing Assistance Administration.

32. COPS, COLOR, AND CULTURE

Presidential Task Force

Certain kinds of work are especially likely to lead to the development of what have been called occupational subcultures, that is, generally agreed-upon standards and procedures, a common language that outsiders do not share or do not employ in the same way, and a common perspective about differences between people who carry out the occupation and outsiders who do not. Among the factors favoring the development of a strong occupational subculture are odd work hours, dangerous work conditions, specialized tasks that people in other occupations either may not be permitted to do or may not be capable of doing, and a visible basis of distinction between the jobholders and other people. At least several of these items apply among printers, miners, railroad engineers, and airline pilots, and also to a number of professional groups like surgeons, astronauts, and career military officers. All of them apply among policemen.

Policemen often feel they are not appreciated or well understood by the civilian public. That is partly because the exigencies of their job lead them to view the world in ordered ways that seem reasonable to them but are not the customary ways in which most people see things. A recent work comments:

> To meet the problems of violation, police culture has fashioned the conceptions that actually predict violation in advance. . . . The police, in dealing with persons, thus have in advance a notion of what a suspect ought to look like, what signifies trouble, and how suspects should be categorized on a police blotter . . . types are assigned argot names and roles, are attributed a modus operandi, and are to be known by

Source: *The President's Commission on Law Enforcement and Administration of Justice* (Washington, D.C.: Government Printing Office, 1967), pp. 144–71.

their dress, posture and manner with police. . . . The police, . . . operating with these deviant typifications, go about ordering deviance. . . . They perceive trouble in accordance with their working definitions of it.[1]

We take it for granted that police *ought* to go about their work impartially. But we also know that their impartiality is compromised by the hunches their occupational subculture tells them they ought to play, as well as by their sharing some widely prevalent and less than objective standards for evaluating different categories of people. Just how prejudiced are they? Do their prejudices affect the way they carry out their work? What steps have been and may be taken to make police operations more impartially effective?

The selection that follows tries to answer those questions. (It does *not* discuss the issues of how much emphasis society ought to place on law and order, or of whether increased police efficiency and control imperil or support civil rights and liberties. Although extraordinarily important issues, they are beyond the scope of this book.) It shows that while most people seem to be satisfied with police performance, black people— especially young black people—think it leaves a lot to be desired. The selection also shows that at least some of the complaints are almost certainly not unwarranted. Any negative feelings black people have toward policemen are clearly reciprocated among the policemen themselves. It shows, too, that even police departments ready to recruit minority-group members have done little or nothing to make up for past educational deficiencies to enable minority candidates to pass examinations or enter training programs. Finally, it shows that the absence of minority-group representation is greatest just where its presence would count the most—at the top.

In the end, remember that policemen are not their own bosses. It is still true, despite thousands of criticisms and as many bad jokes, that the policeman is a public servant. Perhaps the essential question to ask, then, is, "Just what 'publics' does he serve?"

[1] Earl Rubington and Martin L. Weinberg, *Deviance: The Interactionist Perspective* (New York: The Macmillan Company., 1968), p. 112.

PUBLIC ATTITUDES TOWARD THE POLICE

The General Public

Contrary to the belief of many policemen, the overwhelming majority of the public has a high opinion of the work of the police. A national survey conducted by the National Opinion Research Center (NORC) for the Commission produced these answers to the following questions: [1]

Do you think that the police here do an excellent, good, fair, or a poor job of enforcing the laws?

Excellent	22%
Good	45
Fair	24
Poor	8

How good a job do the police do on giving protection to people in the neighborhood?

Very good	42%
Pretty good	35
Not so good	9
No opinion	14

The results of other surveys are substantially consistent with this one. A Louis Harris poll in 1966 found that 76 percent of the public rated Federal agents as good or excellent in law enforcement and the comparable figures for State and local agencies were 70 and 65 percent respectively.[2]

The public generally believes that the police do not engage in serious misconduct. A Gallup poll in 1966 showed that only 9 percent of the public believed "there is any police brutality in this area." The NORC survey found, in answer to the question, "How good a job do the police do on being respectful to

people like yourself?" that the public answered: [3]

Very good	59%
Pretty good	26
Not so good	4
No opinion	10

These studies might seem to suggest that there is no widespread police-community relations problem. And, if the persons showing greatest skepticism toward the police were evenly distributed through all kinds of communities and neighborhoods, this would be true. In fact, however, this is not so.

The Negro Community

Police effectiveness / The NORC survey shows that nonwhites, particularly Negroes, are significantly more negative than whites in evaluating police effectiveness in law enforcement. In describing whether police give protection to citizens, nonwhites give a rating of "very good" only half as often as whites and give a "not so good" rating twice as often. These differences are not merely a function of greater poverty among nonwhites; they exist at all income levels and for both men and women.[4]

Other surveys indicate a similar disparity in views. The Louis Harris poll, for example, shows that 16 percent fewer Negroes than whites—a bare majority of 51 percent—believe that local law enforcement agencies do a good or excellent job on law enforcement.[5] A survey in Watts found that 47 percent of the Negroes believed that the police did an "excellent or pretty good" job while 41 percent thought they were "not so good" or "poor." [6]

A poll in Detroit in 1965 found that 58 percent of Negroes did not believe

---

[1] National Opinion Research Center, "A National Sample Survey Approach to the Study of the Victims of Crimes and Attitudes Toward Law Enforcement and Justice" (Chicago: unpublished, 1966), ch. 8, p. 1.

[2] Louis Harris, "Eye-for-an-Eye Rule Rejected," *The Washington Post*, July 3, 1966, sec. E, p. E-3, col. 4.

[3] NORC, *op. cit.*

[4] *Ibid.*

[5] Harris, *op. cit.*

[6] John F. Kraft, Inc., "Attitudes of Negroes in Various Cities" (New York: John F. Kraft, Inc., 1966), p. 25. Report prepared for the Senate Subcommittee on Executive Reorganization.

	White annual income		Nonwhite annual income	
	$0 to $2,999	$6,000 to $9,000	$0 to $2,999	$6,000 to $9,000
Males:				
Police very good	56%	67%	34%	31%
Police not so good	4	4	22	6
Females:				
Police very good	62	66	28	41
Police not so good	3	1	12	45

that law enforcement was fair, and an earlier poll in 1951 found that 42 percent of Negroes believed that it was "not good" or "definitely bad." [7]

Police discourtesy and misconduct / Negroes show even greater attitude differences from whites with regard to police discourtesy. The NORC national survey found, as to respectfulness to "people like yourselves," the differences shown in the table above between the attitudes of Negroes and whites.

A 1965 Gallup poll showed that only 7 percent of white males but 35 percent of Negro males believed that there was police brutality in their area; 53 percent of Negro males thought that there was none.

A survey of the Watts area of Los Angeles concerning opinions on the existence of "brutality" found: [8]

Existence of police brutality	Total	Age		
		15 to 29	30 to 34	45 and over
A lot	22.2%	24.4%	25.0%	17.1%
A little	24.6	35.6	22.7	14.3
None at all	15.1	17.8	11.4	14.3

Thus, nearly 47 percent of all respon-

[8] Kraft, *op. cit.*
[7] Richard W. Ouderlugs, "How Citizens Rate Police Department on Racial Fairness" *Detroit News,* February 3, 1965, sec. A, p. 1, col. 3.

dents and 60 percent of all those from 15 to 29 years of age believed that there was at least some police brutality. Of those who had answered "a lot" and "a little," approximately half claimed that they had witnessed it.[9]

Another survey of Negroes in the general area of Watts by the University of California at Los Angeles found that a high percentage of those surveyed believed the police engaged in misconduct, said they had observed acts of misconduct, or indicated that such an act had happened to someone they knew or to themselves [10] (see table, p. 386).

This study also shows that males below the age of 35 were most critical of the police. For example, 53 percent of young males reported they had been subjected to insulting language; 44 percent to a roust, frisk, or search without good reason; 22 percent to unnecessary force in being arrested; and 10 percent to being beaten up while in custody. Well over 90 percent of young males believed that each of these kinds of incidents occurred in the area and 45 to 63 percent claimed to have seen at least one of them. There were no substantial differences based on economic levels. Negroes with higher education reported more insults, searches without cause, and stopping of cars without cause.

[9] *Ibid.*
[10] Walter J. Raine, "Los Angeles Riot Study: The Perception of Police Brutality in South Central Los Angeles Following the Revolt of August 1965" (Los Angeles: University of California, 1965), at fig. 1.

Police	Happened in area	Saw it happen	Happened to someone you know	Happened to you
Lack respect or use insulting language	85%	49%	52%	28%
Roust, frisk, or search people without good reason	85	52	48	25
Stop or search cars for no good reason	83	51	49	25
Search homes for no good reason	63	22	30	7
Use unnecessary force in making arrests	86	47	43	9
Beat up people in custody	85	27	46	5

Surveys may not accurately reflect the full extent of minority group dissatisfaction with the police. In-depth interviews with members of minority groups frequently lead to strong statements of hostility, replacing the neutral or even favorable statements which began the interview. For example, a study of 50 boys from the slums of Washington concluded that, as a result of real or perceived excessive force, humiliation, and other police practices, they regarded the police as "the enemy." [11] Attacks on police officers, interference with arrests, disturbances and riots starting with police incidents, and verbal abuse by citizens offer abundant testimony to the strong hostility. The way in which such hostility can become an important factor in a riot is illustrated by the following statement of a resident of Watts to an interviewer: [12]

Two white policemen was beating a pregnant colored lady like a damn dog. They need their heads knocked off. I agree 100 percent for the Negroes going crazy—they should have killed those freaks. Yes, treating niggers like dirty dogs.

This incident, which was thought by many people in Watts to have been the cause of the 1965 Los Angeles riot, never occurred.[13] But many Negroes apparently were prepared to believe that police officers act in such an improper manner.

The characteristics of personnel within a police department have a direct bearing upon police-community relations. If, for example, police departments hire officers who are prejudiced against minority groups or who do not understand minority group problems, serious conflicts will develop. And if police departments, through their hiring or promotion policies, indicate that they have little interest in hiring minority group officers, the minority community is not likely to be sympathetic toward the police.

Psychological stability and racial attitudes / Screening out candidates whose emotional instability makes them clearly unfit for police work—through psychological tests and psychiatric interviews—should also improve the capacity of police forces to improve community relations. Unthinking anger at abuse from a citizen or panic at facing a hostile crowd causes obvious community-relations problems.

A more difficult issue is whether officers should be screened also for racial and other bias. Some police officials believe that officers must be not only emotionally stable but "free of bias or

[11] Paul A. Fine, "Neighbors of the President" (New Brunswick, N.J.: Paul A. Fine Associates, 1963), p. 126. Report prepared for the President's Committee on Juvenile Delinquency and Youth Crime.

[12] Kraft, *op. cit.*

[13] Governor's Commission on the Los Angeles Riots, "Violence in the City—An End or a Beginning?" (Los Angeles: Office of the Governor, 1965), p. 12.

prejudice." Other police experts contend that police officers can be trained and disciplined to overcome personal prejudices by strong department leadership. It is doubtful, however, that the complete exlusion of all persons who are biased is realistic in view of the high proportion of the population generally who have prejudices against certain types of people. Moreover, persons with relatively slight prejudices will probably control them if properly trained and supervised. On the other hand, there is a serious problem as to officers who have strong prejudices.

The precise extent to which prejudice affects the conduct of the officer on the street is not known. Social scientists, however, believe that discriminatory action is influenced not only by individual attitudes, by the social structure, and by the views of the rest of the group, but also by the policies of the organization. This would indicate that policy directives of a department, if enforced, can affect the actions of individual officers. On the other hand, the seriousness of strongly held prejudices by numerous officers should not be minimized.

Few police departments have yet devised systematic methods for screening out biased officers. In one Commission study of police practices in several large northern cities, it was found that a large proportion of officers expressed strong racial prejudice to neutral observers; and the Michigan State survey similarly found that officers often show prejudice in private references to minority groups.[14] Further, a study of juvenile officers in a western police force of particularly high standards found that 18 of 27 officers openly admitted a dislike of Negroes, attributing their attitude to experiences as police officers, and another

study of officers generally in that city found that "hostile feelings toward the Negro are characteristic of policemen in general."[15] And a survey of Philadelphia policemen, made in the 1950's, found that over 59 percent of white patrolmen said that they would object to riding with Negro officers in a patrol car, and over one-third said that they would object to taking orders from a Negro sergeant or captain.[16] The same survey found that some Negro officers were extremely hostile to Negro offenders and have emotions of shame, indignation, and disgrace concerning Negro crime.

Whatever bias an officer has when he joins the force, without adequate training it will often get worse. Officers see the worst side of life and, in view of the higher crime rate, especially the worst side of the ghetto. As a result, their stereotypes of Negroes, as well as of other minority groups, may be strengthened. And such prejudices are likely to become increased by virtue of the large number of other officers who express prejudice.

The study of Philadelphia policemen during the 1950's found that those white officers who were prejudiced—i.e., believed there were too many Negroes on the force, and objected to riding with Negro patrolmen, taking orders from a Negro sergeant, or having Negro patrols in white neighborhoods—believed more often that it was necessary to be stricter with Negro offenders. For example, of officers who objected to riding with Negro patrolmen, 65 percent found it necessary to be stricter with Negro offenders and 32 percent did not. Of those who did not object to riding with a Negro pa-

---

[14] Donald J. Black and Albert J. Riess, Jr., "Patterns of Behavior in Police and Citizen Transactions" (Ann Arbor: University of Michigan, 1967), table 25, report prepared for the President's Commission on Law Enforcement and the Administration of Justice.

[15] Irving Piliavin and Scott Briar, "Police Encounters with Juveniles," *American Journal of Sociology,* 70:206–214, 212; supra, note 1 at p. 82.

[16] William M. Kephart, *Racial Factors and Urban Law Enforcement* (Philadelphia: University of Pennsylvania Press, 1957), pp. 185, 187. The University of California, while making no detailed survey, surmised that prejudice among Philadelphia's police officers had somewhat declined in recent years.

trolman, 29 percent found it necessary to be stricter with Negro offenders and 66 percent did not.[17] The study of a western police department found that racial prejudice did not have any apparent effect as to some assignments. In other assignments, however, including patrol, it had an effect such as in treatment of Negroes as suspects on the basis of a vague description. A study of patrolmen in one city also found that these patrolmen stopped and interrogated Negroes more frequently than other youths, often even in the absence of evidence that an offense had been committed, and Negroes usually received more severe dispositions by the officer for the same violations. One reason for this difference in treatment was long-held prejudice on the part of the individual officer.[18] The Commission's studies in several northern cities, however, found no discriminatory treatment against Negroes in comparison to whites of the same economic level; indeed, if anything, low-income whites received slightly more severe treatment.[19]

With adequate training, supervision, and discipline, officers can often be trained and induced to overcome personal prejudices which exist generally in our society. But this is not enough. It is extremely difficult for the best police leaders to prevent all verbal abuse or, in times of crisis, unnecessary physical force. It is even more difficult to curtail subtle forms of discrimination in the exercise of discretion such as arresting a Negro in situations in which a white man would not be arrested, applying handcuffs tighter to a Puerto Rican, or talking more harshly to a Mexican-American. . . . [Community service officers could help]. . . . They could seek to refer delinquent children to a social service agency. They could—as in the Richmond, Calif., project where five neighborhood aides have been assigned to a juvenile unit—work with juveniles who were in trouble and explain to parents why their children had been arrested. And, as that same project has shown, they could be extremely effective in organizing community meetings to deal with problems relating to the police.[20]

It is essential, however, that the community service officer not be used for all "helping" functions of the police department while police officers are thereby left to concentrate on law enforcement alone. Such a division of functions would make the police officer seem even more isolated than at present.

MINORITY GROUP PERSONNEL

Attraction and Selection

The Need / Police departments in all communities with a substantial minority population must vigorously recruit minority group officers. The very presence of a predominantly white police force in a Negro community can serve as a dangerous irritant as exemplified by the following comment: [21]

Why in the hell—now this is more or less a colored neighborhood—why do we have so many white cops? As if we got to have some-

---

[17] *Ibid.*

[18] Piliavin and Briar, *op. cit.*

[19] Donald J. Black and Albert J. Reiss, Jr., "Police and Citizen Behavior in Field Encounters: Some Comparisons According to the Race and Social Class Status of Citizens" (Ann Arbor: University of Michigan, 1966), p. 10, report prepared for the President's Commission on Law Enforcement and Administration of Justice. This report is a preliminary draft which is being included with the Commission's records in the National Archives. It is presently being revised by the University of Michigan and will be embodied in research studies to be published by the Commission.

[20] Gordon E. Misner, "The Development of 'New Careerist' Positions in the Richmond Police Department" (Walnut Creek, Calif.: Contra Costra Council of Community Services, 1966) pp. 44–45.

[21] Harlem resident, as quoted in Kenneth B. Clark, *Dark Ghetto* (New York: Harper & Row, 1965), p. 4.

body white standing over us. . . . Now if I go to a white neighborhood, I'm not going to see a lot of colored cops in no white neighborhood, standing guard over the white people. I'm not going to see that; and I know it, and I get sick and tired of seeing so many white cops, standing around.

To some extent such a statement is likely to be the result of accumulated resentment by Negroes of white persons generally, and such prejudice appears to be most prevalent among those who are more poorly educated, have the lowest incomes, and live in high-crime neighborhoods. To an even more important degree, however, the problem is symbolic. In neighborhoods filled with people suffering from a sense of social injustice and exclusion, many residents will reach the conclusion that the neighborhood is being policed not for the purpose of maintaining law and order but for the purpose of maintaining the status quo.

In order to gain the general confidence and acceptance of a community, personnel within a police department should be representative of the community as a whole. But the need for competent minority group officers is more than a symbolic one. The frequent contact of white officers with officers from minority groups on an equal basis can help to reduce stereotyping and prejudice of white officers. Minority officers can provide to a department an understanding of minority groups, their languages, and subcultures, that it often does not have today. This obviously has great practical benefits to successful policing. In some cities, for example, the lack of knowledge of Spanish has led to conflicts between the police and Spanish-speaking people.[22] Personal knowledge of minority groups and slum neighborhoods can lead to information not otherwise available, to earlier anticipa-

tion of trouble, and to increased solution of crime.

Police officers have testified to the special competence of Negro officers in Negro neighborhoods. For example, while a study in Philadelphia found that commanding officers were divided as to whether Negro policemen are more effective in Negro neighborhoods than white policemen, more than three-fourths of the patrolmen thought that Negro policemen did better jobs. The reasons given include: they get along better with, and receive more respect from, the Negro residents; they receive less trouble from Negro residents; they can get more information; and they understand Negro citizens better.[23]

· · · · ·

But the same standards for selection which must be demanded of white officers must also be required of minority officers for equivalent positions. While the mere addition of policemen from minority groups will undoubtedly improve police-community relations, it will not end hostility to the police if such officers are prejudiced or abusive. The University of California survey found substantial hostility to Negro officers among Negroes in San Diego and Philadelphia on the ground that they were harsher than white officers.[24] Kephart's study of the Philadelphia Police Department found that many white and Negro officers said that the latter were harsher with Negroes. This study also found that many Negro officers were indignant and ashamed because of the high number of Negro offenders. There is even some evidence that in some places, low-income Negroes prefer white policemen because of the severe conduct of Negro officers.[25] Observations of consultants in

[22] Joseph E. Lohman and Gordon E. Misner, *The Police and the Community* (Berkeley: University of California, 1966).

[23] Kephart, *op. cit.*
[24] Lohman and Misner, *op. cit.*
[25] Elliott M. Rudwick, "The Unequal Badge: Negro Policemen in the South" (Atlanta: Southern Regional Council, 1962), p. 11.

several cities revealed proportionally at least as much physical abuse by Negro officers as by white officers.[26]

The need for greater numbers of qualified minority group officers in nearly all police departments in communities with substantial minority group populations is easily documented. A 1962 survey by the U.S. Civil Rights Commission of all cities with Negro populations of over 5,000 showed that 124 cities in the South and the border States had 1,128 Negro officers. There was 1 Negro officer for every 3,125 Negroes, in contrast to 1 white officer for every 490 whites, a disproportion of over 6 to 1. The number of Negro officers has risen in many southern cities since 1954, but the disproportionate representation of white officers remains extreme.

One hundred and six northern and western cities had a total of 2,937 Negro officers in 1962. This was 1 Negro officer for every 1,351 Negroes, in contrast to 1 white officer for every 442 whites.

The reasons for under-representation / In most large cities, police officials are genuinely interested in attracting more officers from minority groups—Puerto Ricans and Mexican-Americans as well as Negroes. But, there can be little doubt that in many communities, both in the North and South, discrimination in the selection of officers has occurred in the past and exists today. There are very striking and puzzling differences in the percentage of Negroes employed by police departments. For example, in New York City, the standards are approximately the same for employment in the New York City Police Department and for policemen for the City Housing Authority. Yet, the former has approximately 6 percent Negroes, the latter 55 percent. The Illinois State Police had, in 1962, eight times the number of Negro officers as the next highest state police agency.

Furthermore, some police departments have dramatically increased their proportion of officers of minority groups within relatively short periods of time. For example, Philadelphia increased the percentage of Negroes on the force from 3.6 percent in 1952 to 13.6 percent in 1956. In Pittsburgh, the percentage of Negro police doubled between 1952 and 1962. And in Chicago the percentage quadrupled between 1952 and 1961.

Past discrimination or even the belief that discrimination does or has existed has much the same effect as actual, present discrimination. Thus, the President's Commission on Crime in the District of Columbia found that although the Metropolitan Police Department's policy was opposed to discrimination, "we doubt that many Negro citizens believe that the policy is being vigorously implemented." Plainly, such a prevalent view hinders recruitment.

Even in the absence of discrimination, a substantial discrepancy would remain. Of 117 departments with acknowledged difficulty in recruiting nonwhites, 48 said that the problem was too few applicants and 83 noted failure to pass the examination and meet other standards. The same factors underlying the disproportionate failure of members of minority groups in the selective service examination and other written tests operate in police recruitment. In Miami, the number of Negro officers dropped from 85 in 1959 to 74 in 1962, apparently because the recruiting standards for Negroes, which had been lower, were raised to match those for whites. Negro leaders in Miami have reported that one reason for the reduced number of Negroes was that most Negroes cannot meet the present entrance requirements because of

[26] Albert J. Reiss, Jr., "The Use of Physical Force in Police Work" (Ann Arbor: University of Michigan, 1966), p. 10, report prepared for President's Commission on Law Enforcement and Administration of Justice.

inferior economic and educational background.

In Philadelphia, a study completed in 1957 found that about 50 percent of applicants for the police department were Negro. While a somewhat higher percentage of Negroes than whites failed the physical examination or had a criminal record, most of the discrepancy in the relative proportion of Negroes selected was a result of written examination. Some of the key personnel on the Civil Service Commission, which gave the tests, were Negro, and the tests were apparently given fairly. The study concluded that educational deficiencies were the main reason for the failure of Negroes to qualify.

The manner in which discrimination and educational deficiencies can operate together to interfere with increased recruitment of Negroes is shown by a study of selection procedures in Detroit. Of the 1,566 applicants for the Detroit police force in 1959, there were 434 Negroes. This approximated the proportion of Negroes in the city. Of this group, 71 whites and 2 Negroes were eventually selected.

An investigation by the Commission on Community Relations found that 178 whites but only 36 Negroes were allowed to pass the preliminary screening even though they failed to meet one or more qualifying criteria. More than a score of the whites and none of the Negroes from this group were eventually employed. The Commission found that white applicants were favored in this process.

Despite the fact that the anonymity of the individual was maintained in processing the written examination, 49 percent of the whites and 80 percent of the Negroes failed.

Of the remaining 115 whites and 11 Negroes, 4 whites and 4 Negroes were eliminated by preliminary oral interviews. The Commission found that the decision to drop two of the Negroes was questionable. Ten whites and one Negro were then dropped on the basis of a background investigation. Of the 101 whites and 6 Negroes who appeared before the Oral Examination Board, 71 whites and 2 Negroes passed. The Commission again questioned the subjective reasons used to drop two of the Negroes.

Remedies

Any program to increase the proportion of members of minority group police officers must begin by persuading qualified candidates to apply. However, the hostility of Negroes to police forces is so strong that Negro officers are frequently disliked by their fellow Negroes. And Spanish-speaking persons have traditionally regarded policing as not an appropriate occupation. Consequently, the problem of attracting candidates requires police departments to improve all aspects of police relations with minority groups.

On the other hand, the unattractiveness of police work to minority groups should not be overemphasized. Negroes frequently apply in substantial numbers. A recent survey of three precincts in Washington by the Bureau of Social Science Research found that 54 percent of the Negro men responding, in contrast to 50 percent of the white males, disagreed with the statement that "a man would make a mistake if he became a policeman."

Improvement of recruitment techniques / Police forces generally rely heavily upon referrals from their own members as a source for qualified recruits. A study in St. Louis showed that 42 percent of applicants and 57 percent of those appointed were referred by precinct police officers. Since relatively few police officers are from minority groups, referrals are an inadequate source of minority group candidates. Consequently, new recruiting techniques must be developed. Particular effort must be made to recruit minority members from low income areas because differences in attitudes and opinions frequently separate middle- and low-income persons within the same minority groups almost as much as persons of different races.

Promotions

Increasing the number of ranking officers from minority groups is as important as, and closely related to, recruiting new officers of minority group background. Successful recruitment and promotion opportunities are obviously interdependent. For example, in one western city, three Negro officers left a city department after failing to get promotions and joined the county sheriff's department where all were promoted, one reaching the rank of captain. This story is still being told by Negroes as one reason for Negroes not seeking employment in the city department.

There is an even more marked disproportion of minority group supervisory personnel than of minority group officers generally throughout the police service. A survey in 1952–53 of 19 of the 25 largest departments in the country showed that there were only 40 Negro sergeants, 14 lieutenants, and 1 captain. Negroes constituted 3.8 percent of the patrolmen, 1.1 percent of the sergeants, 0.9 percent of the lieutenants, 0.2 percent of the captains, and 0 percent of higher ranks.[27]

The 1962 survey of the Civil Rights Commission of localities with a Negro population of over 5,000 showed that Negroes were still seriously underrepresented at command and supervisory levels. In the southern and border States, 30 departments had a total of 70 Negro sergeants; 8 communities had a total of 9 Negro lieutenants; only St. Louis and Kansas City, Mo., had Negro captains.

The following table compares the the ratio of white supervisory officers to

[27] Kephart, op. cit.

white officers generally and Negro supervisory officers to Negro officers in southern and border State cities:

	Sergeants	Lieutenants	Captains
White	1:8	1:20	1:37
Negro	1:16	1:125	1:246

In the 106 northern cities responding, 6 had a total of 9 Negro captains, 17 had a total of 26 Negro lieutenants, and 48 had a total of 141 Negro sergeants. The following table compares the number of white and Negro supervisory officers to white and Negro officers generally in these cities:

	Sergeants	Lieutenants	Captains
White	1:9	1:25	1:45
Negro	1:20	1:108	1:311

Thus, Negro officers have been unsuccessful in gaining higher rank outside of the South.

Removal of discriminatory policies / The recruitment of minority groups requires that all forms of discrimination in the selection of officers be ended. Indeed, even the appearance of discrimination must be eliminated if members of minority groups are not to be discouraged from applying. This can be accomplished by screening personnel officers with particular care for prejudice. Written examinations should be analyzed to ensure no cultural or other bias against minority groups exist.

Officers from minority groups should participate in the selection process. For example, in Washington, D.C., a Negro physician is on the four-man board which screens for medical and psychological problems; and in New York, two of the three highest ranking Negroes examine all rejections of minority applicants subject to the final determination of the Commissioner. Minority officers should, whenever feasible, serve on personnel interviewing boards both to prevent discrimination and to observe strong points of minority applicants which other officers might miss.

In addition, no recruiting drive can succeed as long as police departments discriminate against their own minority officers. In some police departments the legal powers vested in an officer depend on whether he is white or Negro. For example, a 1961 survey found that 28 police departments (31 percent of those surveyed) restricted the right of Negroes to make felony arrests. In 18 of the departments, the officer could hold a white suspect until a white policeman appeared; if none was available, the Negro officer could make the felony arrest. In 10 others, the Negro officer could not arrest a white suspect at all, although 3 required the Negro policeman to keep the suspect under surveillance. The power of Negro officers to arrest for misdemeanors was even more limited.

In only 11 of 41 sheriffs' departments surveyed in the southern and border States could Negro officers arrest a white felon. In three northern counties, Negro deputies were allowed to arrest white felon suspects only if a white deputy was not immediately available. An earlier survey of the South in 1959, which covered a greater number of small communities, found that over half required Negro officers to call white officers to arrest a white suspect.

As described, many police forces appear to have denied equal opportunity for promotion to members of minority groups. Officers from minority groups have often been segregated by being denied entrance to specialized units, by being usually assigned to Negro areas, by being required to patrol with members of their own race, by being assigned to a separate shift or even by having lockers in a different room. They have often been made to feel unwelcome or have been harassed by other officers. In many communities, Negro officers have been discouraged from participating in policemen's associations or have been completely excluded. All these actions have significantly affected the morale and attitudes of minority officers and have surely served as a negative influence on attracting minority group persons to seek careers in police service.

33. THE POLITICS OF GRAPES

Peter Matthiesson

By summer's end in 1970, Cesar Chavez had led
the United Farm Workers' Organizing Committee to
negotiated contracts with virtually all the wine and
table grape growers in the United States; lettuce growers
were the next group to recognize and negotiate with the union.
Though the total campaign had by no means ended, Chavez'
victories along the way to his goal of obtaining decent wages
and working conditions for all migrant farm workers were the
most significant gains migrant laborers had ever made. They
were also the first example of the successful mass moblization
of Mexican-Americans.

These were no mean accomplishments, despite the
subsequent emergence in urban areas of younger leaders who
sometimes claimed that Chavez had not demanded sufficiently
sweeping changes. Moreover, urban problems were different
from the rural ones, and perhaps Chavez himself had not
devoted enough attention to the prospect that increasing
technological sophistication in agriculture would, over time,
decrease the size of the migrant labor force, adding to the
ranks of the unemployed and underemployed in Mexican-
American ghettoes. Furthermore, though California was
changing, Texas, the state with the second largest Mexican-
American population, had hardly been touched. Perhaps the
formation of a new political entity, *La Raza Unida* (The United
People), could someday consolidate a solidary swing vote
to win concessions there.

In some ways, Chavez' movement has been analogous to
the Southern civil rights movement under Martin Luther King's
leadership. Both placed strong emphasis on nonviolence; both

Source: *Sal Si Puedes: Escape If You Can* (New York: Random
House, 1969), pp. 346–70. Copyright © 1969, by Peter Matthiesson.
Reprinted by permission of the publisher. A substantial porton of this
material originally appeared in *The New Yorker*.
PETER MATTHIESSON is a professional writer and journalist.

had to face the opposition of state authorities and police forces that were clearly aligned on the side of landowners and of entire agricultural industries that were key parts of state economies; both attempted to make changes within the framework of the established socioeconomic order without attempting to overthrow it; and both depended for their successes on the support of outside groups—a few allies in Washington, the leadership of the United Auto Workers, and much larger numbers of sympathetic ordinary people who saw no reason why such naked exploitation and repression should continue. The analogy is not perfect, however. California never depended on naked terror and force as much as, say, Mississippi and Alabama; UFWOC did all of its own organizing work without shock troops, whereas King's Southern Christian Leadership Conference often followed (and sometimes fought with or occasionally held back) the Student National Coordinating Committee; and while King was a well-educated son of a moderately well-off minister, Chavez is literally a man of his people, a son of migrant workers, and an ex-migrant worker himself.

It is quite possible that there will be one more significant similarity. As the civil rights movement shifted to Northern cities, it became replaced by black power, more radical and more self-consciously assertive; as Chicano solidarity shifts from field to ghetto, it gives every indication of being replaced by brown power. Just a few more excessive or careless police actions like those which precipitated the Denver, 1969, and East Los Angeles September, 1970, disturbances will practically guarantee it; and we shall have another opportunity to witness the ambivalence and probable failure of what Oppenheimer, in Selection 4 called the "two-war strategy."

The selection begins with some extracts from the Congressional Record that are useful background materials for placing UFWOC's efforts in full context.

[From the *Congressional Record,* Oct. 11, 1968]

Mr. WILLIAMS of New Jersey.

The growers say that 90 percent of their workers are local people, not migrants, and that they have year-round work in table grapes. The figures of the Farm Labor Service say something else. There are three major work periods in table grapes; in Kern County, Calif., in 1967–68, for example:

Pruning and tieing peak: December 18–January 27, 6 weeks, 3,200 workers needed at peak.

Thinning and girdling peak: May 13–

June 1, 3 weeks, 3,500 workers needed at peak.

Harvest peak: August 7–September 2, 4 weeks, 6,000 workers needed at peak.

There are migrants at work in each of these seasons. At the peak of the harvest approximately 50 percent of the fieldworkers are migrants. At other times of the year there is less work; for example, October 28, 1967: 3,000 workers; December 2, 1967: 200 workers; February 24, 1968: 200 workers; March 30, 1968: 0 workers; July 13, 1968: 800 workers. In the United States, there are well over 1 million migratory seasonal workers. In California, there are over 200,000— about one-third migrants and two-thirds local seasonals.

Opponents of the union say that California grape workers make $2.50 per hour and more. It is true that some workers earn more than $2 per hour during certain parts of the harvest season. Of course, the work is backbreaking. But the harvest season is short and families should live in decency year-around. Through the whole year, day in and day out, hourly wages in California agriculture average $1.62. Even this low wage level has been reached as a result of union pressure for higher wages, and the recent termination of the *bracero* importation program. Add to these low wages the seasonal nature of farm labor and it is then easy to understand why annual income for male farmworkers in California is just under $2,000 and family income is between $2,500 and $3,000 per year.

Average hourly wage for all farmworkers —including year-around hired hands—in 1967 was $1.33 for the entire Nation, and $1.62 for California.

In 1965, average hourly earnings of farmworkers in the United States and California was one-half that of factory workers.

Average annual earnings for migrant workers in the Nation in 1967 was $1,307.

The average migrant only finds 82 days of farmwork a year and supplements his meager income with other low-paid work. Very few workers get any free food, transportation, or housing. Even for those who do, the value does not come close to the paid insurance, vacations, and other fringe benefits common in America.

Growers say that the migrant is surviving and working. Death rates of migrant farmworkers as a percent of the national rates in 1967 are shocking:

Infant mortality: 125 percent higher than the national rate.

Maternal mortality: 125 percent higher than the national rate.

Influenza and pneumonia: 200 percent higher than the national rate.

Tuberculosis and other infectious diseases: 260 percent higher than the national rate.

Accidents: 300 percent higher than the national rate.

Life expectancy for migrants is 49 years, as opposed to 70 for all others.

Wages paid farmhands are only a small part of food costs; for example:

	Cents
Retail price in 1965	
Lettuce (per head)	21
Lemons (per pound)	24
Field labor cost in 1956	
Lettuce (per head)	1.2
Lemons (apiece)	0.8

Farmworkers are specifically excluded from unemployment insurance and collective bargaining laws. They are discriminated against in minimum wage coverage—$1.15 for farmworkers, $1.60 for others—and social security laws. Children working in agriculture are excluded from child labor and school attendance laws. Without contracts, farmworkers do not have protections that other workers take for granted; for example, job security, overtime pay, holidays and vacations with pay, sanitary toilets and drinking water, health insurance, grievance procedure, rest periods, and so forth.

The growers, expecting sympathy from a Nixon Administration, were lobbying for new farm labor legislation, and on April 16 Dolores Huerta, Jerry

Cohen and Robert McMillen, the Union's legislative representative in Washington, appeared before the Subcommittee on Labor of the Senate Committee on Labor and Public Welfare, which was holding hearings on a new bill to include farm workers under the National Labor Relations Act. Other farm workers, from Wisconsin, Texas, Florida and Colorado, also testified. Mrs. Huerta read a general statement by Chavez, who could not be present; he was concerned about the illusory protection that the NLRB would give to farm workers unless the new union was at least temporarily exempted from the Taft-Hartley and Landrum-Griffin amendments, which would deprive it of the only weapons at its disposal, and thus legislate it out of existence. "Under the complex and time-consuming procedures of the National Labor Relations Board, growers can litigate us to death; forced at last by court order to bargain with us in good faith, they can bargain in good faith—around the calendar if need be—unless we are allowed to apply sufficient economic power to make it worth their while to sign.

"We want to be recognized, yes, but not with a glowing epitaph on our tombstone."

Unfortunately, the Union had not publicized its position on the NLRA before the hearings, and Chavez's resistance was misunderstood and resented, even by some segments of the press that had been sympathetic. Inevitably, the growers and their spokesmen ridiculed his fear that the "protection" of the NLRA might legislate his union out of existence. "By opposing various measures newly introduced in Congress to improve the bargaining position of farm workers, the head of UFWOC[1] has shown up his cause for what it is: neither peace-loving nor compassionate, but a ruthless grab for power," cried an editorial in *Barron's* on June 2; in this

same issue, three months after AWFWA[2] had been exposed as a disreputable fake, *Barron's* was still taking it seriously. Meanwhile the growers were spending hundreds of thousands of dollars on anti-Chavez propaganda prepared by expensive advertising firms, including an attack by the president of the California Grape and Tree Fruit League which blamed UFWOC for "the terror tactics visited upon the grocery outlets of this nation"; he referred to the fire bombings at A&P stores in New York City in October 1968 which the Union long ago admitted were probably the work of misguided sympathizers. Out of context, *Barron's* quoted from Chavez's "Marxist" response to the League's attack: "While we do not belittle or underestimate our adversaries, for they are the rich and the powerful and possess the land, we are not afraid or cringe from the confrontation. We welcome it! We have planned for it. We know that our cause is just, that history is a story of social revolution, and that the poor shall inherit the land." The word "revolution" is the key to *Barron's* uneasiness, but the truth is that the United Farm Workers have never asked for land reforms, nor considered revolt against the American Way of Life; they ask only for a share in it.

An example of what *Barron's* means by legislation "newly introduced in Congress to improve the bargaining position of farm workers" is the "Food Profits Protection Act," sponsored by a legislator who has called the farm workers' strike "dishonest."

WASHINGTON, Apr. 30 [1969] (AP)—Senator George Murphy (Rep., Cal.) Tuesday unveiled a plan that he said would protect customers and agriculture from persons he called "of narrow interest, limited vision," such as organizers of the California grape boycott . . .

[1] [United Farm Workers Organizing Committee—Ed.]

[2] [Agricultural Workers Freedom to Work Association, a grower-controlled counterthrust to UFWOC—Ed.]

Murphy said his bill would safeguard production and marketing of food products from labor disputes and provide "an orderly system within which agricultural workers may organize and bargain collectively."

He would prohibit secondary boycotts, efforts to persuade a farmer to join a union or employer organization or to recognize or bargain with an uncertified union, picketing at retail stores, and inducements to employers not to handle or work on an agricultural commodity after it leaves the farm.

"Strikes at farms are not permitted if the strike may reasonably be expected to result in permanent loss or damage to the crop," Murphy said.

He said that he expects to get President Nixon's endorsement of his plan but has not solicited it . . .

President Nixon endorsed instead a plan attributed to his Secretary of Labor, Mr. Schultz, under the terms of which farm workers would remain excluded from the jurisdiction and protection of the NLRB but would be subject to the strike-killing provisions of the Taft-Hartley amendment that forbid secondary boycotts and organizational picketing; a special "Farm Labor Relations Board" could delay any strike at harvest time (in farm labor disputes, a strike at any other time is a waste of effort) with a thirty-day period of grace that could be invoked at the discretion of the grower. After thirty days, when the harvest in any given field would be largely completed, the workers could strike to their heart's content.

The Nixon plan was strongly criticized by Senator Walter Mondale of Minnesota, who had taken over from Senator Harrison Williams as head of the Subcommittee on Migratory Labor, and by Senator Edward Kennedy, who had inherited a vested interest in *la causa* from his brothers. Mondale and Kennedy led the dignitaries who assembled, on May 18, to greet a company of strikers who had trudged one hundred

miles in a 100-degree heat from Coachella to Calexico, to dramatize their protest against the unrestrained importation of poor Mexicans to swamp their own efforts to better their lot. Cesar Chavez addressed the rally in Calexico, and so did Senator Kennedy: a country that could spend $30 billion every year on a senseless war, send men to the moon and present rich farmers with millions of dollars in subsidies for crops they do not grow, Kennedy said, could afford to raise the standard of living of the poor who fed the nation. Both Kennedy and Mondale pledged themselves to a fight for new green-card [3] legislation.

The strike in Coachella began ten days later, on May 28. Over one hundred local workers manned the picket lines, and though the harvest had scarcely started, another two hundred walked out in the first two days. Many signed affidavits of the sort required to certify a strike, and thereby make illegal the importation of scab labor into that field, but this year the two observers from Mr. Schultz's Department of Labor refused to interview striking workers or inspect their affidavits. When David Averbuck, the Union attorney, protested to the department's regional director, he was told that "orders from Washington" forbade the Labor officials to investigate or certify strikes: unless the strikes are decreed official, there is no legal recourse against the wholesale importation of Mexican strikebreakers. Since an estimated fifty thousand workers are available in this border region, with only three thousand needed to harvest the grapes, the strikers would be giving up their jobs for nothing.

Averbuck was also told that the federal men would make no investigations whatever but would base all decisions on the reports of inspectors sent by Governor Reagan. One of the latter declared

[3] [An entry and work permit for Mexican nationals coming as farm laborers to the United States—Ed.]

frankly that the state men would not interview the strikers either. They were willing to accept signed affidavits, which would then be made available to the growers; if the growers used the affidavits to compose a blacklist, that was no concern of theirs.

Averbuck, a cynical young man not easily surprised by perfidy, was stunned. "It's a Nixon-Reagan conspiracy to screw the farm workers and to help the growers recruit workers illegally," he said. "It's so blatant it's unbelievable."

In any case, the Coachella strike got off to a slow start, and the growers, emboldened by open federal and state support, were making the same old arguments. "If my workers wanted me to sit down at the negotiating table, I would," said a Coachella grower interviewed by a *New York Times* reporter in early June. "But my workers don't want Union recognition. If they did, they would have walked out and joined the strike."

But one of his workers, interviewed in the same report, refuted him. "I belong to the Union but I'm working here because I have bills to pay. The Union can't pay them and I can't work anywhere else. A lot of people like me are forced to do this. How can you stand on a picket line when your family is hungry! It's hard for me to work here when the Union is out there picketing, but I can't help it."

By the time I returned to Delano in late July 1969, the strikers were back from the Coachella Valley and were preparing for the harvest in Lamont. Dave Averbuck was convinced that the campaign in Coachella had been a great success, whereas Jim Drake, while acknowledging progress on all fronts (including fair treatment from the Riverside County police, who did much to prevent the violence of the previous year's campaign), was sorry to come back without a contract. Everyone agreed, however, that

most or all of the Coachella Valley would be under Union contract before a single grape was harvested in 1970, and although much the same thing was said last year, the evidence for this year's confidence is much better. Grape sales were off 15 percent, and even those chain stores that were still selling grapes have used the boycott as an excuse for paying the growers so little that many grapes were left unharvested. As a group, the Coachella growers were admitting that they had been badly hurt, though a few still refused to be led from the burning barn. "The Union's boycott has failed," Mike "Bozo" Bozick declared manfully on July 11, the day after the local agricultural commissioner estimated that 750,000 boxes of Coachella grapes had been left in the fields to rot, and one week after eighty-one of his fellow grape growers filed suit against UFWOC, claiming boycott damages of $25 million.

A turning point, not only in the Coachella campaign but in the four-year strike, was a sit-in, in early June, by Filipino strikers at Bozick's Bagdasarian Grape Company's labor camp Number 2 that led to a wave of sit-ins at other ranches. By the time Bozick had the last holdouts evicted and arrested a few days later, the Union had won its most significant victory since the Schenley capitulation in 1966,[4] and Dolores Huerta gave much credit for this to the Filipinos of Bagdasarian. "Their courage, their actions, may have been the final straw that scared the growers into opening discussions," she said.

On Friday the thirteenth of June, ten growers, who claimed to represent 15 percent of the state's table-grape production, held a press conference at Indio at which they declared willingness to negotiate with the Union. Their spokesman was Lionel Steinberg, whose Douglas

[4] [The first major breakthrough on wine, not table, grapes. Wines, of course, are branded, and it is relatively easy for consumers to avoid given brands selectively—Ed.]

Freedman Ranch is the biggest in Coachella. Steinberg, acknowledging publicly that the boycott had been costly, said, "If we have a conference and discussions with the Union and we see that there is a give-and-take attitude on their part, there is no question that we are prepared to recognize UFWOC as the collective-bargaining agent."

Five of the growers were from Arvin-Lamont, the next area to be harvested, and the spokesman for the Arvin group was John J. Kovacevich, who had been holding private talks with Jerry Cohen ever since March. Publicly Kovacevich was still fulminating about the "illegal and immoral boycott," but this did not spare him the damnation of the Delano growers, led by Martin Zaninovich and Jack Pandol, who said that the 93 percent of the table-grape industry that they spoke for would fight Chavez to the end rather than sell out the consumer. The actions of the ten, according to Pandol, were "un-American and un-Christian," an opinion apparently shared by the unknown Christians who attempted to gouge out the eye of one of the ten, William Mosesian, in a night attack outside his house, and burned a stack of wooden grape boxes belonging to another, Milton Karahadian, in the Coachella Valley. Grower Howard Marguleas was warned not to set foot in Delano, John Kovacevich was snubbed by friends in Top's Coffee Shop in Lamont, and Lionel Steinberg, after years of membership, resigned from the California Grape and Tree Fruit League due to the viciousness of the League's attempts to defame the ten growers and sabotage the negotiations.

The Union, of course, had welcomed the meetings, which began on June 20 in the Federal Building in Los Angeles; the negotiations were supervised by three officials of the Federal Mediation and Conciliation Service of the Department of Labor, whose job it was to keep them from breaking down. Most of the ten growers were present at most of the meetings, which continued until July 3; the Union was represented by Jerry Cohen, Dolores Huerta, Larry Itliong and Philip Vera Cruz, and by Irwin de Shettler, an observer for the AFL-CIO. At the last conference, on July 3, the ten were joined by Bruno Dispoto of Delano. Dispoto had been hurt that spring in Arizona, but many Union people felt that he had been sent in by other Delano growers to find out what was going on. Bruno, introduced to Dolores before the meeting, said, "I haven't seen you since the old days on the picket line."

The talks were recessed for the Fourth of July and have not been resumed. There had been inevitable differences (wage scales, Union hiring halls, jurisdiction of workers, safety clauses, and other matters), but the one that derailed the talks was the matter of pesticides. The growers agreed to abide by the lax state and federal laws regarding the use of dangerous chemicals so long as the Union did "not embark on any program which will in any way harm the industry to which the employer is a member." This clause, which also gave immunity to the nonnegotiating growers, would stifle all campaigns by the Union against pesticide abuses, including the matter of chemical residues on grapes; it was presented in the form of an ultimatum by the growers' negotiator, a fruit wholesaler named Al Kaplan, and was promptly rejected by the Union. The growers retired to think things over. At a press conference a week later, they denounced the Union for its bad faith and demanded a new "fact-finding commission," to be appointed by President Nixon. (The growers' charges were excited, but it is true that the Union was not overly accommodating: except on very favorable terms, a settlement with a small part of the industry was simply not worth the inevitable weakening of the boycott.)

The bad news was received in the Union offices with a certain levity—"We were very upset," Cesar says, "but what could we do? We just made jokes." The growers' demand seemed to bear out certain people in the Union who suspected that the breakdown of negotiations had been planned from the start as an excuse to go to the Nixon Administration for help. But Dolores Huerta was convinced that most of the ten growers were serious, and so was Jerry Cohen. "One night, you know, like it was maybe two in the morning, and everybody was worn out, and Kaplan was still abusing us with all this bullshit, and there was this popcorn on the table, so I started to eat popcorn. And finally the things he was saying got so stupid that I started to crunch the popcorn, and the stupider he got, the louder I crunched, you know, just to bug him. Well, our side was trying like hell not to laugh, especially Dolores, and Kaplan was beginning to get sore, and finally this grower named Howard Marguleas couldn't stand it any more—he flipped. He said, 'How can you be so rude! Here we are trying to settle something which is very serious, and you sit there eating popcorn that way, and all you Union people smirking!' So there was this silence for a minute, I was sitting there like I had lockjaw, and then I said, 'Can I swallow, Howard?' Well, this just about broke Dolores up, and the meeting too, but anyway, Howard is usually a pretty calm guy, and the incident told me a lot about the strain they were under and about how serious they were about finding a solution."

In mid-July, as the negotiations broke down, Senator Mondale's subcommittee was advised in Washington that the Department of Defense, by its own estimate, would ship eight times as many grapes to Vietnam in 1969 as in any previous year. Like the chain stores, the Defense Department was getting a bargain on the grapes, but in the opinion of the Union, this was no more the reason for the incredible jump in grape consumption than the dehumanized excuse of "increased troop acceptance" that issued like a machine chit from the Pentagon. Claiming the usual collusion within the military-industrial establishment, the Union filed suit against the Defense Department for taking sides in a labor dispute in contravention of its own stated policies: in effect, using public funds to offer a "market of last resort" to a special-interest group.

The Mondale hearings, which continued until August 1, later heard testimony from Jerry Cohen that the growers were using dangerous chemicals in dangerous ways and in dangerous amounts, among them Thiodan, which caused the recent fish kill in the Rhine, and Amino Triazole, residues of which, ten years before in New Jersey, caused the confiscation of wholesale lots of cranberries. By common estimate, it had taken the cranberry industry nine years to recover from the public scare, and the Union did not introduce this evidence without having given the growers a chance to regulate their own practices and come to some satisfactory arrangement about pesticides without being committed to a Union contract. But the growers had not bothered to respond to this offer from Chavez in January, and when, after negotiations had fallen apart on the pesticide issue, Cohen called John Kovacevich to advise him of his intention to bring up the use of Amino Triazole at the Senate hearings, Kovacevich thanked him for the warning but could not bring the growers to act on it. As Averbuck says, "Sometimes they seem to want us to do exactly what we don't want to do, which is to put them out of business."

Cohen told the senators about reports from Micronesia of decreased cannibal acceptance of American missionaries; the poisonous residues in American bodies had become so great, he said, pointing a finger at Senator Henry Bellmon of Oklahoma, that "you are no longer fit for human consumption." Subsequently, an official of the FDA testified that Mr. Cohen's remarks were accurate enough, but that his agency was ready and able to protect the public against grapes with chemical residues that exceeded the federal tolerance level. Asked by Senator Mondale for the tolerance level on the pesticide known as aldrin, he said, "One tenth of a part per million." The senator then submitted a laboratory report obtained by the Union on two batches of grapes purchased the day before at a Safeway store in Washington, D.C. One batch, carrying the label of Bozo Bozick's Bagdasarian Fruit Company, contained aldrin residues of 1.4 parts per million, or fourteen times the permissible amount; another batch from Bianco Fruit Company carried eighteen parts, or one hundred and eighty times the federal tolerance level.

"They won't understand that we will not compromise on the pesticide issue, that we will give up wage increases first," Chavez said. "They're just not ready yet to negotiate seriously; they need more pressure, and they're going to get it. But I think some of them were serious. Jerry and John Kovacevich were able to talk like human beings, right from the start; if Kovacevich had done their negotiating for them, we might have hammered out a contract in two days."

Like all his people, Chavez was upset by the damage that the growers' recalcitrance is doing to the industry. "The longer the boycott continues, the more damage will be done. We *still* hear of people boycotting Schenley, you know, even after they are told that the Schenley boycott has been over for two and half years."

As of early August, Union people agree that a meaningful settlement of the California grape strike is unlikely in 1969, since contracts could not be written in time to help the growers; even the ones most likely to sign would probably prefer to hold out until the spring of 1970, in the hope of legislative help from the Nixon Administration. If that help is not forthcoming, however, the Coachella growers will probably give in, and once Coachella falls, the Arvin-Lamont area will fall too. The Delano growers have a longer season and are better equipped with cold-storage sheds, but it seems doubtful, even so, that they could compete indefinitely with Union competitors who are not harassed by the boycott (although how the boycott will be made selective without losing its impact remains a problem). And if Delano falls, so will all the ranches to the north, because Delano is the heart of the resistance to its own foremost citizen, Cesar Chavez.

Even if the present talks remain suspended, their implications are momentous for the Union. The precedent for negotiation is a gaping crack in the monolithic wall that the growers have shored up for four years, and that crack can only erode faster and faster. *Hay más tiempo que vida,* as Chavez says, and time is on his side.

34. EPILOGUE TO *LA RAZA*

Stan Steiner

One of the hallmarks of a people's subordination is
the absence of strong, stable organizations involving
many individuals in regular activities and providing
opportunities to share decision-making and leadership;
rather, organizations are short-term and sporadic, involving
individuals on their own behalf. Because strong, stable
organizations do not exist when group consciousness and
solidarity are just beginning to form, new social movements
among the previously dispossessed frequently have to
depend on the personal leadership of a few outstanding
men. A great leader symbolizes his movement. His
followers identify with his courage and strength, feel
confidence and pride through associating with declarations of
principle he formulates for them, find hope and unexpected
reservoirs of resourcefulness as fruits of accomplishments they
win together. Moreover, the leader's outstanding qualities often
help to dispel the negative stereotypes of the group that are
common among majority outsiders.

Yet movements may be vulnerable precisely because they
depend so much on particular individuals. Leaders may sell
out, or may lose their thrust and drive, or may turn dishonest,
or, finally, they may die or be murdered. Therefore, as
movements gain strength, leaders who are farsighted usually
try to build organizations both firm and genuine enough to
continue effective pursuit of the goals for which they were
founded after their originators have passed from the scene.

Rodolfo Gonzales is another Chicano leader who is
attempting to construct a firm autonomous organizational

Source: "The Poet in the Boxing Ring," in *La Raza: The Mexican
Americans* (New York: Harper and Row, 1969), pp. 378–92. Copyright
© 1969, 1970 by Stan Steiner. Reprinted by permission of the publisher
and Rodolfo Gonzales.

STAN STEINER, professional writer and journalist, is also the author
of *The New Indians*.

foundation that the nascent group pride and idenity of his people can build upon. Gonzales' efforts in Denver are already of great importance as a model for what Mexican-Americans have been able to accomplish for themselves in a major urban area. The model will become still more important in the future, as the Chicano population goes on becoming more and more urbanized.

He "lurked like a cat for the kill." The ritual lingo of the boxing ring described the fighting style of a young intellectual who read Lorca in the dressing room, and who fought seventy-five professional bouts and won sixty-five of them. He fought with the desperation of a kid from the barrios. The crowds savored the blood that dripped from his eyes, his lips, his bronzed face. "A crowd pleaser," one boxing buff recalls.

"Rodolfo is a gentle man," his wife says. "He is a poet."

In a poem he wrote later, an epic of the "La Raza revolution" that he titled "I Am Joaquín," the lyrical fighter remembered his own bleeding as a symbol.

I bleed as the vicious gloves of hunger
 cut my face and eyes,
As I fight my way from the stinking barrios
 to the glamor of the Ring
  and lights of fame
   or multilated sorrow.

The Championship of the World was almost his. *Ring Magazine* hailed him as one of the five best boxers of his weight. He was rated the third ranking contender for the World Featherweight title by the National Boxing Association. When Gonzales was still in his teens he had won the National Amateur Championship and the International Championship as well. In the Lysoled corridors of the pugilistic kingdoms of the Mafia he was fingered as the coming "King of the Little Men." He was a "hungry fighter," the connoisseurs of flesh wrote in the sports pages. They did not know he was a poet.

He is a "poet of action" in the ring, the boxing writers wrote unwittingly. Lithe, his mind as quick as his body, he reacted like the reflex of a muscle. He was later to write of a young boxer, Manny, in one of his plays, "His movements are smooth, casual, and catlike." It may have been a self-portrait.

The Golden Boy of the boxing legend, he was to become the new voice of the Chicano movement. He was the idol of his generation, and he shared their frustrations. He was the embodiment of the confused barrio youth, the urban Chicanos.

He quit the ring. In his poem of self-discovery he wrote of the odyssey he embarked upon:

 I am Joaquín
 Lost in a world of confusion,
 Caught up in a whirl of
  Anglo society,
 Confused by the rules,
 Scorned by the attitudes,
 Suppressed by manipulations,
 And destroyed
  by modern life.

Where was he going? He did not know. "It's a long road back to yourself when the society has made you into someone else," he now says. "But I was determined to find my way, to rediscover my roots, to be the man I am, not the emasculated man that the Anglo society wanted me to be."

Rodolfo "Corky" Gonzales lived all the lives that "divide our hearts and emasculate our souls." In his young manhood he became an insurance salesman, a romantic poet, a big-city politician, a campesino in the fields, a soldier, a lumberjack, a playwright, the landlord in the ghetto, the leader of the Poor People's March on Washington, D.C., a high-ranking government official, a lone crusader, the father of eight children, the hero of the newspapers—and the villain, the All-American Boy, the victim of police riots, the descendant of the conquistadors, the "foreign Communist agitator," a political ward heeler, a successful businessman, and a revolutionary.

"The young Chicano is the most complex man in the country." He smiles, self-effacingly. "I guess that means me, too."

He was born in the barrios of Denver, a kid of the streets. Yet he grew up on the earth as well as the cement pavements, for his father was a Mexican emigrant, who worked as a campesino and coal miner in southern Colorado. As a boy he worked in the sugar-beet fields, beside his father, at the age of ten.

"Yes, I am a city man," he says. "But I did a lot of farm work. I have relatives in the villages in the San Luis Valley. Every spring and summer, as a boy, I worked in the fields. Every fall and winter I lived in the city slums."

Schools did not educate him. He learned of life in the fields and barrios. "The teachers taught me how to forget Spanish, to forget my heritage, to forget who I am," he says bitterly. "I went to four grade schools, three junior highs, and two high schools besides, because of our constant moving to the fields and back to the city." Even so, he graduated from high school at sixteen. He remembers working in a slaughterhouse at night and on weekends, so he could afford to go to school. He walked in so much blood that his shoes were always stained.

. . . . .

. . . A hero, Gonzales went into politics, opened a free boxing gymnasium for ghetto youth, was befriended by the mayor, became an after-dinner speaker on inspirational themes. "Like all boys growing up in this society, I identified success by wanting to be an important person loved by everyone."

He became a businessman. In one year he was owner of an automobile insurance agency and owner of a surety-bond business. Within three years, by 1963, he was General Agent for the Summit Fidelity and Surety Company of Colorado.

Once again he was too successful. He was the pride of the barrio. "Corky beat the Anglos with his fists, then he outsmarted them with his brains," a neighbor says. The fair-haired boy wherever he went, the "different" Mexican, he was beckoned with offers of political jobs. Los Voluntarios, a political action group, had been organized in Denver with Gonzales as chairman. "The sleeping giant was awakening."

The poet with scarred eyelids became a ward heeler. He was the first Chicano ever to be a district captain in the Denver Democratic Party at the age of twenty-nine. "Corky has charisma," says a City Hall hanger-on. "He zooms. That boy was a comer." In the presidential election of 1960 he was Colorado coordinator of the "Viva Kennedy" campaign, and his district had the highest Democratic vote in the city. . . .

In no time he was a one-man directory of poverty agencies. He was on the Steering Committee of the Anti-Poverty Program for the Southwest, on the National Board of Jobs for Progress (S.E.R., a major funding group for the barrios), on the Board of the Job Opportunity Center, President of the National

Citizens Committee for Community Relations, and Chairman of the Board of Denver's War on Poverty.

Gonzales was rumored to be in line for state or even national office. The line was long. The Chicano was last in line. On the rising aspirations of the young and pugilistic barrio go-getter there was a political ceiling. And he was not yet poet enough to celebrate his frustrations. The poverty programs had disappointed him, much as party politics had disenchanted him. In the barrios the jobs were just as scarce, the poor just as poor. He attended conferences by the dozens, perhaps feeling the same as he imagined the delegates to the White House's Cabinet Committee hearings on Mexican-American Affairs in El Paso, Texas, felt: "well-meaning, confused, irate, and insulted middle-class Chicanos who knew they were being had when they were asked to swallow and digest the same old soup and cracker disks fed by the politicians, with Johnson and Humphrey at the head of the line. Lacking was any positive direction or militant action. . . . What resulted was a lot of brave words, promises, motions—and no action."

. . . . .

I ride with Revolutionists
against myself.

"The politics of the Anglo emasculates the manhood of a man of La Raza. It makes him impotent, a Tío Taco, an Uncle Tom. I was losing my cool," Gonzales says.

"I was used by the Democratic Party. I was used because I had a rapport with my people. Working in the two-party system I found out one thing, and I found it out very late. My people were exploited and men like I was are . . ." he falters, biting off the sentence. "But I was never bought. I could have accepted a number of payoffs from politicians and administrators. I never accepted them. Our people who get involved become political monsters." He pauses again and says, "Whores."

In his play, *A Cross for Maclovio*, the hero complains, "They're afraid, now they want to buy off our leadership. You stir up people, get them ready for a revolution, and the establishment comes running with a suitcase of pesos." And in his poem, "I Am Joaquín," Gonzales writes:

> I sometimes
> sell my brother out
> and reclaim him
> for my own when society gives me
> token leadership . . .

The Golden Boy was ending his odyssey. When a Denver newspaper attacked him as "almost a thief," it was an insult to his dignity, a betrayal, he thought, of his "manhood." The poverty officials in Washington defended him, denying the accusations, but his friends in City Hall were strangely still. His scathing letter of resignation to the Democratic County Chairman, Dale R. Tooley, reverberated in the barrios of the Southwest.

The individual who makes his way through the political muck of today's world, and more so the minority representatives, suffers from such an immense loss of soul and dignity that the end results are as rewarding as a heart attack, castration, or cancer! . . . You and your cohorts have been accomplices to the destruction of moral man in this society. I can only visualize your goal as complete emasculation of manhood, sterilization of human dignity, and that you not only consciously but purposely are creating a world of lackeys, political bootlickers and prostitutes.

He resigned from the boards and councils of the War on Poverty one by one. He went "home again," he says. "Now I am closer back to home than I ever have been in that I am financially just as bad off as any Chicano," he says.

And now!
I must choose
  Between
the paradox of
Victory of the spirit
despite physical hunger
  Or
to exist in the grasp
of American social neurosis,
sterilization of the soul
and a full stomach.

The odyssey was ended. In an old red-brick building in the condemned barrio of downtown Denver, in 1965, the ex-almost-champion and past-president-of-everything founded *La Crusada Para la Justicia,* the Crusade for Justice. Gonzales declared this was "a movement born out of frustration and determination to secure equality with dignity."

In the politics of the Crusade for Justice there would be no wheeling and dealing. There would be no compromise with stereotypes. "To best serve our particular ethnic and cultural group our organization must be independent, and must not be dependent on the whims and demands of private agencies which are establishment-controlled and dominated. The services offered will not have the taint of paternalism, nor will the feeling of inferiority be felt when securing need, help and guidance."

In a few years, the Crusade was so influential that "the Anglos come to us for our help," Gonzales says. He tells how Archbishop James Casey of Denver came, uninvited, to the Easter "Mexican Dinner" they held. The Archbishop donned a tourist sombrero, told the guests, "Cherish your history, your culture, and preserve your wonderful language," and donated $100 to the Crusade's Building Fund.

The Crusade bought an old church in downtown Denver that resembled a miniature U.S. Treasury. In the colonnaded edifice there is "the most unique Mexican-American center in the country," with a school of "Liberation Classes," a nursery, gymnasium, Mayan Ballroom, Chicano Art Gallery, Mexican shops, library, community dining room and community center, job "skill bank," legal aid service, Barrio Police Review Board, health and housing social workers, athletic leagues, a barrio newspaper [*El Gallo*], a bail bond service, a kitchen and a "Revolutionary Theatre."

"No government money, no grants, no rich angels, no hypocrisy, no begging, no handouts" created El Centro Para La Justicia, boasts Gonzales. "We did it. We can do it. The Crusade is living proof of self-determination. The Crusade is not just an organization; it is the philosophy of nationalism with a human form.

"Nationalism exists in the Southwest, but until now it hasn't been formed into an image people can see. Until now it has been a dream. It has been my job to create a reality out of the dream, to create an ideology out of the longing. Everybody in the barrios is a nationalist, you see, whether he admits it to himself or not. It doesn't matter if he's middle-class, a *vendito,* a sellout, or what his politics may be. He'll come back home, to La Raza, to his heart, if we will build centers of nationalism for him."

In the Southwest, "nationalism is the key to our people liberating themselves," he says.

"Colorado belongs to our people, was named by our people, discovered by our people and worked by our people. We slave in the fields today to put food on your table. We don't preach violence. We preach self-respect and self-defense . . . to reclaim what is ours.

"I am a revolutionary," he says, "because creating life amid death is a revolutionary act. Just as building nationalism in an era of imperialism is a life-giving act. The barrios are beginning to awaken to their own strength. We are an awakening people, an emerging nation, a new breed."

Rodolfo "Corky" Gonzales feels that he has found himself among his people. He is a unique revolutionary in a time of ugliness and hatred in that he devotes his efforts to building his community. He is the happiest revolutionary in the country.

"Now I am my own man. I don't need to prove myself to the Anglos," he says.

"*Machismo* means manhood. To the Mexican man *machismo* means to have the manly traits of honor and dignity. To have courage to fight. To keep his word and protect his name. To run his house, to control his woman, and to direct his children. This is *machismo,*" Gonzales says. "To be a man in your own eyes.

"If you are afraid of the Anglo he is like an animal. The human being is an animal; when you are afraid he attacks you, he punishes you, but if you are not afraid of him he respects you. The Anglo respects you only when you have power and respect yourself.

"We have been withdrawn. We have been quiet. And this has been mistaken for being afraid. We are not afraid. Look at the Congressional Medals of Honor our people have. It shows that when it comes to *machismo* there is no match for La Raza. We have been withdrawn from this society to protect our culture, the values we have—not because we were cowards. Now we have to show them that we are strong. We have to use more forceful methods."

Gonzales is not talking of violence and nonviolence. The luxury of that choice he feels exists for those who have power to control and order their environment. It is meaningless in the barrio, as in the boxing arena, where violence is a normal act of everyday life that people are powerless to halt.

"Power is respected in this society," he says. "The black militants say the Negro needs black power to offset white power, and we need brown power to offset Anglo power.

"Are we endangering the economic system, the political system, by saying that? I think the system should be endangered. It is a system that is built upon racism and imperialism. That is why the low-income people and the minority people across the nation are rebelling. Unless the system changes, there will be more rebellions. Those who advocate change will save the country, not destroy it. Those who are resisting change are destroying the country.

"If there is no change by peaceful assembly, by demonstrations, by sitting down to discuss changes, then there will be frustration. Out of the frustration will come real violence, not riots. Unless everyone gets an equal share in this country, there won't be any country."

In Washington, D.C., during the Poor People's March, where he and Reies Tijerina led the Chicanos of the Southwest, Gonzales created a plan for the future, "the Plan of the Barrio." His words became the poetic demands of the Crusade for Justice to the Government of the United States:

> I am Joaquín
> in a country that has wiped out
> all my history,
> stifled all my pride.

We are basically a communal people . . . in the pattern of our Indian ancestors. Part of our cultural rights and cultural strengths is our communal values. We lived together for over a century and never had to fence our lands. When the gringo came, the first thing he did was to fence land. We opened our houses and hearts to him and trained him to irrigated farming, ranching, stock raising, and mining. He listened carefully and moved quickly, and when we turned around, he had driven us out and kept us out with violence, trickery, legal and court entanglements. The land for all people, the land of the brave became the land for the few and the land of the bully.

> My knees are caked with mud.
> My hands callused from the hoe.
> I have made the Anglo rich.

Robbed of our land, our people were driven to the migrant labor fields and the cities. Poverty and city living under the colonial system of the Anglo has castrated our people's culture, consciousness of our heritage, and language. Because of our cultural rights, which are guaranteed by treaty, and because the U.S. *says* in its constitution that all treaties are the law of the land . . .

> Here I stand
> Poor in money
> Arrogant with pride.

THEREFORE WE DEMAND: HOUSING.

We demand the necessary resources to plan our living accommodations so that it is possible to extend family homes to be situated in a communal style . . . around plazas or parks with plenty of space for the children. We want our living areas to fit the needs of the family and cultural protections, and not the needs of the city pork barrel, the building corporations or the architects.

EDUCATION: We demand that our schools be built in the same communal fashion as our neighborhoods . . . that they be warm and inviting facilities and not jails. We demand a completely free education from kindergarten to college, with no fees, no lunch charge, no supplies charges, no tuition, no dues.

We demand that all teachers live within walking distance of the schools. We demand that from kindergarten through college, Spanish be the first language and English the second language and the textbooks to be rewritten to emphasize the heritage and the contributions of the Mexican-American or Indio-Hispano in the building of the Southwest. We also demand the teaching of the contributions and history of other minorities which have also helped build this country. We also feel that each neighborhood school complex should have its own school board made up of members who live in the community the school serves.

ECONOMIC OPPORTUNITIES: We demand that the businesses serving our community be owned by that community. Seed money is required to start cooperative grocery stores, gas stations, furniture stores, etc. In-stead of our people working in big factories across the city, we want training and low-interest loans to set up small industries in our own communities. These industries would be co-ops with the profits staying in the community.

AGRICULTURAL REFORMS: We demand that not only the land which is our ancestral right be given back to those pueblos, with restitution for mineral, natural resources, grazing and timber used.

We demand compensation for taxes, legal costs, etc., which pueblos and heirs spent trying to save their land.

REDISTRIBUTION OF THE WEALTH: That all citizens of this country share in the wealth of this nation by institution of economic reforms that would provide for all people, and that welfare in the form of subsidies in taxes and payoffs to corporate owners be reverted to the people who in reality are the foundation of the economy and the tax base for this society.

LAND REFORM: A complete re-evaluation of the Homestead Act, to provide people ownership of the natural resources that abound in this country. Birthright should not only place responsibility on the individual but grant him ownership of the land he dies for.

On Palm Sunday, 1969, in the secular temple of La Crusada Para la Justicia the elated Rodolfo "Corky" Gonzales convened a national gathering of barrio youth. He called it, with a flourish, the Chicano Youth Liberation Conference. The young campesino activists, university graduate-school Chicanos, barrio gang members, *vados locos* from the streets, clever young government "Mexican-Americans" incognito, and the wealthy children of the descendants of Spanish dons came to the temple-like building in downtown Denver to attend workshops in philosophy, self-defense, poetry, art, and identity. In all, more than 1,500 Chicanos come from as far away as Alaska, where no one thought there was any La Raza, and from Puerto Rico, and from all the states in between.

They came from one hundred youth and student groups.

The conference of "music, poetry, *actos, embrazos,* tears, *gritos,* and the Chicano cheer: *'Raza, Raza, Raza, Raza,'* " went on for five days and nights. Afterward a youth wrote, "The building is just an ordinary building, but what counts is when you step through its doors. In this building we are not separated by the gringos. We are one."

" 'Conference' is a poor word to describe those five days," wrote Maria Varela, in *El Grito del Norte.* "It was in reality a fiesta: days of celebrating what sings in the blood of a people who, taught to believe they are ugly, discover the true beauty in their souls during years of occupation and intimidation. Coca-Cola, Doris Day, Breck Shampoo, the Playboy Bunny, the Arrow shirt man, the Marlboro heroes, are lies. 'We are beautiful'—this affirmation grew into a *grito,* a roar, among the people gathered in the auditorium of the Crusade's Center."

In the streets of Denver there were cries of youthful pain. The week before the Liberation Conference began some teen-agers walked out of the city's West Side High School to protest the insults of a teacher who had told his class, "Mexicans are dumb because they eat beans. If you eat Mexican food you'll become stupid like Mexicans." Students objected to his sense of humor and requested that the teacher be transferred. After a rally in the park the high school boys and girls tried to re-enter their school to present their demand to their principal. Two hundred and fifty policemen barred their way.

Soon there was "a riot." The ex-boxer hurried to the school. "Fearing the police were going to hurt the students I rushed forward to take a bull horn," Gonzales recalls. "I shouted to the young people to leave. The police were beating men, women, and children, indiscriminately." Gonzales' young daughter was one of those caught in the melee. "I heard my daughter Nita Jo scream. She was being mauled by a six-foot policeman." There were thirty-six Chicanos arrested.

Denver's barrios had never seen the kind of riots that had been desecrating ghettos in other cities. The people of the community walked to the school the following day to protest, in dismay as much as in anger. Some two thousand came, kids and parents, brown and black and white, teachers as well as students.

When the demonstration was over the police began to move in on those who lingered. There were curses hurled. In moments a battle erupted and dozens of police cars, riot police equipped with chemical Mace and a police helicopter, were ordered into the fray against the taunting teen-agers. "Some say it was a riot. It wasn't. It was more like guerrilla warfare," says one eyewitness. The helicopter dropped tear gas on the youths. "But the wind was blowing the wrong way and they [the police] ended up gassing their own men. This also happened with the Mace. The police were practically Macing their own faces," says another eyewitness.

George Seaton, the Denver Chief of Police, reported that twenty-five squad cars were damaged, "some extensively," and at least "seventeen police were assaulted, injured, and hospitalized." It was the worst street fighting in the modern history of the city.

"What took place after many people left was a battle between the West Side 'liberation forces' and the 'occupying army.' The West Side won," said Gonzales. He told the high school students, "You kids don't realize you have made history. We just talk about revolution, but you act it by facing the shotguns, billies, gas, and Mace. You are the real revolutionaries."

It was barely a year before that the Crusade for Justice leader had told me that he thought there would be no riots in the barrios. "The riots across the nation lead to the self-destruction of man. He acts like an animal," Gonzales had said. "I don't think it is in the Mexican temperament to riot, or to hurt your neighbor that way. Our way would be to pinpoint our enemy, where we wanted to attack him—not to riot."

Riots were "circuses," Gonzales had said then. He described the urban upheavals as the products of the "dehumanized cities," where life itself was riotous and people had no hope. "Why do blacks riot? Because they see no way out, because they feel trapped in the ghettos, because that is how mass society acts. I respect the suffering of the blacks. We have both suffered. We work together. But we work differently because we are a different people.

"Our culture is such that we don't like to march, to protest. We don't like to be conspicuous. We don't like to seem ridiculous in the public eye. That is *machismo*. That is a man's sense of self-respect. We are not nonviolent. But in the barrio self-determination means that every man, every people, every barrio has to be able to take care of themselves, with dignity.

"We are men of silent violence," Gonzales had said. "That, too, is *machismo*."

He voiced these thoughts in the summer of 1968, not in the spring of 1969. In the streets of the barrios of Denver something new had happened to the young Chicanos.

In the fiesta of the Chicano Youth Liberation Conference there emerged the "Spiritual Plan of Aztlán" that opened a new road for the odyssey of Rodolfo "Corky" Gonzales. The name of Aztlán had been that of the ancient nation of the Aztecs. Now the young Chicanos

who had come from throughout the Southwest of the United States voted, almost unanimously, to revive the spirit of that defeated nation.

On the flowered and festooned platform the ex-boxer, former politican, and once-successful businessman, who had not so long ago sought so desperately to escape from the barrio, was the heroic host to the "Spiritual Plan of Aztlán":

In the spirit of a new people that is conscious not only of its proud historical heritage but also of the brutal "gringo" invasion of our territories, we, the Chicano inhabitants and civilizers of the northern land of Aztlán, whence came our forefathers, reclaiming the land of their birth and consecrating the determination of our people of the sun, declare that the call of our blood is our power, our responsibility, and our inevitable destiny.

We are free and sovereign to determine those tasks which are justly called for by our house, our land, the sweat of our brows, and our hearts. Aztlán belongs to those who plant the seeds, water the fields, and gather the crops, and not to the foreign Europeans. We do not recognize capricious frontiers on the Bronze Continent.

Brotherhood unites us, and love for our brothers makes us a people whose time has come and who struggles against the foreigner *"gabacho"* who exploits our riches and destroys our culture. With our heart in our hands and our hands in the soil, we declare the Independence of our Mestizo Nation. We are a bronze people with a bronze culture. Before the world, before all of North America, before all our brothers on the Bronze Continent, we are a nation, we are a union of free pueblos, we are Aztlán.

March 1969
Por La Raza Todo   Fuera de la Raza Nada

35. FROM RUMBLE TO REVOLUTION: THE YOUNG LORDS

Frank Browning with Roberta Weintraub

In the same issue of *Ramparts* magazine from which
the present selection has been taken, there appeared (on
p. 52) this statement of policy about the magazine's
editorial intent:

*For us the test of a political tactic, violent or non-violent, is
whether it can be understood and supported by large numbers
of people, whether it leads to heightened political
consciousness and therefore really advances their struggle
for liberation. Does it mobilize large numbers of people
toward their freedom, or does it disorient and demoralize them?
These are the questions that determine the political morality
of a given action. They are hard questions, and not to be
taken lightly whatever kind of action is to be considered.*

Knowing *Ramparts'* position helps to explain several
overstatements in the article reprinted here. For example, is
the Young Lord Health Clinic in Chicago literally ". . . the first
attack on the health problems of the entire Puerto Rican
community?" More generally, open declaration of an editorial
position can make clear where sympathy lies. *Ramparts* clearly
and unabashedly supports underdogs' attempts to use
collective means to accomplish change. Occasional
overstatement is part of a conscious reportorial technique that
does not necessarily seek a balanced perspective. Instead,
such reporting is analogous to a lawyer's presentation in an
adversary proceeding. That is, *Ramparts* tries to present all of
one side's complaints and actions in as favorable a light as
possible, for it assumes that better established and more widely
read periodicals have already presented the testimony and

Source: *Ramparts,* Vol. 9 (October 1970), pp. 19–25. Copyright
Ramparts Magazine, Inc., 1970, by permission of the Editors.

viewpoints of supporters of the status quo. Now, for those who can afford lawyers, courtroom procedures try to guarantee fair hearings to both sides. That is less true of the mass media of communication. True, a few great newspapers do attempt to present balanced accounts of the differing points of view of parties disputing an issue, but even they have better contacts with established community or government agencies than with new citizens' organizations. Moreover, such agencies are usually in a far better position than protesting citizens to supply information about the good they do or about circumstances making their tasks more difficult. Also to be considered is the matter of what Howard Becker has called the "hierarchy of credibility." [1] The term means that under normal conditions people reading or hearing about a disputed issue at a distance are more inclined to accept the judgments of officials (who are assumed to be expert and informed) than of whoever may be complaining about the performances of the officials. The juvenile court judge is supposed to know more and is, in any case, more respectable than the delinquents. The administrator of the state mental hospital is generally assumed to be competent, humane, and rational while his patients are merely crazy and generally poor. The housing administrator can seem to have a more balanced and general perspective than the Housing Authority's tenants.

The present selection sides with militants of the dispossessed. It explains and excuses what some might take to be their excesses, though it touches on some of their weaknesses as well. We might just as well hear what the whole story looks like from their side, for the group will be heard from in any case. We shall hardly find ourselves in a reasonable position to evaluate the group if we know only the attitudes and opinions of the people and agencies against whom it is contending.

[1] Howard Becker, "Whose Side Are We On?" in Jack D. Douglas (ed.), *The Relevance of Sociology* (New York: Appleton-Century-Crofts, 1970).

Ceil Keegan is 27 years old, a widow, the mother of two small children. Deep brown circles appear under her eyes where the bones were crushed during one of the three beatings she has suffered since Christmas. Several months ago Ceil was walking near her home in West- side Chicago when three men drove up, forced her into their car and took her to a party a few blocks away. She was slapped around and beaten for three hours. The three men were plainclothes cops. They stood by smiling. Later they dumped her back at home, nearly dead.

A few weeks after that, just a block from her home six kids from a white gang beat her and left her crumpled in the street, unable to move. Ceil is a target because she works in the headquarters of the Young Lords Organization, a Puerto Rican street gang-turned-political movement.

Today Ceil is probably safe from the intergang warfare which left her lying in the street. Not because she's dropped her work for the Young Lords, but because of the way the Lords are working with street gangs all over Chicago.

The Lords, until 1967 just another gang, have become the most potent revolutionary organization of Puerto Rican youth in the United States. The Lords are not prodigal sons, returned from suburbia to organize the ghetto. Less romantically, they started out operating in fundamentally the same style as in *West Side Story*. That history sets them apart from the vast majority of radical organizations around the country. They have negotiated peace pacts among nearly all of Chicago's white and Latin gangs, convincing them to fight, not against each other, but against the system which oppresses them. Influenced by the Lords, the 3000-member Latin Kings, the city's largest Puerto Rican gang, have begun to organize themselves politically and have started their own breakfast-for-children program. At the same time, the Lords have battered constantly at West Lincoln Park's established institutions to make them serve poor people.

In the fall of 1968 they took over the Armitage Street Methodist Church—now the People's Church—to found their headquarters and begin a day-care program.

In the spring of 1969 they led hundreds of their Puerto Rican brothers down the street to an empty lot which was to be made into $1000-membership private tennis courts, and transformed it into a children's park.

By summer they had built a coalition with several other community organizations to fight an Urban Renewal plan that envisioned West Lincoln Park as an "inner-city suburb" for middle-income whites. That battle still wears on as the Lords and their allies have joined with architects and lawyers to present their own plans for poor people's housing.

Last winter they opened a free health clinic in the basement of the People's Church, initiating the first attack on the health problems of the entire Puerto Rican community.

The Chicago YLO has inspired the formation of similar groups in Puerto Rican communities in other cities. By far the most significant of these is the New York City Young Lords. A political split between the two organizations which occurred in June has so far been free of the usual acrimony. The two groups, as is clearly revealed in their parallel development, are in any case bound together by common roots—a bond which they now express with the phrase "revolutionary compañeros."

GANGS AND REVOLUTION

Once their political conversion began, it took no more than six months to establish YLO's revolutionary outlook. Dennis Cunningham, one of several Movement lawyers in Chicago who have handled cases for the Lords and the Latin Kings for several years, points to the Lords' early and continuing affiliation with the Black Panthers as fundamental to their political development.

Like the Panthers, YLO is organized into ministerial divisions, with specified lines of authority and levels of responsibility. So far the structure has not become highly rigid. The sense of personal loyalty and friendship which pervades the whole collective is probably stronger than the machinery of organizational discipline.

YLO's Field Marshal is a young man named Cosmo. In his job he hangs out on the street, jiving with other gang people. Cosmo recognizes that the Chicago YLO in an important way still is a gang: "You have to understand, man, that even *before*, we were in some ways already revolutionary. Dig? It's not that we were a gang one minute and the next we were all Communists. What we had to realize was that it wasn't no good fightin' each other, but that what we were doing as a gang had to be against the capitalist institutions that are oppressing us."

Up to about six months ago the YLO was completely dependent upon Jose (Cha Cha) Jimenez, chairman and head of the gang since long before its politicization. Cha Cha is 21 and has been in the gang since 1959; as soon as he began to move into the leadership he was shuttled in and out of jail on all the usual charges stemming from "rumbles," petty theft, possession of drugs, disorderly conduct. Now he faces a one-year sentence on a charge of stealing $23 worth of lumber last summer. A companion convicted on the same offense was given 30 days. His YLO brothers are trying desperately to raise money for appeals, but they do not sound optimistic. Besides, Cha Cha went on trial again early in August on a mob action charge stemming from demonstrations against the city's Urban Renewal plans. When that trial is over he faces seven more charges.

While serving time earlier, Cha Cha discovered how full the jails were of Puerto Ricans—not just gang members, but old and middle-aged people, workers and welfare mothers. It became clear to him that the real enemy was not the Latin Kings or the Paragons or the Black Eagles; the real enemy was Daley's Chicago Urban Renewal, local Alderman George McCutcheon, and the U.S. government, whose imperial colonization policy had so mangled Puerto Rico that

he and his family had been forced to leave just to survive.

A year ago last spring, Brother Manuel Ramos was shot to death by an off-duty Chicago cop. The cop crashed a YLO party and when he started badgering one of them, Ramos tried to clear it up. The cop drew his gun and fired dead-on into Ramos's left eye. "I think it was at that point that I became a real revolutionary," Cha Cha says. "Instead of going out and killing a pig, I saw the need to sit down and analyze the ways of getting even. Not with a gun. It wasn't the right time. It still isn't. We have to educate the people before we think about guns."

Cha Cha characterizes most of the early demonstrations as being like gang fights because of their diffuse political character. April 1969 was a real turning-point for the Lords' political demonstrations. Just as a national conclave of Presbyterian ministers opened in Texas, the Lords moved into Presbyterian McCormick Theological Seminary. "Blacks were going down to demand money," Cha Cha reflects, "so we sent a Latin to get money for building houses. At the same time we felt we should do an action here to back him up and make them understand that if they didn't give poor people houses, we were going to take over the offices at McCormick.

"We went into the place, barricaded the doors and set up security with walkie-talkies. At first there were only 40 people.

"We had a press conference and by morning the place was full of poor people and guilty middle-class people. Food was always supplied to us by the people of the neighborhood. People outside tried to make trouble between us and other gangs, and the gangs would come to the gate, but we would rap with them and then they stayed to help and saw that they were political too. Dr. Arthur McKay [president of McCormick] told people he was going to call the police. It was on the news.

"We went back and held a press conference and said no warrant to leave, no piece of paper, was going to evict us anymore. McKay talked to the Board and dropped the charge, and we got a call from Texas saying we had got $600,000 for low-income housing in Lincoln Park. The Board agreed to meet our demands for housing, that their financial records be open, that McCormick join to help community groups, that it publicly oppose the racist policies of Urban Renewal, and that it open its facilities to the use of the community. We were in the building for five days before we got that decision."

If the Lords' activities get results, they also reveal their enemies. The YLO occupied the Armitage Street Methodist Church in November 1968. For six months they had asked the congregation for permission to use the basement as a day-care center. They had the support of the church's minister, Rev. Bruce Johnson. Nevertheless, an exodus of about 15 per cent of the primarily middle-class membership followed the occupation. Those who have remained with the church—now the People's Church—have transformed it into a center for dialogue on the theology of liberation.

The Lords realize that while their old image as a street gang helps identify them to other street people, older people in the community remain fearful. Local power-brokers like District Alderman George McCutcheon and the right-wing Chicago *Tribune* try to dismiss the Lords as just a bunch of rabble-rousing vandals.

The Lords never had much hope of winning the hearts of the landowners and city bureaucrats. Still, for the rest of the community—even for those middle-aged or older working people and welfare mothers who have been forced to move from one tiny apartment to another, one jump ahead of the Urban Renewal bulldozer—the Lords' history as a gang is cause for ambivalence.

But there are signs that the Lords are also reaching out more effectively into the entire community. At least two of their projects have had a profound impact on the whole of Lincoln Park and, if they can maintain organizational solidarity, could make them the most important political force in Chicago's Puerto Rican community.

GETTING IT ON

For the last 15 years, Lincoln Park has been on the urban planners' maps as an ideal spot to create a middle-class enclave, a suburb in the heart of the inner city. Entire blocks on Armitage, Halsted and Larrabee streets now lie bare where Urban Renewal has leveled the homes of Puerto Ricans and poor whites.

Last June the Lords and several other local groups formed a Poor People's Coalition to fight Urban Renewal plans to have the Hartford Company construct middle-income housing. The Lords asked a young architect, Howard Alan, to develop plans to be entered as a contract bid before the Urban Renewal board. (A $3000 architect's fee was paid by McCormick Seminary.) Community Urban Renewal Director George Stone led them to believe that if the Coalition submitted technically adequate plans, they would get the job.

Alan designed a building, working closely with the Poor People's Coalition and various members of the community. There would be three stories, each set back so that the roof of the floor below formed a play terrace for the apartment above. The front walls were all glass, and workrooms were placed next to them so that mothers would be able to work while watching their children play. "The terraces were designed," says Alan, "for poor people's interaction in response to an existing way of life whereby poor people could rely on each other."

The Lincoln Park Establishment seemed not to take the Coalition's project too seriously until the local Daley-appointed Conservation Community Council—a (supposedly representative) local community board selected to participate in Urban Renewal planning —came through with an 11–2 recommendation favoring the Coalition's bid.

No Community Council recommendation on a construction bid had ever been reversed by the Department of Urban Renewal (with one exception— which was overturned by the Chicago City Council). Furthermore, there has always been a policy that DUR meetings provide ample opportunity for public discussion.

As soon as the chairman opened the meeting last February, he asked all those in the packed audience opposed to the Hartford Company to stand. All but about 10 rose. Just then, a member of the five-man DUR board moved that the bid go to a private contractor. An immediate unanimous vote supported his motion, and by the time the crowd realized what had happened, the board members were clearing away their papers and were on their way out. One man jumped from the audience to grab a microphone and was immediately surrounded by a phalanx of police. Next day the Chicago *Tribune* headlined, in six columns, "Renewal Hearing Disrupted."

Under the plan approved by the DUR, 15 per cent of the new housing will go to poor people. The Coalition's plan called for at least 40 per cent.

YLO Minister of Information Omar Lopez refers to the Coalition's defeat as only a skirmish in what is really a war against Urban Renewal. He promises that the Urban Renewal buildings will never go up until they are designed to serve poor people.

Since February, however, the Lords have done little on neighborhood housing—to the dismay of Howard Alan, who is anxious to work up other bids. Mio Villagomez, a lieutenant in the YLO Health Ministry who came to the Lords last winter, sees this as one of the organization's serious problems, stemming mostly from a lack of internal discipline. And he says it shows up elsewhere, when members—perhaps because of the close relationships that grew out of their long association in the gang— fail to concentrate on their own jobs, show up late for meetings, spend too much time bullshitting instead of talking to new people in the streets, or let old programs lapse when a new one has caught their interest.

It is a pattern that will not be easily abolished. One of the things Cosmo notes about street gangs, which has both helped and frustrated the Lords in winning over other gangs to cooperative political work, is a faddish attraction to new styles. For though they may dig what the Lords are doing, it's really hard to develop the tenacity to follow through on organizational detail. That kind of periodic excitement which moves from one new program to another is what Mio criticizes as a lack of self-disciplined democratic centralism.

As long as it was dependent on Cha Cha's gentle-but-tough charismatic style, YLO seemed unlikely to solve this problem. But he has steadily shifted much of the leadership responsibility to his ministers. Friends of the organization believe it is now strong enough to stand without him, should the city's efforts to imprison him succeed. He resigned as chairman in mid-July so that full responsibility for YLO would devolve upon the Central Committee, and "in order to allow the second generation of Lords to assume the burden of responsibility and pleasure of serving people."

Of equal importance to YLO strength are two new people who have come into the Lords during the last year: Omar Lopez and Alberto Chivera. Their personal warmth and serious efficiency have brought them into powerful positions as Ministers of Information and Health, respectively.

Alberto, a third-year medical student at Northwestern University, runs the health clinic, a program of free medical service to the community staffed by doctors, medical and nursing students and professional health workers. The clinic, which opened in February with a handful of patients, now receives nearly 50 people each Saturday afternoon, with services from prenatal care to eye examinations.

At first many women were afraid to go to the clinic. They were wary of the old gang image and frightened by what they had read in the city's newspapers. Then health workers started canvassing door-to-door, asking people if anyone needed medical care and making arrangements for them to come to the clinic. If they failed to appear, they were sent a personal letter inviting them to come in the next week. Sometimes members of the Health Ministry and doctors go to the homes of people who can't come to the clinic.

Alberto expects that eventually the clinic will be run entirely by the community, with only occasional help from the Lords—a real People's Clinic freely offered to and freely run by the people it is designed to serve. There is, of course, a tendency of such programs to deteriorate into the piecemeal style of government welfare: patching together one project here and plugging up another there. But the health clinic can also be a stepping-off point for further action.

The fact that the clinic does work primarily in the neighborhood means that it is tying itself very effectively into the social structure of the community. If the Lords can continue that direct relationship with the Puerto Rican women, who form one of the strongest sources of traditional stability, then their chances of growing into an effective community-wide political organization are greater than ever before.

On the surface the Health Ministry appears to offer nothing more than a slightly better version of the city's welfare program. But the camaraderie and sensitive care that the clinic has come to offer have probably become the Lords' most successful organizing tool. Not only does it go a long way toward eroding their traditional gang image, but it doesn't take too many trips to the clinic —where treatment comes free—for the people to realize that their frustration is rooted in the medical system, especially as it is embodied by Grant Hospital.

When the clinic first opened, Grant had agreed to provide free follow-up examinations upon referral by the clinic's doctors. For a while it worked. Then the hospital started billing patients and initiating collection procedures. By that time, though, enough people were behind the Lords that they could escalate their service demands beyond what Grant would concede while still staying well within the community's reasonable expectations. One especially important demand was that the hospital remove police from the emergency room (police regularly interrogate patients before and during emergency treatment). Grant's intransigence on both counts has in the process heightened older community people's awareness of its inadequacy both as a medical and as a social institution.

Through the health clinic more than any other program, the Lords have been able to strengthen their bonds to the community and stimulate some political awareness of how the established social service institutions work. In addition, local shopowners and businessmen have begun to support the Lords' programs. Most of the food for the breakfasts is given freely by local grocers. One record store owner, a staunch supporter of the Puerto Rican Independence Movement, has given recordings of the Puerto Rican national anthem to be played each morning at the breakfast program.

The Lords, though strong opponents of an apolitical "cultural nationalism," are deeply committed to the liberation of Puerto Rico. They consider themselves revolutionary nationalists and maintain many ties with revolutionary leaders on the island. Before he came to Chicago last February, Communications Deputy Tony Baez was active in the Movement on the island, escaping to Chicago for fear of imprisonment. The Lords see their role as one of making Americans realize that the U.S. government has its own resort colony in just the same manner as the 19th-century European empires. [See RAMPARTS, June 1970]

"We feel it our duty to see that 'Free Puerto Rico Now' will be an issue in the next year, second only to getting out of Vietnam," one Young Lord explains. "Why the stress on a nationalistic feeling for an island so far away? For a Puerto Rican living in Chicago who was forced to come here as a cheap laborer, that rallying point gives a sense of pride and identity. All were brought here because of the systematic destruction of the Puerto Rican economy and the death of jobs and promise."

It is above all this common heritage of continuing oppression which binds the Puerto Ricans living in Chicago or New York, not only to their countrymen in Puerto Rico, but also to each other and to those in other cities around the country.

THE LORDS IN NEW YORK

The New York Young Lords (who since last June's split with the Chicago YLO have constituted themselves the Young Lords Party, or YLP) come out of a community whose conditions and concerns parallel the Chicago group's. Guided by the immediate needs of the people, the YLP has focused on the problems of inadequate health care and housing, malnutrition, institutions refusing to serve the community—the same issues around which the YLO organized in Chicago. At the same time, however, sources of divergency in their development can be seen, especially in organizational and tactical style and in strategic priorities, and perhaps also in the personal backgrounds of the two groups.

The New York Lords' first action was in July 1969. Unable to obtain brooms from the Sanitation Department to clean 110th Street in *El Barrio,* they got together with people in the neighborhood and built a barricade of garbage across Third Avenue at 110th. In the days that followed, the action spread to 111th and 112th Streets. At each location, the Lords held a rally and signed up some of their first recruits. The garbage offensive lasted until September 2. The Lords played a hit-and-run game, block to block, talking and spreading politics as they went. Thousands of Puerto Ricans fought the police that summer. Many joined the Lords or at least became friendly to the struggle.

That fall, the Lords began to work with welfare mothers. In October they started door-to-door lead poisoning detection tests. They found that cases of lead poisoning—due to the illegal use of cheap lead paint by tenement landlords —reached epidemic proportions in their community.

As the health work continued, the Lords themselves learned how to do simple blood tests for iron deficiency anemia, another poverty disease widespread in the community. The lack of proper nutrition convinced them to undertake a free breakfast-for-children program.

For weeks, the Lords visited the First Spanish Methodist Church on 111th Street and Lexington Avenue, trying to convince Humberto Carranzana, the Cuban refugee who ran it, to open the large basement facilities for the breakfast program (the church was in use only a few hours a week, on Sundays). On Sunday, December 7, when the Lords attempted to address the congregation, police were called in and beat and arrested 13 Lords. The women who were in the church fought back just as hard as the men, and the Party points to this as the awakening of its struggle against male chauvinism. The Lords returned to the church on December 28, 1969. This time they took it over, renamed it People's Church and began an 11-day occupation. They established an embattled communal enclave with free breakfasts, free clothing and health services, a day-care center, a liberation school, community dinners, films, and on New Year's Eve a revolutionary service to herald "The Decade of the People."

Over a hundred thousand people passed through the doors of the church during those days. The Lords explained their programs. They invoked the teachings of Jesus as a people's gospel of helping those in need.

The barricaded, barred and chained door of the church gave way to police hammers and chisels at 7:15 A.M., Wednesday, January 7. The occupation ended peacefully—as the Lords had promised, for their part, that it would. All of those busted were charged with civil contempt of a January 2 court injunction against remaining in the church. In March all of the charges were dropped.

Since January, support for the Young Lords in the community has continued to grow rapidly. This was made unmistakably clear at the Puerto Rican Day Parade on June 7: As the Young Lords passed by in their purple berets, hundreds of thousands of people greeted them with cheers and the clenched-fist salute.

Community support was demonstrated in a different way a week later with the arrest of the YLP Chief of Staff, Juan "Fi" Ortiz, 16 years old, on charges of kidnapping, armed robbery and assault. The next day four different newspapers provided four implausibly differing versions of Fi's supposed crime; all of them were variations of the theme that 21-year-old Jack McCall of Newark, New Jersey, was kidnapped on an East Harlem Street, forced into a car at knifepoint, driven to Brooklyn, struck on the head and robbed of $40. McCall escaped and reported the car's license number to police, who within the space of a few hours checked it, located the car and Fi and arrested him.

Fi's bail was set at $1000. The judge apparently found the police story less than convincing for the bail must approach a record low for charges of kidnapping, armed robbery and assault.

The night of the arrest, hundreds of people gathered to protest at a rally called by the Lords in front of the People's Church, which since the occupation had become a symbol of the struggle in El Barrio. YLP Chairman Felipe Luciano told the crowd: "We will not allow the brutalization of our community to go without any response. For every Puerto Rican who is brutalized, there will be a retaliation."

The Lords left the rally to return to their Bronx office to work on the current issue of their paper, *Palante*. The crowd raised YLP banners left over from the Puerto Rican Day parade the previous Sunday and marched through the streets of El Barrio chanting, *"Despierta, Boricua. Defiende lo tuyo"*—"Awake, Puerto Rican. Defend what is yours."

Suddenly, small groups of people broke from the march and fanned out north and south on Third Avenue. The gates of the A&P supermarket were pulled down and people filled up bags of groceries. Men and women gathered merchandise from other stores on the avenue; barricades went up to keep the cops—now with guns drawn—away from the people in the stores. Poverty program offices and welfare centers were also targets. Rocks and bottles pelted patrol cars. A cop was beaten when he tried to make an arrest. A car belonging to the Housing Authority, New York's Municipal Slumlord, was found abandoned on 113th Street. People covered it with garbage and crowned it with trashcans.

THE PEOPLE'S MEDICINE

Lincoln Hospital is located in an industrial sector of the South Bronx, the edge of one of the largest, most run-down Puerto Rican ghettos in the City. At 5:30 on the morning of July 18, a group of about 200 Puerto Rican men and women from the YLP, the Health Revolutionary Unity Movement (a city-wide group of Third World health workers), and the Think Lincoln Committee (made up of workers and patients at Lincoln Hospital), walked into Lincoln with the aim of turning the hospital over to the community. Among their demands were door-to-door health services for preventive care, sanitary control, nutrition, maternal and child care, drug addiction care, day care and senior citizens' services, a 24-hour-a-day grievance table, and a $140 minimum weekly wage for all workers.

Hours later, hundreds of people streamed in through the front door to get free tests for tuberculosis, iron deficiency anemia and lead poisoning. Passersby looking up at the ancient, grimy building that could easily pass for a warehouse were surprised to see the Puerto Rican flag flying and banners in the window proclaiming: *"Bienvenido al hospital del pueblo"*—"Welcome to the People's Hospital."

At 10 A.M. there was a press conference. Yvette Trinidad of Think Lin-

coln answered a question: Why use take-over tactics? "There was garbage piled on the corner of 142nd Street and Cortland right outside of this hospital. We complained, we petitioned, we called the Mayor's office. Nothing was done. Addicts from all over town came over here to search for dirty needles in the rubble. One day we decided to act. We moved the garbage into the office of Dr. Antero Lacot, the hospital administrator; that same day the garbage got removed."

At a political education class at the hospital run by Denise Oliver, YLP's Minister of Finance, three Puerto Ricans, all under 12, told of their experience with medicine.

"My brother broke his arm and had to wait two hours in the hall before a doctor came out."

"My aunt died of a wrong blood transfusion."

"My friend's mother died of hepatitis from a dirty needle."

Negotiations with the Mayor's office over the demands broke down after four and a half hours. By afternoon's end, Tactical Patrol Squad and "Special Events" cops pulled up and parked in front of the hospital. But groups of the Lords and sympathizers, many from gangs like the Bones, the Skulls and the Savage Seven, were leaving the hospital unobtrusively, a few at a time. By the time the 150 helmeted cops marched in formation into Lincoln, there was no one inside except hospital employees. The police captain, paunched and pompous, led his 150 men back out, still in formation. They had removed the Puerto Rican flag from the hospital roof.

The hospital occupation lasted a little over 12 hours. New York radio and TV news broadcasts flashed stories of the terrible conditions at Lincoln all day long. Newspapers across the country carried the story. The AP quoted Hospital Administrator Lacot as saying that the Lords did a service to the community by dramatizing conditions at Lincoln.

ACTIONS AND IDEOLOGY

In discussing the difference which led to the New York-Chicago split in the Young Lords, Omar Lopez, Tony Baez and others in Chicago point to the backgrounds of the individuals involved. The Chicago group is made up largely of high school dropouts and some who didn't finish grammar school. The New York chapter evolved out of a political organization called the Sociedad Albizu Campos, most of whose members had either graduated from or dropped out of college in or around New York. The Chicago people feel that the New Yorkers were preoccupied with ideological refinement, whereas they had neither the time nor the educational background to concentrate on theoretical work.

"Here in Chicago we're more concerned with the immediate needs of the people, but we still understand that the real struggle is not a local one," says Omar. "That's why we entered a coalition with the Panthers and the Young Patriots on a national and international level. Yet if we talk of being the vanguard, we need to be up ahead and still have something behind us too. We're better able to analyze when we're out on the streets talking with the people. Ideas must come after actions, not just from reading Marx, Lenin or Mao."

The New York group does not consider its concerns abstract. In their view, a lack of ideological clarity in Chicago was part and parcel of a number of related problems: lack of organizational discipline, leading to inconsistency in ongoing programs; inadequate internal political education; frequent changes in leadership; erratic publication of the national paper—shortcomings that are to a large extent acknowledged by the Chicago group.

The New Yorkers felt that Chicago YLO was not up to leading a sustained, closely-knit national organization. Last May, after several unsatisfactory meetings, the New Yorkers proposed that the Chicago leadership come East for an extended period to join in forging a new national structure and program. The Chicago people refused. Like the New Yorkers, they were unwilling to leave their local work. The split followed, even though relations remain amicable and Chicago members are "hopeful" that they can continue to "work in a way that will enable us to come together again."

The Lords are trying to confront the problem of how to sustain organizational continuity—a perennial problem on the left. The most long-lived organizations are often the most irrelevant sects. The most vital movements—in campus struggles, for instance—are often plainly ad hoc and ephemeral. Clearly a synthesis is needed, and the experience of the two Young Lords groups will be instructive.

It is no accident that episodic organization is endemic to the left. Not only are groups like the Lords and the Panthers subjected to increasingly ruthless repression, but the left also lacks the access to money, power and friendly media that sustains the established institutions of society. The continuity of radicalism is at bottom a continuity of the suffering and outrage that give rise to it. In time these may find their expression in many different organizations or actions.

At the Lincoln Hospital press conference, a reporter asked how the Lords could go on taking over one thing after another. And Minister of Information Yoruba replied, "Because we serve our people. That's why we could move from People's Church to a TB truck to Lincoln Hospital—and you-all don't know where we're gonna be tomorrow."

36. THE RETURN TO THE CAMPUS

Harry Edwards

Administrator: The University of Rurilia has always had an open admissions policy, depending on the objective estimate of academic capacity alone.

Bultinian student: Impossible. Quite aside from the inferior quality of our Bultinian schools, the close association between social class and past educational performance in Rurilia as a whole demonstrates that what your criteria have been measuring is a reflection of status, and not just the capacity to do high-level academic work.

Administrator: You know that our purposes here are learning, teaching, and gathering knowledge for their own sake.

Bultinian student: Our purpose is too urgent allow such luxury. What we learn should be applicable to the pursuit of social change to improve the situation of Bultinians in Rurilia.

Administrator: But we believe that knowledge and its pursuit are disinterested and applicable to the situation of all men.

Bultinian student: Disinterested? What of your faculty members who do contract research work for the Octagon? . . . Applicable to all men? Where have you listed all your courses on Bultinian art and history all these years? Certainly not in your catalogue.

Administrator: We may be prepared to make additions to the curriculum, but in no case will we lower our standards.

Bultinian student: Who said anything about lowering standards? What we demand is that you do not relegate us to second-rate courses or flunk us out instead of taking steps to make up for whatever past deficiencies we have brought with us, and in the creation or maintenance of which, by the way, you have been a witting or unwitting accomplice. Furthermore,

Source: *Black Students* (New York: The Free Press of Glencoe, 1970), pp. 60–73. Copyright © 1970 by The Free Press, a division of The Macmillan Company. Reprinted by permission of the publisher.

HARRY EDWARDS is with the Department of Sociology at the University of California at Berkeley, and is the author of *The Revolt of the Black Athlete.*

different standards are not the same thing as lowered standards. Therefore, we have the right to insist that in the areas we know better than you, those that concern Bultinian experience in Rurilia, we have the right to decide what the proper standards are.

Administrator: Your interest in Bultinians is admirable, but courses devoted to it must be open to all, for we are a community of scholars whose highest value is free inquiry and the open dissemination of knowledge and ideas.

Bultinian student: Your community, so-called, has in the past been open only to pink Rurilians, for until Bultinians began to have enough power to threaten the arrangements that made it possible for you to pursue your goals, we were virtually excluded. As for your free dissemination of ideas, it frequently doesn't seem to have any room for those who urge actions to overthrow the status quo rather than maintain or reform it. In general, your idea of free is different from mine, for I see no reason why we should be any less free to prevent the expression of racist ideas than the faculty member or guest speaker who is free to mouth or write them.

Administrator: It has been our pursuit of truth, free from the petty conventions that too often crowd and trouble men's minds, that has led us to show more concern over the plight of Bultinian Rurilians than any other institution in the society has shown.

Bultinian student: Your concern did more good for the social scientists who got their salaries paid by the Rurilian Science Foundation that it did for us Bultinians. If you are more concerned now, and at all ready to take some effective steps, it is only because we have shown that you are vulnerable.

Administrator: Vulnerable or not, we have now given you the chance to be full members of the university community, and you should not wish to separate yourselves.

Bultinian student: We are here for ourselves and our people, and not to make you feel warm inside over having done something nice for us. Moreover, we feel more comfortable with one another than we generally do with any of you, for we share experiences that you do not. By the same token, you cannot readily understand what we are trying to accomplish; if you try to be a part of it, you will only slow us down and perhaps be made to feel uncomfortable in the bargain. Finally, we do not wish to be made over to fit your image of the sorts of people who fit neatly into the kind of society that your past alumni have favored. What you call a "chance," we call co-optation or bribery.

Administrator: Nevertheless, we anticipate that your

demands will be only temporary and short-term until the Bultinian adjustment is easier here.

Bultinian student: They will last for as long as they are necessary to win for Bultinians the same hopes of being able to control their destinies that pink Rurilians have had for decades.

When Bultinian or any other people band together with sufficient effectiveness to win something for themselves that they have never had before, they upset old assumptions and old prerogatives. One group's sense of principle may seem to another to be mere expediency. Arguments will be settled by power calling for compromise or conscience for scruple rather than by reason's bright beacon of consensual truth. As Louis Wirth put it a generation ago: "Since every assertion of a 'fact' about the social world touches the interests of some individual or group, one cannot even call attention to the existence of certain 'facts' without courting the objections of those whose every raison d'etre in society rests upon a divergent interpretation of the 'factual' situation." [1]

[1] Louis Wirth, "Preface" to Karl Mannheim, *Ideology and Utopia* (New York: Harcourt, Brace, and World, Harvest Editions, 1936), p. xv.

In 1967 and 1968, it became clear that Black Power had gripped the imaginations of Black students across America. It was equally obvious that the days had passed when Black students would leave the campus to sit-in at some segregated facility or another. Over 90 percent of the sit-ins initiated and implemented by Black students during this two-year period occurred on college campuses and not in segregated facilities in the society at large. And most of these sit-ins were not staged to protest against segregated conditions, but rather in order to pry compliance with Black student demands from white or negro administrators of colleges and universities. Most of these sit-ins, primarily on predominantly white campuses but at negro colleges as well, were designed to satisfy demands that were decidedly separatist in nature.

On the predominantly white college campuses, Black students saw change as necessary if such schools were to provide them with the preparation they needed to carry on as active participants in the Black liberation struggle within its new context. To this end, many individuals who had endured the defeats and victories of the integrationist-oriented phase of the student movement set about establishing Black student "unions" on predominantly white campuses. Regardless of what they have been called—The Association of Black Collegians, The Afro-American Society, The Black Students' Union, United Black Students, and so on—all are geared to provide Black students with a solid, legitimate power base from which they can bring about needed changes in the colleges and universities involved. Black student organizations on predominantly white campuses have demanded separate living, dining, and office facilities for their members. They have called for separate educational facilities and instruction. And, they have demanded standards for college entrance and academic achievement different from those used to measure the academic performance of white students.

Negro college campuses have been spared Black student demands for separate facilities and instruction, because whites are an extremely small minority on these campuses, if they attend those schools at all. Black students have, however, deluged negro and white administrators at these schools with demands for changes in the substance and character of their educational experiences. Here, the demands represent the students' desires to cast off traditionally accepted standards of what constitutes a "good" and "relevant" negro education.

In 1967 and 1968, then, the Black student revolt switched from an emphasis upon confrontations in segregated areas of American life to the college campus. The schools no longer were merely bases of operations and recruitment, as they had been earlier. Now they had become the main battlegrounds in the struggle. Why this "return to the campus"?

First of all, young Blacks saw the need to qualify for positions and responsibilities traditionally assumed by oppressive whites and negroes in Black communities. If Black people were ever going to think seriously of driving the oppressors and exploiters from their communities, then there had to be qualified and competent Blacks to lead them. Black students, responding to the responsibilities spelled out for them by Malcolm X, Stokely Carmichael, and Rap Brown, altered their priorities, for instance, from an emphasis upon such activities as desegregating lunch counters and housing facilities to preparing themselves to operate new Black businesses and build new Black controlled housing facilities in the Black communities of America.

Second, the Black student of the middle 1960's realized, for the first time, that the educational system in America was far from being the shining ideal that white apologists made it out to be.

To the Black students education in America was now just as racist and oppressive as any other institution in the society. It was clear to him that neither Afro-Americans nor educational institutions in America simply were going to disappear. And since Black students had a responsibility to prepare themselves to lead the Black liberation movement, their first task naturally would be to bring about changes in the educational institution that would enable them to pursue such preparations.

Third, Black students saw themselves as constituting a vanguard elite in the Black liberation struggle. As such, true to the mandate presented to them by H. Rap Brown and others, they had a responsibility to legitimize the political activities and actions of Black people in Black communities and on the "block." This task could best be accomplished not simply by their becoming involved in local community political activities, but by conscious and deliberate efforts to express in their educational endeavors and in their actions their support of and the justifications for political acts carried out by Black people at the local level. To the extent that this was to be accomplished, it was necessary for the Black student to transfer to the campus the same brand of radicalism that hitherto had been confined to exposing inequities and injustices in the society at large.

And last, many Black students turned to the campus as the focus of their political activities in the Black liberation struggle, because they were not yet ready to engage in the types of activities which had either augmented or replaced non-violent action in local Black communities as legitimate means of achieving liberation. Although many students were in full sympathy with the new tactics and gave them, much as they do today, verbal support, they themselves were not yet ready to violently engage police, national guardsmen, and state troopers in armed rebellions. They were not yet ready to employ "any means necessary" to bring about freedom, justice, and equality for Afro-Americans. So they returned to the campus, carrying with them their newly found political sophistication, the frustrations of over half a decade of struggle, and their idealism, which had both waxed and waned during the "integrationist" phase of the movement.

What awaited them at the various colleges and universities? What would confront them? What of Black Power, and how would it be realized on predominantly white campuses?

SEPARATION OR "SELF-IMPOSED SEGREGATION"

Many educational administrators, faculty members, and concerned citizens—as well as traditionalist, old-line negro civil rights leaders—are frightened, confused, and intimidated by the widespread demands of Black students for separate facilities and, in general, for the institutionalization of a life style separate from that enjoyed by white students on the predominantly white campus. No less confounding to many are the demands of Black students on negro campuses for Black studies programs and Black cultural facilities. These demands are both justifiable and necessary within the context of the present phase of the Black student revolt. And those who refuse to recognize these justifications and the need for separatism are either ignorant of the Black experience in America or are completely out of

touch with the realities of the Black liberation struggle in the 1960's, or both.

For the Black student on the white campus, there is nothing new in being alone with his own kind. Over the years, and since 1954 in particular, while liberal white administrators and faculty members at northern universities have piously slapped themselves on the back and criticized southern segregated white schools, the Black student has known the truth about the Black experience in the "integrated" predominantly white college. The truth of the matter is that even today, fraternities, sororities, extracurricular activities, and many other facets of life at predominantly white integrated colleges are closed to the Black student. The case of the Black athlete is particularly relevant here. So vicious and widespread has been the racism and injustice in collegiate athletics at predominantly white schools that in 1968 a new front was opened in the Black student revolt, an attack by Black athletes on traditionally racist practices in athletics. (A documentary analysis of this aspect of the more general Black student revolt is presented in Harry Edwards' *The Revolt of the Black Athlete*, Free Press, 1969.) Black students have traditionally eaten alone with their own kind; they have traditionally been assigned to dorm rooms with other Blacks; and they have usually socialized mainly with Blacks on the integrated college campus. Typically, segregation within an ostensibly integrated context has been the rule for the Black student. The fact has been driven home, both subtly and directly, that his presence on the predominantly white campus is primarily maintained at the sufferance of liberal whites and, that beyond this presence, he has little legitimacy—if any—in the college community. In short, the call for a separate community of Black students within the larger academic community of Black students within the larger academic community may be new to the liberal campus in its political implications, but it most certainly is not new in its visible manifestations. For even on the most highly integrated and liberal college campuses, there have always been a Black community and a white community. The Black student today has simply recognized this central fact and moved to capitalize on it in order to realize the goals of the present phase of the Black liberation struggle.

One of the philosophical bases for the Black student's seemingly sudden advocacy of Black separatism in academia is the fundamental distinction which he makes between separation and segregation. Both the conceptual and operational meanings of segregation are, for the Black student, all too clear. Under a segregated system of human relationships, a dominant group defines the limits and boundaries of acceptable behavior, activities, and aspirations for a subordinate group. This usually has the effect of maintaining or reinforcing those advantages enjoyed by the dominant group in the social order. These advantages become, over a period of time, institutionalized within the fabric of practically every aspect of the society, including the political, economic, social, educational, and even the religious spheres of life. For even on Sundays, it is as if some invisible force surged through the nation sending whites to one church and Blacks to another. The results for the subordinate group are usually disastrous—culturally, economically, and politically. Its members, in fact, become inferior, not because they are innately so, but because they are defined as such by their oppressors— and, ultimately, they come to regard themselves as inferior. The subordinate group becomes inferior because its members are treated categorically as inferiors and because they respond to such treatment from a perspective of inferiority. Segregation, then, *has* produced and perpetuated the inferiority complex which

afflicts many people in Black society. But this inferiority complex does not stem solely from the fact that Blacks have not been allowed by their white oppressors to socialize, go to school with, work beside, or otherwise rub elbows with whites. In fact, this contrived inferiority has little to do with the absence of physical intermingling between whites and Blacks. The determining factor in bringing about the inferiority complex, exhibited through both the behavior and attitudes of many in Black society, is the fact that these people have accepted the white racist definition of themselves as having been relegated to a sub-human existence in America because of certain "innately inferior" characteristics supposedly possessed by Black people and not by whites. With Black separatism, an entirely different philosophical perspective is brought to bear on the fact of traditional Black-white estrangement. And, it is this difference which renders separatism different from segregation in both its philosophical and political substance and in its consequences.

Black separatism is neither a manifestation of Black "racism," a cult of Black superiority, or the evidence of Black people's intentions to "do the same thing to whites that whites have done to Blacks for almost four hundred years." In America, *Black* and *racist* are, first of all, mutually contradictory terms. Second, the entire notion of Black separatism being a cultic movement espousing Black superiority is simply fallacious. And, the idea that Blacks who advocate Black separatism are somehow preparing to reciprocate in kind the injustices and humiliations that whites have traditionally heaped upon Blacks is merely evidence of the truth of the old adage that "the guilty flee when no man pursues."

In the present phase of the Black student movement, the advocacy of separatism means that young Black people today are determined to control all aspects of their own environment—social, political, educational, economic, and otherwise—to the advantage of Black people. Unlike segregation, when a subordinate group separates itself categorically from an oppressive dominant group, the former in effect declares a psychological and social sovereignty and legitimacy beyond any that might be ascribed to it by the latter. Such a subordinate group runs its own affairs; it sets its own standards of acceptable behavior and aspirations; and, from its ranks come the people who will be charged with the responsibility of solving the problems facing that group. But most important, it creates its own definitions of itself and its environment. A group that seeks to separate does not attempt to control and exploit other groups in the social order. For its tactic is separation, not the domination that has been the tactic of the white majority in America relative to Blacks. Neither is separation a goal. It is a means of bringing about freedom and justice for Black people in America. Hopefully, Black separatism will develop a more homogeneous and just society, wherein all men can be free and receive justice under a single set of standards. But America is not such a society now, and this is the reality with which Black people are faced. For Blacks, there are separate standards for almost everything. It is this revelation which Afro-Americans have finally come to understand.

Most Black students recognize today that Afro-Americans, as was stated in the last chapter, are not merely Americans who happen to be Black. Theirs is a life style and environmental condition which is distinctively different from those of other groups, owing to a uniquely Black heritage of slavery, oppression, exploitation, and dehumanization stemming from racism. As such, the problems faced by Blacks are not amenable to solutions typically employed by other groups in overcoming problems issuing from attempts to ascend the socio-economic and political ladders of the system. Black people have been *in* America longer than 95 percent of all of the other ethnic groups represented in this society, and still they lie at the bottom. In short, they are still not *of* America. In separatism, Black students see a potentiality for developing the Black communities of America into such an internally controlled power block that Blacks will in fact be able to compete on an equal basis with other groups in the larger society. On an individual level, separatism holds the potential for instilling Black people with the pride and confidence necessary if they are to seek self-fulfillment in America. This aspect of Black separatism is all the more laudable because the possibility of societal disaster being precipitated from within remains a definite reality while members of any group feel themselves to be categorically denied the right to such self-actualization.

SEPARATISM ON THE CAMPUS

There are several basic justifications for the advocacy of Black separatism on the college campus. . . . Calls for Black separatism have run the gamut from demands for separate Black dining facilities and parking lots to cries for separate Black instructional facilities and curricula. Although the specific justification for some of these demands may be peculiar to certain campus atmospheres and conditions, several do conform to philosophical mandates generally accepted throughout the Black student movement.

Today there is considerable evidence to support the assertion that the substance and functioning of traditionally accepted educational activities in America are de facto racist. As such, the educational experiences of Blacks emerge not only as irrelevant—a charge often made by white students—but also as intellectually degrading and racially derogatory. Consequently, Black students have moved to bring about changes that they feel promise more relevant educational experiences as these relate to solving the problems faced by the Black masses in America.

Across America, Blacks have demanded separate educational facilities. Here, the justification is simple. When Blacks and whites have engaged in conversation or discussion about problems facing Black people, there has always been a great deal of discussion back and forth but very little has been resolved. Black students recognize this. They feel that in the latter half of the 1960's, it is a waste of precious time to argue with whites about a fact of the Black experience in America that even a six-year-old Black child would consider trivial or obvious. So rather than waste time arguing with whites about whether or not racism exists in the north, or about whether the racial question revolves around a "negro problem" or a white problem, or about whether Blacks want integration in order to facilitate access to white women, Black students have merely demanded that they be provided with separate educational facilities. The assumption here is that such separate instruction would allow them to move at their own pace toward realizing as much as they possibly can in their pursuit of a relevant education. And this can be done only without the burden of white classmates, who can neither fully understand nor accurately analyze life in America from the Black perspective.

Much of the same argument underlies Black student demands for courses taught by Black instructors. They feel that at the present time neither negro nor white professors, no matter how liberal, can capably and competently teach substantive courses relevant to Black people. Each has too much of a stake in and is too much involved with main-taining the racist status quo in the society. Moreover, neither the negro nor the white teacher understands the Black communities of America. The orientations and perspectives of both have been antithetical to or ignorant of the life styles of Black society. The white professor gains his perspectives of Black people, or lack of same, through racist infested socialization and educational processes. The negro often works hard and deliberately to shed all traces of his Black people. To him, the Black community and its problems are merely isolated, academic facts. Realizing the situation, Black students have demanded that Black professors be hired, with students having some decision-making power in determining which professors are Black and which are negro. Such decisions are usually based upon a particular prospect's reputation, his political activities, the content and character of his writings, and/or the tenor of any pronouncements he may have made prior to his being hired.

Black students have been just as adamant in demanding separate housing and dining facilities on campus. For many years at predominantly white colleges, Black students have literally been used both by white students and faculty members as resource items and informants on almost every aspect of Black life in America. It was not until relatively recently, however, that Blacks realized that they were being used this way by whites who usually have had only a casual interest in solving problems of racism and injustice. In the past, Black students have thought nothing of explaining time-and-time again, over and over, to whites how it feels to be discriminated against or abused by racists. They have wasted hours attempting to "justify" various past civil rights protests and rebellions to whites who had demonstrated little concern about racial injustice until Blacks became aggressive in their liberation efforts. Today, however, Black students are rebelling against this kind of exploitation. They realize that the average white person neither understands nor can truly empathize with the Black masses. And what is more, he is not prepared to accept and act upon Black assessments of life in America even after they have been explained to him.

In line with their new sense of racial and cultural pride, Black students have demanded separate living and dining facilities in order that they might pursue and develop a greater appreciation for their own culture, uninhibited by the constant presence of whites, who can neither understand nor contribute to such an understanding. Blacks in America eat different food, so why subject whites to what has been done to Blacks—that is, subject them to a constant diet which may seem bland or distasteful to them? Why subject whites to ethnocentric styles of behavior, dancing, conversation, and attire, which they may not appreciate or identify with and which they may regard as derogatory, vulgar, or uncouth? Black students have tried to avoid these consequences, not out of a hatred for whites, but out of a determination to pursue what is relevant to Blacks.

If separatism is so desirable, then, why go to a predominantly white school in the first place?

WHY BLACK SEPARATISM ON THE PREDOMINANTLY WHITE CAMPUS?

Since it became clear that Black separatism was to be the central trend on the predominantly white college campuses of America, many have asked why Blacks attend such schools and then seek a separate existence. First, predominantly white schools have the best equipment and facilities available in the educational arena. Unlike negro schools in the south, such institutions of higher learning are not constantly hampered by gross shortages in money, space, and basic educational equipment. And given the magnitude of the problems facing Black society, even the best that American education has to offer may not be sufficient to solve them. So why even consider anything less?

Second, the authorities who control predominantly white schools are not so likely to shut them down in order to stem the political activities of Black students. No such hesitancy constrains the white authorities who run the negro colleges. Here the reprisal is swift—call out the police or shut off the funds. After all, "these kids are only niggers." The authorities used every means at their disposal to keep Columbia University in New York City and San Francisco State College in California open. But predominantly negro Voorhees College in Denmark, South Carolina, was sealed like a tomb. The authorities are extremely wary about using unrestrained force against white students at white schools—as was used against Black students at the negro college in Orangeburg, South Carolina—because often the sons and daughters of important whites attend these colleges and sometimes become involved in confrontations. It is also on the predominantly white campuses of the country—at Cornell, Harvard, Berkeley, Chicago, and the like—that most defense and other types of "vital" research are carried on. Civic and university authorities are not likely to shut these facilities down and set the university off limits to students, some of whom are graduate research assistants working on government projects, simply to curtail the political activities of Black students. This is especially true because, as was brought out in a study in May of 1969, Black students comprise less than 2 percent of the student populations at the nation's eighty largest and most prestigious universities. Black students recognize these facts and therefore not only apply for admittance to predominantly white schools but stay on and carry out their political activities there. The administrators at such schools are thus forced either to meet the demands of Black students or face continual disruptions and confrontations.

Third, a Black student can be "Blacker" at a predominantly white college than at a negro school. Administrators at negro schools are, typically, middle-class in orientation and appointed or controlled by conservative or racist white government officials or boards of trustees. As such, they tend to assume the position of "overseer" at the negro college to see to it that nothing distinguishably "Black" occurs and that the school continues to produce "responsible" and "respectable" negroes. At the negro school, then, there is usually a deliberate effort made to guard against the possibility that anything in the educational process will be relevant to Black people. At the predominantly white schools, such is not the case. The administrators at these schools are usually unaware of what is relevant to Blacks. Most have not the foggiest notion of what Black students mean by a "relevant education." Such notions as a relevant education for Blacks in the context of a predominantly white school have simply never crossed their minds. Under these circumstances, the Black student is much freer to engage in distinguishably Black activities on the predominantly white campus than at the negro school.

And, last, but by no means least, Black students recognize that Afro-Americans are and always will be surrounded by whites as long as they remain in America. To this extent, the close, homogeneous environment offered by the negro college is artificial and unreal. At the predominantly white college, the Black student functions in a situation more closely representative of that which awaits him in the society at large—a minority of Blacks engulfed by a majority of whites who are often hostile, seldom understanding, and almost always racist.

PART V: TO WHAT END LEARNING?

It is common these days to hear students making two kinds of complaints about social science research. One is that the research and the people who carry it out are uninvolved, dispassionate, cold, aseptic—in short, uncommitted. What this complaint often means is that the work of social scientists does not, and is not intended to, demonstrate the veracity or the desirability of some humanitarian value which the critics take as a cardinal theme of their own personal creed. In this form, the argument is one of ends, and therefore extraordinarily difficult to resolve. A social scientist may think that he ought most of all to seek knowledge; the critics, that he ought instead to be primarily concerned with implementing or preserving equality, or liberty, or justice, or any cognate condition that might improve the human situation.

More often, however, the complaint and the consequent argument are not over ends as much as over means. A social scientist may be as committed to a given end as any of his students, may define it in the same way, may even select and plan his studies in the light of his eagerness to see it come about. Yet ultimately his efforts may still strike his students or readers as unsatisfactorily indecisive, distant, withdrawn. There are some important reasons for this outcome.[1] (1) The method of social science does call for honesty. Thus it prevents anyone from carrying out studies that prove just—and only just—what he may have set out to prove. (2) Interpretations and recommendations that outrun data so far as to forget them are worse than worthless. They not only misuse social science, but also sooner or later call into question its very credibility. (3) Most social scientists are men of thought rather than men of action. It is the latter who make the policy decisions and frame the legislation that affect us all. Influence over men of action depends on pressure, on emotional appeal, on whatever may be the prevalent calculus of local or national political cost-benefit analysis. Scientific data matter too, but less than these other factors. Rightly or wrongly, moreover, most social scientists think their professional roles and particular expertise do not extend beyond their scientific tasks. As for the rest of the job of remaking society, most social scientists are no more than citizens, pretty much like most of the rest of us.

[1] There are some other reasons as well, but they have little to do with the social sciences *per se*. For example, some research just doesn't pan out. In addition, although it is true that some fields of study have higher concentrations of bright people than others, within any given field there tends to be a normal distribution. Only a few individuals are very good scholars or researchers; some more are pretty good; most do ordinary work; a few are dull plodders; and a very few are simply pretty bad.

The second kind of criticism is that social science research is irrelevant. I take this complaint to mean that studies are insufficiently responsive to the call of what anyone with half an ear can hear, the angry bellows or the plaintive moans of people involved in what we conventionally call our urgent social problems. An adequate consideration of this matter would demand an inquiry into the very meaning of social science, and more specifically into matters like the place of basic versus applied research, the significance to be attached to technique versus substance, or the weight of quantitative sophistication versus that of qualitative refinement. I shall not attend to those matters here. I lack the space and, in any case, am not inclined to evaluate issues that have recently been very well considered at length elsewhere.[2]

Instead, I ask the reader to consider that the usual sense of the word "irrelevant," as it is hurled at sociology, simply does not apply in the study of race relations. Indeed, there are few issues where demands are so clear for action in hundreds of different forms. Yet "irrelevant" is applied to studies in race relations, too. My own guess as to why this should be the case is that our studies document the obvious (We know what needs to be done, and we have known it for at least a generation); that the studies are not so much irrelevant as they are—or appear to be—ineffectual (Why don't they make anybody do anything?); that they have become a way through which officials put off making decisions (Good idea; let's have a commission look into that); and, finally, that study results, however accurate, too often lead to suggestions that cannot be put into effective practice under present conditions (We just can't bus kids all over this city; or, you can't desegregate when all the whites are moving out of town; or, all this agency needs is $7 billion with no damned federal strings attached).

I share these doubts and the sense of impotence they create in me as a sociologist, and I suspect that Tumin, the author of the single selection that concludes this book, does too. Yet I still argue, as he does, that without honest, dispassionate studies by men who are committed to the idea of greater social justice, we shall have neither new ideas for unraveling institutional knots, nor any securer basis than blind faith for thinking that our social judgments are accurate. Not everyone needs to be or should be led to think that he ought to be a social scientist. But the men who do take that role have to accept the obligations that go with it, or else run the risk of

2 Jack D. Douglas (ed.), *The Relevance of Sociology* (New York: Appleton-Century-Crofts, 1970).

letting their frustration or their passion lend a shoulder to the toppling of a still precarious scaffold that reason is still trying to complete.

Tumin implies at many points that hope remains for finding a way to arrive at a more fully democratic multiracial American society. I am less inclined than he to place so much reliance on integration as a means of reaching that goal. More precisely, I want to make it as clear as I can that I do not disagree one bit with his insistence that the majority groups of this society must open themselves much more than they have until now. Where I do differ with him is with his implicit assumption that change in that direction will have to depend practically exclusively on majority initiatives that will bring about minority uplift.

Some readers may find it helpful if I make my own point of view clear if for no other reason than that comparing Tumin's ideas with mine may serve as a springboard for discussion. I begin by making a few general points, elaborating them later.

1. In order for integration to rapidly bring about a pronounced tendency toward full social and economic equality among different racial groups, not only attitudinal standards specifically governing race relations but also some other American institutions would have to change.

2. If integration cannot bring about these institutional changes as much as it has to depend upon them, it is futile to believe that integration is either a panacea or the only method available for promoting greater equality.

3. Therefore, it may often be more useful to concentrate on tactics aiming at the institutional changes which allow integration to work more effectively than to work exclusively for integration and then wait for the changes it might bring in its wake.

In case it is not clear from the three points themselves, it must be emphasized that integration is not always a goal. The basic, ultimate, reigning goal is equality. Integration is a method, a means, a strategy that can be used as one among many theoretically possible techniques to increase racial equality. Furthermore, using integration as one means does not preclude using other techniques that are ultimately devoted to a similar end. We sacrifice some analytical power if we think of all these different techniques as if they were mutually exclusive alternatives. After all, we know that society is composed of different institutions and different spheres of activity. Some areas or parts of areas are already integrated, like much of the working-class labor market. Others are not, like the overwhelming majority of the housing market. Obvious though the examples may be, they serve to remind us that in the predictable future American society is likely to see neither full integration nor full segregation; neither exclusive reliance upon the technique of integration nor upon those like community control and self-governance.

If you have a strong partisan position about these matters, you may have to back away from it for just a moment to see that integration and self-governance are not necessarily mutually exclusive, but can be and often are complementary. For example, when bright minority youngsters try to increase the number of places open to them in "white" universities, or when minority working men try to break a white stranglehold over membership in a craft union, both are working for more integration. Clearly they do so not merely for the sake of integration itself, but rather to improve their own life chances and/or those of their fellow group members. Yet at the very same time, and for the very same ends, other sectors of the same minority group may be seeking more local control over schools, over housing, over welfare administration. It is true that for some time to come, integration will be the only game in town for many people who are seeking better jobs, advanced education and training, or access to the top levels of power in corporate or governmental America. Those are white-dominated spheres not likely to be seriously challenged by rapid development of parallel non- or off-white structures. Even so, to insist that integration has to be the goal in those areas is *not* to prove either that other techniques depending upon mass minority action may not be useful or necessary steps to take before a greater and more genuine integration can take place, or that more satisfying ways of working and living cannot be found in more autonomous communities.

Tumin does point out that the past and present conditions in which integration has had to operate have not enabled it to work the miracle of rapidly placing newly integrated people on an equal footing with others who have been longer in organizations and positions that had previously been segregated. A handy example comes from a glance at government employment. Higher proportions of minority than of majority people have taken jobs that government has created over the past twenty years. That is integration. However, far higher proportions of minority than of majority people occupy the bottom civil service ranks. That is not equality.

Tumin calls attention to a matter that has been more significant than the remnants of personal prejudice in contributing to that kind of outcome in many similar sorts of situations: the generally lower social-class position of minority people, with all it implies in terms of less formal education, lower skills, different work habits, and the like, makes it harder for them to get good positions even in open organizations. He mentions but in my view does not give due emphasis to another matter: the viscosity of established administrative procedures in government, business, and education that rely upon credential criteria for recruitment, appointment, and promotion. The prevalent assumption has been that these credentials are universal tests and screens that are fairly used when applied to all in the same way. The difficulty with that assumption is that it makes it unnecessary to ponder whether a high grade on any such criterion as the absence of a police record, the possession of a high school diploma, or the experience of a stable work history might have little to do with performing well in a newly available job or educational slot, but a great deal to do with the sediment of generations of relative advantage. (Emphasis on these matters of "hidden" discrimination should not create the impression that I have already forgotten comments I made earlier in the introduction to Part IV. There I tried to show that even though pure and simple personal discrimination may be on the wane, it has far from disappeared. Moreover, minimizing the existence of one kind of discrimination makes it easy to be careless about another. Recent research shows, for example, that executives who believe blacks are not discriminated against are also the people most reluctant to take steps to change established hiring and recruiting procedures.[3] Yet, if these steps were taken, they would help to crack the silent cycle of institutional racism.)

Whatever the entire set of reasons for the initial failure of integration to be able to do more than a gradual job of upgrading minority populations (so gradual, it often seemed, that the continuing mobility of the majority would keep income and residence gaps as great as they had ever been), it became clear to many minority leaders that it was imperative both to find a way of exacting majority resources that had not been freely given and to create a solidary base for continuing minority initiative. It was clear by 1966 that riots were no answer; they could not be taken very seriously as part of long-run strategy except as a background threat. They had been too spontaneous and unprogrammatic; besides, they had

[3] Peter H. Rossi et al., Between White and Black: The Faces of American Institutions in the Ghetto, in Supplemental Studies for the National Advisory Commission on Civil Disorders (Washington, D.C.: Government Printing Office, 1968).

frightened the majority without in the end getting very many concessions from it. Hence the shift to nationalism and community control, to make of minorities informed interest groups with a stake of their own in local economics and politics. The hope was to find a means of consolidating interests, submerging segmental concerns in order to present at least the facade, if not always the fact, of a united movement with enough drive and insistence to win gains for the minority community within the minority community. Were nationalism or community control to succeed by revitalizing slum schools, securing better housing, creating involvement and the pride of accomplishment, one result would be more enriching and healthier ghettoes or barrios. Another would be a larger number of people who some years later would, if they chose, be able to go out from them, integrating on higher levels than before in their work and education, but returning, also if they chose, to their own communities for most of their family and other primary group relations.

Will any of the plans for community control and self-governance work? Cohen, in Selection 30, says that at least as far as the school system is concerned, in a place like New York City there is no other choice but to try them. Blauner, in Selection 5, writes of how and why he thinks they will help end colonization and dependency. He adds that the plans ought to be combined with an integration policy that is as open as possible for those who wish to avail themselves of other opportunities. Rather than repeat in detail the points Cohen and Blauner make, I shall confine myself to three concluding observations.

First, I do not know if either nationalism or community control can come close to doing all that its proponents hope and claim for it. In fact, there is certainly the possibility that relying on either will anger so many whites or allow so many others with guilty consciences to get off the hook, that reservoirs of necessary political toleration and economic support will begin to dry up. However, I am sure that a reliance on integration alone will also suffer from severe handicaps. As I write this, I have in mind the withdrawal of white middle classes from the central city. They take their tax dollars with them as they go; and increasingly, they find places to work that are themselves located in the suburbs. My question overstates the matter, but in view of this, with whom and in what is there to integrate?

Second, our historical record tells us that even if every bar and barrier to full integration were to disappear tomorrow, today's minority people would still want to live among themselves, would still wish to feel the comfort and instant rapport of shared experience, would still seek the sense that an area, a place, was home. In addition, it is a common American desire and belief that people ought to shape their lives for and by themselves. When with these goals in mind people discover and refurbish an identity in which they can take pride; when they begin to feel a sense of shared collective responsibility; when they become strong enough to assert their rights autonomously and no longer have to settle for handouts and reassuring promises; then it seems to me that they have already come up from obscurity to begin to be part of the pluralistic package in which we take so much pride. There will be anger and abrasiveness, not only for all the times when groups do not play fair, but also because some people are trying to get what others do not want to give up. Ghettoes will be jungles tomorrow, too, and the day after that; and liberal majority-group members will go on wondering why so many ghetto-dwellers don't seem to like white people, for changes in the lives and the values of whole peoples do not occur in the blink of an eye. Yet our history also shows us that the judgments we make of any group now will change a good deal after two generations, once the group has awakened, makes the nation aware of its presence, and moves forward in the steps of more and more front-runners who used what increased opportunities could give them by way of training and influence.

Third, assuming that our goal is a democratic multiracial America, how can we expect to reach it if the better fed go on eating the cake and leaving the crumbs? Crumbs are nourishment enough only for undertaking desperate and foredoomed attempts to use physical force to burst the shackles of a hoarding, miserly distributive system governed by people as long in power as they are short in vision. Still, my guess is that repression would defeat rebellion. Time would wash away the stains of spilled blood, and many would be the unknowing as well as the direct victims of a tragic loss. Nations are not like trees; they do not always fall from internal rot.

White America can continue to insist both that genuine group pluralism runs against the national grain and that it is right in maintaining the institutional arrangements that make full and complete and equal integration impossible to attain. Or it can see that there are no necessary and compelling reasons to go on doing either. The chance for choice is there.

37. SOME SOCIAL CONSEQUENCES OF RESEARCH ON RACIAL RELATIONS

Melvin M. Tumin

In introducing this final part of the book, I pointed out one or two places where I disagreed with some of the emphases and interpretations of this concluding selection. Indeed, because the article deals at length with many matters still at the heart of heated controversy, it would not have been difficult to come up with a list of points to dispute or argue about. But I have come to the end of my book, and my chance is over. If I have not been able to make my perspective and judgments clear by this time, I doubt that I could make them much clearer by setting them forth as part of a detailed textual examination of Tumin's article.

Besides, I did not include the article in order to dismiss it. On the contrary, I have found it a useful and important contribution, and not merely because it has stimulated my own thinking. Tumin has skillfully related major studies of American race relations to the social contexts that led to their being carried out. In that sense his work is a fine study in the field known as the sociology of knowledge. Furthermore, unlike most contemporary observers of intergroup relations, he has been able to back away from the studies he cites, not to escape their implications, but to view them more panoramically. Thus, he helps to map the routes research has taken among thickets of human folly and political controversy, and to plot paths it may follow in the future if social scientists continue to use knowledge as well as emotion to cut through the tangled brush

Source: *The American Sociologist,* Vol. 3, No. 2 (May 1968), pp. 117–23. Reprinted by permission of the author and the American Sociological Association.

MELVIN TUMIN is Professor of Sociology at Princeton University. He has written widely in the field of racial and ethnic relations, and social stratification.

of conflicting partisan commitments. However, in calling our attention to the fact that the federal government has sponsored the major studies of race relations of the past several years, Tumin also points out a significant irony about knowledge and its use. Government policy led to knowledge being acquired, but the knowledge gained led to no important policy change. The studies again showed the steps that had to be taken (they had been known for twenty years) if black (and, we should add, other minority) people were to be enabled to make great and rapid strides toward equality. Yet the same studies also showed that those steps were still not likely to be taken, not in the face of resistances and antipathies well entrenched in many of the dominant institutions and organizations.

Minority group members hardly needed new research results to learn that America had not been keeping its promises to them. But the paradox was made even more evident by the study findings, lending still another shoulder to the push of protest, and providing still firmer ground for the new ideologies that were beginning to express and make use of bitterness and anger more consciously and openly.

Tumin thus helps to explain some of the frustration that underlay the suspicion, hostility, and turning aside from the dominant society that struck so many white observers as surprising and unwarranted. Nevertheless, he does not condone those angry black responses, but views them as essentially negative, even though easily understood and perhaps fully expectable under the circumstances. Sticking to his judgment that minority people can find secure and satisfying places only in an open, integrated society, he strongly implies that minority leaders err and run a grave risk whenever their actions threaten to shut themselves and their people off from the rest of the society.

Readers will want to question Tumin's assumption that separatism has been as prevalent in fact as in rhetoric; will wonder about what he means in his references to "legitimate" leadership. They will find it much harder to quarrel with three more of his propositions, which are, to my way of thinking, far more central parts of his work. First, in an open society there would be little basis and less drawing power for hostile resistance and revolutionary fervor. Second, American society's current class and racial arrangements mean that the country cannot be made open without firm commitments not just to equal opportunities, but to equal outcomes for equal efforts. And third, such commitments surely cannot be made effective just by racial minorities, but only by them along with the majority and those elite sectors which, when they have been responsive to populist pressures at all, have until now overwhelmingly answered to the needs and desires of the majority alone.

Quite contrary to ordinary and widespread belief about scientific "ivory towers," there has been a serious and despairful lag between the time that scientists have published crucial research findings and the time, if at all, that public and private policy have moved toward any implementation of these findings. This, of course, renders preposterous the common allegations of ivory-tower escapism by academic scientists.

For there can be no doubt in the minds of anyone familiar with the social science research on race relations that today we would not have a history of recurring riots and civil disorders, nor a menacing threat of continued and unending riots and disorders, participated in by Negroes of all classes and educational levels, if, starting with the 1944 publication of the Myrdal volume on the situation of the American Negro, government and other agencies at federal, state and local levels had been at all responsive in any significant degree to the obvious warnings and danger signs that social science research posted with much vigor and prominence.

One may say, in effect, that a major cause of the enormous foment of hate, anger, and despair in the Negro community today, and of the capacity of a small group of extreme militants to take legitimate leadership away (even if only temporarily) from the most serious, thoughtful, and concerned traditional leadership of the Negro community, has been the failure of the American government and public to respond to Negro needs in precisely the ways in which so-

cial science research since the 1940's, and even before, has indicated that these should be responded to, if we did not want to have what we have today by way of extraordinary intergroup conflict and hostility.

Consider, for instance, the fact that since 1940, and up through 1954, (when, for ten years, social science research on race relations was put into quietus by a shutdown in government and foundation sponsorship), we have had brilliant and detailed documentation of the plight of Negroes in every sector of their lives, political, economic, educational, residential, and in their family structures and in such life chances as infant mortality and early death and high rate of broken family. We had, also, in the 1940's, several major handbooks of methods and techniques for the reduction of prejudice and discrimination, as in the excellent inventories by Robin Williams (1947) and Arnold Rose (1948). In the 1940's, too, we had a masterful analysis of the web of government, and of intergroup relations within that web, conceived in terms of tensions and tension-reductions, by Robert MacIver, in his *The More Perfect Union* (1948). We had, too, the grave warnings regarding the weaknesses and cracks in American character and personality given to us by the studies in authoritarian personality. This is not to mention the more than prolific flow of articles and applied investigations documenting what Negroes felt and wanted and what the resistances were like in the white community.

So, too, if anyone was unclear as to

what the nature of prejudice and the social sources of prejudice and discrimination might be, we had the fertile and seminal 1954 Allport volume on these topics, and a very valuable inventory of the best literature, compiled for the 1954 *Handbook of Social Psychology* by Harding, Kutner, Proshansky and Chein.

And if anyone wanted to know and cared about what was boiling up in Negroes under the pressure of increasingly denigrating and unacceptable circumstances of life, it was there for the reading and understanding in the terribly important and insightful *Mark of Oppression* (1950) by Kardiner and Ovesey.

Finally, and in some sense, firstly, we have had unending documentation since the 1930's of the insignificance and uselessness of skin color as a predictor of abilities and talents, and hence, the certain conclusion of the random interchangeability for all cultural functions of Negroes and whites. Here the works of Otto Klineberg and Ashley Montagu, among others, are outstanding.

One can say, then, with accuracy and exactness, that it was all there for the knowing, and it was all, or in large part, ignored, on three mistaken assumptions: (1) that slow and grudging minor concessions toward a far removed equality and first-class citizenship would suffice to handle things nicely because (2) after all, whites had the power and could dictate the terms and conditions and tempos and (3) after all, Negroes were docile, unorganized, and without leadership or the capacity for militant protest.

Not only were these assumptions wrong (and dangerously so), but, if stupidity is measured by the extent to which action is taken or not taken in spite of all evidence to the contrary, then these assumptions were stupidly mistaken as well.

That stupidity and that danger were compounded several times over by the failure to take advantage of the second chance that was given to the public and

the government by the 1954 Brown *vs* Topeka court decision regarding the inherently unequal character of segregated schools. Normally, history does not give such second chances, nor, except rarely, such third chances as the opportunities and warnings provided by the Montgomery bus strike and the early 1950 sit-ins by Negro college students. It should have been apparent when those Negroes with the best chances of "making it" in America took to civil disobedience that unless real change was initiated by white government and white society, Negroes would take the initiative.

I am not speaking here in the comfort of correct hindsight, like some Monday-morning quarterback. Those of us who have been working and writing and speaking in this field are on record with our researches and our warnings. We take no comfort in having seen and spoken of these things earlier than others. What comfort can there be in "speaking into the wind"? But, perhaps strong and urgent words now may contribute something to movement by government at all levels and by the lay public, quickly, deeply, and significantly enough to reduce some of the likelihood of widespread and ever more dangerous civil disorders that predictably face us from now on in.

Let us put the nonresponsiveness of government to social science research into historic perspective. When one does this, one sees two rather distinct periods.

If we date the effective beginnings of social science research on race relations from the Myrdal report (1944), we have a picture of a first period consisting of a decade of considerable activity from 1944 to 1954.

Then, starting in 1955, there is an apparent hiatus that lasts almost ten years, during which almost no major works in race relations appear. (A modest exception was my own study of readiness for and resistance to desegregation in a North Carolina city 1958.)

Since 1964, however, we have had three major research publications on race: Daniel Moynihan's report on *The Negro Family* (1965); the 1966 Civil Rights Commission Report on *Racial Isolation;* and the extraordinary provocative study by James Coleman and others in 1966 on *Equality of Educational Opportunity.*

It is important to distinguish between these two periods for several reasons. First, we are informed by these dates and facts that substantial research in the field is not much more than twenty years old, and that, of those twenty-two or twenty-three years since the Myrdal report, nearly half were prevented by political considerations from being significant.

Secondly, we are presented with a neat division between two different kinds of works. They differ, first, in the fact that all the important research work in the earlier period was financed either by universities or by foundations, or, in some cases, was done on shoe-string budgets by individual scholars. In sharp contrast, the three major works of the last three years, on the Negro family, Negro isolation, and Negro education, were all sponsored and paid for and published by government agencies: the Department of Labor, the Civil Rights Commission, and the Office of Education.

From this first difference, we draw some inferences for an important second distinction between the two periods. The works of the earlier period seem largely to have arisen partly from the troubled consciences and partly from the scientifically immanent pressures in the academic community. By contrast, the latest documents of the second period seem to have been generated within the government bureaus themselves, as direct and surprisingly rapid responses by government to the tensions and pressures generated by social action in the Negro community (always remembering, of course, the presence in such bureaus of

an increasing number of research people with academic histories or prospects).

These are not opposite tendencies that we are contrasting here. They differ, but they are not in direct contradiction. In the first case, the main feature seems to be one of relative detachment of research from policy, in either possible direction of flow of effects. In the second case, the flow of effects seems to go from social action in the streets to government concern about such action and then, from there, to the expression of that concern by government in the form of policy-related research; then, as we shall see soon, the movement is back to the streets again.

This is the picture we get of contrasting epochs and styles of research and of relationships between research and policy, if we focus alone on the three recent studies of family, isolation and education.

When one narrows his focus in that way, however, he tends to overlook the extraordinary richness of other basic research and policy-relevant documents prepared by individual scholars in the last four or five years. Consider, in this light, the 1964 book by Michael Harrington, *The Other America,* which can truly be said to have helped America and its government rediscover poverty in this country, after Galbraith had almost persuaded us not to give it a second thought. Can one doubt that the Harrington book made poverty respectable, both for public policy action and for social science research? And surely, Negro poverty and its consequences are central to race relations in this country.

Of equal importance, though in quite a different genre, is Samuel Bloom's 1964 book, *Stability and Change in Human Characteristics.* It was this book, more than any other, which alerted the academic, government, education, and lay communities to the dangers of early childhood, cultural, and intellectual deprivation, and documented the enduring consequences of such deprivation. We may worry much, as perhaps we should, about the ways in which Bloom's notion of early retardation has been dramatically and dangerously oversimplified. But we cannot deny the great care and scholarliness of Bloom's work and its significance for a vast array of both basic and applied researches. There may have been programs of higher horizons and cultural enrichment before Bloom's book. But the enthusiastic public support for the development and proliferation of such programs (albeit based on an untested assumption of their absolute indispensability to equality of education) can accurately be dated as coming after and because of this book and its dispersed messages.

Consider, too, the ingenious experimentation from 1962 on, by Robert Rosenthal at Harvard, on the subject of experimenter bias, which is easily translated into teacher bias. This research is outstanding for its demonstration of the types and intensities of distortion in testing outcomes that preconception about such outcomes can produce. Join this work with that of Harry Passow and Miriam Goldberg on homogeneous groupings and tracking, and we have the research matrix out of which vital policy implications for educational reform can and have been drawn. We see, for instance, from these works, how the self-confirming hypothesis and the self-verifying prejudice take on worlds of dangerous meanings when applied to the educational process and when related to early childhood deprivation.

I cite just these few works, two of them by outstanding academics and one by a social reformer and essayist, all of them apparently modest in dimension but decisively significant in their implications, so that I can now indicate that these works did not represent crash efforts, incited and impelled by the actions in the streets of dissident minorities; nor did they represent government responses to political pressures. But in many important senses they are as significant and consequential as the three major works sponsored by government bureaus. And surely of the Bloom and the Rosenthal works one can say that they represent basic rather than applied research, and primary research rather than secondary compilation. Further, whatever their political uses, they represent what the internal demands of developing bodies of scientific thought suggested were important next steps in research. The same remarks can be applied with almost equal force to the Myrdal volume and the earlier work by Franklin Frazier (1932) on the Negro family.

That these basic and primary scientific researches have had applied, secondary and political consequences is certain. One may also venture the judgment that if the political groundwork and setting had not been fertile and receptive to these studies, they would have remained recherché documents, treasured by various segments of the intellectual and academic community, but only occasionally, if at all, seeping into public view in today's mass market of information through the mysterious osmosis in which ladies' journals play a crucial part.

We are saying, in effect, that while these basic and primary researches had evident potential political vitality, that vitality was not expressed until the political ambiance was appropriate, and until, in a rather interesting and perhaps novel way, the implications of the basic research findings were put into politically usable and commanding form in the applied studies by Moynihan, Coleman, and the Civil Rights Commission, under the impulsion of the need of government to make a dramatic and sympathetic response to the agitation in the Negro community regarding the persisting plight of the Negro.

If it is fair to say that the applied researches by government bureaus gave political translation to the basic research materials, it is equally fair and important to note that the applied researches could hardly have been done with any success at all, and indeed might hardly have known what were the relevant questions to ask, if the basic researches had not already been on record. This is not to denigrate the quality of thought that went into the applied researches by the government bureaus, but rather to indicate the extent and quality of their interplay with the basic research materials which underlay them both theoretically and temporally.

If one now raises questions as to what these interrelations of basic and applied science and public policy and action indicate about scientific sensitivity to topical and pressing issues of the day, it is clear from the range of connections just cited that science can and does relate to policy in a variety of ways and that, judging by the dates of the research and applied documents, and by the political issues to which they were relevant, scientists have proven extraordinarily sensitive to what is going on "out there." If anything, they have been perhaps too sensitive and responsive. For, because of their urgent and full political relevance at the time of their appearance, these research materials have tended to get less of the basic scientific evaluation and criticism that all such documents need, and have tended too much to be judged in anti-scientific contexts and by irrelevant political criteria.

In any event, there is little point in debating whether scientists have been alert enough to the needs of the community. The research of the early period was ahead of any public or governmental interest or action, even by the concerned victims themselves. In addition, the newer researches, though admittedly more applied than basic, could hardly have been more timely. Where then is the far-famed and deprecated "ivory tower"?

Perhaps most interesting and most curious and perhaps, too, most important of all, is the way in which the major findings of both the basic and applied researches have been greeted, responded to, and acted upon by the concerned public.

We can see this clearly by indicating first what the basic findings from those researches were, and then comparing the range of reactions expressed to them and actions taken upon them.

Here then are some of the major research findings:

(1) Negroes and whites are, under conditions of equal opportunity and training, interchangeable at random for all cultural roles.

(2) Desegregation and integration of Negroes and whites in all social contexts are indispensable to the achievement of equal opportunity and training for Negroes and for the achievement of stable political order for the society.

(3) Negro social structures, especially Negro families and communities, under prevailing ghetto conditions, require a fundamental reconstruction if they are to function effectively in the contributions our society expects such groups to make to the preparation of the child for adequate and satisfying functioning in the society.

(4) Basic reconstruction of the economy, and the educational system and the polity are unavoidable if the Negro substructures are themselves to be able to be reconstructed adequately.

(5) Until such reconstruction takes place, fundamental repair, compensatory and uplift work must be done to help Negro children overcome the unavoidable disadvantages and deficiencies so many of them incur in their inadequate primary group training and support.

(6) Wholesale reconstruction of the educational process, and reeducation and retraining of teachers are required to enable the schools to work adequately, and with something approaching equal-

ity, for underprivileged and deprived Negro children. Especially crucial here are those structures of relationships and of attitudes which tend to generate stereotypical preconceptions in teachers and other school officials regarding children's abilities or the lack of them and which function to create ceilings of limitations and restrictions on their possible growth.

(7) The circles of miseducation, inadequate preparation, and poverty are interlocking and self-reinforcing. Especially in the economic sphere, the filtering-down effects that economists hope will ensue from a so-called right labor market have not been very visible, insofar as the bottom twenty percent or so of income earners, where the Negroes are primarily located, seem to experience not more than a few droplets of the affluence circulating vigorously in the upper-half of the income brackets. Massive refurbishing of the economy appears, therefore, to be indispensable if the vicious cycle of self-reinforcing poverty is to be broken.

(8) Close collaboration between Negroes and whites is vital to the development and enrichment of the democratic institutions and processes which are indispensable both to the improvement and uplift of the Negro community and to the general welfare of the entire society.

These, then, are some of the main policy implications which may be drawn from the researches. It is not, let us point out, that the researches say that Negroes *should* be made equal, uplifted, freed from poverty, and the like. But if they *are* to be freed from poverty, uplifted, and made equal, then the foregoing eight steps, among others, seem indispensable.

It is quite evident that these policy implications which have been drawn indirectly from the basic researches, and more directly and explicitly formulated and advocated in the applied documents put together by Moynihan, Coleman, and the Civil Rights Commission all were "on the side of the angels" insofar as that side is defined as being in favor of doing everything reasonable and conceivable, within the limits of democratic process, for the improvement of the situation of the Negroes.

It is most curious, indeed, in this light, to see the way in which the Moynihan thesis of the negative role of the often broken and misfunctioning Negro family in the development of Negro children has been seriously attacked by Negroes as a racist document, one, it is alleged, that seeks to displace the blame for the Negro situation onto the shoulders of the Negroes themselves and thus to divest the white community of its responsibility. Any simple reading of the Moynihan document will show that no such implications are to be found in the study. Yet this matter is still hotly debated. All these accusations, and the responses by Moynihan and others to them, and the responses of others to these responses, are documented at great length in the intriguing recent work by Lee Rainwater and William Yancey (1967). It is perfectly clear, from a reading of the ping-pong of controversy that this book recites, that this is one of those cases where one is sure to be damned by someone for something, no matter what he says.

In the same light, consider the recent fate of the Civil Rights Commission report on racial isolation. It has been attacked with great polemic elegance and even careful supplementary research by Joseph Alsop, of all people, on the grounds that it advocates an impossible, and hence dangerous, mandate to place desegregation of the schools first and foremost on the priority of required actions. This mandate was recently given legal force by Judge Skelly Wright's decision regarding the Washington schools, in which Wright ordered desegregation of the schools in the District, where over ninety percent of the students are Negro. Alsop argues persuasively, with supporting data, that this order is simply incapable of being implemented, and that any effort to do so, and thereby to delay focusing upon improving the quality of education without regard to desegregation of the facilities, is not only utopian but is dangerous and harmful to the Negro school child.

The exchanges in the *New Republic* between Alsop (1967) and social scientists (Schwartz et al., 1967), including one who served as chief consultant to the Civil Rights Commission in its study, have served to throw the connection between research and policy into a fearful muddle—or at least even more fearful a muddle than the one in which they already were embroiled. If Alsop's figures regarding likely Negro concentrations in major urban areas are correct, and they seem persuasively so at the moment, then, the whole point of the study of racial isolation, so far as its obviously intended demand for desegregation is concerned, is lost. So, too, the whole force of the Skelly Wright decision is emasculated, if indeed it was not already—even before it was written. Yet the Wright decision is surely the most liberal and far reaching implementation in formal law of the most soundly argued case for desegregation that social science research has been able to support.

How ironic, indeed, that such firmly based research and such courageously formulated law should find themselves arrayed in decisive battle against some of the persons in the interest of whose emancipation they were conceived and executed.

Nor does the case for the irony end there. For now the Coleman report is with us, and with it, the dissemination through the community of interested scholars and participants of the presumed finding that almost nothing about schools seems to make a significant difference in the intellectual functioning of the children who come to the schools.

The exceptions are minor and almost trivial.

As with all scientific findings, one can go in quite opposite action directions with the very same data. Do the schools really not matter? Then forget about them, and especially about the efforts to desegregate them, since while "desegregation" may be somewhat more relevant than other factors, it is hardly worth mentioning itself.

Or, do the schools really not matter? Then, it must be that *as constructed* they do not matter, and what then can we do about reconstructing them so that they *will* matter in significant degree? Or, focusing alone on segregation *vs. desegregation,* if now the amount of desegregation seems to be trivially relevant to the intellectual performance of the children, then let us find out how and under what conditions desegregation might make a difference. Or, if segregation doesn't seem to be intellectually and otherwise any worse for Negro children, then forget about desegregation and try to build quality education in the ghetto schools.

But *will* quality education matter? The Coleman Report is in various quarters being interpreted as saying that even this is of little significance. Yet, in other quarters, the Coleman Report itself is being questioned; not its intent, or the worthiness of its having been accomplished, but rather its methodology and its sample and its instruments and its analysis. Perhaps, it is being suggested, the Report finds that the schools do not matter because the instruments used for testing the consequentiality of differences in schools simply could not detect or grasp those dimensions of educational process and structure which might make very significant differences. And perhaps, too, others are urging, no repair work to the schools can possibly be effective that does not attack and destroy the basic conception of school as a process of competitive movement of differentiated cohorts through fixed curricula. Since the Coleman Report does not compare such drastically different alternative schools, perhaps that is why the schools, no matter how different, do not seem to make much of a difference.

We have, then, in these three most recent major works, instances of government responding to the pressure of events —riots, demonstrations, and the whole mess—by initiating and completing large-scale studies or surveys of the situation which could serve only to highlight with great effect the actual state of affairs. The intention could have been only to dramatize the situation enough to provoke further demand for effective government action and to disarm the likely opposition to such further welfare measures.

And they served their purposes—each of these studies did. They *did* highlight, and they *did* dramatize, and they *did* evoke the clamor for effective action, legislative and otherwise.

What neither they—nor anyone—expected, however, was the kind of Negro reactions they evoked—including most prominently, a reversal to a demand for separatism and grass roots community development and autonomy; in effect, for reinforced segregation. Had these demands been made by any but Negro militants, they would surely have been dubbed racist and white supremacist.

One can say, with some painful humor, that never has social research been so substantial, in the first instance, and so relevant in the second instance to matters of pressing moment, and *so quickly followed up with social action and policy that run directly against the major grain of the research.*

In using the phrase—the "major grain of the research"—I am appearing to imply that the research suggests a direction of social action. But this is not so. The research *per se,* indicates no direction at all and never does, in the nature of the thing called scientific research. The directionality is given, if at all, by the conditions under which the research is initiated and by the obvious intention of the initiators and supporters.

The report on the Negro family could never have been intended for any program other than social reconstruction of the Negro community, through massive intervention by government, to permit implementing decisions and measures Negro families to play more positive functions.

The report on equality of opportunity in education could surely never have been meant to do anything other than 'to retestify to the persistence of segregated schooling and the attendant damages, especially in the education of Negroes, in spite of the 1954 Court decision and the implementing decisions and measures formulated since then.

How then can we account for the adverse and reverse reactions of some portions of the Negro community to these researches? Why, in effect, have some of the Negro leaders chosen to stand the researches upside down, and recommend Negro separatism? Why should the notion of cultural deprivation have come to be considered a slur? Why the emphasis on a so-called indigenous and rich Negro culture? Why the denial of the role of the Negro family and community in the production of deprived and under-privileged children? Why the attack by Negroes on their closest allies in the white communities, the so-called white liberals, and the promulgation of the curious doctrine that it is better to deal with a whole and open racist than with a person who struggles against his own prejudices to act fairly? (Nor will any reading of Kenneth Clark on this subject or any of the other Negroes who have addressed themselves to it, make this any clearer.) Why, too, the active denial and denunciation of the doctrines of competence and fitness as criteria of eligibility for employment, and the substitution, instead, of the demand for quotas of Negroes in this and that place, regardless of competence? Why, above all, the reemergence of color consciousness, anti-white racism, and the insistence on the primacy of color as a criterion of selection and eligibility?

All of these would seem to run directly contrary, not only to what the researches show is necessary to Negro freedom and equality in this country, but what is also indispensable to any chance for a pluralist democratic polity, inside of which the Negro, like all other minority groups, has surely the best chance for a decent chance at a decent life.

There is a clear-cut answer. The Negroes, or at least many of them, simply no longer trust or believe in the efficacy of the slow workings of democracy and its customary slow modes of social change. They are not impressed with the arguments that point to the character of our federal government and its relations to the federation of 50 states, with the implicit set of states rights as obstacles to full equality. Nor do they care how resistant Southern Congressmen or Northerners may be, and how much the political process requires bargaining. Nor do they believe that we can have an all-out domestic effort and, at the same time, a 25 billion dollar-a-year war. They know, now, as never before, that power is as power does and that as humble petitioners they are not likely in their lifetimes to secure that to which they were entitled three hundred years ago.

Are they wrong to react in these ways? Perhaps. But the government, itself, has appeared to prove that they are right. The government, in its three major recent researches, has in fact documented the correctness of the despair and the disbelief of Negroes in the adequacy of American democratic institutions to change their lives significantly.

What an irony indeed! The government pays for major researches which prove that it is really not very worthwhile, nor wise, to trust in that government. What else could Negroes deduce from the fact that the Moynihan Report proves beyond a doubt how enduringly injured and wounded Negro children have been and will be by the broken substructures and primary groups in which they grow, and in which the adults have few, if any, alternatives to the modes of life they conduct?

And how else can we read the study of racial isolation, except as a document that verifies beyond doubt how little has been done to reduce segregation in communities and schools? And can there be any doubt that whatever else the Coleman Report tells us (perhaps wrongly), it unmistakably tells us that the schools, at least as presently structured, simply won't make any real difference in helping Negro children to become first-class citizens of this country?

If, then, Negroes say, because they feel it and have heard it and can see it, that this society has not moved; that its laws have not worked; that its protections have not been provided; that its facilities have not been shared; if this is how it looks to them, and if the Harrington volume, and the isolation study, and the Moynihan and Coleman reports tell them with figures that this is so, can anyone fail to understand why the Negroes draw the inferences they do about the need to secure power, to shake up the society, to dramatize their plight, and, if need be to construct their own society within a society?

The explanation, then, for the reverse and negative interpretations by Negroes of the best and most reliable findings of scientific research initiated on their behalf, must therefore be sought in these politics of despair and anger. It is as though a challenge has been seen by the Negro community: a challenge to "make it in America," against all odds and all existing institutional obstacles to the contrary. From one point of view, this represents an extraordinarily courageous kind of stand. From another point of view, it represents, curiously, the acceptance by the Negro community of the most-hated of white conservative or reactionary demands, namely, "All other groups have made it by themselves and through self-help, so why can't you?"

From still another point of view, the Negro response is a translation into social policy of the doctrine of grass-roots community development, as against the élite, tough-nosed economist model of a developed élite pulling the rest of the community up by its bootstraps.

Whichever way one views these Negro responses, and whatever reasons one sees for them, they are there. Against them, however, must be set the less spectacular reactions of the majority of the Negro community who still, from all available information, pursue their way slowly, painfully, against great odds, through the American maze, searching for some greater margin of political, economic, and educational rights than they have had before; struggling, in short, through the rank order of their demands in just about the way that Myrdal asserted they would and against the same kinds of rank-ordered oppositions that Myrdal predicted they would meet.

Yet, one dares not take comfort in the fact of the peacefulness of the majority of Negroes. For, it takes no more than a tiny minority of determined and embittered men to initiate and sustain widespread civil disorder. And if a significant portion of the leadership of Negro militants comes from the better-educated, middle-class Negro group, let us not forget that there is also a very substantial layer of hating and hated, alienated and impoverished, Negro slum youth and adults for whom the opportunity to attack and wound and destroy any and every symbol of the society that hates and fears them is welcomed with pleasure and glee. For, to destroy that society, or its symbols, is proof of their manhood

as well as serving as a delicious ventilation of their anger, even when they destroy their own houses and stores and streets.

Two facts persist that we must pay attention to, then. First, if Negroes are going to "make it" in American society, they are going to make it within the framework of democratic institutions and through the normal modes of social and economic mobility.

But if they are to have the opportunity to do so, and if they are to be realistically hopeful that they can do so, white society has to be willing, far more willing than it has been, to open the doors of that system of opportunity to Negroes. Failure to do so now, immediately, hugely, and dramatically, will insure that more and more of the peaceful majority of Negroes will pass over to the violent minority and that the momentary unattractiveness and weakness of the legitimate and peaceful Negro leadership will become a quasi-permanent fact.

The fact is that either white society responds appropriately and actively to legitimate Negro demands and needs, or be prepared to meet the certainty of ever-increasing violent insurgence. One way to meet such insurgence, of course, is to wage all-out war against the Negro community. The white community, would, of course, win such a pitched battle, but in the process it just as surely would destroy itself and everything it values.

And what will government do, government at the federal, state and local levels, if in fact, resentful white, ethnic minorities decide to respond to Negro violence with their own counter violent insurgence? Never mind that a majority of whites would not do this. Insurgency needs only small, determined minorities.

These are the warning signs that social science research and Negro political action have once again posted.

As for the future of scientific research in these fields, it is not unlikely that the next phase will find numerous investigators taking up deliberate postures of social action, "justifying" these in the name of scientific obligations, and taking their cues as to tactics from the leads provided by the more militant and anti-intellectual segments of the Negro community.

Indeed, this trend is already in motion. A number of social scientists have become openly avowed partisans of Negro separatism and violence, and are claiming both the scientific propriety and the research support for their orientations. Needless to say, these orientations are neither proper nor supported. But such considerations are likely either to persuade or deter these new partisans. Nor, on the other hand, are their new directions of activity likely to add anything significant to reliable knowledge about race relations, except as other, more dispassionate, observers, come to study them as instances of interesting, relevant, and important social experiments.

I say all this because I do not believe that as scientists we do science or society any good at all by jumping on political bandwagons. If science, for instance, is to serve well its own internal needs as well as the political needs of the community in the period to come, it would seem far wiser for it to be concerned with serious careful study of the why's and wherefore's of the successes and failures of the predictable efforts at Negro self-help and indigenous community development. For, failures there will be —no question—and perhaps even some modest successes. But if we become partisans of this or that cause, we will destroy our credibility and our capacity to function, effectively as scientists, in the analysis of these outcomes.

So, too, if it seems, as it does, that Higher Horizons and Head Start and More Effective Schools do not seem to serve fully or even partly the purposes for which they were intended, perhaps

this finding may lead in the future to investigating why it is that these programs do not work and what kinds of programs will work. For the Bloom and Rosenthal findings, among others, tell us that *some* such programs must work. Their researches show how the opposite works when the opposite forces are put into play, even if only impersonally in a class and color conscious society. That is, degradation, destruction, and restriction of potential are very effective indeed under prevailing circumstances of delayed start, impoverished beginning, and early circumscribed horizons.

I argue for scientific "detachment," too, because the hopes and lives of the people involved in these matters are simply too precious to permit them to be tossed about recklessly by this and that partisan demand that take turns gaining regnancy, not by the persuasiveness of their logic or even the rectitude of their sentiments, but rather by their deliberate and painful indifference to what is politically salutary in a democratic society and to what is needed if genuine equality is ever to be gained for all citizens.

If I see in all this one line of hope and optimism regarding the relation of science to policy, it is in the extraordinary growth of relevance of science, both in fact, as government and social action now operate, and in sentiment and belief, as the public now conceives of the role of science. It would, indeed, be a sad day if in this flush of new-found meaning and acceptance, science were to foul itself and its possible services to democracy and equality by insisting on altering the crucial role it has heretofore played and which has helped secure it prominence and acceptance.

As scientists, we shall probably always be damned by someone, sometimes more loudly than at others. We do ourselves no good by being sensitive to such damnation. We have, after all, our own kind of internal and immanent damnation to deal with. We shall serve everyone, including ourselves, much more effectively if we stick to our own lasts and are guided by our own best lights. These lasts and lights have not failed in the last 25 years to point the way to resolutions of our problems for those who cared to hear it as it really is and to go where the action is.

REFERENCES

Allport, Gordon, 1934 *The Nature of Prejudice.* Cambridge, Mass.: Addison-Wesley Press.

Alsop, Joseph, 1967a "Ghetto Education," *The New Republic* (November 18).

————, 1967b "No more Nonsense about Ghetto Education," *The New Republic* (July 22).

Bloom, Samuel, 1964 *Stability and Change in Human Characteristics.* New York: John Wiley.

Clark, Kenneth B. (no date cited) "Delusions of the White Liberal." Mimeograph.

Coleman, James S. et al., 1966 *Equality of Educational Opportunity.* Office of Education, U.S. Department of Health, Education, and Welfare. Washington, D.C.: U.S. Government Printing Office (OE-38001).

Frazier, E. Franklin, 1932 *The Negro Family in Chicago.* Chicago: University of Chicago Press.

Harding, J. et al., 1954 in Gardner Lindzey (ed.), *Handbook of Social Psychology.* Cambridge, Mass.: Addison-Wesley Press.

Harrington, Michael, 1963 *The Other America.* New York: MacMillan.

Kardiner, Abram and Ovesey, Lionel, 1962 *The Mark of Oppression.* Cleveland: World Publishing (Meridan Books).

Klineberg, Otto, 1935 *Race Differences.* New York: Harper and Row.

MacIver, R. M., 1948 *The More Perfect Union.* New York: MacMillan.

Montagu, Ashley, 1952 *Man's Most Dangerous Myth: The Fallacy of Race.* New York: Harper.

Moynihan, Daniel P., 1965 *The Negro Family: The Case for National Action.* Office of Policy Planning and Research, Department of Labor. Washington, D.C.: U.S. Government Printing Office.

Myrdal, Gunnar, 1944 *An American Dilemma: The Negro Problem and Modern Democracy.* New York: Harper.

Rainwater, Lee and Yancey, William L., 1967 *The Moynihan Report and the Policies of Controversy. A Trans-action Social Science and Public Policy Report.* Cambridge, Mass.: Massachusetts Institute of Technology Press.

Rose, Arnold M., 1948 *Studies in Reduction of Prejudice.* Chicago: American Council on Race Relations.

Rosenthal, Robert, 1963 "On the Social Psychology of the Psychological Experiment: The Experimenter's Hypothesis as Unintended Determinant of Experimental Results." *American Scientist* 51 (June):268–283.

Schwartz, Thomas et al., 1967 "Fake Panaceas." *The New Republic* (September 23).

Tumin, Melvin M., 1958 *Desegregation: Resistance and Readiness.* Princeton: Princeton University Press.

U.S. Commission on Civil Rights, 1967 *Racial Isolation in the Public Schools.* Washington, D.C.: U.S. Government Printing Office.

Williams, Robin M., Jr., 1947 *The Reduction of Intergroup Tensions.* New York: Social Science Research Council.